Television and Radio Announcing

Sixth Edition

Stuart W. Hyde
San Francisco State University

Houghton Mifflin Company   **Boston**

Dallas   Geneva, Illinois   Palo Alto   Princeton, New Jersey

Once again,
to my wife, Allie, and to our children,
Stuart, Jr.,
John Christian, and
Allison Elizabeth Ann

Cover Credit:

Ralph Mercer, Boston, Massachusetts

Text Credits:

Definitions adapted and reprinted by permission from the *American Heritage Dictionary, Second College Edition.* Copyright © 1985 by Houghton Mifflin Company.

Text credits for reprinted material appear on those pages as source lines; credits for adapted material are listed in the author's preface.

Printed in the U.S.A.

Library of Congress Catalog Card Number: 90-83277

ISBN: 0-395-54446-7

ABCDEFGHIJ-AH-9876543210

Contents

Preface   xii

Chapter 1   **Broadcast Announcing**   **1**

The Broadcast Announcer   3
Employment as an Announcer   7
Education and Training   9
Checklist: Taking Courses to Build Your Career   **12**
The Announcer's Responsibility   15
Spotlight: Broadcast Ethics and the Announcer's Responsibility   **16**
Practice: Interviewing a Successful Announcer   **19**
Practice: Establishing Ethical Guidelines   **19**

Chapter 2   **The Announcer as Communicator**   **20**

Principles of Effective Communication   22
Interpreting Copy   24
    Getting the General Meaning   24
Checklist: Analyzing Broadcast Copy   **25**
    Stating the Specific Purpose   25
    Identifying the General Mood   27
    Locating Changes in Mood   29
    Determining the Parts and the Structure   31
    Analyzing the Function of Punctuation   33
    Verifying Meaning and Pronunciation   38
    Reading Aloud   40
    Conveying an Interest in the Material   41
    Talking to the Listener   42
    Getting Some Background   43
    Employing Characterizations   44
Ad-Lib Announcing   44

Checklist: Getting Better at Ad-Lib Announcing   **45**
Spotlight: Every Night's a Party with Arsenio Hall   **46**
Practice: Analyzing Voice Quality   **49**
Practice: Effecting Mood Changes   **49**
Practice: Talking a Script   **49**
Practice: Ad-Lib Announcing   **52**

Chapter 3   **Performance**   **55**

Overcoming Microphone and Camera Fright   56
Spotlight: The Real-Life Appeal of Oprah Winfrey   **57**
     Lack of Experience   59
     Lack of Preparation   59
     Fear of Failure   59
     Lack of Self-Esteem   60
     Lack of Mental Preparation   61
     Dislike of One's Voice or Appearance   61
Microphone Consciousness   62
Camera Consciousness   64
     Hitting Marks   64
     Standing on Camera   65
     Sitting on Camera   66
     Telegraphing Movement   66
     Cheating to the Camera   67
     Addressing the Camera   68
     Holding Props   70
     Holding Scripts   71
     Using Peripheral Vision   72
     Clothing and Makeup   72
     Working with Cue Cards   73
     Working with Prompters   74
Instructions and Cues   77
     Taking a Level   79
     Hand Signals   80
Phonetic Transcription   85
     Wire-Service Phonetics   87
     Diacritical Marks   92
     The International Phonetic Alphabet   93
Performance Skills   94
     Preparing for a Performance   94

Checklist: Preparing to Perform   **95**
  Achieving a Conversational Style   96
  Reading Telephone Numbers   96
  Developing a Sense of Time   97
  Other Tips for Improving Your Performance   98
  Evaluating Performances   99
Practice: Gauging Your Own Performance   **99**
Checklist: Evaluating Radio and Television Performances   **100**
Checklist: Evaluating Television Performances   **101**
Practice: Getting Through an Ad-Lib Challenge   **102**

Chapter 4   **Voice and Diction**   **103**

Pitch   104
  Optimum Pitch   105
  Inflection   107
Volume   107
Tempo   108
Vitality   109
Pronunciation   110
  Pronunciation Problems   110
  Speech Sounds of American English   112
Voice Quality and Articulation   120
  Diagnosing Problems   121
  Improving Voice Quality   122
Spotlight: How a News/Announcing Duo Achieved   **126**
Their Good Sound
  Improving Articulation   129
Practice: Achieving a Low Pitch   **135**
Practice: Varying Your Pitch   **136**
Practice: Varying Your Tempo   **136**
Practice: Pronouncing Diphthongs   **138**
Practice: Working on Nasal Resonance   **139**
Practice: Pronouncing Consonants   **140**

Chapter 5   **American English Usage**   **147**

Age Referents   149
Jargon and Vogue Words   150
Redundancies   152
Clichés   154

Latin and Greek Plurals   157
Nonstandard Expressions and Usage   158
    Slang   158
    Solecisms   159
    Deliberate Misuse of Language   167
Our Changing Language   167
    American English and Ethnicity   168
Spotlight: The Debate Over General American Speech   **169**
    Gender in American English   173
    Nations and Citizens of the World   175
Practice: Improving Vocabulary and Pronunciation   **177**
Practice: Analyzing Regional Accents   **177**

Chapter 6   Broadcast Equipment   178

Microphones   180
    Internal Structure   180
    Pickup Patterns   182
    Intended Use   184
Audio Consoles   185
Cart Machines and CD Players   191
    Cuing and Playing Carts   191
    Cuing and Playing CDs   192
Turntables   193
    Components   193
    Cuing Up   194
Automated Radio Stations   195
Spotlight: Equipping Broadcast Studios for the   **197**
Twenty-First Century
Practice: Comparing the Audio Quality of Microphones **198**
Practice: Surveying Field Equipment   **198**

Chapter 7   Commercials and Public-Service Announcements   199

Radio Station Advertising Practices   200
    Target Audience   200
    Single-Sponsor Programs   200
    Advertising Purchase Plans   202
    Role of Advertising Agencies   203
    In-House Production   204

The Announcer's Role   205
    Analyzing and Marking Commercial Copy   206
    Recording a Commercial in a Studio   214
    Working with Commercials During an On-Air Shift   215
Spotlight: Tips from a Voice-Over Pro   **218**
    Character Voices   220
Radio Public-Service Announcements   221
Television Commercials   225
Checklist: Making Effective Television Commercials   **229**
Practice: Trying Accents and Character Voices   **230**
Practice: Delivering Radio Commercials and PSAs   **248**
Practice: Delivering Television Commercials   **248**
Practice: Producing Your Own Commercial   **249**

Chapter 8   **Interview and Talk Programs**   **250**

Principles of Effective Interviewing   251
    Avoiding Abstraction and Bias   251
    Tips for Conducting Successful Interviews   254
Spotlight: Talk-Radio Guru Bruce Williams   **258**
Checklist: Becoming a Skilled Interviewer   **264**
Announcing at Radio Talk Stations   267
    Preparing for the Shift   268
    Performing as a Talk Show Announcer   270
    Legal and Ethical Concerns   272
    Challenges and Responsibilities   274
Hosting Television Talk Programs   274
    Types of Talk Shows   275
    A Typical Production Effort   275
Practice: Interviewing   **278**

Chapter 9   **Radio News**   **281**

Anchoring Radio News   282
    News Sources   283
    Preparing for a Shift   287
    Writing News   290
Checklist: Writing Effective News Copy   **292**
    Delivering the News   294
The Radio Field Reporter   298
    Live Reporting   298

Voicers, Actualities, Sceners, and Wraps	299
Preparing Feature Reports: Minidocs	302
Spotlight: Top of the News—National Public Radio	**303**
Checklist: Recording Interviews Successfully	**306**
Practice: Reading News Copy Cold	**309**
Practice: Doing Commercials on the Side	**309**

Chapter 10   Television News   310

A Typical News Operation	310
The Field Reporter	314
Preparing a Package on Tape	315
Reporting Live from the Field	320
The News Anchor	322
Working Conditions and Responsibilities	323
A Typical Workday	324
The Weather Reporter	326
Spotlight: High-Tech Weather	**328**
Philosophies of Broadcast Journalism	329
Practice: Comparing Local and National Newscasts	**332**

Chapter 11   Music Announcing   333

The Disc Jockey	333
Working Conditions	333
Standard Station Formats	338
Announcing Styles	343
Working Conditions at Representative Stations	343
Preparing for a Career as a Disc Jockey	347
Checklist: Improving Your Popular Music Announcing Style	**348**
Spotlight: Fifty-Year Legend of Radio Cool, Al "Jazzbeaux" Collins	**350**
The Classical Music Announcer	353
Checklist: Polishing Your Classical Music Announcing	**356**
Practice: Tracking Rate of Delivery for Different Sounds	**357**
Practice: Announcing Popular Music	**357**
Practice: Announcing Classical Music	**358**

Chapter 12 **Sports Announcing** **368**

Working Conditions of Sports Announcers 369
Interviewing Athletes 376
    Tape-Editing Considerations 376
    Tips for Effective Interviewing 378
Sports Reporting 379
    The Television Sports Reporter 379
    The Radio Sports Director 382
The Play-by-Play Announcer 385
    Working Conditions 386
    Preparation for Play-by-Play Announcing 389
    Calling the Game 391
    Additional Tips on Sportscasting 392
Checklist: Becoming a Better Play-by-Play Announcer **395**
The Play Analyst 398
Spotlight: In the Game with Harry Caray **400**
Practice: Play-by-Play Announcing **402**
Practice: Getting Athletes' Names Right **402**

Chapter 13 **Starting a Career in Broadcasting** **403**

Preparing for Your Career 404
Job-Hunting Tools 405
    Résumés 405
Checklist: Assessing Your Career Potential **406**
    The Cover Letter 415
    Audition Tapes 416
Spotlight: Breaking into the Announcing Field **418**
    Answering Machine 422
    Mailing Address and Phone Number 422
Finding Job Openings 422
Applying for a Position as a Disc Jockey 425
Interviewing for a Job 426
Joining a Union 430
Going Where Your Career Takes You 430
Practice: Drafting Your Résumé **432**
Practice: Checking Out the Job Scene **432**

Chapter 14   **The International Phonetic Alphabet**   **433**

Vowel Sounds   435
     The Front Vowels   435
     The Back Vowels   437
     The Vowel Sounds "Er" and "Uh"   437
Diphthongs   438
Consonants   439
     Some Common Consonant Problems   440
     Syllabic Consonants   441
Accent Marks   441
Summary of the IPA   443
Practice: Phonetic Transcription   **447**

Chapter 15   **Foreign Pronunciation**   **448**

Guidelines for Announcers   449
Spanish Pronunciation   451
     Stress   451
     Spanish Vowels   452
     Spanish Diphthongs   452
     Spanish Consonants   453
Italian Pronunciation   458
     Stress   458
     Italian Vowels   458
     Italian Diphthongs   459
     Italian Consonants   461
French Pronunciation   465
     Stress   465
     French Oral Vowels   465
     French Nasal Vowels   466
     French Semivowels   469
     French Consonants   470
German Pronunciation   473
     German Vowels   474
     German Consonants   475
Other Languages   480
Practice: Pronouncing Spanish Words   **485**
Practice: Pronouncing Italian Words   **485**
Practice: Pronouncing French Words   **485**
Practice: Pronouncing German Words   **486**
Practice: Pronouncing Foreign Words   **486**

Appendix A Commercials and PSAs   492

Appendix B Pronunciation Guide   516

Appendix C Revised Job Titles from the   532
U.S. Department of Labor

Appendix D Nations and Citizens of the World   539

Appendix E Suggested Readings   550

Glossary   554

Index   572

Preface

Television and Radio Announcing emphasizes performance skills essential to successful communication through electronic media. Like its predecessors, the Sixth Edition is a comprehensive introduction to the diverse field of broadcast performance, and it covers many topics: analysis of copy and ways to convey the mood and message effectively; instructions for working with microphones, cameras, and studio equipment; guidelines for pronunciation, voice quality, and usage; strategies for interviewing and ad-lib announcing; techniques for specialized announcing; and career options and job seeking within the industry.

Those familiar with earlier editions of *Television and Radio Announcing* are aware that, rather than proposing a single theory of announcing, the book presents several theories of communication. Beyond this foundation of theoretical balance, however, the book takes a very practical approach to the announcing industry, offering throughout tips on the mechanics and techniques of announcing. Because of the flexibility of topical presentation, instructors and students can arrange the material in ways best suited to their needs.

New to This Edition

Chapter on Finding a Job

The Sixth Edition, which has been updated and reorganized, features an all-new chapter, Chapter 13, "Starting a Career in Broadcasting." This chapter shows how to prepare résumés, cover letters, and audition tapes; discusses resources and strategies for job seeking; provides information on performers' unions and relocating for that first job; and includes a self-assessment checklist that helps students determine their own goals and priorities.

New Sections and Organization

The early chapters again focus on aspects of good communication and performance; chapters on voice quality and American English usage follow; after a tour through the average studio's equipment, the book turns to particular announcing specialties, such as commercials, interviewing, radio and television news, and music announcing.

Chapter 1 has expanded material on ethics in broadcast announcing, including a self-evaluatory section on typical ethical dilemmas in the workplace.

In "Broadcast Equipment" (Chapter 6) and elsewhere, new material explains how announcers' jobs have been affected by advanced technology such as digital programming and playback systems, satellite uplinks, and portable cameras and recorders.

A new section in the chapter titled "Commercials and Public-Service Announcements" provides information on accents, dialects, and character voices; the chapter also includes many commercials for student practice.

Material on foreign pronunciation and the International Phonetic Alphabet (IPA), which had previously been integrated with material throughout the book, has been consolidated into two distinct chapters (Chapters 14 and 15) and placed at the end of the book for easy reference.

Finally, the appendixes offer brief guidebooks to pronunciation, official job titles, and nation/nationality terms.

Features on People and Issues

The reader will find a new series of "Spotlight" features on the people and the issues of broadcasting. In some "Spotlight" features, successful announcers share their stories about climbing the competitive career ladder and offer tips on how to sell a radio commercial or how to make sure your résumé gets noticed. Other "Spotlights" track the careers of national figures such as Oprah Winfrey, Harry Caray, and Arsenio Hall; explain the technology of the 1990s for studios and weather reporting; and address topics such as news production at National Public Radio and ethics in broadcast announcing.

Practical Application Guides

Checklists, which offer concise, point-by-point strategies for better broadcast performance, appear throughout the text; they outline tips for analyzing copy, preparing for an interview, getting ready to go on-air, and so on.

Practice sections at the end of chapters put theory into practice by directly applying chapter concepts in projects that the student can perform at home or in the dorm room. (Ideas for group projects are offered in the Instructor's Manual.) Practicing timing and style on audio tape, turning newspaper stories into news copy, and analyzing commercial copy are some of the ways students can begin immediately to apply announcing techniques.

Acknowledgments

In preparing the Sixth Edition of *Television and Radio Announcing*, I consulted with numerous professional broadcasters, colleagues, instructors, career guidance personnel, equipment manufacturers, and advertising agency personnel. To all who helped, I extend sincere thanks for your cooperation and suggestions and your interest in the project.

Among my colleagues who provided special help are Dr. Stanley T. Donner, professor emeritus of the University of Texas at Austin, and Ernie Kreiling, professor of telecommunications and syndicated television columnist. Of great help to me were several colleagues at San Francisco State University, including Chief Engineer Winston Tharp and Professors Herbert L. Zettl, Rick Houlberg, Herb Kaplan, Doug Carroll, and John Hewitt. I am very grateful to the late Professor Paul C. Smith, long-time audio coordinator for the Broadcast Communication Arts Department at San Francisco State. Paul is responsible for most of what I know about audio.

Manuscript for this revision was read and commented upon by professionals from radio and television stations and professors of broadcasting. Their comments, suggestions, and encouragement were extremely helpful to me. I am grateful to these individuals:

Rick Barnes, Southern Ohio College

Sharon Brody, WBCN-FM, Boston

Richard Carvell, Arkansas State University

David Eshelman, University of Arkansas

Douglas Ferguson, Bowling Green University

David Gravel, Miami-Dade Community College

Mark Suppelsa, KSTP-TV, Minneapolis
Donna Walcovy, Framingham State College
Kathleen Whitson, Brookhaven College
Ron Wilson, University of Cincinnati
Robert Wright, Pasadena City College

I also thank Chet Casselman, who once again allowed me to use his excellent suggestions for writing news copy. Peter Cleaveland of ABC Radio News and Wayne Freedman of CBS News shared with me their techniques for producing both radio and television news packages.

Sports directors and announcers who were generous with their help include Don Klein; Art Popham, independent sports producer, Tacoma, Washington; Lon Simmons and Bill King, radio play-by-play announcers for the Oakland A's; and Walt Brown, former play-by-play announcer for the University of Arizona.

Broadcast personnel from KRON-TV who made contributions include Darryl Compton, associate news director for operations; Bob McCarthy, traffic reporter; news anchors Bob Jiminez and Evan White; urban affairs specialist Belva Davis; and political analyst Rollin Post. At KGO-TV, I was helped by news anchors Cheryl Jennings and Don Sanchez. At WBZ-TV, I received assistance from television news publicist Andrew Radin, news anchor Jack Williams, talk show host Buzz Luttrell, and floor director Patsy Wheeler. Producer Andrew Findlayson, reporter Leslie Griffith, and engineering director Ed Cosci of KTVU were very helpful to me. My thanks to Terry Lowry, Eric Greene, Nerissa Azurin, and Cheryl Fong for posing for photos. Terry and Eric were very helpful in discussing their work with me.

Personnel of radio station KFRC were generous in updating my knowledge of popular music broadcasting. My appreciation is extended to chief engineer Philip Lerza, production director Albert Lord, and disc jockey Bobby Ocean. Fritz Kasten of Windham Hill Productions provided information on New Age Music. Dave Sholin, of "The Gavin Report" and formerly program and music director of KFRC, was especially helpful. KTID personnel who influenced this book include general manager Susan Bice, general sales manager Dick Blaustein, chief engineer Tom Howard, and program director Maria Lopez. At KCBS, help was provided by Al Hart, Valerie Coleman, Harvey Steiman, and Barbara Kaufman. Jim Eason of KGO Radio provided ideas on radio talk shows, and Rosie Allen and Ed Baxter contributed information on radio news performance.

Bill Kalbfeld, deputy director and managing editor of the Associated Press, provided detailed information about that organization's services.

Advertising agencies that supplied copy for the book include Allen and Dorward; Ammirati & Puris, Inc.; Ketchum Communications; Cunningham & Walsh, Inc.; Grey Advertising, Inc.; McDonald & Little Advertising; and Ingalls Associates, Inc.

Special assistance also was provided by the following individuals: Jim Deasy, Cindy Mills, Gerry Sher of KABL, Mike Ching of KGO-TV, Scott Singer, and Paul C. Mesches of Backer & Spielvogel Advertising. Gene Chaput of Young & Rubicam/San Francisco made available the outstanding commercial copy from the Lincoln-Mercury Division of the Ford Motor Company. Chuck Blore, of Chuck Blore & Don Richman, Inc., provided some of the most creative copy in the book. Additional thanks to Del Gundlach, creator of Cheep Laffs; freelance announcer Peter Scott; and Troy Alders of TLA Productions. Special thanks to Samantha Paris and Denny Delk, who provided valuable material on performance and job seeking.

S. W. H.

1

Broadcast Announcing

This book is about human communication, with a focus on the electronic media of radio and television. Its purpose is to help you improve your communication skills. Studying how to communicate can be of lasting benefit, whether or not you intend to become a broadcast performer. Confident, effective expression has always been an invaluable tool. The ever-increasing significance of electronic media means that competence in their use may become nearly as important as literacy was a century ago. This book is an aid toward developing media literacy.

In one sense, then, this book is about television and radio announcing. It discusses announcing as a profession, treats both the technical and the performance aspects of the field, covers correct usage of American and Canadian English, describes major areas of specialization within the field, provides broadcast copy for practicing performance skills, and offers job-seeking information and suggestions.

In a broader sense this book is about communication. If you apply yourself, you can look forward to noticeable improvement in your ability to (1) make pleasant speech sounds, (2) clearly articulate the sounds of the English language, (3) vary pitch and volume effectively, (4) pronounce words according to accepted standards, (5) select and use words, phrases, similes, and metaphors effectively, (6) express yourself confidently, (7) interpret copy, (8) speak ad-lib, and (9) communicate ideas lucidly, both orally and nonverbally.

The regular use of audio and video recorders can be of immense help to your development as a broadcast performer. After hearing and seeing yourself perform over a period of several weeks, you should begin to note and correct annoying mannerisms, speech malpractices, voice deficiencies, and personal idiosyncrasies that displease you. Ask others to comment on your performances, because you may fail to detect some of your shortcomings. As you make adjustments and improve, you will gain confidence; this, in turn, should guarantee further improvement.

Although you may have to rely on a department of communication arts, mass communication, or broadcasting for regular practice with a videocassette recorder, you can obtain an audio recorder of adequate quality at a reasonable cost. If you are serious about becoming an effective communicator, you should purchase and use an audio cassette recorder. Choose your recorder carefully, testing it before purchase under the conditions of intended use. For real improvement to take place, you must work with a recorder that does not mislead you. A poor-quality machine can distort your voice or create problems of excessive sibilance and popping. It may cause you to waste time working on nonexistent problems, while failing to alert you to problems that do exist.

You can also work on speech improvement without equipment of any kind. You speak with others for a considerable amount of time each day. Without sounding affected you can practice speaking clearly in ordinary conversations. Many college students tend to slur words as they speak. Make note of the number of times each day someone asks you to repeat what you have just said, often by uttering a monosyllabic "huh?" This is an indication that you are not speaking clearly enough for broadcast voice work.

For improvement of nonverbal communication skills, you can practice in front of a mirror. Note the degree—too pronounced, just right, or too weak—of your facial expressions and head movements. Watch for physical mannerisms that may be annoying or that interfere with clear communication. Through practice you can improve your performance abilities significantly, even without the use of recording equipment.

Closely related to performance ability is **ear training.** It is doubtful that anyone who does not *hear* well can speak well. Develop a critical ear as you listen to television and radio performers. Listen for vowel distortions, mispronunciations, poor interpretation, and other attributes of speech. Decide who impresses you as an outstanding user of spoken language. Identify those speakers who make you snap to attention, as well as those who cause you to tune out. Try to determine the positive and negative characteristics and qualities of speakers, and apply what you learn to your own work. (Speech diagnosis, speech problems, and suggestions for improvement are covered in Chapter 4, "Voice and Diction.")

The Broadcast Announcer

The broadcast announcer is essentially a product of the electronic age, but several related professions have existed for centuries or even millennia. Preliterate storytellers, troubadours, the singers of psalms, town criers, and early newspaper journalists were all forerunners of modern announcers. Each was charged with providing a service to a public. With some the emphasis was on the delivery of information; with others it was on entertainment. Announcers are like storytellers in that they speak directly to their audiences. Radio announcers also resemble writers for the print medium in that they often describe events their audiences have not seen. Television reporters and news anchors, on the other hand, frequently describe events that are simultaneously being viewed live or on tape. As millions around the world watched the 1969 moon landings, the presentation was enhanced by commentators such as Walter Cronkite, who presented facts and explained events that could not be shown. The 1989 prodemocracy demonstrations in Beijing's Tiananmen Square, as well as the 1989–1990 U.S. invasion of Panama, would have been incomprehensible without the comments and explanations of on-the-scene reporters. For **live coverage** of occurrences, there is no model from earlier times for the television announcer. When describing and commenting on taped events, television reporters and news anchors can be compared with the narrators of the newsreels that used to be shown in movie theaters.

Despite the similarities that announcing shares with earlier professions, there are some important differences. Both radio and television reach vast audiences, scattered over thousands of miles. In addition, radio and television are instantaneous media. Radio made it possible for the first time in history to describe to millions of people events as they were occurring. Because of the opportunities radio presented for instantaneous communication over great distances and the fact that radio is a "blind" medium, announcers became indispensable. Radio could not function without the services of people who provide direct oral communication by describing events, introducing entertainers, and reading the news. It was one thing for an oral historian to describe to the people of Macedonia the triumph of Alexander over the Persians months after the event; it was quite another for millions of Americans to see and hear live reports from Eastern Europe as one communist regime after another toppled in late 1989.

On radio the announcer is the clarifying link between the audience and what would otherwise be a jumble of sound, noise, and silence. On television the announcer is the presenter, the communicator, and the interpreter. Without such performers neither radio nor television as we know it would be possible. Obviously, their function is important, and their responsibility considerable. Because announcers usually make direct presentations to their audiences, they also embody economy. No other means of disseminating information is so direct and swift as the word spoken directly to the listener. Small wonder, then, that the radio or television announcer must be equipped with native talent and a broad educational background, and then must undergo intensive training and work diligently at practicing the skill.

Announcers are also referred to as personalities, disc jockeys, hosts, narrators, and reporters. In fact, some people who work in broadcasting do not like to be called announcers and refer to themselves as news anchors, reporters, commentators, sportscasters, or narrators. Specialization and codification have certainly made more precise nomenclature possible, and it should be used when clarity demands it. However, the term *announcer* will be used throughout this book for simplicity whenever the profession is being discussed in general terms.

An **announcer** is anyone who speaks to an audience over radio or television, through cable or other closed-circuit audio or video distribution, or by electronic amplification, as in an auditorium or theater. Singers, actors, and actresses are considered announcers only when they perform that specific function—in commercial presentations, for example. There are many announcing specializations, including the following:

Broadcast journalism
anchors, or news readers

field reporters—special assignment or general assignment

feature reporters (usually taking a humorous or satiric view of a current event)

analysts

commentators

weather reporters

consumer affairs reporters

environmental reporters

science reporters

entertainment reporters

farm news reporters

business news reporters

medical reporters (usually doctors)

traffic reporters

Sports
play-by-play announcers (radio and television)

play and game analysts (radio and television)

sports reporters (radio and television)

Music
radio disc jockeys (DJs or jocks)

music video jockeys

classical music announcers (for both live and recorded performances)

Public affairs
interviewers

panel moderators

Commercials
voice-over announcers (radio and television)

demonstration and commercial announcers (television)

Narration
readers of scripts for film and video documentaries or industrial or corporate presentations

Hosting special programs
hosts of talk shows, interview and phone-in (television and radio) and remote live shows (radio); of magazine shows such as "Evening Magazine" and "Entertainment Tonight" (television); of food, gardening, home repair, and similar specialty shows; of dance and popular music shows (television); of children's programs; and of game shows

introducers of feature films (occasionally also making pertinent comments about the film before or after commercial breaks)

There are also many single-subject specialists who contribute to talk shows or newscasts on topics such as gardening, cooking, exercise, consumerism, science, art, and health. These specialists often work with a station staff announcer who serves as host. (See Chapter 8,

Figure 1.2
One career option for broadcast announcers is radio disc jockey. Here DJ Rohn Steelman produces a taped program from compact discs. (Megan Reisbord, courtesy of KUHF-FM, University of Houston)

Figure 1.3
Sports announcing spans all forms of broadcast media. As shown here, announcers are often paired to give both action and interpretation: play-by-play announcer Don Klein and color announcer Don Heinrich broadcast a professional football game. (Courtesy of *49ers Report*)

"Interview and Talk Programs," for details.) During televised parades (Macy's Thanksgiving Day Parade, the Rose Parade), announcing teams identify the participants, explain float construction, and provide color.[1] As you can see, there are many announcing specializations, any one of which may be well-suited to your personality.

Employment as an Announcer

According to the U.S. Department of Labor, approximately fifty-five thousand men and women are currently employed as broadcast announcers. Most are full-time employees of radio and television stations, cable operations, and broadcast networks. Some are full- or part-time freelance announcers who perform as narrators for both broadcast and nonbroadcast documentaries and instructional tapes. Many freelance announcers work only sporadically; therefore, not

[1]**Color** was coined for radio to mean the description of things of interest that could not be seen by the listeners; today, in both radio and television usage, color announcers are those who provide stories of human interest, as well as anecdotes of an informative, amusing, or offbeat nature.

more than sixty thousand persons earn their full income as radio and television announcers.

The rapid expansion of cable television services has created additional openings for announcers. The applicant who can offer more than announcing skills has a better chance for initial employment and subsequent career advancement than does a narrowly trained specialist. Also, between 80 and 85 percent of all broadcast announcers work for radio stations and networks. Your chances for success as an announcer, then, will be enhanced if you prepare chiefly for radio and if you bring to your job the ability to write and produce local commercials, prepare weather reports, write or rewrite the news, or program the computer at an automated station.

A growing number of men and women work, not in broadcast stations, but in **industrial media,** or **corporate media.** Audiotapes, videocassettes, and slide-tape presentations are made for a variety of purposes, including employee training, introduction of new products, dissemination of information to distant branches, and in-house communication. The term *industrial media* is a loose one, for it applies to the media operations of hospitals, government agencies, schools, prisons, and the military, as well as those of businesses. Few training or media departments can afford the services of a full-time announcer or narrator, so, if such work appeals to you, you should prepare for media writing and producing as well as announcing. One or more courses in **message design and testing** would serve you well. (Chapter 13, "Starting a Career in Broadcasting," provides specific information on job seeking.)

The following chapters describe the working conditions and the kinds of abilities you will need to succeed in each of the major announcing specializations. Most students of announcing are interested in one of three attractive job possibilities: news reporting, sports reporting (including play-by-play announcing), or music announcing. Other students show enthusiasm for commercial delivery or for interviewing. It is important for you to resist the temptation to concentrate on one kind of announcing. It is true that most radio stations follow a single format—all music, all talk, or all news—but the chances are that you will not find your first job at a station that features the format of your choice. You should, therefore, work on every facet of announcing, while emphasizing the area in which you hope to specialize.

Television stations provide multiprogram service, but aside from daily newscasts and interview-talk shows, there are relatively few openings for announcers. Far more employees work in sales, traffic, and engineering than in announcing. Local television stations do produce commercials, and they also run commercials produced by local and regional production companies. This means that even the smallest community with a commercial television station may offer some work for announcers. If this field interests you, you can get specific information about how announcers are hired by calling the production unit of the sales or promotion department of a station. If a talent agency is involved in local production, you should look under "Agencies, Theatrical" in the classified section of the telephone directories for medium to large cities in your area. A call to such an agency will provide you with information about how to present yourself for possible employment.

Education and Training

The subject matter of radio is not *radio,* nor is *television* the content of television. Both of these influential media devote their broadcast hours to news, weather, music, sports, and drama. During your time in college you should not limit yourself to the study of broadcasting. Although the ability to talk knowledgeably about broadcasting, to operate standard broadcast equipment, and to interpret skillfully a script prepared by someone else is necessary for employment, you must be able to offer more to a station and the public. Radio and

Figure 1.4
As the media industries expand, more jobs are created for announcers and narrators in cable and industrial production, local news programs, and specialized formats addressing environmental, political, and consumer issues. (Ken Robert Buck, The Picture Cube)

television have little room for narrowly educated announcers. For one thing, the influence—for good or ill—of radio and television broadcasters is immense and must not be underestimated. Also, the broadcast announcer is being evaluated by increasingly sophisticated listeners. Americans are better informed today than ever before. Informational media are reaching millions of people with more and more messages of critical importance to their future. A television generation has grown up to be quick to spot shallowness or ignorance.

The dramatic explosion of knowledge in the past several years will make announcers who do not grow with the times inadequate for the 1990s. The makers of dictionaries have been adding new entries to their editions at an unprecedented pace; each represents to an announcer not only a new word to pronounce but a new concept, a new technological breakthrough, a newly perceived human condition, or a new phenomenon to know about. Moreover, as radio stations have developed special-appeal formats, they have built up more homogeneous audiences who know and care about the program material being offered. Therefore, the majority of listeners to a single-format radio station are quick to detect and be turned off by an announcer's lack of knowledge.

Finally, on both radio and television the number of broadcast hours devoted to unscripted presentations has increased considerably. Television program hosts, disc jockeys, interviewers, announcers covering sports and special events, and talk show personalities use written material only occasionally; most of the time they are on their own. Radio and television field reporters almost never work from a script.

With such independence comes the need to have much information at hand to share with the audience.

What should you study if you intend to become an announcer? It is not possible to rank courses in any order of importance, because individual employers have their own ideas about what is the best preparation for the position of announcer. Above all, they look for well-educated persons who possess certain basic skills: good writing ability, outstanding proficiency in spoken communication, computational skills (basic math), and critical thinking. They also look for people who are hard-working, self-motivated, and pleasant to be around.

In studying to be a broadcast announcer, obviously you should pursue *subjects that will prepare you for your first announcing job*. You also should select *courses that will qualify you for one or more specializations* beyond straight announcing. Finally, you must obtain *a broad background in the liberal arts and sciences*; if you are serious about an announcing career, your education must have breadth. The courses mentioned in the checklist are arranged under these three categories. You will probably not be able to study all the suggested areas, but you should at least discuss them with an advisor.

Most departments of music offer a course in lyric diction, which teaches principles of pronunciation of French, German, Italian, and

Figure 1.6
Announcers of the 1990s must be trained not only in a wide range of writing, editing, and performing duties but also in operating broadcast equipment. Work at college stations and in local internships is the best way to prepare for success in a first job. Here TV reporter Caroline Chang edits her stories and then transmits them from a bureau to her station in Wilmington, North Carolina. (© 1989 Michael Edrington/The Image Works)

Checklist: Taking Courses to Build Your Career

1. Take courses that give you training in radio and television announcing by focusing on the following subjects: interpretation, articulation, phonation, phonetic transcription, microphone use, camera presence, ad-libbing, script reading, adapting one's personality to the broadcast media, foreign language pronunciation, control room operations, small-format video production and editing, and writing for radio and television.

2. Choose courses to prepare you for specialized duties associated with the following jobs:
   - broadcast journalism—courses in journalism, international relations, political science, economics, history, and geography
   - broadcast sales and advertising—courses in business, marketing, accounting, sales techniques, sales promotion, and audience research
   - sports and play-by-play announcing—courses in the history of sports, sports officiating, and the sociology of sport
   - weather reporting—courses in meteorology, weather analysis, weather forecasting, and geography

3. Take as many courses as you can to further your general education, especially courses that examine the following topics:
   - social, ethical, aesthetic, and historical perspectives on broadcast communication
   - the arts—music, theater, literature, or the graphic and plastic arts
   - social and behavioral sciences—psychology, sociology, urban studies, and ethnic studies
   - quantitative reasoning—essentially mathematics and computational methods
   - critical thinking—the study of skills crucial to clear and constructive thought
   - media law and regulation
   - writing, writing, writing

occasionally Russian or Spanish. Courses in control room operations should include practice in manipulating audio consoles, tape cartridge machines, compact disc players, reel-to-reel tape recorders, and turntables. You need a course in video production and editing because some television stations expect field reporters to be able to tape and edit their own news stories. News anchors must learn to write news-copy. Most stations in medium to small markets expect announcers to write commercial copy and station promotional pieces as well.

Many of the general courses you will take will be required for a liberal arts degree from your college or university. Note that it is not enough to study and practice writing for the media. Departments of English offer courses in expository writing, essay writing, creative writing, and dramatic writing. It is impossible to get too much writing experience.

One area of preparation is important enough to warrant separate mention. Broadcast stations rely heavily on the use of computerized information systems. Computers have been used at automated stations for years, and there are currently few areas of broadcast operations that do not make some use of them. Computers are central to most videotape editing systems, character generators, word processors, graphics systems, scheduling and billing systems, and data-retrieval systems. For most of these applications a specialized language—such as FORTRAN or COBOL—is not required. Some familiarity with information systems is highly desirable, and the ability to type well is mandatory. A course in information science should be selected with care, for most such courses are not geared toward applications common in the broadcasting industry. For most students of announc-ing, the ability to use Macintosh and IBM-compatible computers is sufficient.

You must evaluate these suggestions in the light of your own aptitudes, interests, and career plans. Any college counselor can help you determine the appropriateness of the courses available to you. The important point is that only you can apply your growing knowl-edge to your announcing practice.

The typical community college requires 60 semester hours for an associate in arts or associate in science degree; the typical four-year college or university requires about 125 semester hours for a bachelor's degree. Modern departments of broadcasting invariably require courses in the history of broadcasting, writing for the electronic media, broadcast research, and communication theory. Whether you are en-rolled in a two- or four-year program, it is unlikely that you will be offered more than 6 semester hours of performance courses. You should, therefore, look for performance opportunities wherever they present themselves—on a campus radio station, in television directing and producing classes, or on public access cable stations. Remember, though, that the majority of your class hours will be spent in non-performance courses, all of which are important to your development as a well-rounded broadcaster.

Clearly, announcing encompasses a wide range of activities. Most modern liberal arts colleges and their broadcasting departments are well equipped to help you begin the process of becoming a competent and versatile communicator, which is what you must be if you expect to be able to face challenges such as these:

- You are a staff announcer, and you are to read a commercial for a local restaurant featuring international cuisine. You must pronounce correctly *vichyssoise, coq au vin, paella, saltimbocca alla Romana,* and *hasenpfeffer*.
- You are a staff announcer, and you must read news headlines containing the place names *Sault Sainte Marie, Schleswig-Holstein, Santa Rosa de Copán, São Paulo,* and *Leicester*.
- You are the announcer on a classical music program, and you need to know the meaning and correct pronunciation of *scherzo, andante cantabile, Die Götterdämmerung,* and *L'Après-midi d'un faune*.
- You are a commercial announcer, and the copy for a pharmaceutical company demands that you correctly pronounce *hexachlorophene, prophylaxis,* and *epidermis*.
- You are a play analyst on a sports broadcast, and you need to obtain extensive historical and statistical information on football in order to fill the inevitable moments of inactivity.
- You are the play-by-play announcer for a semipro baseball game, and you must pronounce the names *Martineau, Buchignani, Yturri, Sockolow, Watanabe, Engebrecht,* and *MacLeod*.
- You have been assigned to interview a Nobel Prize winner in astrophysics, and you need to obtain basic information about the field as well as biographical data on the winner.
- You are narrating a documentary, and you must analyze the intent and content of the program to determine the mood, rhythm, structure, and interrelationship of sound, picture, and script.
- You are covering a crowd scene that could deteriorate into a riot. You are expected to assess responsibly the human dynamics of the

scene, while carefully avoiding comments or activities that could precipitate violence in this already dangerous situation.

- You are a radio disc jockey, and you are on duty when word is received of the unexpected death of a great American (a politician, an entertainer, or a scientist). Until the news department can take over, you must ad-lib appropriately.

It is obvious that no one type of course will completely educate you as an announcer.

The Announcer's Responsibility

Before committing yourself to a career as a broadcast announcer, you should recognize that, along with the undeniable privileges and rewards that accrue to people working in this field, there are several areas of responsibility as well. First, and most obvious, there is the obligation any performer owes to an audience—to be informative, objective, fair, accurate, and entertaining. Not everyone who goes before an audience deserves respect. Announcers who are sloppy, unprepared, given to poor usage, or just plain boring may get what they deserve—two-weeks notice. There are also announcers who work hard, possess outstanding skill, and never want for work but, at the same time, pollute the public air. These people make outrageous (and unsubstantiated) statements in order to gain attention, deliberately provoke guests into extreme behavior, sensationalize or slant the news, seriously misrepresent shoddy products, endorse questionable products or services, circulate unfounded rumors, or fan the flames of prejudice by displaying misguided fervor. In our free society such announcers are protected by the First Amendment to the Constitution; the only protection the audience has resides in the integrity of each individual announcer. Most departments of broadcasting offer courses in ethics and social responsibility. A grounding in this subject, together with serious consideration of the effects of mass communication, should be seen as vitally important to your development as a public communicator.

Another area of responsibility for announcers is that of **emergency notification.** When floods, hurricanes, tornadoes, and other natural disasters occur, broadcast announcers are frequently in a position to

Spotlight: Broadcast Ethics and the Announcer's Responsibility

More than textbook theory, ethics comprises a broad range of decisions you will have to make every day on the job. Here are some hypothetical situations in which you might find yourself as a radio or television announcer.

- You are a disc jockey on a free-form radio station where you are allowed to choose some of the music you play on the air. An acquaintance offers you $1,000 to play a record he has produced. Because you think the music is quite good, you accept the $1,000 and play the record at least once during each of your air shifts. You justify your action on the grounds that you would have played the piece even without the gift of money.
- You are a television reporter, and you have been told by a reliable witness that some children at the scene of a disturbance threw rocks at a police car before you arrived with your field camera. You pay the children $5 each to throw rocks again, while you make a videotape of the action. Your position is that you taped an event that actually occurred, and you brought back to the station some high-impact footage for the nightly news.
- You are a talk show host on an early evening radio show. Your guest is an outspoken advocate of free speech on radio, arguing that there should be no language restrictions whatsoever. During your interview, you speak a number of words that are generally considered obscene in order to determine whether your guest is sincere in her (to you) extremist position. You maintain that only by saying the words on the air can you test her conviction.
- Your morning drive-time partner takes a two-week vacation. In order to stir up a little audience interest, you announce that he has been kidnapped. For most of the two-week period, you broadcast regular "flashes" on the status

of the "event." Audience ratings skyrocket as you report on phony ransom notes, police chases, and so on. You feel that your reputation as an on-air jokester justifies this hoax.
- You are a host on a television talk show, and you are insulted and angered by the behavior of a hostile guest. The next day you launch an attack on that person, questioning her integrity, honesty, and character. The reactions of your viewers are very supportive of your attack, and you feel that, having had your revenge, you can let the matter drop.
- As the business reporter for an all-talk radio station, you decide to mention with favor a company in which you own stock. The interest you generate causes listeners to invest in the company, and the value of its stock rises. You feel justified in the favorable comments you made, because you did not receive payment from the company in return.
- As a television reporter, you are given some highly sensitive information about the misdeeds of an important local politician. You report the details as accurately as you can, but in order to protect the person who gave you the information, you invent a fictitious informant.

What all of the scenarios described above have in common is that each violates a law, a regulation, or a provision of a professional code of ethics.

As a broadcast announcer, your words reach and influence vast numbers of people; because of the potential for wrongdoing, your freedoms to speak and act are restricted. Freedom of speech, as guaranteed by the First Amendment to the Constitution, does *not* always apply to those using the public airwaves. Areas of restriction are obscenity, fraud, **defamation** (making libelous statements), bribery (**payola**), slanted news, invasion of privacy, and conflict of interest.

Generally speaking, laws regarding obscenity, indecency, and profanity are governed by the United States Criminal Code. **Obscenity** is loosely defined as words or actions "offensive to accepted standards of decency or modesty." **Indecency** refers to that which is "offensive to public moral values." **Profanity** is defined as "abusive, vulgar, or irreverent language."

Payola and **drugola** refer to the acceptance of money, drugs, or other inducements in return for the playing of specific recordings on the air; **plugola** refers to the favorable mention of a product, company, or service in which the announcer has a financial interest. The acceptance of any sort of bribe in return for favors is prohibited by the FCC.

The *Code of Broadcast News Ethics* of the Radio and Television News Directors Association (RTNDA) specifically labels as irresponsible and unethical such practices as staging news events, misrepresenting the source of a news story, sensationalizing the news, and invading the privacy of those with whom the news deals.

The FCC is the chief regulatory agency for broadcasters. Its fairness doctrine requires that persons who are attacked on the air be furnished with a transcript of the attack within a specified period of time and that provision be made for the attacked person to reply on the air.

The radio and television codes of the National Association of Broadcasters were invalidated by a 1985 court decision, but nearly all broadcasters continue to use the ethics portions of those codes as models for professional and ethical behavior. Among the provisions still widely honored are that prohibiting the broadcasting of any matter that is deemed fraudulent and that requiring the clear identification of sponsored or paid-for material.

Libelous statements (defamation) are not illegal, but an announcer can be sued by persons who claim they were defamed. Laws regarding libel vary from state to state, but in no state is an announcer given total freedom to make accusations against others.

As an announcer, you must be thoroughly aware of the realities of broadcast law and ethics; only by having complete knowledge of the applicable laws and codes can you routinely avoid violating them in your behavior or words.

All announcers exert some influence over the stories and news they present, but talk show hosts are notorious for their strong political views. Boston radio host Charles Laquidara decided to use his show as a forum for a cause in which he strongly believed—using consumer boycotts to protest apartheid in South Africa. The photo on the left shows the onslaught of supportive letters he received from listeners; the photo on the right shows Boston's mayor acknowledging the impact of Laquidara's efforts by launching a citywide boycott of the protested company. (Left: Peter Southwick, Stock Boston; right: courtesy Charles Laquidara)

 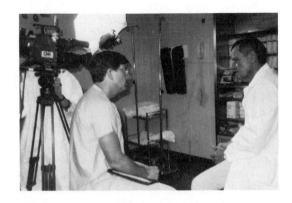

Figure 1.7

Any announcer will be confronted daily with choices concerning news coverage and audience welfare, but some deliberately choose positions of responsibility in specialized reporting of (left) consumer troubleshooting or (right) science and health affairs. (Courtesy of Turner Broadcasting System)

save lives through early warnings. The U.S. government has established an **emergency broadcast system (EBS)** that relies on broadcast licensees to disseminate disaster information. It is imperative that all broadcast announcers study the disaster manual (found at all stations) and be prepared to act swiftly and appropriately in an emergency.

Finally, the area of social responsibility goes beyond the normal responsibility of performer to audience. Nearly all announcers, whether they like it or not, have influence as a result of their visibility and prestige. Years ago, Paul F. Lazarsfeld and Robert K. Merton perceived and described what they called the **status-conferral function** of the mass media. In essence, they said, the general public attaches prestige to people who appear in the mass media, and the average person is more readily influenced by prestigious people than by equals. The public's reasoning is circular: "If you really matter, you will be at the focus of attention; and, if you *are* at the focus of mass attention, then you must really matter." A newscaster, then, is not simply an efficient conveyor of information; as a radio or television star, he or she is trusted and believed as a qualified authority. Even the entertainment show announcer or the disc jockey has automatic, though sometimes unwarranted, authority. As an announcer in any of the broadcast media, you should be aware of your status and measure up to it.

Even those announcers who do have a sense of social commitment are not always in a position to accomplish very much. Nevertheless, you should be aware of the opportunities you may have to either enlighten or confuse the public. As a nation we have been slow to perceive and attack the serious problems of urban deterioration, increasing crime, environmental pollution, racial inequities, world hunger, poverty and homelessness, AIDS, the rise of antidemocratic action groups, and increased use of drugs. If you are committed to using the mass media to make ours a better society, you are already socially responsible and potentially important as the kind of communicator demanded by our times.

Practice: Interviewing a Successful Announcer

Contact a professional announcer whose work you admire, and ask that person for an interview. Questions you might ask include these:

Where did you study for your career?

What was your major in college?

What subjects that you studied have you found to be especially useful to you?

What subjects do you wish you had studied?

How did you get your first job in broadcasting?

Do *not* ask overly personal questions, such as "How much money do you make?" Write up the results of your interview to share with class members. Be sure to follow up by sending a thank-you note to the announcer.

Practice: Establishing Ethical Guidelines

Find copies of various codes that pertain to announcers, such as the Radio and Television News Directors (RTNDA) code, the radio and television codes of the National Association of Broadcasters (NAB), and the ethics code of the American Society of Newspaper Editors (ASNE). Prepare for yourself a list of the most important canons of professional ethics.

2

The Announcer
as Communicator

Your goal as a radio or television announcer is to communicate ideas or feelings effectively to other human beings. This brief and rather obvious statement is the key to success in announcing. Understanding that effective communication ought to be your goal is by no means the same thing as achieving it. For some, the ability to communicate comes easily and is readily adapted to radio or television performing. For most, however, difficulty in being effective, economical, and accurate even in daily conversation is a constant reminder that much work lies ahead. This chapter discusses the communicative process, offers specific advice on interpreting copy, and briefly considers ad-lib announcing.

Unfortunately, some students of announcing feel that they have succeeded when they have developed the ability to "sound like an announcer." American broadcasting has been served by several generations of announcers, and early in the development of radio a particular style of delivery evolved. In its most exaggerated form, this style is represented by Gary Owens on the 1960s television program "Laugh In" and Ted Baxter on "The Mary Tyler Moore Show." If these programs are being aired as reruns in your area, you should watch them, note the delivery of these two performers—and then make certain to avoid sounding like either! Both are *acting* the part of the old-time stereotypical announcer. By contrast, today's stereotypical announcers are not guilty of such obvious affectation; they are usually soft-spoken and are accepted by most listeners as sounding "the way radio announcers are supposed to sound." Actually, they have put aside their individual personalities and developed the ability to act the part of an announcer. They have become capable imitators.

Good announcing is not imitation; it is *communication*. Top announcers retain their individuality as they concentrate on getting their

Figure 2.1
Effective communication is key to the career longevity of well-known announcers, and it involves building a rapport with listening or viewing audiences based on clarity and trust. Jim MacNeil and Robert Lehrer, shown here, have drawn nightly audiences to the MacNeil/Lehrer News Hour for years. (Courtesy of MacNeil Lehrer Productions)

messages across. True communication as an announcer beings when you learn who you are, reflect yourself in your delivery, and realize that you are speaking to individuals, not to a crowd. Merely developing your vocal apparatus or expanding your vocabulary cannot guarantee that you will become an effective communicator. You must try to be constantly aware of two other aspects of successful oral communication: reflecting your personality, and communicating the ideas or feelings inherent in the words you are speaking.

Announcers must be skilled in several modes: ad-libbing, ad-libbing from notes, script reading with preparation, and script reading from **cold copy** (material not seen by the announcer until the very moment of delivery). Typical ad-lib announcers are radio and television field reporters, weather reporters, sports play-by-play announcers, radio disc jockeys, television talk show hosts, and radio phone-in talk show hosts. News anchors often see some of their copy for the first time when it appears on a prompting device. At the other extreme are documentary narrators and readers of recorded commercials; hours—sometimes days—are required for them to achieve the proficiency demanded by a producer. You should practice all four modes until you feel comfortable with them.

One of your most challenging tasks as an announcer is to read in an effective manner copy written by someone else. You are the middle link in a chain that begins with a writer and ends with a listener or viewer. It is your responsibility to ensure that the writer's ideas are faithfully transmitted to the minds of your listeners.

Principles of Effective Communication

Copy begins not as a script but as ideas in the mind of a writer: an advertising agency copywriter, a newswriter, a documentary script-writer, a station sales representative, or some other specialist in broadcast writing. Having conceived the idea, the writer next casts it into the words (and, in television, the pictures) that will best communicate the thoughts. The ability to select fresh, meaningful words and arrange them well is the art of broadcast writing; the ability to communicate these words successfully is the art of announcing.

Radio and television are media of oral communication. As a professional announcer, you can make messages more effective than they would be if communicated directly in writing. Of course, you can only do this if you do not misread or mispronounce words. Beyond this basic level you need to convey an emotion appropriate to your copy—enthusiasm, seriousness, or humor—and thereby provide variety and interpretation for your listeners. On yet another level you

Figure 2.2
Good oral communication requires much more than merely reading a script; one must give tone and interpretation to the words on the printed page. This announcer speaks not just with his voice but with his entire body; the result is an animated, conversational style that sounds like one person talking with another. Note also his use of two tools of the trade: a clean script and an open dictionary. (Gale Zucker, Stock Boston)

can demonstrate the relative importance of the various parts of the message, thereby enhancing its meaning. In short, you present the material in its most persuasive and readily understandable form.

Oral communication, however, can be ineffective when radio or television announcers fail to present their material clearly and convincingly. Too many professional announcers merely read words and consider themselves successful if they avoid stumbling over them. A word is a symbol of an idea; if the idea is not clear in your own mind, or if you lack the ability to transmit it compellingly through your spoken words, you reduce your chances of communicating it to your listeners. Of course, words read by even a poor interpreter convey some of the ideas from writer to listener, but this is not good announcing. Announcers are paid to be effective, and this means they must develop oral reading skills that are far more than adequate.

Make it a point to listen to as many news reporters and popular music announcers as you can, and study their deliveries. Listen especially to those you generally avoid. Decide for yourself who among them are true communicators. In all probability you will discover that you have unconsciously formed the habit of tuning in the announcers who communicate best and tuning out those who communicate least. Laypersons usually do not consciously assess the communicative ability of a given announcer, but they are nonetheless affected by it. They find themselves listening to those who are best able to help them receive and assimilate ideas. At the same time, however, they are being swayed, perhaps without realizing it, to causes, concepts, and products.

Radio announcers who believe that only their voices are important may attempt to project vitality without the accompaniment of body motion. Such playacting is not likely to be convincing. Energy is easy to simulate, but unless the speaker is genuinely motivated by the content of the message, it usually comes across as phony. Uncalled-for enthusiasm hinders communication. To avoid it you should announce for radio as though your listener were in the booth with you. Use your face, hands, and body just as you do in ordinary conversation. Integrating all the tools of communication will help to clarify and intensify the message, despite the fact that your listener cannot see you. Appropriate gesturing for both radio and television is marked by two considerations: honest motivation, and harmony with the importance and the mood of the ideas being expressed. Oversized grins, frowns, and grimaces and sweeping arm movements are seldom appropriate.

If merely reading the words constitutes a low level of oral communication, what is good oral communication? *Good communication occurs when the listener or viewer receives an undistorted and meaningful impression of the ideas of the writer or ad-lib speaker, with proper emphasis given to each of the parts that make up the whole.*

Interpreting Copy

Good interpretation requires a thorough comprehension of the material to be presented. Just as a musician or conductor must understand the intention of the composer, so must an announcer understand the intention of the writer. With the exceptions of such ad-lib announcers as disc jockeys, sports play-by-play announcers, and field reporters, announcers are interpretive artists. Even news anchors who write their own material are still interpreting copy. Those who read scripts serve as a link between creator (writer) and audience. However beautiful your voice and however rapidly and unfalteringly you read copy, you are not truly a good announcer unless you are able to communicate the ideas and values as the writer originally conceived them.

Truly comprehending the intention of the writer is a more difficult and demanding task than is commonly thought. News anchors and disc jockeys very often read their copy without preparation, because the pressures of their work simply do not allow time. But it is no exaggeration to say that their skill in interpreting copy quickly is possible only because, at some time in their careers, they engaged in deliberate and methodical practice. You can establish a solid foundation for the analysis of copy while you still have the luxury of time.

Stanley T. Donner, professor emeritus of the University of Texas at Austin, has prepared an excellent approach to analyzing copy. He suggests that you work on the points in the checklist on the next page when approaching new copy. If you use this checklist for serious analysis of various types of copy, you will develop the ability to size up new copy almost unconsciously. Since this list of considerations suggests much more than might seem obvious at first reading, the following sections will elaborate on Donner's twelve points.

Getting the General Meaning

One problem confronting anyone who spends time and effort preparing for oral delivery of copy is that too much concentration on pro-

---

Checklist: Analyzing Broadcast Copy

1. Read the copy twice to get the general meaning.
2. State the specific purpose of the copy in one brief sentence.
3. Identify the general mood of the copy.
4. Locate any places where the mood changes.
5. Determine the parts of the copy and its structure.
6. Analyze the punctuation to see what help it provides.
7. Note any words you do not fully understand or cannot pronounce.
8. Read the copy aloud.
9. Think about how you can convey an interest in the subject matter of the copy.
10. Visualize your listener. Establish a mental rapport, and imagine you are actually talking to him or her.
11. Find out if there is anything you should know about the origin and background of the copy.
12. Decide whether any characterization is needed.

---

nunciation or timing may obscure the overall meaning and purpose. You should form an impression of the whole piece by silently reading through it at least twice before undertaking any of the more detailed work of preparation. Remember, though, that after these silent readings to determine meaning and purpose, *all subsequent readings should be performed aloud.*

Stating the Specific Purpose

This is the most important item on Donner's checklist. You must decide on the major objective of the copy. Just as it is pointless to begin a trip to some undetermined destination, it is foolish to begin interpreting copy without first knowing its goal. Your job as an oral interpreter is to choose appropriate *means,* but it is first necessary to determine appropriate *ends.* The interpretations of two identical sentences will differ if the sentences are used in different contexts or for different purposes. Similarly, pieces of broadcast copy that seem superficially to call for the same delivery may actually require quite different interpretations. Raising questions about the purpose of the copy will help you determine the most appropriate delivery.

For example, read this commercial and then decide on its specific purpose:

ANNCR: See the all-new Ferrari, on display at the
           Foreign Motorcar Centre, 16th and Grand. You'll
           love its European styling and out-of-this-world
           performance. If you love high-tech automobiles,
           come meet the Ferrari!

If you decided that the purpose of this copy is to awaken curiosity and interest in the new Ferrari, you analyzed it correctly. If you decided that its purpose is to promote the name and address of the sponsor, you were incorrect. The phrase "at the Foreign Motorcar Centre, 16th and Grand" is subordinate to the idea of "the all-new Ferrari." Though it is unusual to subordinate the name and address of the sponsor, in this instance the copy clearly indicates that it should be done. Perhaps the sponsor has the only foreign car agency in town, or perhaps sponsor identification has been built up over a long period of time by other commercials. The moral here is that it is unsafe to take for granted that the name and address of the sponsor is the phrase to be stressed in all commercial copy.

Now read this commercial for the same sponsor:

ANNCR: See the all-new Ferrari at the Foreign Motorcar
           Centre. Serving you since 1933, we offer total
           service and a complete shop and parts department.
           That's the Foreign Motorcar Centre, 16th and
           Grand, downtown River City!

Here phrases from the first commercial have been used, but it is obvious that in this version the name of the automobile is subordinate to the name of the sponsor. If in analyzing this copy you decided that its chief purpose is to impress on the audience the dealer's name, address, and reliability, you were correct.

Identifying the General Mood

Having determined the purpose of the copy, you next identify its mood, which will influence your attitude as you read it. To some extent the number of words in the copy limits the degree to which you can control the mood, especially in commercial copy. The commercials for the Foreign Motorcar Centre require the announcer to read about 36 words in 10 seconds, or 210 words a minute, which is just about as rapidly as one should read aloud. The number of words in this copy determines that the announcer's delivery will approach that of a **pitch-man.** Excluding commercial announcements, which are written with inflexible time limits in mind, copy for radio and television may be shortened or lengthened to allow for a rate of delivery geared to a particular mood. For still other kinds of announcements—the introduction of a musical composition, for example—the length of time taken is not a particularly important consideration, although split-second timing frequently is crucial (as pointed out in Chapter 11 on the disc jockey). In sportscasting, the mood is set by the action of the game.

As indicated earlier, the mood of a piece of copy will determine your attitude. Attitudes are described by adjectives such as ironic, jocular, serious, somber, urgent, sad, light, gloomy, and sarcastic. Read the following news items, and jot down an adjective characterizing an appropriate attitude for each one.

1. (CHICAGO) THE NATIONAL WEATHER SERVICE HAS ISSUED
   TORNADO WARNINGS FOR THE ENTIRE UPPER MIDWEST.
   OFFICIALS SAY THAT CONDITIONS ARE SIMILAR TO
   THOSE THAT ACCOMPANIED THE DEVASTATING STORMS OF
   MAY FIFTEENTH, IN WHICH SEVENTY-ONE PERSONS WERE
   KILLED. SMALL-CRAFT WARNINGS HAVE BEEN RAISED FOR
   LAKE MICHIGAN, AND BOAT OWNERS ARE URGED TO
   SECURE THEIR CRAFTS AGAINST THE EXPECTED HEAVY
   WEATHER.

2. (MIAMI) A COAST GUARD OFFICIAL REPORT SAYS THAT A
   CIVILIAN PILOT HAS REPORTED SIGHTING TWO MORE OIL

SLICKS OFF THE COAST OF FLORIDA NEAR FORT
LAUDERDALE AND WEST PALM BEACH. CLEAN-UP CREWS
ARE STILL AT WORK ON A MASSIVE OIL SLICK THAT
SPREAD ONE WEEK AGO.

3. (WASHINGTON) THE FEDERAL ELECTION COMMISSION HAS
VOTED TO HALT SECRET CONGRESSIONAL ''SLUSH
FUNDS,'' A PRACTICE IN WHICH LAWMAKERS USE
PRIVATE DONATIONS TO PAY PERSONAL AND OFFICE
EXPENSES. THE COMMISSION UNANIMOUSLY VOTED TO
REQUIRE THAT ALL SUCH FUNDS BE PUBLICLY REPORTED.
THE DECISION REQUIRES THAT THE FUNDS COUNT TOWARD
LAWMAKERS' CAMPAIGN SPENDING LIMIT.

4. A BULLETIN HAS JUST BEEN HANDED ME THAT SAYS A
TORNADO HAS BEEN SPOTTED ABOUT TWENTY MILES FROM
DULUTH. THERE ARE NO ADDITIONAL DETAILS AT THIS
TIME.

5. (WASHINGTON) THE GOVERNMENT SAID YESTERDAY THAT
PEOPLE ARE TAKING BETTER CARE OF THEMSELVES NOW
THAN EVER BEFORE, AND THAT THE PROBLEM NOW IS TO
FIND WAYS TO CARE FOR THE LARGE NUMBER OF PEOPLE
WHO LIVE LONGER AS A RESULT. THE REPORT SAID THAT
SOCIETY'S SUCCESS IN KEEPING PEOPLE HEALTHY AND
HELPING THEM TO LIVE LONGER IS PLACING GREAT
STRESS ON THE NATION'S HEALTH CARE RESOURCES.

6. (MONTPELIER, VERMONT) IT TOOK EIGHTEEN DAYS, BUT
SEARCHERS HAVE FINALLY TRANQUILIZED ONE OF THE
BABY ELEPHANTS LOST IN THE WOODS. THE MANAGER OF

Figure 2.3
No news announcer should go on the air without studying the script to establish the pace, tone, and mood of each item. Bessie Moses, the radio announcer shown here, must do more than analyze the news—she also translates it into the Inupiaq Eskimo language. (Courtesy of KICY, Nome, Alaska)

THE CARSON AND BARNES CIRCUS SAYS THE ELEPHANT WILL BE TIED TO A TREE IN AN EFFORT TO LURE THE OTHER OUT OF HIDING.

Here are appropriate attitudes for these stories: (1) urgent, (2) angry, (3) slight note of victory—winning one for the public, (4) very urgent, (5) straightforward, (6) light, slightly humorous. The mood of each item, except the tornado reports, is to be conveyed with only a hint of the emotion mentioned.

Locating Changes in Mood

A long piece of copy may contain several moods, although the dominant one may remain constant. In commercial copy a familiar construction calls for a change from gloom to joy as the announcer first describes a common problem and then tells the listener how Product X can solve it. Spot such changes as you give your copy a preliminary reading, and note them on your script. Unless the script calls for mock-serious delivery, be careful not to exaggerate the moods.

    In an extended television or film documentary or a thirty- or sixty-minute newscast, changes of mood are more numerous and more apparent. The next time you watch a newscast, make it a point to notice such changes, as well as the devices the speaker uses to reflect the shifting moods. In carefully working out such changes in mood, the narrator or announcer contributes to the flow, unity, and overall meaning of the presentation.

    In newscasting, changes in mood usually coincide with the beginnings of news items. But many newscasts begin with brief headlines that call for several changes within a short span of time. Read these headlines, and determine the mood of each:

```
HERE IS THE LATEST NEWS:


OVER EIGHT INCHES OF RAIN HAS FALLEN ON EASTERN

MAINE IN THE LAST TWENTY-FOUR HOURS, AND THERE

ARE REPORTS OF WIDESPREAD DAMAGE AND SOME DEATHS.


A MONTGOMERY WOMAN WHO CLAIMED SHE KILLED HER

HUSBAND IN SELF-DEFENSE AFTER TEN YEARS OF

BEATINGS HAS BEEN ACQUITTED BY AN ALL-MALE JURY.


A FOURTEEN-YEAR-OLD MARYLAND BOY HAS BEEN AWARDED

THE CITY'S HEROISM MEDAL FOR RESCUING AN INFANT

FROM A SWIMMING POOL.


ON THE INTERNATIONAL SCENE, THERE IS RENEWED

FIGHTING IN EL SALVADOR BETWEEN GOVERNMENT TROOPS

AND GUERRILLAS, WITH HEAVY CASUALTIES REPORTED ON

BOTH SIDES.
```

```
A THREATENED STRIKE OF MUSICIANS AND STAGEHANDS

AT THE CITY OPERA HAS BEEN AVERTED, AND THE

SEASON WILL OPEN AS SCHEDULED.


AND, THERE'S JOY AT THE ZOO TONIGHT BECAUSE OF

THE BIRTH OF A LITTER OF LIGERS--OR IS IT

TIGONS?--ANYWAY, THE FATHER IS A LION, AND THE

MOTHER IS A TIGER.


I'LL HAVE DETAILS ON THESE AND OTHER STORIES

AFTER THESE MESSAGES.
```

The varying moods implicit in these headlines require flexibility in delivery, with rapid changes of mood—a challenge that faces news-casters daily.

Determining the Parts and the Structure

Almost any example of well-written copy shows rather clearly differentiated parts. On the most basic level, copy may be broken down into beginning, middle, and end. The beginning is the introduction and customarily is used to gain attention. The middle, or body, contains most of the information. In commercials the middle reveals the advantages of this product over all others. The end is generally used for summing up the most important points. It frequently urges action or repeats the name, address, and telephone number of the sponsor.

In most copy these three parts may be further subdivided. Commercial copy frequently follows this organization:

1. Getting the attention of the listener or viewer
2. Giving some concrete reason for further interest and attention
3. Explaining step by step why this product or service is superior
4. Mentioning or implying a price lower than the listener has been led to expect
5. Repeating some of the selling points
6. Repeating the name and address or phone number of the sponsor

Here is an example of a commercial written according to this formula. Look for the parts, and notice how they conform to the six-part outline. (SFX is short for "sound effects.")

AGENCY: Reist Advertising, Inc.

CLIENT: Mertel's Coffee Mills

LENGTH: 60 seconds

ANNCR: Are you a coffee lover? Most Americans are. Would you like to enter the world of gourmet coffees? Mertel's can help.

SFX: SOUND OF COFFEE BEING POURED INTO CUP

ANNCR: Gourmet coffee begins with whole beans, carefully selected, freshly roasted.

SFX: SOUND OF COFFEE BEANS BEING GROUND

ANNCR: Gourmet coffee is ground at home, just before brewing. Choose your coffee according to your taste, and the time of day. A rich but mild Mocha Java for breakfast. A hearty French Roast for that midday pickup. A nutty Arabian with dinner. And a Colombian decaf before bed. Sound inviting? You bet. Sound expensive? Not so. Mertel's Coffee Mills feature forty types of coffee beans from around the world, and some are only pennies more per pound than canned coffees. And there's always a weekly special. This week, its Celebes Kalossi, at just $7.99 a pound! Remember—if you want gourmet coffee, you must begin with whole beans, and grind them just before brewing. So, come to

```
Mertel's Coffee Mills, and move into the world of
gourmet coffee! We're located at the Eastside
Mall, and on Fifth Street in downtown Russell.
Mertel's Coffee Mills.
```

Outstanding commercials are both subtle and complex. Special consideration will be given to the analysis of superior commercials in Chapter 7.

Analyzing the Function of Punctuation

In addition to the symbols of ideas we call words, writers have at their disposal a number of other marks, which we call punctuation. Punctuation is potentially helpful to the announcer, for it shows the author's intentions regarding mood and meaning. However, although you should pay attention to the punctuation in your copy, you need not be a slave to it. The copy was punctuated by a writer who thought it should be interpreted in a particular way. When you perform it, you need to make the copy your own—to make it true to your particular personality. Therefore, repunctuate as appropriate.

Punctuation marks, like the diacritical marks used to indicate pronunciation, are so small and differ so subtly that they may cause occasional difficulties for an announcer—especially when sight reading of copy is required. Announcers working with written material need near-perfect eyesight; some wear reading glasses during their air shifts or recording sessions even though they need glasses at no other time. Whenever possible, you should review your copy prior to air time and, if you find it helpful or necessary, add to and enlarge the punctuation marks. (Some suggestions for the use of emphatic punctuation marks are found on page 38.)

You probably already have a good grasp of punctuation, but the review that follows will relate that knowledge to broadcast copy. It does not consider every use of each punctuation mark, but rather comments on those that have a direct relationship to oral interpretation.

The period The period is used to mark the end of a sentence or to show that a word has been abbreviated. In written copy abbreviations such as FBI, NATO, and AFL-CIO appear without periods. Some news departments ask writers to place hyphens between letters in abbreviations that are not acronyms, for example, F-B-I. Abbreviations such as Ms and Mr may appear with or without concluding periods.

Periods at the ends of sentences give the reader of the copy places to take a breath. Use periods for this purpose, but let the mood of the copy tell you how long to pause.

The question mark   The question mark appears at the end of a sentence that asks a question. In marking copy you may find it helpful to follow the Spanish practice of placing an upside-down question mark (¿) at the beginning of a question, so that you will know it is interrogatory as you begin to read it.

The exclamation point   The exclamation point is used at the end of a sentence that demands some stress or emphasis. As with the question mark, it is helpful to place an upside-down exclamation point (¡) at the beginning of such a sentence.

Quotation marks   Quotation marks are used in broadcast copy for two different purposes: to indicate that the words between the marks are a word-for-word quotation, and as a substitute for italics. The first use is found extensively in news copy:

```
. . . HE SAID AN ANONYMOUS MALE CALLER TOLD HIM
TO "GET OUT OF THE CASE OR YOU WILL GET BUMPED
OFF."
```

Figure 2.4
Writer Jim Deasy has checked his script for length, counting words and gauging the pauses needed for the various punctuation marks. To tailor his story to the amount of time allotted, he must cut three seconds' worth of copy. (Courtesy of Jim Deasy and TLA Productions, San Francisco)

In reading this sentence, you can indicate the presence of a quotation by the inflection of your voice, or you can add words of your own to make it clear that there is a direct quotation:

. . . HE SAID AN ANONYMOUS MALE CALLER TOLD HIM,

AND THIS IS A QUOTE (or AND I QUOTE), TO "GET OUT

OF THE CASE OR YOU WILL GET BUMPED OFF."

In any event, never say "unquote" at the end of a quotation, because you cannot cancel out the quotation you have just given.

Quotation marks are often used in news copy in place of italics:

. . . HIS NEW BOOK, "READING FOR FUN," HAS BEEN ON

THE <u>TIMES</u> BEST SELLER LIST FOR THREE MONTHS.

The semicolon   The semicolon is used between main clauses that are not joined by *and, or, for, nor,* or *but*.

The little boy dashed away through the night; his feet made no sound on the dry pavement.

In reading a sentence that contains a semicolon, you should pause between the two clauses separated by the mark, but you should also indicate by inflection (in the example, on the words *night* and *his*) that the two thoughts are related.

The colon   The colon is frequently used to introduce a long quotation:

ANNCR: Senator Marble's reply was as follows: "I cannot

conceive of any period in our nation's history

when we were more in need of determined

leadership than at present. We stand, today, at a

crossroads."

A colon is also used before a list of several items, as in this example:

EARTHQUAKES ARE COMMON TO CENTRAL AMERICAN

NATIONS: GUATEMALA, HONDURAS, NICARAGUA, EL

SALVADOR, COSTA RICA, PANAMA, AND BELIZE.

In reading a sentence that contains a colon, you should pause between the two words separated by the colon; but, as with the semi-colon (to which the colon is related), you must indicate by inflection that the two phrases or clauses are related.

The dash   The dash is a straight line, longer than but in the same position as a hyphen. In typewritten copy the dash is customarily represented by two hyphens (--). It indicates hesitancy, an omission of letters or a name, or a sudden break in the line of thought. Here are two examples:

We—we need to know.

He looked around the room, but he couldn't seem to—wait a moment. Wasn't that a figure in the corner?

The dash is also used to summarize a preceding statement:

ANNCR: Senator Marble has never lost sight of one very

important fact of life--national defense.

In reading copy with a dash, you should first determine which of the meanings is intended. If the purpose is to show hesitation or a break in the thought pattern, then the words preceding the dash should be read as though they were going to continue beyond the dash. When the break comes, it should come abruptly, as though you had no idea until you did so that you were going to stop. (An exception to this occurs when the dash is combined with a mood of slowness and deliberation.) In using the dash to summarize a preceding statement, you should read the first part of the sentence as a buildup to the final statement. The final statement should be read, after a pause, as though it were a summation and a crystallization of the entire idea expressed before the dash.

Dashes may be used in pairs to set off a thought that interrupts or needs emphasis within a sentence. In this usage the dashes could be replaced by commas, but the emphasis would be lost.

ANNCR: Senator Marble hoped that nothing--partisan

politics, foreign pressures, or economic

stresses--would cause a reduction in our armed

forces.

When you are reading such a sentence, the phrase set off by dashes should be set apart by pauses, before and after. Also, because the writer set it apart for reasons of emphasis, it should be stressed by manipulating pace, volume, and voice quality.

Parentheses Although parenthetical remarks (remarks that are important but not necessary to the remainder of the sentence) are used occasionally in radio and television copy, the same result is usually achieved with pairs of dashes. Parentheses are used in radio and television copy to set apart the instructions to the audio operator, to indicate music cues, and to contain instructions or interpretations for the announcer, the performer, or the camera director. Words and sentences within parentheses are not to be read aloud by announcers.

Parenthetical remarks sometimes are added to newspaper copy, usually for purposes of clarification, as in this example:

> Senator Johnson said that he called the widow and demanded that she "return my (love) letters immediately."

A reader of this sentence can see that (love) has been added by a reporter or editor. If this copy were used on the air and the announcer did not indicate that (love) had been added by an editor or a writer, the senator's statement could be seriously misrepresented.

Ellipses An ellipsis is an omission of words in a sentence. The punctuation that indicates such an omission is a sequence of three or four periods, called ellipses. These are rarely used in broadcast copy but may be used in newspaper copy, as in the following example:

> Senator Marble stated yesterday, "I do not care what the opposition may think, I . . . want only what is best for my country."

In this example ellipses have been used to indicate that one or several words have been omitted from the original quotation.

Newswriters often use ellipses to mark the ends of sentences and as a substitute for commas, dashes, semicolons, and colons. Here is an example: "The mayor was late to his swearing-in ceremony today . . . He told those who had gathered for the ceremony . . . some two hundred supporters . . . that he had been held up in traffic." This practice is regrettable, but it is so widespread that you can expect to be asked at some time to work from copy so punctuated. And if you should become a newswriter, you may be expected to write copy in this style. Obviously, such punctuation is workable; the problem is that ellipses cannot indicate the shades of meaning conveyed by six other punctuation marks.

The comma   The comma has several specific purposes, but, generally speaking, it indicates a separation of words, phrases, or clauses from others to which they may be related but with which they are not necessarily closely connected in the structure of the sentence. Commas may link main clauses, separate a number of items in a series, separate a nonrestrictive modifier from the remainder of the sentence, indicate the name of a person being addressed or referred to ("I want you, John, to leave"), set apart an interjection ("I want you, let's see, at about five o'clock"), or set apart items in dates or addresses (Lowell, Massachusetts or July 16, 1892).

The comma usually marks a pause in broadcast speech. Although the number of variations in the use of the comma precludes making an exhaustive list, the important point is that the comma frequently gives the announcer an opportunity to pause briefly for breathing.

Marking copy   Because punctuation marks are quite small, most announcers have worked out systems of marking their copy that make use of marks that are much larger and, therefore, more readily seen. These are far from standard, but a few of the more commonly used ones are as follows:

- A slanted line (/), called a **virgule,** is placed between words to approximate the comma.
- Two virgules (//) are placed between sentences or between words to indicate a longer pause.
- Words to be stressed are underlined. (Some announcers mark copy with a colored highlighter to indicate words, phrases, and sentences to be stressed.)
- Question marks and exclamation marks are enlarged.
- An upside-down question mark is placed at the beginning of any sentence that is a question.
- An upside-down exclamation point is written at the beginning of any exclamatory sentence.
- Crescendo (∧) and decrescendo (∨) marks indicate that a passage is to receive an increase or a decrease in stress.

Verifying Meaning and Pronunciation

To interpret someone else's copy, you must understand the meanings of words. You should cultivate the habit of looking up all unfamiliar words in an authoritative dictionary. This means developing a healthy skepticism about your own vocabulary; through years of silent reading you have probably learned to settle for approximate meanings of many words. As a quick test, how many of these words can you define and use correctly?

voilà (French)	impassible
burlesque	ordnance
fulsome	rhetoric
capricious	catholic

Check the definitions of these words in any standard dictionary. Some of them are seen and heard frequently, whereas others only sound or look familiar.

Correct pronunciation of words is as important as accurate understanding. You should, therefore, be skeptical about your ability to pronounce words correctly. Check your pronunciation of each word in Table 2.1 against the correct pronunciation, which is shown there in three ways.

Appendix B is a pronunciation guide for about three hundred often mispronounced words. Use it to strengthen your ability to pronounce words according to accepted principles.

In addition to using and pronouncing words correctly, you must understand **allusions** in your copy. An allusion is an indirect but pointed or meaningful reference. Writers sometimes use phrases from the Bible, mythology, Shakespeare, and other sources from the past.

Table 2.1   Correct Pronunciation of Some Tricky Words

Word	IPA	Diacritics	Wire-Service System
drought	[draʊt]	drout	(DRAWHT)
forehead	[ˈfɔrɪd]	fôrʹĭd	(FOR'-IHD)
toward	[tɔrd]	tôrd	(TAWRD)
diphtheria	[dɪfˈθɪriə]	dĭf-thîrʹē-ə	(DIFF-THIR'-EE-UH)
accessories	[ækˈsɛsəriz]	ăk-sĕsʹər-ēz	(AK-SESS'-UH-REEZ)
quay	[ki]	kē	(KEE)
pestle	[ˈpɛsl̩]	pĕsʹəl	(PES'-UHL)
worsted	[ˈwʊstɪd]	wo͝osʹtĭd	(WUHSS'-TIHD)

Explanations of these phrases can be found in dictionaries, encyclopedias, and collections of well-known myths. A few allusions are given
in the following list. They are not common, but any one of them could
appear in your copy at any time. If you do not know their origins,
search them out.

He was considered a quisling.

She was given to malapropisms.

He had the temper of Hotspur.

He suffered as mightily as Job.

You cannot expect to be familiar with all allusions in every piece
of copy. During your career you may read copy written by hundreds
or even thousands of people, each drawing on a separate fund of
knowledge. You can, however, cultivate the habit of tracking down
allusions not familiar to you. Self-discipline is required, because it is
easy to convince yourself that the context will make an allusion clear
to the audience even if you do not understand it.

Reading Aloud

Because you will perform aloud, you should practice aloud. Copy
written for radio or television differs from copy written for newspapers,
magazines, and books. Good broadcast copy usually makes poor silent
reading. Short, incomplete, or ungrammatical sentences are often
found in perfectly acceptable radio and television scripts. Consider
the following, for example:

```
ANNCR:    Been extra tired lately? You know, sort of logy

          and dull? Tired and weary--maybe a little cranky,

          too? Common enough, this time of year. The time

          of year when colds are going around. And when we

          have to be especially careful of what we eat.

          Vitamin deficiency can be the cause of that

          "down-and-out" feeling. And Supertabs, the

          multiple vitamin, can be the answer. . . .
```

This is quite different from the copy an agency would write to advertise the same product in a newspaper. Reading it correctly requires a kind of skill developed most rapidly by practicing aloud.

Reading a long script aloud can be difficult. You cannot afford to make even the minor errors the silent reader may make, such as skipping over words or sentences, passing over difficult material or unfamiliar words, and resting your eyes when they become tired. As an announcer, you must read for extended periods of time, read everything before you, read it accurately and with appropriate expression, and do all of this with little opportunity to rest your eyes. As your eyes tire, you are more and more likely to make mistakes.

One way of giving your eyes the rest they need is by reading ahead: when your voice is at about *this point,* your eyes should be about *here.* When your eyes have reached the end of the sentence, you should be able to glance away from your script while you finish speaking the words. Practice this, and you should be able to read even lengthy scripts without excessive eyestrain. But as you practice, make certain you do not fall into the irritating habit of many announcers who read ahead—going into a monotonous, decelerating speech pattern at the end of every sentence. Unless you guard against it, you may be unconsciously relaxing your interpretation as you rest your eyes.

Conveying an Interest in the Material

Whatever the purpose or nature of the copy to be read, you must show interest in it if you are to communicate it effectively. In many instances you will have a genuine interest in the subject, such as when delivering the news or narrating a documentary. At other times, for example, when reading a commercial for a product you do not use or perhaps even dislike, it may be difficult for you to feel genuine interest. As a professional, you cannot afford to show disinterest in, or disrespect for, the copy you are paid to read. You must try to put your biases aside. You are an intermediary between people who supply information and people who receive it. You act as a magnifying glass: it is your job to enhance perceptions with the least possible distortion. Of course, if you are asked to perform a commercial for a product you know to be shoddy or misrepresented, then your conscience should take over. And, if you find yourself reading copy that is offensive, find out if it is possible to have it changed.

Even when you are provided with good copy for reputable advertisers, it is impossible to develop a belief in each commercial cause.

The following guidelines, therefore, may be helpful. When you must read a great many commercials for many different products and when it is impossible to develop honest enthusiasm for all of them, the best you can do is read each one with as much effectiveness and interpretive skill as possible. When you are the exclusive speaker for a product or have had a long personal relationship with a sponsor, try to gain firsthand knowledge of the product and communicate your honest belief in it.

Assuming that your announcing copy arouses genuine interest, how can you reflect it in your interpretation? Honest enthusiasm is seldom noisy or obtrusive. It manifests itself in inner vitality and quiet conviction. As a radio or television commercial announcer, you will not be dealing with life-or-death matters, and you will be speaking, in effect, to small groups of people who are only a few feet away. In a sense you are their guest. Your conviction is revealed through a steady focus on your listeners and through your earnestness and your personality. This does not rule out the possibility of a humorous commercial or introduction. Being sincere does not mean being somber!

Talking to the Listener

Several aspects of the problem of communication with a listener have already been mentioned, but one more point should be made. Most of this chapter has emphasized the problems of *reading* scripts. It might be better if you considered your job to be one of *talking* scripts. Even though you work from a script and your listeners know it, they appreciate it when you sound as though you are not merely reading aloud. The best way to achieve a conversational style is to visualize the person to whom you are speaking and "talk" your message to him or her. Of course, some scripts lend themselves more readily to intimate delivery than others.

When asked to interpret a piece of copy, ask yourself several questions:

Who am I as I read this piece?

To whom am I talking?

How many people am I talking to?

How old is the person I am speaking to?

Where am I as I speak?

Figure 2.5
Even highly experienced veterans do not go on the air "cold"; they spend time before each broadcast studying scripts and getting whatever background they need to understand the various stories. Here two television news co-anchors shuffle through their scripts and discuss news stories they are just moments away from broadcasting. (Frank Siteman, Stock Boston)

Getting Some Background

Unlike brief commercials, which tend to be self-explanatory, longer and more complex pieces of copy will often be better interpreted if you know something about the writer and understand the author's intentions.

Think about what you should find out before narrating the following pieces:

A miniseries of television packages on the problems of the inner cities

A program on world hunger

A program on the works of a great painter

An instructional tape on the use of a particular personal computer

Each of these topics requires specialized knowledge and an understanding of the author's motivations. Commercials are quite obviously designed to sell products or services, but what are the purposes of programs such as these? One good way to find out is by talking to writers, producers, and directors. On a basic level, you will learn whether the program is intended to be objective and factual or a position statement. You may also discover the mood the writer intends to convey. You can question passages that puzzle you, suggest improvements (when appropriate), and ultimately do a better job of interpretation.

Figure 2.6
For commercials, industrial videos, or feature productions, you may need to employ characterization to convey different sorts of personalities and voices. Here actress Katie Leigh records a child's voice for a television cartoon series. (Courtesy of Hanna-Barbera Productions)

Employing Characterizations

You may be asked at times to read copy calling for characterization. Courses in acting and participation in plays (both radio and television plays) will help you learn character interpretation. Some commercials call for no real characterization but demand a foreign accent or a regional dialect. However, before starting to practice copy with a dialect, accent, or character voice, make all of your key decisions about the purpose of the copy, the mood of the copy, the person or persons to whom you are speaking, and so on. Characterization alone is insufficient to make a piece of copy effective. First get the interpretation down, and then add the character voice. (A section of Chapter 7, Commercials and Public-Service Announcements, discusses accents, dialects, and character voices in some detail.)

You cannot, of course, apply every one of the points discussed here each time you pick up a piece of copy. In time, however, you should develop a conditioned reflex that allows you to size up a script and interpret it effectively without relying on a checklist. In the meantime, the suggestions given here may help you spot your weaknesses and measure your progress.

Ad-Lib Announcing

Sooner or later, you are sure to find yourself working without a script. Then all your acquired skills of phonation, articulation, and interpretation cannot guarantee effective communication. When you are on your own as an ad-lib announcer, only your ability as a compelling conversationalist will earn you listeners. Much of the broadcast day consists of unscripted shows. Disc jockeys, field reporters, telephone talk show hosts, interviewers, children's show personalities, game show hosts, and panel moderators are among those who seldom see a script and must conduct their programs spontaneously. Field reporters may work from notes, but they almost never work with a complete script.

Ad-lib announcing can be practiced, but it probably cannot be taught. The formula for success is easy to state but difficult to achieve: *know what you are talking about, be interested in what you are saying, be eager to communicate with your listener, and try to develop an attractive personality.* In ad-lib interviews, *show a genuine interest in your subjects and their views.*

Checklist: Getting Better at Ad-Lib Announcing

| █ ▌ ▍

1. Know what you are talking about: do your research on specific topics; read widely to keep up on broader topics.
2. Be interested in what you are saying: keep the material fresh every time you report.

3. Be eager to communicate with your listener: your announcing must reach real people on the other end.
4. Develop an attractive personality: be yourself, and be genuinely interested in others.

An ad-lib announcer has a greater opportunity to show spontaneity than a script reader does; at the same time, the ad-lib announcer runs a greater risk of boring the listener. Scripts are usually tightly written; an ad-lib announcer can wander from point to point. Scripts have specific objectives; the ad-lib announcer is free to ramble without a clear objective. Scripts are often polished and tightened during recording sessions; the ad-lib comments of an announcer cannot be taken back once they have been spoken. Scripts may call for interruptions when there is some motivation for them; ad-lib interviewers may throw in a question just as their guest is about to make an important point in response to the *last* question.

Despite all these potential pitfalls, ad-lib announcing is a craft that must be practiced and perfected by anyone who wants to become a professional announcer. Keeping the formula in mind, practice ad-lib announcing at every opportunity, using a tape recorder for self-evaluation. The following tips should be helpful.

Know what you are talking about   Ordinarily we take this point for granted. We expect a sportscaster to have a thorough knowledge of sports and a disc jockey to know music. The problem arises when an announcer must ad-lib on an unfamiliar topic. As a special-assignment reporter, you may be asked to interview a person about whom you know little and about whose special interests you know nothing at all. Suppose, for example, you are to interview a medical researcher about an important discovery. How would you prepare? Many radio and television stations maintain both a library and a **morgue** (a collection

Spotlight: Every Night's a Party with Arsenio Hall

This generation's prince of nighttime talk shows is the only personality who has been able, since the 1954 launch of the *Tonight Show,* to challenge Johnny Carson. Where Alan Thicke, Joan Rivers, and Pat Sajak failed, a lanky guy from Cleveland, who calls himself "the talk show host for the MTV generation," gave the format a few new twists and ended up a success.

Arsenio Hall, now in his early thirties, grew up in an inner-city neighborhood, where many of his friends later met with violent deaths or landed in jail. As a child, Hall had no time for playing after school or joining the basketball team. A latchkey kid, he would come home alone and, while his mother worked two jobs and took night school courses, sit in front of the television, mesmerized. At 12, Hall told his mother that he wanted to grow up to be Johnny Carson. He took magic lessons and began to perform at neighborhood parties, bar mitzvahs, and weddings; he went to school for the chance to clown around. An only child with one often absent parent, Hall says, "Everyone else had nine brothers and sisters. School was my only audience" (*The New York Times Magazine,* 1 Oct. 1989, p. 31).

Anne Hall worked hard to pay her son's way through college, so after Hall earned a degree in communications from Kent State University, he initially took a "normal" job as an advertising salesperson for Noxell. He lasted one year. "I had a company car and a dental plan and I was making $15,000 a year," he recalls. "When women came to my house I could give them free nail polish. I was happy." But restless. Hall broke the news to his mom that he wanted to test his talent as a comedian and announcer, "I told her that I just didn't want to wake up when I was 60 talking about what I coulda been" (*Essence,* July 1989, p. 98).

Moving to Chicago and beginning as a stand-up comic for $10 a night at clubs and strip joints, Hall had his first break when musician Nancy Wilson spotted him at a club and asked him to open for her concert. A series of concert openings and occasional appearances on ABC's *Half-Hour Comedy Hour* followed; by 1983 he was a regular on *Thicke of the Night* and *Solid Gold.* It wasn't until 1987, when the short-lived Joan Rivers' *The Late Show* was failing and Hall was asked at the last minute by Fox Network to fill in as host for the last thirteen weeks, that he had the chance to really show his stuff. He now says that it was because no one cared about the show, because the producers were distracted elsewhere, that he was able to do whatever he wanted with the format. "I took chances," he says. "I played with the band, took cameras on the street, did improv, sang, wrote sketches, asked provocative questions, so that when it was over maybe somebody would give me a job" (*NYT Magazine,* p. 65).

Hall's career took off from there. After co-starring with Eddie Murphy in the 1988 movie *Coming to America,* Hall got a generous offer from Paramount and then a chance to sit opposite his idol, Johnny Carson. His guest appearance on that show reminded him that "All my life, I've wanted to do what this man does" (*NYT Magazine,* p. 65), and he signed up as executive producer and star of his own show.

The Arsenio Hall Show was an instant phenomenon, earning ratings second only to Carson's. But that has been okay with Hall, who says that he doesn't want to steal away Carson's audience—only their kids.

Hall has done more than gain a share of the existing nighttime audience: his show has attracted new viewers to television during his slot (*Time,* 13 Nov. 1989, p. 92). His style is energy;

he bounds all over the stage and through the aisles of the studio. He may leap up and run over to his studio band, which he calls "my posse," and get the musicians into some impromptu jamming. No two shows are alike: Hall may do skits or fall into his "alter ego," a fat rapper named Chunky A. He interviews everyone from Kirstie Alley and Whoopi Goldberg to Kool Moe Dee, 10,000 Maniacs, and the "Friday the 13th" Jason. Although he has earned a reputation for getting guests to open up, Hall's interviewing trademark is his gentility: he is an old-fashioned, gushy host whose questions are often as harmless as "Let's talk about pet peeves." Beneath the hip talk and occasional racy remarks runs a current of respect. Hall explains, "In the ghetto the game is respect. If I book you, I'm committed to you. I'm an entertainer, not a tough interviewer. My philos-ophy is to leave my ego at the door and get the best out of my guests" (*Time*, p. 95).

In 1989, he co-starred with Eddie Murphy in another movie, *Harlem Nights*. On the movie screen he is hilarious. On the television screen he is easy-going, loose, stylish. He considers his show to be a living room party rather than a formal talk program. In his spare time he watches tapes of his own and others' shows to improve his technique, and he produces antidrug and antiapartheid commercials. He realizes that the audience that loves him today will demand just as much tomorrow: "One bad show, and I'm mentally packing a U-Haul," he quips; looking into the future at a career's necessary end, he muses, "It's scary—someday I'll be the punchline" (*Time*, p. 97).

Arsenio Hall (Courtesy of Paramount Pictures)

Figure 2.7
Announcers in every branch of broadcasting need to know how to ad lib to get through those terrifying blank on-air moments. Major sports and political events especially test one's skill at ad-lib announcing; shown here at a Republican National Convention in New Orleans is INN's reporter Marvin Scott. (Courtesy of Tribune Company)

of newspaper and magazine clippings, news releases, and other published biographical material). You might well begin your research there. More and more stations maintain computers that are tied into information banks. Inquiries typed into the computer via a keyboard will, in less than a minute, provide you with reams of information on almost any topic or famous person.

As a talk show host, you would, of course, not rely on a station library or morgue. To be competent you would have to be a voracious reader of newspapers, newsmagazines, current fiction and nonfiction best sellers, and a number of general-interest periodicals. At a large station you would have the help of a research assistant when specific information was needed about a particular guest or topic. (Chapter 8 discusses the role of radio and television talk show hosts.)

Be interested in what you are saying   This point may seem superfluous, yet anyone who listens attentively to radio or television ad-lib announcers will notice that there are some who seem to have no interest in what they are saying. Among the guilty are certain weather, traffic, and business reporters on radio who make frequent reports throughout the day. It is easy to fall into a routine delivery pattern, to speak too rapidly, and to show no interest in what one is saying.

Be eager to communicate with your listener   Only if you really want to communicate to others should you consider radio or television announcing in the first place. If you want to speak merely for and to yourself, buy a tape recorder and have fun "doing your own thing."

Develop an attractive personality   Very little can be offered on this point. Most people who are attractive to others have found out how to be truly themselves, are able to show their interest in others, and have wide intellectual curiosity. Wit, wisdom, and charm are easily detected and warmly appreciated, but hard to come by.

Practice: Analyzing Voice Quality

Make an audio recording of a radio or television newscast or a talk show, and listen to it as often as necessary to analyze each of these: voice quality of announcers, good or bad articulation, ability to get a point across, ability to hold attention, and ability to communicate appropriate emotions.

Practice: Effecting Mood Changes

Make an audiotape of a news anchor delivering three different stories, each calling for a different mood. Determine the techniques used to change from one mood to another.

Practice: Talking a Script

The following two scripts may be used for practice in talking scripts. The Blue Cross script should be delivered in a very straightforward, matter-of-fact manner. The Six Flags commercial is marvelous for practicing changes in rate of delivery, pitch, and volume, as well as for practicing conversational style. Both commercials defy conventional rules of structure, and both benefit from their originality. Sound effects enhance both.

AGENCY: Allen and Dorward

CLIENT: Blue Cross of Northern California

LENGTH: 60 seconds

MUSIC: LOUD ROCK AND ROLL MUSIC

MOM: Annie . . . would you turn that down, please?

MUSIC: R & R DOWN AND UNDER

MOM: Thank you, dear. I'm a working mother with two teenage girls. Sometimes, it seems that they're at that difficult age. Sometimes, it seems they've been there for years. I've got my own business and we're all healthy. When I opened my shop, I signed up for Blue Cross protection. I looked at other health plans, but it was obvious that the Blue Cross Concept One Hundred Plan had everything we needed . . . and, I can afford it! Last spring, Cindy was in the hospital for a few days. Nothing serious . . . but I know how much it would have cost me. Believe me. Plenty!

START FADE   I just couldn't handle a bill like that alone.

ANNCR: There's no reason for you to handle it alone. Our Blue Cross Concept One Hundred Plan offers a full range of benefits for your growing family. See our ad in this Sunday's magazine section or TV Guide or call eight hundred . . . six, four, eight . . . forty-eight hundred. Blue Cross of Northern California.

MOM: As a single parent, Blue Cross was one of the best decisions I've ever made.

AGENCY: McDonald & Little Advertising

CLIENT: Six Flags

CAMPAIGN: New Season

LENGTH: 60 seconds

TITLE: It Starts Off Slowly

ANNCR: It starts off slowly at first, climbing upward at maybe two miles an hour. Then it hits the crest, picks up speed, and before you know it, it happens. The ground is gone. The world is a blur far below; look down if you dare. And don't think about the fact that you're moving at almost a mile a minute and headed straight down into a lake. Or that you're screaming and laughing at the same time. It's all in good fun. Here on the biggest, fastest, highest roller coaster in the world. The Great American Scream Machine. Just one of the many, many new experiences now at the new Six Flags Over Georgia. There's a whole lot of new to do this year at Six Flags. Things you'll never forget. Because good times here are not forgotten.

Practice: Ad-lib Announcing

The exercises that follow rely on the use of an audio recorder. Most can be adapted to video recording, but the advantages of being able to practice extensively without requiring studio, cameras, and crew make audiotaping more practical for most students.

Do not look at the topics that follow until you are fully prepared to begin practicing. To prepare, get a stopwatch or a clock or watch with a sweep second hand, and find an isolated area that is free from distractions. Cue up a tape on an audio recorder. Then choose a number from 1 to 20. Without looking at any other topics, read the item corresponding to the number you have chosen. Start your stopwatch. Give yourself exactly 1 minute to formulate your thoughts. Make notes, if desired. When the minute is up, reset the stop watch, and start it and the tape recorder simultaneously. Begin your ad-lib performance, and try to speak fluently on your topic for a predetermined time: 1 minute for your first few efforts and 2 minutes after you have become more experienced. Decide on the length of your performance before you look at your topic. Eliminate the number of each topic when you use it so that you will have a fresh challenge each time you practice.

As you form your thoughts, try to think of (1) an appropriate opening, (2) material for the body of your remarks, and (3) a closing statement. Do not stop your commentary because of stumbles, hesitancies, or any other problems. Do not put your recorder on pause while collecting your thoughts. This exercise is valueless unless you work your way through your ad libs in "real time." In order to improve, you must have firsthand knowledge of your shortcomings; the only way to gather this knowledge is to follow these instructions to the letter, regardless of initial failures. It is also helpful to keep all your taped performances so that you can review them and measure your progress.

Some of the ad-lib topics that follow are rather trivial; some are of importance. Some should be approached with humor; others demand a more sober delivery. All of the topics are general, and anyone should be able to find something to say about each. However, remember that, as a broadcast announcer, you will never be asked to ad-lib on topics such as these, but rather on current events, as reflected in a given day's newscasts and newspapers. You may use the topics that follow for initial practice, but eventually you must graduate to more important, current, and realistic topics. To truly test your ad-libbing abilities with important topics, make a list of the week's headlines. A typical week will yield topics as diverse as disarmament proposals, third-world indebtedness, hunger in some parts of the planet, labor negotiations in your community or area, breakthroughs in medicine, important Supreme Court decisions, newly proposed legislation on a variety of issues, election results and their implications, speedups or slowdowns of the economy, and news on the greenhouse effect. List each topic on a separate slip of paper, and follow the instructions for ad-libbing given above, but do not limit yourself to arbitrary time constraints.

1. Give reasons for agreeing or disagreeing with this proposal: "Upon graduating from high school, all students should be required to serve for one year in the Peace Corps or perform some type of community service."
2. Discuss the most influential book you have ever read.
3. Describe your memories of some important holiday during your childhood.
4. Name the most important college course you have taken, and give reasons for your choice.
5. How do you turn down a request for a date?
6. Describe your most embarrassing experience.
7. If you could change one law, what would it be, how would you change it, and why?
8. Tell about your first memorable date.
9. What do you hope to be doing in ten years?
10. Express your feelings about capital punishment (the death penalty).
11. Tell about your most memorable pet.
12. Give reasons for your agreement or disagreement with this statement: "All nuclear power plants, worldwide, should be taken out of service."
13. What turns you on?
14. What turns you off?
15. Tell about your recurring nightmares.
16. How should the government deal with terrorists?
17. What should the government do to be more effective in combating illegal drugs?

18. Tell how you feel about graffiti on buses and public buildings, and, if you disapprove of it, what you think should be done.
19. Describe the characteristics or qualities of a broadcast announcer whose work you admire.
20. What are your strengths and weaknesses?

3

Performance

All your preparation for announcing will culminate in performance, and it is on the basis of your performing ability that you will be judged by your audience and your employer. Of course, you must develop other abilities and qualities, such as competence as a journalist, personableness as a music announcer, and dexterity in the operation of basic items of broadcast equipment. However, your before-camera or on-air work will ultimately determine your success. This chapter concentrates on several performance skills that you must develop, addressing the topics of microphone and camera fright, microphone and camera consciousness, clothing and makeup for television, the use of prompters and cue cards, and miscellaneous tips for performers. (Additional information on performance may be found in Chapter 1, "Broadcast Announcing"; Chapter 4, "Voice and Diction"; Chapter 7, "Commercials and Public-Service Announcements"; Chapter 8, "Interview and Talk Programs"; Chapter 11, "Music Announcing"; and Chapter 12, "Sports Announcing.")

Before we turn to these topics, we must consider another aspect of performance that is of utmost importance: audience rapport. Rick Houlberg, professor of broadcast communication arts at San Francisco State University, made this pertinent comment after concluding a study of viewer preferences concerning newscasters:

> After all the preparation, clothing, hard work, and luck, something more is needed for the on-air broadcaster to be successful. We know what that something is although we haven't been able to fully describe or study it. This something made us believe Walter Cronkite and send birthday presents to soap opera characters; this something makes us choose one television newscaster over another; this something keeps us listening to one rock radio DJ despite a play list which is almost exactly the same as the four

other available rock stations. This something is a connection made between the on-air performer and the audience.[1]

In his research, Houlberg found that most respondents chose the television newscaster they watched because of these factors: "he or she made their problems seem easier," "they would like to know more about the newscaster off the air," "the newscaster is almost like their everyday friends," and "he or she made them feel contented." Of course, audience rapport is not everything. News anchors and reporters must also have significant professional characteristics, including objectivity, reliability, honesty, being qualified, and knowing the local market.

The messages here are clear: after achieving professional competency, and while maintaining the integrity that is required of news personnel, broadcast performers must project an attractive and friendly personality to the audience. *Attractive* in this sense does not refer to physical appearance, for Houlberg found that neither physical appearance nor gender was significantly important to his respondents. Synonyms for *attractive* are *appealing, engaging,* and *charming.* These qualities can be used by a sensitive performer to build audience rapport—a relationship of mutual trust or emotional affinity. It is not likely that every student can be taught these qualities, for they come from within. Being aware of them can, however, help you channel your inner feelings of respect for your audience, concern for people, and dedication to your profession into more effective communication. Audience rapport is a state of mind. It relies heavily on your integrity. It is a reflection of who you are and what you care about.

Overcoming Microphone and Camera Fright

An irrational fear of performing before a microphone or camera is a common reaction for an inexperienced performer. A few students will relish every opportunity to perform and will delight in performance playbacks. For most of us, though, it is normal to have butterflies before and during a performance and to feel disappointment on seeing and hearing the results during taped playbacks.

[1]These comments were made by Professor Houlberg after he had conducted a study of 258 respondents in Ohio. The complete report is in *Journal of Broadcasting*, Fall 1984. Houlberg cites other studies supporting his conclusions.

Spotlight: The Real-Life Appeal of Oprah Winfrey

If you didn't know the childhood history and personal philosophy of Oprah Winfrey, you might think she leads a charmed life. After all, she is only in her mid-thirties, yet she has earned national fame as daytime television's hottest talk show host. About sixteen million people watch *The Oprah Winfrey Show*, during which the vibrant, aggressive Winfrey tackles topics from transvestism to racism.

But Winfrey does more than perform: she owns the show. In 1988 her company, Harpo Productions, gained ownership and control. She secured a guarantee—unprecedented in her field—that ABC would carry the show for the next five years; and she purchased an enormous studio in Chicago, which will serve not only as production facilities for her own show but also as "*the* studio between the coasts," says Harpo's chief operating officer Jeffrey Jacobs.

Winfrey has also starred in the movie features *The Color Purple* and *The Women of Brewster Place* and owns screen rights for two future projects, Toni Morrison's novel *Beloved* and Mark Mathabane's South African autobiography, *Kaffir Boy*. She owns a luxurious condo that looms above downtown Chicago and Lake Michigan, a 162-acre getaway farm in Indiana, and a portion of a Chicago restaurant called *The Eccentric*.

It seems that Winfrey is one announcer who has used her talent to climb steadily to the top, not only in audience popularity but in the financial and managerial control she wields over her own career. But when she blasts welfare mothers for giving in to the system, she also tells them that she started out as a welfare daughter.

Born on a farm in Kosciusko, Mississippi, Winfrey lived there with her grandmother—and a frightening grandfather—until she was 6, when she joined her mother in Milwaukee. She has lived through poverty, repeated sexual abuse, and

a sentence (unserved) to a juvenile delinquent home. Rebellious, Winfrey was sent at 13 to live with her father in Nashville. Vernon Winfrey was a barber, a city councilman, and a strict disciplinarian who soon had Oprah reading a book a week and writing reports on them.

Winfrey's first "performance" was held in a Baptist church where she spent all day every Sunday in Sunday school and services; she often was called on to recite lessons, otherwise known as "going on program." She won Miss Black Tennessee in 1971, attended Tennessee State University, and landed her first broadcast job at age 19, as a reporter-anchor for the CBS affiliate in Nashville. From there she worked as co-anchor for a Baltimore television station, co-host for the show *People Are Talking*, and host of *AM Chicago*. When Quincy Jones caught a glimpse of Winfrey on Chicago television, he called her and asked her to read for the part of Sofia for the film version of Alice Walker's *The Color Purple*. Winfrey, who reads voraciously, especially African-American literature and history, not only knew the book but had coveted that very role.

Soon she had her own nationally syndicated talk show, whose ratings soared. The show has

Oprah Winfrey (Courtesy of HARPO Productions Inc.)

earned several daytime Emmy awards; Winfrey has won an Emmy and been named "Broadcaster of the Year."

Her audience knows nearly everything there is to know about Winfrey—her 67-pound weight loss, her dog and her hairdresser, her childhood of abuse, and her love life. There is little separation between the talk show host and the woman, who candidly presents her views and experiences to support or contrast those of her guests. The message is simple—that nothing happens randomly. Winfrey, who sees her show as her "mission," tries to use the hour both to turn around the lives of her guests and to give viewers a vicarious experience of guilt-cleansing or change. Self-contradictory, opinionated Winfrey challenges the belief-systems and problems of her guests. She believes in fate, that people claim their success or failure; she is convinced that the "root of all evil" is people's lack of self-esteem.

Although guest psychologists still allege that she has a low self-image, Winfrey has risen quite above the rural poverty, broken family, and abuse of her past. Because her announcing style is so personal, she exposes to her audience both her convictions and their contradictions, her glamour and human warmth, her fallible self and the announcing/acting/producing giant. And audiences love it.

Some tension not only is to be expected but can actually help your performance. **Mic fright,** as this phenomenon is traditionally called, results in the release of adrenalin into the bloodstream, which causes one to become more alert and more energetic. A little mic fright can be an asset to a performer. A performer who is keyed up generates more positive energy than one who is routinely working through a piece of copy in an unfeeling manner.

Excessive nervousness, however, can seriously impair a performance. You are suffering from extreme mic fright when any combination of these symptoms is present: physical tension, shallow breathing, constricted throat, dry mouth, and (at an extreme) upset stomach and shaking knees and hands. In terms of your performance, these conditions cause your voice to go up in pitch or to break or make you run out of breath in the middle of a sentence, lose concentration, read or speak at an excessive rate of speed, or adopt a subdued attitude. At its greatest extreme mic fright can render you entirely unable to communicate.

The vocal folds (often called the vocal cords), which are central to good vocal tones, tighten up during times of moderate to extreme nervousness. The tighter the folds, the less they vibrate, and this results in a lowering of resonance and a strident sound to the voice. Hot liquids can help relax the vocal folds. Hot tea, bouillon, coffee, or even hot water can help you achieve a better speaking voice (this is true even after nervousness has been conquered). Make certain that

Figure 3.1
Ultimately, it is the on-air (radio) or before-the-camera (television) performance that determines an announcer's success. ABC's Peter Jennings, known for his ultraprofessional yet friendly personal style, has anchored the leading network news program through the 1980s and into the 1990s. (Capital Cities/ABC, Inc.)

the beverage of your choice is not too hot, however. (Avoid carbonated beverages and any beverage containing milk.)

Generally speaking, mic and/or camera fright is caused by the following conditions.

Lack of Experience

Nothing but time and regular performances will allow you to overcome lack of experience. Performances need not occur on the air or in a class session. Perform a variety of written and ad-libbed assignments, and record them on an audio recorder. Even television performances will benefit from being recorded and played back for evaluation on an audio recorder.

Lack of Preparation

It is not possible to prepare for ad-lib announcing (a news report live from the field or the badinage that is expected of you as a talk show host), but it is possible to practice ad-lib announcing. To gain confidence and to develop a smooth ad-lib delivery, practice by talking aloud to yourself. Walk through your living quarters and describe what you see; when driving, talk about what you are passing. Sharpen your ability to hold your friends' attention as you relate anecdotes or discuss matters of mutual interest.

With written scripts, of course, it is possible to practice. Though time pressures may make it impossible for professional announcers to rehearse, you are under no such strictures. If you want to improve your performances, you must prepare thoroughly.

Fear of Failure

Most of us are more afraid of failing—of making fools of ourselves— than we are of physical dangers. It is necessary for you to conquer this fear and to realize that you can progress only by daring to try a variety of approaches in your announcing work. To remain safely within a comfortable shell and perform in a laid-back, low-key manner is to sacrifice any chance of major improvement. If you are a member of a class in broadcast announcing, keep in mind that you and your classmates are all in the pressure cooker together. Mature students will applaud and encourage one another's efforts to improve.

Almost any performance will benefit from conviction on your part. That is, if you believe in your message and if you sincerely want to communicate it to others, your fear of failure may be pushed aside by your conviction. Professional announcers do not always have the luxury of believing in what they are paid to say, but as a student, you will usually be free to choose messages that are of interest or importance to you.

As you perform, try to concentrate on your message. Forget about self and forget about audience. Assume that you are speaking to one or two people whom you respect and with whom you want to communicate. If you truly have a desire to get your message across, you can overcome your concern about failure.

Lack of Self-Esteem

Some of us simply feel that we are not important enough to take up the time and attention of others. This is an incredibly debilitating attitude, and there is nothing to recommend it. Modesty may be a virtue, but self-effacement is not.

Each of us is a unique creation. You are the only person just like you who has ever lived. Because you are unique, you have something

Figure 3.2
One way to overcome fear of the flashing lights and complex equipment of the studio is to talk with the floor manager before broadcast. *Nightline*'s Ted Koppel discusses an unusual camera shot planned for a segment that is being shot on location and transmitted via satellite back to New York. (Martha Stewart, The Picture Cube)

special to offer. If you respect yourself, you will perform at an acceptable level; if you respect your listeners, you will find something worthwhile to say to them; if you respect your subject matter, you will find ways to get it across. Self, listeners, and topic are interrelated variables that must mesh if you are to communicate successfully. Successful communication will inevitably increase your self-confidence and boost your self-esteem. Enhanced self-esteem will bring about further improvement in performances. Better performances will raise self-esteem—and so on. Believing that what you have to say is worthy of the interest and time of others is the start of a new and healthier attitude toward yourself.

But let's face it: if you are presenting dull material in a lackadaisical manner, you have no right to expect the rapt attention of your listeners. If you conduct a boring interview with a boring guest, there is no reason to try to tell yourself that what you are doing is important. This brings us back to conviction—the belief that what you have to offer is important and valid. To raise your self-esteem, be certain that what you offer your listeners is worthy of their attention.

Lack of Mental Preparation

During the minutes before a performance, you should remove yourself (physically if possible, but at least mentally) from the confusion of a typical production situation. Find a way to relax, to gather your thoughts, to concentrate on the upcoming performance. Think over what it is you have to say or read. Think about mood, about appropriate pace, about the importance of the message, about any potential problems of diction, pronunciation, and so on. Perform physical relaxation exercises. If possible, sit in a comfortable chair. Begin to physically relax—starting with your head, then your neck, your shoulders, and so on. After you have attempted to relax your entire body, imagine that the tension or stress is being discharged from the ends of your fingers. If you try, you can actually feel the tension leaving your body. At this point, think again about your assignment, and keep your message and your objectives clearly in mind as you prepare to perform.

Dislike of One's Voice or Appearance

It is common for students of announcing to dislike the way they sound and look on tape. This is not surprising, because we neither see nor hear ourselves as others do. Most people do not believe that their voice sounds like what comes back to them from an audio recorder. The reason is simple: we hear ourselves speak through both air and bone conduction. The sound waves that emanate from our mouths are what others hear; the physical vibrations that go through the bones of the head to the tympanic apparatus of the ear are heard by the speaker alone. The combination of sounds conducted through air and bone is what we think we sound like to others. Only when we hear ourselves through air conduction alone, as from an audiotape player, do we truly hear ourselves as others hear us.

As for appearance, we are used to seeing ourselves head on, in a mirror. Even when posing for photographs, we typically look straight into the camera lens. We are not nearly as accustomed to seeing ourselves in profile or in one-quarter or three-quarter shots. Television spares us nothing; replays show us how we look to others, but because we are not accustomed to these views, we tend to like them less. Television can also distort one's appearance to some extent. Most of us look heavier on television than in real life.

If you truly understand that audio and video recordings are surprises only to yourself and that others accept your sound and appearance on tape just as they accept you in person, you are well on your way toward overcoming mic or camera fright.

In summary, you can keep your nervousness within bounds if you prepare thoroughly, practice at every opportunity, believe in what you are saying, concentrate on your message, stop analyzing your feelings and emotions, think of your listener, perform relaxation exercises, accept yourself as you are, believe that you can and will succeed, and understand that many of your colleagues are fighting the same battle.

Microphone Consciousness

Microphones are marvelous instruments, but they can do their job only when they are properly used. Improper use sometimes results from inexperience or ignorance but is more often due to a lack of **microphone consciousness**. To be mic conscious is to be always aware that the misuse of a microphone will result in a flawed or failed performance. Typical examples of faulty microphone consciousness include the following:

- Failing to clip on a lavaliere mic before beginning a performance
- Attaching a lavaliere mic improperly—too far away from the mouth or under clothing that will muffle the sound

- Clapping with your hands near a lavaliere mic
- Making unwanted noises near an open mic, such as drumming fingers on a table near a desk mic
- Moving away from a mounted mic or moving out of range of a boom mic
- Failing to properly move a hand-held mic between you and a guest you are interviewing
- Positioning yourself and a guest improperly in relation to a desk mic
- Making sudden and extreme changes in the volume of your voice
- Moving in and out in relation to a mounted mic
- Failing to understand and properly relate to the pickup patterns of microphones
- Wearing jewelry, such as metal bracelets, that clank when moved
- Walking away from the set after a performance without remembering to unclip a lavaliere mic.

One problem is so common that it deserves separate attention. The sound of paper being bent, turned over, or shuffled is the mark of an amateur. Learn to handle scripts in such a way as to avoid paper rattling. Never work from a script that is stapled or held together with a paper clip. Never turn script pages over as you move from one page to another; always slide the pages you are finished with to one side. Obviously, all scripts should be typed on only one side of the paper. When working with practice material from this or other texts, type copies on $8\frac{1}{2}$-by-11-inch paper, with double or even triple spacing. Ordinarily, the cheaper the paper, the softer it is and the less it will rattle. Work with the softest paper you can find.

Despite continual improvement, lavaliere condenser mics must be used carefully to prevent their picking up unwanted noise. A script being thumbed or rattled 3 inches away from the lavaliere will sound as loud as or louder than a voice coming from a foot or more away. Clothing brushing against the surface of the mic will sound like a forest fire. Nervous toying with the cable will transmit scratching and rumbling sounds directly into the microphone. If you tend to produce a popping sound as you pronounce *p*, *t*, or *k* or excessive sibilance with *s* or *sh*, you may benefit from having a windscreen placed over the face of the microphone. Several manufacturers supply open-cell polyurethane foam windscreens that only slightly affect the frequency response by eliminating some of the highs.

During rehearsals and on the air, always assume that your microphone is open (and when performing for television, that the camera is on). Watch what you say and do. Always assume that profanity and backbiting comments about others will be heard by someone, possibly with devastating consequences!

Camera Consciousness

Just as a microphone initiates the process of sending your voice to listeners, a camera is the first element in the transmission of your physical image. **Camera consciousness** begins with understanding the needs and limitations of cameras and recognizing the problems camera operators face. The discussion that follows covers only those technical aspects that are relevant to you as a performer.

A television camera picks up reflected light in much the same way the human eye does. Like the eye, a camera has a lens, an iris (or diaphragm), and a surface on which images are focused—the retina in the eye, a photosensitive surface in the camera pickup tube. The lens focuses the picture, the iris opens or closes to control the amount of light entering the system, and the photosensitive surface converts the light patterns into electrical impulses.

Unlike the human eye, the television camera does not do all its work automatically. Camera operators are responsible for focusing, and video engineers maintain the proper iris opening. (Field production cameras do have automatic iris controls.) Another difference between the eye and the camera is that the eye does not have a built-in zoom. The zoom lens allows a stationary camera to handle anything from a wide shot to an extreme close-up. To the eye a person standing 10 feet away will always be on the medium shot, so to speak. A final difference is that we can rapidly move our heads approximately 180 degrees horizontally, focusing on one object at the start and on another at the end of the head movement, without any sensation of blurring. A television camera cannot do this.

Keep these elementary facts about cameras in mind as you consider the following aspects of television performance.

Hitting Marks

Hitting marks means moving to an exact spot in a studio or in the field marked by a piece of tape or a chalk mark. When a specific movement is called for, it is important to move exactly as required and to come to rest in the predetermined position. There are at least three reasons why precision in hitting marks is critical.

1. The amount of light entering a lens determines the f-stop setting of the iris; the f-stop setting in turn determines the **depth of field**, the extent of the area in front of the camera in which everything is in focus (objects closer or farther away will be blurred). The greater the amount of light entering the lens, the smaller the iris opening and the greater the depth of field. Because zoom lenses have a great deal of glass through which the light must pass, because prompting devices cut down further on light entering the lens system, and because studio lighting is kept to the lowest possible level for the comfort of performers, the iris is generally quite open, and this reduces depth of field considerably. To put it plainly, if you don't hit your marks, you may be out of focus.

2. Another reason for hitting marks precisely is that the camera operator is responsible for the composition of the picture. Where you should stand for the best composition will have been determined earlier, and you must follow through in order to enable the camera operator to do a professional job.

3. A third reason for being meticulous about hitting marks is that studios often feature area lighting, which means that not all parts of the set are illuminated equally. If you miss your mark, you may be outside the area specifically prepared for your presentation.

Standing on Camera

When standing on camera, you must stand still and avoid rocking from side to side. Weaving or rocking from one foot to the other can be distracting on a long shot and disastrous on a close-up. In Figure 3.3 Terry Lowry shows how a little rocking looks on a medium shot and on a close-up. In a television studio a monitor will be placed where you can see it; therefore, you will know whether the camera has you on a wide, medium, or close-up shot and will be aware immediately if you are moving out of the picture. In the field you most likely will not have a monitor, and thus no way of knowing whether you are moving out of the frame.

The moral is to practice standing with a minimum of movement. To reduce a tendency to rock, stand with your feet slightly apart and with one foot turned out to form a 15-to-20-degree angle with the other foot; the turned foot should be 4 or 5 inches in front of the other. Standing in this manner should make it all but impossible to rock.

Figure 3.3
Talk show hostess Terry Lowry shows how rocking from side to side, which may seem a perfectly natural movement for the announcer, looks to viewers in (left) a wide-angle shot and (right) a close-up shot. (Courtesy of KTVU, Oakland)

Sitting on Camera

You will find it easier to avoid excessive random movement when seated, but remember that most movements are exaggerated on television. If you find that you habitually move your upper torso and head in rapid or wide-ranging motions, you should work to reduce such movement—without at the same time seriously lowering your natural energy level. Sideways movement can be very annoying, especially on close-ups. Movement toward and away from the camera can take you in and out of focus.

Telegraphing Movement

When rising or sitting down and when moving from one part of the studio (or exterior location) to another, you must move somewhat more slowly than you ordinarily would, and you must telegraph your movement. To **telegraph a movement** is to begin it with a slow and slight motion followed by a pause before following through with the intended movement. Camera operators are trained to follow even fast-moving athletes, but you should not test their skill unnecessarily. A little thoughtfulness on your part can guarantee that you will not cross them up.

You should not sit down or stand up on camera unless the movement has been planned in advance or signaled by the floor director. When the camera is on a head shot of a standing performer and the performer suddenly sits, the head drops right out of the picture. When the camera is on a head shot of a seated performer who suddenly stands, the result is even worse: the viewer is treated to the infamous crotch shot. In Figure 3.4 Eric Greene shows how this movement looks on television. If you find that you must stand up when no such movement was planned, telegraphing is imperative—it will give the director time to zoom out to a wider and safer shot.

Cheating to the Camera

To **cheat to the camera** is to position yourself so as to create the impression that you are talking to another person (as in an interview) while still presenting a favorable appearance on screen. Such positioning has no relevance to a television performer making a direct address to the camera, as a news anchor does. But when a performer is speaking to a guest or a co-host, two requirements that would be mutually exclusive if it were not for cheating should be satisfied: viewers want to see the faces of both persons, and they want to feel that the two are speaking to one another rather than to the audience. So, instead of presenting only their profiles as they speak, interviewer and guest position themselves at about a 25-degree angle from one another—thereby **opening up to the camera**—while continuing to speak as though they were facing one another directly.

When standing or sitting with another person, when conducting an interview, for example, position yourself nearer the other person than you would if you were talking with that person off-camera. We are all surrounded by an invisible area we consider our own personal space. When talking with others, we usually sit or stand at a com-

Figure 3.4
Television talk show host Eric Greene shows what happens when a performer suddenly rises, without previously telegraphing his movement. (Courtesy of KTVU, Oakland)

fortable distance from them. Television performing, however, is no respecter of this psychological space. The intimacy of television is best exploited when both interviewer and guest can be seen in a medium shot. Sitting or standing too far from another performer forces the director to settle for close-ups and wide shots. In unrehearsed programs the director wants to have an acceptable **cover shot,** a shot that can be used regardless of which person is speaking. If the only cover shot available is a long shot, the director's job is made more difficult.

Addressing the Camera

When directly addressing the camera (the viewer, actually), look straight into the lens, and focus your gaze about a foot behind the glass, for that is where your viewer is.

When searching for a thought or a word, many of us tend to raise our eyes toward the ceiling as we pause for inspiration. This is distracting and unflattering; if you have such a habit, you should work to overcome it.

Make certain you don't try to freeze a smile on your face while waiting for the director to go to black, to another camera, to a taped segment, or to a commercial. Try to make small and natural movements while you wait. In Figure 3.5 Nerissa Azurin demonstrates the look that results when a director stays on a shot too long and the performer attempts to hold a smile. This is called the **egg-on-face look.**

In a studio production you can expect to work with from two to four cameras; three are standard. This means that from time to time you will have to change your attention from one camera to another, on cue. The cuing sequence begins when the floor director points both hands to the **taking camera** (the camera that is on, indicated by an illuminated red light called a tally light). On a signal from the director, the floor director rapidly moves one or both hands to point to the camera to which you are to turn. When you are performing as a news anchor, the procedure is to notice the cue, glance down at your script, and then raise your head in the direction of the second camera. In Figure 3.6 Janet Zappala shows how to make a clean movement from one camera to another.

Do not stare at the camera. Just as staring at a person with whom you are speaking can make that person uncomfortable, staring at the camera lens can have the same effect on your viewers. As you speak

Figure 3.5
Nerissa Azurin, a bit impatient to get out of the limelight, wears the egg-on-face look as she waits for the director to go to a commercial break. (Courtesy of Nerissa Azurin)

Figure 3.6
The floor director is using hand signals to let the anchor know which camera is being used. This allows her to gracefully alter her eye contact to follow the changing camera angles. (Courtesy of KGO-TV, San Francisco)

(read), let your head make small, subtle movements. These should be natural movements, motivated by the words you are speaking.

Examine your appearance closely while viewing playbacks. In addition to watching for such obvious physical problems as poor posture, look at your mouth on a close-up. See if you have developed the unattractive and distracting habit of speaking out of the side of your mouth—in other words, speaking with one side of your mouth noticeably lower than the other. If so, practice straightening out your mouth while performing before a mirror. A lifetime habit of speaking with a crooked mouth may be difficult to overcome, but you must do so to have a future as a television announcer.

Finally, don't forget to use nonverbal communication when performing on camera. Facial expressions and head, hand, and torso movements *that are not overdone* can add much to your communicative abilities.

Holding Props

A **prop,** short for *property*, is an object that a performer holds, displays, or points to. Typical props are goods used in demonstration commercials, the food and utensils used in cooking shows, and books or album covers displayed by talk show hosts.

Hold maps, sketches, books, products, or other props with a steady hand. Chances are the director will want an extreme close-up of the object, and even a slight movement can take it out of focus or off-camera. Position the prop so that the taking camera has a good view of it.

When pointing to an object or a portion of it, move your hand, with the index finger extended, slowly and evenly toward the spot to be highlighted. Then hold that hand as steady as possible. Do not make quick motions here and there—the camera cannot follow them. Always rely on a monitor to check both your positioning and your hand movements.

When holding any object that has a reflective surface, such as the dust cover on a book or an album liner, check your monitor to make sure you are holding it at a correct angle. Studio lights reflected from any glossy object can totally wash out its details. In Figure 3.7 talk show hostess Terry Lowry shows the wrong and the right way to hold a prop with a reflective surface on camera.

When demonstrating a product or a procedure on camera, do not feel compelled to keep up a nonstop narration. Most of us have dif-

Figure 3.7
Talk show hostess Terry Lowry shows (left) the wrong way and (right) the right way to hold a reflective object on camera. (Courtesy of KTVU, Oakland)

ficulty speaking fluently while using our hands to show how something is done or used. Because television is a visual medium, some things are best left to sight alone. Of course, there are times when commentary is helpful or even necessary, so you should practice and perfect the skill of simultaneously speaking and demonstrating. But constant chatter, especially when marred by hesitancy and repetitions, is not good communication.

Holding Scripts

Scripts are used in live television primarily by news anchors. They are usually a backup to a prompting device. If the prompter fails or the person feeding it falls behind or rushes ahead of your delivery, then you can refer to your script. At some stations, however, you will not have a prompter and must work entirely from hand-held scripts. (Working with a prompter is discussed in a later section.)

When working with a script, hold it with both hands, above the desk and tilted toward you at a comfortable angle for reading. There are three important reasons for holding your script above desk level. First, as you look down to the script and then up to the camera, the degree of the up-and-down motion of your head is reduced. Second, as you look from camera to camera, you can move the script so as to keep it in front of you, thereby eliminating diagonal head movements. Also, if the script were flat on the surface of the desk, you would have to bend your head down, which would restrict the air flow and thus impair your vocal quality.

Figure 3.8
It is important to use peripheral vision. Reporter Cheryl Fong shows what happens when a performer on a close-up glances away for a cue. (Courtesy of Cheryl Fong)

Using Peripheral Vision

A periphery is a boundary. If you look straight ahead, you will find that the left and right boundaries of your vision extend in an arc of about 150 degrees. This is the range of your **peripheral vision,** and you should be able to pick up movements, such as hand signals, given to you within this area. Actually, you will need to use only about a 45-degree arc of your peripheral vision, because floor directors will give you signals as close as possible to the camera you are addressing. When receiving signals, do not allow your head or even your eyes to turn toward the signaler. In Figure 3.8 Cheryl Fong shows how even a slight movement of the eyes to pick up a cue can look on camera.

Clothing and Makeup

When performing on television, plan your clothing carefully. If your station's system uses chroma-keying, you should avoid wearing any shade of the color used for the mattes (blue or green in most instances). **Chroma-keying** is a process that allows a picture from one camera to be keyed in to a portion of the picture from another camera. If blue is the color of the chroma-key backdrops and you were to wear a blue shirt or blouse, the second picture would appear in the area of your blue clothing whenever a chroma-key matte was used.

Avoid any article of clothing that has small checks or narrow stripes. The television cameras cannot handle fine, high-contrast patterns, and a wavy, shimmering look, called the **moiré effect,** results. Also avoid black-and-white clothing; it can be accommodated by the television camera system if both lighting and background are compatible, but it makes problems for engineers. Pastel colors are best for nearly all broadcast purposes and are complimentary to people of all skin shades. Performers with extremely dark faces should wear clothing somewhat darker than that worn by people with light skin tones. The principle you should follow is to avoid excessive contrast between your face and your clothing and avoid clothing that is the same shade and color as your skin.

Jewelry can cause video problems, as can sequins. Studio lights reflected directly into the camera lens cause **flaring** (a flash on the television screen caused by signal overload due to light reflected from a highly polished object). This effect may be used to assert the glamour of a particular guest, but it is very distracting if created regularly by a program host.

If your vision needs correction, contact lenses will usually give you your best on-camera appearance. If you prefer wearing glasses, have their lenses treated with an anti-glare coating. The frames you choose are an important aspect of your appearance, so look for frames that are flattering and suit your on-air personality. Generally speaking, frames should not be so unusual as to call attention to themselves. Eyeglass frames made of metal may cause flaring, so choose plastic frames.

Makeup for television performers is usually quite simple and quickly applied. Makeup is used to reduce skin shine, eliminate five-o'clock shadow, improve skin color, and hide minor blemishes. It is seldom intended to drastically change the appearance of a television performer. Close-ups are too revealing of any such attempts to change basic facial features. If your complexion is very sallow, you must be careful to cover your entire face, neck, and ears with makeup, because the contrast between the near-white of uncovered skin and almost any color of makeup would be most noticeable. Some men, even when freshly shaven, show a dark cast in the beard and mustache area. Although pancake makeup helps cover five-o'clock shadow, there is also a special beard-stick that eliminates the problem in nearly all cases.

Always have powder or pancake makeup near you. Most sets are brightly lit, and the heat from lighting instruments may cause you to perspire. Check frequently to make sure you are not perspiring; if you are, apply powder during times you are off-camera.

Working with Cue Cards

Cue cards are used at most television stations to give the script of a short announcement to be made by an on-air performer; to list items to be ad-libbed, such as the names and professions of program guests; or to supply some bit of information to the performer, such as a telephone number to be given or a reminder to mention an upcoming segment of the show. For lengthy messages that must be read by on-air announcers, electronic prompters are used by nearly all television stations, large and small.

Some college departments of broadcasting do not own prompting devices, and students who must deliver lengthy messages word for word must rely on memorization or cue cards. Memorization involves a greater risk of disaster. The pressure of performing before one's peers along with the normal distractions of the television studio—

bright lights in one's face, time cues, signals from a floor director to change cameras—makes concentration on a memorized script quite difficult. For most learners cue cards are the best option.

Cue cards are generally made in one of two configurations. If the message is brief enough, the cue card will be a single sheet of poster board measuring 28 by 44 inches. The script is written on the card with a black felt marker. During rehearsals and performance a floor director holds the card to the right of the camera lens; as the performer reads the card, it is slowly moved upward so that the line being spoken is always alongside the lens. Although standard poster board is 28 inches wide, wide margins are generally left so that the reader/performer will have to employ a minimum of left-to-right head movement.

For longer messages smaller cue cards are used. These are generally wider than 24 inches and no more than 12 to 15 inches high. Less information can be placed on each of these smaller cards—a 30-second commercial will require several of them—but they help the performer maintain better eye contact with the viewer than is possible with the larger cards. Cards should be held as close to the lens as possible; the best placement is just below the lens, because this allows the performer to look directly at the viewer. If the script calls for a switch from one camera to another, either the cards must be duplicated, with one set held at each camera, or they must be divided according to the lines that are to be addressed to each camera.

When working with cue cards—especially with multiple ones—it is imperative that you practice with the person or persons who will be holding them during your performance. Even a slight hesitation in changing the cards can cause you to stop in midsentence. As you read from cue cards, practice looking as directly as possible into the lens, using your peripheral vision to its greatest degree. It isn't easy, but with regular practice you can develop this skill.

Working with Prompters

Most television stations use prompting devices to enable performers to maintain eye contact with viewers. Some prompters are entirely electronic; scripts are typed on a word processor, stored, and transmitted to a display terminal. Other prompters are combinations of mechanical and electronic components; a script made of pieces of paper taped together is run under the lens of a fixed camera. With both systems the image appears on a black-and-white monitor attached to each television camera; a mirror reflects this image onto a sheet of glass mounted at a 45-degree angle in front of the camera lens. The performer sees the script while looking directly at the lens. The speed of the moving script is regulated to match the reading speed of the performer. Also, with both systems **hard copy**—a script printed on sheets of 8½-by-11-inch paper—is generated for use by producers, directors, news anchors, and others. The script may be typed on an electronic keyboard and then duplicated in the number of copies required for production, or it may be typed directly onto **copy sets,** multipart forms that yield as many as eight copies, each of a different color. Copies go to each of the co-anchors, the producer, the director, the prompter operator, the tape librarian, and the station management, and one copy goes in the files.

Prompters are used most extensively on television newscasts. On talk, interview, game, variety, and other types of programs that are predominantly ad-libbed, prompters are used only for short messages that must be delivered verbatim (word for word) and, in some operations, to pass on information such as the nature of an upcoming program segment.

When delivering a commercial or a station editorial, you will seldom have a script in your hands or on a desk in front of you. Nearly all such performances are taped and can be repeated if the prompter malfunctions. During a live newscast, on the other hand, it is imperative that you have a complete script to turn to in the event that the prompter ceases to work or gets out of phase with your reading.

When you go on the air for a 60-minute newscast, you will have a complete script, but you can expect it to be revised or replaced during the broadcast. Runners will bring new copy to you and to the prompter operator. Instructions to toss to a reporter in the field or to a co-anchor in the newsroom will be given to you by the director or producer over an **IFB** (interrupted foldback), a small earpiece that contains a speaker.[2] You will also receive instructions passed on by the floor manager during commercial breaks, reports from the field, or taped stories.

Because you will not have had an opportunity to study those portions of your script that are written and delivered after the start of the newscast, skill in sight reading is extremely important. You may have a chance to skim the new copy for names of people, places, or things that you may have trouble pronouncing, but there is no guar-

---

[2]To **toss** is to give a brief ad-libbed introduction to another announcer, such as a co-anchor or a weather reporter.

antee that anyone in the studio or control room will be able to help you with the pronunciation. For this reason, you should establish an understanding with the newswriters, assignment editors, and associate producers that unusual words or names will be phoneticized on the copy that goes to you and the prompter. As an example, your script may read

```
THE EAST AFRICAN NATION OF DJIBOUTI

(JEE-BOO'-TEE) HAS BEEN HIT BY A SEVERE PLAGUE

OF LOCUSTS.
```

In this instance, the newswriter took the phoneticized spelling from the pronouncer included in the wire-service copy from which the story was taken. **Pronouncer** is the term used by news services for the phonetic transcriptions of words and names that have been inserted in wire-service copy.

In the above example the wire-service pronouncer appears in all capital letters, with an apostrophe to indicate the syllable to be stressed. A second style of wire-service phonetics has stressed syllables in upper case and the unstressed syllables in lower case, as in the following example:

```
WASHINGTON-A DIETARY SUPPLEMENT THAT MAY CAUSE

A FATAL BLOOD DISORDER HAS BEEN REMOVED FROM

SALE BY ITS MANUFACTURER. L-TRYPTOPHAN

(el-TRIP-toe-fan) HAS BEEN LINKED TO THE

POTENTIALLY FATAL BLOOD DISEASE EOSINOPHILIA

(EE-uh-sin-uh-FEEL-ee-yuh). A NATIONAL CONSUMER

ORGANIZATION PRAISED THE MANUFACTURER'S DECISION,

AND CALLED THE HALT IN SALES A QUOTE, ''PRUDENT

AND CAUTIOUS COURSE OF ACTION.''
```

If you type your own script, make certain that each sentence is indented four or five spaces. This will enable you to more quickly spot the part of the story you are reading in the event of prompter failure. As you read from the prompter, slowly move your right thumb down the side of your hand-held script. With practice, you can eventually become quite precise in keeping your thumb positioned at the point of the story as it is read from the prompter.

Never hyphenate a word at the end of a typewritten line in a script. An announcer must be able to see entire words without having to shift the eyes back to the beginning of a new line for the conclusion of a word. If, for example, a line ended with *con*, there would be no way for an announcer reading along to know whether the rest of the word were *tinuous*, *tinent*, or *vict*.

When working with a prompter, make sure that the camera is at least 10 to 15 feet in front of you. Eye movement as you scan the projected script will be less noticeable at that distance. Glance down at the script frequently. This not only eliminates the staring look but keeps you in touch with the ongoing script—a necessity in case the prompter fails.

Instructions and Cues

Many radio and television announcers work as members of teams and must therefore develop harmonious relationships and efficient means of communicating. Disc jockeys and others who work solo do not, of course, have the same kinds of communication needs. Because you cannot be certain that you will always work independently, you should learn to coordinate your efforts with those of others.

Instructions and cues are given to television performers by floor directors and producers. Floor directors use either oral or visual means of communicating, depending on whether the instruction comes at a time when oral communication is feasible. Television producers communicate by way of an IFB. On-air radio announcers and performers working in a recording studio may receive instructions from an engineer or a producer. These instructions may be given orally over an intercom connecting a control room with a studio, through a headset, or as hand signals. In general, instructions from floor directors and engineers are confined to details such as cuing, indicating an upcoming program break, and signaling the improper use of equipment or (in television) of lights. Producers usually concern themselves with matters of interpretation or changes of plan, such as dropping a news story. Regardless of who issues the instructions, it is your responsibility to carry them out promptly and effectively.

Figure 3.9
Cooperation is vital between on-air personnel and production staff. Every radio or television station has its own system of cues and signals to help announcers stay aware of the show's timing and camera angles. News co-anchors Don Sanchez and Cheryl Jennings wait for the cue that will let them know when to go back on-air after a commercial break. (Courtesy of KGO-TV, San Francisco)

Several considerations are involved in developing good working relationships. First, as an announcer you are not expected to act like a mindless automaton. There will be ample opportunity for you to talk over your ideas and concepts with others. However, while a program is being broadcast is not the time to exercise independent judgment. Follow the instructions you have been issued; if appropriate, discuss them later.

Second, when rehearsing or when making a number of takes of a performance under the coaching of a producer or a director (for example, when recording the narrative for a documentary or when recording commercials), do your best to implement suggestions. If your director welcomes it, you may discuss alternative ways to deliver lines, but always remember that the producer's word is final. One effective way to express your opinion is to say "What if I tried it this way?" This approach is tactful and nonthreatening and will most likely be productive.

During rehearsals, do not feel compelled to continually explain why you did something this or that way or why you made a mistake. No one is really interested, and alibis and explanations only delay the project.

During rehearsals and performances, always remain alert for cues and instructions. Sometimes you will wait an eternity for a problem, usually a technical one, to be ironed out. This is no time for day-dreaming and certainly no time to leave your position. When the problem is corrected, you will be needed—at once.

Always treat every member of the production team with respect. No one is unimportant, and your success—and that of the show—depends on the degree of commitment and the quality of performance of every member.

Taking a Level

Before nearly every performance you will be asked to take a level. The purpose is to give the audio engineer an opportunity to adjust the volume control associated with your microphone. Because so much time can be wasted in taking voice levels and because getting faulty results will be detrimental to the announcer and the production, it is necessary for you to understand this procedure.

Before taping or going on the air, the engineer must know the volume level of all audio inputs. In the simplest production this means the volume level of the announcer; in elaborate productions it might mean the levels of several voices, music, and sound effects. The engineer's job is to mix or blend audio inputs in the proper proportions

Figure 3.10
Prior to a broadcast, a radio or television announcer often works with an audio engineer to take a level. (Courtesy of Turner Broadcasting System)

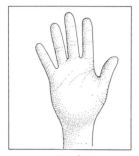

attention

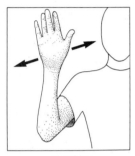

stand-by

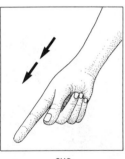

cue

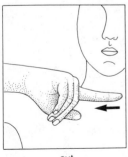

cut

and with optimum quality. When taking a level, an engineer can tell you if you are off-mic, if you are too loud or too soft, or if you are popping or creating excessive sibilance. **Popping** is an air blast when plosives are sounded; plosives are the consonants *p*, *b*, *t*, *d*, *k* and *g*. **Sibilance** is the hissing sound made when the letter *s*, and sometimes *sh* or *z*, is sounded. You cannot sound your best if you are misusing your mic. An audio engineer can help you make the most effective use of your voice, but you must cooperate. When you are asked to take a level, *it is imperative that you read from the actual script to be used* (*or, if ad-libbing, that you speak at exactly the same volume you will use during the performance*), *that you position yourself in relation to the mic exactly as you will during the show, and that you continue reading or ad-libbing until the engineer is satisfied with the result.*

In taking a level, follow this procedure.

1. As you sit or stand before a mic or after a lavaliere mic has been clipped on, remain silent. Unnecessary chatter is distracting and potentially embarrassing if your mic is open.
2. Wait patiently and alertly for a signal to take a level; the signal will probably be given orally by a floor director (television) or by an engineer over an intercom (radio). If you must depend on a visual signal, keep watching the engineer.
3. On receiving the signal, move into the exact position and posture you will use during the performance, *and read or speak exactly as you will later on.*
4. When working with a script, read from that script, using all of the vitality, emotion, and other qualities you intend to use in actual performance. Do not hold back, thinking that it is wise to save yourself for the real thing.
5. As you read or speak, remain alert for any hand signals given by the floor director or engineer, which might indicate "louder," "softer," or "move closer to (or away from) the mic."
6. As you make the suggested adjustments (if any), continue to speak until the signal is given that everything is satisfactory.

Hand Signals

In radio and television hand signals are sometimes used for communication between members of a working team. Hand signals were developed in the early days of radio because soundproof glass partitions separated directors and engineeers from performers. As radio turned to recorded music, most music announcers began doing their

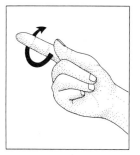

speed up

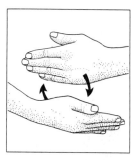

wrap up

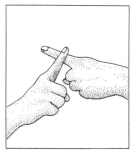

30 seconds

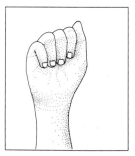

15 seconds

own engineering. Today, many radio stations do not even have a control room adjacent to the announce booth or studio. Despite this, some hand signals are still used in radio and in television, and students of announcing should understand and be able to use them.

Most of the signals that follow are standard throughout the industry, but their use may vary from station to station. Some signals are used only in radio, some only in television, and others in both.

Radio and television signals

- The **attention signal**, a simple waving of the hand, usually precedes the stand-by signal. In radio it is given by an engineer, in television by the floor director.
- The **standby signal** is made by holding the hand slightly above the head, palm toward the announcer. The standby signal is given at any time when the announcer cannot judge the precise moment at which to pick up a cue, such as at the beginning of a program. (A different standby signal is used in television when cuing the anchor from one camera to another.) At some stations the standby signal is given by the operator of the camera that will go live next.
- The **cue signal** is made by rapidly lowering the hand from the standby position, with the index finger extended and pointing directly at the person being cued. The cue signal nearly always follows the standby signal; neither signal is normally given alone. At some television stations the cue signal is thrown toward the camera that is going on the air. In some radio operations the cue signal is given as often by the announcer as by the engineer. Music and fast-paced news programming require timing to the split second, and cues are given by the person who is in the best position to coordinate the elements of production.
- The **cut signal** is made by drawing the index finger across the throat. This signals an emergency; on receiving it, stop speaking at once. After stopping your performance, wait for oral or visual signals before beginning again.
- The **slow-down or stretch signal** is given by a television floor director or an audio engineer or director. It is made by pulling the hands apart, as though pulling taffy. Because *slow down* and *stretch* mean two different things, you must rely on the context in which the signal is given to know how to interpret it. When you are reading from a script, the signal means to slow the pace of your delivery; when you are ad-libbing, it means to stretch (in other words, to keep talking until a further signal is given).

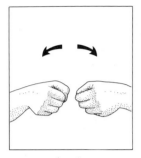

break

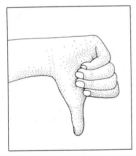

introduce report

drop report

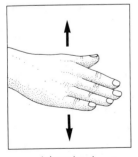

take a level

- The **speed-up signal** is given by holding the hand before the body, index finger extended, and then rotating the hand. On receiving this signal, you should increase the pace of your delivery. The signal is imprecise; it does not tell you how much you should speed up or for how long. Later directions or signals will give you this information. You must be careful not to confuse this signal with the wrap-up sign.
- The **wrap-up signal** is made by holding both hands in front of the torso and then rotating them about 8 inches apart so that first one hand and then the other is on top. On receiving this signal, you should bring the program or the segment to a close as soon as possible in a smooth and natural way.
- As a program nears its conclusion or as a segment of a program nears a station break, it is important for an announcer to know the exact number of minutes or seconds remaining. Time signals are given in the same manner for both radio and television, though they are used much more in television. They are as follows:

   three-minute signal—three fingers held up and waved slowly

   two-minute signal—two fingers held up and waved slowly

   one-minute signal—the index finger held up and waved slowly

   thirty-second signal—the right and left arms crossed (television) or the index finger of one hand crossed with the index finger of the other (radio)

   fifteen-second signal—a clenched fist held upright and near the head

   ten-to-zero signal—all fingers on both hands held up and then lowered one at a time as the seconds are counted down

   five-to-zero signal—the fingers on one held up and then lowered one by one

Television signals
- The **stand-by signal**, most often used in newscasts, tells the anchor to prepare to be waved from one camera to another. It is made by holding both hands next to the lens of the taking camera. Figure 3.5 shows this signal.
- The **switch-camera signal** tells you to look immediately toward the camera to which you have been waved. The floor director will have

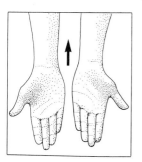

louder

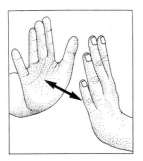

softer

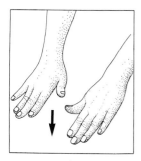

move closer to mic

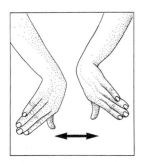

move back from mic

progressed from the stand-by signal to the switch-camera signal by moving one or both hands from the first to the second camera. An earlier section of this chapter, "Addressing the Camera," tells how this transition is best made when working with a script.

- The **break signal**, used chiefly on interview and talk programs, tells you that you should wrap up the present segment for a commercial break. The signal is made by holding the hands as though they were grasping a brick or a stick of wood and then making a breaking motion.
- The **introduce-report signal** consists of a thumbs-up sign given to a news anchor to indicate that a planned report from the field is ready to go on the air. The **drop-report signal** is a thumbs-down sign meaning that the report is not to be introduced. Reports may be dropped because of technical difficulties or because of time pressures.

Radio signals (also used in some audio recording studios)

- The **take-a-level signal** is generally made by holding the hand palm down and then moving it back and forth as though smoothing a pile of sand. In some operations the signal is given by holding a hand at face level, with the tip of the thumb touching the fingers, and then opening and closing the hand rapidly, as though to say "go on and gab." This usage should be discouraged because it can be confused with the signal for an upcoming tape. The signal to take a level is not often used; an oral cue is preferred by most audio engineers. At times it can be used with the following four hand signals for efficiently directing a performer to make the best use of a microphone.
- The **louder signal** tells the performer to increase volume and is made by holding the hand before the body, palm up, and then raising the hand.
- The **softer signal** tells the performer to reduce volume and is made by holding the hand before the body, palm down and then lowering the hand.
- The **move-closer-to-the-mic signal** is made in two ways. In the first, the hands are held apart, palms toward each other, and then moved so as to bring them together. (This version is sometimes used in television to tell a performer to move closer to another person on the set.) The alternative way to make this signal is to hold a hand at face level, the palm toward the mouth, and then move the hand toward the mouth.

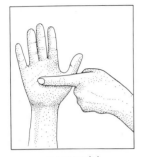

commercial

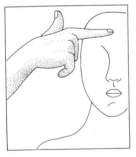

cart

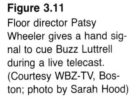

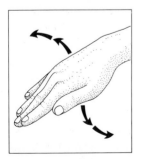

headlines

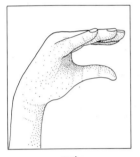

sounder

- The **move-back-from-the-mic signal** also has two versions. In the first, the hands are held close to one another in front of the body, with the backs facing one another, and then moved further apart. The second version is to hold a hand at face level, with the back toward the mouth, and then move it away from the face.

- The **commercial signal** is made by touching the index finger of one hand to the palm of the other. It may be given by an engineer or an announcer to indicate that a recorded commercial will follow.

- The **cart signal** is made by holding up one hand in the shape of a U or a C, as though the hand were holding a tape cartridge. (Cart is an abbreviation for tape cartridge.) In news operations the cart signal indicates that the news item coming up includes a carted segment, usually a recorded report from a reporter in the field.

- The **headlines signal** is made either by drawing the index finger across the forehead or by tapping the top of the head. The signal is given by the announcer to tell the engineer that news headlines will follow the news item then being read. The engineer is to play the headlines sounder. **Sounders,** also called **logos** or **IDs,** are musical jingles that introduce sports reports, consumer action reports, business news, and similar regular features.

Figure 3.11
Floor director Patsy Wheeler gives a hand signal to cue Buzz Luttrell during a live telecast. (Courtesy WBZ-TV, Boston; photo by Sarah Hood)

• The **sounder signal** is made by holding the hand flat, palm down, and moving it from right to left while simultaneously making it flutter. The signal is given by the announcer to tell the engineer that the next scheduled feature is coming up and that the appropriate sounder is to be played on cue.

There is a natural tendency to acknowledge that one has received and understood a hand signal. Experienced performers working with professional crews do not send back a signal indicating "message received, will comply." At some stations, however, and especially when new, unrehearsed, or unusually complex programs are being produced, performers are asked to acknowledge hand signals. In some instances this acknowledgment is conveyed by an unobtrusive hand or finger movement; in others it may involve a larger gesture. Follow the practice preferred by the director or producer of the show.

Phonetic Transcription

As an announcer, you face unique and challenging problems in pronunciation. In reading news, commercial, and classical music copy, you will frequently encounter words of foreign origin, and you will be expected to read them fluently and correctly. As a newscaster, you will be expected not only to pronounce foreign words and names with accuracy and authority, but also to know when and how to Americanize many of them. Although British announcers are allowed to Anglicize categorically, you would be seen as odd or incompetent if you said DON KWICKS-OAT for Don Quixote or DON JEW-UN for Don Juan, as they do.

Because English pronunciation is subject to few general rules, English is one of the most difficult languages to learn. In Spanish the letters *ch* are always pronounced as in the name *Charles*; in American English *ch* may be pronounced in the following ways:

sh as in *Cheyenne*

tch as in *champion*

k as in *chemist*

two separate sounds, as in the name *MacHeath*

There are many other examples. In the sentence "I usually used to use this," the letter *s* is sounded differently in the words *usually*, *used*, and *use*. The letter *a* is pronounced differently in the words *cap*, *father*, *mate*, *care*, *call*, *boat*, and *about*. Similar variations are seen for all other vowel sounds and most consonants as well. For example, *th* is pronounced differently in *Thomas*, *though*, and *then*; *r* is pronounced differently in *run*, *fire*, and *boor*. Letters may at times be silent, as in *mnemonic*, *Worcester*, and *Wednesday*. At other times, and for no apparent reason, a word is correctly pronounced only when all letters in it receive some value, as in *misunderstood* and *circumstances*. The letters *ie* are sometimes pronounced "eye," as in *pie*, and sometimes "ee," as in *piece*. Two words with almost identical spellings, such as *said* and *maid*, can have quite different pronunciations. In short, the only constant in spoken American English is variation.

The whole problem of English pronunciation was reduced to its most obvious absurdity by George Bernard Shaw, who wrote *ghoti* and asked how this manufactured word was to be pronounced. After all attempts had failed, Shaw revealed that it was to be pronounced "fish": the *gh* to be pronounced "f" as in *enough*, the *o* to be pronounced "ih" as in *women*, and the *ti* to be pronounced "sh" as in *motion*.

Of course, common words do not cause pronunciation problems. But try to determine the correct pronunciation of the following words—some quite familiar, others less so—according to your knowledge of language and any rules of pronunciation you may have learned:

quay	flaccid	dais
mortgage	interstices	gunwale
medieval	forecastle	brooch
egregious	cliché	phthisic

Now look up the correct pronunciation of these words in any standard dictionary. After checking the pronunciation, you will certainly agree that no amount of puzzling over them, and no rules of pronunciation, would have helped.

Correct American pronunciation of English not only is inherently illogical but also changes with time and common usage, generally tending toward simpler forms. It is becoming more and more acceptable, for example, to pronounce *clothes* as KLOZ, to leave the first *r* out of *February*, and to slide over the slight "y" sound in *news* so that it becomes NOOZ.

If you have difficulty pronouncing words whose spelling offers little help, you may be doubly perplexed by American personal names and place names that are derived from foreign originals. As a sportscaster, for example, you cannot assume that a player named Braun gives his own name the correct German pronunciation, "Brown." He may pronounce it "Brawn" or "Brahn." If, as a sportscaster, you tried to pronounce every foreign-derived name as it would be pronounced in the country of origin, your audience would wince every time you failed to use the established pronunciation.

American place names present the same problem. In Nebraska, *Beatrice* is pronounced BEE-AT'-RIS. In South Dakota, *Pierre* is pronounced PEER. In California, *Delano* is pronounced DUH-LANE'-O. In Kentucky, *Versailles* is pronounced VER-SALES'. In Georgia, *Vienna* is pronounced VYE-EN'-UH. In the Southwest, Spanish place names are conventionally pronounced neither as the Spanish original nor as they seem to be spelled. For example, in California, the *San* in *San Jose* is pronounced as in *sand* rather than as Spanish speakers would pronounce it (as in *sonnet*), and HO-ZAY is used rather than the Americanized JO-ZAY or the Spanish HO-SAY.

Because the only standard for pronouncing place names is the common practice of the natives of the region, you must be on guard to avoid error. All American and Canadian communities have special and capricious ways of pronouncing the names of streets, suburbs, nearby towns, and geographic landmarks. Radio and television announcers who are new to an area and consistently offend listeners with mispronunciations may not be around long enough to learn regional preferences. Bostonians may not care if you mispronounce *Pago Pago* (PANG'-GO PANG'-GO), but they will be outraged if you pronounce *Quincy* as QUIN-CEE' rather than QUINZ'-EE.

It is not surprising that the problems inherent in the pronunciation of American English have given rise to various systems of phonetic transcription. Two of these systems are outlined here, and the third—the International Phonetic Alphabet—is introduced here and discussed fully in Chapter 14.

Wire-Service Phonetics

Several news agencies provide radio and television stations with news stories, sending them via satellite and telephone lines to teleprinters and computer terminals. When a word or a name that might cause pronunciation problems is transmitted, that word often is phoneticized—given a pronouncer—as in this example.

```
(SYDNEY, AUSTRALIA) THE ISLAND NATION OF

VANUATU (VAHN-OO-AH'-TOO)-FORMERLY THE NEW

HEBRIDES (HEB'-RIH-DEEZ)-WAS HIT TODAY BY A

STRONG EARTHQUAKE.
```

Pronouncers are useful, but you should not rely on them completely. They are sometimes ambiguous and occasionally inaccurate. A few sounds defy accurate transcription. Wherever possible, check pronunciations in dictionaries, atlases, or other appropriate sources.

All of the symbols of wire-service phonetics appear in Table 3.1 arranged in the same order in which they appear in the International Phonetic Alphabet. (Since we are dealing with speech sounds, alphabetic arrangement has no relevance.) Key words have been chosen for clarity, so most are quite commonplace. Two symbols are sometimes given for a single sound. For example, for the second vowel sound listed, I works well for the word *impel*, but IH works better for *Bethesda*. If this word were transcribed as BI-THEZ'-DUH instead of BIH-THEZ'-DUH, a reader might pronounce the first syllable as the English word *by*.

With a little practice—and some ingenuity—you can make wire-service phonetics into a useful tool. The consonants are easiest to learn because most of them represent only one sound; the symbols T, D, S, Z, and M, for instance, can hardly cause confusion. Other consonant sounds need two letters to represent them, for example, TH (THIN), CH (CHAT), and SH (SHOP). One symbol, Y, is used for two sounds, one a consonant and the other a diphthong. As a consonant, it appears in the word *yeoman* (YO'-MUN); as a diphthong, it represents an entirely different sound, as in *sleight* (SLYT). The symbol TH is the most troublesome, for it represents the initial sounds in *think* and *then*. Context can help in some instances, but not all. It works for *hearth* (HAHRTH), but not *calisthenics*. Anyone seeing KAL-UHS-THEN'-IKS might read THEN as the common English word, and this is not the correct sound.

Some vowel sounds are a bit troublesome, but they usually can be differentiated by their contexts. The letters OO, for example stand

Table 3.1   Symbols of Wire-Service Phonetics

	Symbol	Key Word	Phonetic Transcription
Vowels	EE	*believe*	(BIH-LEEV′)
	I or IH	*impel, Bethesda*	(IM-PEL′) (BIH-THEZ′-DUH)
	AY	*bait*	(BAYT)
	E or EH	*pester, beret*	(PEST′-ER) (BEH-RAY′)
	A	*can*	(KAN)
	AH	*comma*	(KAH′-MUH)
	AW	*lost*	(LAWST)
	O	*host*	(HOST)
	OO	*mooring*	(MOOR′-ING)
	OO	*pool*	(POOL)
	ER	*early*	(ER′-LEE)
	UH	*sofa*	(SO′-FUH)
Diphthongs	Y	*lighting*	(LYT′-ING)
	AU	*grouse*	(GRAUS)
	OY	*oiling*	(OY′-LING)
	YU	*using*	(YUZ′-ING)
Consonants*	TH	*think*	(THINGK)
	TH	*then*	(THEN)
	SH	*clash*	(KLASH)
	ZH	*measure*	(MAYZH′-ER)
	CH	*church*	(CHERCH)
	J	*adjust*	(UH-JUST′)
	NG	*singing*	(SING′-ING)
	Y	*yeoman*	(YO′-MUN)

*The consonants P, B, T, D, K, G, F, V, S, Z, H, M, N, L, W, and R are pronounced as in English and therefore are not listed. The symbol G is always as in *green*, never as in *Gene*.

for vowel sounds in *food* and *poor*, which are not, of course, the same. Here is how context can help distinguish between them:

buoy (BOO′-EE)   Purim (POOR′-IHM)

In these examples, the common words *boo* and *poor* tell which sound to give OO.

It is not for common words that wire-service phonetics were developed. Here are some typical words that might be given pronouncers by a wire service:

Beirut (BAY-ROOT')   Sidon (SYD'-UN)

Bayreuth (BY'-ROYT)   Coelho (KWAY'-LO)

Clio (KLY'-O)   Ojai (O'-HY)

Schuylkill (SKUHL'-KIL)   Yosemite (YO-SEM'-IH-TEE)

Faneuil (FAN'-UHL)   Hamtramck (HAM-TRAM'-IK)

Obviously, your use of such phonetic transcription will be reserved for the few names and words in your copy that require you to turn to a dictionary, gazetteer, or similar reference work. Table 3.2 offers suggested sources for correct pronunciations in several different problem categories.

At times you will have to read a news story for which no pronouncers are given. In a rip-and-read operation you will have to attempt difficult copy without adequate preparation time.[3] When time permits, you should do your own transcribing of difficult words, as in this example, done easily and quickly on a word processor:

```
(NASHVILLE, TENNESSEE) MEDICAL RESEARCHERS TODAY

REVEALED A STUDY SHOWING THAT AS FEW AS TWO CUPS

OF COFFEE CAN CUT THE BLOOD FLOW TO YOUR BRAIN BY

10 TO 20 PERCENT. DR. WILLIAM WILSON, ASSISTANT

PROFESSOR OF PSYCHIATRY AT VANDERBILT UNIVERSITY,

AND CO-AUTHOR OF THE STUDY, SAID: ''WHILE THE

BLOOD-FLOW REDUCTION DOES NOT SEEM SEVERE ENOUGH

TO CAUSE PROBLEMS IN NORMAL INDIVIDUALS, IT

IS UNCLEAR WHETHER IT MAY INCREASE THE RISK

OF TRANSIENT ISCHEMIC (IZ-KEE'-MIK) ATTACKS
```

[3]**Rip and read** refers to the practice of tearing wire-service copy off a printer and almost immediately reading it on the air, without taking time to look for typos or pronunciation problems or to decide on interpretation.

Table 3.2 Sources for Correct Pronunciations of Names and Place Names

Category	Source
Names of persons	The individual featured in the story; failing that, members of the family or associates
Foreign names	Appropriate embassy or consulate
Foreign place names	*Columbia Lippincott Gazetteer of the World*
State or regional place names	State or regional historical societies or the state police or highway patrol
Names of members of legislatures	Clerk of the legislature

```
AND CEREBRAL INFARCTIONS (SEH-REE'-BRUHL

IN-FARK'-SHUNZ) IN HIGH-RISK INDIVIDUALS OR

THOSE RECOVERING FROM CEREBROVASCULAR

(SEH-REE'-BRO-VAS'-KYU-LER) ACCIDENTS."

CAFFEINE COULD ALSO MAGNIFY THE

EFFECTS OF CERTAIN DRUGS, SUCH AS

THE DIET DRUG PHENYLPROPANOLAMINE

(FEN'-UHL-PRO-PAN-OHL'-UH-MEEN), WHICH ALREADY

CONTAINS CAFFEINE.
```

   Wire-service phonetics work well in this example, but there are times when the system will not work. There is simply no foolproof way to use the twenty-six letters of the English language to represent more than forty speech sounds. Furthermore, the wire-service system does not include symbols for most foreign speech sounds that do not occur in English. Until a few years ago, teletype machines were limited to the same symbols found on an ordinary typewriter. Today's teleprinters, however, could be programmed to reproduce any symbol desired, so the time may come when additional pronunciation symbols will be added to the twenty-six letters now in use. A good starting point would be to add these symbols from the International Phonetic Alphabet:

[ð] for the initial sound in *then*
[ʊ] for the vowel sound in *good*

At the end of Chapter 15, "Foreign Pronunciation," there is news and commercial copy featuring names and words in a variety of foreign languages. For practice you should transcribe these names and words into wire-service phonetics and then read the copy aloud. Work with this and other practice copy until you find it easy to do phonetic transcriptions and can read them without errors or hesitation.

Diacritical Marks

Dictionaries use a system of phonetic transcription that features small marks placed above the vowels *a*, *e*, *i*, *o*, and *u*, along with a few additional symbols for sounds such as *th* in *thin* and *zh* in *vision*. The *American Heritage Dictionary* uses these symbols:

ă pat	ā pay	â care	ä father
ĕ pet	ē be		
ĭ pit	ī pie	î pier	
ŏ pot	ō toe	ô paw	
o͞o took	o͞o boot		
th thin	*th* this		
ŭ cut	û urge		
zh vision			
ə about			

The diacritical marks are not totally standardized; there are variations from dictionary to dictionary. The *American Heritage Dictionary* uses seventeen symbols to indicate the vowel sounds of the English language. *Webster's Collegiate Dictionary*, on the other hand, uses thirty symbols. If you decide to use diacritical marks to indicate correct pronunciation on your scripts, it is important to adopt one system of marks and stick with it. Going from one dictionary to another would be very confusing.

The system of phonetic transcription used in dictionaries has at least three important limitations. First, diacritical marks are rather difficult to learn and to remember. The publishers of English-language dictionaries recognize this fact and place a guide to pronunciation at the bottom of every page. A second disadvantage is that diacritical marks were not designed for use by oral readers. The marks are small and vary only slightly in their configurations. When accuracy under pressure is demanded, diacritical marks often fail to meet the test. A final limitation of the method of transcription used in dictionaries is that the key words used may vary in pronunciation from area to area. To learn that *fog* is pronounced as *dog* tells a Texan that "fawg" rhymes with "dawg" and a Rhode Islander that "fahg" rhymes with "dahg."

Some modern dictionary publishers have developed rather sophisticated pronunciation guides. They have eliminated some ambiguity through the use of more standardized key words. Fairly extensive discussions of pronunciation, symbols to indicate foreign speech sounds not heard in the English language, and a few symbols from more sophisticated systems of phonetic transcription have been added.

The International Phonetic Alphabet

The International Phonetic Alphabet (IPA) was devised to overcome the ambiguities of earlier systems of speech transcription. Like any other system that attempts to transcribe sounds into written symbols, it is not totally accurate. It does, however, come closer to perfection than any other system. Like diacritics, the IPA uses key words to indicate pronunciation, so if you speak with a regional accent, you may have difficulty making the IPA work for you.

The International Phonetic Association has assigned individual written symbols to all the speech sounds of the major languages of the world. Whether the language is French, German, or English, the symbol [e] is always pronounced "ay" as in *bait*. Speech sounds not found in English have distinct symbols: for example, [x] represents the sound *ch* in the German word *ach*, and [y] represents the sound *u* in the French word *lune*.

The IPA is not difficult to learn, but few professional announcers use or have even heard of it. Most broadcast announcers get by with wire-service phonetics or diacritics, but those who want to excel in certain areas of news or sports announcing (international coverage or competitions) should learn and continue to practice with the IPA. The same is certainly true for classical music announcers.

Chapter 14 presents a detailed exposition of the IPA. With the help of the IPA, you can learn the principles of French, German, Spanish, and Italian pronunciation, as presented in Chapter 15.

Performance Skills

Preparing for a Performance

Conscientious preparation for a performance is necessary for all but the most seasoned veterans, and proper preparation involves several considerations. Once you have worked in the field for many years, announcing will be as natural as breathing. Until then, follow the suggestions in this section to prepare for smooth and confident performances.

First, if you are working with a script, you should study and mark it. Underline words to be stressed. Write, in phonetics, the correct pronunciation of difficult words or names. Note any words that might be mistaken for others; for example, the following words are sometimes confused because of similar spellings:

though—through

county—country

uniformed—uninformed

united—untied

mediation—meditation

complaint—compliant

impudent—imprudent

To eliminate the possibility of reading such words incorrectly, mark your copy. You might write *tho* and *thru* for the first pair of words and use hyphens for the others: *coun-ty*, *coun-try*; *un-in-formed*, *uni-formed*; *u-nited*, *un-tied*; and so on.

The final 10 minutes before a performance are critical. You must try to separate yourself from any distracting activities and concentrate on your upcoming performance. If you are excessively nervous, try to relax; if you are apathetic, try to psych yourself up to an appropriate degree of energy.

If your performance is to be ad-lib, go over its objectives, and make determinations about how you will structure your ideas within the allotted time. How much time will you give to your opening? How much will you give to your conclusion? How much time does this leave for the body of your presentation?

Note the placement of microphones and, for a television presentation, the cameras. Note where you will sit or stand, and decide

Checklist: Preparing to Perform

1. Study the script; mark it for correct pronunciation of and distinction among words
2. Use the final 10 minutes before your performance to separate yourself from all distractions; concentrate on calming your nerves and psyching up your energy level.
3. Note the placement of microphones in the studio. Note where you will sit, and decide how you will hold your script. For video performances, check lighting and the range within which you may move without retreating into shadows. Check with the floor director about which camera(s) will be used and whether any unusual camera shots will be taken.
4. Practice holding and demonstrating any objects that will be part of your performance; find out to which camera you will be presenting the object.
5. Remind yourself to speak slowly, and to continue gracefully with your broadcast if you should stumble.

where you will hold or place your script. For television, check out the lighting, and determine exactly where you will stand or sit and how far you may be able to move in each direction without moving into shadows. If necessary, check with the floor director to be sure you know which camera is to be called up to open the scene, and be sure you know about any critical or unusual camera shots.

If you are to hold or demonstrate an object, decide exactly where and how you will hold it and to which camera you will present it.

Finally, remind yourself that you are going to control any tendency you have to speak too rapidly; that if you make an error, you will correct it as naturally and unobtrusively as possible and continue; and that if you stumble, you will move on, putting the error behind you (dwelling on it will divide your attention and make further stumbles almost inevitable). Above all, do *not* stop to ask if you may begin again, unless such a possibility has been agreed to in advance. Even if your performance will never actually leave the classroom or studio, always adopt the attitude that it is going out live over the airwaves.

Achieving a Conversational Style

A conversational style is one that is natural to you, is appropriate to the intimacy of the broadcast media, and sounds as though you are talking rather than reading from a script. You can best achieve a conversational style by remembering a few simple principles.

First, don't hesitate to smile or laugh when it is appropriate. Don't be afraid to pause as you silently grope for an idea or a word because this is perfectly natural. Fear of pausing can lead either to "ers" and "uhs" (vocalized pauses) or to spouting inanities as you try to fight your way back to where you left off.

Conversational quality is totally destroyed by reading "ay" instead of "uh" for the article *a*. Read this sentence, pronouncing the article as "ay":

> A good way for a person to make a fortune is to open a savings account in a bank.

Now read the sentence again, substituting the sound "uh" for "ay." Do not stress any of the "uhs." Note how stilted the sentence sounded the first time you read it and how much more natural and conversational it was when you used "uh" for the article *a*.

The article *the* is sometimes pronounced "thee" and sometimes "thuh." The general rule is to say "thee" before a word beginning with a vowel sound and "thuh" before a word beginning with a consonant:

> SCRIPT: The appetite is the best gauge of the health of the average person.
>
> READ AS: THEE appetite is THUH best gauge of THUH health of THEE average person.

At times this general rule is broken for purposes of emphasis, as in "It is THEE best buy of thuh year!"

Reading Telephone Numbers

When reading a telephone number that includes an area code, read it with a pause after each part:

> SCRIPT: Phone (332) 575-6666.
>
> READ AS: Phone area code three-three-two / five-seven-five / six-six-six-six.

When reading a telephone number that includes zeros, do not say "oh" or "ought."

SCRIPT: Phone 924-0087.
READ AS: Phone nine-two-four / zero-zero-eight-seven.

When you repeat a number, you can vary the way you say it:

SCRIPT: Phone 344-8200; that's 344-8200.
READ AS: Phone three-four-four / eight-two-zero-zero; that's three-four-four / eighty-two hundred.

Some sponsors have special numbers that must be treated in a certain way. Part or all of the number may spell out a word, as in 332-SAVE. Often such numbers are given twice: once with the word(s) and then in the all-number version.

Toll-free telephone numbers should be read with the beginning given as "one-eight-hundred."

Developing a Sense of Time

Announcers must develop a keen sense of time, for split-second timing is a part of every radio or television broadcast. Delivery of the live portion of a radio commercial must be brought off in exactly the allotted time. Disc jockeys must often provide an ad-libbed introduction to a song that will end exactly when the vocal portion begins. Newscasters and engineers must work together so that there will be neither unwanted pauses nor overlaps when going from announcer to tape or vice versa.

In television you will be given time signals by a floor manager or floor director. In a newscast or an interview-talk show, you will often be given a countdown as you introduce videotaped stories. The floor director will first hold up the correct number of fingers and then, on instructions from the director, will lower the fingers one at a time. When the countdown is completed, the director has gone to tape.

At other times during a program, you may be given a hand signal meaning that you have 10 seconds in which to wrap up, or that there are 3 minutes, then 2 minutes, then 1 minute left in the program or in a segment of it. It is important to develop a sense of how long these periods of time are. Smooth transitions and unhurried endings require accurate timing. To develop this sense, you must practice extensively, using a stopwatch. Without looking at the watch, start it and then stop it when you think that a given number of seconds has passed. At first, you will typically think that a minute has passed when the actual elapsed time is closer to 30 or 40 seconds. With practice you should become quite accurate at estimating elapsed times. Then you must practice speaking and reading lead-ins and program closings, matching your words with a predetermined number of seconds.

Other Tips for Improving Your Performance

First, there is no substitute for practice. Theoretical knowledge of broadcasting is important, and such knowledge will enhance your development, but without practice you will never become truly professional. You do not need to confine your practice to class assignments. You can practice nearly anywhere, and you can practice without a single item of equipment. When reading newspapers, magazines, and books, isolate yourself from others and read at least some of the printed material aloud.

Second, invest in a few basic items of equipment. Most practical is a good-quality cassette recorder. With it, you can practice any type of announcing that appeals to you—news, interviewing, sports play-by-play, music announcing, or commercial delivery. Before investing in a tape recorder, check it out through actual use. A recorder that cannot accurately record and play back your voice clearly is of little use to you. Be sure the recorder can accept an external microphone. A good-quality microphone might be your next purchase.

Third, become honestly self-critical. As you listen to playbacks, imagine the voice you hear is that of another person. Listen for communicative values. Listen for voice quality, precise diction, and correct pronunciation. Experiment. Try different styles of delivery, levels of energy, and rates of delivery. You should not try these things in imitation of another performer; rather you should experiment to find ways of bringing out the best that is in *you*.

When performing in a newscast, commercial, or interview, do not do takeoffs unless the assignment calls for you to do so. You may amuse yourself and others by burlesquing your material, but it really affords you no useful practice—unless, of course, you intend to make a career of doing spoofs and takeoffs. This does not rule out humorous commercials or humor-oriented interviews, as long as they are realistically related to your growth as an announcer.

You can practice television delivery with or without equipment. In most cases, unless you are working to improve your facial expressions, performing before a mirror will only distract you. Instead, place some object on a wall (a drawing of a television lens will serve you well) and use it to practice eye contact. Although there is no perfect substitute for performing before a camera, with subsequent playbacks for critical evaluations, an audio recorder can help you with television practice. If possible, volunteer as talent on the projects of others. Perhaps you can even get on-camera experience at a local cable station.

Finally, save your recordings and review them from time to time to measure your progress. When you compare performances made four or five months apart, your improvement will be both impressive and encouraging—*if you have practiced!*

Evaluating Performances

Critical self-evaluation is the mark of the true professional in any of the performing arts. Here *critical* does not mean disparaging; it means careful, objective, and exact. Self-evaluation also involves the development of a mature attitude toward one's performance. A superior performance does not make you a superior person, any more than a wretched performance makes you a wretched person. Learn to distinguish between yourself as a person and your performance on any given assignment. Growth and improvement depend on your ability to learn from your mistakes rather than being disheartened by them.

Of the two checklists presented on the following pages, the first may be used to measure vocal performance for both radio and television. The second covers the physical aspects of television performance.

Practice: Gauging Your Own Performance

Consult a daily news source (newspaper or radio or television newscast), and write your own version of a local or national story. Prepare a script that will take 2 to $2\frac{1}{2}$ minutes to read. Read through your copy as you would if someone else wrote it, marking for emphasis, pronunciation, and so on. Read it aloud several times. When you are ready, tape your performance. Use the audio checklist to evaluate all aspects of your performance. If a video recorder is available, record the same story as a television report. Evaluate your performance with the video checklist.

Checklist: Evaluating Radio and Television Performances

1. Pitch
   Good_____   Too low_____   Too high_____
2. Pitch variety
   Good_____   Too little_____   Too much_____
3. Volume
   Good_____   Too weak_____   Too loud_____
4. Tempo
   Good_____   Too slow_____   Too fast_____
5. Tempo variety
   Good_____   Too little_____   Inappropriate variations_____
6. Vitality
   Good_____   Too little_____   Too much_____
7. Articulation
   Good_____   Underarticulated_____   Overarticulated_____
8. Voice quality
   Good_____   Nasal_____   Husky_____   Thin_____
   Other_____
9. Sibilance
   Good_____   Excessive_____
10. Plosives
    Good_____   Popping_____
11. Use of microphone
    Good_____   Note any problems_____
    _____
    _____
    _____

12. Note any mispronounced words._____
    _____
    _____
    _____

13. Give performance an overall evaluation._____
    _____
    _____
    _____

14. Note specific things to work on._____
    _____
    _____
    _____

Checklist: Evaluating Television Performances

1. Eye contact
   Good_____ Needs work_____
2. Use of peripheral vision
   Good_____ Needs work_____
3. Posture
   Good_____ Needs work_____
4. Standing on camera
   Steady_____ Rocking_____
5. Moving on camera
   Telegraphed movement?_____
   Moved smoothly?_____
   Sat correctly?_____
6. Were transitions smooth when switching cameras?_____
7. Were props held correctly for cameras?_____
8. Was pointing clear and even?_____
9. Was eye contact with camera maintained while using cue cards?_____
10. Were cues correctly responded to?_____
11. Was dress appropriate?_____
12. Facial animation
    Appropriate?_____ Too much?_____ Too little?_____
13. Note specific things to work on._____
    _____
    _____
    _____

14. Note areas that showed improvement._____
    _____
    _____
    _____

Practice: Getting Through an Ad-Lib Challenge

Imagine that you are a news reporter for a television station in a small to medium market. Your city's mayoral race is on, and the election campaign has been so full of gossip, attack, and counterattack that voters have almost no idea where the party nominees stand on local issues. Now it is election night, and you are on location at City Hall, where votes are being counted and only 2 hours remain until the polls close. Your anchor, back at the station, has just turned the show over to you. The campaign manager who agreed to be interviewed has not shown up, so you must carry on—with a live ad-libbed report from the steps of City Hall.

Using a stopwatch and audiotaping your performances, create ad-lib reports that span 10, 30, and 60 seconds. Invent candidate names and specific issues, and address questions you think your viewers would ask.

Listen to your three performances and rate yourself. Note phrases or words that recur annoyingly, expressions of apology or uncertainty that seep through, and places where you delivered useful information to the viewing audience.

4

Voice and Diction

Your voice is the most important instrument of communication you possess. Whether or not you intend to enter the field of broadcast announcing, you will use your voice daily for the rest of your life. Thus, you should make every effort to refine your speaking voice, to eliminate harsh or shrill sounds, and to enunciate words clearly; in short, to develop the most pleasant and effective speaking voice you are capable of producing. Although you may not have an innately pleasant voice, you can improve its quality. Just as some people exercise to strengthen their biceps or thigh muscles, you can exercise to strengthen your voice. Most authorities on voice improvement suggest that students read nearly everything—newspapers, magazines, textbooks—aloud. As you exercise your voice in this manner, you will find that you are able to speak without strain for long periods of time (some air shifts are four or more hours in duration) and that your vocal range has increased by at least half an octave.

Most professional broadcast announcers have excellent voices. Both male and female announcers tend to have rather low, resonant voices. They speak at an ideal rate of speed for easy comprehension, and they articulate words and phrases with clarity and precision. Some sports announcers, disc jockeys, and commercial **pitchmen** (announcers of commercials, always men, who speak at a rate in excess of 200 words a minute) are exceptions to the general rule, but news anchors and reporters, talk show hosts, interviewers, and announcers on classical and most popular music stations must have pleasant voices and use them well.

As a radio announcer, you will rely totally on your voice for the communication of messages; in television announcing your voice is only slightly less important. It is, therefore, imperative that you protect this instrument. Smoking and yelling yourself hoarse at sports events

are two ways of losing or seriously impairing your voice. In addition
to affecting voice quality, smoking cigarettes will decrease your lung
capacity, and this, in turn, will negatively affect your breathing. At
worst, smoking can cause a permanently hoarse voice, a rasping cough,
and, eventually, lung cancer. If you have a smoking habit yet want
to succeed as a professional announcer, you should seriously reasses
your priorities. Quitting smoking becomes more and more difficult
as you grow older. There has never been a better time to quit than
now!

This chapter will help you identify problems of voice or diction
and provides exercises for speech improvement. It is not designed as
a substitute for speech therapy where significant problems exist. In
the discussion of the speech sounds of American English, the symbols
of wire-service transcription, diacritical marks, and the International
Phonetic Alphabet (IPA) will be used. However, this entire chapter
(and, indeed, the entire book) can be studied without knowledge of
the IPA.

Your **speech personality** is the way you sound, that which makes
you instantly recognizable when you speak to a friend on the telephone. The speech personality is made up of seven variables: (1) pitch,
including pitch range, (2) volume (degree of loudness), (3) tempo, or
rate of delivery, (4) vitality, or enthusiasm, (5) pronunciation, (6)
voice quality, including timbre and tone, and (7) articulation (the
movement of speech organs to make speech sounds). All of these
qualities and characteristics can, to a degree, be isolated and worked
on for overall speech improvement. Using appropriate exercises, you
can concentrate on your pitch, for example, without at the same time
working on volume or tempo. Eventually, however, your efforts must
come together if your speech is to avoid affectation and to blend
successfully into the aural representation of the personality you want
to project to others. You may not like some aspects of the speech
personality you have acquired, but one of the most positive results
you can expect through your study of announcing is a considerable
improvement in your speech.

Pitch

Pitch is that property of a tone that is determined by the frequency
of vibration of the sound waves. Generally speaking, low-pitched
voices are more pleasant than high-pitched voices. An exception is

Figure 4.1
Opera singers must be masters of perfect vocal pitch, but announcers, too, must work for the right level for their speaking voices and just enough variation of tone. (Photo of Ghena Dimitrova, by Catherine Ursillo)

when a voice is pushed so far down the pitch scale as to sound guttural, unnatural, or even grotesque. While avoiding this extreme, you should speak near the lowest pitch level that is comfortable. Whatever your pitch, you should make sure that you do not consistently speak at your lowest pitch, because good speech demands variety in pitch. If you always speak at your lowest level, you have no way of lowering your pitch for selected words. Furthermore, a voice that remains "in the cellar" sounds strained and monotonous.

Pitch is determined by the rate of vibration of the vocal folds, sometimes referred to as the vocal cords; the faster they vibrate, the higher the pitch. The vocal folds of a mature women generally vibrate about twice as fast as those of a mature man, so male voices are generally about an octave lower than female voices.

Optimum Pitch

To make the best use of your voice, you should find and develop your **optimum pitch**—the pitch at which you feel most comfortable and are able to produce the most pleasant sounds. Most of us sound best when we are speaking in the lower half of our available pitch range. Although careless speakers make little use of their available range, with practice nearly everyone can achieve a range of between one and two octaves.

There are several methods for determining your optimum pitch. One effective system is based on the theory that the optimum pitch is that level where the greatest amount of **resonance** is produced. Resonance is the intensification of vocal tones during speech as the result of vibrations in the nose and cheekbones. When you resonate, you can feel these vibrations alongside your nose. Place your palms on your cheekbones and your fingers on the sides of your nose. Now read a series of short sentences, each at a different pitch level. You should be able to feel it when you hit your optimum pitch. By recording and playing back the test sentences, you will be able to hear, without the distraction of bone-conducted sound, what you sound like when you are at or very near your optimum pitch.

Another useful method for determining optimum pitch involves a piano. Sitting at the piano, sing the scale as low and as high as you comfortably can, striking the note that corresponds with each sound. If your singing voice covers two octaves, your optimum speaking voice should be at about the midpoint in the lower of the two octaves. In other words, optimum pitch is very close to a quarter of the way up from your bottom to your top pitch. Having determined the note that corresponds to your optimum pitch, start reading a prose passage. When you reach a vowel sound that can be prolonged, hold the tone and strike the note that matches your optimum pitch. You can easily tell if you are consistently above, on, or below your optimum pitch level.

Figure 4.2
Vocal sounds are emitted through the vocal folds (cords), shown (left) open and relaxed and (right) tensed and closed. Vocal folds are small bands of tissue that stretch across the larynx. When you begin to speak, larynx muscles pull on the vocal folds, narrowing the opening. Air emerging from the lungs vibrates against the tensed folds and forms the sounds you produce.

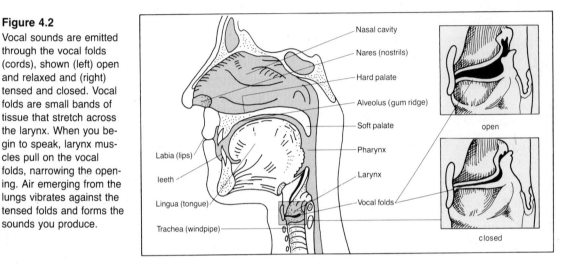

Nasal cavity

Nares (nostrils)

Hard palate

Alveolus (gum ridge)

Soft palate

Pharynx

Larynx

Vocal folds

open

closed

Labia (lips)

Teeth

Lingua (tongue)

Trachea (windpipe)

Because the vocal folds are actually two muscles, they are subject to contraction. In a taut, contracted state, they vibrate at a more rapid rate than when they are relaxed; and the faster they vibrate, the higher the pitch. Therefore, some degree of speech improvement can be achieved by relaxing the vocal folds. This cannot be done in an isolated way, however. To relax the throat muscles, you must simultaneously relax the rest of your body. Because an announcer is a performer, and because performing usually causes tension, it is important that you learn to relax. A professional announcer with several years of work experience usually has no problem with nervousness. But the inexperienced student of announcing, performing before an instructor and fellow students or auditioning for that coveted first job, can expect to experience nervousness. Mic fright, stumbling over words, or a raised pitch may be the result. (To help you confront and control mic and camera fright, a section of Chapter 3 discusses causes and cures of these common maladies.)

Some radio and television announcers speak above their optimum pitch level for a variety of reasons. Many sports reporters apparently believe that a loud, frenetic, mile-a-minute delivery enhances the significance of their reports, and both the frenzy and the volume level tend to raise their pitch. On-the-scene reporters, sending in an eye-witness story amid a high level of ambient noise, sometimes must raise their volume level (and with it, their pitch) in order to be heard. And some television performers unconsciously attempt to project their voices to the camera rather than to the lavaliere mic that is only 10 or 12 inches from their mouths, thereby throwing their voices 10 or 15 feet. This raises the volume level and, in turn, the pitch. Use your medium; electronic communication does not usually require high volume. Speak softly, and the pitch of your voice should remain pleasantly low.

Inflection

Inflection refers to the altering of the pitch or tone of the voice. Repetitious inflection makes some voices sing-song, and lack of inflection causes others to speak in a monotone. Good speech avoids the extremes and reaches a happy medium. Untrained speakers often fail to use variations in pitch sufficiently, whereas some overtrained speakers sound pretentious. You should be very self-critical about the degree and style of your pitch variations. Listen intently to tape recordings of your speech. If you feel that improvement is needed, use the exercises at the end of this chapter, always speaking aloud, and always taping, replaying, and noting your progress. For additional practice in increasing your pitch range, see the drill material in Appendix A.

Volume

Volume level is seldom a problem in broadcast speech, except for laypersons who do not know how to use microphones and reporters or sportscasters who are covering events that produce a high level of ambient noise. In a studio or control room, sensitive microphones pick up and amplify all but the weakest of voices. An audio console, properly operated, will ensure that the proper volume of speech is going through the board and on to the transmitter. Always remember that your listener is very close to you and speak in a normal voice, as you would in a face-to-face conversation.

Outside the studio environment, volume level can be a problem. The noise from a parade, a political convention, or a sports event may make it necessary to use a louder voice. Under these circumstances the best results may be obtained by moving closer to the mic and actually reducing your volume level. On the other hand, if conveying the excitement of the event dictates an increased volume, back away from the mic and speak up. Your pitch may go up as you do so, but that might enhance the excitement of your report.

Most radio and television speech is at its best when it is delivered at conversational level. Because this level remains relatively constant for all of us, there is an optimum distance from mouth to mic to achieve speech whose quality is suited to the event. A weak voice, too distant from the microphone, will require an increase in the gain (volume level) of the console or tape recorder; this in turn will increase the volume of the ambient noise. On the other hand, a speaker with a high volume level who is positioned too close to a microphone is likely to produce popping, excessive sibilance, or an unpleasant aspirate quality. A windscreen will eliminate popping, but it also will eliminate the higher frequencies. Sibilance is a characteristic of all who speak the English language, and totally avoiding it will lead to a lisp. The microphone tends to exaggerate sibilant sounds, so it is important to avoid excessive sibilance. To **aspirate** is to release a puff of breath, as when saying the word *unhitch*. Like sibilant sounds, aspirate sounds are a part of our spoken language and tend to be exaggerated by microphones. (If you find that you pop on microphone, practice with the exercises given at the end of this chapter for the plosives. Practice with the exercises for the fricatives to overcome excessive sibilance. Use the exercises that are given for the (h) sound to work on problems of overaspiration.)

Establishing your optimum volume level and microphone placement (distance from the mouth) should be one of your first priorities as a student of announcing. Because microphones vary in sensitivity, pickup pattern, and tonal reproduction, it is important to experiment with each type of microphone you are likely to use.

Tempo

Your **tempo**, or rate of delivery, is often determined by the number of words to be read in a given period of time. In general, newscasts and hard-sell commercials are read quite rapidly, whereas documentary narration, classical music copy, announcements on many popular music stations, and institutional commercials are read more slowly. When ad-libbing, you must judge what speed is appropriate to the mood of the event (whether it is an interview, a live report from the

Figure 4.3
Although voice volume is rarely a problem inside a radio or television studio, an announcer in an outdoor setting may have to work harder to be heard. As this public speaker in Missouri could tell you, an announcer at a special event such as a parade or political convention may have to work against poor acoustics and ambient noise. (Nick Sapieha, Stock Boston)

field, or a description of a sports event) and adjust your rate of delivery accordingly.

There is no single correct rate at which to speak or read. When no time limit is imposed, gear your reading speed to the mood of the copy. But keep in mind that most of us speak too rapidly much of the time. Speed is often the enemy of clear articulation. If read at too rapid a rate, the sentence "So give to the college of your choice" becomes "Sgive tuhthukallage uvyer choice." There is an absolute limit to the reading speed you can achieve without sacrificing good articulation. Few of us are good judges of our own speech; this is doubly true when it comes to judging tempo. Aside from soliciting help from others, the best way to learn to achieve your optimum speaking or reading rate is by continually using an audiotape recorder. Isolate the one problem of tempo, and work on it until a good speed becomes automatic.

Aside from a good basic rate of delivery, you should also work for variety in speed. Speeding up for throwaway phrases and slowing down for emphatic words or phrases will help give more meaning to your message. Throwaway phrases include "member, FDIC," "substantial penalty for early withdrawal," and "your mileage may vary."

In the diagnostic reading called "William and His Friends" (page 121), there are two rather obvious "speed traps" that may cause you to trip over your tongue. There are other, less obvious traps in the piece, so if you read it too fast, you may find yourself slurring. Your challenge is to keep your reading moving, while avoiding stumbles.

Vitality

Two speakers with nearly identical speech qualities may sound quite different if they vary greatly in **vitality**, or enthusiasm. Though a sense of vitality is often communicated by rapid speaking or reading, it is not necessary to rush your delivery to communicate vitality. Many speakers are able to communicate a feeling of energy or enthusiasm even when speaking slowly; other speakers may be fast but unenthusiastic. Many disc jockeys speak with a fairly low volume level but attain a feeling of vitality by speaking more rapidly than most of us do.

You should strive for two objectives with respect to the vitality of your announcing: you should use a degree of vitality that is appropriate to your personality, and you should gear the degree of vitality to the mood of the event being described. Above all, do not push yourself up to a level of vitality that is forced, unnatural to you, or inappropriate to the occasion. Most announcers are at their best when they are being themselves. You may need years of study and practice to develop your latent speaking potential, but you will certainly waste your time if you try to substitute someone else's personality for your own.

On the other hand, many beginning students of announcing are more subdued (and therefore less vital) in performing assignments than they are in their normal, out-of-class behavior. Your objective might well be to lift yourself up to your customary level of vitality.

Pronunciation

To pronounce means to form speech sounds by moving the articulators of speech—chiefly the jaw, tongue, lips, and glottis. There are many different but acceptable ways of pronouncing American English, because the language is spoken differently in various parts of the United States and Canada. Think of the differences in the speech of a native-born Georgian, a Texan, a New Englander, a New Yorker, a Hoosier (Indianian), and a person from British Columbia. Despite the richness represented by regional differences in pronunciation, broadcasters have always favored **General American**—roughly defined as the native speech of well-educated Americans and Canadians of the Midwest and Far West. One hears General American spoken by broadcast announcers in every part of the United States.

Figure 4.4
Based on the content of the copy, an announcer will adjust the tempo to match the mood—quick and light, slower and grave, or punchy and businesslike. This economics reporter in Houston keeps his tempo measured to match the financial news of the day. (KUHF-FM, Houston)

There are signs of change (most noticeable at the local station level), and it is now possible to hear—occasionally, at least—voices that are identifiably African-American, Hispanic, Southern, or from Down East. This trend will undoubtedly continue and accelerate, but your chances of succeeding as a professional announcer will still be enhanced if you employ General American. As a student of announcing, you must consider the question of pronunciation: if you do not speak General American, you must decide whether you want to cultivate it. Because overall pronunciation is an important part of your speech personality, a decision to change it should not be made lightly.

Pronunciation Problems

If regional variations in speech are not substandard (except in the eyes of many broadcast executives), what *does* constitute incorrect pronunciation? One or more of the following problems can cause mispronunciation.

Sloppy or incorrect articulation   If you say AIR for *error* or WIH-YUM for *William*, you are mispronouncing because of laziness in the use of your articulators. Say the words *air* and *error* aloud. Note that *air* can be sounded by a simple closing of the mouth and a drawing back of the tongue; *error*, however, requires more effort—two distinct movements of the lips and two movements of the tongue. Other words often mispronounced because of sloppy articulation include *variable* pronounced VAR'-UH-BUHL instead of VAR'-EE-UH-BUHL, and *government* pronounced as GUV'-MUNT instead of GOV'-ERN-MENT. Articulation, which is related to pronunciation, is discussed in some detail later in this chapter. If you are guilty of sloppy articulation, you should work extensively with the practice exercises on voice quality and articulation.

Physical impairment   Missing teeth, a fissure in the upper lip, a cleft palate, nasal blockage, or any degree of facial paralysis may make it impossible for a speaker to pronounce words correctly. If you have a correctable physical impairment, such as missing teeth, you should consult an appropriate specialist.

Misreading   Mispronunciations may result from a simple mistake, such as reading *amenable* for *amendable*, *outrage* for *outage*, or *through* for *though*. If you are a consistent misreader of words, you may have a learning impairment or a problem with your vision; either condition calls for consultation with a specialist.

Affectation   Some Americans who employ General American for nearly all their speech pick up a Britishism here and there, and this practice can be jarring to a listener. Saying EYE'-THUH for *either* works well with New England or Southern speech, but it sounds out of place when used by a Westerner or a Midwesterner. Affectation can be worked on and eliminated, but this requires a keen ear and, in many instances, calls for the help of a qualified speech teacher.

Ignorance of correct pronunciation   Most of us have a reading vocabulary that is far more extensive than our speaking vocabulary. From time to time, we err when we attempt to use a word known to us only through our eyes. The word *coup* (pronounced KOO), for example, might be pronounced KOOP by one who knew it only from the printed

Figure 4.5

Vitality, that elusive quality that gives life to the sound of a broadcast, is the forte of many actors, as in this portrayal of Shakespeare's King Lear. Most announcers, however, relish the overlap of drama with voice performance. (Ellis Herwig, The Picture Cube)

page. Ignorance of correct pronunciation may be due to having a limited speaking vocabulary, to having grown up in a home where American English was poorly pronounced, or to having learned English as a second language. It can be overcome only by a systematic effort to become somewhat of a linguist.

To be truly professional, you must develop an extensive vocabulary and cultivate accuracy and consistency in pronunciation. There are many books that can help you build your vocabulary, but be sure you are not simply adding to your reading vocabulary. Appendix B provides a list of about 300 words that are often mispronounced or are uncommon words that might turn up in broadcast copy.

Vowel and diphthong distortion Some people have grown up in environments where scores of words were mispronounced because of the distortion of vowels and diphthongs. Those who say MELK for *milk* or BE-KUZ for *because* are guilty of vowel distortion. To say KAWL for *coil* is to distort a diphthong. Vowel and diphthong distortions can be corrected, but first they must be identified. Both are discussed later in this chapter.

Speech Sounds of American English

Much of the remainder of this chapter deals with the speech sounds of American English. Wire-service phonetics and diacritical marks are used to illustrate the sounds. For the benefit of those who have learned—or are learning—the IPA, those symbols are also given. Wire-service phonetic symbols are always enclosed in parentheses: (PUH-REN′-THUH-SEEZ). Diacritical marks appear between virgules: /vûr′gyo͞olz/.[1] IPA symbols are enclosed in brackets: [′brækəts].

Speech sounds may be classifed as vowels, diphthongs, and consonants. You may have been taught that the English language uses five vowel sounds—*a, e, i, o, u*—but this is misleading. Our language actually requires us to manufacture twelve vowel sounds. A **vowel** is defined as a pure phonated (sounded) tone that does not use the articulators and can be held indefinitely without changing. If you say aloud the vowel (AH) /ä/ [ɑ] as in *father*, you will notice that you can hold it as long as your breath lasts without substantial change in its sound. If you say the diphthong (OY) /oi/ [ɔɪ] as in *toy*, you will

---

[1]The diacritical marks used by the *American Heritage Dictionary* are followed in this textbook.

notice that it glides from (AW) /ô/ [ɔ] to (IH) /ĭ/ [ɪ] and that you cannot hold its entire sound. You *can* hold the last part of this diphthong indefinitely, but only because it is actually the pure vowel (IH) /ĭ/ [ɪ] as in *it*.

Now try to say aloud the consonant *p*. You will notice that you cannot do so unless you add some vowel sound, such as *o*. The *p* sound is merely exploded air and cannot be prolonged. Other consonants, such as *n*, can be prolonged; but as soon as you stop using your articulators (in the case of *n*, the tip of the tongue has been placed on the gum ridge behind the upper front teeth), the sound turns into a vowel sound such as (UH) /ə/ [ə]. Consonants, then, may or may not require phonation but always involve use of the articulators.

There is a point at which it becomes impossible to say whether an unacceptably uttered word has been mispronounced or sloppily articulated. Saying MIRR for *mirror*, for example, could be the result of either not knowing the correct pronunciation or simply not bothering to force the articulators to do their job. Many so-called pronunciation problems can be overcome by frequent use of the articulation exercises at the end of this chapter.

Vowels   The English language contains twelve vowel sounds if we ignore the three or four sounds that lie between some of these twelve and occur rarely—and only regionally—in American speech. Vowel sounds are usually classified according to the placement of the tongue in the mouth, the tongue being the only articulator that materially affects their production. The **front vowels** are produced through the vibration of the vocal folds in the throat and are articulated by the tongue and teeth near the front of the mouth. The **back vowels** are produced in nearly the same manner but are articulated by the tongue and the opening in the rear of the mouth.

The front vowels are as follows:

(EE) /ē/ [i] as in *beet*
(IH) /ĭ/ [ɪ] as in *bit*
(AY) /ā/ [e] as in *bait*
(EH) /ĕ/ [ɛ] as in *bet*
(AAH) /ă/ [æ] as in *bat*

If you pronounce each of these sounds in turn, beginning at the top of the list and running to the bottom, you will find your mouth opening

Figure 4.6
Listening to the last moment of music before she goes on-air for her next introduction, this announcer concentrates so as to get all aspects of voice quality just right: the timing of her voice just after the end of the music, the pitch and tone to match the last notes of the piece, and correct pronunciation and articulation. (David Krathwohl, Stock Boston)

wider as you move from one sound to the next. As your mouth opens, your tongue is lowered and becomes increasingly relaxed.

Here are the back vowels:

(AH) /ä/ [ɑ] as in *bomb*

(AW) /ô/ [ɔ] as in *bought*

(OH) /ō/ [o] as in *boat*

(OOH) /o͝o/ [ʊ] as in *book*

(OO) /o͞o/ [u] as in *boot*

If you pronounce each of these vowel sounds in turn, you will find your mouth closing more and more and the sound being controlled at a progressively forward position in your mouth.

There are two more vowel sounds that are not classified as front or back: the (UH) sound, as in *fun* (FUHN), and the (ER) sound, as in *her* (HER). In the IPA two symbols are used for the (ER) sound: one when the sound is stressed, as in *bird* [bɝd], and the other when the sound is unstressed, as in *bitter* [ˈbɪtɚ]. The IPA also has two symbols for the (UH) sound: one when the sound is stressed, as in *sun* [sʌn], and the other when the sound is unstressed, as in *sofa* [ˈsofə].

The twelve vowel sounds can be described according to the way each is manufactured. This is done in Table 4.1.

It is not uncommon for speakers of American English to distort one or more vowel sounds. This does not refer to those who speak with regional accents. It is not incorrect for an Easterner or a Southerner to say AN-SUH(R) for *answer*, but it is substandard for speakers of American English anywhere to say FER-GIVE for *forgive* or JIST for *JUST*. This type of vowel distortion is the concern here. Throughout this section General American (or broadcast speech, as it is sometimes called) will be used.

Five vowel distortions occur with some regularity among Americans in any part of the United States and Canada, and several others occur less frequently. It is not surprising that these distortions take place between vowel sounds that are next to one another in the list that arranges them according to place of production in the mouth.

The five chief vowel distortions are discussed below. The readings given with them will help you discover whether you have problems and provide you with exercises to overcome such problems.

Table 4.1 How the Twelve Vowel Sounds Are Produced

Front Vowels

(EE), as in *beet*, is formed by holding the mouth slightly open, placing the tip of the tongue on the back surface of the lower front teeth, and arching the tongue toward the front of the mouth so that the sides of the tongue are in contact with the molars.

(IH), as in *bit*, is formed by placing the tip of the tongue on the back surface of the lower front teeth and lowering and relaxing the tongue slightly more than for (EE).

(AY), as in *bait*, is formed in much the same way as the (IH) sound, but the mouth is in a more open position and the tongue lies almost flat in the mouth.

(EH), as in *bet*, is formed with the mouth open still further than for the (AY) sound but with the tongue in just about the same relative position.

(AAH), as in *bat*, is formed with the mouth quite open and the tongue lying flat on the bottom of the mouth. A certain tenseness in the jaws is noticeable.

Back Vowels

(AH), as in *bomb*, is formed with the mouth quite open and the tongue lying flat and relaxed in the mouth.

(AW), as in *bought*, is formed by holding the lips open (but not rounded) and raising the tongue slightly in the rear. The tip of the tongue lies low on the gum ridge under the lower front teeth.

(OH), as in *boat*, is made by rounding the lips and raising the tongue slightly in the rear of the mouth.

(OOH), as in *book*, is formed in much the same way as (OO), except that the lips are more relaxed and slightly more open.

(OO), as in *boot*, is formed by holding the front of the tongue in approximately the same position as for the (EE) sound and the rear of the tongue in a raised position. The lips are rounded and extended.

ER and UH

(ER), as in *bird* and *bitter*, is formed by holding the mouth slightly open and holding the tongue back in the mouth, with the tip poised somewhere about the midpoint between the hard palate and the floor of the mouth.

(UH), as in *sun* and *sofa*, is formed by holding the mouth slightly open with the tongue quite relaxed and flat on the bottom of the mouth.

Five major vowel distortions

1. (EH) for (AY)   /ĕ/ for /ā/   [ε] for [e]

Those who distort the (AY) /ā/ [e] sound, turning it into (EH) /ĕ/ [ε], usually do so only when it is followed by an (UL) sound. This is because it is quite easy to sound the (AY) in a word such as *pay* but more difficult to sound it in the word *pail*. Say, in turn, the words *pail* and *pell*, and you will see why some speakers slip into the easier of the two and thus distort the vowel sound of this and similar words.

> The pale graduate of Yale hailed the mail delivery daily. She failed to go sailing, for fear of gales and whales, but she availed herself of the tall tales told her by the mail deliverer. "I shot a quail out of season and was sent to jail," he wailed," but a female friend put up bail, so they failed to nail me." The pale Yale graduate did not fail to hail the mail deliverer's tale.

2. (AAH) for (EH)   /ă/ for /ĕ/   [æ] for [ε]

Unlike the problem just described, this distortion tends to be of regional or ethnic origin and is not brought about because one manner of pronunciation is easier than another. Those from cities or areas where there is a sizable population of German ancestry are most prone to make this vowel distortion. *FANCE* for *fence* and *TALEPHONE* for *telephone* are examples.

> My friend, who is well but elderly, helped me mend my fence. I telephoned him to let him know when to get here, but he didn't answer the bell, so I guess he'd left. He's a mellow friend who never bellows, but he sometimes questions everything a fellow does. He took some lessons on television about fence mending, or else he wouldn't be able to help me mend my fence.

3. (EH) for (AAH)   /ĕ/ for /ă/   [ε] for [æ]

Many Americans do not distinguish between the vowel sounds in the words *Mary* and *merry*, giving both the (EH) /ĕ/ [ε] sound. It was because of widespread distortion of these two vowel sounds that *catsup* became *ketchup* in common usage. Whereas (AAH) /ă/ [æ] is not often a source of trouble in the sounding of words such as *bat*, *champion*, and *sedan*, it often slips into (EH) /ĕ/ [ε] in words in which it is more difficult to sound the (AAH), such as *shall*.

> Mary left the Caribbean to visit Paris. She carried her clothes in a caramel-colored carriage. Mary tarried at the narrow entrance

of the barracks. There was a caricature of Mary that chilled her marrow. Mary said, "I shall never tarry in Paris again."

Note the difficulty of hitting the (AAH) /ă/ [æ] sound when many words using this sound appear in rapid succession. Note, too, how the passage begins to sound foreign to American ears. The (AAH) sound will remain in American English speech, but there is no doubt that it is gradually disappearing for words in which its manufacture is difficult.

4. (AH) for (AW)   /ä/ for /ô/   [ɑ] for [ɔ]

Some speakers do not distinguish between these sounds, giving the same vowel sound to the words *bought* and *bomb*. Of the following readings the first uses words for which the (AW) sound is correct, the second mixes words using both sounds.

We all talked about the day in the fall when Loretta sawed off the longest stalk. Our jaws dropped in awe of her raw courage. She caught the stalk in a bolt of gauze and waited for the dawn to prevent the loss of all her awful, morbid, haunted house of horror.

I saw them haul the bomb from the bottom of the waterfall. All around, I saw the awesome possibility of large-scale horror. Lost souls watched in a state of shock. The bomb slowly fought its way clear of the pond. Water dripped from the bottom of the bomb. I lost my fear, for I saw that the bomb was not awfully large.

5. (IH) for (EE)   /ĭ/ for /ē/   [ɪ] for [i]

Sounding (EE) before an *l* calls for slightly more effort than sounding (IH) in the same construction. For this reason, some speakers habitually say RIH-LY for *really* and FIHL for *feel*.

Sheila Fielding had a really strong feeling that something really bad would come of her deal to have the keel of her boat sealed. She wanted to shield the keel, so that peeling paint wouldn't be a really big deal. Sheila really hit the ceiling when she saw the bill. As Sheila reeled, she took the wheel and dragged the keel with the peeling paint across the pier and into the field, where her feelings were really healed.

Aside from these major problems of vowel distortion, several others are occasionally heard. Speakers who commit these distortions (with some exceptions) tend to be quite consistent. Table 4.2 lists these distortions with examples of correct and incorrect pronunciation.

Table 4.2   Some Vowel Distortions

Vowel Sound	Word	Correct Pronunciation	Distortion
(AW) for (OOH) /ô/ for /oo/ [ɔ] for [ʊ] as in *book*	*poor*	(POOHR) /poor/ [pʊr]	(PAWR) /pôr/ [pɔr]
	your	(YOOHR) /yoor/ [jʊr]	(YAWHR) /yôr/ [jɔr]
	sure	(SHOOHR) /shoor/ [ʃʊr]	(SHAWHR) /shôr/ [ʃɔr]
	tourist	(TOOHR′-IST) /toor′ĭst/ [′tʊr,ɪst]	(TAWR′-IST) /tôr′ĭst/ [′tɔr,ɪst]
	jury	(JOOHR′-EE) /joor′ē/ [′dʒʊr,i]	(JAWHR′-EE) /jôr′ē/ [′dʒɔr,i]
(ER) for (OOH) /ûr/ for /oo/ [ɝ] for [ʊ] as in *book*	*jury*	(JOOHR′-EE) /joor′ē/ [′dʒʊr,i]	(JER′-EE) /jûr′ē/ [′dʒɝ·i]
	sure	(SHOOHR) /shoor/ [ʃʊr]	(SHER) /shûr/ [ʃɝ]
	insurance	(IN-SHOOHR′-UNS) /ĭn-shoor′əns/ [ɪn′ʃʊrəns]	(IN-SHER′-UNS) /ĭn-shûr′əns/ [ɪn′ʃɝ·əns]
	assure	(UH-SHOOHR′) /ə-shoor′/ [ə′ʃʊr]	(UH-SHER′) /ə-shûr′/ [ə′ʃɝ]
(IH) for (EH) /ĭ/ for /ĕ/ [ɪ] for [ɛ]	*tender*	(TEN′-DER) /tĕn′dər/ [′tɛndɚ]	(TIHN′-DER) /tĭn′dər/ [′tɪndɚ]
	get	(GEHT) /gĕt/ [gɛt]	(GIT) /gĭt/ [gɪt]
	send	(SEND) /sĕnd/ [sɛnd]	(SIHND) /sĭnd/ [sɪnd]
	engine	(EN′-JUHN) /ĕn′jən/ [′ɛndʒən]	(IHN′-JUHN) /ĭn′jən/ [′ɪndʒən]
	friend	(FREHND) /frĕnd/ [frɛnd]	(FRIHND) /frĭnd/ [frɪnd]

Table 4.2 *(continued)*

Vowel Sound	Word	Correct Pronunciation	Distortion
(ER) for (UH), (AW), or (IH) /ûr/ for /ə/, /ô/, or /ĭ/ [ɝ] for [ə], [ɔ], or [ɪ]	*familiar*	(FUH-MIL′-YER) /fə-mĭl′-yər/ [fə′mɪljɚ]	(FER-MIL′-YER) /fûr-mĭl′-yər/ [fɚ′mɪljɚ]
	forget	(FAWR-GET′)/fôr-gĕt′/ [fɔr′gɛt]	(FER-GET′) /fûr-gĕt′/ [fɚ′gɪt]
	congregate	(KANG′-GRIH-GAYT) /käng′grĭ-gāt/ [′kaŋgrɪget]	(KANG′-GER-GAYT) /käng′gûr-gāt/ [′kaŋgɚget]
	garage	(GUH-RAHZH′) /gə-räzh′/ [gə′raʒ]	(GER-AHZH′) /gûr-äzh′/ [gɚ′aʒ]
	lubricate	(LOO′-BRIH-KAYT) /lōō′brĭ-kāt/ [′lubrɪkæt]	(LOO′-BER-KAYT) /lōō′bûr-kāt/ [′lubɚket]
(EH) for (IH) /ĕ/ for /ĭ/ [ɛ] for [ɪ]	*milk*	(MIHLK) /mĭlk/ [mɪlk]	(MEHLK) /mĕlk/ [mɛlk]
	since	(SINSS) /sĭns/ [sɪns]	(SENSE) /sĕns/ [sɛns]
	fill	(FIHL) /fĭl/ [fɪl]	(FELL) /fĕl/ [fɛl]
	think	(THINGK) /thĭngk/ [θɪŋk]	(THENGK) /thĕngk/ [θɛŋk]
(IH) for (EH) /ĭ/ for /e/ [ɪ] for [ɛ]	*cent*	(SENT) /sĕnt/ [sɛnt]	(SIHNT) /sĭnt/ [sɪnt]
	men	(MEHN) /mĕn/ [mɛn]	(MIHN) /mĭn/ [mɪn]
	helicopter	(HEL′-IH-KAHP-TER) /hĕl′ĭ-kŏp′tər/ [′hɛlɪkaptɚ]	(HIL′-IH-KAHP-TER) /hĭl′ĭ-kŏp′tər/ [′hɪlɪkaptɚ]
	many	(MEHN′-EE) /mĕn′ē/ [′mɛn,i]	(MIHN′-EE) /mĭn′ē/ [′mɪn,i]
(UH) for (IH) /ə/ for /ĭ/ [ə] for [ɪ]	*it* (as in *get it?*) becomes *uht* (as in *get uht?*)		
(UH) for (AW) /ə/ for /ô/ [ə] for [ɔ]	*because* becomes *be-kuz*		

Diphthongs The **diphthong**, or glide, as it is sometimes called, is a combination of two vowel sounds, spoken in rapid order and with a glide from one to the other. The diphthongs are represented as follows:

(Y) /ī/ [aɪ] as in *bite* (BYTE) /bīt/ [baɪt]
(AU) /ou/ [aʊ] as in *bout* (BAUT) /bout/ [baʊt]
(OY) /oi/ [ɔɪ] as in *boy* (BOY) /boi/ [bɔɪ]
(YU) /yoo͞/ [ju] as in *beauty* (BYU'-TEE) /byoo͞'tē/ ['bju,ti]

The vowel sound (AY) /ā/ [e], as you may detect by saying it aloud, is actually a glide; it quite definitely goes from (AY) to (IH). It is therefore sometimes considered a diphthong and given the symbol [eɪ] in the IPA.

Diphthongs are a source of trouble for some speakers. Diphthong distortion tends to be regional and, though not necessarily substandard, is not compatible with General American speech. Table 4.3 gives a few common diphthong distortions.

Voice Quality and Articulation

The remainder of this chapter discusses voice quality and articulation, the two most important and demanding aspects of human speech. Speech is the process of making meaningful sounds. The sounds of the English language are created by vibrations of the vocal folds, nasal resonance, and exploded air. Speech sounds are controlled and patterned by the degree of closure of the throat, the placement of the tongue, and the use of the teeth, lips, and nasal passages. Improper use of vocal folds and resonance cavities gives rise to problems of

Table 4.3 Some Diphthong Distortions

Diphthong	Word	Correct Pronunciation	Distortion
(Y) /ī/ [aɪ]	*bike*	(BYKE) /bīk/ [baɪk]	(BAHK) /bäk/ [bak]
(AU) /ou/ [aʊ]	*cow*	(KAU) /kou/ [kaʊ]	(KA'-OW) /ka'oo/ ['kæ,aʊ]
(OY) /oi/ [ɔɪ]	*toy*	(TOY) /toi/ [tɔɪ]	(TAW) /tô/ [tɔ]
(AY) /ā/ [eɪ]	*pail*	(PAY'-UL) /pāl/ ['peəl]	(PELL) /pĕl/ [pɛl]

voice quality; improper placement or use of the articulators gives rise to problems of articulation.

Diagnosing Problems

The following readings are designed to help you discover minor problems in your voice quality and articulation. Each speech sound of American English appears in initial, medial, and final positions in each reading, unless a sound is not used in a given position in English. Each sound is given at least once; the more common sources of speech difficulty appear at least twice. The passages may seem nonsensical, but you should read them as though they make a great deal of sense. Try to use your regular patterns of inflection and stress and your normal rate of delivery; only by doing so can you detect errors in voice quality and articulation. It is highly recommended that you record your reading so that, after making a diagnosis of your problems, you can retain the tape to use in measuring your progress.

WILLIAM AND HIS FRIENDS

This is the story of a little boy named William. He lived in a small town called Marshville. Friends he had galore, if one may judge by the vast numbers of children who visited his abode (UH-BODE'). Every day after school through the pathway leading to his house, the little boys and girls trudged along, singing as though in church. Out into the yard they came, a vision of juvenile (JOOV'-UH-NUHL) happiness. But, joyous though they were, they served only to work little William up into a lather. For, although he assuaged (UH-SWAYDGD') his pain with comic books and the drinking of milk, William abhorred the daily routine. Even Zero, his dog, was aghast at the daily appearance of the running, singing, shuffling, open-mouthed fellows and girls. Beautiful though the sight may have been, William felt that they used the avenue leading to his abode as an awesome item of lush malfeasance (MAL-FEEZ'-UNCE). Their little oily voices only added fuel to. the fire, for William hated music. "Oooo," he would say, "they mew like cats, baa like sheep, and moo like a cow. My nerves are raw." Then back into his menage (MAY-NAZH') the little gigolo (JIG'-UH-LOW) would scamper, fast action earnestly being his desire.

THE BATTLE OF ATTERBURY

The big battle was on! Cannons thundered and machine guns chattered. The troops, weary after months of constant struggle, found themselves rejuvenated by a vision of triumph. Atterbury, the junction of three main roads, was on the horizon. Using whatever annoying tricks he could, Jacques Deatheridge, the former millionaire playboy, was much in charge as he eyed the oil capital of the feudal republic. Few men would say that the Beige Berets had not cashed in on Jacques's flash of genius. Then the rather uncommon English fellow, a zany half-wit to many who now would writhe in agony, looked puzzled for a moment; the mob on top of Manhasset Hill was frantically throwing him a signal. He snatched the message from the courier. "My gracious," he muttered. "Atterbury is our own capital!" Elated, nonetheless, he invited his overawed band to play in his honor. After a solo on the drums, Jacques spoke to the multitude. "Rejoice, my fellow citizens! All is not bad! At least our troops have won *one* victory!"

Improving Voice Quality

The most common problems associated with voice quality are nasality, huskiness, and thinness (lack of resonance). Each can be worked on, and all can be overcome to some extent. The first step is to diagnose your problems. You will probably need help with this, for few of us are objective about the sound of our own voices. Once you have identified specific problems of voice quality, you should follow the suggestions and exercises that apply to your case.

Nasality and denasality **Nasality** is caused by allowing air to exit through the nose, rather than the mouth, when sounding *m*, *n*, and *ng*. **Denasality** is caused by a blocked nasal passage, and often is present when one is suffering from a cold. Pinch your nostrils and speak a sentence or two; you will find that by preventing air from passing through your nose, you have produced a certain vocal quality—this is denasality. Now, without holding your nose, try to speak with a nasal tone. You will find that the sound can be generated only by forcing air up through the nasal passage—this is nasality.

Proper use of the nasal passage involves selectively closing off sound—with the lips or the front or rear of the tongue—to force it through the nasal cavity. If you say, in turn, *sim*, *sin*, and *sing*, holding on to the last sound of each word, you will find that for *sim* your lips close off the (M) sound, for *sin* the front of your tongue against the upper gum ridge (alveolus) creates the (N) sound, and for *sing* the rear of your tongue against the soft palate (or velum) produces the (NG) sound. These are the three nasal sounds, and they are properly produced only by the correct placement of your articulators and an unblocked nasal passage.

If you have a nasal voice quality, your first problem is to determine whether it is caused by not properly sending the (M), (N), and (NG) sounds up through your nose or whether it is the result of sending non-nasal sounds through the nasal passage. The following sentence should help you do this. Read it very slowly, pausing to prolong every vowel sound that can be held without change. Record and play back the results.

Many men and women can do this in many differing manners.

All the sustained (M), (N), and (NG) sounds should have nasal resonance associated with them (as a matter of fact, unless these sounds are allowed to pass through the nose, they can barely be sustained). All non-nasal vowels should have no taint of nasality.

You can check for nasal resonance by placing the tips of your fingers lightly on either side of your nose. When holding a nasal consonant, you should feel a distinct vibration; when prolonging a non-nasal vowel, you should not. If you speak the word *women*, for example, the first prolonged vowel sound, "wiiii," should not have nasal resonance, and therefore you should not feel any vibration. The "wiiiii" gives way to "wimmmmm," and this should produce nasal vibration. The next vowel sound is "ihhhhhh," which should be free from vibration. The final sound, "nnnnnnn," should bring back the vibration. If you find that your nose does not produce vibrations on the nasal consonants, your problem is representative of the most common type of nasality. If, on the other hand, you find that you are nasalizing vowels that should not be nasalized, you have a less common and more difficult problem to work on.

If you are not nasalizing the nasal consonants *m, n,* and *ng,* your problem may be physiological, or you may simply be experiencing nasal congestion. In either case, there is no point in working on speech exercises as long as the blockage exists. Do whatever is appropriate to end the blockage, even if this means a trip to a speech therapist, a nasopharyngologist, or an allergist. If you have no physiological problem or congestion and still lack resonance on the nasal consonants, the exercises on resonance at the end of this chapter should help. If your problem is nasalization of non-nasal vowels, those exercises should still help. Work to avoid any nasal resonance in non-nasal words, but do not try to eliminate it from the words that legit-imately call for nasality.

Huskiness   A husky, or excessively hoarse, voice is usually the result of a medical problem. Laryngitis, smoker's throat, infected tonsils, or infected sinuses can cause a husky voice. Obviously, you should seek medical attention for these conditions, for they are a handicap in radio and television work. To some extent, huskiness can arise as the result of excessive nervous tension. If yours is an unpleasantly husky voice and if there is no medical explanation for it, you might improve your performance by using relaxing exercises as described in Chapter 3. Speaking exercises will help you overcome excessive huskiness or hoarseness only if your problem is the result of a gross misuse of your speech organs.

Thinness, or lack of resonance   A good voice for the electronic media is one with resonance (an intensification of vocal tones during artic-ulation). A sensitive, top-quality microphone, such as a condenser mic, can enhance your natural resonance. But even the best equipment can work only with what you give it, and a voice that is thin or lacking in resonance can be significantly improved only by its owner. The sound vibrations that emanate from your vocal folds are weak and colorless. They need resonators to strengthen and improve the quality of sound. The chief resonators are the bones of the chest and face, the windpipe (trachea), the larynx (connecting the trachea and the pharynx and containing the vocal folds), the pharynx (between the mouth and the nasal passages), the mouth, the nose, and the sinuses.

   In general, thinness of voice is caused by one or more of three factors: shallow, weak breathing; speaking at too high a pitch (in general, the higher the pitch, the less the resonance); and inadequate use of the resonators that can be moved (the pharynx, the larynx, and the tongue).

   As with any other speech problem, the first step is diagnosing it. Do you have a thin voice? What causes it? What do you need to do about it? The following passage is provided for diagnostic purposes. Read it slowly, working for your most resonant quality. Record it, using a sensitive professional microphone and a top-quality tape re-corder. If possible, seek the help of a person qualified in assessing both voice quality and the apparent causes of thinness. Begin this reading approximately 5 feet from the microphone, using a volume level appropriate to that distance. At each number, move forward about 6 inches, until you are reading the final sentence about 8 inches from the mic. Lower your volume as you move in. On playback, determine whether your resonance is significantly affected by distance and volume level. Unless other negative qualities interfere (excessive sibilance, popping, nasality), this process should allow you to find and use your optimum microphone position to bring out resonance.

1. Johnny has an IQ of 170, but he can't read. The words are jumbled, upside down. Mirrored.
2. He has dyslexia. A learning disability that affects one out of every ten children.
3. Johnny goes to school and faces frustration, humiliation, and ridicule.
4. It's a tragedy because the techniques are there to help the dyslexic child. He can learn to read and write. And survive in school.
5. He can even go to college. If—and only if—dyslexia is diagnosed early. And dealt with.
6. Today, there are over a dozen centers in Massachusetts that can diagnose dyslexia—even among preschoolers.
7. To find out more, call 1-555-6880.
8. 1-555-6880.
9. One out of every ten kids has dyslexia.
10. And every one of them needs help.[2]

If yours is a thin, colorless voice, you should be able to increase resonance by following these suggestions:

- Practice deep breathing. Learn to breathe from the diaphragm. While you speak or read, consciously try to increase the force of air coming from your lungs.
- Make sure you are moving your articulators. (Use the exercises given later in this chapter to work on an exaggerated use of tongue and lips.)
- Make sure that there is no blockage of your nasal passages.
- Try to lower your pitch. (See the suggestions given earlier in this chapter.)
- Read passages that emphasize vowel sounds (nineteenth-century British poetry is excellent for this), prolonging those sounds when they occur and trying to keep your throat as open as possible.

[2]Courtesy Ingalls Associates, Boston, Massachusetts.

Spotlight: How a News/Announcing Duo Achieved Their Good Sound

When they first went on the air in 1985, announcer Mary Ann Nichols and news director/anchor Laura Carlo were the only all-female team on the air during morning drive time in the Boston area. Letters poured in: listeners liked their sound, Nichols's mellow voice introducing classical music selections and the pleasant, no-nonsense voice of Carlo giving the hourly news reports.

But neither announcer strode directly from the college classroom to the announcing booth. When Nichols was in college in Washington, D.C., in the 1970s, she was majoring in speech and drama and playing the viola for the university orchestra. She had no idea she'd end up as a DJ in Boston (where she moved to earn a master's degree), first at a small AM station with a Latino/ Black format, later at two major-market commercial classical FM stations. Her work in the theatre, she believes, prepared her for the vocal control and energy now required of her every weekday morning from 6 to 10 A.M.

For Nichols, the combination of classical music and the chance to use her most important dramatic tool—her voice—created just the niche she was looking for in a permanent career. Although she still participates in professional theatre and does industrial voice-over and commercial characterization work, Nichols thoroughly enjoys her morning shift on WCRB. "I'm not one of those classical music nerdy types," she laughs. "I just like playing it."

Not only does she play the selections, she also does all her own programming, struggling to achieve variety within limited chunks of time between morning news and weather reports. "I try to program light, more melodic pieces on my shift," she explains, "because I think that in the morning people enjoy familiar music."

She begins broadcasting at 6 A.M., wraps up her show by 10, and completes the next day's preparation by 11. But Nichols remembers her early days on the job. "The idea of pacing was terrifying," she recalls. "I mean, what do you say in a block of 30 seconds? How in the world do you manage to meet the news exactly on the hour?" She learned to bring her pitch down a few notches, to a level that was more comfortable both to speak and to hear. A veteran announcer told her to smile at all times while on the air, to reduce the sibilance to which women are especially prone. She began to sit up straight "to get an uninterrupted column of air," to "pick up" her voice, and to slow herself down to a pace appropriate to a classical station's sound.

Studying the style and technique of both newswriting and announcing was one way Laura Carlo taught herself good voice quality. Thrown cold into news reporting at a small-market station where no one took the time to teach her anything, Carlo spent her evenings studying the way her major competitor ("I didn't like him at all but I knew he was good") put together news stories into scripts. "He put this [fact] here and this [portion] there, but why?" she asked herself. For good female vocal sound, she studied then-famous TV anchor Jessica Savitch, the only female announcer whose voice she found appealing, "not frilly or sexy." Carlo would sit in front of the television, taping news reports, and then playing them back again and again, until she could emulate the style, pitch, and tone she wanted for herself.

When Carlo entered college in the late 1970s, her primary interest was in political science; she found her way into news announcing as a way to combine a performance medium with the current issues about which she cared. An educational bill that would affect tuition levels for students in her state was currently being debated; when Carlo asked the college radio station manager if she could interview local politicians concerning this bill, she landed her own radio show. For four years, Carlo hosted a weekly talk show, interviewing a range of guests from mayors and senators to dress designers and sports color announcers.

Carlo's first job provided a tough initiation into real-life broadcast announcing. When she walked into the 1000-watt AM talk/news station in a city south of Boston, she faced a roomful of veteran reporters, all of whom were men. "There I was in my proper grey flannel suit and my crisp white blouse, so young and eager to do well," she retells. "When I looked around the room I saw five men, all middle-aged—no kidding, it was like [TV's] Lou Grant times five." Carlo may laugh ruefully now, but at age 21, within five minutes of starting her first day on the job, she was out on the streets of an unfamiliar city to track down her first story. "A lead came in on the police scanner about a murder/suicide," she explains. "I hadn't even taken off my coat—my new boss looked at me and said, 'Well', what are you waiting for?' Luckily I had bought a map just the night before, thinking that it might be nice sometime to get to know my new 'beat'." She found her way to the cocktail bar where the shooting had occurred and interviewed the bartender and witnesses.

Returning to the station with what turned out to be a good story, Carlo had a hard time finding anyone who was willing to show her how to transcribe recorded quotes to cart or to operate equipment she had never encountered in college. Also, having never written a news story before, Carlo wrote a long story packed with every detail she'd learned, only to have her editor slash paragraphs and paragraphs of her effort. The story turned out to be a scoop, however, and in the next three years Carlo covered major breaking stories and won several UPI awards, working her way up to news director of a six-person staff.

Both Nichols and Carlo have come a long way, but they still work hard to retain the good vocal sound for which they have become well-known. For Nichols, in announcing classical music, "the greatest nightmare is mispronouncing foreign names"; so she spends time researching all her copy and verifying the station's preferred style of pronunciation. Carlo inspects her daily news copy for local terms and names, which she has to pronounce according to regional style.

Today's audiences, insists Nichols, want to hear a voice "that sounds like a real person." She thinks that announcing style may have been more stiff and pedantic years ago but has become increasingly conversational. "Audiences want you to be more human," she explains.

Know the music, advises Nichols; know your story, says Carlo. Concentrate. Practice reading a piece of copy until it doesn't sound as though you're reading it anymore; make it your own. Preread all material, but be able to ad-lib, too. Be confident about your material, advises Carlo—if the story is good enough, the voice quality "will all come from the material." She recommends Spanish as a good second language for U.S. news broadcasting and warns students to "get rid of any and all regionalities" (accents and sayings). Both announcers keep an eye on the electronic meter in order to gauge their volume, and both let the material or music determine not only volume but pitch and tone.

They both recommend spending hours with a cassette recorder, taping and analyzing your voice, and using a microphone, getting comfortable with vocal performance. College radio, they agree, is a great place to start—"a great place to make all your mistakes." Years later, like Carlo and Nichols, you'll make it look effortless.

Announcers Laura Carlo (left) and Mary Ann Nichols (right). (Courtesy of WCRB, Boston)

- If you have a choice of microphones, discover the best instrument for your voice, and establish your optimum distance from it. (A ribbon mic will generally make your voice sound more resonant than a dynamic mic will.)

Correct breathing and breathing exercises Correct breathing requires that you maintain good posture, that your neck, shoulders, and face be relaxed, and that you breathe from the diaphragm. Good posture means sitting or standing with a straight spine and with your shoulders drawn back. It is impossible to breathe properly when you are hunched over. Check your posture frequently throughout the day, every day. Become aware of when you are standing or sitting erect, as opposed to slumping in your seat or slouching. In time, you should become so conscious of your posture that your common bearing will be one that demonstrates good posture. When speaking or reading aloud, first check your posture, and then eliminate any tension that may be present in your neck, shoulders, or face.

Your diaphragm is a muscular membrane that separates your stomach from your chest cavity (lungs). Place your fingers just at the point where your upper abdomen meets your lowest ribs. When you breathe in, you should be able to feel movement outward, as air fills the lungs. When you speak, you should try to "push" your voice all the way up from your diaphragm. You simply cannot have a strong, resonant voice if you are manufacturing your speech sounds entirely in your mouth. Speech sounds other than sibilants and plosives are initiated by the vibration of the vocal folds. These sounds are then broken up into speech by the articulators. To produce a strong and healthy voice, the air stream that vibrates the vocal folds must be strong, and that in turn means that the stream should be forced up by the diaphragm.

To begin a regimen of breathing exercises, you need only to count aloud and see how many numbers you can say without effort. As you practice this several times each day, you should soon find yourself able to count to 30 before beginning to run out of breath. Along with the counting exercise, begin to read aloud as often as you can. You can work to strengthen your breathing by always checking to see whether you are, indeed, pushing your voice up from your diaphragm.

Other exercises to develop good breathing habits may be found in a number of texts on speech improvement, including those mentioned as suggested readings in Appendix E.

Improving Articulation

Articulation problems arise from too fast a rate of delivery and from improper placement or faulty use of the articulators (the jaw, the tongue, and the lips). Read the brief selection that follows, and see if you have difficulty sounding all of the syllables of each word.

THE DIAGNOSTIC CENTER
This is undeniably the most conscientiously designed diagnostic center imaginable. I recognize that, from an architectural standpoint, the building is magnificent. It also is strategically placed. At the same time, however, is it environmentally sound? Does it mirror our civilization's preoccupation with transcendental human competencies? Looking at the phenomenon from an unexpectedly malevolent point of view, we probably should ultimately find an alternative.

Because many North American speakers suffer from poor articulation, many of the exercises at the end of this chapter are intended to improve articulation. Analysis of your performance with the diagnostic readings "William and His Friends," "The Battle of Atterbury," and "The Diagnostic Center" should tell you if you have inarticulate speech or if you have difficulty with any of the speech sounds. If you find that you have problems, you should do the appropriate exercises daily for as long as necessary. The exercises will do you no good, however, unless you read the material aloud, making a conscious effort to form successfully every syllable of every sentence. It is wise to exaggerate articulation at first, gradually moving toward normally articulated speech.

Consonant sounds   There are twenty-five consonant sounds (phonemes) in the English language. They may be classified in a number of ways, the most basic of which is according to whether or not they are voiced. Thus, the letter *b*, spoken with a vibration of the vocal folds, is called a **voiced consonant**, whereas *p*, formed in exactly the same way but not phonated, is called an **unvoiced consonant**.

A more detailed and more useful system, based on how the sound is formed, classifies the consonants as follows:

Plosives begin with the air from the throat blocked off, and the sound is formed with a release of the air. The plosive consonants are *p*, *b*, *t*, *d*, *k*, and *g*.

Fricatives are created by the friction generated when air moves through a restricted air passage. The fricative consonants are *f*, *v*, *th* (as in *thin*), *th* (as in *the*), *z*, *s*, *sh* (as in *shoe*), *zh* (as in *vision*), *y* (as in *yellow*), and *h* and *hw* (as in *when*).

Nasals are resonated in the nasal cavity. The nasal consonants are *m*, *n*, and *ng* (as in *sing*).

Semivowels are similar to the true vowels in their resonance patterns. The consonants *w*, *r*, and *l* are the semivowels.

Affricates combine a plosive with a fricative. The consonants *ch* (as in *choose*) and *j* (as in *jump*) are the affricates.

Still another system classifies consonants according to their place of articulation.[3]

Labial, or **bilabial, consonants**   *Labia* is Latin for "lip." The lips are primarily responsible for the labial consonants, *p*, *b*, *m*, *w*, and, in a less obvious way, *hw*.

Labiodental consonants   For these sounds the lower lip is in proximity to the upper teeth (hence-*dental*). The labiodental consonants are *f* and *v*.

Interdental, or **linguadental, consonants**   For these sounds the tongue (*lingua*) is between the upper and lower teeth. The interdental consonants are *th* (as in *thin*) and *th* (as in *then*).

Lingua-alveolar consonants   For these sounds the tip of the tongue is placed against the upper gum ridge (*alveolus*). The lingua-alveolar consonants are *n*, *t*, *d*, *s*, *z*, and *l*.

Linguapalatal consonants   For these sounds the tip of the tongue touches (or nearly touches) the hard palate just behind the gum ridge. The linguapalatal consonants are *y* (as in *yellow*), *r* (as in *rain*), *sh* (as in *shoe*), *zh* (as in *vision*), *ch* (as in *chew*), and *j* (as in *jump*).

Linguavelar consonants   For these sounds the rear of the tongue is raised against the soft palate (*velum*), and the tip of the tongue is lowered to the bottom of the mouth. The linguavelar consonants are *k*, *g*, and *ng* (as in *sing*).

Glottal consonant   The glottal consonant, *h*, is formed by the passage of air between the vocal folds without vibration of those folds.

These methods of classification are quite helpful, because they accurately describe the most significant characteristics of the consonants.

[3]The terms used in this classification system generally derive from Latin.

b   The consonant *b* is a voiced labial plosive. It is formed by first stopping the flow of air by closing the lips and then releasing the built-up air as though in an explosion.

p   The consonant *p* is an unvoiced labial plosive. It is formed like *b*, except that it is unvoiced and, therefore, merely exploded air.

t   The consonant *t* is an unvoiced lingua-alveolar plosive. As this description suggests, *t* is formed by the release of unvoiced air that has been temporarily blocked off by the pressure of the tip of the tongue against the upper gum ridge. Note that *t*, like *p*, is best softened for radio and television speech.

The medial *t* is a problem for many American speakers. In the West and Midwest, it is often turned into a *d*, as in saying BAD'-UL for *battle*. In some parts of the East Coast, it is turned into a glottal stop, as in saying BAH-UL' for *bottle*.[4] To help you determine whether you have a medial *t* problem, record and listen to this reading:

> The metal kettle was a little more than half full. I settled for a little bit of the better stuff and waited while an Irish setter begged for a pitiful allotment of the fatter part of the kettle's contents. The setter left, disgusted and a little bitter over the matter of the lost battle for more of the beetle stew.

For extra work with the medial (*t*) try saying the following with increasing speed: *beetle, bittle, bayttle, bettle, battle, bottle, bootle, berttle, buttle.*

d   The consonant *d* is a voiced lingua-alveolar plosive. Except for being voiced, it is the same as *t*. (Say *tot* and then *dod*, and you will find that your articulators repeat the same positions and movements. Deaf people who read lips cannot detect any difference between voiced and unvoiced pairs and must therefore rely on context for understanding.)

k   The consonant *k* is an unvoiced linguavelar plosive. It is formed by releasing unphonated air that has been blocked momentarily from passage by the pressure of the top of the rear of the tongue against the hard palate.

g   The consonant *g* is a voiced linguavelar plosive, formed like the unvoiced *k*.

f   The consonant *f* is an unvoiced labiodental fricative. It is formed by releasing air through a restricted passage between the front teeth and the lower lip.

---

[4]A **glottal stop** is a speech sound produced by a momentary but complete closure of the throat passage, followed by an explosive release.

v

The consonant *v* is a voiced labiodental fricative, formed like *f* except for being phonated.

th

The consonant (TH) /th/ [θ] (as in *thin*) is an unvoiced interdental fricative. This sound is frequently a source of trouble, because the microphone tends to amplify any slight whistle that may be present. In making this sound, place the tongue up to, but not into, the space between the upper and lower teeth, which are held about an eighth of an inch apart. Air passing over the top of the tongue and between its tip and the upper front teeth makes the (TH) sound.

The consonant (TH) /*th*/ [ð] (as in *them*) is a voiced interdental fricative, formed the same as the sound in *thin* but phonated.

s

The consonant *s* is an unvoiced lingua-alveolar fricative. It is one of the more common sources of trouble for the announcer. A slight misplacement of the articulators may cause a whistle, a thick fuzzy sound, or a lisp. There are two methods of producing *s*, neither of which seems clearly superior to the other. In the first, the sides of the tongue are in contact with the upper teeth as far forward as the incisors. The tip of the tongue is held rather high in the mouth, and a fine stream of air is directed at the tips of the upper front teeth. The teeth, meanwhile, are held slightly apart. In the second method of making *s*, the tongue is fairly low in the mouth at the rear and at the tip and is raised just behind the tip to make near contact with the gum ridge. A fine stream of air is permitted to flow through this passage, down toward the front teeth, which are held slightly apart. Because most microphones tend to exaggerate any slight whistle or excessive sibilance, work for a softened *s*.

Because the sibilant *s* is a common source of trouble to announcers, a diagnostic exercise is included here. Read the following passage into a tape recorder, play it back, and determine whether you have the problem of excessive sibilance. Before working to soften this sound, however, you should experiment with microphone placement and even the use of a windscreen or pop filter, for you may find that the problem is with the equipment or the way you are using it, rather than in your speech.

How long has it been since you saw a first-rate sideshow? Some of us certainly should be sad over the disappearance of the classic circus sideshow, once a staple of civic celebrations. Six or seven acts, set forth in circumstances that seemed awesome, or at least mysterious. Certainly, sideshows were sometimes scandalous, and sometimes in questionable taste, but they served to keep our curiosity in a steady state of astonishment.

If you do produce excessive sibilance, use the exercises at the end of this chapter.

z   The consonant *z* (as in *zoom*) is a voiced lingua-alveolar fricative formed like *s*, except for phonation.

sh   The consonant (SH) /sh/ [ʃ] (as in *shoe*) is an unvoiced lingua-palatal fricative. It is made by allowing unvoiced air to escape with friction from between the tip of the tongue and the gum ridge behind the upper front teeth. Although this sound is not a common source of difficulty, you should guard against its becoming a thick, unpleasing sound. To form (SH), make certain that air does not escape around the sides of the tongue, and keep the central portion of the tongue fairly low in the mouth.

zh   The consonant (ZH) /zh/ [ʒ] (as in *vision*) is a voiced linguapalatal fricative and is formed the same way as (SH) but with phonation. It is seldom found in an initial position in English.

h   The consonant *h* (as in *healthy*) is an unvoiced glottal fricative. It is seldom a source of difficulty, although many announcers tend to drop this sound in certain combinations. Note that the *h* is definitely present in most words beginning with *wh*. Note also that this sound depends entirely on the sound that follows it and cannot, therefore, be articulated at the end of a word.

ch   The consonant (CH) /ch/ [tʃ] (as in *charm*) is an unvoiced linguapalatal affricate. It is, by definition, formed with the tongue against the gum ridge behind the upper teeth with both the release of pent-up air of the plosive and the friction of the fricative.

j   The consonant (J) /j/ [dʒ] (as in *justice*) is a voiced linguapalatal affricate, formed like (CH) but with phonation.

m   The consonant *m* (as in *major*) is a voiced labial nasal. It is articulated with the lips completely closed. When *m* occurs in a final position, the mouth remains closed. When it occurs in an initial position, the mouth must open, not to sound *m* but to move immediately to the sound that follows.

n   The consonant *n* (as in *nothing*) is a voiced lingua-alveolar nasal. Unlike *m*, it can be sounded with the mouth open, because the tongue, rather than the lips, blocks off the air and forces it through the nasal cavity. The sounding of *n* is responsible for much of the excessive nasality characteristic of many irritating voices. If you detect, or someone detects for you, a tendency to overnasalize such sounds, spend several sessions with a tape recorder learning how it feels to soften them.

ng   The consonant (NG) /ng/ [ŋ] (as in *sing*) is a voiced linguavelar nasal. It is formed much as the consonant *g* is, but it lacks the plosive quality of that sound. One of the most common problems with (NG) involves turning this sound into "in" in words that end with *ing*. Each announcer must, of course, determine whether it is appropriate to do this. A newscaster will undoubtedly decide not to. Disc jockeys and sports announcers, depending on their speech personality, may decide that it is permissible. A less common pronunciation problem involving this sound is the practice in some parts of the East of adding *g* in the middle of a word such as *singing* (SING'-GING) ['sɪŋgɪŋ].

l

The consonant *l* is a voiced lingua-alveolar semivowel, formed by placing the tip of the tongue against the upper gum ridge and allowing phonated air to escape around the sides of the tongue. This sound presents little difficulty when in an initial or final position in a word, but is frequently a source of trouble in a medial position. If you say aloud the word *William*, you will notice that the tip of the tongue is placed low in the mouth for *Wi*, raised to the upper gum ridge for *ll*, and returned to the floor of the mouth for *iam*. Obviously, it is easier to speak this name without moving the tongue at all, but then it sounds like WIH-YUM, and the *l* sound is completely lost. Unlike some English speech sounds that may in informal delivery be softened or dropped without loss of effectiveness, the lost medial *l* is definitely substandard and should never occur in an announcer's speech.

Here is a diagnostic reading for the medial *l*.

> Millions of Italians filled the hilly sector of Milan. The willing celebrants whirled all along the palisades, down by the roiling river. The lilting lullabies, trilled by Italian altos, thrilled the millions as they willingly milled along the boulevard. "It's really thrilling," said William Miller, a celebrant from Valley Forge. "I willingly call this the most illustrious fellowship in all of Italy.

If you have difficulty with the medial *l*, practice with the exercises given at the end of this chapter.

w

The consonant *w* (as in *willow*) is a voiced labial semivowel, formed by moving the lips from a rounded, nearly closed position to an open position. The tongue is not in any particular position for *w* but is placed to produce the following vowel sound. A common speech fault is insufficient movement of the lips in making *w*.

hw

The consonant (HW) /hw/ [hw] (as in *where*) is an unvoiced labial fricative. It is a combination of the two consonants *h* and *w* and is achieved by forming the lips for *w* but releasing the air that makes *h* first; then the (W) sound follows immediately, so the (H) sound is barely heard. Although the (HW) sound in words such as *when* is lost by most speakers, radio and television announcers should include it, at least until it drops out of our language altogether.

y The consonant (Y) /y/ [j] (as in *yellow*) is a voiced linguapalatal fricative. As with *l*, *w*, and *r*, a slight glide is necessary during the delivery of this sound. Although *y* causes little difficulty when in the initial position in a word, the medial *y* frequently follows a double *l* and is therefore sometimes involved in the speech problem that arises from dropping the medial *l*. Americans often mispronounce million as MIH-YUN'.

r The consonant *r* (as in *runner*) is a voiced linguapalatal semivowel. In certain areas of the United States and in England, *r* is frequently softened or completely dropped. In General American speech, however, all *r*'s are sounded, though they need not and should not be prolonged or formed too far back in the throat. A voice described as harsh is frequently one that overstresses *r* sounds. However, in attempting to soften your *r*'s be careful to avoid affectation; a pseudo-British accent is unbecoming to Americans and Canadians. Few speakers can successfully change only one speech sound. The slight softening of *r* should be only one part of a general softening of all harsh sounds in your speech.

Practice: Achieving a Low Pitch

Use the following commercial to try to achieve a low pitch. If you have a very low voice, make sure that you do not creep along the bottom. Remember to work for variety in pitch. In addition to concentrating on pitch, try to read the commercial in exactly 30 seconds. If you read it in less time, you are probably not savoring the key selling words, and your speed may be interfering with the achievement of optimum pitch.

> Mellow. Smooth and mellow. That's the way to describe Dairyland Longhorn Cheese. We use the finest grade A milk from happy cows. Nothing but pure, natural ingredients. We take our time, letting the cheese age to the peak of perfect taste. We package Dairyland Longhorn in cheesecloth and wax, just like in the old days. And we speed it to your grocer, so that you get it at its flavorful best. Dairyland Longhorn Cheese. It's smooth and mellow.

Practice: Varying Your Pitch

Say these sentences, inflecting on the italicized word or words:

When did *you* get here?	When did you *get* here?
I *hope* you're right.	I hope you're *right*.
Which *one* is it?	*Which* one is it?
Which one *is* it?	Which one is *it*?
We *lost* the *game*!	*We* lost the game!
Don't say *that*.	Don't *say* that.
She found the key.	She *found* the key.
The *dog* ate the steak.	The dog ate the *steak*.

Inflect these words in isolation:

What?	Tremendous!
Certainly!	Ridiculous!
Maybe.	Surely.
Awful!	Life?
Sure!	How?
Try!	Stop.
Go!	Caught?

Note that the challenge is greatest with one-syllable words. The word *Life*, for example, asked as a question, can accommodate both an upward and a downward inflection without becoming a two- or three-syllable word.

Practice: Varying Your Tempo

The following commercial provides good opportunities for employing shifts in reading speed. (SFX is the standard abbreviation for sound effects.)

SFX: SOUND OF GRIZZLY MOTORCYCLE IN DISTANCE,
GRADUALLY APPROACHING.

ANNCR: I can hear it in the distance. (PAUSE) Can you?
(PAUSE) The "grrrr-ing" of the Grizzly motor
bike. (PAUSE) No, not a "purring," a "grrr-
ing." What's the difference? A "purr" comes from
a contented cat--a "grrr" is made by a hefty
Grizzly, looking for adventure. Cats are great,
but they're usually gentle. The Grizzly is wild,
but not unmanageable.

SFX: GRIZZLY VOLUME CONTINUES TO INCREASE.

ANNCR: The Grizzly doesn't "putt-putt," and it doesn't
purr. It has a warm, furry sound, as befits a
creature of the wild. (PAUSE) Here's the Grizzly,
speaking for itself. (PAUSE)

SFX: SOUND UP FULL, THEN BEGIN FADE.

ANNCR: There it goes! (PAUSE) "Grrrr-ing" its way to
where it's going. Hear the "grrrr"? You can own
the "grrrr"--if you don't want a pussycat and
think you can tame a Grizzly. Check us out.
(PAUSE) We're in the Yellow Pages. The Grizzly.
(PAUSE) It's for people who want something on the
wild side.

SFX: SOUND OF GRIZZLY TO CLOSE.

Practice: Pronouncing Diphthongs

If you have trouble with diphthongs, practice making each of the vowel sounds that form them and then speak the two sounds consecutively with increasing rapidity. The following exercises will help only if you are producing the sounds of the diphthongs correctly.

Read these sentences to practice the diphthong (EYE) /ī/ [aɪ].

1. I like my bike.
2. Lie in the silo on your side.
3. Fine nights for sighing breezes.
4. Why try to lie in the blinding light?
5. Cy tried to fly his kite.
6. My fine wife likes to fly in my glider.
7. Try my pie—I like it fine.
8. Shy guys find they like to cry.
9. My sly friend likes to be wined and dined.
10. Like all fine and right-minded guys, Mr. Wright liked best to try to find the slightest excuse to lie about his life.

These sentences allow you to focus on the (AU) /ou/ [aʊ] sound.

1. Flounce into my mouse's house.
2. Cows allow just about too much proudness about them.
3. Round and round went the loudly shouting lout.
4. A mouse is somewhat louder than a louse in a house.
5. A bounding hound went out on the bounding main.
6. Grouse are lousy bets when abounding results are found.
7. A cow and a mouse lived in a house.
8. The louder they proudly cried, the more the crowd delighted in seeing them trounced.
9. They plowed the drought-stricken cow pasture.
10. Allow the grouse to shout louder and louder, and you just about drown out the proud cows.

Use the following sentences to practice the diphthong (OY) /oi/ [ɔɪ].

1. A toy needs oiling.
2. The soybeans are joyously coiling.

3. Floyd oiled the squeaky toy.
4. Goya painted Troy in oils.
5. His annoying voice was boiling mad.
6. The oyster exploited the joyous foil.
7. Roy and Lloyd soiled the toys.
8. Joy, like a spoiled boy, exploited her friends.
9. What kind of noise annoys an oyster? A noisy noise annoys an oyster.

Read these sentences for practice with the (YU) /yo͞o/ [ju] sound.

1. I used to refuse to use abusive news.
2. The kitten mewed, but I refused to go.
3. The music was used to imbue us with enthusiasm.
4. The beautiful view used to confuse.
5. June was beautiful.
6. The newest pupil was wearing his suit.
7. The cute kitten mewed.
8. He eschewed responsibility for the news.
9. The few new musical numbers were confusing to the beautiful girl.
10. A few beautiful girls are using perfume.

Practice: Working on Nasal Resonance

Speak each pair of nasal and non-nasal words, keeping the tips of your fingers lightly touching the sides of your nose. Work for vibration with the first word of each pair and for lack of it with the second.

(M)

aim—aid	beam—beet
arm—art	farmer—father
atom—attar	bump—butt
balm—back	summer—Sutter
calm—cot	ram—rat

(N)

earn—earth	bend—bet
barn—bard	bin—bit
bane—bathe	win—will
fawn—fall	own—oath
band—bat	friend—Fred

(NG)

link—lick	bunko—bucko
bank—back	tongue—tuck
blank—black	ming—mick
wink—wick	manx—Max
singer—sinner	trunk—truck

Practice: Pronouncing Consonants

The exercises that follow are based on the correct sounding of consonants. Note, however, that vowel and diphthong sounds (which have already been discussed) are present in every exercise and must be sounded correctly in order to achieve good American English speech. Voiced and unvoiced consonants formed in the same way are considered together.

b   Use these sentences to practice sounding the consonant *b*.

1. Big Bill bent the bulky box.
2. The Boston bull was bigger than the boy.
3. Libby lobbed the sobbing lobster.
4. The ribbing was robbed from the jobber.
5. Bob could rob the mob.
6. The boxer baited the big boy, while the mobster hobbled about the sobbing, crabby boy named Bob.

p   These sentences can be used to practice the *p* sound.

1. Paula peeked past the platform.
2. Peter Piper picked a peck of pickled peppers.

3. Happy people appear to approach unhappiness happily.
4. Approximately opposed in position are Dopey and Happy.
5. Stop the cap from hitting the top.
6. Apparently the perfect approach to happiness is practiced by the popular purveyor of apoplexy, Pappy Perkins.

t

The following sentences allow you to practice the consonant *t*.

1. Tiny Tim tripped toward the towering Titan.
2. The tall Texan tried to teach the taxi driver twenty tall tales of Texas.
3. Attractive though Patty was, the battling fighters hesitated to attempt to please her.
4. The bottled beetles were getting fatter.
5. The fat cat sat in the fast-moving draft.
6. Herbert hit the fat brat with the short bat.

d

Use these sentences as exercises for practicing the consonant *d*.

1. Don dragged the dull, drab dump truck up to the door.
2. The dry, dusty den was dirtier than Denny's delightful diggings.
3. The ladder added to the indeterminate agenda.
4. The sadly padded widow in the middle looked addled.
5. Around the lad the red-colored rope was twined.
6. Glad to lead the band, Fred allowed his sad friend to parade around.

k

These sentences can be used to practice sounding *k*.

1. Keep Kim close to the clothes closet.
2. A call came for Karen, but Karen wasn't caring.
3. Accolades were accorded to the picnicking dockworkers.
4. Action-back suits were accepted on occasion by the actors playing stock comedy characters.
5. Like it or not, the sick man was picked.
6. Rick kept count of the black sacks.

g

The following sentences are useful for practicing the consonant *g*.

1. The good girl with the grand guy glanced at the ground.
2. One glimpse of the good green earth, and the goose decided to go.
3. Agog with ague, the agonizing laggard stood agape.

4. Slogging along, the haggard sagging band lagged behind.
5. 'Twas brillig, and the rig did sag.
6. The rag bag was big and full, but the sagging trigger was clogged with glue.

f   Use these sentences to practice sounding *f*.

1. The fish fry was a fairly fashionable affair.
2. Flying for fun, Freddy found the first fairly fast flying machine.
3. Affairs of affection are affable.
4. The affected aficionado was afraid of Africa.
5. The laugh graph showed a half-laugh.
6. The rough toff was off with his calf.

v   You can use these sentences to practice sounding *v*.

1. Victor is a vision of vim, vigor, and vitality.
2. Viola was victorious with Vladimir's violin.
3. Avarice, averred the maverick on the avenue, is to be avoided.
4. An aversion to lavender obviously prevents the inveterate invalid from involving himself avidly in mauve.
5. A vivid avarice was obviously invested in the avoidance of the man on the avenue.
6. Live, live, cried the five live jivesters.

th   The following sentences can be used to practice the unvoiced (TH) sound.

1. Think through thirty-three things.
2. Thoughts are thrifty when thinking through problems.
3. Cotton Mather lathed his bath house.
4. The pathway to the wrathful heath.
5. The thought of the myth was cutting as a scythe.
6. Thirty-three thinking mythological monsters, wearing pith helmets, wrathfully thought that Theobald was through.

th   Use these sentences for practicing the voiced (TH) sound.

1. This, the man said, is older than thou.
2. The man therein was thereby less than the man who was theretofore therein.
3. Other people lather their faces further.
4. I'd rather gather heather than feathers.

5. Wreathe my brow with heather.
6. I seethe and breathe the truths of yore.

sibilance

The following sentences should help you reduce excessive sibilance.

1. Should Samson slink past the sly, singing Delilah?
2. Swimming seems to survive as a sport despite some circumstances.
3. Lessons on wrestling are absurd, asserted Tessie.
4. Assurances concerning some practices of misguided misogynists are extremely hysterical.
5. The glass case sits in the purse of the lass.
6. Past the last sign for Sixth Place, the bus lost its best chance to rest.

z

You can use these sentences to practice sounding *z*.

1. The zippy little xylophone had a zany sound.
2. The zoological gardens were zoned by Zola for the zebras.
3. The fuzzy, buzzing bees were nuzzling the trees.
4. He used the music to arouse enthusiasm in the buzzards.
5. Was the buzz that comes from the trees caused by the limbs or the bees?
6. His clothes were rags, his arms were bare; yet his features caused his admirers to gaze as though his misery were a blessing.

sh

Use these sentences to practice the (SH) sound.

1. Shortly after shearing a sheep, I shot a wolf.
2. The shapely Sharon shared her chateau with Charmaine.
3. Mashed potatoes and hashed cashews are flashy rations.
4. The lashing gale thrashed; lightning flashed, and the Hessian troops gnashed their teeth.
5. A flash flood mashed the cash into trash.
6. Fish wish that fishermen would wash their shoes.

zh

These sentences allow you to practice the (ZH) sound.

1. Jeanne d'Arc saw visions in the azure sky.
2. *Measure for Measure* is not the usually pleasurable Shakespearean play.
3. A hidden treasure was pleasurably unearthed from the beige hill with great precision.

4. The seizure was leisurely measured.
5. The edges of his incision had the *noblesse oblige* to form an elision.

h   You can use these sentences to practice with the consonant *h*.

1. The huge hat was held on Henrietta's head by heaps of string.
2. Halfway home, the happy Herman had to have a hamburger.
3. Manhattan abhors one-half the upheaval of Manhasset.
4. "Ha-ha-ha," said the behemoth, as he unhitched the horse.

ch   The following sentences are useful for practicing the (CH) sound.

1. Chew your chilly chop before you choke.
2. Choose your chums as cheerfully as children.
3. An itching action follows alfalfa pitching.
4. The richly endowed Mitchells latched onto much money.

j   Use these sentences for practicing with the consonant *j*.

1. The junk man just couldn't joust with justice.
2. Joan jumped back in justifiable panic as Jud jettisoned the jet-black jetty.
3. Adjutant-General Edgewater adjusted his midget glasses.
4. The edgy fledgling was judged unjustifiably.
5. The edge of the ledge was where Madge did lodge.
6. Trudge through the sedge and bridge the hedge.

m   The following sentences are helpful for practicing the consonant *m*.

1. Miranda meant more than my miserable money.
2. Merton moved my midget mailbox more to my right.
3. Eminent employers emulate immense amateurs.
4. Among amiable emigrants, Kimball admitted to mother and me his inestimable immaturity.
5. Slim Jim and Sam climbed the trim limb.
6. Rhythm hymns they perform for them.

n   You can use these sentences to practice the sounding of *n*.

1. Ned's nice neighbor knew nothing about Neil.
2. Now the new niece needed Nancy's needle.
3. Indigestion invariably incapacitated Manny after dinner.

4. Many wonderful and intricate incidentals indirectly antagonized Fanny.
5. Nine men were seen in the fine mountain cabin.
6. Susan won the clean garden award and soon ran to plan again.

ng

Use these sentences to practice the (NG) sound.

1. The English singer was winning the long contest.
2. He mingled with winged, gaily singing songbirds.
3. The long, strong rope rang the gong.
4. Running and skipping, the ringleader led the gang.
5. Among his long songs, Engel mingled some lilting things.
6. Along the winding stream, the swimming and fishing were finding many fans.

l

The following exercises will allow you to practice sounding the medial *l*.

1. A million silly swallows filled their bills with squiggling worms.
2. Willy Wallace willingly wiggled William's million-dollar bill.
3. Lilly and Milly met two willing fellows from the hills.
4. A little melon was willingly volunteered by Ellen and William.
5. Bill filled the lily pot with a million gallons of water.
6. The mill filled the foolish little children's order for willow leaves.
7. William wanted a million dollars, but he seldom was willing to stop his silly shilly-shallying and work.
8. Phillip really liked Italian children, although he seldom was willing to speak Italian.
9. Enrolling in college really was thrilling for William, even though a million pillow fights were in store for the silly fellow.
10. Billy Bellnap shilled for millions of collegians, even though his colleagues collected alibis galore in the Alleghenies at Miller's celebration.

w

You can use these sentences to practice the *w* sound.

1. Worried Willy wouldn't waste one wonderful word.
2. The wild wind wound round the woody wilderness.
3. The wishing well was once wanted by Wally Williams.
4. Wouldn't it be wonderful if one walrus would wallow in the water?
5. Walter wanted to wash away the worrisome watermark.
6. Always sewing, Eloise wished the wonderful woman would want one more wash dress.

hw   The following sentences are useful for practicing the (HW) sound.

1. Mr. Wheeler waited at the wharf.
2. Wherever the whippoorwill whistled, Whitby waited.
3. Why whisper when we don't know whether or not Mr. White's whelp is a whiz?
4. "Why not whet your knife?" whispered the white-bearded Whig.
5. Whitney whittled the white-headed whistle.
6. On Whitsun, Whittier was whipping Whitman on a whim.

y   You can use these sentences to practice with the consonant *y*.

1. Young Yancy used yellow utensils.
2. The millionaire abused the useful William.
3. Yesterday the youthful Tillyard yelled "Yes."
4. The Yukon used to yen for yokels.
5. Yorick yielded to the yodeler from Yonkers.
6. The yegg yelled at William.

r   Use these sentences to practice the consonant *r*.

1. Rather than run rapidly, Rupert relied on rhythm.
2. Robert rose to revive Reginald's rule of order.
3. Apparently a miracle occurred to Herman.
4. Large and cumbersome, the barge was a dirty hull.
5. Afraid of fire and sure of war, the rear admiral was far away.
6. The bore on the lower floor left his chair and went out the door.

5

American English Usage

To be an announcer is to be a user of words. Thus, every serious student of announcing will undertake a systematic study of American English. This means engaging in several different but related studies. It means making a lifelong habit of consulting dictionaries. It means becoming sensitized to nuances of language and striving to find the precise, rather than the approximate, word. It means changing your vocabulary as changes in our language occur. It means cultivating and practicing the art of plain talk. And it means perfecting your pronunciation of both American English and foreign words. This chapter examines American English usage from the standpoint of the broadcast announcer and discusses our changing language. Appendix B provides a list of frequently mispronounced words. Chapter 15 reviews the principles of pronunciation of some of the major languages of the world.

Top professional announcers use words with precision and manage to sound conversational while honoring the rules of grammar. Unfortunately, some broadcast announcers are far from perfect, and listeners and viewers suffer daily from a variety of errors in usage. During a randomly chosen two-week period, the following mistakes were made by announcers at local and network levels:

"The French farmers have thrown up barrages across the major highways leading out of Paris." The announcer meant *barricades*, not *barrages*.

"The deputy sheriffs are still out on strike, and it doesn't look like they'll be back to work before long." *Soon* would be acceptable in place of *before long*.

"General ———, who last year authored an unsuccessful coup, . . . " *Author* is a noun, not a transitive verb; even if it were, it is doubtful that the announcer meant that the general "wrote" an unsuccessful coup.

"The fishing boat was loaded to the gills." Fish may possibly be loaded to the gills, but boats are loaded to the *gunwales* (pronounced GUN′-UHLZ).

"The little girl was found in the company of an unidentified man." Does the announcer mean that the man's identity was unknown or that his identity was not disclosed?

"The secretary of state reportedly will visit South America late this summer." There are many kinds of visits—long visits, brief visits, surreptitious visits—but no one can make a reported visit. The announcer meant "It is reported that the secretary of state . . ."

"Three kids died when their house slid down a hill during the storm." *Kids* is slang, acceptable under some circumstances but not when reporting a tragedy.

"After being surrounded by the policemen, the suspect came out with his hands up." The term *policemen* has been replaced by *police officers* according to standards issued by the U.S. Department of Labor.

"Firefighters rescued an elderly Oriental man . . ." Using the word *Oriental* when referring to a person is offensive to most people of Asian ancestry.

"The government of Kenya (KEEN′-YUH) is making a serious effort to eliminate poaching in its national parks." The citizens of this nation call it KEN′-YUH and consider KEEN′-YUH an unwelcome reminder of colonial days.

"The A's won MVP honors three consecutive years in a row." *Consecutive* means basically the same thing as *in a row*; this is a case of redundancy.

"The U.S. was outcompeted last year to the tune of 1.5 billion dollars." The United States may have had a 1.5-billion-dollar trade deficit, but the nonword *outcompeted* does not stand up to linguistic logic or rules of grammar.

News reporters, interviewers, commentators, disc jockeys, talk show hosts, sportscasters, and weather, environmental, and consumer reporters must frame their own thoughts into words and must choose those words well and pronounce them correctly. To do this, they must be experts with their language. The sections that follow cover a portion of the territory that is the province of professional announcers.

Age Referents

It is as offensive to a young adult to be called a boy or a girl as it is to a middle-aged person to be called elderly. Announcers must be sensitive to the feelings of those described by age classifications and of listeners and viewers who may object to such classifications. Age is, of course, not always an appropriate referent. In a report that a musician triumphed at a concert, it is not necessary to give the musician's age—unless he or she was extremely young or very old. On the other hand, in a report of the death of a well-known person, age is a legitimate item of information. When the age of a person is known, and when age is of some significance (as with athletes, prodigies, or people who have reached an unusual age, such as 100), give the correct age and avoid using an age category.

At times it is appropriate to state that a given person is within a recognized age group. Use the criteria in Table 5.1 as a guide.

Elderly people are often referred to as *senior citizens*, but many do not like the term. *Senior* is somewhat more acceptable, though

Table 5.1   Guidelines for Using Age Referents

Label	Appropriate Age Range
child	between birth and puberty (approximately 12 or 13)
boy or *girl*	before puberty
youth	between puberty and legal age (approximately 13 to 18)
young adult	between 18 and 21
juvenile	between 13 and 18
adolescent	approximately 13 to 19
teen-ager	13 through 19, inclusive
man or *woman*	over 18
adult	over 18
middle-aged	approximately 40 to 65
elderly	beyond late middle age (above 70)
old	advanced years (above 75)
senior	beyond retirement age (usually above 70)

there always will be some individuals who resent being classified by an age category.

The word *kid*, meaning a young person, is sometimes acceptable and at other times in poor taste. You are safe when speaking of a kid sister or brother or in saying "Your kids will love this!" When your focus becomes narrower and you speak of a specific person, you run the risk of provoking resentment: a child up to the age of 12 or 13 probably will accept the label *kid*; adolescents gradually begin to object as they approach the age of 14 or 15. The term is never appropriate when describing a tragedy. In general, slang words or words that seem flippant should never be used when reporting a story that involves suffering or death.

Jargon and Vogue Words

Every profession and social group has a private or semiprivate vocabulary. Some words and phrases from such groups enter the mainstream of public communication. It is useful and enriching when expressions such as *gridlock*, *agribusiness*, *software*, or *hostile takeover* (the world of business) are added to the general vocabulary. As an announcer, you should guard against picking up and overusing expressions that are trite, precious, deliberately distorting, or pretentious. Here are a few recent vogue words and phrases with translations into plain English (slightly facetious in some cases).

From the military
de-escalate to give up on a lost war
balance of power a dangerous stand-off
nuclear deterrent the means by which war can be deterred when antagonistic nations possess enough nuclear weapons to destroy the world
debrief to ask questions of someone

From government
at home and abroad everywhere
nonproliferation monopolization of nuclear weapons
disadvantaged poor people
Department of Human Resources Development the unemployment office
decriminalize to make legal

Figure 5.1
Talk show hosts must use age referents such as *elderly* or *senior* with accuracy and sensitivity. Phil Donahue is a master at using language with care as he maintains a fast-paced ad-lib presentation. (Al Satterwhite, The Image Bank)

From academe
operant conditioning learning by trial and error
quantum leap a breakthrough
de-aestheticize to take the beauty out of art
dishabituate to break a bad habit
dehire to fire someone
microencapsulate to put into a small capsule
found art someone else's junk
megastructure a large building

A few words that should be used precisely and sparingly, if at all, are *rhetoric* (when the meaning is "empty and angry talk"), *charisma*, *relevant*, *obviate*, *facility* (when referring to a building), *viable*, and *meaningful*. Vogue phrases that have already become clichés should be avoided; some of these are *a can of worms*, *a breakdown in communication*, *head honcho*, and *generation gap*.

Tacking the suffix *-wise* onto nouns in awkward ways is possibly one of the most offensive speech habits that has arisen in the past several years. Here are some familiar examples:

Culturewise, the people are . . .
Foodwise, your best buy is . . .
National-securitywise, we should . . .

Violations of correct American English are perpetrated by people who have found such usages an effortless means of avoiding correct sentence construction. The suffix *-wise* does, of course, have a proper use in words such as *lengthwise* and *counterclockwise*.

Three particularly contagious vogue words that seem to strike their victims as a team are *like*, *man*, and *y'know*. Obviously, such words replace *uh* and other annoying affectations in the speech of many who find a need for verbalized pauses to compensate for lack of fluency. Make certain that these words are used by you only when appropriate. *Like* and *man* have their obvious places in our language; *y'know* would be fitting only in very conversational chatter, such as that used by a disc jockey.

Boring and ineffective speech is not the exclusive property of any particular group. Linguistic fashions spread alarmingly through our society. Awareness of your speech patterns, together with an adequate vocabulary, should help you eliminate most vogue words from your speech.

Redundancies

To be redundant is to be repetitive. At times, in a commercial, for example, redundancy may be useful in driving home a point or a product advantage. At most times, however, redundancy is needless repetition. *Close proximity* is redundant because *close* and *proximity* (or *proximate*) mean the same thing. A *necessary requisite* is redundant because requisite contains the meaning of *necessary*. Spoken English is plagued with unnecessary redundancy, and constant watchfulness is required to avoid it.

Here are some redundancies heard far too often on radio and television:

abundant wealth *Wealth* means having a great amount.

an old antique There can be no such thing as a new antique.

both alike, both at once, both equal *Both* refers to two people or things, and *alike*, *at once*, and *equal* all imply some kind of duality.

completely surround, completely abandon, completely eliminate To *surround*, to *abandon*, and to *eliminate* are done completely, if they are done at all.

cooperate together To *cooperate* means that two or more work together.

divide up, *end up*, *finish up*, *rest up*, *pay up*, *settle up* All of these are burdened by unnecessary *ups*.

Easter Sunday Easter occurs, by definition, only on a Sunday (the first Sunday following the full moon that occurs on or next after March 21).

equally as expensive If something costs what another thing does, then inevitably their costs are equal. (The correct form is *equally expensive* or *as expensive as*.)

excess verbiage Because *verbiage* means "wordiness," it contains the concept of excess.

exchanged with each other An exchange is necessarily between one and another.

general consensus *Consensus* means "general agreement."

Hallowe'en evening *Hallowe'en* includes *evening* in an abbreviated form.

I thought to myself Barring telepathy, there is no one else one can think to.

joint partnership *Partnership* includes the concept of *joint*.

knots per hour A knot is a nautical mile per hour, so *per hour* is redundant.

Figure 5.2
Left: "Hip" jargon was a trend of the 1970s and 1980s, but even today there are rock radio stations across the country at which phrases and words that are unique to a certain age group or geographic area are tossed about between songs. Right: In contrast, the precise, correct language of announcers such as PBS's Alistair Cooke remains timeless and universally understood. (Left: Jack Spratt, Picture Group; right: courtesy of WGBH, Boston)

more preferable Use this only if you are comparing two preferences.

most outstanding, *most perfect*, *most unique* A thing is outstanding, perfect, or unique, or it is not. There are no degrees of any of these qualities.

novel innovation To be innovative is to be novel; this essentially says a "new new thing."

Sahara Desert Sahara means "desert."

serious crisis It is not a crisis unless it has already become serious.

set a new record All records are new when they are set.

Sierra Nevada Mountains Sierra means "rugged mountains."

still remains If something *remains*, it must be there *still*.

totally annihilated Annihilate means "to destroy totally."

true facts There can be no untrue facts.

visible to the eye There is no other way a thing can be visible.

Develop a keen ear for redundancies. Recognizing errors in usage is the first step toward avoiding them in your own speech.

Clichés

A **cliché** is an overused expression or idea. Most popular clichés were once innovative and effective. They became clichés by being overused and, in most instances, misapplied by people who were not aware of their original meanings. Many who use the cliché *as rich as Croesus* have no idea who Croesus was or the degree of his wealth. Similarly, the expression *as slow as molasses in January* may be used by some who are not familiar with the properties of molasses.

Many clichés reflect our rural past. We say "mad as a wet hen," "fat as a pig," "stubborn as a mule," "silly as a goose," "strong as an ox," and other similar expressions. Most of these **similes** have been learned by rote and are used by people who have never associated with creatures of the barnyard. For most of us these expressions should be replaced by similes that reflect our own experiences.

Good use of language demands that we think before we fall back on the first cliché that comes to mind. Commonly used clichés include these:

as sharp as a tack   *bright as a button*

quick as a flash or   *quiet as a grave* or
   quick as a wink   *quiet as a tomb*

dead as a doornail   *as common as dirt*

dry as a bone   *as cool as a cucumber*

mad as a hatter or   *as hungry as a bear*
   mad as a March hare   *as new as tomorrow*

fresh as a daisy

The effectiveness of the similes listed here and dozens more like them has simply been worn out by endless repetition. Good broadcast speech is by no means measured by the ability to produce new and more effective images, but from time to time creative metaphorical expression can make for memorable communication. See what a little thought and time can do to help you use language creatively. How would you complete the followimg similes to make novel and effective images?

as awkward as _____

as barren as _____

as deceptive as _____

as friendly as _____

as quiet as _____

as strange as _____

In addition to overworked similes and metaphors, many other words and phrases have become hackneyed through overuse. Many clichés can be heard on daily newscasts. If you intend to become a news reporter or newscaster, you should make a careful and constant study of words that have become meaningless and replace them with meaningful synonyms. Here are a few examples:

Overworked phrase	*Suggested alternative*
has branded as ridiculous	*has called ridiculous*
a shroud of secrecy	*kept secret*
deem it advisable	*consider it advisable*
was held in abeyance	*was suspended*
informed sources at the White House	*White House aides*

Overworked phrase	*Suggested alternative*
has earmarked several million dollars	*has set aside several million*
stated in no uncertain terms	*was definite about*
tantamount to election	*ensured election*
a flurry of activity	*sudden activity*

One cliché of the newsroom that deserves special attention is *pending notification of next of kin*. This is a stilted and clumsy way of saying "until relatives have been notified."

Many speakers and writers use clichés without knowing their precise meaning. In doing so, it is easy to fall into error. For example, the adjectives *jerry-built* and *jury-rigged* sometimes become "jerry-rigged" and "jury-built" when used by people unaware that the first adjective means "shoddily built" and the second is a nautical term meaning "rigged for emergency use."

It is also important to avoid incorrect quotations from or allusions to works of literature. The following are some examples of this type of mistake.

"Far from the maddening crowd" is the incorrect version of "far from the madding crowd's ignoble strife," which is from Thomas Gray's "Elegy Written in a Country Churchyard."

The phrase "suffer, little children" or "suffer the little children" has been used recently to mean "let the little children suffer." The original expression, in the King James version of Mark 10:14, is "Suffer the little children to come unto me." In this context *suffer* means "allow": "Allow the little children to come unto me."

"Alas, poor Yorick, I knew him well." This is both corrupt and incomplete. The line from *Hamlet*, Act V, scene i, reads: "Alas, poor Yorick! I knew him, Horatio: a fellow of infinite jest."

The misquotation "Music hath charms to soothe the savage beast" is an inelegant version of a line from the play *The Mourning Bride* by William Congreve, and the original version is "Music hath charms to soothe the savage breast."

The all-too-familiar question "Wherefore art thou Romeo?" is consistently misused by people who think that *wherefore* means "where." The question asks "*Why* are you Romeo?" not "*Where* are you, Romeo?"

"Pride goeth before a fall" is actually, in the King James version of Proverbs (16:18), "Pride goeth before destruction, and an haughty spirit before a fall."

"A little knowledge is a dangerous thing" is close, but not close enough, to what Alexander Pope actually wrote: "A little learning is a dangerous thing."

"It takes a heap o' livin t' make a house a home." Edgar Guest's poem opens with "It takes a heap o' livin in a house t' make it a home." The corrupt version is probably an attempt to improve the original.

"I have nothing to offer but blood, sweat, and tears." Winston Churchill really said, "I have nothing to offer but blood, toil, tears, and sweat."

These are but a few of many common misquotations. As a broadcast announcer, you should routinely check original sources. A handy source for checking the accuracy of quoted phrases is *Bartlett's Familiar Quotations*. But only use a quotation if it truly belongs in your work. When in doubt, skip the cliché—even correctly cited clichés are still clichés.

Latin and Greek Plurals

People who care about broadcast media should be meticulous in using *medium* for the singular and *media* for the plural. Radio is a medium. Radio and television are media. We can speak of the news media but not of television news media. If people who work in broadcast media do not reinstate correct usage, no one else will, and the incorrectly used plural *media* will take over for the singular form.

Data is another Latin plural that is commonly misused as the singular, as in "What is your data?" This sentence should be "What *are* your data?" The sentence "What is your datum?" is correct if the singular is intended.

Many other words of Latin and Greek origin are subject to similar misuse. Here are some of the more important of these (note that the Greek words end in *-on* and the Latin words end in *-um*):

Singular	*Plural*
addendum	addenda
criterion	criteria
memorandum	memoranda
phenomenon	phenomena
stratum	strata
syllabus	syllabi

The words referring to graduates of schools are a more complicated matter, for both gender and number must be considered:

Female singular: *alumna*, "She is an alumna of State College."

Female plural: *alumnae*, pronounced (UH-LUM′-NEE) /ə-lŭm′nē/ [ə′lʌmni], "These women are alumnae of State College."

Male singular: *alumnus*, "He is an alumnus of State College."

Male plural: *alumni*, pronounced (UH-LUM′-NY) /ə-lŭm′nī/ [ə′lʌmnaɪ], "These men are alumni of State College."

Male and female plural: *alumni*, pronounced as the male plural, "These men and women are alumni of State College."

Nonstandard Expressions and Usage

Slang

Slang, the nonstandard vocabulary of a given culture or subculture, is often brilliantly effective. Expressions such as *crash pad* for a place where a person could sleep without fee or invitation and *glitch* for a mishap or, in television, a type of visual interference on the screen are descriptive and, in the proper context, useful additions to our language. Other recent additions include *humongous*, *gridlock*, *rad* (derived from "radical" and meaning "far out," but definitely in a positive sense), *good* or *bad vibes*, and *high fives*.

The word *attitude* is presently widely used in the construction "he really gave me attitude." Its meaning in this usage is imprecise but negative. On the other hand, "lots of attitude" can mean cocky self-confidence. As an announcer, you must develop sensitivity to when and how language that is nonstandard—or not yet standard—adds to or detracts from your message. What might be appropriate in a commercial may be out of place in a newscast.

It is important to remember that one person's slang may not fit another's speech personality. Many expressions used by African-Americans may sound pretentious or condescending when spoken by whites. Similarly, words of foreign origin, such as *mensch* or *schlepping*, may sound out of place when spoken by someone who has only a vague notion of their meaning and uses them in inappropriate contexts. Some users of in-group expressions resent outsiders who take over their language.

Especially to be avoided are words from the world of crime and drugs. Terms such as *ripped off* to mean stole or *busted* to mean arrested are devised to remove the onus from the object or activity being described. "He was busted for smack" sounds far more innocent and trivial than the straightforward translation, "He was arrested for possession of heroin." To rip someone off is to steal from a person, and theft is not an activity to be condoned by removing from the language the words that connote its illegality; the slang only attempts to make the action seem less serious than it is and, perhaps, even a little humorous. Though you should in general avoid using street expressions, you should be aware that a few stations encourage—or even require—announcers to use such language. At such a station an announcer might be directed to use terms appropriate to a certain type of tabloid journalism, such as saying that someone was butchered rather than killed or murdered.

Solecisms

A **solecism** is a nonstandard or ungrammatical usage. It is related to a barbarism (a word or phrase not in accepted use), and both should be avoided by broadcast announcers. Surely you do not need to be told that *ain't* is unacceptable or that *anywheres* is not used by educated speakers. A number of words and phrases that we pick up in early childhood are substandard, but survive to plague us if we do not become aware of them. These include the following.

Foot for *feet*, as in "She was five foot tall." Five is more than one, and it demands the plural *feet*: "She was five feet tall."

Enthused over for *was enthusiastic about*

Guess as a substitute for *think* or *suppose*, as in "I guess I'd better read a commercial."

Expect for *suppose* or *suspect*, as in "I expect he's on the scene by now."

Try and for *try to*, as in "She's going to try and break the record."

Unloosen for *loosen*, as in "He unloosened the knot."

Hung for *hanged*, as in "The lynch mob hung the cattle rustler." *Hung* is the past tense of *hang* in every meaning other than as applied to a human being. Correct usages are "I hung my coat on the hook" and "He was hanged in 1884."

Outside of for *aside from*, as in "Outside of that, I enjoyed the movie."

Real for *really*, as in "I was real pleased."

Lay and *lie* are problem words for some speakers of English. *Lie* is an intransitive verb (does not require a direct object) meaning "to recline." It is used correctly in the following examples.

Present tense: I will lie down.

Past tense: I lay down.

Past participle: "I had lain down."

Lay is a transitive verb (requiring a direct object) that means "to place."

Present tense: "I will lay it down."

Past tense: "I laid it down."

Past participle: "I had laid it down."

Hens *lay* eggs, but they also *lie* down from time to time. A parent can *lay* a baby on a blanket and then *lie* next to her.

Hopefully, *reportedly*, and *allegedly* are among several adverbs misused so pervasively and for so long that some modern dictionaries now sanction their misuse. Adverbs modify verbs, adjectives, and other adverbs; in other words, adverbs tell us how something happened. In the sentence "He runs rapidly," *rapidly* is the adverb, and it modifies the verb *runs*. The adverb tells how he ran. *Hopefully* means "with hope" or "in a hopeful manner." To say "Hopefully, we will win" is not the same as saying "We hope we will win." The former implies that hope is the means by which we will win. *Hopefully* is used properly in these sentences: "She entered college hopefully," "He approached the customer hopefully."

There is no proper use of *reportedly*. This quasi-adverb is of recent origin and does not stand up to linguistic logic because there is no way to do something in a reported manner. To say "He was reportedly killed at the scene" is not to say "It is reported that he was killed at the scene." "He was reportedly killed" means that he was killed in a reported manner.

The adverb *allegedly* is widely misused. It is impossible for a person to steal, kill, or lie in an alleged way. "Twenty people were allegedly killed or injured by the crazed gunman" makes no grammatical sense. *Allegedly* and *alleged* (the adjective) are perhaps the most overworked and misused words in modern broadcast journalism. One may assume that their proliferation stems from announcers' prudence and sense of fairness. To state on a newscast that "Jones allegedly stole eighty typewriters" may make you guilty of poor grammar, but it shows your virtue in having indicated that Jones may be innocent of grand theft. Many newswriters, news directors and station managers believe that the use of *alleged* protects the station from legal charges of defamation, but such is not always the case. The only sound reason for using any of the derivatives of *allegation* is that to do so helps preserve the notion that all people are innocent until proven guilty. There are, however, correct and incorrect ways of using these words. Here are a few misuses recently noticed:

"The bullet, allegedly fired at the president . . ."

"Jones also will stand trial for alleged auto theft." The notion of a trial carries with it the allegation, by a district attorney, of guilt. *Alleged* is unnecessary in this sentence.

"The experts have examined the alleged bullets used in the assassination." There are many kinds of bullets, but no one has ever examined an alleged one.

When considering the use of any term of allegation, ask yourself these questions: (1) Is the word necessary to qualify the statement? (2) Am I using it correctly? Clearly, *allegedly* and *alleged* are superfluous in the three examples above. Is it possible or useful to say who is doing the alleging? "Jones is alleged by his estranged wife to have set fire to the store" is longer and more cumbersome than "Jones, the alleged arsonist," but it contains more useful information and is fairer to Jones than the shorter version. Here are some correct and incorrect uses of these terms:

Figure 5.3
One of the most often misused words in broadcast journalism, *allegedly* is mistakenly used to describe a crime that seems to have been committed or a person who appears to be guilty. In a live news broadcast such as this, the temptation is great for an announcer to seek an easy way to cover herself legally for whatever the outcome of the story may later be. But people do not commit crimes in an *alleged* manner; rather, they *allege* that someone else did. (Spencer Grant, Stock Boston)

Correct	*Incorrect*
The principal alleged that the striking teachers destroyed their attendance records.	The striking teachers allegedly destroyed their attendance records.
Benson is alleged to be an undercover agent for a foreign power.	Benson is allegedly an undercover agent.
Lindsay is reported to be set to buy the hockey team at the end of the season.	Lindsay allegedly is set to buy the hockey team at the end of the season. (Note that this is wrong in two ways: it is not possible to buy anything in an alleged manner, and terms of allegation should be reserved for instances in which there is possible wrongdoing.)

Allegedly, like *hopefully* and *reportedly*, is a poor reporter's cop-out. These words fail to tell us who is doing the alleging, the hoping, or the reporting. To say "The negotiators are reportedly near an agreement" is only slightly worse than saying "The negotiators are reported to be near an agreement." The second statement is proper grammar, but it would be far better as a news item if it included the source of the information. As a newswriter, you may not know who is doing the alleging, the hoping, or the reporting, but it is part of your job as a field reporter to gather such information and include it in your report.

Adverbs such as these three represent a special problem to announcers: should you go along with conventional misuse? One argument in favor of this says that everyone understands what is meant. An argument against it says that widespread misuse of adverbs undermines the entire structure of grammar, making it increasingly difficult for us to think through grammatical problems. Because any sentence can be spoken conversationally without misusing adverbs, it is to be hoped that you will use adverbs correctly.

Other words often misused are discussed in the following paragraphs.

Do not say *anxious* when you mean *eager* or *desirous*. *Anxious* means "worried" or "strained" and is associated with anxiety.

Connive, *conspire*, and *contrive* are sometimes confused. To *connive* is to "feign ignorance of a wrong," literally to close one's eyes to something. To *conspire* is to "plan together secretly"; one person cannot conspire, because a conspiracy is an agreement between two or more persons. To *contrive* is to "scheme or plot with evil intent"; one person is capable of contriving.

Contemptible is sometimes confused with *contemptuous*. *Contemptible* is an adjective meaning "despicable." *Contemptuous* is an adjective meaning "scornful" or "disdainful." You may say "The killer is contemptible" or "He is contemptuous of the rights of others."

Continual and *continuous* are used by many speakers as interchangeable synonyms, but their meanings are not the same. *Continual* means "repeated regularly and frequently"; *continuous* means "prolonged without interruption or cessation." A foghorn may sound continually; it does not sound continuously unless it is broken. A siren may sound continuously, but it does not sound continually unless it is going off every five minutes (or every half-hour or every hour).

Convince and *persuade* are used interchangeably by many announcers. In some constructions either word will do. A problem arises when *convince* is linked with *to*, as in this incorrect sentence: "He believes that he can convince the Smithsonian directors to give him the collection." The correct word to use in this sentence is *persuade*. *Convince* is to be followed by *of* or a clause beginning with *that*, as in "I could not convince him of my sincerity" or "I could not convince him that I was honest." The sentence "I could not convince him to trust me" is incorrect. In the following sentence, recently heard on a network newscast, *persuade* should have been used: "He did not know whether or not the president could convince them to change their minds."

Distinct and *distinctive* are not interchangeable. *Distinct* means "not identical" or "different"; *distinctive* means "distinguishing" or "characteristic." A distinct odor is one that cannot be overlooked; a distinctive odor is one that can be identified.

Emanate means to "come forth," "proceed," or "issue." You may say "The light emanated from a hole in the drape." Note that only light, air, aromas, ideas, and other such phenomena can emanate. Objects such as rivers, automobiles, or peaches cannot emanate from mountains, a factory, or an orchard.

Farther and *farthest* are used for literal distance, as in "The tree is farther away than the mailbox." But *further* and *furthest* are used for figurative distance, as in "further in debt."

Feasible is often used interchangeably with five other words: *possible*, *practical*, *practicable*, *workable*, and *viable*. These words should be differentiated by people who want to be precise in their use of American English.

Feasible means "clearly possible or applicable": "The plan was feasible" or "Her excuse was feasible."

Possible means "capable of happening": "It is possible that the plan will work."

Practical refers to the prudence, efficiency, or economy of an act or thing: "This is a practical plan" or "He is a practical person."

Practicable means "capable of being done": "The plan is hardly practicable at this time." Note that *practicable* never refers to persons.

Workable means "capable of being worked or dealt with": "The plan is workable." Note that *workable* implies a future act.

Viable means "capable of living, growing, or developing": "That is a viable tomato plant." Recently *viable* has replaced *feasible* in many applications. You should avoid using this overworked word. If you remember that it is derived from the Old French *vie* and the Latin *vita*, both of which mean "life," it is unlikely that you will speak of "viable plans."

Flaunt and *flout* are often used interchangeably and thus incorrectly. To *flaunt* is to "exhibit ostentatiously" or to "show off." To *flout* is to "show contempt for" or to "scorn." You may say "He flaunted his coat of arms" or "He flouted the officials."

Fulsome originally meant "abundant," but over the years it has come to mean "offensively excessive" or "insincere." The *American Heritage Dictionary* advises against using this word in a positive sense, as in "fulsome praise," stating that this usage is obsolete.

Implicit means "implied" or "understood"; *explicit* means "expressed with precision" or "specific." "He made an implicit promise" means that the promise was understood but was not actually stated. "His promise was explicit" means that the promise was very clearly stated.

To *imply* is to "suggest by logical necessity" or to "intimate"; to *infer* is to "draw a conclusion based on facts or indications." You may say "Her grades imply a fine mind" or "From examining her grades, I infer that she has a fine mind." Avoid the common practice of using one of these words to mean the other.

Libel means "any written, printed, or pictorial statement that damages by defaming character or by exposing a person to ridicule." *Slander* means "the utterance of defamatory statements injurious to the reputation of a person." *Defamation* is a more general term meaning both libel and slander. Libel is associated with defamation by means of a permanent medium; slander is associated with transient spoken statements.

A *loan* is "anything lent for temporary use"; to *lend* is to "give out or allow the temporary use of something." *Loan* is a noun, and *lend* is a verb. You may say "She applied for a loan" or "He lent me his rake" or "Do not lend money to friends." Avoid using *loan* as a verb, as in "Do not loan money to friends."

The suffix *-ology* means "theory of." *Methodology* is not the same as method; it is the theory of methods. *Technology* is not the same as the manufacturing of products; it is the theory of technical applications of scientific knowledge. Broadcast announcers can avoid compounding confusion by obtaining precise definitions of all the words ending in *-ology* they habitually use.

Oral means "spoken." *Verbal* means "of, pertaining to, or associated with words." *Aural* means "of, pertaining to, or perceived by the ear." *Verbal* is less precise than *oral*, because it can mean spoken or written; for this reason, the phrase "oral agreement" rather than "verbal agreement" should be used if the meaning is that the agreement was not written. Although *oral* and *aural* are pronounced the same, they are used in different senses: "She taught oral interpretation" but "He had diminished aural perception."

People (not *persons*) should be used in referring to a large group: "People should vote in every election." *Persons* and *person* should be used for small groups and for individuals: "Five persons were involved" and "The person spoke on the telephone." A *personage* is an important or noteworthy person. A *personality* is a pattern of behavior. It is technically incorrect to call a disc jockey a "personality," even though the term has wide acceptance.

Most dictionaries indicate that *prison* and *jail* can be used interchangeably, but strictly speaking a jail is maintained by a town, city, or county, whereas prisons are maintained by states and the federal government. Jails are usually used to confine prisoners for periods of less than a year; prisons or penitentiaries are for confinement of people with longer sentences.

Repulsion is the act of driving back or repelling; *revulsion* is a feeling of disgust or loathing. Do not say, "His breath repelled me," unless you mean that his breath physically forced you backward.

Reticent means "silent"; *reluctant* means "unwilling." Do not say "She was reticent to leave" when you mean "She was reluctant to leave."

Rhetoric is the art of oratory or the study of the language elements used in literature and public speaking. *Rhetoric* is not a synonym for *bombast*, *cant*, or *harangue*. *Rhetoric* is a neutral term and should not be used in a negative sense to mean empty and threatening speech.

A *robber* unlawfully takes something belonging to another by violence or intimidation; a *burglar* breaks into a house or store to steal valuable goods. Although both actions are felonies, they are different crimes, so *robber* and *burglar* should not be used interchangeably.

Xerox is the trademark of a corporation that makes copying machines. The company specifies that *Xerox* is the name of the company or, if followed by a model number, a specific machine. A photocopy made by that or any other machine is not "a Xerox."

This review of common usage errors is necessarily limited, but it may be adequate to alert you to the problem. If you habitually make errors such as those described here, you should undertake a study of English usage.

Deliberate Misuse of Language

As an announcer, you will at times have to read copy that is ungram-matical, includes poor usage, or requires deliberate mispronunciation. Here are a few examples: "So, buy ———. There's no toothpaste like it!" If there is no toothpaste like it, the advertised product itself does not exist; the correct expression is "There's no *other* toothpaste like it." In "So, gift her with flowers on Mother's Day!" the word *gift*, which is a noun, has been used ungrammatically as a transitive verb. You can give her flowers on Mother's Day, but unless all stan-dards of grammar are abandoned, you cannot *gift* her. You may be asked to pronounce the Italian island KUH-PREE′ instead of the correct KAP′-REE. When you are asked to commit these and other errors as an announcer, what should you do?

You may resent the advertising agency that asks you to foist poor examples of American speech or pronunciation on the public. Al-though some errors in usage are made by copywriters through igno-rance, do not assume that all copywriters are unaware of correct standards of grammar or pronunciation; many of the mistakes in their copy are deliberate. Poor grammar, advertising copywriters believe, is more colloquial and less stilted than correct grammar. Poor usage causes controversy, and to attract attention is to succeed in the primary objective of any commercial message. Mispronunciations are often asked for because the American public, for any of several reasons, has adopted them.

You may be obliged to make deliberate mistakes when they are requested of you, and this is a problem because your audience will assume either that the mistake is yours or that the poor usage or mispronunciation actually is correct! You should use language prop-erly in all broadcast circumstances you control; when you are asked to read ungrammatical copy exactly as it is written, you should, if possible, ask the writer or the agency if it can be changed.

Our Changing Language

American English is a dynamic, ever-changing language. Although change is slow during periods of relative stability, it is more or less constant. During times of upheaval, whether political, economic, or social, rapid changes in our language take place. World War II, for example, created many new words, among them *blitz, fellow traveler, fifth column*, *radar*, and *quisling*. More recently, *cryogenics*, *dashiki*, and *apartheid*, and many terms from the world of computers have been added to our language.

During the 1960s and 1970s three separate movements brought about many changes in both spoken and written American English. First, there was the rise of African-American awareness, followed by similar movements among other ethnic groups. Among many other changes, ethnic consciousness demanded that new terms replace *Negro*, *American Indian*, and other labels.

Second, the decline of colonialism saw the emergence of new nations—Tanzania, Namibia, and Sri Lanka, to name just three—and the nouns and adjectives used to identify them and their citizens brought about important changes in our language.

Finally, the women's movement of the 1970s and later made obsolete—or at least inappropriate—words such as *mankind*, *manpower*, and *chairman*. Broadcast announcers must be in the forefront as far as knowledge of our ever developing language is concerned; professional communicators are expected to reflect the best contemporary usage and to set an example.

American English and Ethnicity

Changes in designation have been sought by several ethnic groups during the past twenty or thirty years. Some of these changes—from *Negro* to *black*, for example—occurred easily and in a relatively brief period of time. In other cases, change has been hindered because of a lack of consensus on preferred usage. For example, some Americans of Filipino ancestry want to be called *Pilipinos*, but it is not yet clear whether this term will gain general acceptance.[1] As a broadcast announcer, you must carefully watch this and similar movements in our evolving language, so that your speech reflects contemporary usage. The discussion that follows gives general principles of usage. You should always check to see if they apply in your geographic area. You also should be alert for further changes as time goes by.

Some members of non-European ethnic groups in the United States resent being given a hyphenated status, such as Chinese-American. Preferring to be regarded simply as Americans, they point out that Americans of European descent are not identified in news stories as "German-Americans" or "Italian-Americans" and that the U.S.

[1]There is no *f* in Tagalog, the official language of the Philippines.

Spotlight: The Debate Over General American Speech

If you have a regional dialect, you should be aware of the fact that your announcing opportunities may be limited. For better or worse, broadcasters all over the United States favor announcers who speak General American over those with regional accents. The following brief history of broadcast speech in America gives the background to this situation.

From the very beginning of radio broadcasting in the United States, attempts were made to force standardized pronunciation on announcers. In 1929, less than a decade after the first radio broadcast, the American Academy of Arts and Letters began the yearly award of a gold medal to that radio announcer who best exemplified the kind of speech of which the Academy approved. In awarding the 1930 medal to Alwyn Bach of NBC, the Academy commented, "We believe the radio announcer can not only aid the European immigrant to acquire a knowledge of good English, but he can influence the speech of isolated communities whose young people have no other means of comparing their own accent with the cultivated speech of those who have had the advantage of travel and education." ("Broadcast Announcing Styles of the 1920's," Michael Biel, a paper presented at the convention of the Broadcast Education Association, March 16, 1974.)

In taking the position that one style of American English speech was superior to others, the Academy was following a European model. England and France each had a great variety of dialects within their borders. But not all those ways of speaking were considered "proper." Cockney, Midlands, and Cornish dialects in England and the speech of the people of Marseille and Strasbourg in France were looked down upon by those who spoke with "correct" pronunciation. Also, during the eighteenth and nineteenth centuries, many small European kingdoms, duchies, provinces, church-owned lands, and independent cities were consolidated into the nations of Germany and Italy. The boundaries of these nations coincided roughly with language groupings. But the German that was spoken in Berlin was quite different from that spoken in Bavaria, and the Italian spoken in Genoa was not the same as that spoken in Sicily. Before long, there were established "correct" or "official" ways of pronouncing the language in these newly formed nations. From this action it was but a short step to social discrimination based on regional accent or dialect.

Many feel that the United States, the land of equal opportunity and upward mobility re-

Joan Rivers is one successful performer who has a regional accent. (Harry Langdon, courtesy of Joan Rivers)

gardless of origins, had no reason to follow Europe's lead. Until the advent of radio broadcasting, there were two standards for correct American pronunciation. The first was platform speech, an overarticulated, oratorical manner of speaking, with a strong Oxford-British flavor. The second was the speech used by "the enlightened members of the community." This phrase is significant, for it sanctions regional differences in pronunciation. Correct American speech could therefore vary—being that spoken by educated persons in New England, the South, the Midwest, or the West Coast.

This acceptance of regional differences in pronunciation has been maintained by linguists and those who compile dictionaries, but was abandoned by broadcasters during the early years of radio broadcasting. Platform speech was precisely what the American Academy of Arts and Letters was promoting, as spelled out in its statement of criteria for good radio speech: "first, clear articulation; second, correct pronunciation; third, freedom from *disagreeable local accent*, fourth, pleasing tone color; fifth, evidence of cultivated taste" (from Biel, "Broadcast Announcing Styles of the 1920's," italics added for emphasis).

By the mid-1930s, objections to the stilted, quasi-English manner of speaking began to force change. However, despite the change to a more natural and conversational style of speech, the objective of standardized pronunciation remained. General American speech became the standard for announcers all over the United States and Canada. General American is thought to be pleasant, easily understood, and more common than any other regional accent. Even though it is not the only style of American speech that is pleasant and effective, for years those with Southern, New England, Eastern, or Southwestern accents (as well as those with Asian, Latin American, or Middle Eastern accents) have been under-represented on announcing staffs. A few exceptions may be noted: New England accents have long been accepted for the announcing of symphonic and operatic music; Southern and Eastern accents have been heard on many sportscasts; and nearly all regional accents have been accepted for news reporters, analysts, and commentators. All regional accents have been heard on commercials and talk shows.

Some significant breakthroughs have occurred. Joan Rivers, George Plimpton, and Dinah Shore are but three examples of successful performers with regional accents. Peter Jennings speaks General American in almost all instances but still uses the Canadian *out* and *about*. Announcers who speak with identifiable Southern, Eastern, and New England accents may be heard on many stations and some networks. It may be that this trend will continue, and even accelerate. Regional pride may some day bring to the American radio and television public that full richness of our language in all its variations.

government does not apply ethnic terms to such people, lumping them together for most purposes as "whites." There is no consensus on this among any major ethnic group, however, and any metropolitan telephone directory may list organizations under such headings as "Japanese-American . . . ," "Mexican-American . . . ," and "Afro-American . . . ."

In broadcasting the racial or national background of Americans is irrelevant in most circumstances, though not all. For instance, if a person of Mexican heritage is interviewed on the subject of soccer or rapid transit, that person's heritage is not an essential or even appropriate item of comment. On the other hand, if the same person were being interviewed on the subject of bilingual education or the working conditions of Mexican-American farmworkers, mentioning the person's heritage would be a legitimate means of establishing his or her interest in, and special knowledge of, those topics. There are times, then, when an announcer may legitimately refer to the ethnic background of a person or group. The general rule is to ignore ethnicity when it has nothing to do with the subject at hand. There is a corollary: do refer to ethnic background when it helps promote understanding.

You must also be accurate in using ethnic terms. Nowhere is the task of correct identification more difficult than in designating the large group of people often referred to in U.S. government documents as "Spanish surnamed." The difficulty arises from the diversity of their ancestry, which may be Spanish, Filipino, Cuban, Mexican, Puerto Rican, Central American, or South American. "Spanish surnamed" embraces all these different cultures and races, but it is both too cumbersome and too general for broadcast use. More specific terms must be applied. For Americans who come from or owe their ancestry to Mexico, the Caribbean, or Central or South America, the term *Latin*, or *Latin American*, is appropriate; the derivatives *Latina* and *Latino* may be used to designate female and male, respectively. *Mexican-American* is acceptable to all or nearly all members of that ethnic group. Some use *Chicano* and *Chicana*, *La Raza*, or *Mexican* to describe themselves, but not all members of Mexican-American communities find these terms acceptable.

A person from Cuba may be referred to as either a *Cuban* or a *Cuban-American*, depending on whether that person is a resident alien or a naturalized citizen. Puerto Ricans, because they are citizens of the United States, should not have *American* tacked onto their designation. *Spanish-American* and *Filipino-American* are correct designations for people originally from Spain or the Philippines.

In referring to Americans whose names are of Spanish origin, do not assume that a person from the Southwest is of Mexican ancestry, that a person from Florida is Cuban, or that a person who lives in New York is Puerto Rican. Where ethnic or national background cannot be ascertained, it is better to avoid using a specific term than to guess.

The original inhabitants of the United States were named Indians by early European explorers. Five hundred years later, we still have not agreed on the designation of this group of citizens. The federal government classifies them as "Native-Americans" in many demographic and statistical reports, yet it continues to operate the Bureau of Indian Affairs. Some resent the term *Indian*, yet refer to themselves as members of the American Indian Movement. *American Indian* is acceptable in some parts of the United States but considered derogatory in others. You would be wise to check on sensitivities in your area. It is generally acceptable to use Anglicized tribal designations—Sioux, Navajo, Nez Perce, Apache, and Zuñi, for example.

Black Americans prefer the term *black*, *African-American*, or *Afro-American*. *Negro* and *colored person* are presently offensive to most African-Americans, but note that many of them, as well as many Asian-Americans and Native Americans, refer to themselves as "people of color."

The term *Chinaman* is seldom heard today. It is extremely insulting and must be avoided. Americans of Chinese heritage may be referred to as *Chinese*, *Chinese-Americans*, *Sino-Americans*, *Asians*, or *Asian-Americans*. Use *Asian* when referring to people who came from Asia or whose ancestors came from Asia. *Oriental* is no longer acceptable when referring to a person; you may speak of an Oriental rug but not of an Oriental man.

It is not only Americans of color who are concerned about their designations. Others are offended from time to time by insensitive announcers. Scots bridle when they are referred to as "Scotch." People from Scotland are *Scots*, *Scottish*, or *Scotsmen* and *Scotswomen*. Scotch is an alcoholic beverage manufactured by the Scots. Scots may sometimes drink Scotch. *Scotch* should not, of course, be used as a synonym for stingy because it is both as offensive and as false as most stereotypes.

People from Canada are *Canadians* and should never be referred to as "Canucks." Those living near the border between Canada and the United States know this, but others living far from Canada may not realize that Canuck is considered derogatory by French Canadians. A professional Canadian hockey team is named the Vancouver Canucks, but it is one thing to call oneself a Canuck and another to be called that by a stranger.

People of Polish ancestry are never "Polacks"; a person of Polish ancestry is a *Pole* or a *Polish-American*. Announcers should never say "Polack," even in jest.

You should refer to citizens of Iran as *Iranians*, but never as *Arabs*. Iranians share Islamic faith with their Arabian neighbors, but Iranians are not Arabs.

Do not use *Welsh* to mean a failure to pay a debt. Do not say *Irish* or *Dutch* to mean hot-tempered. Do not use the word *Turk* in any construction indicating that a person so labeled is brutal or tyrannical, such as "young Turk." Avoid the term *Dutch* in any of several derogatory connotations: *Dutch bargain*, to mean a transaction settled when both parties were drinking; *Dutch courage*, meaning courage from drinking liquor; *Dutch treat*, where each person pays for his or her share; and *Dutchman*, a term used to describe something that conceals faulty construction.

Other offensive terms are *Indian giving*, meaning to give something and then take or demand it back, and *Scotch verdict*, meaning an inconclusive judgment. No list of dos and don'ts can substitute for sensitivity and consideration. If you use phrases such as *Mexican standoff*, *French leave*, or *Chinese fire drill*, you could find yourself in serious trouble as an announcer.

Gender in American English

The women's movement brought about significant changes in the terminology we use for a great many acts, objects, and occupations. The historic male orientation of our language was the source of three general areas of discontent. The first was the use of *man* and *mankind* to refer to the entire human race. The second was the group of nouns and verbs that have "maleness" built into them; *chairman*, *spokesman*, and *manning the picket lines* are examples. The third was the generic use of *he* and *his* when both sexes are meant, as in "Everyone must pay his taxes."

Over the centuries the male orientation of our language gradually increased. Originally, *man* was used to refer to the entire human race. In the proto–Indo-European language, the prehistoric base for many modern languages, including English, the word for man was *wiros* and the word for woman was *gwena*. *Manu* meant human being. As the centuries passed and as language changed, *man* came to be used for both males and the human race. Many of us speak of the man in the street, the working man, and manpower. Many of us are accustomed to saying that all men are created equal and that we believe in the common man.

Because words help determine and define reality, terminology had to be changed to eliminate the male bias in our everyday language. One tangible sign of this was reflected in the U.S. Department of Labor's *Dictionary of Occupational Titles*, 4th edition (1977), in which the official terminology for nearly 3,500 occupations was changed to eliminate discriminatory referents. Publishing houses prepared guidelines for authors with instructions and suggestions for removing male bias from their writings. Linguists seriously proposed that the rules of grammar be changed, so that "Everyone must pay their taxes" would become correct usage.

A number of words that are thought by some to be sexist actually are not. The Latin word *manus* means "hand," and it formed the basis of a great many English words, including *manacle*, *manage*, *manager*, *manner*, *manual*, *manicure*, *manifest*, *manipulate*, *manufacture*, and *manuscript*.

Faced with the need to eliminate male bias, announcers have a challenging responsibility. Colloquial speech, which is standard for most announcers, does not lend itself to some of the changes that have been proposed. To substitute *humankind* for *mankind* or *human being* for *man* is necessary until something less affected comes along, but it *is* awkward.

It is necessary to phase out nouns such as *chairman* and *spokesman*, even though the proposed substitutes, *chairperson* and *spokesperson*, are longer and somewhat awkward. *Chair* is heard increasingly to mean the moderator of a group, as in "the chair of the PTA," and *speaker* might be an acceptable substitute for *spokesman* or *spokesperson*, but these and other changes must become generally accepted before this linguistic problem can be considered solved. Broadcast announcers must work with accepted usage, try to coin better expressions to replace those they do not like, and be alert for the many changes yet to come.

One way of avoiding the use of male-oriented terminology when the intent is to include people of both sexes is to use the plural. An awkward statement such as "Everyone should send in his or her entry so that he or she will be eligible for a prize" can easily be turned into "All listeners must send in their entries to be eligible for prizes." Another way is to use the second person: "Send in your entry so you'll be eligible for a prize." Also, because television and radio are intimate media, the use of the second person helps establish a direct link between announcer and listener.

Changes in usage to avoid male bias in language have been rapid and widespread. Few announcers need to be told that *flight attendant* has replaced both *airline steward* and *stewardess*, that *firemen* and *policemen* are now *fire fighters* and *police officers*, that *camera operator* has replaced *cameraman*, and that the *mailman* has become the *mail carrier*. If, however, you find that you are using obsolete terms for workers in any field, you should make a conscious effort to change this practice. Using terms that indicate a male bias is, for a broadcast announcer, a definite handicap.

Nations and Citizens of the World

Broadcast announcers, and especially news anchors and reporters, can expect to refer at one time or another to nearly every nation in the world. If you were asked to read a news story from Belau or some other new nation, where would you turn to learn the correct pronunciation of the name? And, although you undoubtedly know that a citizen of Turkey is a Turk, how would you refer to a citizen of San Marino? [Belau is pronounced BAY-LAU', and a citizen of San Marino is a San Marinese (SAHN MAHR-EE-NAY'-SAY).] Announcers cannot be expected to know pronunciation and terminology for all the nations of the world, but they are expected to know where to find the information.

Appendix D provides the name and its correct pronunciation for every nation of the world.[2] It also gives the correct noun and adjective to be used when referring to citizens of these nations, for example, "He is a Lao" (noun) and "She is Laotian" (adjective). If both noun and adjective are the same, as for Omani, only one term is given. Refer to Appendix D whenever you are unsure of the pronunciation of a nation's name or of the correct noun or adjective for its citizens. If Appendix D is not available to you, you can obtain correct pronunciations of foreign names and place names by phoning the appropriate consulate or embassy.

Note that we Americanize the names of many nations. The country we call Albania is properly Republika Popullore e Shqiperise (SCHK'YEE-PUH-REE'-ZUH). The Ivory Coast is actually Republique de Cote d'Ivoire (RAY-POO-BLEEK' DIH COAT DEE-VWAR'). Because we have Americanized the names of nearly all nations, you should try for correct American pronunciation rather than attempting to pronounce the name as a native of the country would pronounce it. This is true even for countries for which we have not changed the spelling. Remember, though, that pronunciation changes over the years. Moreover, there is a growing trend toward giving correct or nearly correct Spanish pronunciation to the names of nations such as Uruguay, Colombia, and Costa Rica. If you are a

---

[2]Names of nations change from time to time, so it should be noted that the names of nations and their citizens listed in Appendix D are correct as of 1990.

Figure 5.4
Just as important as using respectful terms to describe U.S. citizens' age, ethnicity, and gender is the ability to cover international stories with the same consideration. When announcing such stories from the studio or on location, as CNN's Bernard Shaw is doing here as he reports for *The International Hour* from Moscow, one must research unfamiliar pronunciations for names of people and places and correct terms for citizens of various nations. (Courtesy of Turner Broadcasting)

Spanish-speaking American announcer, correct pronunciation of such names is acceptable and may even be preferred by your audience and supervisors.

This chapter ends much as it began, with a brief compilation of some usage errors recently heard on radio and television. The sentences that follow have one thing in common—all are *incorrect*.

"The odds against them overtaking the Democrats are astronomical."

"But what really sold my wife and I was the guarantee."

"And they'll put on a new muffler within thirty minutes or less."

"The _____ remain clustered in their suburban mansion." The reporter meant *cloistered*.

"The Cuban refugees claim that an invasion of Cuba is eminent." The correct word is *imminent*.

"He said he does not believe that such riots are in the offering." He should have said "in the *offing*."

"They amuse themselves by hurtling insults at each other." We *hurtle* through the field, but *hurl* insults.

"A barge with a large wench is on its way to the scene of the accident." (It is unlikely that even a *huge* wench could lift a truck from the bay.)

"He ran it in a ship-shod manner." The word is *slipshod*.

This list of errors in usage is brief, to be sure, but it exemplifies the kinds of mistakes made by professional speakers who should be providing models of correct speech. If you make mistakes such as these or if you confuse *who* and *whom*, *shall* and *will*, *like* and *as*, and *which* and *that*, this chapter should serve as notice to you that you should undertake a serious study of American English. The suggested readings in Appendix E include several works on American English usage that should be a part of every announcer's library.

Practice: Improving Vocabulary and Pronunciation

Turn to Appendix B. Choose 50 words that have unfamiliar meanings or pronunciations. Using a cassette recorder and the pronunciation guides provided, record each word. Repeat it until you are comfortable with the sound of its correct pronunciation. Then, consulting a dictionary, read and record the word's most common definition(s).

Practice: Analyzing Regional Accents

Watch several local, PBS, and network newscasts, and determine the percentage of news reporters, anchors, and weather, sports, or environmental reporters who employ General American, compared to those who speak with regional accents. Jot down at least ten regional differences in speech patterns, and guess as to the origin of the accents.

6

Broadcast Equipment

This chapter provides basic information about broadcast equipment generally regarded as standard by most radio stations in the early 1990s. Many items long considered indispensable in on-air announce booths are rapidly being replaced. These include turntables for playing vinyl discs (records) and reel-to-reel audiotape recorders and players. Other types of equipment recently developed and put into service by radio stations, such as compact disc (CD) players, may eventually be replaced by new products. In years to come, CDs, tape cartridges (carts), and vinyl records may be replaced by digitally recorded music stored on tape or computer chips. Audio consoles may be replaced by computerized workstations resembling present-day word processors. Broadcast technology constantly evolves; and as it does, equipment tends to become more compact, easier to operate, and of higher fidelity.

At present, however, radio station managers agree that you should prepare for your career by learning how to utilize and operate the equipment that is now or has been standard in one application or another in radio broadcasting: microphones, audio consoles, CD players, audiotape cartridge recorders and players (cart machines), turntables for 45-rpm and $33\frac{1}{3}$-rpm records, audiocassette players, and open-reel tape players for $\frac{1}{4}$-inch audiotapes.

The text briefly discusses automated radio. Satellite radio programming, a phenomenon that is rapidly gaining acceptance and is increasingly replacing automated radio systems, is essentially a distribution system, and therefore it is not discussed. (Tips about television equipment are found in Chapters 3, 8, and 10.)

As a radio announcer, and especially as a beginner, you must master many aspects of broadcasting in addition to good delivery. Some of these skills are identifying and properly using microphones,

Figure 6.1

From the old indispensables (record turntables) to the new conveniences (computerized programming systems), a radio announcer will work with a variety of broadcast equipment.

cuing and playing CDs, records, and carts, operating audio consoles, and performing the special functions required at automated radio stations.

As a radio announcer, you will be surrounded by costly and delicate equipment; if you abuse or improperly operate it, you can defeat your best announcing efforts. Improper use of a microphone can result in excessive sibilance, popping, or voice distortion. Improper use of an audio console can result in poor broadcast sound quality and even damage to the equipment.

Television announcers seldom touch broadcast equipment, but they must know how to conduct themselves in the presence of cameras and microphones. Radio announcers, on the other hand, are normally expected to operate the equipment in a station's on-air studio. Although turntables and open-reel, rack-mounted ¼-inch tape recorders are disappearing from most on-air studios, they remain in use at many smaller-market stations, as well as in nearly every station's **production studio**. At small- and medium-market radio stations, announcers are expected to spend some of their working time in the production of commercials, public service announcements (PSAs), and station promotional features. To do so requires the ability to operate several types of broadcast equipment.

RCA 77-DX ribbon
microphone

Beyer M 500 dynamic
ribbon microphone

Electro-Voice DO56, a
dynamic omnidirectional
microphone
(Photos courtesy of RCA;
Beyer Dynamic, Inc.; and
Electro-Voice, Inc.)

This chapter is an elementary introduction to radio equipment. You should supplement your reading with practice, for no book can develop your manipulative skills or train your ears to make audio judgments.

Microphones

When sound waves enter a microphone, they set in motion a chain of events culminating in the apparent re-creation of the sound by a radio or a television set. As the first link in the chain, the microphone is of primary importance. If a microphone is improperly selected, improperly used, or damaged, the sound will be adversely affected throughout the remainder of its trip to the listener and will appear distorted.

Microphones transform sound waves into electric energy. This transformation of energy is called **transduction**. Ribbon and dynamic microphones transduce sound waves into magnetic voltage (electromagnetic) variations; condenser microphones transduce sound waves into voltage (electrostatic) variations.

Microphones are usually classified according to internal structure, pickup pattern, and intended use. As an announcer, you probably will not select the microphones you use, but you should be able to recognize the types given to you so that you can use each to your best advantage.

Internal Structure

Ribbon, or velocity, microphones The **ribbon, or velocity, microphone** contains a metallic ribbon, supported at the ends and passing between the poles of a permanent magnet. The ribbon moves when sound waves strike it, generating voltage that is immediately relayed to the audio console. This type of microphone is extremely sensitive to all sounds within a great frequency range, flattering to the human voice, and unaffected by changes in air pressure, humidity, and temperature. In addition, it is not prone to picking up reflected sound.

When using a ribbon mic, it is best to stand or sit 8 inches to 1 foot from it and speak directly into it. This range usually makes voice quality deeper with a ribbon mic. If you find you have voice reproduction problems at close range, speak at an oblique angle across the mic's front screen.

Neuman U 87 and U 89, multidirectional condenser microphones

Shure switchable PE2 microphone (Photos courtesy of Gotham Audio Corporation, and Shure Brothers, Inc.)

The RCA 77-DX, a very old design, is still widely used in radio. It can be adjusted to a variety of pickup patterns and sound characteristics. Your work will be affected by the way it is set. This ribbon mic is significantly more flattering for voice work when the set screws are turned to "Voice 1" and "Bidirectional."

Dynamic, or pressure, microphones In the **dynamic, or pressure, microphones**, a lightweight molded diaphragm attached to a small wire coil is suspended in a magnetic field. Sound waves striking the diaphragm are relayed to the coil, and the movement of the coil within the magnetic field transforms physical energy into electrical impulses. The dynamic microphone has a number of advantages. It is more rugged than other types, can be used outdoors with less wind blast, can be as small as a person's fingertip, and can perform better in a wider range of applications than any other type of mic. Only a well-trained audio operator is likely to be bothered by the fact that it does not reproduce the subtle colorations achieved by a high-quality ribbon or condenser mic.

When using a dynamic mic, you should stand or sit 6–10 inches away from and to one side of the front screen of the instrument. By talking slightly across the screened surface, you should project your voice quality at its best; this is especially true if you speak at high volume or are given to excessive sibilance or popping.

Condenser, or electrostatic, microphones This type of microphone is often found in professional recording studios and at stereo FM stations. The **condenser, or electrostatic, microphone** is similar to the pressure mic in that it has a diaphragm, but instead of a coiled wire it has an electrode as a backplate. A capacitance between the diaphragm and the electrode varies with the minute movements of the diaphragm as they reflect the sound waves.

If you are asked to work with a high-quality condenser mic, you should treat it as you would a dynamic mic. If you find that the extreme sensitivity of the condenser mic is creating sibilance or popping problems, try working farther away from it and/or speaking into it at an angle. One or both of these adjustments should correct the problem. Condenser mics require a battery for their operation. If you experience problems with a condenser mic, first check to make sure that the battery is there, is inserted in the proper position, and is not dead.

The **pressure zone microphone (PZM)** is a condenser mic that is designed to allow direct and reflected sound waves to enter the mi-

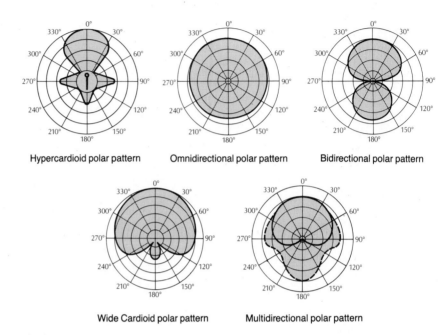

Hypercardioid polar pattern   Omnidirectional polar pattern   Bidirectional polar pattern

Wide Cardioid polar pattern   Multidirectional polar pattern

Figure 6.2
Microphone polar patterns show how sounds are absorbed in different shapes, depending on what type of mic you use. Note that these pickup patterns are actually three-dimensional and that the shapes alter with the changing relationship between the instrument and voice.

crophone at the same time.[1] Other mics pick up both direct and reflected sound but with a slight lag between the two due to varying distances of sound source to mic. The PZM eliminates this lag and has very little sound distortion.

Pickup Patterns

The **pickup, or polar, pattern** of a microphone is the shape of the area around it from which it can accept and transmit sounds with the maximum fidelity and optimal volume. **Fidelity** refers to the degree to which the electronically produced sound corresponds to the original sound. Nearly all microphones can pick up sounds from areas outside their ideal pattern, but the quality of those sounds is not as good. For best results, you as speaker (sound source) should be positioned within

[1]PZM is a copyrighted trademark of Crown International Inc.

the pickup pattern, generating enough volume so that the volume control knob can be kept at a minimal level. If you are **off-mic** (out of the pattern) or if you speak too softly, the volume control will have to be turned up, and the microphone will automatically distort your voice and transmit unwanted sounds from outside the pattern. When you use a stand, hand-held, or control room mic, you cannot ignore the pickup pattern of the instrument. You have to position yourself properly and adjust your voice level to optimize the sound.

Manufacturers classify microphones according to four pickup patterns:

1. **unidirectional**, meaning only one side of the microphone is live
2. **bidirectional** (or figure eight), meaning two sides of the mic are live
3. **omnidirectional** (also called nondirectional or spherical), meaning the mic is live in all directions
4. **multidirectional** (polydirectional or switchable), meaning two or more patterns can be achieved by adjusting a control

Nearly all unidirectional microphones have pickup patterns that are **cardioid** (heart-shaped). Cardioid patterns range from wide to narrow (or tight) to **hypercardioid** (or **supercardioid**). Hypercardioid mics are used chiefly as boom mics in television studios. They have a narrow front angle of sound acceptance and pick up very little sound from the sides.

The pickup pattern of the PZM is **hemispheric**, meaning that, when the mic is placed on a flat surface such as a table, the area of sound acceptance is one-half of a sphere, like the Northern Hemisphere of the globe.

Descriptions and engineering diagrams (see Figure 6.2) of microphone pickup patterns are inadvertently misleading because they do not show the three-dimensionality of the pattern and do not indicate that the pattern changes when the relationship between instrument and sound source changes. Because cardioid mics can be placed in every conceivable position with respect to the sound source, their pickup patterns vary in design and are especially difficult to understand from engineering diagrams. The cardioid pattern shown in two dimensions on engineering data sheets will differ significantly depending on whether the mic is hand-held or stand-mounted at a 30-degree angle. The data sheet shows whether a particular cardioid microphone has a narrow or a wide angle of front sound acceptance, as well as

Electro-Voice RE20
dynamic cardioid
microphone

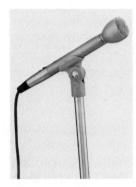

Electro-Voice 635A
dynamic omnidirectional
microphone

Beyer Dynamic MCE-5
Electret condenser
microphone
(Photos courtesy of
Electro-Voice, Inc., and
Beyer Dynamic, Inc.)

designating the areas of rear acceptance and rejection, but only actual practice with cardioid mics will teach you how to position them.

As you study the pickup patterns of cardioid mics shown in Figure 6.2, assume that the microphone is exactly in the center of the circle in each instance. Also remember that the actual pattern is three-dimensional.

Intended Use

Radio utilizes diverse production methods, so microphones have become increasingly specialized. They can therefore be classified according to intended, or best, use.[2] A microphone of one design may be ideal for one kind of work but inappropriate for another. One dynamic omnidirectional mic may have been designed to be hand held and another to be permanently mounted above an audio console.

Announce microphones   These microphones are found in radio station announce booths and are also used for off-camera film and television narration. Typical announce mics are the Sony C-37P, the Electro-Voice RE15, RE20, and 635A, and the RCA 77-DX.

Stand microphones   These microphones are used for off-camera television narration and in the production of radio commercials. The RCA 77-DX and Shure SM33 are examples.

Hand-held microphones   These microphones are versatile: they can be used indoors or out and can be fitted into a desk mount. The Electro-Voice 635A and RE55 are widely used models.

Headset microphones   Miniaturized microphones connected to headsets are standard for play-by-play sports announcers. Both dynamic and condenser mics are used with headsets, but they must be designed to include a honeycomb pop filter in front of the diaphragm.

Wireless microphones   These microphones are practical for work at remote locations and for studio work when performers need to move without the restraints of a mic cable. This type of mic, as well as studio boom mics and lavaliere mics, is widely used in television production.

Advances in microphones are constantly being made, and instruments not even mentioned here will most likely be in use by the time

---

[2]Some of the popular microphones described here are no longer manufactured, but they will remain in use for many years to come.

Swintek wireless
microphone

Crown PZM-3LV lavaliere
microphone
(Photos courtesy of
Swintek Enterprises, Inc.,
and Crown International,
Inc.)

you enter the field of radio performance. But regardless of progress in miniaturization, sensitivity, and fidelity, the principles of microphone use will remain the same for many years.

Audio Consoles

Most radio announcers will, at one time or another, operate an **audio console**, or **board**. Disc jockeys almost always work their own boards. Announcers making station breaks, news bulletins, or live commercials work in an on-air studio and operate a console. Announcers on some all-news radio stations and hosts of radio talk shows seldom work the board, but they almost certainly were required to do so at some earlier point in their career.

The audio console picks up the electrical impulses coming from microphones, cart machines, turntables, and other sound sources. It mixes the sounds in proper proportions when more than one signal is coming in, controls the amplitude (strength) of the electrical impulses, and sends them, by means of another amplifier, to the transmitter. A microphone suspended from an adjustable arm is positioned in front of the console. Several cart machines and CD players are placed within reach of the console operator; turntables and open-reel tape recorders may also be positioned nearby. The physical arrangement of the on-air studio may vary in small details (see Figures 11.1, 11.3, 11.4, and 11.5).

Audio consoles may seem a bit intimidating at first glance, but they are actually simple to operate. On-air boards (those used by DJs) require the operation of only a few controls. Production boards are more complex, and those who operate them must have special training. **Production consoles** are equipped with controls for equalization, compression, and noise-reduction and assorted features for sweetening that make possible the production of high-quality commercials, station promos, musical IDs or logos, and other program material. **Sweetening** is the process of using equalization, reverberation, and other electronic effects to improve the quality of recorded sound. A sophisticated production console, as well as other production equipment, is shown in Figure 6.3.

As an announcer at a major-market station, you probably will not have occasion to operate a production console. As an announcer-engineer, however, especially at a smaller station, you very likely will be asked to operate the production board. Combining engineering and announcing is called **working combo**.

This section cannot give you all the details concerning audio control and sound mixing; if you are heading toward a career that may require sophistication in audio production, you should enroll in appropriate courses.

Most boards, however different they may seem at first glance, have essentially the same features. On-air boards are either monaural or stereo. These two general types are further distinguished according to whether their volume controls (**potentiometers**, or **pots**) are rotating knobs or **vertical faders**. Rotating knobs can be seen on the console in Figure 11.1 or 11.3; vertical faders are shown in Figure 11.5. Most boards with rotating pots are constructed as a single unit; most boards with vertical faders are made up of several plug-in modules, and elements can be shifted as desired. A pot is also known as a **fader**, **mixer**, **attenuator**, or **gain control**.

Each station uses the input potential of its board in a unique way, so you should not merely learn to operate one board by rote. If you understand the reasons for doing what you do, you will be able to transfer your skills to other consoles with little additional instruction.

Figure 6.3
A typical radio station production studio. Here the production director operates an ABX-34 production console, Technics turntables, Tomcat tape cart machines, Tascam cassette machines, Otari reel-to-reel tape recorders, and Sennheiser 441 microphones. (Courtesy of Albert Lord and KFRC, San Francisco)

As a typical example, let us look closely at the features of an audio console serving a station of moderate size that broadcasts in both AM mono and FM stereo. The station has four production areas: (1) an on-air studio, where the board will be housed, (2) a newsroom, (3) a talk studio that can accommodate three microphones for interviews and panel discussions, and (4) a small production studio, with its own production console. Note that the following description of a stereo console and its inputs is based on the maximum anticipated needs of a local music-oriented station. The description stresses functions rather than electronics, so you can see how the board relates to your work.

The sounds of radio begin with the electrical impulses from microphones, CD players, cart machines, turntables, and other sound sources. Music originates on CDs, carts, 45- and $33\frac{1}{3}$-rpm records, and reel-to-reel tapes. Commercials are all carted. The station broadcasts hourly feeds from an affiliated news network and signals from the Emergency Broadcast System (EBS) and regularly puts telephone callers on the air with special music requests. Provision, therefore, must be made for a number of signals to be selected, go through, and be regulated by the board. Signals to be provided for include those from two microphones, an on-air studio mic and a newsroom mic (the three talk studio mics are mixed on a board in that studio); two CD players; six cart machines; two turntables; two reel-to-reel tape players; a telephone line; a line for the EBS signal; a line for the audio feed from the news network; two remote lines for occasional remote broadcasts; and two spare lines for unforeseen needs. This is a total of twenty-one signal sources.

To accommodate the twenty-one sound sources, there would seem to be a need for twenty-one inputs with associated volume controls. It is possible to economize by installing **input selector switches**, which allow feeding more than one signal through each input channel.[3] The two microphones need to have their own input channels; the other nineteen sound sources can be paired up and fed through eight input channels. With the two mic channels, this makes a total of ten input channels to handle twenty-one signal sources. Table 6.1 (on the next page) shows how the sources and channels might be assigned.

Mics generate weak signals, so their output must be **boosted**, or amplified, before being fed into the board. The amplifiers that receive and boost signals from mics are called **preamplifiers** (or **preamps**); the

---

[3]Another way of reducing the number of pots needed is to use a patch panel and a board that allows the routing of signals to be varied.

Table 6.1   Typical Configuration on a Radio Station Board

Sound Source	Input Channel
on-air announce mic	1
newsroom mic	2
cart #1 and turntable #1	3
cart #2 and turntable #2	4
cart #3 and tape recorder #1	5
cart #4, tape recorder #2, and network news feed	6
cart #5 and EBS line	7
cart #6 and remote line	8
CD #1, mobile van, and spare	9
CD #2 and spare	10

one that collects, boosts, and sends the sounds to the transmitter or tape recorder is the **program amplifier**.

Controls are needed to vary the volume of sound and to open and close microphones. The volume is regulated by a pot for each input channel. For the two microphones the board has three-position selector switches, with the positions designated as "on," "off," and "spare" (for some unanticipated future use). Each of the other input channels has a four-position selector switch, with one position for "off" and three for channels for sending signals. Each of the three channels has its own program amplifier, so there are five amplifiers for the board: two preamps for the microphones and three program amplifiers. This board is therefore a two-channel stereo audio console.

So that the operator will be able to assess the volume level of the sound, the board has a **level indicator** that gives a picture of the sound. This indicator may be an **LED** (**light-emitting diode**), a series of dots, arranged either vertically or horizontally, that are illuminated according to the strength of the signal. Many portable AM/FM cassette players use LED indicators.

Another type of level indicator is a meter with a swinging needle, called a **VU** (**volume unit**) **meter**, or **VI** (**volume indicator**) **meter**. The needle registers the volume level on a calibrated scale marked off in units from 1 to 100 along the black part of a semicircular line; above 100 the line becomes red. Readings that are too low on the

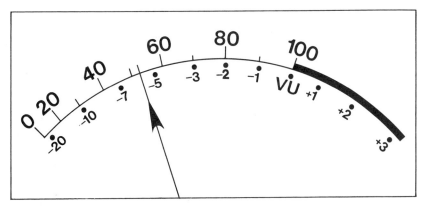

Figure 6.4
The reading on a VU or VI meter should be neither too low nor too high.

scale are said to be "in the mud," and those that are too high are "bending the needle," "in the red," or "spilling over." If the volume peaks too high on the scale, the signal may be distorted (an effect called **overmodulation**), and the equipment may be damaged. Three meters, one each for the left and right stereo channels and another to show the monaural signal that is being received by listeners to the AM station, are positioned at the top and center of the board, where they are easily visible.

A **muting relay** cuts the sound of the monitor speakers in the booth whenever the announce mic is open. This prevents **feedback**, the loud squeal produced when the sound of a speaker re-enters an open mic.

The controls described so far enable the operator to pick up sounds from the mics and other sound sources and send them through the board to the transmitter or a tape recorder. The operator can open and close the mics, mix the signals from the various sources, boost the signal strength of the mics, and monitor and adjust the volume level.

The difficulties that would arise in manually balancing the input of more than one sound source are eliminated by the **master pot**, which can raise or lower at the same time the volume of all sounds being mixed. This pot is generally left in a fixed position, but it can be used when necessary.

Stereo boards also have a **panoramic potentiometer** (abbreviated **pan pot**). This control allows the operator to shift a mono sound source, such as from a single mic, from the left channel to the right (or vice versa), in order to place it in proper position on the "stereo stage." Stereo recordings are already balanced, so the operator does not need to correct them on the board.

To allow the operator to hear material being broadcast, two **monitor speakers** are hooked up, one to monitor each of the two channels. If the program channels are patched to the transmitter, the announcer can listen to the programming on the program monitor speakers. The audition monitor speakers can be used to audition material for possible future use or to listen to material being recorded for later broadcast. The amplifiers for the monitor speakers must be of higher power than the program amplifiers to boost the signal to the level needed to drive the loudspeakers. Each set of speakers has its own **monitor pot**, used to raise and lower the volume of sound in the control room. There is also a **monitor select switch**, used to selectively monitor program and audition outputs.

Although records may seldom be played directly over the air, the console should be versatile enough to perform in all eventualities. This means that it should provide for the cuing up of records, which, in turn, means that the operator must be able to hear them without broadcasting the sound. A **cue speaker** or **cue box** has its own amplifier fed by all nonmicrophone pots. When each of these pots is turned to an extreme counterclockwise position (or, in the case of slider pots, all the way to the bottom) the cue amplifier and speaker are automatically activated. There are other arrangements, but this one seems best. With a turntable or tape pot turned completely into cue, there is no possibility of accidentally sending cuing sounds out over the air—unless, of course, the control room mic happened to be open at the same time. To make sure that cuing sounds will not be confused with program sounds, the monitor speakers and the cue speaker are placed in different parts of the control room.

Finally, a **headphone jack** allows the operator to listen to either program or audition without having sound emanate from the monitor or cue speakers; both speakers automatically cut off when the announce mic is open. This feature allows the announcer to talk over music on the air or to listen to the balance between voice and music without using the monitor speaker, which, of course, would create feedback. Announcers also use headphones to cue records when working combo.

The audio console described here is not the most sophisticated available, but nothing more is really needed for most modern radio station applications. Many radio stations are installing far simpler

Figure 6.5
Auditronics 700 Series audio mixing console—otherwise known as a production board. (Courtesy of Auditronics, Inc.)

consoles, but you cannot reasonably expect to find such a model at every station. The board described here is a practical compromise between the extremes of on-air board simplicity and the complexity that is characteristic of production boards.

Cart Machines and CD Players

Nearly all disc jockeys must cue up and play music recorded on both carts and CDs and play music, commercials, and station promotions that are recorded on carts.

Cuing and Playing Carts

The cuing and playing of carts can be learned in a few minutes. A cart is loaded with a looped, endless audiotape that automatically rewinds as it plays. Each tape contains only one audio item—one song, one commercial, or one station ID, for example. To play a cart, you insert it into the slot in the **cart machine** (or **playback machine**), and a red light comes on highlighting the word STOP. This tells you that the cart is cued. When you are ready to play it, you press a button, usually square, to start the tape. This button may be on the cart player itself, or it may have been **remoted** to the board. In the latter case, the button will be adjacent to the pot used to control the cart player's volume. After the tape has played, allow it to run until it stops automatically; it will then be recued and ready for the next playing. If you stop the tape before it recues, you will get **dead air** (a noticeable period of silence) at the start of the next playing.

At some stations—including many campus radio stations—there is an insufficient number of cart machines to allow you to play a number of carts in succession while allowing each to play through and recue. You will have to remove carts before they have recued, stack them, and recue them at a later time.

Cuing and Playing CDs

Some or even all of the music played by a radio station may be recorded on compact discs. CDs are small, and they are encoded with digitally recorded music on one side only. In digital recording, sound is translated by a computer into on/off pulses. A CD is played through decoding of such pulses by a laser beam. Because there is no contact with the disc's surface, there is an absence of surface noise. The disc spins at speeds ranging from 200 to 500 revolutions per minute (rpm) and gets up to speed almost instantly.

If you are familiar with a home CD player, learning how to operate a professional model requires getting familiar with only a few additional features. Although professional CD players vary somewhat in features offered and in the layout of controls, the Harman Kardon HD 800 is typical. It includes controls that allow you to open the record compartment, load the disc, close the compartment, select the cut you want to play, and, when ready, start the disc. Labeled displays show the cut being played, the elapsed and remaining time for the track, and the elapsed and remaining time for the disc. (This CD player is shown in Figure 11.1.)

To use the Harman Kardon HD 800, you follow these steps:

1. Press the button labeled OPEN/CLOSE, and the disc compartment will open.
2. Load the disc into the disc compartment, and again press the OPEN/CLOSE button to close it.
3. To cue up a particular **cut** (a term that comes from a time when records actually were cut with a recording stylus), press the double arrows pointing to the right on the display labeled SKIP, and continue pressing until the number of the cut you want—5, for instance—appears on the multi-display.
4. Press the PLAY/PAUSE button twice: first to acknowledge that the cut is the correct selection, and again to keep the disc from playing at that moment. When the elapsed-time indicator reads

0:00, you know that the disc is ready to play. Pressing the PRO-GRAM button then will set up the player to stop after playing the selected cut.

5. Press the PLAY/PAUSE button once more, and turn up the volume on the audio console.

CD players other than the one described here may have their controls arranged differently or have features not mentioned above. Nonetheless, the principles and operating practices are essentially the same.

Turntables

As an announcer for a medium- to small-market music radio station, you will likely spend part of your time cuing up and playing records. Even if a station plays only **carted music** (music that has been dubbed to cartridges), a part of your workday may be spent doing the dubbing to carts, and this means that you must know how to cue up and play both 45- and 33⅓-rpm records.

Components

Most broadcast turntables have seven components: a rotating table that is connected to the motor, a pickup arm (or tone arm), a pickup cartridge with stylus, an off-on switch, a variable equalizer, a speed-selector switch, and an attachment for playing large-holed 45-rpm discs.

The **rotating table** (or **turntable**) is usually made of metal and may be covered by a felt or rubber pad. The pad is not attached to the metal, and some announcers cue the record, hold the pad, turn on the power, and release the pad (and the record on it) when it is time to play the music. This is called **slip starting**. If you feel that there is friction of the pad against the turntable, you should not slip-start records at all.

A direct-drive turntable is, in effect, an electric motor. Motors are composed of a stationary part, called the stator, and a rotating part, called the rotor. The rotating table is the rotor on direct-drive turntables. Older turntables may have a rim-driven mechanism, but most of these old-timers have been phased out.

The **pickup, or tone, arms** used for broadcasting are both counterbalanced and damped to prevent damage to records. The tone arm is adjusted to put less than 1 gram of pressure on the grooves of the record; and viscous damping, which uses fluid silicone in a hydraulic mechanism, prevents the arm from making sharp or sudden movements.

The **pickup cartridges** for turntables are of a plug-in style. **Styluses** are spherical or elliptical in shape. Spherical styluses are generally found on home equipment, but elliptical styluses are preferred in broadcast applications.

All turntables are equipped with an **off-on switch** for controlling power to the turntable. Most disc jockeys now start records by pressing this switch on instead of slip-starting them.

Some older turntables are equipped with **variable equalizers**, or filters, that allow the announcer to control the frequencies being transmitted. Discs that were poorly recorded or pressed can be made to sound better by eliminating high frequencies. At most stations, records in need of equalization are dubbed to tape carts with the appropriate corrections being made through the board.

Almost all turntables have a **speed-selector switch**, offering a choice of $33\frac{1}{3}$ or 45 rpm.

Many turntables have a recessed metal hub in the center. By turning this hub, you can raise it to accommodate large-holed 45-rpm discs. Some turntables require an adapter that fits over the center spindle.

Cuing Up

Records have dead grooves before the sound begins. Because you do not want several seconds of dead air between your announcement and the start of the music, you must **cue up** records. This involves the following steps:

1. While one record is being broadcast, place the next selection on another turntable.
2. Using a control on the audio console, activate the cue box or cue speaker.
3. Place the stylus on the record's surface in the groove just before the desired cut.
4. Disengage the drive mechanism so that the table spins freely.
5. Spin the table clockwise until you hear the start of the sound on the cue speaker.
6. Stop the table and turn the record counterclockwise.
7. When you hear the music being played backwards stop, continue

spinning the record a short distance into the dead groove. Turntables are not standardized, but on most you will go back one-quarter of a turn before the music begins.
8. Engage the drive mechanism at the proper operating speed.
9. To play the cut on the air, open the volume control and turn on the power switch.

The purpose of turning the record back to a point in the dead grooves is to allow the turntable to reach its operating speed before the sound begins. All turntables need a little time to go from zero rpm to operating speed; until they have reached operating speed, sound is distorted. This **wowing** is as unacceptable as several seconds of dead air. A little practice with a particular turntable should enable you to cue records unerringly.

Automated Radio Stations

In the past twenty-five years, many radio stations have become automated. Most of this automation has been in FM or AM stereo stations, although some monaural AM stations have been automated. Although many automated stations have lately switched to a satellite programming service, others remain on the air.

Automation provides several advantages for station owners: stations can be operated with fewer employees; owners of both AM and FM stations can use the AM staff to program the FM station; a small station can have a "big city" sound; and disc jockeys can do their day's announcing work in less than an hour, which helps them sustain energetic delivery.

Opponents of automated radio are offended by the sacrifice of instantaneousness, long thought to be radio's most valuable characteristic. Opponents also claim that automated radio sounds canned, and that even the most sophisticated equipment and the most skilled operators cannot make an automated station sound live. Overweighing these aesthetic considerations for many opponents of automated radio is one based on economics: automated radio means fewer jobs for announcers.

Although some stations that became automated many years ago have returned to live programming or signed up with a syndicated satellite service, automated radio will be with us for some time, so you should become familiar with its essentials. Because several automated systems are in use today, you will have to learn the details of a particular system on the job. This brief overview is designed simply to provide you with an idea of how an automated station works and to expose you to some of the terms used in automated radio.

Most automated systems rely on three components: a **controller** (a computer, sometimes called the **brain**) is programmed by an operator; a series of reel-to-reel tape reproducers play the station's music; and a bank of cart machines stores commercials, public-service announcements, voice-track program openers, station jingles, time announcements, news headlines, weather reports, and network access announcements. Such systems also include an automatic logging device and an internal clock programmed to give accurate time signals that can be used to join and leave a parent network's hourly newscasts.

The controller's chief function is to intersperse music with other program elements. An adult/contemporary station might use four large music reels: one containing music from the current charts, a second playing golden hits from the past, a third containing up-tempo music to be played at the start of each hour following station identification, and a fourth made up of the music director's favorites. Nearly all automated stations have a rigid format that is repeated hourly.

As an announcer for an automated station, you will be expected to spend some of your workday programming the controller and the rest performing a variety of tasks. These include recording music introductions, weather reports, commercials, and newscasts; loading the cart machines and replacing carts that have served their purpose; and providing preventive maintenance for the equipment.[4] However, unless you have a background in electronics, this maintenance may simply involve cleaning tape heads and performing other nontechnical chores.

This chapter on broadcast equipment gives an overview of the equipment and production practices that are more or less standard. Two points should be made in conclusion: first, no amount of reading about equipment and procedures by itself can teach you to be competent—one or more hands-on courses in radio production are necessary to help you develop the requisite skills; second, because radio technology continues to develop at a rapid pace, you should make an ongoing effort to keep up with its constantly evolving world.

---

[4]Both recorded weather reports and newscasts are recorded just prior to being broadcast.

Spotlight: Equipping Broadcast Studios for the Twenty-first Century

Imagine sitting in the news anchor's chair and gazing out on a studio filled with cameras but containing no human operators. Or setting up (and storing for later network playback) thousands of cable features and commercial spots on your computerized cart machine. Or programming a 24-hour radio format that may or may not utilize a live announcer and for which the songs are transmitted from on-line rather than the playing of CDs.

From the phonograph that was used in the first radio broadcast (in 1906 from Brant Rock, Massachusetts, by Reginald Fessenden) to the sound boards, multi-CD players, and lighting systems of today, broadcast equipment continues to evolve. And, though most television and radio stations operate on a shoestring budget—getting by with outdated equipment—the few that can afford to are already testing the electronic devices of the twenty-first century.

At NBC News for the past few years, anchor Tom Brokaw has made eye contact with unassisted cameras. Three free-wheeling robotic cameras, supplemented by two wall-mounted cameras, have replaced a camera crew of six people, who earned a combined $600,000 per year.

Bonneville desktop radio programming system. (Courtesy of Bonneville Broadcasting System)

The first generation of camera robots were a bit constrained by their rail tracks, which allowed them to move only back and forth along a fixed path. But newer robots, being used also by the NBC studios in Burbank, California, and the Cable News Network of Turner Broadcasting System, are mounted on wheeled pedestals and can roam freely about the studio, using laser scanning with a system of reflectors to stay on course. They can be set for either preprogrammed camera angles or remote-controlled maneuverability.

Radio has long depended on cart machines to store program and commercial segments, but now cable television is benefitting from advances in audio/video electronic cart machines, called MERPS (multi-event recorder/player systems). MERPS's memory and storage capacity allow for

Roboped camera robot. (Courtesy of A.F. Associates)

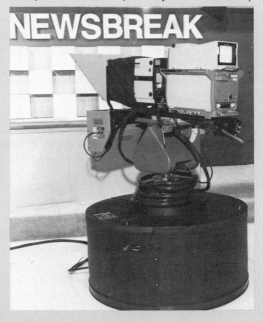

network playback at various times, back-to-back programming of even the shortest promotional segments, and transmission from the computerized cart machine itself rather than a master reel.

Many medium- and large-market radio stations in the United States have already changed the way they do programming. New equipment allows all of a station's recordings to be categorized on disk (by theme, composer/group, or length of piece), assembled into a day's program, compared with programming of the recent past, and sometimes played directly from computer to airwaves. One broadcasting system (see photo) offers a computer system with a researched library of Adult Contemporary and Easy Listening songs, which can be combined in any order and played directly from on-line, with or without a DJ. Other companies have developed software systems such as Selector and MusicScan, which offer increased precision and flexibility in hourly and daily music programming, scheduling jingles to "match" corresponding music selections, and indexing and cross-indexing music for any programming challenge that may arise.

As we approach the twenty-first century, computerized broadcast equipment will become more sophisticated and more widely available to smaller radio and television stations. Presumably, though, there will always be humans behind the designing and the programming of these devices—and humans in front of the microphones and cameras.

Practice: Comparing the Audio Quality of Microphones

If appropriate equipment is available, make an audio recording of your voice reading copy into a dynamic, a condenser, and a ribbon mic. Compare the results, and determine which type of instrument gives your voice its most pleasing sound.

Practice: Surveying Field Equipment

Arrange to interview someone who operates some item(s) of technical equipment: television cameras, video recorders, audio consoles, television switchers, character generators, or videotape editing consoles. Ask such questions as these: Where did you learn to do what you do? What should a person study to prepare for this work? What special challenges does your job present? Also, ask the interviewee to describe some of the newer equipment he or she works with. How have advances in broadcast technology altered everyday work? Share your findings with your class.

7

Commercials and Public-Service Announcements

Radio announcers at small-market stations sometimes combine announcing duties with the selling of commercial time and the production of radio commercials (also referred to as **spots**). Because a knowledge of time selling can provide an entrée to an announcing job, this chapter offers an introduction to the advertising side of broadcasting. The first section gives an overview of radio advertising practices; the second covers the announcer's role with respect to radio commercials; the third discusses public-service announcements (PSAs); and the last section provides information on delivering television commercials.

Advertising is the lifeblood of American commercial broadcasting. Radio and television would be far different if there were no commercial advertising. One has only to look at the broadcast services in nations in which tax-supported systems predominate to see that advertising has brought the American public many more radio and television stations, more daily hours of broadcast, and a much greater range of program material. Although commercials are sometimes maligned, they do furnish useful information, help fuel our economy, and provide work for writers, producers, directors, audio engineers, sales personnel, and announcers. Because of the commercial orientation of broadcasting in this country, your future as an announcer will be more secure if you develop the ability to sell products.

Public-service announcements (PSAs) resemble commercials in many respects. Both are brief announcements; both are informational in nature; and both are considered nonentertainment. Radio commercials and PSAs differ considerably from those on television, so the challenges presented by the two media will be discussed separately. Note, however, that the suggestions for analyzing and marking copy apply to both.

Radio Station Advertising Practices

This section outlines current advertising practices at commercial radio stations. As one hoping to enter the world of commercial broadcasting, you should have some understanding of sales practices and the responsibilities of sales personnel. Reading and studying this material will not, of course, qualify you for a sales position. But you may be able to undertake an internship with the sales department of a nearby radio station, giving you an opportunity to see in operation the practices outlined in this section. This would help prepare you for a combined announcing-sales job upon completion of your studies.

Target Audience

Aside from hourly newscasts, which may come through an audio feed from a parent network or a wire service, nearly all radio broadcasts originate and are heard in a fairly restricted geographical area. This means that most radio commercials, except for national spots, are placed by local merchants and service agencies and are designed to be heard within a specific station's signal range. Thus, radio stations rely heavily on local retailers, many commercials are written and produced at the local station level, and commercials are geared to the age, taste, interests, socioeconomic profile, ethnic background, and gender of the intended audience (these characteristics are called **audience demographics**). Advertisers are careful to scrutinize the demographics of a station's audience before committing advertising money. A product used chiefly by people middle-aged and older will not be advertised on a station that caters to young adults. The commercial approach on a station featuring country music may be quite different from that used for the very same product when it is advertised on a Black/Urban Contemporary station. What all this means to you is that in writing and delivering radio commercials, you must know the **target audience** and adapt your presentation to it.

Single-Sponsor Programs

Programs supported by a single sponsor are the exception on radio, but they occupy a portion of the day on some foreign-language stations and all-religion stations, and are sometimes heard on classical music stations when a local music store or record outlet sponsors "Opera Classics" or "Symphonic Masterpieces." At times, a company will

Figure 7.1
Some commercials go beyond consumer products to advertise stations themselves. This announcer and station staff member are producing a television spot to advertise a weekly Tuesday "giveaway" by a Baltimore station. (Courtesy of WPOC, Baltimore)

sponsor an hour of popular music on a rock station. A brief program format that is also subject to single sponsorship is typified by "Business Briefs," "Farm Report," or "Report from the Produce Mart." Advertisers for such reports want their commercials broadcast at a precise time each day in order to reach a particular audience. For example, a brokerage house may sponsor a business feature weekdays at 7:35 A.M., hoping to reach commuters during early-morning drive time. A farm products company may sponsor a five-minute program of agricultural news at 5:30 or 6:00 A.M., intended to reach farmers, who rise early. A chain of food stores may sponsor a daily report on the best produce buys of the day at 10:00 A.M., in the belief that shoppers will be listening at home before setting out to buy groceries. Each of these times is chosen on the basis of assumptions about the listening habits of the target audience.

Specialized phone-in radio programs featuring experts on cooking, gardening, home repair, investment, or real estate attract advertisers who believe their potential customers make up a good portion of the listening audience. Thus, grocery stores and specialty shops sponsor cooking shows, hardware stores sponsor home repair shows, and so on.

Advertising Purchase Plans

Other local advertisers buy time according to one of several plans offered by a given radio station. Typically, a station will divide its broadcast day into dayparts. A **daypart** is simply a portion of the broadcast day, and the advertising value of each such time segment is based on its audience size. A station may designate its dayparts as shown in Table 7.1, where the categories are listed in order of decreasing cost per spot. This cost is directly related to audience size.

Using its established dayparts as a base, a station may then offer a variety of purchase plans. There are several common types: Total Audience Plan (TAP), Run of Station (ROS), and Best Times Available (BTA).

Total Audience Plan (TAP) distributes advertising spots over three or more dayparts. A typical distribution would be one-third of the spots played during drive times, one-third during midday, and one-third in the evening. This plan gives an advertiser maximum audience coverage at less than the cost of placing all of the spots during drive time. If, for example, a spot in drive time sells for $100, a midday spot for $55, and an evening spot for $25, the cost for the TAP would be $60 a spot, regardless of when it is played.

Run of Station (ROS) and **Best Times Available (BTA)** are much cheaper than Total Audience Plan, but offer no guarantee as to when

Table 7.1   Typical Dayparts

Traditional Category	Current Designation	Time Period
AAA	Morning drive time	usually 6:00–9:00 A.M., though often expanded to 5:30–10:00 A.M. in major markets with heavy and extended commutes
AA	Afternoon drive time	usually 4:00–6:00 P.M., though often expanded to 3:00–7:00 P.M. in major markets
A	Midday	either 9:00 A.M.–4:00 P.M. or 10:00 A.M.–3:00 P.M.
B	Nighttime	6:00 (or 7:00) P.M.–midnight
C	Overnight	midnight–5:30 (or 6:00) A.M.

spots bought will be broadcast. Normally, except during peak advertising periods such as pre-Christmas, stations attempt to give ROS and BTA buyers enough good placements to attract their year-round advertising support.

A client's spots in any daypart may be **rotated**, or **orbited**, meaning the station plays the spots according to a formula that is designed to reach listeners at a variety of times within a given daypart. For example, a spot will be played between 6:00 and 7:00 A.M. on Monday, between 7:00 and 8:00 A.M. on Tuesday, between 8:00 and 9:00 A.M. on Wednesday, and between 9:00 and 10:00 A.M. on Thursday. On Friday, the spot will return to the 6:00–7:00 A.M. interval, so that it does not move to a time when the audience falls off.

Spots may also be scheduled on a horizontal or a vertical basis. **Horizontal spots** are scheduled across the days of the week; **vertical spots** are scheduled at various times on a given day.

Wild spots are more common than rotating spots because they are easier for stations to schedule. A **wild spot** comes with a guarantee that it will be played sometime within a specified daypart.

Role of Advertising Agencies

A radio spot gets to a station and into a program schedule in any of several different ways. In major and medium markets advertising agencies are usually involved to a fairly large extent.

- An agency may send a station a recorded commercial for which the announcing and other production work has been done at a recording studio.
- An advertising agency time buyer buys time on the station, and a written script is sent to the station to be read or ad-libbed by a staff announcer. In most such cases the commercials are carted, rather than performed live.
- An agency sends a script and a recording, and the announcer reads the written copy live during the appropriate daypart.

Commercials with a script and a recorded portion are often **cart with live tag**. This means that the commercial begins with the playing of the cart, which may be only a jingle or music with recorded speech, and the station announcer comes in at the end to provide a tag that gives local or extra information, such as the current price or a local phone number. In other instances, the recorded portion of such commercials may begin with a brief jingle and then fade under while the announcer reads the entire sales pitch. **Donut commercials** are similar. A jingle opens the spot, the music fades down for a pitch by the announcer and then is faded up just as the announcer completes the message. The term *donut* arose because music begins and ends such a commercial, with the announcer filling in the middle.

Recorded commercials prepared by advertising agencies come to a station on one-fourth-inch reel-to-reel tapes, and station production personnel dub these to tape carts. Carts are not produced at advertising agencies because there are several different cart formats, and each is playable only on the machine for which it was designed.

In-House Production

In smaller markets advertising agencies may supply only 10 percent of the commercials broadcast; the other 90 percent are written and produced by station staff for local merchants. Here are common practices in these markets:

- A station sales representative (or an announcer in some cases) sells time to a client, is given essential information (nature of the business and specific objectives of the spot), and may write the commercial copy. Few small radio stations employ full-time **continuity writers**, so scripts are written by management personnel, time sellers, announcers, or production specialists. A production specialist, who may be the production director, then works from the script and produces a commercial using a **music bed** (recorded music), sound

Figure 7.2
Every aspect must be perfect: producer Cindy Mills times a "take" during the recording of a radio commercial. They will keep working through a dozen takes before they get sound and timing that are broadcast quality. (Courtesy of Allen and Dorward Advertising, San Francisco)

effects, voices, and any other appropriate elements. Voicing of such spots almost always is done by the station's on-air personnel. At larger stations, full-time account executives sell time and write and produce commercials, often using station personnel as talent.

- A local merchant comes to the station to deliver a commercial and is recorded by station personnel for later editing (if necessary), carting, and scheduling.
- A local merchant is taped on location at that person's place of business, often an auto dealership or furniture store.

The Announcer's Role

Most radio announcers deliver commercials as part of a job that includes other duties, such as music announcing (DJ work), sportscasting, or performing as talk show host. Some staff announcers—particularly DJs on highly rated stations—receive extra payment beyond their salaries if they can perform well as commercial announcers; they may receive an additional $100 or more a week for working a stipulated number of hours in the production of carted commercials. Especially valuable to a production manager responsible for recording such spots are announcers who can act, including those who can do dialects. Many staff announcers earn additional money by doing freelance work at professional recording studios. These announcers are represented by talent agencies and are hired by advertising agencies.

More than 90 percent of the commercials broadcast by most radio stations are on tape carts. As an announcer, you will have to read some commercials live, however, and your work usually will leave you very little time to study the commercial copy. As a professional, you will be expected to sight-read without stumbling or misreading. Sight-reading in an authoritative and convincing manner is difficult. Take advantage of any and all spare moments to look over the copy you are given to read, even if this means arriving for work earlier than scheduled. And, when you go over the copy prior to reading it on the air, *read it aloud*!

Much commercial copy used on radio, especially that written without the help of a professional agency, is uninspired. Most merchants want a straightforward catalogue of items and prices, which is hardly designed to bring out the best in any announcer. Commercial announcing at many (perhaps most) radio stations demands skill in reading unfamiliar copy, concentration during performance, and the expenditure of time in **woodshedding**—a longstanding radio term meaning reading, rehearsing aloud, and marking copy. If you are fortunate enough to work for a classical music station, a low-key FM station, or any station at which commercials are limited in frequency, your chances of being effective are greatly improved. Take advantage of such ideal working conditions to woodshed. The results will benefit you, your station, your client, and your listeners.

Analyzing and Marking Commercial Copy

Chapter 2 presented analyses of several types of broadcast copy, including commercial copy. Because commercials are much shorter than other types of broadcast material, such as newscasts or documentaries, they present a unique challenge to announcers. Both the structure and the mood of a commercial must be effectively communicated in 60 seconds or less. Announcers are better able to do this if they have analyzed and marked the copy for a commercial.

Analyzing the structure   The first thing an announcer considers is the **structure** of a commercial. Most outstanding commercials are both subtle and complex. Chapter 2 provided some analysis of the structure of copy; the discussion here adds one more consideration—the **rule of three**. This long-recognized principle says that the sharpness and punch of one's comments are diluted by going beyond three words or phrases in a given sequence. Note how the rule of three applies to the following commercial script.

```
  AGENCY:  Ketchum Advertising, San Francisco
  CLIENT:  The Potato Board
 PRODUCT:  Potatoes
   TITLE:  "Versatile"
  LENGTH:  60 seconds

   ANNCR:  Here's another message from The Potato Board.
           Don't we Americans love food? Fast food . . .
           slow food . . . all kinds? But, above all, don't
           we love that good food--the potato? Today, the
           potato stands alone as the number one vegetable
```

of versatility. And our friends at The Potato
Board remind us that Americans crave potatoes in
any and every form, for every meal. Why,
Americans love potatoes as appetizers, in soups
and salads, as entrees and side dishes, and . . .
yes . . . even as desserts. The Potato Board says
any way you serve the all—American potato, you'll
be getting an economical vegetable that has lots
of nutrition, but not——I repeat not——lots of
calories. So, whether you serve potatoes
scalloped, hashed, or mashed . . . sliced or
diced . . . french fried, boiled, or baked, in
all their delicious versatility, The Potato Board
says potatoes are America's favorite vegetable.
Well, aren't they in your house?

Note that in this commercial the first grouping of three comes
early: "Fast food . . . slow food . . . all kinds?" Also note that the first
three sentences (beginning with "Here's another—" and ending with
"—the potato?") form a complete expository unit and should be
read in such a way as to give a sense of a beginning, a middle, and an
ending—though not so obvious an ending as to make what follows seem
tacked on.

The next set of three is less obvious. Here are the three parts of
this segment of the Potato Board commercial:

1. "Why, Americans love potatoes as appetizers,—"
2. "—in soups and salads,—"
3. "—as entrees and side dishes,—"

Then comes what seems to be a fourth element, ". . . even as desserts," but the ellipses indicate that this is to be set apart from the
preceding sequence of three by a pause. These words become a group
of three in themselves if you pause slightly between each word—

". . . even . . . as . . . desserts." In analyzing and marking this copy, you should not see "appetizers," "soups," "salads," "entrees," "side dishes," and "desserts" as six points receiving equal stress.

The final set of three consists of the phrases "scalloped, hashed, or mashed," "sliced or diced," and "french fried, boiled, or baked." Two of the three phrases in this sequence are made up of three units each.

Now, consider another outstanding commercial, one that requires a British accent. This Schweppes commercial has a Monty Python quality, and you should enjoy it as an exercise in mock disdain. Be sure to avoid a Cockney dialect—it calls for your best Oxonian accent.

AGENCY: Ammirati & Puris, Inc.

CLIENT: Schweppes

LENGTH: 60 seconds

ANNCR: (BRITISH) I have before me a bottle of Schweppes
           Bitter Lemon. The soft drink loved by half of
           England. We British love the way it looks: a
           fine, sophisticated mist, with morsels of crushed
           whole lemon. We love the way it sounds: (BOTTLE
           OPENS) a particularly masterful rendering of
           Schweppes cheeky little bubbles. And we
           especially love the way it tastes: (POURS)
           refreshingly brisk, cultivatedly crisp and
           thoroughly Schweppervescent. It's no wonder that
           Bitter Lemon is adored by half of England.
           Now, what about the other half, you might ask?
           The half that doesn't adore Bitter Lemon? Well,
           let me assure you, they're all whining children,
           grubby little urchins whose opinion is completely

and totally insignificant. They are youthful
upstarts and, as such, absolutely incapable of
appreciating anything as forthrightly crisp as
Bitter Lemon. The frightfully grown-up soft drink
from Schweppes. The Great British Bubbly.

Note that the first 60 percent of this commercial is to be read in a precise, dignified, and restrained manner. Then, beginning with "Now, what about the other half," you must begin to build in emotion, intensity, volume, and rate of delivery. As you reach the end of the third-to-last sentence, begin decelerating on "as forthrightly crisp as Bitter Lemon." The last two sentences should see you returning to the dignified mood with which you began.

Note how this copy applies the rule of three three times. The first group is:

1. "We British love the way it looks"
2. "We love the way it sounds"
3. "We especially love the way it tastes"

Near the middle is this sequence of three:

1. "refreshingly brisk"
2. "cultivatedly crisp"
3. "thoroughly Schweppervescent"

Then, finally, the children are

1. "whining children"
2. "grubby little urchins"
3. "youthful upstarts"

In analyzing copy, always look for structure as revealed by the parts.

Analyzing the mood Read the following two commercials and the brief analysis that follows them; then practice them aloud, attempting clearly differentiated moods.

AGENCY: Yamashiro Associates
CLIENT: Webster's Department Stores
LENGTH: 60 seconds

ANNCR: Webster's has you in mind!
MUSIC: UP-TEMPO INSTRUMENTAL, UP AND UNDER
ANNCR: Webster's announces the sale of the year! Up to
         one-half off on thousands of items! Arrow and Van
         Heusen men's shirts, 50 percent off. All shoes in
         stock, one-third off. One dollar above our cost for
         men's three-piece, all wool suits. Save dollars
         on neckties, belts, socks, and sport shirts. In
         the women's department, one-third to one-half off
         on designer pants, blouses, and blazers. Entire
         dress inventory reduced by 50 percent. Even
         homewares are going at all-time low prices. Rag
         rugs from India--were $69, now only $39. Bath and
         beach towels, all prices cut in half. Fifty-piece
         stainless tableware, down by one-third. All
         radios, portable TVs, and home recorders, just
         dollars above our cost. Now's the time to take
         advantage of low, low prices, while enjoying the
         traditional high value of Webster's! Three stores
         to serve you. Sorry, at these prices, no free
         delivery and no layaways. Come see us today.
         Webster's has you in mind! Webster's, where
         you'll save dollars, with no sacrifice of quality!

AGENCY: Ketchum Advertising
CLIENT: Lindsay Olives
LENGTH: 60 seconds

MUSIC: FRIENDLY MUSIC IN BACKGROUND
ANNCR: (FRIENDLY OLIVE) Hi! Hi! How are ya? Good. I'm Ted. I'm a friendly olive. In fact, most of my true-blue friends are olives, too. Yeah, yeah, sure they are. Now, my friends are all mature—strictly high-quality guys. That's why they're Lindsay Olives. We were all very close friends on our branch. We did everything together: soaked up the sun, talked to the girl olives, read the classics. Yeah. Honest. We read the classics. I told you we were high-quality olives. Well, one day the Lindsay picker came for the final inspection. He took all my friends, but rejected me. He said I had a bruise. Yeah, a bruise. I don't know how I got it—but I got it. We all argued, but the inspector wouldn't take a flawed olive for Lindsay. Well, I was quite upset. Upset! 'Cause I knew some day I'd end up like this in some obscure can of olives, and all my pals would be Lindsays.
ANNCR: (FEMALE VOICE) An olive is just an olive, unless it's a Lindsay.
ANNCR: (FRIENDLY OLIVE) Hey, you look friendly. Let's have lunch sometime.

Note the striking difference of mood in these two examples. The first, for Webster's, is designed to hold attention through vitality and the illusion of importance. Every effort is made to encourage direct and rapid action from the listener. The second commercial, for Lindsay Olives, is light, humorous, and wistful. Both pieces of copy contain the same number of words (182), which means that both must be read rather rapidly. Be careful to avoid turning the Lindsay Olive spot into a hard-sell commercial.

Marking commercial copy   After the analysis of structure and mood comes the marking of copy. As a disc jockey, you will have little or no time for marking copy; but as a free-lance announcer working with other professionals in a recording studio, you will mark your copy both before and during the recording session.

The copy that follows was marked by a professional announcer after arriving at the recording studio. Read it aloud according to the indications made for pauses and stresses. One virgule (/) means a brief pause; two virgules (//) mean a longer pause. One line under a word means some stress; two lines indicate fairly heavy stress. Note, though, that this is a soft-sell commercial; even your heaviest stress should be consistent with the mood and style of the piece. (SFX is the abbreviation for sound effects; UP means the volume is raised; VO is the abbreviation for voice-over.)

AGENCY: Ingalls Associates, Inc.

CLIENT: Middlesex Bank

SUBJECT: Home Improvement Loans

LENGTH: 60 seconds

SFX: CHILLING WIND SOUNDS

VO: This harsh and untimely interruption of summer/ is

brought to you by/ Middlesex Bank. As a reminder

that this summer is no time to forget about/ next

winter.

SFX: UP

VO: The heating. Those storm windows. That leaking

ventilating system. If your house could use a

little <u>winterizing</u>, <u>summer</u> is the time to do it.
Because right now, the <u>prices</u> are <u>right</u>.
<u>And</u>/right now, Middlesex Bank is standing by,
ready with a <u>home</u> <u>improvement</u> <u>loan</u>.// We interrupt
this interruption of <u>winter</u>/with <u>summer</u>.

SFX: SPLASHES OF SWIMMING POOL

VO: As a reminder, that with <u>gas</u> prices the way they
are, you might even consider turning your house
into a <u>summer</u> place . . .// by putting in a
<u>swimming</u> <u>pool</u>. No matter what part of your home
you'd like to improve, we've got a <u>Home</u>
<u>Improvement</u> <u>Loan</u> to help you do it. We're
<u>Middlesex</u>. The Little/<u>Big</u> Bank.

Now read the following commerical, and note how it was marked
during a recording session (note also how this commercial follows the
rule of three).

AGENCY: Allen and Dorward

CLIENT: New Century Beverage Co.

LENGTH: 60 seconds

ANNCR: Wherever you go in San Francisco/(SFX: FOG
HORNS), the executive <u>bistros</u>/(MUSIC:
CONTEMPORARY)/ in the bustling <u>financial</u>
<u>district</u>, the elegant homes of <u>Pacific</u> <u>Heights</u>
and Sea Cliff, or the lavish rooms of the major
hotels, you'll hear the inviting sound of
<u>Schweppervescence</u>. // (SFX: HISS AND POUR) That
curiously refreshing sound when the mixer meets

the ice, is an <u>irresistible</u> call to pleasure./And
whether you're pouring Schweppes Tonic Water,
Club Soda, or Ginger Ale, the sound is the same.//
(SFX: HISS AND POUR) But <u>each</u> has a taste <u>all</u> <u>its</u>
<u>own</u>./You'll find the unchanging quality of
Schweppervescence <u>immediately</u> apparent in the
company of kindred spirits or/<u>straightaway</u>. That
<u>curiously</u> refreshing sensation found only in
Schweppes that makes your drink <u>so</u> extraordinary.
San Franciscans are not alone in their refreshing
appreciation of Schweppes, for Schweppes Mixers
are accepted around the world by those with a
taste for quality. The <u>great</u> <u>taste</u> of Schweppes
Mixers <u>cannot</u> be silenced (SFX: HISS AND POUR)
<u>Tonic</u> <u>Water</u>, <u>Club</u> <u>Soda</u>, <u>Ginger</u> <u>Ale</u>. Listen to the
sound of <u>Schweppervescence</u>. Call for Schweppes.
Curiously refreshing since 1783. (SFX: FADE OUT
HISS)

Recording a Commercial in a Studio

Despite the analyzing and copy marking you have done just before
the recording session, be prepared to make changes during the ten,
twenty, or more **takes** that will be necessary before the person producing the commercial is satisfied. A typical recording setup for a
radio commercial requires from three to five persons: one or two
announcers, an agency producer, an audio engineer, and, at times,
the writer of the commercial. Music is recorded in advance and added
by the engineer.

As each take is recorded, instructions are given to the announcer
by the producer or writer as to changes to be made: to eliminate
awkward phrases, to delete or alter sentences with too many sibilant

sounds ("That's because Bonnie's citrus scouts search the finest orange groves"), to change the emphasis of words or phrases, and, most often, to delete words or short phrases to conform to time limits. The producer or writer may also offer suggestions for interpreting the copy. The producer will inform an announcer who is going too fast or too slow, is mispronouncing a word, or is slurring or having some other articulation problem. The writer (if the writer is not also the producer) will decide what words to change or cut. As the announcer, you are expected to follow all instructions without comment or argument.

Not all agency representatives are equally competent in coaching performers. Some will give you vague instructions such as "give me more" or "try it another way." As a freelance voice-over performer, you will work with many different producers, and only some will be able to give you clear and helpful directions. There may be times when you would like to offer suggestions, and to do so is appropriate *if* you are confident that the producer feels secure and is open to your ideas. Remember, though, that even constructive suggestions from you are unwelcome by some agency writers and producers. Feel your way carefully as you attempt to sense when it is safe to offer suggestions for changes in commercial copy.

If, when being recorded, you stumble or slur a word, pause, say "pickup," pause again, and begin reading from the beginning of the sentence in which you stumbled. This practice will make it easy for the audio engineer to edit the tape.

Working with Commercials During an On-Air Shift

As an announcer on a music or talk radio station, most of your commercial announcing will occur during a regular on-air shift, unless you work extensively with the production department to record commercials on carts. This section describes the on-air procedures you are most likely to encounter.

The commercial copy for your entire shift will have been logged by the **traffic department**, and you will have a copy of that log.[1] The log indicates the order of the commercials, whether a given commercial is recorded or is to be read live, the cart number for carted commercials, and the time each commercial is to be broadcast. If your station

---

[1]The traffic department—sometimes consisting of only a sales manager—is responsible for scheduling commercials.

has a tight format, the times will be precise; if the format is casual and relaxed, the times will be approximate.

If you are working at a large station, chances are there will be (in addition to the log) a **copy book**, sometimes called a **continuity book**. Seven such books are prepared weekly by the traffic department, one for each day of the week. Each book will contain, in the order of presentation, the commercial copy for spots to be read live, as well as indications of the spots that are carted. Your job in working from a copy book is not difficult; you merely keep track of the sequential placement of the commercials, entering a mark on the program log as each commercial is broadcast. A turn of the page brings you to the next commercial.

At smaller stations, where limited budgets dictate fewer staff members, the procedure is somewhat more complicated. There is one copy book. Commercials are inserted alphabetically by sponsor name. The program log contains an entry such as "live #4, Malagani Tires" or "cart #23, Red Boy Pizza." The first of these examples indicates that you should look up the Malagani copy, commercial number 4, in the alphabetically arranged copy book and read it at the appropriate time. The second indicates that, assuming you are working combo, you should locate cart number 23 and play it at the correct time.

In working with commercials that are part live and part recorded, it is necessary to develop split-second timing. A script for a cart with live tag follows.

CLIENT:	Bellach's Furniture
LENGTH:	60 seconds
TYPE:	Cart with live tag
CART #:	L-66
BEGIN:	8/12
JINGLE:	(5)
VOICE:	"Chicago's newest shopping mall"
CART CLOSE AND TAG CUE	
VOICE:	"Open Tuesdays 'til nine."
SFX:	(1)

```
TAG IN AT:    (45)

LIVE TAG:     Visit the home furnishings display at Bellach's.

              Fine leather sofas and lounge chairs are on sale

              at 25% off! Bedroom sets by Heritage now marked

              down a full 30%! Lamps, end tables, occasional

              chairs, and desks--all on sale at prices you have

              to see to believe! Bellach's, at the Stonestown

              Mall!
```

How do you work from this script? First, you must understand the symbols used. The numbers following CART # identify the particular cart to be played. BEGIN: 8/12 gives the starting date for air play. JINGLE: (5) identifies the specific musical identification cart to be played. CART CLOSE means that at this point, the recorded portion of the spot concludes. TAG CUE and VOICE indicate that the last line of the recorded portion is "Open Tuesdays 'til nine."

Figure 7.3
Advertising agencies make frequent use of freelance performers. Here Peter Scott reads a script for a radio commercial. (Courtesy of Peter Scott)

Spotlight: Tips from a Voice-Over Pro

Samantha Paris works at the top of the voice-over profession. From her home base in Marin County, California, just north of San Francisco's Golden Gate Bridge, she earns a living doing what she loves: performing for radio commercials, dubbing voices for cartoons, and narrating corporate/industrial and documentary films. Occasionally she is hired to **loop** a voice for a commercial feature film (her voice is edited in to replace the voice of an actor whose vocal quality does not match her appearance).

Some of Paris's workdays are spent at home rehearsing scripts that she receives by fax, making audition tapes in her in-home studio, and sending out cassettes to agents who have asked her to read for a part. Other days are spent in recording sessions in the city; about once a week she flies to Los Angeles for production work.

Under the surface of today's success, however, lies a foundation of years and years of effort. Paris is one of those people who always knew exactly what she wanted to do; at fifteen she began taking voice-over lessons four evenings per week. While her high-school peers were socializing after school, Paris was immersed in her lessons, spending extra hours each week practicing. What she learned then has carried her through many high-pressure situations: how to size up a piece of copy in seconds, how to make instant decisions about character and mood, and how to adapt her voice quality and personality to the job

at hand. Two years after Paris began her lessons, an agent visited her class and told her she had promise; at seventeen, she began to audition for every feature film and video commercial in the area.

Although she became adept at video work, Paris realized that she derived the most satisfaction from using her voice. Although she worked as an agent "to see how the other side of the business works," that lasted only six months. Promoting others' voice talent only made her more certain that she "could do this so much better!" She wondered, "Why'd I ever give it up?" So, after six years of intense training, another five years of occasional work that didn't pay the bills, and then a steady succession of jobs that built her repertoire and reputation, Paris is now in constant demand by producers and talent agents.

Paris is the first to admit that establishing oneself in this profession isn't easy. "There have been lots and lots of tears," she says. "But you can't give up. If you want it badly enough, you've just got to believe that you're good, and you can't give up. . . . Sometimes it's painful, but you've just got to stay with it and keep the faith."

Warning today's announcing students not to expect anything, Paris advises, "When you're first studying, you can't be looking down the road, wondering, 'Well, how long is it going to take?' You have to love what you are doing, and just enjoy the journey."

SFX: (1) identifies the sound effects cut to be played. TAG IN AT: (45) tells you to begin the closing live tag 45 seconds into the commercial, which means that you have 15 seconds to read the tag. In practicing this commercial, use a stopwatch (preferably a digital one) and work until you are able to read the tag in exactly 15 seconds.

Most radio announce booths are equipped with a mounted stopwatch or an electronic digital clock that can be programmed to show

Now that she has studied the field and performed well within it, Paris teaches voice-over acting herself. Following are some suggestions she offers to help performers achieve their highest potential:

- Read, read, read aloud. Use anything from actual scripts to newspaper articles. Do *not* record and play back your performances on your own. Concentrate on your work, and rely on qualified teachers and coaches to judge your taped performances. We all sound pretty bad to our own ears.
- Newspaper articles are difficult to deliver orally, so reading them aloud is good practice for cold readings at auditions.
- Always have a clear picture of who you are, to whom you are talking, and where you are.
- Make sure that each listener feels that you are talking only to her or him.
- Choose an *attitude* before you choose a character. Characterization comes only after all other decisions as to purpose, place, mood, nature of listener, and so forth have been made. The decision about attitude must be precise: *motherly* is not the same as *caring*; *caring* is not the same as *neighborly*; *neighborly* is not the same as *friendly*.
- It isn't nearly enough to decide that in your performance you will be, for example, a middle-aged mother. You have to go deeper than that. As a mother, how do you feel about the child you are addressing? Are you talking to one child or two? How old are the children? How old are you? What is the setting in which you speak to the children?
- When you are given a technical direction such as "I want you to really punch that word," make sure that your attempt to carry out the instruction fits your attitude and character. Make it believable.
- Techniques eventually come into play. For example, emphasis can be accomplished by intonation, by pauses before and after the words of importance, by a break in delivery, or by a change in rhythm or volume. However, before you even think about such techniques, make sure to establish your attitude, your objectives, and your character.

Voice-over actress Samantha Paris records a commercial in her home studio. (Courtesy of Samantha Paris)

either elapsed time or remaining time. In reading commercials of any kind, time is important. Use a stopwatch or clock each time you practice. Split-second timing is most important for carts with tags and donuts; time is what radio stations sell, and clients expect precisely what they pay for.

Donut commercials require the most accurate timing of all, because just enough seconds have been provided for the reading of the copy before the musical background is faded back up. A typical donut begins with music, often with lyrics, and at a specific second the volume is lowered for you to read your copy. At exactly the time indicated on the script, the volume of the music is raised to full, and the song or jingle is repeated until the end of the commercial. If you read too rapidly, you will finish while the background music is playing at reduced volume. If you read too slowly or if you stumble and have to repeat a portion of your script, the music will return to full volume while you are still reading. As a professional, you should work for perfection in reading donuts, for you will be judged on your timing abilities.

Some radio stations have developed a practice that makes split-second timing on donuts unnecessary. The first part of a donut commercial is recorded on one cart and the last part on another. The first cart typically includes the opening jingle and the reduced-volume musical bed; the second cart begins with the start of the concluding jingle. The way you would work with two carts is obvious, and it is equally apparent that this system eliminates almost all possibility of timing error. But you cannot be sure that your station will allow the time it takes to dub donuts onto two carts, so you should practice and perfect the skill of reading them to the exact times indicated.

Character Voices

General American or Standard English has been the accepted manner of speaking by both men and women announcers since the beginning of radio broadcasting in the United States. However, broadcasters have also used foreign accents, regional dialects, and character voices in some dramas and in a great many commercials. If you have a good ear for speech sounds and find that you are able to perform competently while using a character voice, you may want to develop a number of dialect specializations. This is especially true if you intend to become a freelance performer of commercials.

Many commercials, especially those produced for Saturday morning television shows, are done as cartoons with voice-overs. The types of voices that are used in cartoon spots include pretend animal voices (such as that of Garfield), monsters, aliens from other planets, and superheroes and heroines, to name a few.

In addition to foreign accents and regional dialects, commercial copy—and especially that written for radio—often asks for a specific type of speech personality, such as the nag, the wimp, or the bully.

Some commercials call for a speaker who can speak at a very rapid rate or who has an unusual voice. Nonstandard styles of speech may be grouped in the following categories: (1) Unusually rapid delivery, (2) unusually low or high pitch, (3) unusual voice quality, (4) unusual personality type, (5) stage English, (6) regional dialects, and (7) foreign accents. As Table 7.2 (on the next page) shows, some of these are performed only by men, some only by women, and some by both. These categories are, of course, stereotypes, but that is precisely why they are used—they quickly identify types of persons to an audience that has been conditioned to associate character traits with certain voice qualities.

Radio Public-Service Announcements

Nearly all commercially licensed broadcast stations provide free time for the reading or the playing of recorded public-service announcements (PSAs). The Federal Communications Commission (FCC) defines a PSA as follows:

> A public-service announcement is an announcement for which no charge is made and which promotes programs, activities, or services of federal, state or local governments (e.g., recruiting, sales of bonds, etc.) or the programs, activities or services of non-profit organizations (e.g., UGF, Red Cross Blood Donations, etc.), and other announcements regarded as serving community interests, excluding time signals, routine weather announcements and promotional announcements.

Most broadcast stations limit PSAs to organizations that enjoy tax-exempt status, as defined by the Internal Revenue Service. Despite deregulation, nearly all radio stations continue to carry PSAs. Station management knows that the goodwill of community members is important to the success of the station. There also is a long tradition of community service on the part of broadcasters.

Some announcements of community interest are paid for by local merchants, who realize that their interests are served by supporting important local causes. These are not truly PSAs, because PSAs are broadcast without charge; but, except for the mention of the sponsor, they read like PSAs. Such a sponsored announcement will be broadcast during any daypart the sponsor pays for, because it is treated like

Table 7.2 Nonstandard Styles of Speech Used in Commercials

Category	Example(s)	Gender of Announcer
rapid delivery	pitchmen, speaking at over 200 words a minute; can be loud ("used car salesman") or soft-spoken	man
unusually low- or high-pitched voices	gravel-voiced "he-man," often heard on commercials for "muscle" cars	man
	"in the cellar," as in many commercials for financial institutions	man
	children's voices performed by adults	woman
unusual voice quality	breathy, as in spots for perfumes	woman
	breathy, as in spots for some luxury automobiles	man
unusual personality type	the whiner	man or woman
	the wimp	man
	the dumbell	man or woman
	the crab	man or woman
	the nag	usually a woman
	the bully	man
stage english	sinister	man or woman
	pretentious	man or woman
	authoritative	man or woman
regional dialects	folksy-country, New England, New York, Southern, drawled Southern, Hoosier (Indianian), Western, harsh Midwestern, Texan, country bumpkin	man or woman
foreign accents	German, French, Italian, Mexican, Greek, Russian, other Slavic, Chinese, Japanese, Southeast Asian, Filipino, English (both Cockney and Oxford), Scandanavian, Australian, Arabic, and Transylvanian (often associated with Dracula)	man or woman

Figure 7.4
Public-service announce-
ments are an important
tool for increasing public
awareness of issues and
events while advancing a
station's image, but an announcer often has little to
work with in terms of
script. Here DJ Bill Monihan reads from a 3-by-5-
inch card, ad libbing to fill
in the sketchy facts.
(Courtesy of KTID, San
Rafael, CA)

a commercial. Here is an announcement paid for by a brake and tire service.

> ANNCR: Brandon's Brake and Tire reminds you that, with the opening of the school year, it's extra important to keep alert on the road. A child often forgets all the safety rules that are taught by parents and teachers. Drive carefully and cautiously, and be prepared to stop in a hurry if you see a ball bounce into the street—a child may be right behind it. As adults, we need to do some thinking for children. This message is brought to you by Brandon's Brake and Tire, Clement and 14th Streets, in Madison.

PSAs and commercials have much in common, but there are some differences: PSAs tend to be shorter, some constituting only a brief mention on a community billboard feature; PSAs seldom are aug- mented by elaborate production, such as music, sound effects, and so forth; and PSAs are more likely to be broadcast during **off hours**, those times of the day that are least attractive to advertisers. More important differences lie in the objectives and in the motivational devices used. Many commercials present rational arguments to sell a product or a service, such as a spot for a supermarket that lists the weekend specials. Other commercials are designed to arouse the emotions of fear, greed, or insecurity. Public-service announcements must shun such tactics. Fear, greed, and insecurity are basic human emotions, and it is rather easy to exploit them. A campaign for famine relief or one to save the whales may indeed appeal to basic human emotions, but the producers of PSAs for such causes traditionally avoid emotional overkill. Because of these considerations, you should give PSAs an unadorned, straightforward delivery in nearly all instances.

At a large-market station the PSAs that you are to read will be neatly typed, duplicated, and placed in your copy book. At small-market stations PSAs will come to you in a variety of ways. Where there is a staff member assigned to public affairs, PSAs may be typed on three-by-five index cards. At regular intervals you will read two or three of the brief messages as a community calendar. The following is typical of such notices.

MISSION HOSPITAL   out: Apr. 5
The Sunrise Unit of Mission Hospital will present the film "Chalk Talk" and a discussion on alcoholism on April 5th, 6:30 P.M., at the hospital.   info: 924-9333

At times, you may have to ad-lib an announcement based on a fact sheet, such as that in Figure 7.5. Obviously, skill in ad-libbing is required when working from such a fact sheet to deliver the message effectively.

Here are some suggestions for practicing the delivery of radio commercials and PSAs.

- Practice reading aloud and recording 10-, 20-, 30-, and 60-second commercials as well as 10-, 20-, and 30-second PSAs, always working with a stopwatch. Listen carefully to playbacks. Ask yourself these questions: Does this voice please me? Does the piece hold my attention? Does the meaning come through? Is the rate of delivery too fast or too slow? Is there variety in pitch, rate, and emphasis? And, most important, am I sold on the product or the cause?
- As you practice ad-libbing PSAs from brief fact sheets, try to get the essential information across in 10 seconds.
- Produce on audiotape commercials that require sound effects, music, and/or dramatization.

Dixie School
1818 Morgan Drive
Outland, MI

Dear Friends:

   I would appreciate having the following announcement read during your community billboard.

Parental Stress Workshop
Wednesday, February 24
7:30 p.m.
Dixie School   Room 23

*Child care   *Refreshments

Thank you!

Janice Hicks

544-3321 (school)
544-5467 (home)

- Ask a radio station or advertising agency for copies of taped donut commercials, complete with copies of their scripts, and practice with them until your timing becomes razor sharp.

Television Commercials

Television commercials differ from radio commercials in several ways. They are usually briefer than most radio commercials, running from 15 to 30 seconds; they use music and sound effects more often; and they are almost never performed live. Because television is a visual medium, most advertisers want to show their products or services, and this means that the majority of television commercials feature voice-over narration. The face of a television commercial announcer seldom appears on the screen. Even in commercials that do show an announcer, the appearance is usually confined to a few moments of introduction at the beginning.

As a television commerical announcer, you will not have to cope with the problem of reading copy cold, which challenges many radio disc jockeys. There will be time to prepare and even to discuss interpretation with a copywriter or agency producer—and tape recording will give you a margin of safety.

Television commercials reach the air by processes similar to those for radio commercials. Some are sent to a station, almost always on videotape, by an advertising agency; some are produced by a nearby production company and sent to a station by the advertiser; others are produced by the retail services unit of a station and are played on that station and sent to other stations. If you are an announcer specializing in television commercials, you probably will receive your assignments through a talent agency. You will perform in one of these

Figure 7.6
If it is to have high audio quality and credible, appealing visual images, a television commercial requires much planning and production time. During a moment between takes, a performer checks back through his script and gets a refreshed look from the makeup artist.
(Photo courtesy of Cellular One, Cincinnati, Ohio)

settings: a sound recording studio (for voice-over commercials), a television station studio, a video or film studio, or in the field with an **EFP (electronic field production) crew**.

Many television commercials that appear to be produced locally actually originate in major production centers and are offered to local merchants as cooperative commercials. A **cooperative commercial** is one for which a national advertiser pays the cost of production and then shares the cost of broadcast with a local merchant. The bulk of such a commercial is on tape by the time it reaches the local station or local production house, where a closing tag on behalf of the local merchant is added. The following is a script for a cooperative commercial produced by Serta.

```
   AGENCY:   Allen and Dorward
   CLIENT:   Breuner's
  PRODUCT:   Serta Mattresses
   LENGTH:   60 seconds
```

VIDEO	AUDIO
MUSIC UNDER: WOMAN TOSSING AND TURNING IN A TRAIN SLEEPING COMPARTMENT	SHE: I want my Serta! ANNCR (VO): Here's why people want their Serta--why they're spoiled for any other mattress--
ANNOUNCER STANDING NEXT TO SERTA MATTRESS	Only Serta goes beyond just being firm, beyond what others do.
SUPER: SERTA PERFECT SLEEPER	We top our support with the extra comfortable Serta surface--
SHOTS OF COILS AND TOP SURFACE	a unique difference you can feel in a Serta Perfect Sleeper

```
ART CARD: SERTA LOGO "I WANT MY        BREUNER'S ANNCR (VO): Save 50%
SERTA"                                 off original prices on the
                                       clearance of all Serta Perfect
PERFECT SLEEPER HOTEL 50% OFF          Sleeper Hotel sleep sets, with
(DISSOLVE) NO PAYMENTS UNTIL           no payments 'til November!
NOVEMBER
(DISSOLVE) BREUNER'S FINE HOME
FURNISHINGS SINCE 1856
```

As either a radio or a television announcer, you may pick up extra money by freelancing as a television commercial announcer. Network news anchors and reporters are barred by contract from advertising a product, but most other television performers are free to **moonlight** (to work at a second job during one's spare time, often at night). Television commercial announcing at the national level pays well, but it is a difficult field to enter. Most performers in national spots live in New York, Chicago, San Francisco, or the Hollywood area, and a small number of them dominate the field.

Locally produced television commercials offer employment to many performers, mostly in voice-over roles. Portable electronic field production equipment, along with character generators, graphics generators, digital video effects (DVE) equipment, and chroma-keying, makes it possible for even small local stations to create elaborate and effective commercials. Videotapes can be made on location—at a carpet store, an auto parts dealer, a tire and brake service, or a grocery store. Then, during **postproduction**, station personnel add written information (character generator), draw images onto the screen (graphics generator), create and manipulate **multi-images**, such as changing a picture into a mosaic or swinging a picture through space (DVE equipment), or key two or more pictures onto the same screen (chroma-keying). A typical locally produced television commercial will show an announcer at or near the beginning of the spot and then show images of products or services, while the announcer continues with voice-over narration.

Voice-over narration for television commercials differs from radio commercial delivery only in that the words must be timed to match

Checklist: Making Effective Television Commercials

1. When performing on camera, dress as you would if you had been hired to deliver the commercial.
2. Try to understand and convey the impression the sponsor wants to create.
3. In handling props or pointing to signs or products, make your movements slow, deliberate, and economical.
4. If television equipment is available, try to simulate actual broadcast conditions.
5. Make sure you adhere scrupulously to the time limits of the commercial.
6. When appropriate, look directly into the camera lens, but don't stare.
7. In on-camera performance, practice switching smoothly from one camera to another on cue.
8. Do not do a parody or a burlesque of a commercial unless the assignment calls for it. There is no way to judge your ability to sell a product or a service if you turn your performance into a lampoon.
9. *Communicate!*

the pictures being seen by the viewers. This coordination is achieved through one of three production routines:

1. The announcer reads the script, and the pictures are timed to match the words in postproduction.
2. The visual portion of the commercial is shown on a monitor, and the announcer matches the words to the pictures.
3. The audiotaped performance is edited to match the pictures, again during postproduction.

In most instances the announcer is long gone before the commercial is completed, and perhaps may never see the finished product.

Some television commercials are produced in the field, with the announcer playing a visible role, as in the showing of furniture or automobiles in a showroom. To perform in this type of commercial, you have to memorize your lines or ad-lib from cue cards, and make a direct address to the camera. Although on-camera commercial delivery is rare, it is worth practicing. Elsewhere in this book, particularly in the chapters on performance, interviewing, and television news, many suggestions are offered for improving your on-camera performance. Nearly all these suggestions apply to on-camera commercial announcing.

In addition, the checklist presented in this section has some tips that apply to performing commercials in the classroom or studio.

As you deliver radio and television commercials, try to reflect your own personality. Some commercials call for a slow, relaxed delivery, others for a hard-sell approach; often sponsors will ask for a particular style of delivery. But appropriately changing pace, volume, and level of energy does not mean you have to transform yourself totally each time the style or mood of a commercial changes. If you do not maintain and project your own personality, you run the risk of sounding like an impersonator rather than a communicator.

Practice: Trying Accents and Character Voices

The commercial scripts that follow are offered for your practice. No suggestions on how to speak with an accent, dialect, or character voice are given because written instructions are of little or no help. Commercially prepared audiotapes are available featuring announcers performing a variety of character voices, as well as foreign-born speakers conversing in English. Your audiovisual department or learning resources center may very well stock some of these tapes. As you work with these scripts, make taped recordings and listen critically to the results. If you are not truly outstanding at doing a particular voice, abandon it in favor of others that you can do with authority.

The Pitchman

AGENCY: Client's Copy

CLIENT: Compesi's Meat Locker

LENGTH: 60 seconds

ANNCR: How would you like to save <u>dollars</u>, while serving

          your family the best in beef, pork, chicken, and

lamb? Sounds impossible? Well, it isn't, <u>if</u> you
own a home freezer and buy your meats wholesale
at Compesi's Meat Locker. Hundreds of families
have discovered that it actually costs less to
serve prime rib, steaks, and chops than it does
to scrimp along on bargain hamburger and tough
cuts. The secret? Buy your meat in quantity from
Compesi's. Imagine—one hundred pounds of prime
beef steaks and roasts for less than $2.00 a
pound! Save even more by purchasing a quarter or
a side. With every side of beef, Compesi's throws
in twenty pounds of chicken, ten pounds of bacon,
and a leg of spring lamb—absolutely free! If you
don't own a freezer, Compesi's will get you
started in style. Buy any of their 300-pound
freezers, and Compesi's will give you a <u>freezer</u>
<u>full</u> of <u>frozen</u> <u>food</u> <u>free</u>! Meat, vegetables, even
frozen gourmet casseroles, all free with the
purchase of a new freezer. Prices for freezers
start at $299, and terms can be arranged. Beat
the high cost of living! Come into Compesi's and
see which plan is best for your family. Compesi's
has two locations—in the Lakeport Shopping
Center, and downtown at 1338 Fifth Street.

The Wimp

AGENCY: Allen and Dorward
CLIENT: New Century Beverage Company

LENGTH: 60 seconds

ANNCR: Here is your one-minute wombat training lesson for today. The common wombat is an Australian marsupial. That means she carries her young in a pouch. She is powerful and tough and built like a fireplug. She has no tail, weighs up to eighty pounds, and loves to dig tunnels. Boring. The wombat can dig faster than a Hollywood reporter. Always keep your wombat off the grass. The first trick to teach her is "Keep off the grass." If she digs in, you may have to settle for a sunken garden. Stop the lesson and pour yourself a frosty, ice-cold Mug Old-Fashioned Root Beer. Mug Root Beer is the ideal drink for wombat trainers and former wombat trainers. Ice-cold Mug Old-Fashioned Root Beer. Regular or Diet. You haven't tasted root beer like this in years.

The He-Man

IN-HOUSE: Channel 7

TITLE: 3:30 Movie, Macho Men tease

MUSIC: MACHO HEAVY MUSIC

ANNCR: We're going to be tough on you this week on Channel 7's "3:30 Movie."

Yeah . . . it's those tough Macho Men beginning Monday and Tuesday when Rock Hudson and the Duke—John Wayne—star in "The Undefeated."

Wednesday, one of the toughest of them all, Charles Bronson, has Ursula Andress in his arms in "Red Sun." Thursday and Friday, Steve McQueen and Ali McGraw are up to their ears in stolen cash in "The Getaway." The Macho Men take over Monday on Channel 7's "3:30 Movie."

Low-Pitched Voice

IN—HOUSE: Channel 7

TITLE: 3:30 Movie, Creepy Creature Tease

AUDIO EFFECTS	COPY
(MUSIC: "THE DAY TIME ENDED")	Hello. Afraid of those creepy things that go bump in the
(STING ON "NIGHT")[2]	night? Well, I wouldn't watch Channel 7's "3:30 Movie," because we've got a whole week of creepy creatures.
	Monday, it's Ray Milland and his
(SFX: LOUD FROG)	giant (SFX) "Frogs." (SLIGHT PAUSE)
	Tuesday, Hank Fonda is all wrapped up in "Tentacles."
(SFX: MALE SCREAM)	(SFX)
	Wednesday, it's back to those old days, with prehistoric

[2]A **sting** (short for stinger) is a sharp musical chord used to highlight a transition or draw attention.

(SFX: ELEPHANT TRUMPET, BACKWARDS)

creatures in "The People Time Forgot."

Thursday, little gnomes (GUH-NOMES) are after a luscious young wife in "Don't Be Afraid of the Dark."

Finally, Friday—-if you haven't had enough—-it's a submarine full of snakes in "Fer-de-Lance."

(SFX: WOLF HOWL)

Creepy Creatures starts Monday on Channel 7's "3:30 Movie."

High-Pitched Voice

AGENCY: Annette Lai Creative Services

CLIENT: Allison's Pet Center

LENGTH: 60 seconds

MUSIC: INSTRUMENTAL VERSION OF "RUDOLPH, THE RED-NOSED REINDEER" UP AND UNDER TO CLOSE

ANNCR: (HIGH-PITCHED AND ELFLIKE) Hi! I'm Herman, one of Santa's helpers. Rudolph would have been here, too, but he's getting the light bulb in his nose replaced right now. We're inviting you to Allison's Pet Center for their annual and spectacular Christmas sale! Every year, kids send letters to Santa asking for puppies and kittens, monkeys and mice—-and, to top it off, some ask for aquariums, too! Can you imagine what the back of Santa's sleigh looks like? Come on, give Santa a break! I don't want to baby-sit all those animals and fishes until Christmas Eve——I want to go back to building dollhouses! Come to Allison's, and save on household pets, and presents for your pets. Get a head start on your Christmas shopping. The sale starts on Saturday, and runs through Christmas Eve. Allison's is located at the corner of Fulton and North Streets, in Petaluma. And, a Meow-y Christmas, and a Hoppy New Year from Allison's Pet Center!

Authoritative Voice

AGENCY: Post-U-Chair, Inc.

CLIENT: Post-U-Chair

LENGTH: 60 seconds

ANNCR: Orthopedic specialists will tell you that backaches are often the result of poor posture. Standing or sitting with the spine in a curved position can weaken muscles and cartilage and make you susceptible to backache and spinal injury. The Post-U-Chair has been designed to help avoid an unnatural curvature of your sacroiliac (SAK-RO-ILL'-EE-AK). Post-U-Chair and regular exercise can help prevent lumbago (LUM-

BAY'-GO), sciatica (SY-AT'-IK-UH), and other
aches and pains associated with back trouble. Of
course, Post-U-Chair can't do the job alone--
knowing the correct way to stand, walk, and lift
is important, too--but, Post-U-Chair can keep
your back in a straight line while resting,
reading, or watching television. Send for our
free booklet, "Caring for Your Back," and see how
the Post-U-Chair can combine with exercise and
common sense to give you a strong, trouble-free
back. Send a card to P.O. Box 333, Ames, Iowa,
and Post-U-Chair will send the booklet by return
mail.

Folksy-Country Accent

AGENCY: Ketchum Communications
CLIENT: CIBA-Geigy Corp.
LENGTH: 60 seconds

MUSIC: UP AND UNDER THROUGHOUT
ANNCR: Harvest time in sorghum country. The air is dry
         and dusty--thick with the smell of diesel. A
         combine pauses in a field of deep red sorghum,
         having gathered its first load of the day.
         This is the finest sorghum grown, kept clean and
         free of weeds and grasses with Bicep herbicide
         and Concep II safened seed--the most cost-

effective weed control program available.
Concep II provides the protective shield for
young sorghum. Bicep provides the tough control
of weeds and grasses--like pigweed, crabgrass,
signal grass and barnyard grass. Nothing works
better. Nothing lasts longer. So you get nothing
but sorghum--with no danger to crops, no tank
mixing, and no broadleaf weeds or grasses--a
clean, healthy harvest. With Bicep and Concep II,
sorghum growers' first choice for cleaner, more
profitable sorghum.

Southern Accent

AGENCY:	McDonald & Little Advertising
CLIENT:	McDonald's
PRODUCT:	Egg McMuffin
TITLE:	"Breakfast Is a Big Thing"

ANNCR: You know, down in Willacoochee where I hail from
          breakfast is a big thing with grits and fried
          steak of lean and all, but the other day I had a
          different kind of breakfast. I went to a
          McDonald's store. It was right after 7 in the
          morning, and they were cooking breakfast like I
          never saw. They take this muffin, it's not like
          biscuits, I suppose it's what people over in
          England sop syrup with, cause it's called an

English muffin. But they take this foreign muffin
and heat it up, and flat dab on it they put a
yard egg, and this bacon that's more like ham,
but they call it Canadian bacon. And right there
on top of all of it they put a piece of cheese.
And I'm telling you that it sure is mighty
delicious. I never did have a breakfast before
that you could hold in your hand. But that would
get kinda messy with grits.

New York Accent

CLIENT: Sol's Deli[3]

LENGTH: 60 seconds

MUSIC: INSTRUMENTAL FROM "FIDDLER ON THE ROOF"

ANNCR: Ah ha, it's a New York flavor in music . . . and
at Sol's you'll get the true New York flavor in
deli. How can the true taste be transferred to
Omaha? It's simple. You just serve true Eastern
beef, cured and pickled to Sol's unmatched
palate, and sliced to your order. Of course,
there's hot New York corned beef . . . hot
pastrami . . . Hebrew National salami and baloney
. . . lox . . . bagels . . . and much much more--
all with Sol's taste buds controlling the taste
that has not been in Omaha until now. At Sol's

[3]Script courtesy of Gerry Sher, Accounts Executive, KABL Radio.

when you taste the kosher pickles and the sour
tomatoes you'll remember those days. How about a
knish—-potato, kasha, or beef? If you've never
had a Sol's knish, then you're in for a gourmet's
delight. Actually, Sol's wife makes them, but
where would Sol be without her anyway . . . Mrs.
Sol also makes the matzo ball soup, the borscht,
and the change. Sol's isn't easy to find . . .
but it's worth the look. To find Sol's, first
find the Flatiron Building, and there,
practically in its shadow on Oak Street, is Sol's
. . . actually, it's next to Logan's Irish Pub.
Sol's—-777 Oak Street . . . A New York tradition
in Omaha.

British Accent (Oxford)

AGENCY: Ammirati & Puris, Inc.

CLIENT: Schweppes

LENGTH: 60 seconds

MUSIC: BRITISH MARCHING MUSIC UNDER

ANNCR: For many years it seemed, if there were a place
in the world far too hot and altogether too
sunny, then we British would inevitably make it a
part of our empire. In fact, we practically
cornered the market on deserts. Making us, if not
enormously wealthy, enormously thirsty. Thus

creating a brisk demand for Schweppes Tonic
Water, the great British bubbly. From the parched
outback of Australia, where thirst-crazed kiwi
hunters virtually subsisted on Schweppes Tonic
Water. To the Saharan Tungsten Mines, where we
British would gratefully relish its cheeky little
bubbles. To the Manchurian Gobi Desert, where
plucky yak traders would linger over its savory
taste of lemons and Seville oranges. Schweppes
Tonic Water turned out to be just the thing.
So refreshing and Schweppervescent. So
thirst-quenching, that even after we gave back
all those blasted deserts, we British still
thoroughly enjoy Schweppes Tonic Water. The great
British bubbly.

British Accent (Cockney)

AGENCY: Ammirati & Puris, Inc.

CLIENT: Schweppes Ginger Ale

LENGTH: 60 seconds

MUSIC: GUITAR MUSIC AND TUNING UP UNDER VOICE

COCKNEY: Years ago, if a fellow gargled with floor
            sweepings, he'd be called crazy. But today, it's
            just one of the things we've got to do to be
            heavy metal stars here in England. In fact, we
            scream our flippin' lungs out. Makes us awfully

parched and thirsty. Which is why me and the
boys, the Sleeze-Hunks, keep a lot of Schweppes
Ginger Ale on stage. You see, for all our
obscene wealth, there's still nothing like
Schweppes Ginger Ale's cheeky little bubbles and
thirst-quenching Schweppervescence to make sure
our voices don't crack and the windows do.
(LAUGH) Here, take this little ditty we whipped
up, for instance:
(MUSIC, HE SINGS)

> "Coat-check woman--You make me sore!
> When I got back, I found my coat on the
> floor!"

See what I mean? Totally taxing to the old vocal
cords. Not to mention thirst-building. So it's no
wonder this Schweppes Ginger Ale, made with real
Jamaican ginger, is so popular with us Brits. I
like it so much, I had my hair dyed that lovely
green on the label. (LAUGH)

ANNCR: Schweppes Ginger Ale. The great British bubbly.

Transylvanian Accent

AGENCY: Scott Singer
CLIENT: Partytime Novelties
LENGTH: 30 seconds

(SCARY MUSIC) (BELA LUGOSI IMITATION) Good
evening. You are probably expecting me to say

that my name is Count Dracula, and that I am a vampire. Do you know what makes a vampire? Do you . . . really? It's not the hair--bah! greasy kid's stuff! It's not the cape, made from your sister's satin bed sheets. No! It is the fangs that make the vampire. Now, you too can have the fangs. Dress up for parties--frighten the trick-or-treaters on Halloween. These plastic marvels fit over your regular teeth, but once there-- you'll be the hit of the party. Amaze and delight your ghoul friend. It is so much fun! I know. So, send for your fangs today. Send $2.98 to "FANG," Box 1001, Central City, Tennessee. Or dial toll-free: 800-DRA-CULA. Order before midnight tonight. That's an order!

Spanish Pronunciation

AGENCY: Miller and Stein, Advertising
CLIENT: Su Casa
LENGTH: 60 seconds

MUSIC: MEXICAN HARP, UPBEAT TEMPO, IN AND UNDER TO CLOSE
ANNCR: Ole, Amigos! (OH-LAY' AH-MEE'-GOS) Su Casa (SOO-KAH'-SAH) means "your home," and that's what Ramona wants you to feel when you visit her at San Antonio's most elegant Mexican restaurant. Su Casa. Ramona features the most popular dishes

from Mexico, including enchiladas verde or
rancheros (EN-CHIL-AH'-DAS VEHR'-DAY or RAHN-
CHER'-OHS), chile con queso (CHEE'-LAY KAHN KAY'-
SO), and chimichangos (CHEE'-MEE-CHANG'-GOS).
But, Ramona also has special family recipes that
you won't find anywhere else. Try Pescado en
Concha (PES-KAH'-DO EN COHN'-CHAH), chunks of
sole in a rich cream and cheddar cheese sauce,
served in scallop shells. Or Scallops La Jolla
(LAH-HOY'-UH), prepared with wine, lemon juice,
and three kinds of cheeses. Or Baked Swordfish
Manzanillo (MAHN-ZAH-NEE'-OH). See Ramona today,
where _her_ home is _your_ home. Su Casa!

German Accent

The two award-winning commercials that follow feature Dieter
(DEET'-ER), a German imported car salesman. These commercials
were improvised, so the scripts were actually typed after the fact.[4]

AGENCY:	Young & Rubicam
CLIENT:	Lincoln-Mercury Dealers
LENGTH:	60 seconds
TITLE:	"Dieter 5"

DIETER:	Pull over and help me, please, my car is . . . .
WEAVER:	Hi, Dieter.
DIETER:	Hello, Mr. Weaver.

[4]The three Lincoln-Mercury commercials presented here were supplied by their
creator, Gene Chaput, of Young & Rubicam.

WEAVER: Having a little trouble with that fine European
           sedan, huh?

DIETER: Having a little lunch.

WEAVER: Yeah, the hood's up.

DIETER: Heating my bratwurst on the engine block.

WEAVER: It must be done; it's smoking.

DIETER: It's smoked bratwurst.

WEAVER: Hmm, some kind of hot purple liquid's dripping
           out of there.

DIETER: Smoked fruit punch.

WEAVER: Uh huh, you know I haven't had any trouble since
           I traded in that car you sold me for this Mercury
           Cougar, Dieter.

DIETER: Mercury Cougar, it's a very fine car.

WEAVER: Oh, it's a lovely car, Dieter.

DIETER: Could you give me a ride in the Mercury Cougar to
           the mechanical?

WEAVER: Oh, I want to give you more than a ride, Dieter.
           I want to give you a push.

DIETER: I don't want a push.

WEAVER: Get in the car, Dieter.

DIETER: My car is moving.

WEAVER: Turn the flashers on. I want people to see this.

DIETER: Let me get in there.

WEAVER: Clear the way.

DIETER: (LOUDLY, OUT THE CAR WINDOW) He's not pushing me
           . . . I'm pulling him!

ANNCR: The Mercury Cougar. Compare the performance with luxury European imports. Compare the styling with the luxury European imports. Even before you compare the price.

WEAVER: Okay, Dieter, you're on your own.

DIETER: Wait, this isn't a service station; it's a Lincoln—Mercury dealership.

WEAVER: Think about it, Dieter.

ANNCR: The Mercury Cougar. See your Lincoln—Mercury dealer today, at the sign of the cat.

AGENCY: Young and Rubicam

CLIENT: Lincoln—Mercury Dealers

LENGTH: 30 seconds

TITLE: "Dieter/Law"

DIETER: Mr. Weaver, I have something for you.

WEAVER: What is this, Dieter, a flyer? Are you having a sale?

DIETER: It's a subpoena. I'm suing you.

WEAVER: Suing me? For what?

DIETER: I'm no longer just Dieter Eidotter, car salesman. You're dealing with Dieter Eidotter, third week law student.

WEAVER: What is this? "Defamation of car"?

DIETER: You told people that the Mercury Cougar was better looking than the car I sell.

WEAVER: It's a fact.

DIETER: It's an opinion.

WEAVER: "Alienation of affection"?

DIETER: Well, the people who found out that the Mercury Cougar costs one-half as much as the car I sell don't come into the showroom anymore.

WEAVER: You're blowing more smoke than one of those diesels you sell.

DIETER: Oh, now you're into the murky legal area of libel, and slander, and torts.

WEAVER: What's a tort?

DIETER: Well, right now, it's a chocolate cake. But when I find out what it is . . .

WEAVER: You're not even a real lawyer. I don't have to put up with this. Here is what I think of this thing, right back at you!

DIETER: This could be second-degree littering, Mister.

ANNCR: The Mercury advantage. Compared to the imports, Mercury gives you more style, more features, more for your money. See your Lincoln-Mercury dealer.

Swedish Accent

AGENCY: Young & Rubicam

CLIENT: Lincoln-Mercury Dealers

LENGTH: 60 seconds

```
   TITLE:   "Swedish Designers"

INTERVW:    I'm with the crack Swedish design team of . . .
   NILS:    Nils.
INGEMAR:    I'm Ingemar.
INTERVW:    Apparently you gentlemen specialize in the design
            of station wagons for the American market.
   NILS:    Yes, the boxy . . .
INGEMAR:    Square ones . . .
INVERVW:    On purpose?
   NILS:    Dumpy . . . Oh sure, yes.
INGEMAR:    To punish the wife!
INTERVW:    Punish the wife?
   NILS:    Yes, because the husband wants to keep her at
            home, you know.
INGEMAR:    That's right, she's embarrassed to be seen in an
            ugly car like that, you know. The Mercury Sable,
            on the total other hand . . .
INTERVW:    The Mercury Sable?
INGEMAR:    It's got them swoopey-doopey lines.
   NILS:    Very pretty car, you know.
INGEMAR:    Once the wife gets inside, she don't look back.
   NILS:    No, she just drop him at the train and just keep
            going all the way the other direction.
  ANNCR:    The Mercury Sable wagon.
INTERVW:    We noticed that even your lowest-priced wagon
            sells for more than the Mercury Sable wagon in
```

America. Must be very profitable for you guys,
though.

INGEMAR: You kidding me?

NILS: We make a lot of money; look at these boots.

INGEMAR: Yeah, you got a closet that turn into a sauna at
the flick of a switch? We have one.

NILS: You get Ludefisk two, three times a day?

INTERVW: No.

ANNCR: Before you get yourself in a box, see the Mercury
Sable wagon. Now with special factory cash
incentives. The Mercury Sable wagon looks better
than ever. Visit your Lincoln—Mercury dealer.
It's worth it!

Practice: Delivering Radio Commercials and PSAs

Appendix A offers a number of commercial and PSA scripts as well
as several fact sheets. These materials provide practice with most of
the types of commercials and PSAs heard on radio today. You are
encouraged to find additional practice material and to write some of
your own. Fact sheets should be used for ad-lib practice, but you can
also write and record commercials based on the fact sheets found in
Appendix A.

Practice: Delivering Television Commercials

Because television commercials usually involve elaborate visual effects, students of announcing have difficulty finding opportunities for

realistic practice. Appendix A provides many radio scripts and a few television scripts. Some of the practice commercials call for animation, film inserts, or properties that may not be available. There is no ideal way of working with such commercials, but they are included here because they form a large part of broadcast commercials today and it would be unrealistic to exclude them. You can adapt some of the radio scripts for television performance, but you will generally be limited to a straight, on-camera presentation.

The following exercises should make it possible for you to achieve satisfactory results with a minimum of production support.

1. Practice on-camera delivery with some of the simple presentational commercials included in Appendix A. Use demonstration commercials and those incorporating **studio cards** or one or two slides instead of those that involve elaborate production. Work for exact timing as well as camera presence. Practice with cue cards or a prompting device.
2. Prepare slides and adapt a 30-second or 60-second radio commercial for voice-over presentation. Practice synchronizing your off-camera delivery with the visual images as they appear on the screen.
3. Videotape commercials currently being broadcast. Write out a script of the spoken portions of each commercial. Then, with the sound turned off, run the tape and practice voice-over delivery.
4. Produce a demonstration commercial with one person on-camera while you are off-camera, delivering the voice-over narration.

Practice: Producing Your Own Commercial

Ask a local merchant—the owner of an independently owned small grocery store, a restaurant, a flower shop, or a gift shop, for example— if he or she will help you fulfill a class assignment. Make sure that the merchant does not think that you have something to sell. Take with you a note pad on which to write basic information about something the merchant would want to promote if he or she were going to have commercials written, produced, and broadcast. Prepare one or more commercials based on the fact sheet, and return to get the reactions of the merchant.

8 ▮ ▮ ▮ ▮ ▮ ▮ ▮

Interview and Talk Programs

The word *interview* comes from the French and means, roughly, "to see one another." Interviews fill a great many hours of every broadcast day. Some are brief, such as a 10-second actuality or sound bite on a news broadcast.[1] Others are longer and constitute the substance of hour-long talk programs. Interviewing eyewitnesses and spokespersons at the scene of a fire, an airplane crash, or a similar event for a news broadcast is only a minor aspect of the news-gathering responsibilities of reporters; on the other hand, conducting interviews is the chief activity of hosts of talk and interview shows. Interviewing for news broadcasts is discussed in Chapters 9 and 10. This chapter is devoted to practices and techniques appropriate to radio call-in shows, television interview programs, and community affairs programs.

Some interviews are essentially question-and-answer sessions, often with controversial guests; others are low-key conversations. The difference is in technique, and technique is determined by purpose. Every interview has a purpose, and it is important to determine that purpose before beginning an interview. Some interviews, for example, those with outstanding storytellers, are intended to entertain, so your approach should be lighthearted. When interviewing a gifted teller of anecdotes, you should be prepared to let the guest relate humorous or otherwise entertaining stories with little interruption. In interviews with writers who have a book to promote, your aim should be to provide your audience with enough information about the book to form a decision as to its purchase; at the same time, you must keep the interview from becoming merely a puff piece for the author. Interviews on serious societal problems should be geared to providing useful information on critical issues and should be approached with a

---

[1] **Actuality** is the radio term for a brief report featuring someone other than station personnel. **Sound bite** is the television term for the same feature.

serious, but not somber, attitude. Establishing the purpose of an interview before starting it is one of the most important decisions you can make as a talk show host.[2]

Talk programs are important features of American broadcasting. Although television makes almost exclusive use of studio guests for such programs and radio utilizes both guests and telephone callers, the two media are alike in that the key to success is the interviewing ability of the program host. The intimacy of talk shows makes them naturals for radio and television. Also, they present contemporary issues, are entertaining and informative, offer variety, and often directly involve listeners or viewers. They are inexpensive to produce and require a minimum of preparation time.

Jobs as talk show hosts are not numerous, but they are rewarding and challenging. You may or may not succeed in having your own talk show, but the skills you acquire as you work toward that goal will be useful to you in a range of announcing specializations. Some of those skills can be practiced; others cannot. You can practice interviewing, discussing music, sports reporting, commercial delivery, and news reporting—all of which will help you become competent as a talk show host—but the true measure of your effectiveness will be how well you can put it all together on a live broadcast. Talk show hosts are among the few announcers whose auditions usually coincide with their first air experience in that capacity. You may not be able to practice in an integrated way all the skills you need for the job, but you can study the practices and procedures you would encounter if you were to work as a radio or television talk show host.

Principles of Effective Interviewing

Avoiding Abstraction and Bias

Two fundamental aspects of interviewing affect every interviewer's approach. The first concerns what semanticist S. I. Hayakawa calls the "ladder of abstraction." This refers to the fact that several terms are usually available for the same phenomenon, and some are precise and some general. Take, for example, *food*, *fruit*, and *apple*. An apple is a specific fruit and is also a food, so all three terms are accurate.

[2]The term *host* is now customarily used to identify both males and females who perform as interviewers on talk shows. *Hostess* is no longer necessary or appropriate when identifying a female host.

Figure 8.1
Called one of the best interviewers on television, Larry King is well-known for his thought-provoking questions to famous politicians, artists, and thinkers. (Courtesy of Turner Broadcasting System)

The term *food* is a high-level abstraction; *fruit* is below it on the ladder; *apple* is quite specific and is, therefore, at the lowest rung on the ladder. Some interviewees consistently speak at a level that is high on the ladder of abstraction; that is, they consistently use vague and general terms rather than precise ones. It is up to you as the interviewer to "pull" such guests down the ladder of abstraction, when appropriate. For example, consider this exchange:

> ANNCR: And just what does the administration intend to do about the problems of the inner cities?
>
> GUEST: We're extremely aware of the seriousness of the situation. We feel that the development of human resources in our cities must come before we can expect to overcome the problems of the physical environment.

What this guest is saying in an abstract way is quite simple: we need to find jobs for people before we can hope to clean up and rebuild. The interviewer's problem is to find a way to get the guest to say this in clear, specific language. One approach is to ask directly for clarification of terms:

> ANNCR: And just what do you mean by "the development of human resources"?

A later question would steer the guest toward an explanation of the phrase "the problems of the physical environment."

The second basic consideration for any interviewer is that of bias. When interviewing a person on a controversial or extremely important subject, one has a natural tendency to accept without question comments that one agrees with. This is not a problem when the unsubstantiated statement is a matter of common knowledge or of record, as in this example:

> ANNCR: How do today's students compare with students of twenty years ago?
> GUEST: Well, standardized test scores of college-bound seniors have fallen pretty regularly over the past two decades.

On the other hand, statements by a guest may be opinions or theories:

> ANNCR: And how do you explain the drop?
> GUEST: Television viewing is the primary culprit.

Assume that you believe this. As a responsible interviewer, you have an obligation to ask further questions to bring out any factual evidence that may have led your guest to the conclusion reached. Probing may reveal that the statement is based on hard fact—or that it is simply an unsubstantiated hunch. Whatever the outcome, you owe it to your listeners to question undocumented assertions.

Figure 8.2
Food and wine expert Harvey Steiman works with host Al Hart on the "KCBS Kitchen." Callers ask questions about food preparation, restaurant recommendations, and wine vintages. (Courtesy of Harvey Steiman and KCBS Radio, San Francisco)

Tips for Conducting Successful Interviews

Ernie Kreiling, a syndicated television columnist, has compiled a list
of dos and don'ts that are especially helpful to radio or television talk
show interviewers. These suggestions provide an excellent framework
for discussing interviewing and are therefore used as subheads in this
section. You need not memorize these points or follow them reli-
giously. Think about them and work them into your practice where
appropriate. It is also helpful to refer to them after each interview.

Note that the tips cover three general areas: the first group concerns the guest (interviewee), the second the topic to be covered, and
the third the interviewer's strategy and contributions.

*Carefully research the guest's background, accomplishments, atti-
tudes, beliefs, and positions*   You will generally know from one to
several days in advance who your guest will be, so you will have enough
time to do some research. If your guest has written a book, and if the
interview is to focus on it, obviously you should read the book, make
notes, and read some reviews. Among the many sources of information
about well-known persons and important topics are *Who's Who* (in
politics, in education, in medicine, and so on), the *Europa Yearbook*,
the *Book of the States*, and the *Municipal Yearbook*. You can find
articles by checking the listings in the *Reader's Guide to Periodical
Literature* and the *New York Times Index*. Many radio and television
stations have access to computerized data banks that will provide
information on nearly anyone of importance. If your guest is not a
person of national prominence, you may find background information
through local newspapers, libraries, or chambers of commerce. If your
guest has been scheduled by a booking agent, you will be provided
with a press kit containing useful information.

When time and circumstances permit, researching your guest's
background is as important as all other factors combined. No amount
of style, personality, smooth performance, or perfect timing can compensate for a lack of such knowledge.

*During the interview, listen attentively to the guest's replies and react
with appropriate interest*   Next to preparation, this is the most important aspect discussed in this section. If you do not listen carefully,
you will certainly fail to follow up important statements with appropriate questions. Also, do not feign interest. If your interest is not
genuine, you are either conducting a bad interview or not listening to
your guest's responses.

Make the guest feel at home   Introduce your guests to studio and control room personnel when it is convenient. Show your guests the area where the interview will take place and give them an idea of what is going to happen. Such hospitality should help relax your guests and induce them to be cooperative. With **seasoned guests** (people used to being interviewed), you can plunge right into the interview. With inexperienced interviewees, it helps to spend a few minutes explaining how you will conduct the interview and what you expect of them.

Do not submit questions in advance, unless you would lose an important interview by refusing to do so   Hostile guests and some politicians may ask you to submit your questions in advance. This is a bad practice, for spontaneity demands that guests not rehearse their answers. On the other hand, it is good practice to let an interviewee know the general areas to be covered. To help relax an inexperienced guest, you might even reveal your first question slightly in advance.

There is one exception to this rule: if you are going to ask a guest for his or her most interesting, funniest, or most unusual experience, advance notice will provide time for reflection. Most interviewees draw a blank when asked such a question abruptly, but a little advance notice may make the answer the highlight of the interview.

Never refer to conversations held before air time   Ideally, you will have an opportunity to chat with your guest before air time, and this will help you determine areas of questioning, the general mood you want to establish, and other matters of importance. At the same time, an audience will feel excluded by a question such as "Well, Pat, I'm sure the folks would find interesting that new hobby you were telling me about just before we went on the air. Will you tell them about it?" Listeners or viewers want to feel in on the interview, not as if most of it has already taken place.

Establish the guest's credentials at the start of the interview   Station personnel have usually selected guests because they believe them to be knowledgeable and responsible; the audience should know how and why they are qualified to speak on a particular subject. The significance of a partisan statement about heart transplants differs depending on whether it is made by a heart surgeon, religious leader, heart recipient, or politician. One opinion is not necessarily better or more newsworthy than another, but your audience must be aware of the specific credentials of the speaker in order to assess statements in a meaningful way.

Occasionally and indirectly re-establish the guest's name and credentials   On television guests are identified periodically with **supers** at the bottom of the screen. It is also customary to mention a guest's name when breaking for a commercial—"We'll be back with Annie LaMott right after these messages." On radio, of course, reminders must be done orally, and, because listeners cannot see the guest, frequent reintroductions are essential. Because the television audience can see a guest, reintroductions are unnecessary if the guest is well known.

Seek out a guest's deep convictions   Do not settle for mentally rehearsed platitudes and clichés. Probing usually means that you must reveal something of yourself. Your guest is not likely to open up unless you do.

Be tenacious   Do not be put off with evasive answers. Keep probing until you see that you cannot get any further. Then drop the line of questioning and turn to something else.

Do not interrupt with meaningless comments   "I see," "Uh huh," "Oh, yes," and "That's very interesting" add nothing to an interview and actually detract from what your guest is saying. All announcers should cure themselves of the habit of using vocal reinforcement as they interview. Practice giving nonverbal reinforcement—a smile or a nod of the head—and work to eliminate voiced encouragement. At the same time, because a good interview frequently is a conversation, do not be afraid to make meaningful responses that are appropriate to the interchange, such as "I can't believe you didn't know about your nomination."

There is a practical reason for not peppering an interview with "uh huhs." Some interviews are intended for editing (usually for newscasts or documentaries), and the words of the interviewer will be edited out and replaced with narration. You always will know in advance whether or not an interview will be edited, so you will be able to differentiate between times when interjections are acceptable and times when they are not. The nature of the interview will determine the extent to which you should speak up.

Do not patronize your guest, and do not be obsequious   Avoid phrases such as "I'm sure our viewers would like to know" and "Do you mind if I ask?" Some people are reluctant or hostile, to be sure, but most have come to be interviewed and need no coddling.

Keep cool Interviewing is your specialization, and you should feel at ease. Your guest may be a stranger to the interviewing situation and may be awed by the equipment, a bit afraid of you, and worried about saying something wrong. If you fail to remain calm or are distracted by the signals of floor managers or others, you will only rattle your guest further.

Discuss the subject with the guest Do not cross-examine or otherwise bully guests. Because they may be nervous, it is up to you, no matter how much you may dislike or disagree with them, to put them at ease. If you show hostility, unfairness, or lack of common hospitality, both your guests and your audience will resent it.

There are, to be sure, a few talk show hosts who make it a practice to bully their guests and who thrive on dissension. Several such hosts have appeared in the last few years, giving rise to the term **trash television** to describe their efforts. These hosts are willing to ask any question, however tasteless, and to make any statement, however outrageous. You should always remember that viewers or listeners do not see a talk show host as an actor, playing a role; to them your role is the real you. If you value your reputation, you will treat guests with respect.

Remember that the guest is the star Very rarely is the interviewer of more interest to the audience than the guest. One famous wit and raconteur consistently upstaged his guests, and the audience loved it. In general, however, dominating an interview is not only contrary to the purpose, which is drawing the guest out, but also simply rude.

Remember that the guest is the expert At times, of course, you will be an authority on the subject under discussion and will be able to debate it with your guest. In most cases, though, your guest will be the expert. (But also keep in mind the next tip.)

Keep control of the interview Experienced interviewers, particularly politicians, can take over and use an interview for their own purposes. Keep the questions coming so that guests do not have time to digress from the subject or the opportunity to indulge in speechmaking.

On television, do not have the guest address the camera The most effective television interviews give the illusion that the two participants are so absorbed in their conversation that the camera is eavesdropping.

At the conclusion of the interview, thank the guest warmly but briefly Do not be effusive. Move on quickly to your concluding comments.

Spotlight: Talk-Radio Guru Bruce Williams

It's early evening at NBC Radio's Talknet studios in Manhattan, and Bruce Williams is ready to talk. He leans back in a red leather chair, his antelope cowboy boots propped up on a desk, and reaches for his customary can of diet Coke. "Hey Pittsburgh, what's on your mind?" asks Williams as he commences his three-hour call-in radio show.

A sweet-voiced woman, fresh out of college, wants Williams to help her manage her finances. "Don't go out and buy a lot of expensive furniture," he advises. "What you thought was cool at 21, you wouldn't want to put in front of your house at 30 because people might think you *liked* that stuff!" Next on is a 33-year-old woman who fears she is being discriminated against in an office full of men. "The only way you won't be discriminated against is if you ask for no concessions," says Williams. "In the meantime, you've got to outwork them."

Every weekday night, the avuncular, reassuring tones of Bruce Williams draw some 3 million advice seekers in all 50 states to the radio. Williams, 57, commands the largest talk show audience in the country.

Most nights Williams dispenses advice on financial topics ranging from mortgages to liability suits, but he has coolly tackled such disparate subjects as suicide, prisoners' problems and kids' conflicts with their parents. Indeed, as he once said, he'll talk about "everything but wine and sex." Williams' guileless approach has been so successful that he has created a cottage industry around the show. He does at least 40 personal appearances a year where fans flock to hear him hold forth on investing in the stock market, drawing up a will or avoiding being fleeced by sleazy salesmen. There are Bruce Williams instructional tapes, and a second book filled with Williams's folksy wisdom is due out later this year. He owns several businesses, including flower and gift shops, two radio stations and a barbershop, and lends his name to ads for banks and other products. Williams does not think his endorsements compromise his credibility as a consumer adviser. "Radio is a commerical enterprise," he says. "If I thought the endorsements were damaging, I wouldn't do them."

But Williams's first concern is still the person on the other end of the line during his immensely popular show. "Nothing on your mind? That's cool," he says to his audience in a soft voice. "Just sit back and eavesdrop." If you do manage to get him on the phone (only one of every 15 callers gets on the air), don't expect to be coddled. "Look, it's a conversation between two people," says Williams. "It's not a professional counseling session where I'm gonna puff on a briar pipe and say, 'Tell me more.' It's not only what you say; the inflection in your voice has to leave no doubt that you agree or disagree with the listener."

On the rare occasions when Williams is stumped by a request, his listeners often help each other out. A caller in L.A. who once wrote a book about Jerry Lee Lewis lost all the copies of a Lewis biography in a fire and couldn't find his own book anywhere. "Ten minutes later," remembers Williams, "one of the major collectors of Jerry Lee Lewis memorabilia calls and says he has a copy that he would mail to the guy." A woman wanted to know what a medal from the 1890s, which she found in her backyard, was worth. A distant relative of the decorated soldier who received the badge of honor dialed 800-TALK-NET and said she knew something about it.

Williams's greatest resources are common sense and a keen mind. His appeal lies mainly in the fact that he is a Regular Guy and not some rarefied financial expert. He doesn't have an M.B.A. or a journalism background, and he says he never prepares for a show. He does read the *Wall Street Journal*, but he is proud to point out, "I also read the local weekly in Franklin Township, N.J."

Williams describes himself as a hustler growing up in East Orange, N.J. His father had a profitable shoe salon in New York City and "made a considerable amount of money" until the Depression. "He worked hard but never recovered financially," says Williams. The younger of two boys, Williams became a businessman himself at age 11 when, toward the end of World War II, he began making his own toy soldiers and selling them. "I used to melt down lead pipe in the coal furnace in the basement, cast the soldiers and dip 'em in olive drab paint," he says.

In 1951, after attending New Jersey's Upsala College for a semester, Williams joined the Air Force. He saw action in Korea, served a total of four years there and in the U.S. and then returned to New Jersey to earn a degree in education at Kean College. In 1957 he married Ruthann Burns. Four years later they started a private kindergarten called Lane Robbins in Somerset, N.J., and raised their own five children in the same community.

Williams was on the Franklin Township council from 1967 to 1975, served as Mayor for a year, and, after an unsuccessful bid for the state assembly, he decided to try working behind a microphone.

Bruce Williams (Photo by Michael A. Smith/*People Weekly*/The Times Inc. Magazine Co.)

His first radio show, *At Your Service*, in New Brunswick, N.J., became a local hit. A year later he set his sights on New York City and began "assaulting" WMCA with letters and phone calls. After two years, Williams reports, "this guy calls and says, 'Christ, I'm so tired of seeing these messages on my desk. Would you be willing to work on a Sunday afternoon?' I said, 'Done.'"

The response was so overwhelming that the station asked him to work six days a week, and in 1981 Williams was hired away by Talknet, which is a nightly package of advice-oriented talk shows. Today he earns a salary which is "a good deal more than minimum wage" but nowhere near the $2.6 million-a-year figure he has seen reported. "You gotta be kidding me," he says with a laugh.

Source: Abridged from an article in *People Weekly*, "Radio Guru Bruce Williams Offers Soothing Advice On-Air," by Andrew Abrahams, 9 October 1989, pp. 119–122. Reprinted with permission.

Be sure the subject to be discussed is of interest or importance
Although a dull guest can make even the most exciting subject boring, an interview always benefits if the topic itself is truly interesting or important.

When practicing interviewing as a student, do not settle for the most readily obtainable guest. Interviews with parents, siblings, classmates, and others you know well are seldom of interest to anyone, the participants included. A special energy is generated when you interview people who are strangers to you, and an even greater intensity develops when you interview people of real accomplishment.

Where appropriate, limit the number of topics discussed so that they can be discussed in depth   Depending on the intended length of the interview, it is best to explore only as many topics as can be dealt with in some depth. The least interesting interviews are those that randomly skim the surface of one topic after another.

Establish the importance of the topic   Topics that are obviously noteworthy need no special buildup, but others may require brief amplification. People are interested in almost anything that directly affects them, so your interview will increase in significance if you can establish its relevance to your listeners or viewers. One simple way of doing this is to ask your guest early in the session why the issue is important.

Write out, or at least make notes on, the introduction and conclusion   Writing out or outlining the beginning and ending of an interview will free you during air time to focus on its body. Note, however, that unless you are able to read your opening and closing in a totally conversational manner, the shift from reading to ad-lib speaking will be quite noticeable. In most instances the conclusion should include a summary of important or interesting information revealed during the interview; this cannot, of course, be written in advance, but your prepared conclusion can indicate the point at which you will ad-lib this summary.

Try to build an interview toward a high point or climax   Hold back an especially interesting or provocative question until near the end of the interview. If your skill allows you to lead up to that question, so much the better. Be on guard, however, against springing an important question too late; it is unacceptable to abruptly cut off the answer to a significant question because you have run out of time.

Plan at least a few questions to get the interview started and to fill awkward gaps Few sights are more pathetic than an interviewer at a loss for a question. (Note the next tip, however.)

In general, base questions on the guest's previous statements Do not hesitate to dispense with preplanned questions if more interesting ones arise naturally from the discussion. The following dialogue is an exaggerated example of failure to switch to a new topic.

> ANNCR: Now, Mayor, your opponent has charged you with a willful and illegal conflict of interest in the city's purchase of the new park. What is your answer?
>
> MAYOR: Well, it hasn't been revealed yet, but I have evidence that my opponent is a parole violator from out of state who served five years as a common purse-snatcher.
>
> ANNCR: The *News-Democrat* claims to have copies of the deeds of sale and is ready to ask for your resignation. Will you tell us your side of the story on the park purchase?

Clinging to a predetermined question when a far more important topic clamors for recognition may result from insensitivity, rigidity, or inattention to your guest's answers. In assessing taped practice interviews, be on the alert for moments when you have sacrificed interest or effectiveness to a previously determined plan. Have a plan, but do not be a slave to it.

In particular, follow up on important contradictions Public figures, especially politicians, often make contradictory statements that can be developed into good dialogue. Be wary, however; if you perceive that your guest is going to be evasive, adopt another line of questioning.

Make logical, smooth transitions to new subjects Here is a bad example of making a transition:

> ANNCR: You said a few moments ago that your most memorable experience was the time you nearly drowned. Are you into any other sports besides swimming?

Always be ready with your next question, but do not allow this to distract you from the comments your guest is making Be prepared to alter your plan on the basis of an unexpected answer, but don't be caught with no question at all in mind. The problem of thinking ahead to the next question without tuning out the present can be solved only with practice and experience.

On television, check your notes openly, rather than furtively There is no reason to try to hide your notes; their use does not in any way detract from a good discussion.

Make questions brief and to the point, but do not be rude or brusque Do not be afraid to ask more detailed questions when the circumstances warrant, but avoid rambling questions such as the following:

> ANNCR: Pat, I remember when you won the Academy Award for *Broken Hearts*—that was '84, I believe—and at that time you said you wanted to give up motion picture directing and do something on the Broadway stage. That's when you got involved in directing a modern-dress version of *Uncle Tom's Cabin*, and I guess they'll never let you forget that disaster. Well, looking back, is there any one moment you consider to be the turning point in your career? Any moment when you should have done something other than what you did?
>
> PAT: Z-z-z-z-z-z . . .

Don't ask questions that invite yes or no answers Try instead to draw your guest into an amplified response. Here is an example of phrasing to avoid:

> ANNCR: Are you working on a book now?
> AUTHOR: Yes.

This is a better way of asking essentially the same question:

> ANNCR: Tell me about the present. Are you working on a book an article, or what?

Even if the author were not writing at the time, it would be impossible to respond to this question with a simple yes or no. If your guest *does* answer yes or no, and the point is of significance, ask for an explanation of the response.

Ask questions a layperson would ask Don't be afraid to ask some questions that are fundamental. Most of your listeners will need basic information on the topic. (However, see the next point.)

Go a step further, and ask interesting questions most laypersons would not think of The outstanding interviewer will bring out information that members of the audience want but do not know that they want.

Avoid obvious questions For example, do not ask a famous baseball player, "You were a baseball player, weren't you?"

Try to avoid predictable questions Word some of your questions from a point of view that is opposite to that of your guest. Fresh and unexpected questions are necessary in two common circumstances: when the guest is someone who regularly appears on interview shows and whose opinions are, therefore, widely known; and when the topic has been so thoroughly chewed over by experts and amateurs alike that the audience can anticipate what questions are likely to be asked. Because your primary task is to give your audience something of value (interesting, useful information), try to break away from the known, the obvious, and the redundant.

Point up and emphasize important answers But do not parrot responses. Here is a good example of how a significant answer is given emphasis:

> ANNCR: Senator, if you were offered your party's nomination, would you accept it?
> SENATOR: I've given much thought to that possibility, and my present inclination is to accept such a call, provided that it was a mandate from the rank and file as well as the party leaders.
> ANNCR: Senator, you've just said—for the first time, I believe—that you are willing to run for the presidency. That sounds firm and unconditional. Am I right in drawing that conclusion?

On the other hand, you should avoid the meaningless repetition of answers, as in the following:

> ANNCR: You've been married five times. If you had your life to live over, would you try to stick with one of your wives?
> MILLAR: No, I wouldn't do anything differently.
> ANNCR: You wouldn't do anything differently. Well, which of your five partners did you love the most?
> MILLAR: I loved every one of them.
> ANNCR: You loved every one of them. Does that include spouse number three, with whom you lived for only two days?

Do not follow a guest's statements with meaningless comments before launching into the next question It is distracting to constantly repeat "I see" or "That's very interesting" after guests' responses.

Checklist: Becoming a Skilled Interviewer

The Guest

1. Carefully research the guest's background, accomplishments, attitudes, beliefs, and positions.
2. During the interview, listen attentively to the guest's replies and react with appropriate interest.
3. Make the guest feel at home.
4. Do not submit questions in advance, unless you would lose an important interview by refusing to do so.

Interacting on the Air

5. Never refer to conversations held before air time.
6. Establish the guest's credentials at the start of the interview.
7. Occasionally and indirectly reestablish the guest's name and credentials.
8. Seek out a guest's deep convictions.
9. Be tenacious.
10. Do not interrupt with meaningless comments.
11. Do not patronize your guest, and do not be obsequious.
12. Keep cool.
13. Discuss the subject with the guest.
14. Remember that the guest is the star.
15. Remember that the guest is the expert.
16. Keep control of the interview.
17. On television, do not have the guest address the camera.
18. At the conclusion of the interview, thank the guest warmly but briefly.

The Subject

19. Be sure the subject to be discussed is of interest or importance.
20. Where appropriate, limit the number of topics discussed so that they can be discussed in depth.
21. Establish the importance of the topic.
22. Write out, or at least make notes on, the introduction and conclusion.

The Interviewer's Strategy and Contributions

23. Try to build an interview toward a high point or climax.
24. Plan at least a few questions to get the interview started and to fill awkward gaps.
25. In general, base questions on the guest's previous statements.
26. In particular, follow up on important contradictions.
27. Make logical, smooth transitions to new subjects.
28. Always be ready with your next question, but do not allow this to distract you from the comments your guest is making.
29. On television, check your notes openly, not furtively.
30. Make questions brief and to the point, but do not be rude or brusque.

31. Don't ask questions that invite yes or no answers.
32. Ask questions that a layperson would ask.
33. Go a step futher, and ask interesting questions most laypersons would not think of.
34. Avoid obvious questions.
35. Try to avoid predictable questions.
36. Point up and emphasize important answers.
37. Do not follow a guest's statements with meaningless comments before launching into the next question.
38. Do not answer the question as you ask it.
39. Do not make an interview merely a Q & A session.
40. Do not feel compelled to jump in with a question the second a guest stops talking.
41. Do not ask more than one question at a time.
42. Question jargon unless its use is so widespread that you are sure the audience will understand it.
43. Before ending an interview— and especially if you have run out of questions—ask the guest whether he or she has anything to add.
44. Never end an interview with "Well, I see our time is up."

ANNCR: How old are you, Robin?
ROBIN: Fifteen.
ANNCR: I see. And yet you've already graduated from college?
ROBIN: Yep.
ANNCR: I see. And what are your plans for the future?

Do not answer the question as you ask it   For example, what could the senator say in response to the following question except "That's right"?

ANNCR: Senator, you voted against the treaty. Just what were your feelings about it? Your statement to the news media indicated that you felt we were giving up more than we were gaining.

Do not make an interview merely a question-and-answer session
Questions are essential to an interview, but if you simply move from one question to another without revealing *your* feelings about the answers, you run the risk of seeming indifferent or unimpressed by what your guest is saying. Feel free to express honest reactions, including laughter when appropriate.

Do not feel compelled to jump in with a question the second a guest stops talking   Some interviewers feel that any dead air is unacceptable. One popular talk show host was notorious for interrupting guests in the middle of amusing anecdotes out of a fear of a moment of silence. Because good interviews are conversations, pauses are appropriate. Additionally, silence, together with an expectant expression, will often encourage a guest to continue in more detail.

Do not ask more than one question at a time   It is a poor practice to combine questions into a multipart form, as in this example:

> ANNCR: Where did you get your inspiration for "Moonlight on the Ohio," and is it true that "Love Song" was inspired by your first wife?

A guest may be able to handle such multiple questions, but there is a good chance that you will end up with a muddled answer.

Question jargon unless its use is so widespread that you are sure the audience will understand it   The term *jargon* has several negative connotations, but it also has a neutral meaning, "the specialized or technical language of a trade, profession, or fellowship." When guests use jargon, you may need to elicit clarification so that the audience will not feel confused.

> ANNCR: And what did you find?
> GUEST: There wasn't a single P.F.D. in the boat.
> ANNCR: P.F.D.? I'm not sure what that is . . .
> GUEST: A personal flotation device.
> ANNCR: What I would call a life jacket?
> GUEST: Yes.
> GUEST: He showed negative life signs.
> ANNCR: You mean he was dead?
> GUEST: Correct.

During an interview, you will often find it necessary to make quick decisions about asking for clarification of jargon, or in-group terminology. When interviewing a nurse, you may hear "ICU," and you may decide almost at once that most of your listeners (especially in a hospital context) will know that this means "Intensive Care Unit." On the other hand, if the nurse speaks of "NIC units," you most likely will decide to ask (without interrupting the flow of the nurse's comments) what this term means (Newborn Intensive Care).

Before ending an interview—and especially if you have run out of questions—ask the guest whether he or she has anything to add   Aside from its obvious value when you are unable to come up with another question, this practice often enables a guest to express something interesting or important that has not come out earlier in the interview.

Never end an interview with "Well, I see our time is up" This broadcasting cliché is unnecessary. Your audience knows you are stopping because the time is up!

Announcing at Radio Talk Stations

More than four hundred radio stations in the United States and approximately twenty in Canada are classified as **talk stations**.[3] This classification may mean a number of things; here are some variations of talk formats:

- Station A is a public broadcasting station, playing classical music, contemporary music, and rhythm and blues and also carrying many discussion programs and news commentaries, most of them provided by National Public Radio (NPR).
- Station B is a middle-of-the-road station that places heavy emphasis on the talk of its announcers and on in-depth news reporting. It also provides play-by-play coverage of several major sports, which, of course, is also a form of "talk radio."
- Station C is a major-market station that features locally produced news during commuting hours, network news at the top of the hour, and a number of locally produced call-in shows at all other times. Some of these call-in shows are general interest, whereas others are confined to a single topic such as gardening, cooking, or home repair.
- Station D is a small- to medium-market station that features several locally produced talk shows, including restaurant reviews, a home and garden call-in program, two or more daily general interest call-in programs, a daily remote talk show from local restaurants, hotel lobbies, or shopping malls, regular news reports from a national news service, and a number of syndicated talk programs, such as those featuring Dr. Dean Edell, Sally Jessy Raphael, and Rush Limbaugh.

Of these, only Stations C and D are truly talk stations. Stations that have only one talk show a week or specialize in programming

[3]Radio and television station formats are listed annually in *Broadcasting Yearbook* (Washington, DC: Broadcasting Publications, Inc.).

that is religious or focus on farming or sports do not differ significantly from all-talk stations in the procedures they use for production or performance of talk programs.

As an announcer for a talk program, you need to develop two major related skills: conducting interesting and informative interviews (or conversations) with studio guests, and conversing engagingly with the full spectrum of strangers who call in on the telephone.[4]

Preparing for the Shift

At a typical talk station, you may expect to work a two- to four-hour air shift, five or six days a week. If you work on weekends or on the **graveyard shift** (from midnight on), longer hours may be assigned. Most stations, however, choose to limit talk show announcers to a maximum of four hours, which is about as long as anyone can be expected to remain sharp, energetic, articulate, and patient. Despite what may seem to be short working hours, talk show announcers must work many additional hours a day preparing for their air time.

As a talk show announcer, you will work with a program director or operations manager, a producer, a phone screener, and (at most stations) an engineer. The program director or other designated administrator will suggest guests, will in some cases instruct you to schedule a certain guest, and will evaluate your work frequently. The producer will assist you in selecting and scheduling guests, will handle correspondence, and will act as traffic director for arriving and departing guests. The **phone screener**, who may in some operations be the producer, will handle all incoming calls during your air shift, will cut off obvious cranks or other undesirables, and will line up calls in order of their calling or according to some station policy. The engineer will play carted commercials and station logos, will cut in the network, if any, and will operate the **time-delay system**.[5] Only at stations at which talk programs are broadcast in **real time** do announcers work without an engineer.

[4]The suggestions offered here come from a variety of talk stations, but primary emphasis has been placed on the practices of a successful station in San Francisco—KGO Radio, Newstalk 81.
[5]A time-delay system records the voices of both caller and program host and delays their comments for several seconds. The recording medium may be an audiotape loop or chips in a digital unit.

Your first task in preparing for a shift is to develop at least three or four timely, universally interesting, or controversial topics for discussion. Whether or not you have guests, you must open your program with talk that will stimulate listeners' interest and motivate them to phone in to offer their opinions. Naturally, you will not speak about all your prepared topics at the outset of your program. You will begin with the most logical one and save the others to be used in case the first topic bombs.

In order to be timely and interesting on the air, you must be widely read and conversant with an extremely broad range of topics. There is an absolute limit to the number of times that you will be able to get away with saying "never heard of it." Unless you are hired specifically to do a sports or other specialized talk show, you must be a generalist. You can expect to find yourself discussing local politics at one moment, conservation at another, and the details of a new and important book at still another. This means that you must read several newspapers and magazines regularly and must keep abreast of television, movies, books (both fiction and nonfiction), and other important media. Jim Eason, popular talk show host for KGO radio in San Francisco, provides this information about his reading schedule: each weekday he reads two local newspapers, as well as *USA Today* and

Figure 8.3
The personalities behind successful radio talk shows become famous or infamous—but invariably have a loyal following. Boston host Jerry Williams, who is highly opinionated and intentionally rude, has been on the airwaves for three decades. His station promotes him as "radio's last angry man." (Photo from *The Boston Globe*)

the *Christian Science Monitor*; on Sundays, he reads the *New York Times* and the *Los Angeles Times*, as well as two local newspapers; each week he reads *Newsweek*, *Time*, *Reader's Digest*, *The National Review*, *New Republic*, and *TV Guide*. He also reads (mostly by skimming) three to five books a week.

Although having studio guests is not imperative, they are frequently used by radio talk show announcers to add variety to a program. Guests, including the most famous and sought-after, are seldom paid for appearances on talk shows; they therefore constitute a cost-effective source of program material. Most guests, of course, agree to appear on a program because they see it as an opportunity to promote a book, a film, or a cause. There is nothing inherently wrong in such a trade-off, as long as both parties understand the conditions and as long as the announcer stays in control of the show. Well-known guests are usually on a circuit, appearing on both radio and television talk programs in a number of markets across the country. Such guests know or soon learn that they will be welcome only as long as they help their hosts deliver an engaging program. If you take time to explain to your guests the nature of your show, the kinds of listeners you are attempting to reach (your audience demographics), and any station policies that may be relevant, you should have little trouble in gaining their full cooperation.

When you schedule guests, you will be expected to inform your station several days in advance. This will give the promotion department time to publicize appearances, generally by writing promotion copy to be read by other talk show announcers at your station during their shifts.

Some stations maintain a log to keep control over the appearances of guests. They want to avoid overexposing guests as well as repetitiveness in the type of guest or subject covered. A **debriefing log** is used for entering postbroadcast comments. Such evaluation of a guest's performance usually consists of answers to these questions:

What actually was covered by the guest?

Did the material covered match the preshow expectations?

How well did the guest perform?

How much interest did the guest generate as measured by phone calls?

Performing as a Talk Show Announcer

As a talk show announcer, you will sit in a small studio immediately adjacent to a control room that houses the engineer and phone screener. You will not use a telephone for your conversations with callers; their voices will be amplified so that you can hear them over a special speaker. You will speak directly into an ordinary mic. A soundproof separation of studio and control room is absolutely necessary. Because a time delay is used as a precaution against the broadcasting of profanity and slander, it is imperative that you not be distracted by the sound of your own voice and your guests' voices as they go out over the air approximately seven seconds after the words have been spoken. In addition, the screener will be carrying on conversations with callers who want to talk with you; this potential distraction must also be kept from your ears.

In most cases the studio will have a special telephone console. It will handle several incoming lines, from which you select the caller you want to speak with next by punching the appropriate **bus** on the phone base. Calls are fed to this base by the screener after they have been sifted to eliminate cranks; a light illuminating a bus tells you that you have a caller on that particular line. The lines are usually identified by geographical location; for example, as a hypothetical case line 1 may be the South Side, line 2 Oak Manor, and line 3 Outer Woburn. Some radio talk show hosts use fax (facsimile transmission) machines, allowing listeners to send hard copies of newspaper stories, letters, or other material that they want to comment on.

At the start of your shift, you will ad-lib your introduction along predetermined lines, including an identification of yourself, the station, the length of your program segment, the guests who will appear later, the telephone numbers to call, and the opening topic for discussion.

Stations have many policies for performance; these are not standardized, but do tend to be similar. Most stations ask talk show hosts not to talk at the start of the program for more than a certain number of minutes before taking a phone call. This obviously means that your opening comments must generate listener interest; no interest means no calls. A related policy insists that you never talk for more than a certain number of minutes during your segment without taking a call, even when you have a fascinating guest. Your station may want more and shorter calls, and if you ask "more and shorter than what?" the answer may be "more than you're taking and shorter than you're allowing." The aim of talk radio is maximum listener involvement.

Talk stations cluster their commercial announcements. Unlike a top-40 station, where program segments (songs) last three minutes or less, talk shows cannot tolerate constant interruptions. A **commercial cluster** may consist of three or more commercials. It is mandatory that you, as the organizer and director of your own show, not get so carried away by the ongoing dialogue that you lose sight of the need to deliver the commercial clusters at the times designated. All commercials must be read or played—after all, the sponsors pay for the programming— and they should be properly spaced to avoid piling up toward the end of your shift. Trying to cram too many commercials into too little time can result in your being forced to read live 60-second commercials in 40 or 50 seconds—a sure way to invite the wrath of your supervisor. Finally, all radio announcers work with a log—called the **program log** by people in programming but referred to as the **billing log** by the sales department—and it is your responsibility to initial all commercial and public-service announcements as they are broadcast. Program logs are no longer required by the FCC, but most stations continue to maintain them.

Legal and Ethical Concerns

Despite deregulation of radio by the FCC, broadcasters continue to be legally responsible for what is sent over the airwaves by their stations. Many stations give talk show hosts detailed instructions on their legal and ethical responsibilities. Information typically contained in such instructions is summarized in this section.

Talk shows are, by their nature, often controversial. Talk show hosts should not avoid controversy, but they must be aware of what is and what is not allowed by their station and the FCC.

Figure 8.4
Co-hosts Eric Greene and Terry Lowry give a live tease 5 minutes before the start of their television news and interview show, "2 at Noon." (Courtesy of KTVU, Channel 2, Oakland)

A **personal attack** is an attack on the honesty, character, integrity, or similar personal quality of an identified person or group made during presentation of views on a controversial issue of public importance. The station must act to notify the person (or group) attacked within one week of the broadcast of the attack. The individual must be told the time and date of the attack and must be offered a tape or a script, together with an opportunity to respond. Exceptions to this requirement are (1) attacks on foreign groups or foreign public figures and (2) attacks by legally qualified candidates, their authorized spokespersons, or campaign associates on other candidates, their authorized spokespersons, or campaign associates. It is not the talk show host's responsibility to attempt to decide whether a personal attack has in fact occurred. The host should contact the operations manager or program director any time he or she believes a personal attack may have taken place.

All persons contacted by phone must be informed that they will be on the air before putting them on the air.

All on-air personnel have the responsibility to present representative contrasting viewpoints on controversial issues of public importance. (This policy is known as the **fairness doctrine**.) A related responsibility is the provision of **equal time**, which arises only in connection with political figures during political campaigns.[6] There are two station policies with respect to equal time. First, station management decides which offices and issues will be given air time. Second, all requests for or inquiries about the provision of equal time must be channeled through the program director to the operations manager.

Payola and plugola are illegal practices. **Payola** refers to the presentation of particular programming in return for money or gifts. **Plugola** refers to the on-air mention of commercial services, products, or events outside of the normal broadcasting of commercials. Such mentions violate federal regulations and subject an individual to a potential fine of $10,000 or imprisonment for one year or both. Plugola is prohibited, whether the talk show host receives money or other favors for the plug or has a financial interest in the commercial services, products, or events being mentioned.

---

[6]The fairness doctrine is a policy of the FCC that requires stations to devote air time, in addition to regular newscasts, to the discussion of public affairs and to provide time for opposing viewpoints. The equal time provision exists in law as part of the Communications Act. A thorough discussion of these policies is found in *Broadcasting in America*, by Sydney W. Head and Christopher H. Sterling.

Challenges and Responsibilities

One of your challenges as a radio talk show announcer will be to motivate many new or infrequent callers. To guarantee fresh call-in talent, you must repeat the phone numbers often on the air and tell your listeners from time to time which lines are open. No matter how desultory the response to your invitations and encouragement, do not beg people to phone in. If the telephone lines are dead and cannot be resuscitated by your best efforts, you may conclude that one of the following problems exists: (1) Your comments are so fascinating that your listeners do not want to interrupt. (2) You are so dull and un-inspiring that no one is motivated to call. (3) The transmitter has shorted out.

Occasionally callers may use profane language, mention the names of people other than public figures in a derogatory way, or make defamatory statements. Because your station's license is at stake in such cases, you must develop quick reflexes with the **panic button**, which takes the offending comment off the air and replaces it with a beeping sound or a prerecorded warning about such utterances. It is far better to overreact in questionable situations than to let a caller's comments go beyond the point of safety. You can always apologize if your finger was too quick on the button, but there is little you can do constructively once things have gone past the point of no return. You will, of course, be extensively briefed on dos and don'ts.

One of your responsibilities will be to call your audience's attention to other segments of your station's broadcast day. In some cases this will mean promoting the news, the music, contests, sports, or special features such as farm information. In other instances it will mean speaking favorably of people who have comparable shows—that is, people who might in some ways be considered your competition. Unless there is some station-endorsed feud or mock feud between talk show announcers, you will be expected to do a conscientious job of fairly promoting your co-workers.

Hosting Television Talk Programs

Television talk shows can be seen at nearly every hour of the broadcast day. At both the network and the local level, talk shows are usually broadcast live, even though some segments may have been taped in advance. Local stations also rely on taped talk programs that have been syndicated for distribution. Network programs are early-morning and late-night offerings; most local talk shows are broadcast in mid-morning or afternoon.

As a television talk show announcer, you will face constant demands on your abilities to ad-lib, to quickly cover for slip-ups, to concentrate in the face of multiple distractions, and to help produce a smooth show without scripts or rehearsals.

Types of Talk Shows

Network and nationally syndicated talk shows are produced by large staffs. Guests are booked well in advance, and transportation and lodging are arranged for them. Staff members thoroughly research each guest's background and provide the program host with copious notes. Other staff members procure photos or tapes. The result is a fast-paced, smoothly produced program with enough variety to please the audience.

Locally produced television talk shows are put together with small staffs and limited budgets. Small-market stations provide little support for the host. It is likely that you will spend the first several years of your career as a talk show host at a station with very limited resources. At some small stations there is not even a floor crew; instead there may be two cameras locked in fixed positions and a director sitting at the **switcher**, cutting from one camera to another as appropriate. Working at such a station will allow you to learn every aspect of talk show performance and production, preparing you for a move to a station in a larger market. Medium-market stations offer more support, but resources are still somewhat limited. Program quality need not suffer because of modest support, but interview programs require great effort and adaptability from all members of the team.

Some television talk shows concentrate on interviews. A few intersperse talk with performances by singers or comedians appearing in local clubs and theatres. A third type has a combined format offering both interviews and news. This type is represented by "2 at Noon," on station KTVU, Channel 2, Oakland, California. This program serves as the model for the discussion that follows.

A Typical Production Effort

Locally produced television talk programs, such as "2 at Noon," usually run 60 minutes. The staff consists of camera operators, technical directors, and others who work in the engineering department plus

Figure 8.5
Talk show host Eric Greene conducts an interview via satellite. Eric can see guest J. D. Roth (host of Disney Studios' "Fun House") on a television monitor, at the far right next to the blank chroma-key screen in the photo on the left. What the home audience sees, shown in the photo on the right, is both Eric and his guest on the keyed-in frame. (Courtesy of KTVU, Oakland)

two hosts, an executive or senior producer, two segment producers, a director, and two or more floor directors, one of whom is the crew chief. The show "2 at Noon" has a program producer and two segment producers, one for news and another for interviews. Producer Andrew Finlayson calculates that 30 minutes of production work is required for every minute on the air.

Here is a typical day's routine for Eric Greene, interview host of "2 at Noon." Eric arrives at the station by 8:00 A.M. Because interview guests are scheduled in advance, Eric has had a chance to do some preliminary research on the day's guests, to scan one or more books (if his guests are authors), and to think through some of the areas of questioning that seem logical.

On arriving at the station, Eric is given a **format sheet**, which provides in abbreviated form an indication of what is to take place during each of the show's seven segments, including the interview portions. A format sheet may consist of only one or two pages; that for "2 at Noon" is one sheet of $8\frac{1}{2}$-by-14-inch paper. The hosts, as well as all others working on the program, know the meanings of the numerous script abbreviations. Some of the script symbols used by the staff of "2 at Noon" are fairly universal—including BB for billboard and VT for videotape.[7] Others—such as TX for theme music on audiotape cartridge—are not known or used at some stations.

[7]To **billboard** is to mention an upcoming feature or program in such a way as to capture audience interest. The intent is to keep viewers tuned in or motivate them to watch the next day or week.

At 8:30 A.M. Eric meets with the interview producer, and they spend the next half-hour discussing the day's guests. Taped material concerning guests is sometimes available and may be viewed and discussed. The viewed tapes are either accepted or rejected; if accepted, they often must be edited and always must be inserted into the running order of the show. On some occasions Eric conducts a taped interview by satellite in advance of the day's program. This is done only occasionally, and usually for superstars who have something to promote but who are unable or unwilling to travel the promotional circuit.

At 9:00 A.M. there is a preproduction meeting attended by both Eric and Terry Lowry, who is news anchor for the program, as well as the station's news director, program producer, segment producers, television director, assignment editor, and newswriters. The upcoming show is gone over in meticulous detail, and any necessary last-minute changes are made.

At 10:00 A.M. both program hosts arrive on the set to deliver one live tease and three taped teases for the day's show. Between the end of this taping and the opening of the show at noon, Eric and Terry continue their preparations. Voice-over comments are written by Eric to accompany videotapes that feature the day's guests. Occasionally, a guest will arrive early, giving Eric a chance to discuss the upcoming interview and perhaps uncover interesting angles not revealed by the handouts or videotapes that have been provided by the press agent.

At about 11:50 A.M. the hosts arrive on the set and are outfitted with lavaliere microphones and IFB earphones. At around 11:55 they do a live tease, followed by a commercial break and station identification. The show begins precisely at noon.

Ideally, when time permits, Eric meets his guests in the station's green room, 5 or 10 minutes before leading them to the set.[8] The general nature of the program and specific topics to be covered are discussed. In practice, however, because the show moves so quickly, Eric often meets his guests only a minute or so before the interview goes on the air. Figure 8.5 shows Eric on the set interviewing—via satellite hook-up—a guest who is at a remote location.

Exactly an hour after the taped program opener, the closing credits are rolled. Today's show is history.

Preparation for the next day's program begins shortly after the program ends. Following a brief (5–10 minutes) taping session, during

---

[8]A **green room** is a lounge found in broadcast stations, theaters, and concert halls, for the use of performers and guests.

which 10-second teases for the next day's show are taped, the production team retires to a conference room for a brief **postmortem** of the show just completed. The executive producer and segment producers review with the hosts what did and did not work and why. The postmortem is followed by a discussion of the next day's show.

Practice: Interviewing

It should be apparent that interviews serve several different ends. The exercises that follow cover interviewing for talk show programs and person-in-the-street features. (Many stations continue to refer to these as man-in-the-street, or MOS, interviews.) A practice section at the end of the chapter on radio news suggests interviews for news packages and documentaries.

Before beginning any interview, decide on its purpose, for this will tell you the general approach to be taken (guarded or open, light or somber), the approximate length of the interview, and whether you should stay with one topic or go into two or more areas of discussion. Generally speaking, multiple-topic interviews are appropriate when your guest is a many-faceted celebrity who can talk on several subjects; single-topic interviews are proper when your guest is a specialist in some area, such as pediatrics, investments, or gardening. Single-topic interviews are mandatory when doing person-on-the-street interviews, as well as when conducting interviews for later use in a documentary.

Like most other exercises in this book, those that follow are designed for the simplest possible production, using only a portable audio recorder. Any of these exercises can be adapted to studio or field television production.

1. For a multiple-topic interview, select a person you believe to be unusually interesting. Make sure you do some research about your guest so that you have at least a general idea of what there is to be discovered and discussed. Notes on areas to be explored are almost a necessity for this type of interview. Plan to interview without stopping your tape recorder for at least 10, and preferably 20, minutes.
2. For a single-topic interview, choose a specialist whose field is of great interest to you, and interview at length without significantly

Figure 8.6

Two students create a makeshift talk show set by gathering table and chairs in a corner of the college's television studio. They are going to tape a live interview on current campus issues for their communications class. (Photo from Spencer Grant, Stock Boston)

changing the subject. A list of possible questions should help keep you on course.

3. Choose a topic, and conduct person-in-the-street interviews. Here are a few suggested questions:

What is the most useless gadget on the market?

What job would you most like to have?

What is the worst advice you've ever received?

Have you ever been fired from a job?

Of course, you can also obtain samples of public opinion by asking more serious questions, such as probing people's feelings about an item in the news. Editing the responses and organizing them into packages, with appropriate opening and closing remarks, will complete this exercise.

4. Occasionally, it is effective to conduct an interview for which all or most of the questions have been written out in advance. An example of such an occasion is when you want to pin down an interviewee to answering a string of precisely worded questions, like these:

Why did you vote against the treaty?

Last May, in your Tulsa speech, did you not say that you favored the treaty?

On May 20th, the *Tulsa Record* printed this quote: "I fully support the administration, and therefore I support the proposed treaty." Do you still maintain that you never expressed support for the treaty?

Here is a quote from the *Dallas Advance*, dated May 30th: "Senator James stated that, while he had some minor reservations about the treaty, he would support it when it came to a vote." Did the *Advance* also misquote you?

Select an interviewee and a topic that lend themselves to a scripted approach and practice this unusual, but sometimes very effective, interview technique.

9

Radio News

Radio news ranges from in-depth coverage around the clock to brief hourly summaries, or even no news at all on some stations. Many popular music stations have no news director or reporters and broadcast news reports only in emergencies. At some talk and music stations, news reports are provided by a national news service such as Associated Press Radio, Mutual Radio News, or the UPI Audio Network. At other stations, reports from a wire service are taken directly from a teleprinter and are read without being edited. Announcing at such **rip-and-read operations** requires considerable skill in sight reading, but no journalism skills. This chapter discusses news operations at radio stations where news is taken seriously and where specialized news personnel are employed full-time.

Nearly every broadcast market now has, or can receive signals from, one or more radio stations that feature news. Some of these stations have an all-news format, some provide news during morning and evening drive times, and some give hourly reports researched and written by a news staff. All these news operations rely to some extent on news from these sources: station field reporters, wire services, audio feeds from news services, and a parent network. The most important effort at any station that takes news seriously is that made by its field reporters, newswriters, and anchors.

The all-news stations, such as those owned and operated by CBS, offer far more than news. Typical features are stock market and other business reports, sports reports, theatre and movie reviews, traffic information, and a community billboard. Some stations also feature hour-long special-interest programs, such as a cooking program featuring local chefs or food and wine specialists or a call-for-action consumer complaint program. Some special-interest programs are performed by station news personnel; others feature outside specialists, with a station announcer serving as host.

As an announcer at a news-oriented station, you may find yourself working in the field, collecting news reports and telephoning them in; you might spend your time in a newsroom and an on-air studio, first writing the news and then delivering it; or you might read news stories written by others and spend several hours of your workday recording short features for play during other newscasters' shifts. As a field reporter, you could spend four hours a day in the field gathering, recording, and sending reports by conventional telephone, cellular phone, or shortwave radio. Then you would spend the remainder of your workday at the station, obtaining telephone interviews and editing, writing, and carting them for use by the news anchors.

As you read this discussion of performance and production aspects of radio broadcasting at the local station level, keep in mind that only larger stations have the resources to provide the support described.

Anchoring Radio News

At most news radio stations, anchors prepare much of the copy they read. There are many advantages to this practice. First, if you write (or rewrite from wire-service copy) the script you are to read, it is less likely to contain the typographical errors that crop up from time to time in wire copy. Second, as you write copy, you have an opportunity to contact sources that will give you the correct pronunciation of any names or words that might otherwise be a problem to you during delivery. Third, in writing the copy, you gain familiarity with the story, and this will be reflected in better interpretation and clearer communication. Finally, writing your own copy will help you develop into a journalist, rather than a mere reader of news scripts.

In preparing a news script, you will work with a news editor who will determine what news stories will be broadcast and establish the order of their delivery. You will have access to a log that shows the sequence of the elements that will make up the newscast during your shift. Most news-oriented stations follow a cyclical format—called a **clock**, or **newswheel**—repeated on an hourly basis. Some news clocks divide a drive-time hour into forty or more segments. A typical clock, or newswheel, is shown in Figure 9.2. The meanings of the terms used in the example are given in Table 9.1. A typical format begins each hour with five minutes of network news, provides national and world news headlines at or near the half-hour, and has features such as sports, weather, stock market reports, and local headlines at regularly

Figure 9.1
At many radio stations the news director is also the announcer. Here news director Jeffrey Schaub reads his top-of-the-hour broadcast. (Courtesy of KTID-FM, San Rafael, CA)

established intervals. Commercials are also scheduled at stipulated times. The log plus the material given you by the news editor will determine your task as you prepare for your air shift.

News Sources

Most radio newscasters and reporters are successful because, in addition to other skills, they have good news judgment. As you face the task of writing and assembling materials for a radio newscast, you can expect to receive news from the following sources:

Audio reports, both live and taped, from station, field, and special assignment reporters

AP and UPI news wires

AP Radio Network news feeds

A city wire service, which may be supervised by a major news service or independently owned and operated

Interviews or news reports received by telephone

Wire copy and voiced news reports in Spanish from the Hispanic-American News Service or news from the Black Radio Network

The Associated Press (AP) and United Press International (UPI) provide international, national, and local news services. Although they differ in many respects, the services offered by them are similar enough that the following description of the AP services will give you the general idea.

Figure 9.2
The program clock is a radio station's strategic tool for gaining and keeping audiences; the schedule for each hour is carefully divided into segments of news, sports, weather, headlines, and features. This one-hour clock, from an all-news, commercial AM station, shows the broadcast schedule during morning drive time.

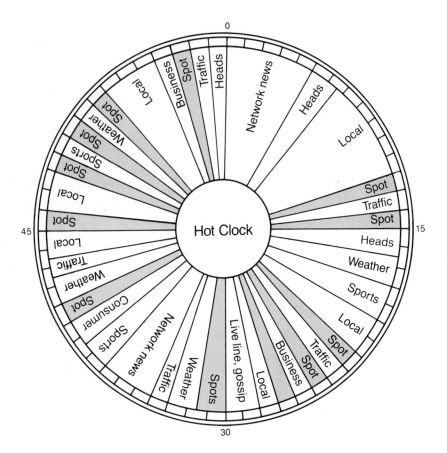

The Associated Press provides AP NewsPower, subscribed to by many radio stations and smaller television stations. News is sent to stations by AP from computer to computer at 1,200 words per minute. News directors select categories of stories that interest them from a **menu**, a list of features such as state news, national news, international news, farm news, business stories, sports scores and stories, and weather reports. Features not chosen from the menu are not received. News stories in selected categories can be printed directly on paper or stored in a station's computer and printed after a decision has been made as to whether or not to use them. An all-news station, a rock station, and a classical music station can choose different assortments of news stories appropriate to their differing formats.

Another feature of AP NewsPower (and UPI CustomNews Service) allows a station's newswriter to summon up a story paragraph

Table 9.1 Terms Used on a Newswheel

Term	Meaning
net news	network news
heads	news headlines
local	local news stories
spot	commercial
traffic	traffic reports
weather	weather report from station's meteorologist
sports	sports briefs from station's sports reporter
business	business report from station's business reporter
live line, gossip, etc.	special features done by news anchors, just for fun
national	national news reported by local anchors
consumer/medical	either a consumer report from station's consumer reporter or a medical report by an M.D.

by paragraph. At the push of a button, the paragraph from the news service moves to one side of the video display terminal, permitting the operator to paraphrase it by typing the story on the unoccupied portion of the screen. The push of another button directs the computer to print the rewritten story.

AP NewsPower also sends timely features throughout the year, including special reports on income tax tips, holidays such as Valentine's Day or Thanksgiving, the new television season, new automobiles, and a year-end review. NewsPower also sends complete newscasts, developing news stories, bulletins, and 60- and 90-second features on such topics as consumerism, health and medicine, physical fitness, entertainment, and home computers.

The Associated Press also maintains APTV, a service mainly used by television stations but also subscribed to by the largest radio stations. This service carries some of the same written material as AP NewsPower, as well as in-depth newspaper-style stories. Stations using APTV are furnished with far more copy on each story than is provided by NewsPower, and this gives them a wealth of source material to augment their local coverage.

The AP Radio Network delivers five-minute audio newscasts at the top of the hour, twenty-four hours a day, as well as a two-minute newscast at the bottom of the hour, from the start of morning drive time until the end of afternoon drive time each weekday. It also provides an hourly business program, sportscasts, and many daily features. These reports can be inserted into locally produced newscasts and thereby provide expanded coverage to stations that cannot afford teams of national and international correspondents.

When using stories from the wire services, you have four options:

1. Read the story as you find it.
2. Leave the story unaltered but add a lead-in of your own.
3. Edit the story to shorten it, sharpen it, or give it a local angle.
4. Completely rewrite the story.

Whatever you decide, the story must be properly entered in the running sequence of the newscast. At some stations this means making a copy for the engineer and adding the original copy to a loose-leaf book with which you will work while on the air. At most stations engineers work only with the log and the ongoing directions of the anchor.

Most radio stations that feature news ask reporters to work the **beat check** (also called the **phone beat**, or the **phone check**). This assignment consists of making telephone calls to agencies and persons who are most likely to provide news items regularly. A typical beat list includes the phone numbers and names of contacts for all nearby police, sheriff, disaster, fire, and weather departments; the FBI, the Secret Service, the Alcohol, Tobacco, and Firearms Bureau, civil defense headquarters, and the National Guard; local and nearby jails and prisons; all local hospitals; all nearby airport control towers; and specialized agencies important to listeners in your community (farm bureau, earthquake stations).

When working the beat check, plan to call each listed agency at the same time each day. Try to establish a personal relationship with the individual who is the contact there. Discover how each contact prefers to work with you—whether you are allowed to tape the conversation or are permitted only to paraphrase statements. If it fits the news report, give credit to the people who supply your station with news items; most people are pleased to hear their names on the air. At the same time, you must respect requests for anonymity.

A related assignment for newsroom personnel is taping recorded messages prepared daily by a variety of government agencies. By telephoning Washington, D.C., you can record feeds from agencies such as the Department of Agriculture, NASA, and both houses of Congress. Similar services are offered by the U.S. Chamber of Commerce. These sources, of course, have their own purposes to serve, and controversial information should be checked against other sources.

Preparing for a Shift

When preparing for a news shift that will keep you on the air for two to four hours, you will typically write, rewrite, and assemble about two hours' worth of material, including live copy, recorded reports, features, and commercials. While you are performing, a newswriter will be writing and assembling material for the remaining hours of your shift.

The checklist prepared for you by the news editor will include the stories to be featured, the order in which they should be given, and the **sounds** with which you will work. Sounds are different from sounders (short musical IDs or logos that identify a particular feature such as a traffic or sports report) and are of several types:

An **actuality** is a brief statement made by someone other than station personnel, such as a newsmaker or an eyewitness. It is recorded in

Figure 9.3
Working in the newsroom before going on-air, a radio news announcer must digest evolving news stories from wire services and other sources, write and rewrite copy, edit recorded reports and actualities, and work with engineers to cart tapes. In the CNN Radio newsroom personnel are involved in the reception of news and the processing of stories into what will become an original radio broadcast. (Courtesy of Turner Broadcasting System)

the field on a battery-operated cassette recorder or at the station by way of a telephone.

A **wrap**, or wraparound, begins with the voice of a reporter leading into an actuality and ends with the reporter's closing comments. The conclusion may be a brief summary, a commentary, or only a tag line such as "Bill Hillman, KZZZ News."

A **voicer** is a report from a field reporter, usually sent to the station by shortwave radio, a conventional phone, or a cellular phone.

A **scener** is a report on a breaking event. It is usually broadcast live, but may also be taped for incorporation into a later broadcast.

Raw sound refers to what may be called "news noise"—protesters chanting or funeral music with no reporter commentary.

Actualities and wraps need lead-ins and lead-outs, sometimes called **intros** and **outros**. During your preparation time for a shift as news anchor, you will have listened to the sounds with which you will work and will have written introductions and ending statements, as appropriate. In preparing lead-ins and lead-outs, you must follow established practice at your station. Practices vary from station to station, but you may expect something like the following.

First, you will make decisions about the editing of the actualities, voicers, and wraps with which you will work, as well as any taped sceners that are to be repeated following their earlier live presentation. As you listen to each tape, you will make decisions about the ten, fifteen, thirty, or more seconds, you would like to use on the newscast. Some of these will have been previously edited and carted by a field reporter, a newswriter, or another newscaster, so you may add them to your on-air material without alteration.

If your shift occurs during drive time (also called **prime time**), you may edit and cart your tapes with the help of an engineer. If your shift is during off hours, such as in the middle of the night or on the weekend, you most likely will rely on tapes prepared by others, because your shift will be longer and fewer station personnel will be on hand to help you prepare or furnish you with updated material.

Most tapes used in newscasts, aside from taped feature reports, are edited electronically rather than manually. Whether or not you work with an engineer, the tape excerpts you intend to use must be dubbed to carts. One actuality or taped telephone interview often provides several sounds for a newscast. On your script you will indicate the words that close each segment of the report so that the announcer who uses the tapes will know the **out cues**.

You will also write a log, giving the numbers of the carts to be used, the general nature of each actuality, the running time of each, and their out cues, or end cues. Figure 9.4 shows one example of current practice in logging actualities. The log shows that the editor (who was also the reporter) was able to get three brief actualities from one recorded telephone conversation with a forest ranger. The general nature of each actuality is given under SUBJECT to enable the person writing the lead-in and lead-out to identify the content, and the end cues are given so that the newscaster can pick up immediately when the cart ends. When the precise end cue is also spoken earlier in the actuality, the person preparing the log writes "double out" in the END CUE column to indicate that fact. For example, if the phrase

Figure 9.4

An actuality log such as this is prepared by a reporter or editor as an aid to a newscaster.

RADIO NEWS ACTUALITY LOG   EDITOR:HEWITT
STORY AND REPORTER: Forest Fire, Hewitt

CART #	SUBJECT	TIME	END CUE
N–35	Mt. Sakea forest ranger James Cleary–– fire has burned over 3,000 acres	:16	"as of now."
N–99	No evidence as to cause. Arson not ruled out. Man seen leaving area at high speed in green sports car.	:11	"in a green sports car."
N–83	Should have it surrounded by tonight, and contained by midday tomorrow–– depending on the weather.	:15	"a lot of tired fire-fighters will be able to go home."

"as of now" had been used by the ranger twice in the first actuality, "double out" would have warned the newscaster against picking up the cue prematurely.

In preparing for a newscast, you must have a fairly accurate idea of the number of lines or pages you will read in the allotted time. To determine how much copy will add up to how many minutes of air time, count the number of lines on a typical page of copy, then time yourself as you read aloud at your most comfortable and effective speed. If you read at about 180 words per minute, you will read the following numbers of lines in the given time:

15 seconds = 4 lines
30 seconds = 8 lines
45 seconds = 12 lines
60 seconds = 16 lines

If a page of copy has 32 lines, for example, you will read a page in about 2 minutes.

With such information it is easy to project the number of lines of copy needed for a newscast of a particular length. (Note, however, that these figures must be modified to suit the time you will actually spend reading news copy on a given broadcast. Commercials and stories from reporters will obviously reduce the amount of copy you will actually read.)

Of course, a time chart is useful only for developing a sense of the relation between space (the physical copy) and time (the newscast). Seasoned reporters have so developed this sense that they can prepare newscasts without conscious thought of lines per minute or of their reading speed. Again, as you work with a time chart, remember that actualities, commercials, and sounds—as well as your desire to vary your pace of reading to match the moods of the stories—will complicate your timing.

Writing News

As a radio journalist, you will be expected to write well and rapidly. To help you develop the necessary writing skills, Chet Casselman, a highly experienced news director and formerly national president of the Radio and Television News Directors Association, offers the following guidelines.[1] They are for the most part equally applicable to writing news for television.

[1]Chet Casselman, *KSFO News Style Book* (San Francisco: Golden West Broadcasters, 1967), pp. 4–7.

Write for the ear rather than the eye   Your audience does not see the script; it only hears it. Sentences should be relatively short, the vocabulary should be geared to a heterogeneous audience, and potentially confusing statistics should be simplified. Some specific rules are as follows:

- Say it the simple way. Eliminate unnecessary ages, middle initials, addresses, occupations, unfamiliar or obscure names, precise or involved numbers, incidental information, and anything else that slows down or clutters up the story.

- Convert precise or involved numbers to a simplified form. For example, change 1,572 to "almost sixteen hundred," 2.6 million to "slightly more than two and a half million," and 35.7 percent to "nearly 36 percent." Unless a number is an essential part of the story, it should be dropped.

- Express names of famous people and their relatives carefully to avoid confusion. For instance, "The wife of famous architect Sydney Nolan is dead; Mary Nolan died today in Chicago of heart failure" is much clearer than "Mary Nolan, 67, wife of famous architect Sydney Nolan, died today in Chicago." (Note, also, that a news story should not begin with a name unless that name is known to nearly everybody.)

- Avoid indiscriminate use of personal pronouns. Repeat the name(s) of the person(s) in the story rather than using *he*, *she*, or *they* whenever there is the slightest chance that the reference may be misunderstood.

- Report that a person pleads "innocent" rather than "not guilty." The latter may be too easily misunderstood as its opposite.

- Avoid the words *latter*, *former*, and *respectively*, which are acceptable in print but should not be used on the air because the listener has no way of referring to the original comment.

- Avoid hackneyed expressions common to newscasts but seldom heard in everyday conversation. Say *run* instead of *flee*, *looking for* instead of *seeking*, and *killed* or *murdered* instead of *slain*.

- Change direct quotations from first person to third person whenever the change will help the listener understand. It is clearer to say "The mayor says she's going to get to the bottom of the matter" than to say "The mayor says, and these are her words, 'I'm going to get to the bottom of the matter,' end of quote."

- Always use contractions, unless the two words are needed for emphasis.

Checklist: Writing Effective News Copy

1. Write for the ear rather than the eye.
2. Avoid confusing words and statements.
3. Avoid excessive redundancy.
4. Use the present tense and the active voice.
5. Avoid initials.
6. Do not give addresses.
7. Use official job titles.
8. Proofread for badly cast sentences.
9. Avoid using we to refer to yourself.
10. Do not refer to a suspect's past criminal record.

Avoid confusing words and statements   The following lead-in to a news story is seriously misleading: "We have good news tonight for some veterans and their families. A House committee has approved a 6 percent cost-of-living increase." People unfamiliar with the legislative process might assume that the money was as good as in the bank. Confusion can also arise from using a word pronounced the same as one with a different meaning; for example, *expatriate* might

Figure 9.5
The writing of news copy is more efficient now than in the days of clacking mechanical typewriters. Using a computer terminal tied in to her station's mainframe, reporter Lois Melkonian can type almost as fast as she can think, and she can send finished copy directly to a printer. (Courtesy of KCBS, San Francisco)

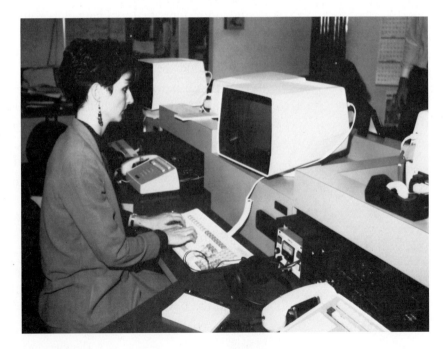

easily be interpreted by a listener as "ex-patriot," with embarrassing consequences.

Avoid excessive redundancy   Repeating salient facts is advisable, but too frequent repetition is dull. As a bad example, a newscaster might say, "Senator Muncey has called the recent hike in the prime lending rate outrageous," and then go to an actuality in which we hear the senator say, "The latest hike in the prime lending rate is, in my opinion, outrageous." Work always for lead-ins that promote interest but do not duplicate the story to follow.

Use the present tense and the active voice   Because the electronic media can report events as they happen, the present tense is appropriate. It automatically gives the news an air of immediacy. The active voice uses verbs that give sentences power. Instead of writing "the passenger ship was rammed by a submarine in Hampton Roads," write "A submarine rammed a passenger ship in Hampton Roads."

Avoid initials   Use initials only when they are so well-known that no ambiguity is possible. A few standard abbreviations are readily identifiable enough to be usable on broadcasts; examples are FBI, U.S., YMCA, and CIA. Most abbreviations should be replaced with a recognizable title, followed later in the story with a qualifying phrase such as "the teachers' association" or "the service group."

Do not give addresses in news copy   You may give them if they are famous or essential to the story. "Ten Downing Street," the home of the British prime minister, is a safe address to broadcast. The address of a murder suspect or an assault victim is not.

Be careful to use official job titles   Use *fire fighters*, *police officers*, *mail carriers*, and *stevedores* rather than *firemen*, *policemen*, *mailmen*, and *longshoremen*.

Be wary of badly cast sentences   This example from a wire-service bulletin shows the peril of careless writing:

```
DETECTIVES FOUND 2½ POUNDS OF ORIENTAL AND

MEXICAN HEROIN IN A LARGE WOMAN'S HANDBAG WHEN

THE CAR WAS STOPPED IN SOUTH CENTRAL LOS ANGELES
```

Listeners probably missed the next two news items while trying to decide whether the heroin was found in the handbag of a large woman or in a woman's large handbag.

When referring to yourself, use I not we   Such use of *we* is inaccurate and pretentious. No one person can be "we" (but monarchs and high church officials have traditionally used *we* this way).

Do not refer to a suspect's past criminal record   Also do not refer to any history of mental illness or treatment unless the information is essential to the story and has been checked for accuracy. Not only may the reporting of such information be defamatory; it may also prejudice the public against the person accused of, but not tried and convicted of, a crime.

A simple and excellent method for checking the clarity of your broadcast newswriting has been developed by Irving Fang, who calls his system the **easy listening formula (ELF)**.[2] It is applied by counting, in each sentence, each syllable above one per word. For example, the sentence "The quick brown fox jumped over the lazy dog" has an ELF score of 2, that is, 1 for the second syllable in *over* and 1 for the second syllable in *lazy*. To find the total ELF score for a script, compute the ELF scores of all the sentences and average them.

Fang's investigation of a wide variety of broadcast news scripts showed that the ELF scores of the most highly rated newswriters average below twelve. If your sentences score consistently above that figure, you may not be writing well for aural comprehension. Fang points out, however, that no mechanical system of measuring language is infallible. Common sense must be applied at all times in using his formula, because "it is easy to devise a confusing sentence with a low ELF score, just as it is easy to devise a simple sentence with a high ELF score . . . . What the easy listening formula shows is tendency and trend."

Delivering the News

Once you have written and rewritten the copy you will use during your air shift, and once the sounds have been assembled, logged, and delivered to the engineer, you are ready to go on the air. As you sit in the on-air studio, you will have before you the following items:

The **running log**, which follows the established format of your station and indicates the times at which you will give headlines, features, time checks, commercials, and other newscast elements or the times at which they will be played by the engineer

[2]Irving E. Fang, "The Easy Listening Formula," *Journal of Broadcasting*. (Winter, 1967), pp. 67–69.

Figure 9.6
When delivering the news, an announcer must be completely comfortable and at the peak of concentration. A student announcer at a university station tunes out the rest of the world while she reads news copy she wrote earlier in her shift. (Photo by Christopher Morrow, Stock Boston)

The **continuity book**, which contains any commercial copy you will read live, as well as notations of recorded commercials to be played by the engineer

Your **news script**, which will be loose sheets

An **elapsed-time clock**, which you can start and stop to help you time the commercials you will read

Switches, or **buses**, that allow you to open and close your announce mic, to open and close the intercom or talkback mic, and to open a mic in the newsroom for feeding out a news bulletin

One or more lights used to communicate information to you while you are on the air (For example, a red light might be used to indicate that the newsroom has a bulletin to be read. A yellow light might be used to tell you that the station's traffic reporter has a traffic alert.)

   The on-air studio will be equipped with a comfortable chair without armrests that would restrict movement and with castered legs that enable you to scoot in and out or from side to side with little effort. The chair may be designed to promote good posture, but no chair alone can make anyone sit up straight. The quality of your voice is directly affected by your posture; remember to sit comfortably, but try to keep your spine as straight as possible. A slumping person cannot breathe correctly, and weakened abdominal muscles and diaphragm cannot push air from your lungs through your phonators and articulators with optimal strength.

Position yourself so that you can easily reach the script, the continuity book, and the controls of both the elapsed-time clock and your mic. You will be checking off commercials, PSAs, and other program elements as they occur, so make sure that you also are in a position to reach the running log with your pencil. Unless you have an unusual voice or speech personality, you should position yourself 6 to 10 inches from the mic. If you experience problems with excessive sibilance or popping, or if your voice sounds thin or strident, work with a station engineer to find a better way of using your mic.

When you are on the air with the news, you are the anchor. This means that you coordinate the elements of the newscast and act as director. When it is time for a sounder (musical ID), you insert the correct cart into a playback machine and press the start button. When working with an engineer, you first give the hand signal for cart and then throw the cue for the sounder for the weather, the traffic report, or some other feature. The engineer, who has the log to work from, takes this and similar cues from you. At times you may be joined in the booth by a feature reporter, a field reporter who has returned from the scene of a news event, or a **co-anchor** (a second newscaster who will alternate with you in the reading of news stories).

Most news announcers read copy at 175 to 200 words a minute. This is considered fast enough to give the appropriate degree of importance to the material, yet slow enough to be easily understood. When you read news for a station that features news infrequently and briefly, you may be requested to read at a much faster rate. The overall sound of the station will determine this. To prepare for all eventualities, you should practice reading news in at least four different ways.

1. Practice reading the news slowly and casually, as is preferred by many low-key stations.
2. Read the news at the rate you feel brings out the best in your voice, interpretive abilities, and personality.
3. Practice at a rate of approximately 200 words a minute; this is the rate that may be expected of you.
4. Practice reading at your absolute maximum rate, with the realization that if you stumble, slur words, have trouble maintaining controlled breathing, have forced your voice into stridency, or have lost significant comprehensibility, you are reading too fast.

As you read, be prepared for mistakes you may make from misreading or stumbling over words, introducing the wrong cart, or cuing prematurely. Some argue that mistakes should be covered up rather than acknowledged, but the best contemporary practice is to acknowledge mistakes as frankly but unobtrusively as possible. Here is an example of a weak cover-up:

> ANNCR: . . . and they'll have your car ready in a half-hour—or an hour and a half, whichever comes sooner.

The script said "in an hour and a half." The cover-up is inappropriate because it gives false information. This is another example:

> ANNCR: The press secretary delayed and relayed the president's statement on the meeting.

Here the cover-up is so obvious that it would have been far better to have said "The press secretary delayed—sorry, *relayed*—the president's . . ."

When giving cues to an engineer or to a co-anchor, stop talking after throwing the cue; if you ramble on, you will talk over someone else's opening words. No well-run station will tolerate such sloppiness. In throwing cues, do not think it is amateurish to make your gestures big, clean, and precise. The best professionals never lapse into practices detrimental to the program or their own performance.

You will be handling a great deal of paper during your air shift, so develop skill in shifting papers without allowing the sound of rattling paper to be picked up by your mic. Necessary paper movements will be those to lift script pages from the pile in front of you, to move them to one side, and to turn script pages in the continuity book. No materials should be stapled together. There should be no need to turn over pages while on the air.

There will be many times during a normal shift when you will have an opportunity to talk directly with your producer, co-anchor, and/or engineer, for instance, during the playing of taped materials or while the network news is being broadcast. Use these opportunities for consultation wisely, but not too often; it is important that you not lose track of what your audience is hearing at such times. Check details that might prevent errors; tell the producer or engineer that you are going to shorten or dump a story because you are running late; if in doubt, ask what the next sound is to be. But remain attentive at all times to what is going out over the air. More than one announcer has followed a tragic actuality with an inappropriate wisecrack. Also, there is the possibility that the wrong cart has been played. If neither you nor your engineer is listening, you cannot possibly correct the mistake.

Be prepared to make constructive use of the minutes you have during your shift when you are not actually on the air. During breaks of 30 to 60 seconds, bring your logging up to date; check out the next few sounds you will introduce or cue; go over the next commercial you will read and make mental notes about its style, content, and the speed with which you will read it; see whether you are running ahead of, behind, or right on schedule. During longer breaks, you may have to write intros to actualities or voicers that have just been received and edited while you were on the air.

Three- or four-hour shifts are not uncommon at stations that feature news. It takes a healthy speech mechanism to continue to perform well day after day. You will very quickly become aware of any misuse of your vocal apparatus because you will suffer from hoarseness, sore throats, or similar afflictions. Obviously, such symptoms should be checked out by a doctor.

Long before you apply for a position as a news anchor, you should practice performing as you will be expected to perform on the job. This means not only learning to work with all the elements of a contemporary newscast, but also reading the news for extended periods of time. Such practice cannot ordinarily be accomplished in a classroom, and you are encouraged to look for opportunities to perform wherever they present themselves. College radio stations offer realistic challenges to students preparing for careers as radio news personnel.

The Radio Field Reporter

Field reporters are responsible for (1) live coverage of events as they occur, (2) taped actualities, voicers, and wraps, and (3) occasional research for and production of **minidocs**, brief documentaries presented as a series, usually over several days. Radio field reporters are sometimes called general-assignment reporters, correspondents, or special-assignment reporters. Their work is similar to that of their television counterparts, with obvious variations dictated by differences in electronic technology.

Live Reporting

It is the live reporter's responsibility to create a word picture of a scene, including sights, sounds, smells, tension in the air, and factual details—for example, the extent of a blaze, the names of the victims, or the value of stolen goods. When reporting live, you may be equipped with a portable shortwave radio, either in a small suitcase or in a station-supplied automobile. You will use this radio to indicate when you are ready to give your report, and you will hear your cue to begin as the program line is fed to you. Even when you are describing events as they occur (a live scener), as opposed to reporting at the conclusion of an event, you may work from notes that you scribbled as you collected information.

As you give a live report, keep these suggestions in mind:

- Do not report rumors, unless they are essential to the story—and then report them *only as rumors.*
- Do not make unsubstantiated guesses as to facts such as numbers of people injured or the value of a gutted building.
- Control your emotions. Remember, though, that a bit of *genuine* excitement in your voice will enhance the significance of your report.
- Do not identify yourself at the start of the report because this will have been done by the anchor. Do identify yourself at the close of the story, following the policy set down by your station.
- In the event of physical danger—a police siege or a confrontation between rival groups or street gangs—do not become so absorbed in your story that you endanger yourself or your station's equipment.
- Be prepared to discuss the event with the anchor. This means doing sufficient investigation prior to going on the air to prepare you to answer questions.

Voicers, Actualities, Sceners, and Wraps

Most of your work as a field reporter will not culminate in live reports, but rather in the making of **packages**, consisting of wraps, voicers, and edited sceners. When recording in the field, you will use a cassette tape recorder; when making packages at the station, the engineer will record on $\frac{1}{4}$-inch tape. After having been edited, if editing is necessary, the tape will be dubbed to one or more carts. These will be the sounds introduced by news anchors during their shifts.

Field voicers are transmitted to the station by shortwave radio or by telephone. After making notes, you notify the station engineer that you are ready to file a report. The engineer either cues up a reel-to-reel tape or inserts a cart into a cart recorder and places an index

Figure 9.7

A radio field reporter must go where the stories are—anywhere from the local courthouse to a cocktail lounge. Reporter Pat Shaer brings notepaper and a tape recorder to do a field interview for a Texas radio station. (Karen Westley, courtesy of KUHF Radio, University of Houston)

finger on the start button. You give a brief countdown—"three, two, one"—and start your report; the engineer starts the tape just after hearing "one." If all goes well, the tape and your voice begin at the same time. Voicers made at the station are produced in essentially the same way, although you will typically work in a small announce booth and have eye contact with the engineer.

Some field reporters must use a telephone to send in voicers. If you are reporting live, the station engineer simply directs your voice to the transmitter. The process becomes more complicated when you are sending a report that you have previously recorded. Your recorded material may be of two kinds: complete reports that you have recorded at the scene of a news event (voicers), or recorded statements made by nonstation personnel (actualities). An actuality to which you have given a lead-in and lead-out is a wrap.

To phone in a *voicer*, follow these steps:

1. Cue up the cassette.
2. Plug your microphone into the recorder with the mic switch on.
3. Depress the record key. This activates the recorder as a transmitting device, but the tape will not roll because you have not also depressed the play key.

Figure 9.8
The Marantz PMD201 portable tape recorder is a popular model. (Courtesy of Marantz)

4. Insert a cable plug into the jack of the recorder labeled "out" or "aux."

5. When you are ready to send your report, dial the station engineer and, using your microphone to speak and the telephone earpiece to listen, tell the engineer that you have a voicer to deliver. When the engineer is ready, count down and begin playing your taped report by hitting the play key. This automatically releases the record key, so the tape rolls and plays without danger of being erased.

If you are reporting from one of your station's "bureaus," such as city hall, the court house, or the police station, you will probably use a telephone that has been rewired by a station engineer. The handset will have been outfitted with a miniplug that allows the cable from your recorder to bypass the telephone's built-in microphone and pass directly over the line to your station. The signal quality is excellent. If you have no such telephone, you may be able to find an older model phone with a mouthpiece that can be screwed off. The cable you would use in this instance comes out of the recorder and culminates in two small alligator clips. The telephone diaphragm (microphone) is lifted out, and the alligator clips are connected to the two wire terminals of the telephone.

A *wrap* is phoned in basically the same way as a voicer is, except for this difference: When all elements are connected, your tape is cued, you mic switch is on, and the record key is depressed, you give the countdown and begin your introduction to the actuality live. When you finish, you depress the play key and the tape rolls. When the actuality is completed, you hit the record key; this cancels the play key, so the tape stops rolling while you give your closing tag live.

If you cannot send a wrap directly to the station as described above, you will have to speak into the mouthpiece of a conventional or cellular phone, roll your tape, quickly move the telephone's mouthpiece down to the speaker of your recorder to send the bulk of your report, and then move the handset up to your mouth to make your closing comments and tag.

If possible, use your recorder even for phoning in reports that could be done without it. Sending a live telephone report through your recorder eliminates the small telephone microphone, and this improves audio quality. Some stations, because of union regulations or station policy, require procedures different from those just described. Be prepared to adapt to the requirements of working situations that vary from the norm.

In making voicers at the station, you will first write a script. In this case the log will simply indicate "script attached," the duration of the voicer in seconds, and the end cue, which is nearly always your name followed by the call letters of your station. In making wraps at the station, you begin by making and recording telephone calls. If there is a news story on an impending strike, for example, your phone calls may be to the union leader, the speaker for the company or agency being threatened, and a labor negotiator. From the telephone interviews you should be able to make several usable wraps—carted, timed, and ready to be logged.

Preparing Feature Reports: Minidocs

Radio stations that emphasize news often vary their programming by broadcasting feature reports or short documentaries. These may be a series of three- or four-minute programs, including as few as three or as many as ten individual segments, each focusing on a different aspect of a topic. Feature reports deal with people, problems, events, or anything else that is of general interest but lacks the "hard news" character that warrants coverage on a regular newscast. News events, in fact, frequently inspire feature reports, but such reports differ from news stories in that they provide much more detail, offer greater perspective, and often express a point of view.

Preparing a series of feature reports begins with the selection of a topic. Once you have chosen or been assigned a topic, your responsibilities will include researching the subject, identifying and interviewing people who will contribute most of the information the public eventually will receive, editing and organizing the taped materials, writing the connective and interpretive narration, voicing the narration, and producing the final mixed versions of the program segments. The steps in creating a series are illustrated in the following example, whose topic is the homeless.

Researching the topic   Your research plan is essential to the success of the series. Developing a personal system for doing research can save hours, reduce the possibility of mistakes, and result in a superior product. You may want to begin your research in a library. If your station subscribes to an on-line information service, however, you may be able to do all your preliminary research at its keyboard. One such system, NEXIS, encodes over 160 newspapers, nearly all popular magazines, government documents, encyclopedias, and many other information sources. The system operates on the basis of key words. In searching for information on the homeless, you type that word on

Spotlight: Top of the News— National Public Radio

The idea of public radio as an alternative to commercial formats has been around since the advent of radio broadcasting in 1920. First called "educational radio," it was meant to offer news, culture, and information not available in the imitative, market-driven commercial realm. But public radio stations were few in number in the first half of the century; these independent entities operated on shoestring budgets and broadcast whenever they could. Not until the inception in 1967 of the government-backed Corporation for Public Broadcasting did public radio have a chance to flourish. The result was the National Public Radio (NPR) network.

NPR, founded in 1970, was ready to go on-air by 1971. With financial support from the U.S. government, nationwide affiliated stations, and corporate sponsors, NPR acts as a producer of radio programs that are then transmitted to member stations. These member stations, which also receive training and promotion from NPR, control which programs they broadcast—and when—and how those NPR-produced programs ought to be promoted and distributed for their particular listening audience.

Now over twenty years old, NPR has almost 400 member stations and about 12 million weekly listeners. Its news program *Morning Edition*, for example, draws an audience equal to that of NBC-TV's *Today* show. Hosted since its inception in 1979 by Bob Edwards, *Morning Edition* is a two-hour magazine of straight news and news-related interviews; features on arts, culture, sports, science, and business; and commentary on social, political, and musical topics. Edwards wakes up at 1:30 A.M. in his Virginia home to get to the Washington, D.C. studio by 2:30; he reads newswire copy and writes stories until time to go on the air at 6:00. He strives to tell listeners "what's so special about today" (*The Atlanta Journal and Constitution*, Nov. 2, 1989).

Listeners to *Morning Edition* have been

called "informationaholics," and perhaps the same is true of those drawn at other times to NPR's spot on the local dial for the magazine-format program *All Things Considered* and the two weekend programs called *Weekend Edition*. *All Things Considered*, which is broadcast in the afternoon drive time and co-hosted by Linda Wertheimer, Robert Siegel, and Noah Adams, features reports from NPR's U.S. news bureaus, worldwide affiliated stations, and freelance journalists about the direction world events have taken during that business day. Listeners, most of whom have at least a 30-minute commute home from work, develop a certain loyalty to the program; their letters are sometimes read on the air, and their influence is felt at the local member-station level.

Besides news, NPR produces and distributes a continuous flow of arts and cultural programs. The best-known daytime program is *Performance Today*, a two-hour program of classical music and arts information. In the evenings, NPR airwaves fill with chamber music, symphonies, opera, folk,

NPR staff (Photo courtesy of Paula Darte, NPR)

and jazz. Perhaps the two most popular music shows are *Afropop Worldwide*, which features African music and its global variations, and *Bluesstage*, a forum for rhythm and blues.

And remember radio drama? NPR not only rebroadcasts old favorites but also produces contemporary shows, such as an all-radio rendition of *Star Wars*, Stephen King's "The Mist," and short stories of Ray Bradbury. An experiment with on-air auto advice, called *Car Talk* and hosted by two expert and jovial auto mechanics, became immediately popular with listeners. And in 1990 NPR launched its attempt to compete with late-night television: a program of interviews and performance called *HEAT with John Hockenberry*.

Even with 90-minutes daily of *All Things Considered*, listeners wanted more news. "News had been getting smaller and smaller," said former producer Jay Kernis, "[on commercial stations they were] down to 1-minute and 2-minute spots, and our NPR stations wanted some sustained reporting in depth."

In fact, news is what drew host Bob Edwards to NPR. Although he could make a much higher salary working on TV, he says, "I'm still affected by the illusion of radio, the illusion that the person on the radio is talking only to me. . . . If you're watching Leslie Stahl on television and she's doing a stand-up somewhere, chances are you're looking at her, thinking [something like] 'Hasn't she done something to her hair?' and you're not listening to her. You're distracted. We don't have that" (*The Los Angeles Times*, Nov. 2, 1989). Edwards calls his co-workers—producers and announcers alike—"news junkies." And what keeps him crawling out of bed at 1:30 A.M. is the "endless variety of subjects" explored on public radio. "You can indulge your interests in all different fields, even fields you don't know anything about," asserts Edwards (*Los Angeles Times*). And then there is the challenge of translating those current culture and news events into stories and interviews that will give listeners something to care about. In the business of news, the most perishable of announcing media, the challenge is new every day because yesterday never matters.

the keyboard, and the display will show how many articles are available. Because the number is staggering, you begin to narrow it down—by city or state, age, socioeconomic group, or some other criterion. Eventually, you will select a number of articles and activate a printer to produce hard copy.

If you must do your research at a library, start with the *Reader's Guide to Periodical Literature*, which will provide you with a list of stories on the subject. *Facts on File* or a similar reference service will give you statistics. In a few hours you will have learned some of the basic facts and opinions about homelessness, or any other topic.

Outlining the series   Having read several articles and compiled some basic statistics about your topic, you are ready to make some tentative decisions about the series. If you and the news director agree that the topic is important and complex, perhaps five or six segments will be needed to cover it adequately. You may decide that your final segment will provide explicit recommendations. You will also decide on the number of people to be interviewed and their specializations.

Segment 1—background for the series. Basic facts about the topic and statistics. To make listeners aware that the problem of homelessness is large and growing and that any person of any age or physical condition could, under certain circumstances, become homeless.

Segment 2—what a homeless person goes through. Made up of edited comments by several homeless people, recorded in a park, under a viaduct, or wherever they congregate.

Segment 3—a police view of the homeless. Features the edited comments of a police officer as well as one or more police officials.

Segment 4—attitudes of neighbors, tourists, and businesspersons. Shows a range of attitudes held by people who are not themselves homeless but who nonetheless are affected by homelessness.

Segment 5—the causes of homelessness. Includes comments made by social workers, psychiatrists, or other authorities on the subject.

Segment 6—what society should do to help the homeless. Consists of suggestions offered by each of the persons interviewed for the series.

Recording interviews Because all your interviews will be in the field, you will need a high-quality, lightweight, battery-operated tape recorder. You will also need a top-quality microphone. Some unions will not allow you to purchase your own microphones, but where there is no such prohibition, you will be wise to invest in the best equipment you can afford.

Before making dates for interviews, speak with the people you have tentatively selected for the program. Tell them that you want ideas and information, but do not invite them to be interviewed until you are satisfied that they are articulate, knowledgeable, and cooperative. You may find that you must look further for your talent. Of course, you would not be able to phone homeless people to screen them or set up appointments, so there is no reason to delay taping them. Obtain their permission to tape, then roll your cassette and start asking questions.

Before each recording session, prepare a list of questions. Be as thorough as possible in your preparation, for the audio quality of your program will suffer if you must record the same person on two or more occasions or in different locations. Ambient noise and acoustics should be as consistent as possible within each of the program segments. Use your prepared questions, but do not be a slave to them.

Tips on interviewing are given in Chapter 8; the following adds some suggestions pertinent to recording material for feature reports.

Test your equipment before beginning the interview, no matter how experienced you are. Even professionals sometimes complete

---

**Checklist: Recording
Interviews Successfully**

1. Test your equipment before beginning an interview.
2. Explain your taping and editing procedures to the interviewee.
3. When you are ready to begin, ask the interviewee to remain silent and then start recording.
4. Avoid giving vocal reinforcements such as "uh-huh" during the guest's remarks.
5. Keep the recorder running.
6. Limit your recording sessions to a reasonable length.
7. Keep your station's format restrictions in mind.
8. If there is ambient noise, keep the mic close to the interviewee's mouth.

---

interviews only to discover that their batteries were weak, the machine was not recording, the volume level was too high or too low, or the absence of a windscreen on the mic resulted in excessive wind blast. Try to test your equipment under the exact conditions and in the precise location of the interview.

Take the time to explain taping and editing procedures to the interviewee. It is important for your guest to know that all your comments and questions will be removed from the tape and replaced by narration recorded in the studio. This means that he or she should make direct, complete statements not preceded by references to the questions. To illustrate, here are two responses to the same question.

ANNCR: What do you feel should be done to combat homelessness in America?

ANSWER 1: I don't really have the answers. It seems like an almost hopeless situation.

ANSWER 2: To come to grips with the problem of homelessness, we first need a study to find out just who the homeless people are and how they became homeless.

It is obvious that the second answer will be easier to edit, will provide more precise information than the first answer, and will allow a smoother flow from narration to statement. You cannot expect every person you interview to overcome a lifetime of conversational habit, but you can expect reasonable cooperation.

When you are ready to begin the interview, ask the interviewee to remain silent and then start recording. Record about 30 seconds of dead air. This precaution provides you with ambient sound for insertion at any point at which you want an undetectable pause. All rooms other than those designed for scientific tests have ambient noise, and no two rooms are alike. You cannot splice in the ambient sound from another interview, and you certainly cannot splice in blank tape, for either would be noticeable to any attentive listener. It is likely that the ambient sound you record will be needed only infrequently, but when it is you will be grateful for having developed the habit of recording it before every interview.

It is also good practice to allow the tape recorder to run for a few seconds after your guest has stopped speaking. Later, when you are editing and script writing, you may want to ask for a **fade-out** at the end of one or another of your guest's comments. If you have abruptly stopped the recorder immediately upon the conclusion of your guest's remarks, there is no way to do a fade.

As you interview, avoid giving your guest vocal reinforcement, such as "uh-huh" or "I see." Such expressions will be impossible to edit out when assembling the program. Nonverbal support—nods of the head or smiles—is sufficient to encourage a guest to continue.

During the interview, try to keep the recorder running. Do not hesitate to stop it, however, if the session is going badly. The reason for an uninterrupted take is that most people are more alert and energized when they feel that what they are saying will be heard later on the air. Constant stopping and starting saps energy and reduces concentration.

Keep your taping sessions to a reasonable length. A 90-minute interview to be edited as part of a 3-minute program segment will cost you hours of production time. Therefore, work for interviews that are long enough to supply you with the material you will need but not so long as to saddle you with hours of editing.

As you interview, keep the format of your station's feature reports in mind. If, for example, your station prefers to use both your questions and your guest's answers on the final tape, your interviewing technique should reflect that fact. You will not then have to ask guests to answer your questions in the form of self-explanatory statements.

Train yourself to detect slurring speech patterns. Some people run words together so habitually and consistently that it is impossible to edit their comments effectively and efficiently. This is often not discovered until time for editing, and by then it is too late. When you hear that you are working with a slurrer, do your best to slow the person down. If this fails, ask the guest to repeat single phrases and sentences that seem to constitute the most important contributions you will later use in your report.

When recording at any location that has a high level of ambient sound (machinery, traffic, crowds), keep your mic close to your guest's mouth. Authentic background sounds can enhance the realism of your report, but they must not be so loud as to interfere with your guest's remarks. If you will later edit out your questions, you need not move the mic back and forth between you and your guest. If, on the other hand, you are to retain even some of your questions or comments, then you must develop skill in moving the mic. To avoid noise due to handling of the mic, wrap the cord around your wrist. Such noises are especially troublesome because they can be heard only on playback or by monitoring during the interview, a practice seldom engaged in by people working solo.

After completing each interview, transfer it from cassette to a reel of ¼-inch audiotape. Cassettes are fine for recording, but they are impossible to edit precisely. When you have finished dubbing the interview, you should make a rough electronically edited version of it by dubbing to a second reel-to-reel machine only those portions of the interview that will conceivably be used in the final report. The rough edit will give you a manageable amount of material with which to begin writing your report. You can, of course, do your rough editing directly from the cassette to ¼-inch tape, but cassettes are extremely difficult to cue up. They give only the roughest indication of where you are on the tape. Because today's ¼-inch tape recorders lose almost no quality when speech is dubbed, you can easily go to three or four generations without detectable loss of quality.

If time permits, make a typescript of the roughly edited interview, preferably on a word processor that allows you to cut and paste. The written word is far easier to identify, retrieve, manipulate, and edit than are words on an audiotape. When writing the narrative script, you will find it easier to develop a smooth flow and precise lead-ins when working in print. Making a typescript may actually save time.

Having completed the script, do the fine editing of the rough dub. This should be done by manually cutting and splicing the tape. Electronic editing is done when you have little time to cut and splice, but it has serious drawbacks. Manual editing allows you to remove unwanted pauses, "ers" and "uhs," or even single words. It also allows you to take a portion of an answer from one part of the interview and join it to an answer from another. *It is critical that such editing preserve the sense of your guest's comments and never be used for any purpose other than clarifying your guest's position and making your report as factually honest as it can be.*

When you cut your tape, you may find that some statements that looked good in the written script do not come out well in sound. Be prepared, therefore, to go back to the roughly edited version to look for substitutes or to rewrite your script to make the narrative sound better or clearer.

As you cut and splice, splice in leader tape between all segments of the edited tape; this will make it extremely easy for you or an engineer to find and cue up each of the statements on the tape. Naturally, you should arrange the edited statements in the sequence in which they will occur in the completed production.

Finally, record your narration. This often means sitting in an announce booth or a small production room and doing a real-time recording, with an engineer alternately feeding your voice and the edited statements to a reel-to-reel tape recorder. It is possible for you to record all your narration without the edited inserts and to have an engineer later mix the entire report, but doing so wastes time and effort. It is also detrimental to your interpretation; despite all the technology of tape editing, there is still something to be said for real-time radio—even when it is on tape.

> ### *Practice: Reading News Copy Cold*

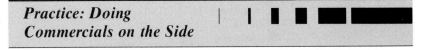

If you or your instructor can obtain printouts of wire-service copy, practice reading 5-minute summaries cold (without looking them over first). Also practice rewriting such copy for a better news sound.

> ### *Practice: Doing Commercials on the Side*

Some stations have policies that prohibit news reporters or newscasters from reading commercials; most do not. To practice delivery of commercial copy, choose three scripts from Appendix A, and read them aloud until you feel confident enough to record your performance. Listen to the tape closely, noting pacing, tone, and pronunciation. Decide what types of commercials your voice is best suited for.

i0 Television News

News on television varies from brief voice-over slide bulletins to the 24-hour coverage of Cable News Network (CNN). Most large television stations produce two or three news programs daily, some 30 minutes in length and some lasting an hour. These are typically broadcast at noon, at the dinner hour, and at ten or eleven at night. Except for stations in small markets, most news departments are large in relation to a station's total employment. Departments range from about a dozen to more than a hundred employees. Television news programs are put together by reporters, anchors, newswriters, videotape crews, mobile van operators, operators of special-effects generators and computer graphics systems, tape editors, and a production crew working in the studio, the control room, and the videotape room.

A Typical News Operation

There is a discernible pattern to a daily television news operation. In the newsroom, hours of anticipation, accompanied by mounting tension, are followed by sudden quiet—as the action moves to the news set and the control room. As the show goes on the air, there follows an hour of concentrated effort, often mixed with some anxiety. As the closing credits roll, there is satisfaction, relaxation, and even exhilaration, as members of the team slowly return to the newsroom.

The following description of a half-day in the life of a television newsroom is not definitive, but the mood and the rhythms are typical. The sketch describes the preparation, broadcast, and follow-up of a one-hour noontime broadcast that alternates between news reports and in-depth studio interviews. The interview portion of such a program was described in Chapter 8. This discussion focuses on the news component.

The scene: A television newsroom

The event: The preparation and broadcast of a one-hour news program

7:00 A.M.: At the start of the workday, the first to arrive is an assistant news producer, who comes in to watch national television news, check and clear the wire-service teleprinters, activate the police, fire, sheriff, and other emergency frequencies, and generally get things rolling.

7:00–8:00 A.M.: Other members of the large team trickle in—the assignment editor and desk assistants, the news director, the program producer, the news producer and assistants, field reporters, the anchor, the on-air camera director and assistant director, programmers and operators of the character generator, videotape editors, newswriters, and news interns. For a time everyone seems to be doing his or her own thing, with only occasional interactions. Gradually, as each team member completes preliminary preparations, small groups begin to form. The pace accelerates, but there is no confusion, no random movements. All team members know their duties and carry out their preparations without receiving instructions.

8:00 A.M.: The news anchor arrives at the newsroom.

8:00–8:30 A.M.: The anchor checks the status of the most important

Figure 10.1

Putting together a television news broadcast involves writing, research, interviewing, filming, editing, and production before the actual show, adding up to many hours of team effort. The staff in a typical local television newsroom may begin work at 7:00 A.M., drafting scripts and assembling video segments for the half-hour broadcast at noon. (Photo by Frank Siteman, Stock Boston) news stories and makes preliminary preparations for the planning meeting with the news producer. Both have been listening to news reports on the radio at home and in their cars since awakening, so they have an awareness of both local and world events.

8:30–9:00 A.M.: The anchor meets with the news producer and two or more newswriters to discuss the day's stories. The group views sound bites and packages—from the station's own reporters, from CNN's NEWSOURCE, from INDX (a news feed for independent stations), and from the parent network. The news producer may check for late developments with the assignment editor. A preliminary determination is made as to which stories will be covered and the order in which they will be reported. The producer then assigns writing responsibilities to the anchor and the newswriters. One writer is assigned to do videotape editing and assembling.

9:00 A.M.: A preproduction meeting is called by the station's news director. Present are the program producer, the news producer, the anchor, the on-air camera director, and other key members of the team.

9:30–10:00 A.M.: Anchor and newswriters write scripts, while other members of the news operation edit tapes and keep up with developing stories from both reporters in the field and other news sources, such as wire services, police radio, and so forth.

10:00 A.M.: Anchor and interview host deliver a live tease on fixed camera in the newsroom, and then tape three more teases to be played between 10:05 and 11:45.

10:05–11:50 A.M.: Anchor and writers continue developing their scripts, while changes are constantly being made as new information or new stories come into the newsroom.

10:30–11:45 A.M.: News scripts begin to be assembled, and stories are arranged in a sequence based on the news producer's judgment as to their significance, viewer interest, and other factors. Stories and pages are numbered. Pages go to the news producer and anchor for editing. The anchor marks copy for interpretation or pronunciation. The director marks copy for camera directions. Other copies go to the prompter operator, the character generator operator, and the script file.

11:45 A.M.: The newsroom suddenly falls quiet. Only a few people remain there: the assignment editor, two assistants, a newswriter, and two news interns. The interns serve as runners, standing by to replace script pages as the show is rewritten on the basis of new or updated stories. The action has moved to the control room and the news set. In the control room the production team has assembled. The team includes the program producer, the news producer, the program director, an assistant director, a technical director (a **switcher**), a camera operator (responsible for rolling tapes and calling up slides), a character generator operator, and two **news runners** (who move back and forth between the newsroom and the control room, bringing in updated script pages). On the set the anchor and the interview host have taken their places to tease the upcoming broadcast.

11:55 A.M.: Anchor and interview host give a live tease from the news set.

12:00 noon: The taped program intro is rolled, followed by a cue from the floor director to the anchor, "You're on the air." For an entire hour—which can seem much, much longer—the news program unfolds. As revised scripts are brought into the control room, they are noted by the producer and assistant director, who make changes during commercial breaks and give instructions for the changes to the news anchor and the prompter operator (who, of course, have also been given the revised pages). The noise in the control room is considerable—the audio feed of the ongoing newscast is played at a high enough volume to be clearly heard above the sounds of ringing telephones, telephone conversations between producer and newsroom personnel, the director's orders, and occasional announcements from the producer, such as "We're losing the feed from Yosemite, so we'll have to kill it—tell talent to stretch."

12:59:50 P.M.: The taped closing credits roll. Earpieces and headset microphones are removed. On the set lights are dimmed. In the control room there is little sound.

1:00–1:30 P.M.: The show has kept team members in a state of tension and even anxiety for over an hour, including the build-up to air time. One by one, the team members drift back to the newsroom—some to relax, others to pick up personal items on their way to the parking lot and home.[1] The news producer, assignment editor, anchor, and other key personnel meet with the program producer for a brief **postmortem** (a discussion of what worked, what did not work, and why).

---

[1]The talent, director, switcher, and floor crew usually remain on the set to tape promos for the next day's program.

As the last members of the noon news staff depart, they meet early arrivals who begin to prepare for the evening newscast. The newsroom will not be completely quiet until nearly midnight.

The Field Reporter

Journalists who work away from the station are called **field reporters**, or **general-assignment reporters**. Reporters who are stationed some distance away are called **correspondents**. As a **special-assignment reporter**, you might cover a regular beat, such as crime, politics, or a particular section of a large city. However, few stations can afford such specialists; most put field reporters on special assignment from time to time.

As a field or general-assignment reporter, you will be given your daily schedule by an assignment editor. Some assignments will involve covering **hard news**—serious accidents or crimes, fires, explosions, chemical spills, tornadoes, and similar unanticipated events; others will be concerned with **soft news**—meetings, trials, briefings, hearings, news conferences, and so on. News departments maintain a **future file**, consisting of 31 folders (for the days of the month) into which is placed information about scheduled soft news events. As notices of events reach the station, they are placed in the folder bearing the appropriate date. Each day, the assignment editor searches the file for the most promising news stories and schedules reporters and camera operators to cover them. Scheduled coverage of soft news is often dropped at the last minute in favor of late-breaking hard news.

As a field reporter, you will work both live and on tape. When working on tape, you will have an opportunity to plan your coverage, engage in on-site investigation, think through and write your opening and closing stand-ups, and record a second or third take if the first effort falls apart. A **stand-up** is an on-camera statement made by a reporter that may come at any point in a taped story but nearly always closes it. When reporting live by way of microwave or satellite transmission, you will report events as they are happening, and this precludes scriptwriting and reshooting. The ability to ad-lib an unfolding news event in an accurate, effective manner is the key to success in live reporting.

Taped and live field reports on television newscasts are often longer than similar stories prepared for radio. Television coverage is much more expensive than radio coverage, and the technical com-

Figure 10.2

Television reporter Caroline Chang, on assignment for an NBC-affiliate in North Carolina, arrives at the site of a local high school to follow up on a lead for a story. Making only $15,000 annually, Chang acts as camera operator, field reporter, and editor for all of her stories. (Photos © Michael Edrington/The Image Works)

plexities are greater. Therefore, you will be expected to cover only one to three stories in a given workday. You must not assume that your field reports will dominate a newscast, however, for most stories from the field run between 30 seconds and 3 minutes in length. To create a usable 60-second report, you may have to spend several hours, both in the field and back at your station. Time must be devoted to investigation of the story, lining up witnesses or others you may want to interview, conducting the interviews, making notes for your stand-ups, and taping the story. Travel time to the stories' locations and back to the station can be substantial.

Preparing a Package on Tape

The reporter's job is usually not over when the field coverage is completed. Although a messenger can take a tape to the station to be edited by an assistant producer, the customary practice is for the reporter to complete a **package** (a report that will need only a lead-in by a news anchor).

As a reporter, you will follow certain steps in making a news package. Each day at the station, the assignment editor (the **desk**) gives you your assignment. If it is a slow news day, you may be given a soft news story to cover, and in this case you may be asked for ideas. On the other hand, if much hard news is breaking, you can expect to be told what you are to cover. After receiving the assignment, you leave the station with an **ENG (electronic news gathering) operator**.[2]

---

[2]Reporters at smaller stations often do their own ENG work.

You may travel in a station wagon with little equipment, in a van that has equipment for viewing tapes en route, or in a truck equipped to send picture and sound back to the station via microwave transmission. **Uplink equipment** bounces the program material off a satellite to a receiver at the station.

On arriving at the scene of the story, you undertake relevant research to learn what has happened, who is involved, what is going on at the moment, why the event is happening—in other words, you pursue answers to the traditional *who*, *what*, *when*, *where*, and *why* of journalism. As you investigate, the ENG operator is setting up to tape whatever is essential or desirable to tell the story. Sometimes you ask the ENG operator to tape this or that person or object; usually, however, you rely on the operator, whose professionalism will lead to sound judgments. As you gather information, you take notes. At this stage you will not have decided how you will structure the report, so almost anything that turns up must be committed to paper. When you and the ENG operator are ready, you interview selected persons on tape. Later the interviews will be edited as **sound bites**, the television equivalent of radio actualities. After all notes have been taken and all visual material taped, you do your stand-ups. You may begin your report on the scene and on camera, and you may make one or more on-camera comments to be edited into the completed package; then you do an on-camera summary and toss for the close.

Figure 10.3
Inside a local high school gymnasium, field reporter Caroline Chang interviews a basketball coach about the outcome of an important game. Like many small- and medium-market television reporters, Chang does double duty as she juggles camera and mic while conducting her interview. Later, back at the studio, she edits this and other stories in preparation for the evening news broadcast. (Photos © Michael Edrington/The Image Works)

Before leaving the scene of your report, you ask the ENG operator to tape material to be used as **cutaway shots**, or **cutaways**. Cutaways are a form of insurance used to avoid a **jump cut**. When editing an interview, you may want to cut out some comments for which the camera was focused on the speaker. The insertion of a brief shot of yourself apparently listening to the speaker will camouflage this kind of cut, keeping viewers from noticing any change in position of the speaker between comments. To prepare for the anticipated need of cutaways, you will ask your ENG operator to tape you as you look into the camera lens after the interview. If possible, do your cutaways while the person you have interviewed is still present. Also, remember that because a cutaway is not an actual, real-time shot of you listening to the speaker, it is imperative that your reactions be as true to the spirit of the interview as possible. A popular motion picture of 1988, *Broadcast News*, made a contrived cutaway shot the focus of its condemnation of unethical journalistic practices.

You view the tapes and make notes on the drive back to the station. There you will write a script that will be used by an editor to mix stand-ups and sound bites into a package. At times you will have to make an audio recording of voice-over narration, which you will do in a small announce booth equipped with a microphone and perhaps an equalizer. You will have worked with a station engineer to learn how to adjust the equalizer so that your voice will sound as close as possible to the way it sounds when recorded in the field.

In writing a script, you will use a conventional format and certain abbreviations. Many of the abbreviations used in television scripts are listed in Table 10.1.

As you prepare a package, you should keep in mind the visual effects that are available to you. In general, visuals are available from a character generator, a design computer, videotape recorders, and switchers. The appropriate use of these resources can make your stories more comprehensible, more informative, and more eye-appealing.

The **character generator** prints out names to identify persons and places and creates pie charts and bar graphs, including animated graphs, and **keys** (images, usually lettering, keyed into a background image). The character generator can also produce reveals, hot changes, and rolls. A **reveal** flashes key terms on the screen to highlight the points being made by the speaker. A **hot change** occurs when words or statements are flashed on the screen for a moment and then replaced. A **roll** occurs when information moves from bottom to top and off the screen as the speaker voices it.

Table 10.1   Abbreviations Used in Television Scripts

Abbreviation	Meaning
TS	tight shot
CU	close-up
MCU	medium close-up
ECU or XCU	extreme close-up
MS	medium shot
WS or LS	wide shot or long shot
ELS or XLS	extreme long shot
OS	over-the-shoulder shot (usually over the reporter's shoulder and showing the person being interviewed face-on)
RS	reverse shot (reporter listening to person being interviewed)
TWO-SHOT	a shot with two people in the frame
PAN	camera moves right to left or left to right
TILT	camera moves up or down
SOT	sound on tape
SLO-MO	slow motion
VO	voice-over
CUT	a brief scene on tape—an actuality, a voicer, or a wrap
IN:	indicates the words that open a sound bite
OUT:	indicates the words that end a sound bite
SLUG	the slug line, a brief title given to a news story for identification purposes
TRT	total running time

The **design computer** features a keyboard, a design monitor, an electronic tablet with stylus, and a menu (a list of effects that can be produced by the computer). The stylus, or electronic pen, works by completing an electrical connection when it touches the tablet. Among other effects the design computer can generate many styles of lettering, boxes, circles, and other shapes, and animated graphics.

Videotape recorders can provide material taped off a parent network or from a satellite feed and can store both file materials and bumpers. **Bumpers** are stills or moving shots, usually with lettering, that bump the story from one scene to another.

The **switcher** can move video images anywhere on the screen and can key in **box graphics**—pictures and words that symbolize the story and are usually placed in the upper left or upper right portion of the screen. A switcher can also produce a great variety of wipes. A **wipe** occurs when one picture gradually replaces another; the first picture is wiped, or pushed off the screen. Wipes may have a number of configurations, but the simplest—and most often used—are horizontal and vertical.

The script you will prepare for each package will list all the cuts (scenes) to be used, identified by tape number and time code address. The **time code** is an electronic readout that gives an address (number) for each frame. The portion of a script in Figure 10.4 illustrates both script abbreviations and time code notations. (The letters WF are the initials of the reporter, Wayne Freedman.) As you can see, the total running time of the package is 2 minutes and 47 seconds. The title, or slug line, is DEMOLITION. This portion of the script lists two cuts featuring the reporter and three sound-on-tape excerpts—two are the wrecker's ball smashing into the building, and one is a sound bite, whose in- and out-cues are given.

You work with a tape editor in the sound bay until the entire package is completed, with sound bites, cutaways, visuals and graphics prepared at the station, your on-camera stand-up closing comments, and your voice-over intros and transitions dubbed to a single tape. When the package has been properly labeled, it is ready to be sent to the videotape room, where it is held for playing during the newscast.

A variation of the foregoing procedures is to perform all the steps taken to produce the package except for doing the stand-ups. After the package has been edited, you return to the scene of the story during the newscast to do a live introduction and close. At a small television station you may do your own camera work. You go to the scene of a story, conduct your investigation, and record sound bites, including interviews; before leaving the scene, you place the camera on a tripod, start the recorder, walk to a position in front of the camera lens, and do your stand-up. When you return to the station, you write the script and edit and assemble your package.

Figure 10.4
A script for a video package identifies the cuts
used by tape number and
time code address.

```
SLUG            VIDEO       WRITER       TRT

DEMOLITION                  FREEDMAN     2:47
```

```
                    WF CUT
It is the urban American way. Every

day we commute to the city, find our

little niche of office space . . .

and do something constructive.

(SMASH INSIDE)

SOT (#1; 16:16)

IN: Well, it's constructive . . .

OUT: In another . . .

WF CUT

This is the Kodak Building. . . .

At least, it used to be.

SOT (#1; 14:51)

(CRASH FROM EXTERIOR)
```

Reporting Live from the Field

Most television news operations make use of one or more remote vans
equipped with ENG equipment: **minicams** (miniaturized cameras),
portable tape recorders, microwave transmitters, and, in some cases,
an uplink to a satellite. These vans are sometimes used for conventional coverage of a news story (taping a report in the field), but their
chief purpose is to enable reporters to cover events and transmit their
stories directly to the station, often live during a newscast. Only those
reporters who are excellent journalists, have widespread knowledge
of many subjects, and can ad-lib fluently and informatively are successful at live reporting.

Studying journalism in college will prepare you to quickly size up a story, make judgments about its potential news value, identify the most salient points about the event, and organize that information so that it is readily comprehensible to the public. When you are covering slow-breaking stories (in fact, whenever time permits), your background in journalism will enable you to engage in investigative, or depth, reporting. Knowing how and where to look for hidden information is essential for depth reporting. Finally, journalism courses will familiarize you with the laws regarding libel, contempt, constitutional guarantees, access to public records, the invasion of privacy, and copyrights. All reporters should be competent journalists, of course, but those who report the news live must be especially well prepared. If a defamatory statement is made on a live broadcast, there is simply no way to undo it.

Extensive knowledge of many subjects is also a prerequisite for reporters and, again, especially for those who report live. It is customary for anchors to end a live report with a **question-and-answer (Q & A) session** with the reporter. The stories you report may vary from a demonstration at a nuclear power plant to the birth of a rare animal at the zoo. In a Q & A session it is often necessary to speak

Figure 10.5
When reporting live from the field, a news announcer must be prepared to ad-lib through a report when little information has yet become available. This reporter in Portland, Maine is delivering a remote on a story he is following; although he holds his notes in his left hand, he speaks directly into the camera. (Photo by W. Mark Bernsau/The Image Works)

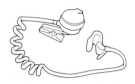

Figure 10.6
An essential piece of many reporters' and anchors' wardrobes is this earphone, called an interrupted foldback (IFB). It is used to convey cues and instructions from a producer or director.

knowledgeably about the general subject area of the story being reported. Blank looks, incorrect information, and the response "I don't know" are unacceptable. Reporters should have a broad education in the arts and sciences and should consider themselves lifelong students. The reading of selected new books, several newsmagazines, and two or more daily papers should be routine for those preparing to work as reporters.

When reporting live during a newscast, you must be able to concentrate under pressure and sometimes in the midst of confusion, to speak smoothly, coherently, and in an organized fashion. Sometimes you will address the camera amidst high levels of ambient noise; you may be distracted by onlookers; you may even be in a position of danger. You will work without a script or a prompter, but you will hear the words of the director and anchor on an earpiece, an IFB (an interrupted foldback).[3] You can expect to face an additional problem when your communication with the anchor is by way of satellite. A delay of about $1\frac{1}{2}$ seconds occurs between the time the anchor speaks and the time you hear the anchor's voice. It is necessary to pick up cues as rapidly as possible to make this delay less noticeable. You can also expect to hear your own voice coming back to your ear a second and a half after you have spoken. Engineers can **minus out** your voice so the anchor and the viewers hear it but you do not; but when no such technical adjustment has been made, you must be able to give your reports smoothly despite the distraction of hearing your words on delay.

The News Anchor

For a news anchor, performance abilities are as important as journalistic skills. News directors look for anchors who are physically appealing (which need not be construed as handsome in the conventional sense), have pleasing voices, are skilled in interpreting copy, can work equally well with or without a prompting device, and can ad-lib smoothly and intelligently. In addition to on-camera performance ability, nearly all successful news anchors have a solid background in field reporting.

---

[3]*Foldback* is the term for an earphone system; *interrupted* indicates that with this system a producer or director can interrupt the announcer with questions or instructions.

Figure 10.7
Despite the perfectly groomed look of news anchors as they deliver calm, authoritative newscasts, their job requires a good deal of behind-the-scenes work. Most anchors write about half their copy, cover stories out in the field, work on feature reports, and develop programming strategy with station management. Many anchors work several hours prior to show time, deliver a newscast, and then work the next shift in preparation for a later newscast. (Photo by Larry Kolvoord/The Image Works)

The chapters that discuss interviewing, voice and diction, principles of communication, language usage, and foreign pronunciation provide suggestions and exercises that will help you perform well as an anchor. Some of the discussion of radio news, especially the section on newswriting, can be applied to the work of the television anchor. This section will not repeat material presented elsewhere but will concentrate instead on aspects of preparation and performance that are unique to television news anchors.

Working Conditions and Responsibilities

Working conditions vary from station to station, but at a typical medium-market or large-market television station, a news anchor's job may involve (1) writing between 25 and 50 percent of the copy read on the air, (2) covering some stories in the field, (3) preparing occasional feature reports, (4) working with a co-anchor as well as sports and weather reporters, (5) preparing and delivering two newscasts daily, five days a week, and (6) meeting with newsroom management as the final makeup and running order of the newscasts are determined. As a novice, you might be called upon to combine some weekday field reporting or newswriting with anchoring weekend newscasts.

As an anchor, you will work with materials from a variety of sources: field reporters, newswriters, wire-service agencies, a parent network, and even local newspapers. Final decisions on the content of newscasts rest with the news director (or may be delegated to the news producer), but the anchor is involved in nearly every step in the preparation for a broadcast. You will have been hired partly because of your journalistic judgment, so you will keep abreast of developing stories. You will check with reporters as they leave on assignment and as they return; you will scan wire reports and a number of newspapers; you will confer at regular intervals with your producer; and you will view taped reports, both to determine their usability and to write lead-ins for those selected.

At a few stations, you may be expected only to show up in time to go over your script, apply your pancake makeup, insert your contact lenses, and spend the next half-hour playing the part of a broadcast journalist. But if you want something better for yourself and your viewers, preparation for a newscast demands that you *be* a journalist— that you know the technological possibilities and demands of your medium, that you be a strong writer, that you learn to cope with confusion and last-minute changes, that you learn to work with all members of the production staff, and that you develop your own style of performance.

A Typical Workday

The following description of a typical day's preparation by a television anchor for a 30-minute newscast reflects conditions at a medium or large station with a well-supported news department.

Before going to work, you talk by phone three or four times with the news producer, who discusses with you the latest developments concerning a possible strike by city bus drivers, a large drug arrest, a new police tactic in dealing with panhandlers, an escape from the women's jail, and an appeal for large quantities of blood for a child with hemophilia who will soon need an operation. As time goes by, it becomes obvious that the bus drivers' strike will be the lead story. You place several calls from your home to union leaders, the city manager, the president of the board of supervisors, and a few bus drivers. When you arrive at the station, you will have about two hours to prepare for the newscast; it is imperative that you keep abreast throughout the day of developments in news stories you will be reporting.

When you arrive at the station (at 2:00 or 3:00 P.M. to prepare for the 6:00 P.M. news), you already have a good idea of what will make up the newscast. The news producer gives you a rundown of the program, which is subject to change if late-breaking news demands it. The rundown sheet gives the running order of the show, item by item. It indicates which anchor is responsible for each story (if there are co-anchors), the running time of each segment, whether the visuals are live or taped, the slug lines for each story, the initials of the field reporter responsible for each story, and the placement of commercial breaks.

The ingredients for a newscast may originate from any of a number of sources: videotape or live transmission from an ENG unit, network videotape, UPI Unifax, live phoned-in beeper reports, or the in-studio report of a field reporter who has just returned from the scene of a developing news event. As anchor, you need to work effectively with all program inputs.

Your preparation is, in general, similar to that of a radio news anchor. You will write lead-ins for packages, voice-over narration, and straight news stories to be delivered without pictorial embellishment and will make notes for teases. A **tease** comes just before a commercial break and is designed to hold viewer interest by headlining a news item to be delivered after the break. Teases must be planned but are seldom written out. A **toss** is a brief introduction to the weather or sports reporter, consumer affairs consultant, or other member of the news team. Tosses are indicated on the script, but they are delivered ad-lib. You toss the program to someone else by simply turning to that person and making a smooth and quick transition to the next segment.

Be sure to review any news item or feature you tease; viewers are resentful of teases that keep them watching yet do not live up to their advance billing. Viewers also resent teases if they feel that the information itself should have been given instead. Wouldn't anyone object to hearing "And you'd better be on the lookout for an escaped lion— details at eleven"?

In writing your share of the newscript, you begin with the standard opening used by your station on all newscasts, for example, "These are the top stories this hour." The opening is followed by headlines of the major stories of the day. As you write your copy, you may decide you need graphics. An anchor sometimes has the responsibility of determining when a graphic aid is appropriate.

You may use a special typewriter that features a **bulletin font** (oversized letters) or a word processor with a video display terminal. Such computers are very flexible, and they make adding or dropping stories quite simple. They also allow you to move a wire-service story to the side or to the top of the screen, leaving room for you to paraphrase the story in your own style. Hard copy (a printed script) is made whether a typewriter or a word processor is used. The script is printed on **copy sets**, prepared forms with six or more sheets, each of a different color. When the entire script has been written and printed out on these forms, the sheets are separated, and complete scripts are given to you, your co-anchor, the director, the prompter operator, the producer, and anyone else who needs to work from a script. Your script pages will be in two colors: one for the segments you will read and the other for those read by your co-anchor. Most news scripts are typed in capital letters only, and the left side of the script is used for video information, the right side for audio. The video column is seldom marked by anyone other than the director, who indicates the shots to be taken.

When your script is assembled, you will have time to review it and mark it as necessary. You may need to mark unfamiliar words or names so that you can transcribe them into your personal phonetic system, to reword a sentence or two to avoid tongue-twisters, and to underline words to be stressed. Most television anchors work with a prompting device fed by a computer. Hard copy is generated in advance of the broadcast, allowing the anchor to read and mark it. However, the copy that appears on the prompter will not have the underlinings, phoneticized words, and other markings, unless they were entered as the stories were being typed into the computer.

The Weather Reporter

Weather reporting on regularly scheduled newscasts is handled in three ways by television stations. At small or low-budget stations the anchor delivers the weather report. Larger stations retain a professional meteorologist who not only reports the weather but explains the causes of meteorological phenomena, subtly and continually educating the audience. Many meteorologists engage in television reporting as only part of their professional careers. At some stations a professional announcer who is not a trained meteorologist may become a specialist in weather reporting.

Nearly all television stations use chroma-keyed maps and satellite photos for weather information. The weather reporter stands before a large blank screen, usually of a medium shade of blue, and points out salient features of the day's weather while looking at a monitor that carries a picture of the reporter and the weather map.

Weather maps are stored in the station's computer. After determining weather patterns from the complex information sent by the U.S. Weather Bureau, the meteorologist goes to the art department and tells the operator where to place graphics showing weather fronts, storms, high and low temperatures, and similar information. Satellite photos are received directly from the Weather Bureau's satellite service and are stored in the computer until used.

As a weather reporter, you may be asked to do special features from time to time. If there is a snowstorm of unusual proportions, if snow falls at a time of year when it is not expected, or if there is prolonged rain or a drought, you may be asked to do street interviews to assess public opinion. In doing so, you follow essentially the same techniques as for any other interview of random passersby, but unless the weather news is serious or tragic, you look for humorous or offbeat comments.

When reporting the national weather, remember that most people do not really care what the weather is anywhere other than where they are, where they may be traveling, or where they have come from. Unless a weather report from two thousand miles away is unusual, it is not news at all. Although people in Georgia may care nothing about the weather in Kansas, they do care about the price of wheat and

Figure 10.8
Prior to broadcasts, weather reporters spend time interpreting weather data, which may come from several different database and wire sources, and preparing weather graphics, which grow increasingly colorful and dramatic as electronic equipment evolves. In Atlanta, weather reporter Kirk Mellish studies a color radar scope, adjusting the radar beam to track down particular storm cells. (Courtesy of Cox Enterprises, Inc.)

Spotlight: High-Tech Weather

Weathercasters of the 1980s knew the frustration of trying to illustrate weather patterns with barely decipherable black-and-white satellite images, with perhaps a few arrows stenciled in. But advances in computer technology, notably in high-powered PCs, have enabled the $50-million weather graphics industry to leap forward into the 1990s. A television newsroom can now be equipped with graphics software that runs on PC hardware, workstations combining software and hardware, or workstations hooked into satellite imaging and data services.

The companies providing computerized weather programs include Kavouras, Accu-Weather, Environmental Satellite Data (ESD), and Colorgraphics. Most of their packages offer

Live Line 5 Weather Graphics System.
(Courtesy of Colorgraphics Inc., Madison, WI.)

sophisticated wipe styles (a wipe is a transitional animation from one image to another), high-resolution images (which make for a sharper, clearer weather map), and advanced paint-box techniques (which allow for creative touches, such as putting sunglasses on the sun). One system, Art Paint by Kavouras, boasts faster data transmission because its information is conveyed directly via satellite rather than over telephone lines. Other packages offer pre-made maps and graphic images, radar images, and lightning data.

Weather workstations, such as Colorgraphics' LiveLine, interface with other companies' satellite feeds, and allow weathercasters to create their own graphics on-screen. Other workstations, such as Accu-Weather's, combine graphics programs with data services, so a weather announcer can use one system to get forecast information and then create graphic images for it.

Not only are weather forecasts an increasingly long segment of any newscast—which reflects their importance to viewers and thus to ratings—but they get more visually complex all the time. Rob Fowler, chief weathercaster of ABC-affiliate WCBD in Charleston, South Carolina, uses computerized weather graphics but warns against packing forecasts with too many gimmicks. "Too many bells and whistles can bother people," he says. "Most of the time, they just want to know whether or not to take their umbrella."

Source: Abridged from an article, "Changes in the Weather," by Michael Burgi, in *Channels*, January 1990, p. 74. Reprinted with permission.

pork. Therefore, whenever possible, tie weather reports to something people care about. In other words, when reporting the weather from distant places, try to arouse interest by interpreting its significance.

It is obvious that weather is newsworthy when it is violent. Tornadoes, hurricanes, exceptional snowfalls, and floods must simply be accurately reported to serve the interest of viewers and listeners. However, slow-developing conditions brought on by weather, such as a two-year drought, must also be reported, and they cannot be adequately covered by a mere recitation of statistics. To best serve the public, you must go beyond the kind of weather news traditionally offered by wire services. In a drought, for example, you could periodically record telephone interviews with a variety of experts on a range of drought-related problems. Ask a representative of the Audubon Society about the effects of the drought on birds in your area. Ask a fish and wildlife expert about the prospects for survival of fish and wild mammals. Ask the farm bureau about the effects on farming. Get drought information from professional gardeners, and share plant-saving tips with your listeners.

In short, as a weather reporter, you should use your imagination and constantly ask yourself these questions: Why should my listeners be interested in today's weather report? What am I telling them that will be of use? Too often weather reports become routine recitations of fronts, temperatures, inches of precipitation, and predictions for tomorrow. Most viewers and listeners find this of some interest but, aside from frost, flood, or storm warnings, there is really nothing useful about the information. Always strive to make your weather reports useful to your audience.

Philosophies of Broadcast Journalism

As a broadcast journalist working for a television or radio station, you will make important decisions daily. Your means of reporting stories will influence the attitudes and actions of your listeners and viewers. Therefore, it is imperative that you develop a working philosophy of broadcast journalism.

In a democracy there are only two theories of the press worthy of consideration. The first, the **libertarian theory**, is based on the belief that, except for defamation, obscenity, or wartime sedition, there should be no censorship or suppression of news whatsoever. The sec-

Figure 10.9
News reporters generally hold views about the role of broadcasting in society, but some announcers deliberately choose positions that involve daily questions of ethics. As a consumer service reporter in Washington, D.C., Betsy Ashton must decide how deep her investigations should delve, which evidence is reliable enough to broadcast, and how much to tell the consumer. (Courtesy of Karl Cook, WJLA)

ond theory, which Wilbur Schramm named the **social responsibility theory**, maintains that journalists must exercise judgment as to whether a particular story should be covered or ignored and, if covered, how it will be covered.[4]

The libertarian theory of the press grew out of democratic movements in England near the end of the seventeenth century and received renewed impetus a hundred years later from the writings and speeches of Thomas Paine, Thomas Jefferson, and other American revolutionaries. Essentially, the libertarian theory was a response to centuries of suppression and censorship by church and state. Jefferson believed that the only security a democratic people have is grounded in a fully informed electorate. "If a nation expects to be ignorant and free, in a state of civilization, it expects what never was and never will be," wrote Jefferson in 1816. The implication of this statement is clear: allow full and free publication of all shades of opinion and all items of information. The basic premise of the libertarians was (and is) that a free people in full possession of the facts will act responsibly.

[4]Wilbur Schramm, *Responsibility in Mass Communication*, New York: Harper & Row, 1957.

The social responsibility theory of the press was a response to what many saw as shortcomings in the idealistic libertarian theory. In practice, the public simply was not receiving all of the facts necessary to make responsible decisions. In the wake of the civil disorders of the late 1960s, a presidential commission called attention to what was perceived to be the failure of the press to adequately inform the public. "Disorders are only one aspect of the dilemmas and difficulties of race relations in America. In defining, explaining, and reporting this broader, more complex and ultimately far more fundamental subject, the communications media, ironically, have failed to communicate."[5] A libertarian defense of riot coverage was unacceptable to the commission for several reasons: reported facts may have been exceptional rather than typical; disclosing some facts may have caused even more serious incidents; and, although the reported fact indeed may have happened, it may have occurred only because the news media were encouraging certain actions by their very presence. The social responsibility theory of the press asks that journalists report not only the facts, but also the truth behind the facts.

The concerns expressed over a libertarian approach to journalism are understandable when one thinks of serious news events such as riots, wars, or insurrections. But the social responsibility theory demands that journalists apply their best judgment and weigh their conduct on a daily basis without regard to the nature or scope of the story being covered. To practice journalism as a socially responsible person, one must start with good intentions, but they are not enough. Only a solid education in broadcast and journalistic law, ethics, and investigative reporting can lead to your success as a responsible broadcast journalist.

[5]*Report of the National Advisory Commission on Civil Disorders*, New York: Bantam, 1968, pp. 382–383.

Practice: Comparing Local and National Newscasts

Make a videotape of a local and a national newscast, that of one of the three major networks or Cable News Network (CNN). Study the taped performances, and list the ways local television news differs from national coverage. Omit obvious differences such as "national newscasts feature reports from all over the world." Look instead for differences in length of stories, use of visuals and computer-generated graphics, and inclusion of specialized reporters focusing on the environment, business, weather, sports, and entertainment.

11

Music Announcing

American radio is heavily oriented toward recorded popular music. There are nearly 12,000 AM and FM radio stations in the United States, and more than 9,000 of these are all-music or nearly all-music stations. Approximately 350 of these stations play classical music, and most of these are noncommercial.

The term *disc jockey* is used for a great range of announcing styles, from rapid delivery to casual, or laid back, but it is associated only with popular music. Announcers on classical music stations are not included under this term, even though their work has much in common with that of disc jockeys. This chapter discusses the work of both the disc jockey and the classical music announcer.

The Disc Jockey

The person who identifies the songs and provides pertinent comments on a popular music station is called a **disc jockey**, a **jock**, or a **DJ** (sometimes spelled **deejay**). Some who perform this function prefer to be called **personalities** or **on-air talent**, even though these terms refer to qualities and not to people.[1]

Working Conditions

As a disc jockey, you can expect working conditions to vary widely from station to station. If you are talented and lucky enough to become a popular disc jockey on a prosperous major-market station, your on-

---

[1]*Personage* is the correct term for which *personality* has been substituted, but it is unlikely that any announcer would want to be referred to as a personage.

Figure 11.1

Although half of a disc jockey's daily work hours are generally spent in duties related to production, programming, and promotion, the 4-hour on-air shift is the payoff. DJ Maria Lopez, having just finished an introduction to her next rock selection, presses the play button on the CD player. (Courtesy of KTID-FM, San Rafael, CA)

air hours will be few, and your salary will be in five or even six figures.[2] If, on the other hand, you begin or end up at a small-market station or at a marginal station in a medium or large market, you can expect to work a 4-hour air shift and to perform other duties for an additional 4 hours each day. In either situation your job will be demanding, because many hours a week of off-duty preparation are required for continued success. Successful DJs at both large and small stations spend considerable time each week reading music trade magazines, making promotional appearances, and writing and recording humorous pieces for their shows.

At a small station you may work an air shift of 4 hours and spend an additional 4 hours selling time, writing commercials, producing commercials for local retailers, auditioning and selecting music, dubbing music from albums to carts, and/or reporting news and weather. You will work in a combined announce booth and control room, called an **on-air studio**, and you will perform the combined functions of announcer and engineer. This is called **working combo.** You may be responsible for preparing and delivering hourly 5-minute newscasts,

---

[2]A **major market** is one with a potential audience of over 1,000,000; a **secondary market** is one having between 200,000 and 1,000,000 potential listeners or viewers; a **smaller market** has a potential audience of fewer than 200,000.

for playing and then refiling musical selections recorded on CDs or carts, for reading commercials and public-service announcements, for playing carted commercials and station IDs, for keeping both the program and engineering logs, and, in some operations, especially on weekends and holidays, for answering the telephone.[3] While doing all this, you are expected to be alert, witty, and personable.

If you watch a disc jockey at work as a combo operator, you will be impressed with the skill and concentration that are required. Should you work combo at a popular music station, a few minutes of your workday might be spent as follows.

3:00 P.M.: You read a 5-minute newscast, complete with one live and one carted commercial. The news is from a wire service and was selected, edited, and rough-timed by you before the start of your shift at 3:00 P.M. The report includes a brief update on regional weather, based on a phone call to the National Weather Service.

3:05:10 P.M.: You identify the next musical selection and **headline**, or tease, some upcoming numbers. You begin to play a **music sweep** (several songs—usually three or four—played without interruption). While the music plays, you check your program log to line up the next carted commercials, and you arrange in order the music carts and CDs that you will play later on.

3:12:30 P.M.: You **back-announce** the music just played, making a few appropriate comments about the music or the performers. If any of the artists are appearing locally, you mention this. After you back-announce, you sight-read a 30-second commercial for a local tire-recapping company and play two carted commercials back to back. You introduce and start a carted musical number.

3:14:50 P.M.: You make a brief comment about the song just played and then read two or three brief PSAs from three-by-five file cards prepared by your public affairs director. You play a carted commercial and then introduce the next cut.

3:18:10 P.M.: You have $3\frac{1}{2}$ minutes (the playing time of the disc being broadcast) to find and cue up the next CD. You check the copy book and the log to see which live and carted commercials are coming up. You take readings on the remote transmitter monitor and make entries in the station log; you check the emergency broadcast system to make sure it is working and make entries in the program log.

[3]The FCC no longer requires radio stations to maintain program logs, but nearly all stations continue to do so for billing purposes.

3:21:40 P.M.: You play a carted commercial for a drugstore and give the local temperature. You announce the control room phone number so that requests may be phoned in, and you then read a commercial for a pizza parlor. You begin, without prior announcement, a music sweep of three numbers. While these are playing, you select the next several cuts (CDs or carts) to be played, refile music already played, look over copy for the next commercial to be delivered live, take two phone calls, and make a note of the selections requested.

3:32:00 P.M.: You back-announce the music played on the sweep and then **segue** into a carted commercial.[4] After that, referring to a bi-weekly almanac called "Wireless Flash," you comment on some trivial but amusing fact, such as "This is National Sauerkraut Month," or "In 1979 a bed-pushing record of 3,233 miles was set." You then start the next carted musical number. Now you have time to gather several music selections, pulling from the cart library those requested by call-ers. You refile tape carts and CDs played so far and check area traffic conditions with the highway patrol, so you can give an ad-lib report when the record ends.

There are a number of variations to this kind of demanding sched-ule. Many stations subscribe to an audio news feed such as UPI Audio, so DJs do not prepare or read newscasts. Some stations still play music directly from albums, and at such stations your work would include the cueing up of records. Some DJs spend relatively more time reading and playing commercials, giving weather reports, making announce-ments of concerts, and making brief humorous or informational com-ments between numbers.

At most popular music stations, the program director develops a clock or wheel that divides each hour of a particular time period into sixteen or more segments; this clock is posted above the audio console. Each segment specifies a certain activity for the DJ: in one segment, a particular type of music is to be played; in another a commercial cluster is to be run; in yet another, a contest is to be announced; and in several segments, weather updates are to be given. Music is cate-gorized, according to the program director's concept of competitive programming, as instrumental, vocal, up-tempo, top 10, top 5, nos-talgia, easy listening, and so on. The clock or wheel may be color-coded, with its colors matching dots on file cards for all musical se-

---

[4]To segue (pronounced SEG'-WAY) is to go directly from the end of one record or cart to the beginning of a second, without a pause or commentary between.

lections. At some stations a DJ is free to select music as long as it is on the current **playlist** and the dot on its card fits the color code for the given segment. After starting to play a selection, the DJ enters the time and date, initials the card, and refiles it.

As a disc jockey on a larger station, you will have some of the same problems and challenges as your counterpart on a small station. However, generally speaking, you will have more help. Even though you will probably work combo, all music selections will be on CDs or will have been carted. A traffic department will have arranged your program log and your commercial copy in the most readily retrievable manner. The days of 6-hour air shifts will be behind you; you are likely, however, to have collateral duties that, with your daily 3- or 4-hour shift, may add up to a solid 8-hour workday.

Regardless of variations, the skills involved in the mechanical part of disc jockey work can be acquired in a few weeks. The challenge is

Figure 11.2
Popular music stations often use a clock as a programming tool, to ensure a balance of music, news, commercials, and features. This clock, which was created for the afternoon drive time, reflects the importance of frequent traffic updates. But clocks do more than manage what gets broadcast when; if entered into a computer, a clock can be altered daily to keep listeners alert and competing stations confused.

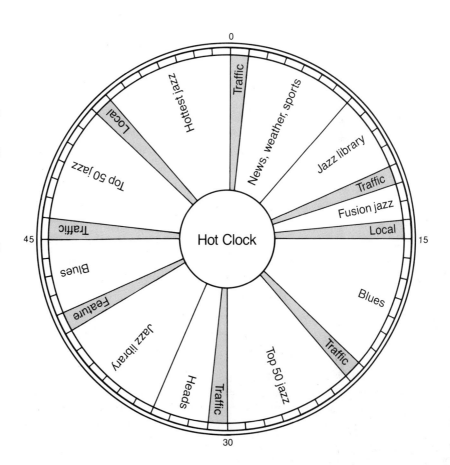

to perform all of the routine duties well and to be energized and articulate during the few minutes each hour when you are in direct communication with your listeners.

Standard Station Formats

Music stations range from those that play one narrowly defined type of music to those that play a broader spectrum of genres. The style of music featured by a station is called its **format**.[5] Music stations describe their formats in a number of ways. A country music station may call itself "Bluegrass"; a Big Band station may advertise itself as "Nostalgia Radio."

Until a few years ago, most popular music station formats fit into one of a number of clearly defined categories. Recently, however, stations have tended more toward mixing their offerings. A station that calls itself Adult Contemporary may play 80 percent soft rock and ballads of the past 30 years and 20 percent jazz and New Age. Other stations mix nostalgia and novelty songs of the past with new releases that fit their sound. A few music stations have play policies that do not fit any standard format. These include contemporary religious, gospel-inspirational, and the even more unusual country-Spanish.

The eleven formats described below are neither rigid nor unchanging. Nearly any type may be automated and may be found in a market of any size; most types are heard on both AM and FM. Nearly all stations operate from a wheel, or clock, such as that shown in Figure 11.2. The clock tells the jock what kinds of music to play during a typical broadcast hour. Most stations have more than one clock— for morning drive time, midday, evening drive time, and nighttime.

Adult Contemporary (A/C) stations   These stations play soft to moderate rock, ballads, and hits by such artists as Johnnie Mathis, Linda Ronstadt, Madonna, Paul McCartney, and Nat "King" Cole. They typically provide hourly news reports, traffic information during peak drive times, sports reports, business reports, and live play-by-play coverage of professional baseball and football games. Adult Contemporary stations are tightly formatted—that is, all music is selected and programmed by a music director—but disc jockeys are allowed to

[5]*Format* is used in several ways in the broadcasting field. A television talk show outline is called a *format*. In radio, *format* refers to the kind of programming provided by a station (all-talk format or country music format) A *tight format* or a *loose format* refers not to types of music but to the degree of restrictions placed on DJs as to choice of music, amount of talk, and sequence of songs played.

chatter with few restrictions on time or topics. Success at an A/C station is tied to a DJ's ability to develop a personal following.

Middle-of-the-Road (MOR) stations   Stations featuring middle-of-the-road music may refer to their format as Bright, Up Tempo, Good Listening, Easy Listening, Standards, or Entertainment. MOR stations are almost indistinguishable from A/C stations but tend to be more conservative in their musical selections. In addition to soft rock, MOR stations play the music of Barry Manilow, Frank Sinatra, and Barbra Streisand. MOR stations often provide the same nonmusic features as A/C stations and usually feature popular DJs who are free to talk on any topic, at greater length than on most other music stations.

Country stations   Also known as Bluegrass, Contemporary Country, or Modern Country, stations featuring country music tend to be moderately paced, even though they are as tightly formatted as Adult Contemporary stations. Country music is incompatible with a frenetic pace. Country stations feature love songs, ballads of drifters and truckers, and songs of love affairs gone bad. Few of these stations project a folksy image through their disc jockeys, preferring instead to appeal to a heterogeneous audience made up of city dwellers as well as those living in rural areas.

Contemporary Hit Radio (CHR) stations   Also known as Top 40 stations, these stations may call their format Contemporary, Rock, Request, Popular Music, or Hit Parade. A typical CHR station rotates

Figure 11.3
Much of the success of a music station depends on the personality of its DJs, who can draw a very large following. This Easy Listening DJ speaks to an unseen audience from a studio in Newport Beach, California. (Photo by Spencer Grant, Stock Boston)

the top twelve to twenty hits of the day with some golden oldies interspersed according to a formula. Station policies vary, but most repeat all the current hits within 90 to 150 minutes of broadcast time. Disc jockeys on CHR stations generally are upbeat, with a rapid rate of delivery but without the piercing high-volume frenzy of earlier days. Most CHR stations limit the amount of DJ talk and feature a seamless sound—one with no gaps or pauses between program elements.

Album-Oriented Rock (AOR) stations   AOR stations may also be called Progressive, Progressive Rock, Underground, Alternative, Hard Rock, or Free-Form. AOR stations play rock music from the latest charts, as well as some golden oldies. The more progressive AOR stations permit DJs to play virtually anything they like, but what they play is expected to add up to an overall identifiable station sound. Most AOR stations, however, are tightly formatted, with all music chosen by a music director.

Urban Contemporary (UC) stations   Also called Rhythm and Blues (R & B) or Soul, UC stations tend to reflect the ethnic makeup of the urban areas they serve. In some markets a black sound predominates, featuring contemporary hits—vocal and instrumental—by African-American artists and groups. In other areas a Latin sound may prevail, with reggae mixing with rhythm and blues, soft rock, and jazz. Most UC stations are programmed much like a Top 40 station (rotation of current hits, with inclusion by formula of hits of the past) and are fast-paced, with little chatter from the DJs.

Golden Oldies stations   The Golden Oldies format is also known as Classic Hits, Rock 'n Roll Classics, Nostalgia, Old Gold, Solid Gold, or Classic Gold. These stations play hits from the early 1960s to the recent past. Songs by the Honeycombs, the Byrds, the Rolling Stones, Blood, Sweat and Tears, the Beatles, the Supremes, the Ronettes, Sonny and Cher, and the Righteous Brothers are typical offerings of these stations. Jocks at most stations of this type are expected to build a personal following and demonstrate in-depth knowledge of the music they play.

Easy Listening stations   The Easy Listening format is also called Beautiful Music, Good Music, or Instrumental Music. These stations feature music (often instrumental) that is soothing to the ear. Its detractors call it supermarket, or elevator, music, but it has many fans. The format calls for low-key arrangements of recent hits, musical comedy songs, standards, and some light classics. Many of these stations are automated, and even hourly news summaries are recorded just before being broadcast. Good Music, once used only to describe the format of stations playing classical music, has been taken over by stations of this type. In recent years New Age music, by artists such as Philip Aaberg, Jim Chappell, and Michael Manring, has replaced the traditional Easy Listening play list on many radio stations.

Jazz stations   There are two types of all-jazz station. The first plays only classic jazz from the past, focusing on the 1920s through the 1950s. The second type plays these hits as occasional reference points but features contemporary jazz by artists such as Steve Rawlins, Grover Washington, Sonny Rollins, Ramsey Lewis, Herbie Mann, and Anita Gravine. Both Dixieland jazz and the music of greats such as Louis Armstrong, Django Reinhardt, Billie Holiday, and Oscar Peterson may be heard on both types of stations.

Big Band stations   These stations feature the music of Artie Shaw, Duke Ellington, Benny Goodman, Glenn Miller, Tommy Dorsey, Count Basie, and Stan Kenton. This format is also known as Nostalgia and can be heard in most parts of the United States, though the station numbers are few. Many Big Band stations, like Jazz stations, encourage their DJs to talk about the music and the artists. Others do not identify the music or the artists and use DJs only to promote contests, billboard features, and give station IDs.

Spanish stations   Spanish-language stations play music appropriate to the origin of their listeners. Stations in Florida favor Cuban music; stations in the Southwest generally feature music from Mexico; and those in areas with a sizable population of Central Americans—Gua-

Figure 11.4
Special-format stations include many possibilities; these disc jockeys are at work at (left) an all-Beatles station and (right) Cuban Radio/Miami. (Photos from AP/Wide World Photos, left; and Bohdan Hrynewych, Stock Boston, right)

temalans, Costa Ricans, Salvadorans, Hondurans, Nicaraguans, or Panamanians—feature music of those countries. Spanish stations generally provide more nonmusic programming than do English-language music stations. They may carry baseball games from Latin America, U.S. games broadcast in Spanish, and interview and religious programs.

A breakdown by format of popular music stations in the United States should be of interest to anyone who is thinking of a career as a disc jockey. As you look at the information in Table 11.1, keep these points in mind. First, radio is a dynamic field, and changes in musical taste are quickly reflected by changes in programming and station format. Second, the information has been supplied by broadcasters, some of whom have been known to subtly misrepresent their formats to make their air time seem more attractive to time buyers.

It should also be noted that there are more than 1,000 religious radio stations in the United States, some of which feature music of a

Table 11.1   Popular Music Formats in the United States

Music Type	Number of U.S. Stations	Percentage of Total
Country	2,496	27.0 percent
Adult Contemporary (A/C)	2,307	25.0 percent
Contemporary Hit Radio (CHR)	972	10.5 percent
Oldies/Classic Hits	723	7.8 percent
Middle-of-the-Road (MOR)	595	6.4 percent
Album-Oriented Rock (AOR)	491	5.3 percent
Urban Contemporary/Black	382	4.1 percent
Beautiful Music (BM)	372	4.0 percent
Jazz	297	3.2 percent
Spanish	261	2.8 percent
Big Band	169	1.8 percent
Classic Rock	159	1.7 percent
Miscellaneous, including New Age, Progressive, Nostalgia, Blues, and Disco	289	3.1 percent

The figures and the names given to the formats are from *Broadcasting Yearbook, 1990* (Washington, DC: Broadcasting Publications, Inc.). All percentages are approximate. The percentages add up to 107 because popular music stations sometimes qualify for more than one category.

spiritual nature. Popular music stations in Canada feature most of the same categories, with Adult Contemporary, Middle-of-the-Road, Country, Contemporary Hit Radio, and Album-Oriented Rock making up nearly 90 percent of the station formats.

Though approximate and subject to change, the percentages in the table are clear in their implications. Country is the single most prevalent format in the United States, but Adult Contemporary and Middle-of-the-Road stations—which are nearly identical in music played and style of announcing—represent over 30 percent of all U.S. popular music stations. Big Band, Jazz, Golden Oldies, and Urban Contemporary account for only about 15 percent. There is probably some correlation between numbers of stations and numbers of DJs employed, so these percentages should give you a rough guide to employment opportunities.

Announcing Styles

You may remember the fast-talking, "punched-up" disc jockeys of a few years back. The frenetic delivery of the early and mid-1980s has given way almost entirely to a more conversational manner that seems better suited to the mood of the 1990s. Many music stations—including those formatted as Easy Listening, New Age, Adult Contemporary, Country, or Oldies—feature DJs with a conversational style of delivery, with a minimum of "chatter." Top 40, or CHR, stations ask DJs to project more energy, but the vitality is expressed in a moderate-volume, rapid-paced delivery. Urban Contemporary stations, featuring music by African-American and Latino artists, often ask for a low-pitched, conversational, noticeably masculine style of delivery.

Because there is a range of announcing styles on the air, you would do well to practice a number of stylistic approaches to popular music announcing. At the same time, it is important to *be yourself*. You certainly can retain your individuality while speaking at different rates and levels of intensity.

Working Conditions at Representative Stations

Just as there is no typical radio station, there is no typical popular music station. There are, however, stations that are fairly representative of popular music stations. The following profiles describe a range of radio station types and give you an idea of the working conditions you might encounter there.

WKKK-AM and FM   These MOR stations are located 35 miles from a major market, and they are the only stations serving the Southern county in which they are located. The daytime-only AM station operates with a 1,000-watt signal, and the FM station, licensed to operate 24 hours a day, broadcasts with 1,900 watts. When both stations are on the air, they **simulcast**; the FM station alone broadcasts from sunset to sunrise.

As a DJ at this station, you are a member of a staff of six full-time announcers, each of whom works a 4-hour on-air shift five days a week. In addition, several part-time DJs work 6-hour shifts to fill in between midnight and 6:00 A.M. seven days a week and during the daytime and evening hours on weekends. These part-timers also fill in when regulars are on vacation or absent because of illness. The six full-time announcers have collateral duties: one is the program director; one is the music director, who also specializes in weather; two do the news during the prime hours when they are not working the board; the remaining two sell time and write and produce commercials.

The announcing style on these stations is geared to the slower pace of a rural area. The DJs are known to their listeners by name and are expected to be visible in the community through civic organizations and appearances at malls and fairs. All music is on CDs and albums, and DJs work combo, pulling, cueing, and playing music and carted commercials.

KMMM   This Country Music station is located in a community of 25,000, about 60 miles from a major market. Although it receives some competition from stations in the large city, the sometimes poor reception of those stations gives it an advantage in its own area. This station is not automated. It has a power of 1,000 watts and is licensed for full operation, though it is permitted to beam its signal in only one direction after sundown. To serve the specific interests of its listeners, KMMM features camping news, fishing and boating information, and commodity reports.

As an announcer on this station, you work a 3-hour on-air shift six days a week. You spend another 3 hours daily in one of several ways: as a writer of commercial copy for local retailers, as a producer of commercials, or as a newscaster. At this station you work from a playlist developed by the music director. You operate your own board and play music and commercials on turntables and cart machines. To succeed at this station, you must know and enjoy country music.

KQQQ   This metropolitan CHR station is located in a large Western city. It operates with a 5,000-watt nondirectional signal and broadcasts

24 hours a day. KQQQ has a tight format featuring current hits from the charts plus regularly scheduled hits of the past. The station categorizes music as current, power gold, regular gold, recurrent, image, or stash. **Recurrent** refers to songs just off the playlist; **image** refers to numbers chosen to provide a change of pace and enhance the station's image, songs by Mick Jagger or the Beatles, for example; **stash** refers to songs that are not on the playlist but are occasionally played. Some music on the play list at this station is **dayparted**, which means that it is to be played only during a specified daypart (a segment of the broadcast day). A novelty song, for example, may be dayparted to morning drive time, and a teen hit may be dayparted to nighttime.

As a DJ on KQQQ, you are required to maintain a fast pace between carted music selections. You ad-lib between songs or sets of songs, but you need to keep your remarks brief. You also are expected to demonstrate a good sense of humor. Once each quarter-hour you work from **liner notes**, prepared by the program or music director, to promote upcoming station features, such as a weekend of 1960s British hits, a contest, or a plug for another disc jockey. You work combo at KQQQ, operating an elaborate console and banks of cart machines. To generate energy, you stand throughout your shift. All selections are dubbed to carts. At KQQQ you work a 3-hour shift, five days a week. The pay is excellent, working conditions are good, and the competition is keen.

WSSS-AM and FM These stations, located in a large Midwestern city, have a Beautiful Music format. The AM station operates at 5,000 watts with a directional antenna, and the FM station operates at 100,000 watts. Both are on the air 24 hours a day, and they simulcast from 4:00 A.M. to 10:00 A.M. daily. Both stations are automated and have tight formats. They play soundtracks from movies, instrumental arrangements of old standards, and music from operettas and musicals.

As an announcer on WSSS, you are given explicit instructions about every detail of your work—for example, you are told to say "Lake Island has 74 degrees," not "The temperature at Lake Island is 74 degrees." All music intros, commercials, and PSAs are taped by you and other announcers, and only the weather summaries and the hourly news capsules are delivered live. The announcers for WSSS are not known by name to their audience. You were hired because you sounded like others already employed by the station, and the desired sound is low, mellifluous, and resonant—just like the music.

KMZ KMZ is an Urban Contemporary (UC) station in a large Western metropolitan area. It operates 24 hours a day, with a power of

5,000 watts. It plays 90 percent rhythm and blues and 10 percent gospel music. KMZ is one of only two African-American–oriented stations in an area with a large African-American population. Public-service announcements and community issues of importance to this community must be broadcast by KMZ, or chances are they will not reach their intended audience at all.

KMZ features eight DJs who have collateral duties. In addition to a 4-hour air shift five days a week, announcers must spend an additional 4 hours daily in production: writing and recording on carts some of the hundreds of PSAs produced by the station each year, working on the production of local commercials, and carting the musical selections. As a disc jockey for KMZ, you are expected to know rhythm and blues, soul, jazz, and black rock music. You are also expected to volunteer time to youth, social, and civic organizations in the community.

WPPP   This 5,000-watt AOR station is located in a major Eastern market. It has solid **cumes** (an abbreviation of cumulative ratings, which indicate the number of listeners at a given time), and its prosperity allows considerable specialization. KPPP maintains a news staff of two, a full-time sales staff, and programming, engineering, and traffic departments. The DJs work combo, with both carts and CDs. The music director selects all the music.

As a DJ on WPPP, you are allowed to play selections from the play list in any order you choose. Your ideas about music are solicited and given objective consideration. As an announcer (or personality) on this station, you are known to your listeners by name, and you are expected to build and maintain a personal following. You have no official duties beyond your 3-hour air shift, but maintaining name and voice recognition virtually demands your presence at a variety of events: softball games to raise funds for recreational programs, charity auctions, telethons, and opening-day ceremonies at county fairs and the Little League season. Your abilities and your popularity create opportunities for extra income. When the station's sales staff sells a commercial package to a local merchant, the spots are written and produced by station personnel, with you as talent. You receive a weekly fee for your voice work on commercials. If you bring in new clients who buy air time, you receive a finder's fee.

WDDD-AM and FM   This Adult Contemporary (A/C) station is a daytime-only, 5,000-watt station located in a farming area. The FM station has an effective radiated power of 3,000 watts, both horizontal and vertical, and broadcasts from 6:00 A.M. to midnight. Having no local competition, this station attempts to meet a great range of interests by broadcasting soft rock, ballads, and hits from the 1950s to the present; local news at the top of the hour and national news at the bottom, with expanded newscasts four times daily; weather summaries every 15 minutes, with expanded weather reports three times daily; a twice-weekly telephone call-in show; a daily 15-minute call-in swap show; and local seasonal sports events presented live.

As a disc jockey for WDDD, you are expected to handle a number of the station's special features in addition to your music chores. As at all but the largest and wealthiest of stations, you work a full 40-hour week. Specialization in weather, sports, farming, or news would help any announcer's chances of employment at this station.

KHHH-FM This station broadcasts 16 hours a day in Spanish and makes the remaining blocks of time available for broadcasts in other foreign languages. Located in a metropolitan area with many ethnic Europeans, it is the only station on which homesick Serbs, Bohemians, Swedes, or Germans can hear their native tongue and the music of their culture.

All announcers on KHHH-FM must be fluent in Spanish (sponsors of programs in other languages supply their own announcers), and they must be able to perform as remote announcers for parades, sports contests, and live broadcasts of Mexican and Central American music. As an announcer on this station, you also work as a time seller and a writer and producer of local commercials. You are expected to have a sound knowledge of both contemporary and standard Latin music.

WZZZ This Big Band station, located in a small resort community in the East, is a daytime-only station. It operates with 500 watts of power and is automated. Music of the Big Band era is featured, but a few more modern groups, such as Blood, Sweat and Tears and Chicago, are occasionally played. WZZZ is run by three employees.

As an announcer at this station, you sell time, write and produce commercials, program and service the automation equipment, record voiced intros to the music, keep the various station logs, and perform as a newscaster on live hourly news summaries.

Preparing for a Career as a Disc Jockey

In preparing for a career as a disc jockey, you should work to develop the ability to operate audio consoles of varying degrees of complexity,

Checklist: Improving Your Popular Music Announcing Style

| | | | | | | | |

1. Become an authority on the type of music you intend to announce.
2. Work to develop an engaging and unique on-air personality.
3. Cultivate your sense of humor.
4. Learn to operate audio equipment efficiently.
5. Practice announcing for several types of formats.
6. Practice delivering commercials, PSAs, and station promos.
7. Work on your ad-libbing skills.
8. Learn to match music and chatter to a specific station sound.

turntables, tape cartridge machines, compact disc players, and reel-to-reel tape recorders; you should also become an authority on the type of music you intend to announce. Beyond this, work to develop an engaging air personality. Concentrate on the sections in this book that discuss performance, interpreting copy, ad-lib announcing, commercial interpretation and delivery, newswriting, news delivery, and interviewing.

Although your chances of success as a disc jockey will be greatest if you develop a unique air personality, it is helpful for beginners to listen to a wide range of successful announcers. This can best be done by listening to all the popular music stations in your reception area, rather than concentrating on the one or two stations you prefer. For a serious study of music announcing types, you can buy airchecks from companies that specialize in this service.[6]

Successful disc jockeys have a well-developed sense of humor, usually of the "off-the-wall" variety. It is unlikely that a person without a sense of humor can develop one after reaching adulthood, but it is possible to improve one's skills in almost anything, including the area of comedy. An analysis of puns, jokes, and one-liners that you find funny can tell you much about the nature of your sense of humor. Even professional disc jockeys need help now and then, and there are companies that sell jokes for use by DJs. Gags used on radio must be

---

[6]An **aircheck** is a sample of an announcer's on-air performance. Airchecks are discussed in Chapter 13.

Figure 11.5

A music announcer must strive throughout a career to maintain a fresh and energetic approach to the work. One way DJ Bobby Ocean achieves this is to stand up, alert and poised, during his entire on-air shift. (Courtesy of Bobby Ocean, Inc., and KFRC, San Francisco)

very brief, such as these two examples: "People tell me I have a great face for radio," and "This day in history! In 1776 George Washington crossed the Delaware, not to attack the British, as we were taught in school, but because he was a cheapskate and wanted to find the dollar he'd thrown across the river a few weeks earlier."[7] These jokes are typical of the kind expected of disc jockeys on some fast-paced popular music stations. It may be helpful to you to see what kinds of gags you can invent and test their effectiveness on your friends.

Disc jockeys also need considerable knowledge of music and musicians, including historical facts, trivia, and current developments. This is best gained by reading on a regular basis several trade magazines and newspapers. Among the most useful are *Billboard*, *R&R (Radio and Records)*, *The Gavin Report*, and a variety of tip sheets.

If you do not have an opportunity to do on-air work as a DJ, you can still practice introductions to recorded music and the kind of humorous chatter required of DJs. There is a practice section at the end of this chapter explaining how to do this.

[7]These examples of DJ humor are from a subscription service, CHEEP LAFFS. Del Gundlach is the writer and publisher of the service.

Spotlight: Fifty-Year Legend of Radio Cool, Al "Jazzbeaux" Collins

In the world of radio, Al "Jazzbeaux" Collins is one of the most famous and well traveled personalities of all time.

He's been on the air in all the big league markets—New York, Chicago, L.A. . . . San Francisco.

And the man has endured. He's been doing this for nearly 50 years—since 1941.

"I'm one of the old Tyrannosuarus rexes left on the plain, man," he says. "I don't wanna feel the tar pit getting soft under my feet."

As you can hear, Collins hasn't lost his cool school bop talk, a hip patois that he picked up from black jazz musicians.

In the book "The Catalog of Cool," his announcing style is described as "so laid back it was four winks west of Sominex, but so *hip*."

Ask him about that and he just shrugs it off.

"What's cool for you would be warm to someone else," he says.

He likes to take people on little mental excursions, so when they're grooving on his wave length, they become, to use one of his patented words, "majuberized."

"It's from majuber, meaning the essence of everything creative and good," he says. "It's a seed. It lets your brain get unstuck."

Collins has been unsticking his listeners' brains for six decades now, using a simple formula that's hardly a secret.

"The thing for me is getting down with people," he says. "People send me pictures of their cats and their grandmother's automobile. I once

had people tearing the knobs off their radios and sending them to me, on the theory that if they were listening to me, they didn't need the knobs anymore. I had a beautiful mahogany board covered with knobs. Things like that give people a chance to participate actively in my program."

Collins has always been a joyous self promoter with a distinctive and offbeat personal style.

He still wears his trademark beatnik goatee, black horn-rimmed glasses, jumpsuits, and a brush down haircut with a little curl on his forehead. He calls his hairdo the "baby seal" . . .

Although he's decidedly off center, Collins has always avoided controversy, which he believes has helped him to maintain his popularity.

Al "Jazzbeaux" Collins (Photo by Scott Henry)

At some stations announcers speak during a sweep, or **set** (two or more songs played back to back without interruption), speaking from the moment the vocal ends on the first selection until just before the vocal begins on the second selection. Practice doing this with dubs made to an audiotape unless you have two turntables at your disposal.

"I never talked about Vietnam or dope," he says. "I only talk about fun things that I like, like motorcycles and airplanes."

And cars.

Collins once had a Datsun king cab pickup made to look like a Peterbilt truck. In the '60s, when he was really hot in Bay Area radio and TV, he drove a '65 Porsche 356C covered with black velvet.

"The whole thing was flocked, man," he says. "Promotion. I live for it."

Although he will go down as one of the greats in radio, he's no stranger to television. He had his own morning TV show on KGO in San Francisco from 1960 to '62. It came on right after Crusader Rabbit and just before Jack LaLanne.

Collins' biggest moment on television was a 13-week stint as host of the "Tonight Show" in New York between the reigns of Steve Allen and Jack Paar.

"It was fun for me, but it was never what I'd really call *me* from a personality standpoint," he says. "On the last night, I had a big moving van pull up and everybody on the show got in. I had Jonathan Winters and Steve McQueen as guests. The tailgate swung up and a sign said, 'That's all, folks.' Then we drove down 49th Street and that was the end of that."

Collins grew up in Florida, and got turned on to radio when he was a student at the University of Miami. He once drove a professor down to the local radio station on his motorcycle for an interview, and when the regular student announcer didn't show up, Collins had to fill in.

On the spur of the moment while on the air, he christened the program "What's New at the U." That lit the spark. He was on his way from there.

"In that 15-minute period I had the revelation," he remembers. "On the radio, I felt like something special. I wanted more of that feeling."

After he graduated with a degree in broadcasting, he went off to West Virginia for his first radio job at $18 a week.

A few years later, at WIND in Chicago in 1945, he picked up his nickname. Collins was a jazz buff, so a station engineer suggested he call himself "jazzbow," which was what they used to call clip on neckties.

"I said, 'OK, I'l! do it,' " he recalls. "I went on the air and said, 'Hello, folks, this is Jazzbeaux.' It had a good sound. I was good on people's ears. People were calling in, saying 'Who's this Jazzbeaux?' "

Collins used to love food almost as much as jazz. He was particularly fond of hot dogs from the King Papaya restaurant in Manhattan. Now he has to watch his diet, but he's in good health and raring to go on the radio again.

"I had four-way bypass surgery and a stroke a few years ago," he says. "I got those things out of the way. I feel good. Age really is a state of mind, man. I got all the vibrancy going on the right planes for me."

Source: Abridged from an article, "The King of Cool Comes Home," by Paul Liberatore, in *Marin Independent Journal*, 14 May 1990, p. D1. Reprinted by permission.

Practice announcing for both fast-paced and more relaxed station formats. Some stations want a laid-back, intimate, and informative performance. This is especially true of Jazz, Big Band, Adult Contemporary, Country, and Golden Oldies stations. Do some research on the music you are playing: find out when a recording was made, who some of the key artists are, and anything of significance about the recording techniques used or the occasion on which a live recording was made. Refer to a news service, such as *R&R*, for information such as important anniversary dates (the Woodstock concert, the breakup of Led Zeppelin, the death of John Lennon, for example) and music happenings of one, five, and ten years ago. Publications such as *R&R* are expensive, but you may be able to examine a back issue at a local radio station. Once you are on a station's payroll, you will have regular access to a number of trade publications.

Here are a few more suggestions for practicing DJ work.

- In selecting music to introduce and play, choose music you know and like. Look especially for music you can talk about. You will not have the opportunity to select your own music on most radio stations, but it is good practice to begin with the easiest possible challenge.
- When practicing, actually play your records, and play them all the way through. Correct pacing and mood demand that you and your music work together for a total impression.
- Practice headlining songs you will play later. This is a realistic practice used to hold listeners who otherwise might switch to another station.
- Give the name of the song and the performers at the start or the conclusion of each selection. All stations have policies on music identification and you will have to conform to them, but as you practice, aim for the communication of a maximum amount of information.
- Practice delivering commercials, public-service announcements, and station promos. It is unrealistic not to do so.
- Practice cueing records. As a disc jockey, you may later work only with carts or compact discs, which are cued automatically, but you must be prepared to work with older-format discs.
- Practice working with an audio console. You almost certainly will be expected to operate your own console as a professional disc jockey.
- Practice doing intros by first timing the music between the start of the record and the start of the vocal; then work to introduce the number so that your voice ceases just as the vocal begins. Although you may not appreciate DJs who talk over music, some stations require it.

- Practice ad-libbing about the music, the day's events, or ideas that intrigue you. You may have little chance to ad-lib on a station with a tight format, but other stations will consider you for a job only if you are able to entertain in a spontaneous, ad-lib manner.
- Introduce records ad-lib. Scripts (other than for commercials, PSAs, and newscasts) are unknown to the disc jockey.
- Avoid corny clichés. Try to develop your own announcing style. The idiosyncrasies of popular disc jockeys' expressions become the clichés of unimaginative and unoriginal announcers.
- Before engaging in practice sessions, remember that all music stations work to achieve a particular sound. A station's sound is the end result of a number of factors: the type of music played, the voices and personalities of the announcers, their energy level, the kinds of things they say, whether they speak over instrumental introductions or endings of songs, and the general pace of music and speech. Useful practice will include an initial determination of the specific sound you are attempting to achieve and selection of music appropriate to that sound.

For information on job seeking, see Chapter 13. Above all, remember that there *are* jobs available if you are well trained, have native talent, and are willing to begin at a modest salary and work hard. Your chances of succeeding once you have a job will be improved if you continue to grow with experience.

The Classical Music Announcer

There are classical music stations in all parts of the United States and Canada, though they add up to only 1 to 2 percent of radio stations that feature music.[8] With fewer than two hundred classical music sta-

[8]*Classical* is not really the best label for stations featuring concert and operatic music. An important period in music history, roughly the last half of the eighteenth century, is known as the classical period; the music of that time—represented by Haydn and Mozart, among others—is, strictly speaking, classical music. *Classic*, which means "of the highest or best order," is a better choice to name stations of this type. One such station calls itself "your classic music station," but most stations that feature operatic and concert music refer to themselves as classical music stations. Because the usage is widespread, it will be followed here.

tions on the air, it should be apparent that job opportunities in this demanding specialization are limited. You should not single-mindedly prepare yourself for a career strictly as an announcer on a classical music station unless your love of both classical music and radio is so strong that you are willing to put practical considerations aside. On the other hand, preparing for classical music announcing as part of your study of the entire field of broadcast announcing can be of considerable benefit. Exploring the great treasure of music, learning musical terms, and practicing the foreign pronunciation that is required of all announcers on classical music stations will enrich your life and make you more competent in any announcing specialization.

As an announcer on a classical music station, you will have some duties in common with a disc jockey. At most stations you will cue up and play CDs, follow and sign the program log, operate an audio console, ad-lib introductions to musical selections (usually from information contained on three-by-five cards), and read public-service announcements and commercials or play them on tape cart machines. Because a high percentage of classical music stations are noncommercial, you may not deliver commercials as part of your work. You will, however, have a number of other collateral duties such as carting music from records, preparing newscasts and summaries, and maintaining the operating log.

Unlike a disc jockey, you will not be concerned with hit records. You will, however, be expected to keep abreast of new recordings of standards, releases of music not previously recorded, and a small output of new works. You will be required to have an extensive knowledge of classical music and to be accurate in pronouncing French, Italian, German, Spanish, and Russian.

As an announcer on a classical music station, your name might be known to your listeners, but it is unlikely that you will be expected to build a personal following. If you were assigned to or developed a specialty program (a music quiz, a telephone talk show centering on classical music, or a program featuring the best of the new releases), you might become well-known to your listeners, but such prominence is rare. Most classical music fans turn to stations because of the music, not because of the announcers.

No ladder extends from the small classical music station to the big time. Most classical music stations are noncommercial FM stations, and working conditions and salaries tend to be uniform. There are highly profitable AM and FM classical music stations in major met-

Figure 11.6
Classical music stations provide a haven for lovers of broadcast announcing, fine arts, and fine music. Classical music announcer Howard Cornelsen is shown here (left) at work in the announce booth and (right) amid the shelves of the studio's extensive CD library. (*Tony Bullard, courtesy of KUHF, Houston*)

ropolitan areas, and salaries there are quite good, but those stations employ only a small percentage of professional radio announcers.

Your announcing work at a classical music station will be more relaxed than that of a disc jockey on a popular music station. The musical selections are longer than most popular songs, many running from 30 minutes to as long as $2\frac{1}{2}$ hours. You will spend most of your time announcing general music programs, consisting, for example, of a Bach fugue, followed by a Strauss tone poem, a Vivaldi concerto, and a Mozart symphony, rounded off by ballet music by Tchaikovsky.

The announcers seldom select the music or even the specific recordings. This is done by the music director, who is responsible for the total sound of the station. There usually is a coherent plan to a broadcast day: brisk and lively short works are played during morning drive time (especially true of commercial classical music stations), concert programs during midday, shorter works again during evening

Checklist: Polishing Your Classical Music Announcing

1. Perfect your foreign pronunciation.
2. Perfect your use of phonetic transcription. Although wire-service phonetics may be adequate for most announcers, as a classical music announcer, you should master the International Phonetic Alphabet.
3. Practice reading and ad-libbing PSAs.
4. Practice cueing up and playing the records or tapes you introduce.
5. Create music programs. Invent titles, write openings and closings, select theme music, and make sample program offerings.
6. Practice ad-libbing with only album liners as your source of information.
7. Practice reading news headlines and 5-minute news summaries, because this is a typical part of a classical music announcer's broadcast day.

drive time, and longer works—including complete operas, masses, and oratorios—throughout the evening. Music directors keep a list of all musical selections played, complete with date and time of each playing. Most stations have a policy requiring the lapse of a certain number of weeks or months between playings.

Concert music usually is introduced by giving the name of the composer, the selection, the orchestra (or other musical group), the conductor, and, when appropriate, the soloist (as in a concerto or an aria). At some stations you will be asked to add the name of the record company. When introducing opera, you will most likely give a résumé of each act or scene and identify the leading singers. The *Schwann Record and Tape Guide*, published monthly, provides up-to-date information on new listings and the albums, tapes, and compact discs that are currently available. Schwann furnishes birth and death dates of composers and, where known, the date of composition of each selection listed.

As you practice classical music announcing, keep the suggestions in the checklist in mind.

The most important requirements for employment as a classical music announcer are impeccable foreign pronunciation and a thorough knowledge and appreciation of classical music. If you choose to specialize in this type of announcing, you should enroll in as many general courses in music as are offered to nonmajors. Of course, if you are a musician, more specialized courses will be available to you. Listen to classical music broadcasts, collect records and tapes, practice aloud the introductions to musical selections, and learn to use at least some of the source books mentioned under Chapter 11 in Appendix E.

Practice: Tracking Rate of Delivery for Different Sounds

Make audiotape recordings of several popular music announcers, each selected to represent a different sound: one from a low-key noncommercial station; the second from a fast-paced CHR station; the third from a Country station; and the fourth from an MOR station. Play each tape, and make a typescript of any 60-second portion of the performance. Count the number of words delivered during the 60 seconds. Compare rates of delivery according to types of stations.

Practice: Announcing Popular Music

To practice ad-lib music announcing, you need a record player or cassette deck for playing music and a second machine (cassette or reel-to-reel) for recording your performance. A stopwatch is also essential. First, select and time your records. Time the entire selection as well as the instrumental introduction from its start to the time the vocal begins. If the instrumental intro lasts 11 seconds, then you have just short of 11 seconds to make appropriate comments about the

song. End your comments a split second before the vocal begins. As
you gain experience in this, make your timing more detailed. If the
intro is 11 seconds and a horn or a drum roll is heard after 6 seconds,
make note of that, for you will want to pause in your comments at
that precise moment.

*Practice: Announcing
Classical Music*

The following are scripts for the introduction of classical music, featuring Spanish, Italian, French, and German names and words. Begin
to practice with these scripts, and then move on to scripts of your own
creation and to ad-lib introductions.

Spanish Music Copy

```
Manuel de Falla inherited the role of Spain's
first composer with the death of Granados in
1916. De Falla, who died in 1946, fulfilled his
mission well, and even outshone his mentor in
popularity outside of Spain. We hear seven
''Canciones populares Españolas'': ''El paño
moruno,'' ''Seguidilla murciana,'' ''Austuriana,''
''Jota,'' ''Nana,'' ''Canción,'' and ''Polo.''
Victoria de Los Angeles now sings seven
''Canciones populares Españolas'' by Manuel de
Falla.
```

```
Our featured work tonight is an out-of-print
recording of the Spanish operetta ''La boda de
```

Luís Alonso," by Giménez. Soloists are Carlos
Munguia as Luís Alonso, Inés Rivandeneira as
María Jesús, Gregorio Gil singing the part of
Paco, Raphael Maldonado as Miguelito, and Ana
María Fernández as Picúa. The Gran Orquesta
Sinfónica of Madrid and the Coros Cantores de
Madrid are directed by Ataúlfo Argenta. We hear
now "La boda de Luís Alonso" by Giménez.

Now for music of the bull ring. We will hear the
"Banda Taurina" of the Plaza de Toros of Mexico
City. The music is a typical group of selections
played at appropriate points during a corrida.
The musical selections we will hear today are
"Las toreras," a dedication to lady bull
fighters; "Canero"; "Toque cuadrillas," a
signal for the assistants to capture the
attention of the bull; "Purificación," played at
the moment of the killing; "Toque banderillas,"
a signal for the placing of the darts; "El
imponente," a sign of respect for a very big
bull; "Canitas," played for a bull that has
earned much respect; "Gualvidal," a musical
selection played for a famous matador; "Toque de
muerte," the signal of death; "Dianas," musical
applause played after a successful encounter; and
"Porque te quiero," played whenever the company

enters or leaves the arena. And now, music of the bull ring.

Italian Music Copy

Gaetano Donizetti's "L'elisir d'amore," "The Elixir of Love," begins in the fields of Adina's farm. It is harvest time, and the chorus of farm workers sings "Bel conforto al mietitore"—— "What comfort to the harvester." Nemorino, who is secretly in love with Adina, then sings the aria "Quanto è bella, quanto è cara!"——"How beautiful she is! How dear!" Adina, who has been reading the story of Tristan and Isolde, laughs aloud, and is asked by the workers to share the source of her good humor. As she tells the story of the love potion, all present——but especially Nemorino——wish for a similar potion. Our cast features Rosanna Carteri as Adina, Luigi Alva as Nemorino, Rolando Panerai as Belcore, Giuseppe Taddei as Il Dottor Dulcamara, and Angela Vercelli as Giannetta. The chorus and orchestra of Teatro alla Scala of Milan are conducted by Tullio Serafin. And now, Act One of Donizetti's "L'elisir d'amore."

On tonight's program, we will hear three overtures by Gioacchino Rossini. The first is the overture to "L'Italiana in Algeri," first performed in 1813. Following that, we will hear the overture to "La Cambiale di Matrimonio," written in 1810. The third of Rossini's overtures is that written for the opera "La Cenerentola," first presented in 1817. Fernando Previtali conducts the Orchestra Dell'Accademia de Santa Cecilia in three overtures by Gioacchino Rossini.

This afternoon on "Musical Echoes" we will hear nine arias sung by the legendary Enrico Caruso. During the first portion of the program, we will hear the aria "Chi mi frena in tal momento," from "Lucia di Lammermoor," by Gaetano Donizetti; "Siciliana," from "Cavalleria rusticana," by Pietro Mascagni; "La donna è mobile," from "Rigoletto," by Giuseppi Verdi; and "Invano Alvaro," from "La forza del destino," also by Verdi.

Following the news, we will hear the great Caruso singing the traditional song "Santa Lucia." The four arias in this part of the program are: "Cielo e mar," from "La Gioconda," by Amilcare Ponchielli; "Vesti la giubba," from "I pagliacci," by Ruggero Leoncavallo; "Recondita armonia," from "Tosca," by Giacomo

Puccini; and "Brindisi," from "Cavalleria rusticana," by Pietro Mascagni. And now, Enrico Caruso sings "Chi mi frena in tal momento," from "Lucia di Lammermoor," by Gaetano Donizetti.

French Music Copy

Maurice Ravel, one of the giants of modern French music, died in 1937. He left behind him such masterpieces as "Pavanne pour une infante défunte," "La valse," and "Daphnis et Chloë." Tonight we will hear one of Ravel's lesser known works, "L'enfant et les sortilèges."
Suzanne Danco, soprano, and Hugues Cuénod, tenor, are accompanied by the Orchestre de la Suisse Romande, conducted by Ernest Ansermet.

Georges Bizet wrote his opera "Les pêcheurs de perles"--"The Pearl Fishers"--in 1863. Since that time it has had its ups and downs, but has never become a staple with opera companies around the world. Despite this, "Les pêcheurs de perles" contains some of Bizet's most inspired music. This afternoon we will hear the opera in its entirety. The cast includes Janine Michaeu, Nicolai Gedda, and Ernest Blanc. The chorus and orchestra of the Opéra-Comique de Paris are

conducted by Pierre Dervaux. "The Pearl
Fishers," by Georges Bizet.

Next we will hear some delightful ballet music by
the French composer André Grétry. The
compositions are "Céphale et Procris," "La
caravane du Caire," and "Lépreuve villageoise."
Raymond Leppard conducts the English Chamber
Orchestra.

Marc—Antoine Charpentier's seldom heard "Messe
pour plusieurs instruments au lieu des orgues" is
our next selection on "Musical Masterpieces."
Jean—Claude Malgoire conducts the Grand Ecurie et
la Chambre du Roy.

German Music Copy

"Die Dreigroschenoper" was first presented to
the public in 1928. The success of this work,
which is neither opera nor musical comedy,
established a new genre of musical theater. Its
authors, Kurt Weill and Bertolt Brecht, took the
200—year—old "Beggar's Opera," by John Gay, as
their model, and fashioned a biting satire on the
Germany of the 1920s. Tonight we will hear three
selections from "Die Dreigroschenoper," as

performed by Lotte Lenya, Wolfgang Neuss, Willy
Trenk–Trebitsch, and Inge Wolffberg. First will
be "Die Moritat von Mackie Messer," followed by
"Die Unsicherheit Menschlicher Verhältnisse."
The concluding selection is "Die Ballade vom
Angenehmen Leben." The orchestra and chorus are
conducted by Wilhelm Brückner–Rüggeberg. Three
selections from "Die Dreigroschenoper."

Wolfgang Amadeus Mozart wrote "Die Entführung aus
dem Serail"––"The Abduction from the Seraglio"––
in 1782, when he was 26 years old. Often
considered Mozart's happiest comedy, the opera
contains some of his most beautiful arias. Today
we will hear excerpts from the third act. First,
Gerhard Unger, in the role of Pedrillo, sings the
romantic "Im Mohrenland gefangen war," followed
by Gottlob Frick in the role of Osmin singing "O,
wie will ich triumphieren." Finally, Anneliese
Rothenberger as Constanze, and Nicolai Gedda as
Belmonte, sing the duet, "Welche ein Geschik! O
Qual der Seele!" The Vienna Philharmonic
Orchestra is conducted by Josef Krips. Three
excerpts from Mozart's "Die Entführung aus dem
Serail."

Next on the "Musical Stage" we will hear the complete "Merry Widow." "Die lustige Witwe," as it is called in German, was written by Franz Lehar in 1905, and has been popular with audiences all over the world since that time. In tonight's performance, the part of Hanna Glawari is sung by Hilde Güden, the Graf Danilo Danilowitsch is sung by Per Gruden, Waldemar Kmentt sings the part of Camille de Rosillon, and Emmy Loose is Valencienne. The Vienna State Opera Chorus and Orchestra is conducted by Robert Stolz. We hear now, without interruption, the complete "Merry Widow," by Franz Lehar.

Mixed-Language Music Copy

Welcome to "Music 'til Dawn." During the next five hours we will hear works from opera and the concert stage. This morning's program features works from Italian, Spanish, German, and French masters.

Our program begins with excerpts from Wolfgang Amadeus Mozart's opera "The Marriage of Figaro." Featured are Hilda Güden as the Countess, Hermann Prey as the Count, Anneliese Rothenberger as Susanna, Walter Berry as Figaro, and Edith Mathis

as Cherubino. The Dresden State Orchestra and
Chorus is directed by Otmar Suitner.

We then will hear excerpts from Handel's
seldom performed oratorio "Belshazzar." Featured
are Sylvia Stahlman, soprano, and Helen Raab,
contralto, with Helmuth Rilling conducting the
Stuttgart Kirchenmusiktage Orchestra.

Andrés Segovia will then perform as soloist in
the "Concierto del Sur," by Manuel Ponce. André
Previn conducts the London Symphony Orchestra.

During the third hour, we will hear George
Bizet's "Jeux d'enfants," with Jean Martinon
conducting the Orchestre de la Société des
Concerts du Conservatoire de Paris.

Following will be Gabriel Fauré's "Masques et
bergamasques." The Orchestra de la Suisse Romande
is conducted by Ernest Ansermet.

Vincent D'Indy's "Symphony on a French
Mountain Air" will bring us to our intermission,
during which we will present a news summary.

In the fourth hour, we will hear "Lieder und
Gesänge aus der Jugendzeit," by Gustav Mahler.
This is sung by Dietrich Fischer-Dieskau,
baritone.

Gioacchino Rossini's overtures to "L'Italiana
in Algeri" and "Il Signor Bruschino" will hail
the final hour of our concert, which features

music from the Italian opera. Our first operatic excerpts will be from Gaetano Donizetti's "L'elisir d'amore." Featured in the cast are Rosanna Carteri, soprano, Giuseppe Taddei, baritone, and Luigi Alva, tenor. Tullio Serafin conducts La Scala Orchestra.

The last selection on "Music 'til Dawn" will be excerpts from the opera "La Favorita," by Gaetano Donizetti. The cast includes Giuletta Simionato, mezzosoprano, Gianni Poggi, tenor, and Ettore Bastianini, baritone. The Maggio Musicale Fiorentino is conducted by Alberto Erede.

i2

Sports Announcing

Sports announcing is very competitive, and years of dedicated effort must be invested before there is any likelihood of significant reward. Despite this, the attraction of spending a career in close association with the world of sports is compelling enough to motivate scores of young people to undertake the struggle. To become a successful sports announcer, you must have a passion for your work. You may find yourself traveling with a team, which means living out of a suitcase, putting in long hours, eating in restaurants and sandwich shops, and leaving your family for extended periods of time. Only a passion for your work can sustain you in such a job. Sports reporters who do not travel outside their immediate geographical area still work long hours and seldom have a day off.

Sports announcing includes sports reporting, play-by-play coverage, and play analysis. Some sports announcers become expert in one or two of these specialties; nearly all beginning sports announcers must become competent at all three. Interviewing and delivering commercials are additional challenges that you must manage well in order to succeed in sports announcing.

The Entertainment and Sports Programming Network (ESPN) has considerably expanded the range of sports events shown on television. ESPN covers traditional, mainline sports such as golf, baseball, and tennis. In addition, in order to fill its many hours of daily broadcast, it also televises such events as bicycle racing (the Tour de France, for example), rodeos, billiards, volleyball, horse-show jumping, body-building championships, surfing, gymnastics, hydroplane racing, and even tractor-pulling contests. All of its programming is produced by ESPN in much the same way as sports telecasts are produced by the regular broadcast networks.

In addition to ESPN, several regional radio and television sports networks offer employment to sports announcers. NESN (New England Sports Network) and PSN (Pacific Sports Network) are but two of a growing number of television cable networks devoted entirely to sports broadcasting.

Working Conditions of Sports Announcers

As a sports announcer, you will work for a radio or television station (perhaps both), a broadcast or cable network, a cable system, or an athletic team. Your working conditions, responsibilities, and income will be determined by your affiliation.

Network sports announcers, whether play-by-play sportscasters, analysts, or reporters, are generally at the top of the salary range and have the least strenuous schedules. Network sportscasters seldom broadcast more than one game a week, and even those who add reporting chores to their schedules are responsible for only a few minutes of sports news a day. Sports announcers for national or regional cable systems are well rewarded, but their work schedule is heavy: they may find themselves calling several games a week during basketball and baseball seasons.

Sports reporters who work for radio stations are usually responsible for delivering one or two hourly reports during their shifts, as well as taping additional reports to be broadcast after they have left the station. Television sports reporters produce several minutes of

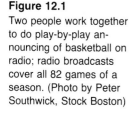

Figure 12.1
Two people work together to do play-by-play announcing of basketball on radio; radio broadcasts cover all 82 games of a season. (Photo by Peter Southwick, Stock Boston)

of visually informative sports news each day and also produce taped sports features to be used on weekends.

Sports announcers who work for athletic teams have the most strenuous, but perhaps also the most exciting and rewarding, job. As an employee of a professional baseball, basketball, football, or hockey team, you will travel with the club. You owe loyalty to your employer, even though you may occasionally find it difficult to reconcile your judgment with that of your boss. Most team owners require that their sportscasters advertise special promotions days and push ticket sales; some demand that their play-by-play sportscasters openly root for their team; some ask their announcers to favor their team but to do so with discretion. Other owners make no demands on the play-by-play staff but expect announcers as well as all other members of the organization to maintain loyalty to the team, especially when the team is in a losing streak. Even when working for the most benign or aloof owner, you will not have as much freedom as the reporter who works for a newspaper or a radio or television station.

Most sports announcers fill a variety of professional roles. The simplest combination is doing play-by-play baseball during its long season and basketball, football, or hockey during the winter. Other sports announcers combine five days a week of sports reporting for a station with weekend play-by-play reporting of college sports. If you become a sports announcer, you most likely will begin at a small-market radio station, doing some sports announcing along with other duties, such as reading hourly news reports or performing as a DJ. If you succeed, you may move into full-time sports reporting and play-by-play announcing. You also may move to a larger-market station and, perhaps, from radio to television.

If you are successful in becoming a full-time sports professional for the electronic media, your work schedule and job description might well conform to one of the following models.

Sports reporter for an all-news network-affiliated radio station in a major market   You are responsible for eight to ten live reports each day and four carted reports to be played after you have left the station. In addition, your popularity has opened up supplemental jobs that do not conflict with your station work: you do football play-by-play for a major university; you announce play-by-play during the football preseason for a professional team in your area; you prepare periodic reports for your network's sports programs, which are broadcast nationally; and you record commercials for a variety of clients, including a chain of sporting goods stores.

Your work schedule is extremely demanding. Aside from the rigors of a six- to seven-day week, you must constantly keep up with developments in all major sports at amateur and professional levels, and this means hours each week spent reading several newspapers, *Sporting News*, *Sports Illustrated*, and a number of other specialized sports publications. There are also team receptions and banquets, news conferences, and civic functions at which you have been asked to speak. You schedule yourself to cover as many sports events as possible. You do postgame interviews for use on your daily sports reports, and you make notes as you watch the game from the press box so that you can give a firsthand review the following day.

Sports director for a popular music-sports radio station   You prepare and perform a daily 10-minute sports show, which is followed by a 2-hour phone-in talk show on sports. You prepare and send one to three weekly feeds to the network, each of which centers on local teams or athletes. Your station carries play-by-play broadcasts of local college and professional football games as well as professional basketball and hockey. You do not do play-by-play regularly, but you do produce locker room features before and after these games. You work freelance to increase your income and your exposure, and this brings you jobs such as preseason play-by-play, postseason tournament and bowl play-by-play, and vacation relief sports reporting for a local television station. Because you cannot predict the kinds of questions and comments that will arise on your telephone talk show, you read constantly to develop an encyclopedic knowledge of sports.

Sports director for a network-owned-and-operated (O&O) television station   You prepare sports news for the daily 6:00 and 11:00 P.M. newscasts. This necessitates viewing and editing tapes of sports action, selecting sports photos sent by wire services, and writing two 3- to 5-minute segments for the newscasts each day. You spend much of your time attending sports events with an ENG operator. Pregame and postgame interviews with players and coaches make up a good portion of your nightly sportscast. On a number of weekends, you spend hours at the station watching games on network television. With the help of a station engineer, you select and have **dubbed off** certain key plays that you may want to use later on the air. A 3-hour game may provide you with as much as 30 minutes of dubbed action, from which you will choose a maximum of 3 minutes for use on your two sports segments.

Your day's work leaves little time for moonlighting. You attend from three to five sports events each week to see nontelevised events firsthand and to tape interviews. You regularly spend early afternoons covering a sports story, accompanied by an ENG operator. You arrive at the station at 3:00 P.M. This leaves you 3 hours in which to view or review all available tape, make your selections, review sports news from the wire services, write your script, and prepare for on-air performance during the six o'-clock news. Between the 6:00 and 11:00 P.M. newscasts, you eat dinner, prepare for your second sportscast, and review sports scores as they come in on the wire-service machines. Your workday ends after the 11:00 P.M. news, but it will begin the next day long before you tape your sports news story of the day. Mornings are spent arranging interviews, reading several sports magazines and the sports sections of newspapers, and perhaps answering requests for information about the life of a sports reporter sent by high school and college students who would like to have your job.

Sports director for a medium-market radio station   You focus on high school, college, and minor league sports events. You work for the station and for the AAA baseball team whose games are broadcast over a three-station network. When not on the road with the team, you do play-by-play descriptions of the most important high school football and basketball games. You work with a group of students you have recruited and trained to phone in ongoing scores of the games not being broadcast. You do play-by-play announcing of home football games for a nearby university. You provide several brief sports reports each day for the hourly 5-minute newscasts. You act as spotter for play-by-play sportscasters when university sports events are regionally telecast. And as time allows, you do play-by-play of newsworthy local sports events, such as tennis and golf tournaments, hockey and soccer championship play-offs, Little League, Babe Ruth, and Pop Warner championships, and track and field meets.

Sportscaster for a television network   You owe no allegiance to owners, managers, teams, or players; your responsibility is to your viewers, and they expect accurate, balanced, and entertaining reports of the games they watch. Because your continued success depends on perfection, you limit moonlighting and other commitments that might cut down on the hours of careful preparation necessary for a first-rate sportscast. Your schedule requires play-by-play work one day a week, which translates into a minimum of 25 baseball games during the season plus preseason and postseason games and 16 professional football games plus divisional play-off games and the Super Bowl.

Figure 12.2
Many types of sports events are covered by television networks. This NBC special reporter is traveling with the American relay team to Seoul, South Korea. (Photo by Bob Daemmrich, Stock Boston)

This schedule adds up to nearly a game a week for the calendar year, depending on the duration of play-offs, but it is possible to succeed at this because you are able to spend several days a week memorizing players by appearance, number, and position and to rely on a professional support staff that includes a play and game analyst, a statistician, and (in the case of football) spotters. The travel schedule is demanding, but you are able to return home for at least a portion of each week. Your salary is very high, and this increases the number of aspiring sportscasters coveting your job. This competition alone is reason enough for you to apply yourself constantly to perfecting and maintaining your skills.

Play-by-play announcer for a professional major league baseball team You are employed jointly by a baseball organization and a radio station. You lead a life similar to that of the athletes in many respects. You travel with the team, so you do not have to make separate arrangements for transportation or lodging. A traveling secretary handles all details, and this eases the rigors of travel considerably. You spend early spring in a training camp. If your team is one of two ultimate survivors in its division, you spend early October covering play-offs; if your team wins, you continue as a guest announcer for the radio or television coverage of the World Series.

Including spring practice games and games that are rained out before the end of the fifth inning and must be replayed, but not including divisional play-offs or World Series games, you call more than 170 games during the season. You work with a partner, who

regularly calls three innings of games broadcast on radio only, and
you may move to the television announce booth for a number of
televised games during the season, while your partner covers all innings of these games for radio.

You make nine or ten road trips a season, each lasting seven to
fourteen days. The longer trips find you visiting as many as four cities
and spending three or four days in each one. By the time you have
settled into your hotel room, sent out your laundry, spent time brushing up on the names, numbers, and positions of your team's opponents, and reviewed the press information kit furnished by the
publicity director of the home team, you have little time left for sight-
seeing or for visiting friends in the area.

***Play-by-play announcer for a minor league professional baseball
team***   You call fewer games each season than your major league
counterpart, but both travel and play-by-play announcing are more
rigorous. One of the ways underfunded minor league teams manage
to survive is by economizing on travel. Buses are used for travel
whenever possible. The team remains in each town for five or six days,
and you must call six games during a five-day visit. This schedule
includes Sunday doubleheaders, made somewhat easier for you (and,
of course, the players) because one game of each doubleheader is
scheduled for only seven innings. You may or may not have the assistance of an engineer. You call every inning of every game and serve
as play analyst and statistician as well.

You stay in motels, and your per diem allowance barely covers
your expenses on the road. Broadcast booths, with some exceptions,
are substandard, and broadcast equipment is quite primitive. The
cheapest phone lines are used to send your sportscasts back home.
Despite mediocre audio quality, you have many loyal listeners, and
you are in demand as a banquet speaker and as an auctioneer at many
charitable events.

Play-by-play announcer for a professional football team   Your working life is quite different from that of a baseball, basketball, or hockey
announcer. Not counting preseason and postseason games, your team
plays sixteen games a season, a week apart. You broadcast mainly on
radio, except when games are carried by a regional television network
or by a cable network on a fee-per-game basis. When your team is
featured on a national network telecast, you do the radio play-by-play
while the announce and production teams of the network handle the
television broadcast.

Obviously, eight away games spread over a sixteen-week season demand little in the way of travel stamina. You stay in comfortable hotels, your per diem allowance is more than adequate, and all travel arrangements are made for you by the team's traveling secretary. At the same time, your work is extremely demanding in other respects. You spend a minimum of 20 hours a week memorizing names, numbers, positions, and basic statistical data and studying the kinds of offensive and defensive strategies your team's opponents have relied on during the season.

Play-by-play announcer for a university football team You call about eleven games each season, assuming that funds are available for you to make road trips with the team. Most universities offer free transportation to away games on charter flights but do not furnish announcers with per diem money. If a radio station, the university, and one or more advertisers put together a commercial package for broadcasting an entire season, then your full travel expenses are met. Both home and away games are radio-only broadcasts, except the big game that concludes the regular season. This game may be shown live or on videotape delay, and it gives you your one experience each year to do television play-by-play.

Play-by-play announcer for a professional basketball team You are part of a four-person announcing staff. You and a partner do television play-by-play, while radio coverage is provided by the two other members of the team's broadcasting staff.[1] The radio broadcasts are regular and frequent—all 82 games, both home and away, are broadcast live over a regional network. Telecasts are furnished to fans in a less regular manner. All home games are carried on cable, and 35 away games are telecast over a local commercial station. As is true of announcing employees of all major professional sports teams, you and your colleagues travel with the team. A typical road trip sees your team involved in five matches in as many cities over twelve days.

Play-by-play announcer for a professional hockey team Your traveling and broadcasting schedule is nearly identical to that of your basketball counterpart. Your team plays 80 games, not counting preseason and play-off games. A typical road trip involves five matches in five cities spread over twelve days. Your friends who do play-by-

[1]Professional basketball announcing staffs range from four members to one. Typical is a team of two, who work together during radio-only broadcasts and separately when a game is covered by both radio and television.

play for minor-league hockey teams call fewer games each season, but they must cope with more demanding travel schedules.

Interviewing Athletes

Interviews are an important resource for nearly all sports reporters. The chapter on interviewing will help you develop a general approach to interviewing. This section offers additional comments directed at sports reporting.

As a sports announcer, you will generally interview players, coaches, managers, trainers, and owners. Your interviews will usually be conducted on one of two occasions: at a sports event or at a news conference. Pregame and postgame interviews are common to all sports. As you approach such interviews, asking yourself certain questions will increase your chances of obtaining worthwhile material for an actuality or sound bite:

What is the overriding significance of the game to be played or just concluded?

Is there an interesting one-on-one player match-up?

Is there something unique in the playing ability or game strategy of the person you interview?

Has the athlete been on a hot or cold streak?

Is there an unusually important or interesting game coming up?

Is there any information about trades or free agents that might be newsworthy?

Interviews with athletes can sometimes be frustrating. The code of the locker room seems to demand that athletes, except for professional tennis players, wrestlers, and boxers, be modest about their own accomplishments and praise their teammates or opponents, regardless of the facts. Moreover, athletes are preoccupied before a game and exhausted afterward. Finally, the noise and confusion in dugouts and locker rooms and on the playing field can make sensible, coherent conversation difficult.

Tape-Editing Considerations

When interviewing for later editing into several individual actualities, clearly determine in advance whether your questions will remain on the tape to be heard by your listeners. This is important because the questions you ask and the answers you receive must be guided by the way you will later edit the tape. The following question and answer would be difficult to use if the question were not included in the actuality when it was broadcast.

Q: You were in foul trouble early tonight. Do you think the refs were blowing a quick whistle?

A: Well, I guess we had a little difference of opinion on that. I thought they were overeager. Talk of the possibility of some revenge for the last game probably had them uptight.

Without the question the answer makes little sense. Of course, you could cut the question and write a lead-in that serves the same purpose:

LEAD-IN: I asked Matty if he thought his early fouls came because the refs were blowing a quick whistle.

This works, but it would have been better if you and Matty had understood from the beginning of the interview that you wanted complete statements that included the question as well as the answer. In that event Matty's response might have begun like this:

MATTY: I got into foul trouble early, and I think the reason might have been . . .

Figure 12.3
A common sight is several reporters clustering around the winner after a match. As a sports announcer, most of your interviews will be conducted in the locker room; here radio sports reporters interview boxer Mike Tyson. (Photo by Martin Benjamin, The Image Works)

Tips for Effective Interviewing

When interviewing sports stars, keep the following points in mind.

Assume that your audience is interested in and capable of understanding complex, precise discussions about training and technique   Avoid asking superficial, predictable questions. Your audience probably already knows a lot about the sport and the athlete and wants to find out more, without hearing the same old things. Followers of tennis, golf, and Olympic performances such as gymnastics, diving, and equestrian events are less tolerant of superficial interviews than most other sports fans. They have come to expect precise analytical comments, and they feel cheated if interviews with participants do not add to their understanding of complexities and strategies. Basketball and football have developed increasingly complex offenses and defenses, and fans have been educated to understand and appreciate detailed information about them. Baseball, one of the most subtly complex of all major sports, is seldom explained or discussed in an enlightened fashion through interviews, but this should not deter you from seeking the answers to complex questions.

Work up to controversial or critical questions with care   If you ask a big question without any preliminaries, you are likely to get a routine statement "for the record" from athletes and coaches. Sports figures are interviewed so often that most of them can supply the questions as well as the answers. They tend to rely on safe explanations for most common questions. If you want more than this, lead up to big questions with a sequence of less controversial ones. If you begin an interview with a football coach by asking whether the coach approves of a trade recently made by the club's owners, the coach is naturally going to say "yes" and avoid elaborating. Begin instead by talking about the team and its strengths and weaknesses. Move to a question about the playing abilities of the traded player. Ask specific questions about the player's strong and weak points. Finally, ask the coach to explain how the loss of this player will affect the team. A coach will seldom criticize the decisions of the club's owners, but you will have a better chance of getting more than a vague response if you do not ask the big question straight out. Give your guest a chance to comment informatively as well as loyally.

Get to know the athletes you are likely to be interviewing   This will help you to get some idea of the kinds of questions they can and cannot handle. Many sportscasters and some reporters travel with teams, visit locker rooms, and are invited to opening-day parties, victory celebrations, and promotional luncheons. If you have such opportunities, use them to become acquainted with the athletes who attend.

Listen to conversations among athletes and coaches   A good way to discover what they think is timely and important is simply to listen to their conversations. Though time pressures sometimes require you to enter into these conversations yourself in order to come up with a story or anecdote for your program, you can often learn more by just listening. If you are lucky enough to have meals with athletes and be accepted in clubhouses or locker rooms, try to be a silent observer. You will be amazed at the spontaneous insights that will emerge.

Sports Reporting

At some smaller radio and television stations, the title *sports reporter* is synonymous with *sports director*. Only prosperous stations can afford the services of more than one sports specialist. Radio station sports directors are usually responsible for both live and carted reports. In addition, they prepare a set of instructions to be followed by nonspecialist announcers who must at times report sports news and regularly give in-progress scores and final results.

A television sports reporter is less likely to see double duty as reporter and director. It is common to find three or more sports specialists at television stations: a sports director, who may or may not appear before cameras, and two or more reporters who prepare and deliver sports reports during regular newscasts. Typically, one sports reporter does the Monday-through-Friday newscasts, and the second works weekends. Both cover sports events with camera crews and prepare taped material for the sports segments of the station's newscasts.

The Television Sports Reporter

As a sports reporter for a local television station, you may find yourself preparing and delivering three sports features daily—for the 5:00, 6:00, and 11:00 P.M. newscasts—plus a taped feature for weekend broadcast. In another common arrangement one reporter performs for the 5:00 P.M. news, with the second featured on the 6:00 and 11:00 P.M. newscasts. The first reporter does weekend sports.

As a sports reporter for a medium- or major-market television station, you can expect to have these resources available to you:

an ENG operator for taping sports action and pregame and postgame interviews

videotapes of complete sports events

videotaped sports highlights from a parent network

tapes and slides from professional and university athletic organizations

sports news, photos, and slides from AP and/or UPI

sports magazines and the sports section of newspapers

press information kits and media guides from all major professional and university athletic organizations

a telephone–audio recorder setup that allows you to make audio recordings of telephone interviews

AP and UPI provide extensive material for sports reporters in addition to regional and national reporting of both sports news items and up-to-the-minute scores. Here is a sample of the extra sports services provided by UPI.

Daily throughout the year—"Broadcast Sports Calendar Today," "Sports Headlines" (eight 1-minute packages, containing scores and

Figure 12.4

As audiences' appetites for sports entertainment grow, so do the number of high-school and college games broadcast locally and the number of nationwide events broadcast on cable networks. Announcing duo Charles and Hickman report sports for the Cable News Network (CNN). (Courtesy of Turner Broadcasting System)

top sports news), "Sports Roundup" (five 5-minute sports packages), sports advisories,[2] urgent and bulletin material, "Snap Scores" (college and pro, as they come in), and "Scoreboard" (standings, last night's scores, and today's calendar)

January—"Sizing up the Super Bowl"

March—"Sizing Up the Majors"

April—"Sizing Up the Masters"

May—"Sizing Up the Derby"

May—"Sizing Up the Indy 500"

June—"Sizing Up the U.S. Open"

August—"Sizing Up the PGA"

August—"Sizing Up College Football" and "Sizing Up Pro Football"

Football season—"Football Prophet," "Pro Prophet," and "Football Periscope"

October—"Sizing Up the World Series"

Weekly from November through April— "Ski World"

December—"The Year in Sports," "Athlete of the Year," and "Sizing up the College Football Bowls"

Every four years—"Sizing Up the Olympics"

Team media guides are the best sources of information. Each player's sports career is outlined in detail; statistics are given for individuals, the team, and the team's opponents; each major player's photograph is included to make recognition easier. Both statistics and significant facts are provided to help you give your narrative a sense of authority and interest.

Your job consists mainly of collecting, selecting, editing, and organizing the materials available to you into a cohesive, action-oriented package for each of the evening's newscasts and of writing an entertaining and informative script. One of your tasks is to log significant plays as you watch games on television. The log is later used to edit the major plays for your sports reports.

Using essentially the same visual materials and sports news items, you must prepare as many as three different sports reports each day. The trick is to organize and write your reports to avoid unnecessary

[2]A sports advisory is a brief mention of some happening in sports—a no-hitter, a track record, or a key injury, for example—with a statement that a complete story will follow.

redundancy. Many of your viewers will see two of your nightly reports, and a few will see all three, so all reports must provide fresh information for addicted fans.

You will be under constant pressure from your sports director to make your reports more visual. Because you are working on television, they will obviously be visual; what the director wants is a great deal of illustrative material (videotaped inserts, even still photos) to avoid using the kind of shots known as **talking heads**. Your judgment may tell you that, at times, a series of taped shots may be more confusing than enlightening or that some important stories should be narrated directly into a taking camera. Since it is doubtful that your judgment will prevail, you will sometimes have to make a special effort to tie words and pictures cohesively. On television, when words and pictures do not reinforce one another, the sound tends to fade from the viewer's awareness. Confine your remarks to the few essential comments needed to enhance understanding of what the viewers are seeing.

The Radio Sports Director

As sports director for a medium-market or major-market radio station, you will have many of the same responsibilities as your television counterpart. You will be expected to produce several fast-moving sports reports each day, you will produce material to be broadcast later, and you will establish and supervise station policy concerning sports. This last responsibility will require you to prepare an instruction sheet or manual for use by general or staff announcers. In the manual you will indicate how sports bulletins are to be handled, how the sports news section of general newscasts is to be structured, and the order and manner of reporting scores and outcomes of games. Depending on your geographical region, you might ask that a certain sport be given priority in reporting. In the Northeast, hockey often comes before basketball; in Indiana, basketball usually comes before baseball; in Chicago, baseball almost always comes before tennis; and in Florida, tennis inevitably comes before hockey. If your town has a minor league baseball team, you might ask that its scores be given priority over major league results.

As a radio sports director, you are likely to use the following resources:

a high-quality cassette audio recorder on which you can record (without the services of an engineer) interviews and news conferences for later editing and broadcasting

the services of a studio engineer for the final carting of tapes

Figure 12.5
Veteran sports announcer Lon Simmons being interviewed in the announce booth at the Oakland Coliseum. Radio sports announcers are responsible for recorded actualities, but they must also interview newsworthy sports figures as material for their commentaries. (Courtesy of Lon Simmons and the Oakland A's)

sports news and scores from the news wire services

audio feeds from the wire services and perhaps from a parent network

special wire-service sports features (listed earlier in this chapter)

a telephone beeper for recording phone interviews

press books and other sources of factual information from professional and university sports organizations

a variety of newspapers and magazines to which your station subscribes.

One of your most time-consuming jobs will be to prepare the audiotape carts for your broadcasts. This includes gathering the recorded material, determining the items you will use, writing a script to accompany the recorded inserts, supervising the editing of the excerpts, and providing the on-air engineer the information needed to reduce the chances of error. Because modern radio practice demands extensive use of carted inserts, the procedures followed by one outstanding sports director, Don Klein of KCBS Radio, San Francisco, are outlined here.

Don Klein records most of his taped material without assistance. He attends many sports events and news conferences, accompanied at all times by a high-quality audiocassette recorder with a first-class microphone. He obtains additional recorded material from telephone interviews. Arriving at the station a few hours before his first report is scheduled, he listens to his tapes and writes a script to accompany the portions he wants to use. From the script, he prepares a cut sheet for the station engineer. The **cut sheet** tells the engineer how to edit the tapes for broadcast. A typical sheet is shown in Figure 12.6.

Figure 12.6
The cut sheet prepared by a sports announcer tells the engineer back at the station how to edit the audiotapes.

```
   Raider Quarterback
1. why New England tougher
   ST: they've gotten players in there
   OUT: :16 "stands for itself"
2. added pressure even for 13-1 team
   ST: we've gone into play-offs before
   OUT: :32 "team that's going to win"
3. overcame early injuries and adjusted
   ST: early in the year, our defense
   (double in)
   OUT: :33 "sign of a good team"
4. effect of the NE victory
   ST: I don't think there's any carry-over
   OUT: :27 "the third down plays"
5. what impressed you with NE defense
   ST: they don't give you anything cheap
   OUT: :13 "think they are"
6. what went wrong at Foxboro
   ST: Well, we had three called back
   OUT: :22 "happened to us"
7. key to victory against NE
   ST: pass protection's going to be
   OUT: :24 "pass protection" (double out)
```

This cut sheet tells the engineer to prepare seven carts for broadcast. All are brief, ranging from 13 to 33 seconds. The cut sheet gives the in-cue for each excerpt (marked ST for start) and the out-cue for each (marked OUT). The first notation ("why New England tougher") summarizes the point to be made in the comment that follows. The words following ST are the first words of the excerpt. "Double in" (in cut 3) warns the engineer that the person interviewed repeated the words "early in the year" so that the engineer will record from the first rather than the second stating of the phrase. "Double out" (in cut 7) warns the recording and on-air engineers that the speaker repeats the words "pass protection" in the statement and that the excerpt is to end the second time the words are used. An excerpt requiring a "triple out" on the cut sheet is not uncommon.

In carting the excerpts, the engineer will dub from cassettes or reel-to-reel tapes to seven individual carts, each labeled with the cart number and the information on the cut sheet. The tape carts are stacked in order and turned over to Don Klein, who hands them and his script to the on-air engineer just before his broadcast. Split-second timing and perfect coordination between Don and his engineer are required to avoid the twin sins of letting dead air stand between live and recorded portions of the sportscast or having Don talking over a cart.

Don Klein does six live sports reports daily and records three more for later use. Each report lasts $2\frac{1}{2}$ to 3 minutes. His personal formula calls for 90 seconds of hard sports news or important sports results plus two features or actualities, each lasting 45 seconds. He is responsible for between 22 and 27 minutes of broadcast material a day. For this, he spends a minimum of 8 hours in preparation.

The Play-by-Play Announcer

Play-by-play coverage of football, basketball, hockey, and baseball games accounts for most of the many hours of sports reporting on radio and television. Other events given such coverage are important golf and tennis tournaments, several popular horse racing events each year, boxing, auto racing, the quadrennial summer and winter Olympics, soccer matches, and a number of nonstandard sports such as wrist wrestling, "hot dog" skiing, and lumberjack championships. The person who calls the game, race, match, or event is known as the **play-by-play announcer**, even though in sports such as track and field

Figure 12.7
SportsTicker brings
scores of other ongoing
games right into the
booth, so the announcer
can give fans up-to-the-
minute sports news.
(Courtesy of SportsTicker)

there are no actual plays. For many types of sports events, the play-by-play announcer works with a play or game analyst, whose role is described in the next section.

Working Conditions

If you are a sportscaster for a team playing many games during a long season, you will easily accumulate the kind of information you need for intelligent ad-libbed commentary. Your association with league players will make player identification routine, and your exclusive involvement with a single sport should give you plenty of material for illuminating analyses of tactics and game trends.

At the highest levels of professional sports broadcasting, you will have help from a broadcast staff and the team management. Each broadcast day you will be given a press information kit updating all relevant statistics. During the game, a sports wire, such as Sports-Ticker, Inc., will give you the scores and details of other games. Perhaps a full-time statistician will work with you, unearthing and bringing to your attention significant records or events you can incorporate into your running commentary. You may also have an engineer to continuously balance your voice with crowd sounds to add drama to your narrative. If you telecast a game, you will have instant replay to enrich the coverage. A famous athlete or manager may be at your side, giving evaluations and predictions that will add another dimension to the broadcast. It is demanding work, but at least you have budget, personnel, and working conditions in your favor. However, overlapping and ever expanding seasons as well as competition from single-sport specialists will require you to focus on no more than two or possibly three major sports.

If you work for a smaller station and must announce a wide variety of games—ranging from high school to college and semipro—your job will be much more difficult. You can expect to cover all sports. Rules of play may not be standardized, players may be unknown to you, press information kits may not exist, and you can expect little help and a low budget.

The booth setup will vary with the sport. Football usually demands the services of a team of four: a play-by-play announcer, a play analyst, and two spotters. If you are doing play-by-play, you will sit between the two spotters, and the analyst will sit next to one of the spotters. For high school, college, and some professional games, the analyst is likely to be quite familiar with the home team, so his or her proper position is next to the spotter who points for the visiting team.

The spotting charts are two-sided. One side lists the offensive players, the other the defensive. Pins are usually used to indicate the players that are in the game at any given moment. Playing positions are arranged in ranks that reflect the positioning of the players on the field. The offense side shows one straight line of six players: left tackle, left guard, center, right guard, right tackle, and tight end. Two spaces for wide receivers are outboard of this line of six. Behind the center of the line is a space for the quarterback and, behind the quarterback, two spaces for the running backs. The defensive side of the chart shows a front line of five players: two tackles, two ends, and a linebacker. There are two spaces behind and outboard of the front line for two more linebackers and four additional spaces directly behind the front line for defensive players such as cornerbacks and strong and free safety.

Each spotting chart also has three words written on it: *rush*, *beat*, and *tackle*. As appropriate, the spotters will point to one or another of these words and then point to a player's name. *Rush* is used to indicate the key players on a rush; *beat*, to show who beat whom in

Figure 12.8
Before, during, and after the game, sports announcers spend hours researching team and player histories, statistics, and interesting sidelights. Play-by-play announcer Bill King goes over his detailed stat book just before the start of a game. (Courtesy of Bill King and the Oakland A's)

a one-on-one situation; and *tackle* to indicate players who made or missed key tackles.

Because football, especially at the professional level, is an extremely complex game, the spotting charts do not provide adequate flexibility to cover offensive and defensive realignments. As the play-by-play announcer, you will be concentrating on the handling of the football, so the spotters are responsible for showing changes in the lineups. For example, the defense spotter will hold up five fingers to indicate a nickel defense, or the offensive spotter will hold up three fingers to indicate three wide receivers in the game. In general, you should use spotters for the things you cannot see for yourself. It is your job to follow the football, so leave other details of each play up to your spotters.

The booth setup for baseball can be as simple as one play-by-play announcer sitting with a remote mixer, a microphone, and the array of information sheets and scoring charts needed to call the game. Some radio and most television broadcasts are enhanced by adding two others to the announcing team: a second play-by-play announcer, and a game analyst who also may serve as statistician. The three-person team is positioned with the statistician on the left and the two play-by-play announcers to the statistician's right. Typically, one announcer will call six innings, and the other will call three. Before them are at least three cards or sheets of paper: a diagram of the baseball field with the names of the defensive players written in, and two score sheets, one for each team.

Another setup for baseball broadcasts calls for two announcers, who take turns doing play-by-play and analysis, and an audio engineer. The engineer serves as booth producer of the broadcast and also adjusts the volume on the remote mixer, gives cues when returning to the booth after a break, hands on scores of games in progress, and reminds the announcers to call for breaks for station identification.

Basketball and hockey move so fast and have so few players that play-by-play announcers have neither time nor need for spotters. A name and position chart with pins indicating the players in the game at any given moment may be helpful at times, but in general there is little time to refer to it. The booth setups for basketball and hockey are simple and quite similar. When two-person announcing teams are used, the second announcer provides analysis (or color on radio). Water polo coverage is in most respects similar to coverage of hockey and basketball.

Boxing, golf, tennis, speed and figure skating, skiing and ski jumping, and gymnastics present no problems of competitor recognition. Spotting is unnecessary, and many of the complexities that make football, basketball, and hockey difficult to call are not present. But most of these sports require in-depth knowledge, and fans have come to expect reporters to have superior comprehension and judgment. It has become common for sports generalists to introduce, talk around, and summarize gymnastics, skiing and skating, with the actual play-by-play provided by a former practitioner of the sport. Boxing, golf, and tennis are covered by announcers who may or may not have competed in those sports but who have made long and intense study of them. Announce booths may be lacking altogether at the sites of these sports; at the opposite extreme, during the Olympic Games, a highly sophisticated electronic center is created for media coverage.

Preparation for Play-by-Play Announcing

Preparation as a student   As a novice, you should practice play-by-play announcing at every opportunity, even though your voice may be going nowhere but into a cassette recorder. Attend every sports event you can, not only the major sports, but tennis, track and field, gymnastics, and skiing—anything, in short, that is recognized as a sport and is the subject of radio or television broadcasts. Practice calling games or events into the mic of a battery-operated cassette recorder. Set your tapes aside until your memory of the game has faded, then listen to them to see whether they paint a clear picture of the game. If you find your reporting incomplete, inaccurate, tedious, or marred by numerous corrections, then work on eliminating the flaws. Note any improvement. Improvement builds confidence, and confidence guarantees further improvement.

It is difficult for a student of sports announcing to practice play-by-play for television. Practice with an audio recorder will help prepare you for telecasting, but there are important differences in style, quantity of information given, nature of information provided, and use of resources available to you, including instant replay. Your apprenticeship for the challenge of televised play-by-play will probably be served by observing others as they call games. If you can, obtain permission to be a silent and unobtrusive witness in announce booths during the telecasts of games in your area. If this is not possible, begin to view games on television with a critical eye and ear. Make notes of your observations. Analyze moments of exceptionally competent and exceptionally incompetent play-by-play narrative. Decide for yourself how much description is illuminating, and learn to sense the moment at which announce booth chatter begins to take away from your enjoyment of the game. Most professional play-by-play announcers maintain voluminous notebooks full of facts about players and teams, so that they can enrich the listener's experience with pertinent information that goes beyond the immediate contest.

Preparation on the job   Preparation is the key to successful sportscasting. As Don Klein says, "The two to three hours spent in calling a game is the easiest part of a play-by-play announcer's work. Preparation for most major sportscasts requires up to twenty hours of study." This, of course, refers to covering contests between teams that are unknown or only slightly known to the announcer; less preparation of a different kind is appropriate for play-by-play announcers who work for a team that plays the same opponent as many as thirteen times a season—as in major league baseball and basketball. Here the problem of player recognition is minimized, so preparation focuses on making each sportscast unique.

Before even entering the announce booth, you should ask yourself a number of questions: Is there anything unusual about this game? Is either team or any player on a streak of any sort? Are there any interesting rivalries in this match-up? How might the weather affect the game? Is there a home-team advantage? How have these teams fared during the season and over the past few years? Pondering the answers to these and similar questions should make you ready to call an interesting game.

In preparing for the coverage of a game when at least one of the teams is unknown to you, you should begin your preparation as far in advance as possible. Your resources are team media guides, press information kits, official yearbooks, newspaper stories and columns, wire-service reports, and specialized sports magazines. Preparation includes memorizing all players by name and position and, if possible, appearance. In football, players' numbers are often important. Preparation includes making notes, usually on three-by-five file cards, of information you feel might be useful during the game. Preparation also requires spotting charts, scoring sheets, and any similar materials appropriate to the sport.

Arrive early on the day of the game. Check starting lineups. If in doubt, check on the pronunciation of players' names with assistant managers or team captains. If possible, spend time with the players before the game; your effectiveness in describing the game will be enhanced by understanding how the players feel. Enter the booth long before game time. Lay out your spotting charts, scoring sheets, file cards of statistical and anecdotal information, and whatever notebooks or other materials you plan to use during the game. Check out your broadcast equipment. For either radio or television sportscasts, commercials, station promotions, and promotions of ticket sales are likely to have been recorded before game time. This practice reduces pressure during the game and gives you many moments during which you can take off your headset and make or read notes.

Plan ahead. Think about everything you will need and make sure you have it all with you when you arrive at the booth. Aside from the spotting charts, scoring sheets, and information cards, you will need pencils, erasers, pins for the chart (if the sport is football), water or some other beverage, binoculars, and perhaps even an electric heater to keep your teeth from chattering!

Calling the Game

In covering any sport as a member of a two-person team, it is helpful to develop and use simple nonverbal signals to avoid confusion. A sportscast can be deadly for listeners if you and your partner are continually interrupting each other or starting to speak at the same time. The general rule is that the play-by-play announcer is the booth director. As play-by-play announcer, you will do all the talking except when you invite your play analyst or statistician to contribute. Play analysts indicate that they have a comment to make by raising a hand; if you decide to allow the comment, you throw a cue by pointing an index finger when you come to the end of your own remarks. Analysts must always complete their remarks well ahead of the time when you must again pick up the play-by-play. Hand signals (except for "you're on" cues) are unnecessary when sportscasters have worked together for long periods of time and can sense when it is safe to interject a comment.

In calling a football game, you might benefit from standing rather than sitting. Walt Brown, formerly sports director and play-by-play announcer for KTVK-TV, Phoenix, stands to broadcast any sport if possible. Not only does he feel much more energy—which is communicated to his listeners—but he cites practical reasons as well. When standing, he finds it is easier to move, as needed, to relate to the field, the television monitor, spotter's charts, and the play analyst.

When calling any game, you must keep many important principles in mind. First, you must truly believe that your chief responsibility is to your viewers or listeners. This will be difficult to hold to at times. Unreasonable owners, broadcast station managers, outraged players, and others who have a stake in your broadcasts may make irrational demands. In the long run, though, you will prosper best if you have a loyal following of viewers or listeners who have developed faith in your ability and your integrity and who know you are not merely a shill for a profit-hungry sports organization.

Second, remember that it is your responsibility to report, entertain, and sell. Your reports must be accurate and fair. As an entertainer, you must attract and hold the fans' attention for up to 3 hours at a time. Selling means selling the sport more than the team. It means selling yourself as a credible reporter, communicating the natural enthusiasm you feel, and avoiding hypocrisy, condescension, forced enthusiasm, and any other trait that will cause listeners to question your values.

Finally, avoid home-team bias. **Homers** are not unknown to sportscasting, and some have managed to capitalize on their lack of objectivity and maintain popularity with fans. But there are practical reasons for avoiding home-team bias, and one stands out as supremely important: bias will blind an announcer to the actual events taking place. Regardless of affiliation or loyalties, it is the play-by-play announcer's responsibility to provide fans with a clear, accurate, and fair account of the game. This responsibility is somewhat more pertinent if you do play-by-play for radio. Television fans can compare your work with what they see, and this operates as a governor on what otherwise might be unchecked subjectivity. But as the eyes of radio listeners, you have an obligation to report with objectivity; your account is almost their total experience of the event.

Additional Tips on Sportscasting

Some of the following suggestions are appropriate to all sports; others apply to one or two.

Communicate the important events in a game and provide interpretation when appropriate   A game is more than a series of individual plays or events. Plays are part of a process that adds up to an overall pattern. If you are perceptive and deeply involved in the event, you will be able to point out crucial plays and turning points immediately after they occur. It is your responsibility to comprehend the significance of plays or incidents and then to communicate your awareness to your viewers or listeners. The importance will be transmitted not only by what you say but also by how you say it. Some critical situations will be apparent to any reasonably sophisticated fan, but at times it will be necessary for you to be so tuned in to the game that your interpretation transcends common knowledge.

When doing play-by-play on radio, provide listeners with relatively more information than is necessary for a telecast   Listeners need to know, for example, what the weather is like, how the stadium or court looks, how the fans are behaving, whether players are right- or left-handed, the wind direction, what the score is, who's on first, how many yards for a first down, how many outs or minutes left in the game, and whether a particular play was routine or outstanding.

When doing baseball play-by-play, always be ready to talk intelligently and entertainingly during rain delays   Baseball fans love baseball lore, and well-prepared announcers who can discuss historical aspects of the sport and provide a wealth of amusing or amazing anecdotes can make a rain delay one of the highlights of a game.

Never make events in a game seem more important than they are   A dull game creates a natural temptation to entertain by exaggerating. Avoid this.

Do not overuse sports clichés   It is not possible to avoid sports clichés entirely, because there are a limited number of ways of describing things that happen over and over in a given sport. But you should be conscious of clichés and try to avoid their overuse. Here are several overused sports expressions:

ducks on the pond	off to a running start
in tonight's action	odds-on favorite
Over in the NBA, over in the American League	off to a shaky start
	sparked the win
all the action is under the lights	suffered a sixth setback
	raised the record to
he was in complete charge	went the distance
he got all of it	

Some familiar sports expressions are clear, direct, and uncomplicated and can hardly be improved on: *loaded the bases, gave up a walk, got the hat trick, finished within one stroke of,* and *lost the decision.* Be wary of time-worn clichés but do not be afraid to use common expressions if you are not able to improve on them. In general, although clichés cannot—and should not—be completely avoided, the variety of play-by-play delivery is improved by the use of several ways of naming the same events or incidents.

Have statistics in front of you or firmly in mind before you start to talk about them   If you make an error, you can correct it, of course: "That's the fourth walk allowed by Rollins—hold it, it's the *third* walk." Taken alone, there is nothing wrong with this. It becomes annoying, however, if you find yourself repeatedly making such corrections.

On television, concentrate on interpreting the events and adding comments about things not clearly shown by the camera   The television viewer does not necessarily see everything that a trained observer sees. With your commentary and the help of instant replay, viewers can be given a myriad of specific details that will illuminate, instruct, and entertain.

When doing play-by-play on television, avoid the extremes of too much or too little commentary   Avoid extraneous chatter that confuses and distracts viewers. On the other hand, do not go to the opposite extreme and assume that your viewers or listeners have been with you throughout the entire game and therefore know everything important that has occurred. From time to time, review key plays, injuries, and other pertinent facts.

When a player is injured, never guess about the nature or severity of the injury   If you consider it important to report on the details of the injury, send an assistant to the team trainer or physician. Inaccurate information about an injury can cause unnecessary worry for friends and family.

Do not ignore fights, but do not sensationalize them   Hockey and football are often violent, and fights between players are not uncommon. If you dwell on them, you may foment both aggression by fans (thrown bottles, for example) and attempts by players to get revenge.

If you are not sure about information, do not guess   Wait as long as necessary to give official verdicts on whether a ball was fair or foul,

---

Checklist: Becoming a Better Play-by-Play Announcer

1. Communicate the important events in a game and provide interpretation when appropriate.
2. Provide a radio audience with more information than is necessary for a telecast.
3. Be prepared to talk intelligently and entertainingly during rain delays of baseball games.
4. Never make events in a game seem more important than they are.
5. Do not overuse sports clichés.
6. Do not talk about statistics unless you have them in front of you or firmly in mind.
7. On television, concentrate on interpreting the events and adding comments about things not clearly shown by the cameras.
8. When doing television play-by-play, avoid the extremes of too much or too little commentary.
9. When a player is injured, never guess about the nature or severity of the injury.
10. Do not ignore fights, but do not sensationalize them.
11. If you are not sure about information, do not guess.
12. Repeat the score at frequent intervals.
13. Give scores of other games without interfering with the announcing of the game at hand.
14. Take care of first things first.
15. Do not keep telling the audience how great the game is.
16. If you cannot immediately identify a player, cover the play without mentioning names and give the name when you are sure of it.
17. Learn where to look for the information you need.
18. Do not rely on scoreboard information.
19. Give statistics and records.
20. Avoid adopting meaningless catch phrases.
21. Avoid overuse of the word *situation*.
22. Use background sounds to your advantage.
23. When working with a play analyst, reach an agreement on the pronunciation of names.

---

whether a goal was scored, and whether a first down was made. Constant corrections of such errors are annoying to the fans.

Repeat the score of the game at frequent intervals Tell a baseball audience what inning it is as you give the score. Tell football, basketball, and hockey audiences which period it is and how much time is left. Football audiences need to be reminded frequently of who has the ball, where the ball is, and what down is coming up. It is all but impossible to give such information too often.

Give scores of other games, but never allow this to interfere with the game at hand   When telecasting, remember that your viewers are being bombarded with information not only from you, the play analyst, and the camera coverage of the game, but also from **supers** called up by the director for providing statistical information, identifying the game, promoting a program or another sportscast coming up, and so on. Because of this overload, you must be careful not to further distract viewers from the game they are watching. Give scores of other games but be discreet.

Take care of first things first   Before going to an analysis of a play, make sure that you have told your audience what it most wants to know. In baseball, do not describe the double play until you have told the fans whether or not the player on third scored. In football, do not start talking about key blocks or sensational catches until you have indicated whether or not a first down was made on the play.

Do not keep telling your audience how great the game is   If it is a great game, the events and the way you report them will speak for themselves. If it is not a great game, no amount of wishful thinking will make it exciting.

If you cannot immediately identify a player, cover the play without mentioning names and give the name when you are sure of it   Here is a poor example of identifying players:

> ANNCR: The ball is taken by Richards . . . He's back in the pocket to pass . . . He's being rushed . . . He barely gets it away and it's intercepted by Pappas . . . no, I think it's Harrison . . . He has it on the twenty-five, the thirty, the thirty-five . . . and he's brought down on the thirty-seven. Yes, that was Pappas, the All-American defensive back.

This is a better example:

> ANNCR: The ball is taken by Richards . . . He's back in the pocket to pass . . . He's being rushed . . . He barely gets it away and it's intercepted on the twenty . . . back to the thirty, the thirty-five, and all the way to the thirty-seven. A beautiful interception by Charley Pappas, the All-American defensive back.

Learn where to look for the information you need   In baseball, watch the outfielders instead of a fly ball to see whether the ball will be caught, fielded, or lost over the fence. Watch line umpires to see whether a ball is fair or foul. In football, watch the quarterback unless you clearly see a handoff or a pass, then watch the ball. Let your spotters or analyst watch the defense and the offensive ends.

Do not rely on scoreboard information   Keep your own notebook and record the data appropriate to the sport you are covering. For football, note the time when possession begins, the location of the ball after each play, the nature of each play, and the manner in which the drive ends. This will help you summarize each drive and will single out the most important plays. For baseball, keep a regular scoring chart and learn to read it quickly and accurately. For basketball and hockey, rely on a statistician for data such as goals attempted and fouls and penalties assessed.

Give statistics and records   Baseball fans are always interested in batting and earned-run averages, fielding percentages, strike-out records, and comparative statistics. Track and field followers are obsessed with distance and speed records. Statistics are of only slightly less importance to followers of football, basketball, hockey, and golf.

Avoid adopting meaningless catch phrases   Perhaps the most prevalent and annoying habit of sports announcers is the interjection of the phrase *of course* into statements when the information being given is not necessarily known by all who are listening, as in "Wilson, of course, has run for over a hundred yards in each of his last seven games." Even when the information is widely known, *of course* adds nothing to most statements: "Jose Canseco, of course, was Rookie of the Year in 1986."

Eliminate or control the use of the word **situation**   With some sports announcers, nearly everything is a situation: "It's a passing situation," "It's a bunting situation," "It's a third-and-three situation." The constant repetition of this word can become very tiresome.

Use background sounds to your advantage   In most sports there are moments of action that precipitate an enthusiastic response from the crowd. The sounds of cheering fans can enhance your game coverage. Do not be afraid to remain silent while the fans convey the excitement of the game for you.

When working with a play analyst, make sure you and your partner agree on the pronunciation of names that could be pronounced in different ways During a recent professional football telecast, the play-by-play announcer and play analyst pronounced the names of three players in very different ways:

Mc Mahon: (MUK-MAN′) versus (MUK-MAY′-UN)

Lippett: (LIP′-UHT) versus (LIH-PET′)

Clayborn: (KLAY′-BORN) versus (KLY′-BERN)

These differences probably went unnoticed by most listeners, but you always should aim for the acceptance of your most attentive listeners and viewers.

The Play Analyst

A **play analyst** interprets individual plays and overall strategies and developments as they unfold. Analysts are, without significant exception, former athletes of the sports they describe. Auto racers, skiers, baseball and football players and coaches, swimmers, gymnasts, golfers, tennis players, and others who have gained fame in sports can now be heard giving in-depth analysis during sportscasts. Play and game analysis is highly specialized, and proper preparation requires devoting oneself fully to the sport itself.

A play analyst provides information and interpretation that complements rather than duplicates what is offered by the play-by-play announcer. The analyst must have clear instructions about what to look for and how to report it. In football, the analyst looks for key blocks, tackles, and similar events of importance. In baseball, hockey, and basketball, the analyst (when one is used) usually performs as a statistician and analyzes the whole game rather than individual plays. In these sports, the analyst sees little or nothing that is not seen by the play-by-play announcer, so information such as "that was Ponce's twenty-first inning without giving up a walk" or "Garrett's 41 points are a season high for him, but they're a long way from the record set by Wilt Chamberlain—he scored 100 points in a game in 1962" is the kind of contribution expected of a play analyst. Hockey and basketball move so fast that opportunities for play analysis are limited, and when interesting points are brought up at all, it is the play-by-play announcer who discusses them.

Gymnastics, figure skating, diving, and similar sports of a strongly aesthetic nature are usually described by experts in the event. Analysis is the primary responsibility of the people who cover sports in which points are assigned by judges, because the vast majority of the viewers have little precise knowledge of the pluses and the minuses of individual performances.

Here are a few tips on play and game analysis.

- Never repeat either exactly or by paraphrase what the play-by-play announcer has just said.
- Do not feel compelled to comment after every play of a football game or after every pitch of a baseball game. If you have nothing significant to report, remain silent
- Be precise in the comments you make "What a great catch" is neither useful nor informative. "Frick has just gone over the 100-yard mark for the eighth time this season" is precise and useful.
- Do your homework on both teams. The play-by-play announcer will also have prepared, but in the heat of the game it may fall to you to remember facts or statistics forgotten by your partner. Make notes of key moments of the game.
- Your major contribution is to see the game with an objectivity not always possible for a play-by-play announcer. Look for the dramatic structure of the contest and report it when appropriate. Do not overdramatize, however.
- Never correct the play-by-play announcer on the air. If an important mistake has been made, write and pass a note. Listeners and viewers become uncomfortable when they sense conflict between members of the announcing team.
- A discussion between play-by-play announcer and analyst in which different points of view are expressed can be useful to fans. As long as the discussion is friendly, there should be no reason to avoid or prematurely terminate it.
- Be careful what questions you ask of your partner. Even the most seasoned veteran can draw a blank when concentrating on a game.
- Follow the rules set down by your play-by-play partner. You will probably be required to ask for an opportunity to speak and to speak only when your partner gives you your cue. If your agreement with the play-by-play announcer calls for it, be prepared to make intelligent comments during time-outs and intermissions in basketball and hockey contests.
- Always be sure to end your comments before the next play begins.

Spotlight: In the Game with Harry Caray

Baseball just isn't baseball without hot dogs, peanuts, and beer. At Chicago's Wrigley Field, a Cubs game just isn't a Cubs game without Harry Caray's taking the microphone during the seventh-inning stretch and leading the fans in a rendition of "Take Me Out to the Ball Game."

"A One! A two! A three!" he yells as 37,000-plus roaring fans take deep breaths.

Take me out to the ball game;
Take me out with the crowd.
Buy me some peanuts and Cracker Jack
I don't care if I never get back. . . .

Caray's voice is nearly muffled by the crowd. "But that's the whole idea," he said after singing his tune. "I'm so bad that they have to sing loud enough to drown me out."

The ditty has become a trademark of the blustery Chicago Cubs broadcaster. Every home game during the season, Caray goes to the "Friendly Confines" of Wrigley Field and revs up the crowd. He doesn't eat peanuts or Cracker Jacks, but if he had his way, he would never get back.

"I have the best job I could possibly have," Caray said from his summer home at the Ambassador East Hotel in downtown Chicago. "I love baseball, and I love the fans. And I love the Cubs. I haven't found a better way to make as much money and have as much fun."

The 45-year veteran announcer has been the voice of the Chicago Cubs on WGN-TV and WGN-AM radio since 1982. Caray's major league broadcasting career began with the St. Louis Cardinals, bringing him his first taste of national fame. After 25 years of doing the Cardinals games, he spent a year with the Oakland Athletics before moving to the Chicago White Sox. After a decade, Caray quit when the management

broke up his longtime partnership with the controversial Jimmy Piersall. He also spoke out against moving the White Sox broadcasts to cable television while the Cubs broadcast their games locally for free.

"I told them that it was crazy," Caray said. "So I picked up the phone and called the Cubs. The Cubs, within a day, had hired me. That's where I am now, and that's where I plan to be for a while."

The move from Comiskey Park to Wrigley Field boosted Caray's already-prospering career. Budweiser commercials with Caray on the dance floor singing "I'm a Cub fan! I'm a Bud man!" have appeared nationally on television and in magazines. The fishing net he waves from the broadcast booth to catch foul balls attracts cameras each game. Then there is his boisterous "Holy Cow!" after each Cubs home run. Viewers expect it, and other sportscasters mimic it. A soft drink was even named after it.

Baseball inducted Caray into the broadcasters' wing of the National Baseball Hall of Fame in 1989 in Cooperstown, New York. Now in his early seventies, the announcer called his trip to Cooperstown long overdue: "I don't know what took them so long, but I don't really care. I know I have offended plenty of people in my broadcasts because I am political, even with my own team. But I've never felt that I worked for the guy who owns the team, or the manager or the general manager or the star players. I feel I work for the fan."

He claims to have been the first to condemn the home team during games. He has criticized umpires' calls, has attacked players' performances, and has even spoken out against the commissioner of baseball. He's not afraid of anyone, he says, not even his boss.

His ability to make the game interesting, even if the Cubs are being blown out in the top of the eighth inning, is an attribute. During lulls in the ball games, he announces birthdays and anniversaries of dozens of fans in the crowd, baseball's version of Willard Scott's routine.

Each game day, Caray, his broadcast partner Steve Stone, and a production assistant cram into the tiny WGN booth overlooking Chicago's north side. Just minutes later, it's time for Caray to go on the air for a pregame message.

Stone and the assistant leave to make way for the cameraman. Caray clears his throat. Every few seconds he speaks into the microphone in reply to a message he hears through his earplug. He clears his throat again; this time it's louder. Finally he says, "Let's do it." Caray's smile and a spotlight suddenly brighten up the room.

"Gooooooood afternoon, Cub fans! Harry Caray here from Wrigley Field. What a beau-uuutiful day for baseball," Caray exclaimed before a sold-out June game with the New York Mets. "What are you doing at home? You should be at the ballpark. Don't you know Dwight Gooden is pitching for the Mets? The Cubbies are going for their third straight win against the New Yorkers. . . ."

After the promo, Stone and the assistant take their places for the first pitch. Caray arranges his score sheet, Mets roster, birthdays and anniversaries, and the *Chicago Tribune* sports section.

Caray's face isn't seen again until that seventh-inning stretch. But his voice booms. Three times in one inning Caray reacts wildly. Two hits and a home run bring a rollicking "Hooolllyyy Cooowww!" Following every yell, sportswriters and broadcasters in adjoining press boxes turn toward Caray and wave, applaud, or just laugh.

"I am just a big fan. I don't realize what I do," Caray said. "If there's any appeal I have to the people it's that people consider me one of them. I show the same disgust in my voice when

Chicago Cubs announcer Harry Caray (Photo courtesy of WGN Television, Chicago.)

something disgusting happens; I'm ecstatic when something good happens. I think the average fan thinks I'm doing the game the way he'd be doing it. I'm talking fan-to-fan."

His ability to talk fan-to-fan is a rarity in a field dominated by former players. Meanwhile, Caray points out, trained broadcasters struggle at small-town radio stations. "I really feel sorry for the young guy who wants and really tries to make it in broadcasting," he said. "There are so many talented young people who are working in small stations developing their style and vocabulary and their personality waiting for a chance to break into the major leagues. They're never going to get that chance, though.

"My advice to the college student who wants to become a broadcaster is to become an all-American football player or a baseball player. Get into the professional ranks, play ten years, and then they'll put you in the television booth."

Source: Abridged from an article, "Holy Cow! It's Harry Caray," by Charles P. Miller. In *The Saturday Evening Post*, October 1989, pp. 54+. Reprinted with permission from *The Saturday Evening Post*. © 1989 BFL&MS, Inc.

It may be difficult to maintain harmonious relations with your partner, but it is imperative. Fans appreciate listening to announcing teams that complement each other and work together to present the sports experience competently and completely.

If you hope to become a professional sports announcer of any kind—reporter, play-by-play, analyst—you should build your own sports library and become knowledgeable about as many sports as possible. And remember that there is no substitute for practicing your skills.

Practice: Play-By-Play Announcing

Using a battery-operated audiotape recorder, do play-by-play announcing for a baseball, football, basketball, or hockey game (or any other sport you prefer). Put the tape aside for a week or two, and then listen to it critically. Are you able to visualize the game from the words you spoke and recorded?

Practice: Getting Athletes' Names Right

Prior to an amateur sports event of any kind, obtain a list of players' names. Mark any whose pronunciation is not obvious—you may be sure of the pronunciation of Smith but not of the preferred pronunciation of Smythe. Then, depending on where you are allowed access, visit the locker room, the dugout, or other area where team officials may be found, and ask to be told the pronunciation of names in question. As you are given the information, use your favored system of phonetic transcription (wire-service, diacritics, or IPA) to denote the correct pronunciation on the list.

i3

Starting a Career in Broadcasting

This chapter is designed to help you start your career as a broadcast announcer. Its focus is on college students who have not held a paying job as an announcer, but feel that they are ready for professional employment. Most of the information in this chapter is also applicable to those who have had some professional experience, who received their training in workshops conducted by professionals, or who have developed their abilities through self-study.

This chapter assumes that you are looking for a job as an announcer in one of these categores:

popular music announcing

news reporting and/or anchor work

news-related announcing as an environmental, consumer information, or entertainment news reporter

radio or television talk show hosting

sports reporting and/or play-by-play announcing

weather reporting for either radio or television

radio commercial announcing as a freelance performer

on-camera television commercial performance

voice-over television work for commercials, documentaries, or training tapes

This chapter also assumes that you have become capable, though not necessarily completely proficient, in the announcing specialization of your choice. As indicated in Chapter 1, merely taking a course or two in broadcast performance cannot make you a competent journalist, sports reporter, or talk show host. It is assumed that you have augmented your education with practice and that you have completed course work in the subject area of your specialization.

Preparing for Your Career

If you have determined that you want to be a broadcast announcer, you undoubtedly have identified many positive reasons for your choice. To be an announcer is to be important. Broadcasting is an exciting and dynamic field. Electronic communication will unquestionably become more and more influential as the years go by. There are noteworthy rewards of fame and wealth for those who make it to—or near—the top of this profession. Finally, the opportunity to inform or entertain vast numbers of people is surely a substantial motivation.

Before committing yourself to a career as a broadcast performer, however, you should make an honest assessment of yourself—of your strengths, your skills, your areas of specialized knowledge, your interests, and your values. No one else can do this for you, but it is important that the appraisal be made. It will clarify a number of things for you, including what type of job or freelance work coincides with your career interests and abilities, exactly what type of work you are equipped to perform, what kinds of working conditions are necessary for you to receive job satisfaction, the salary you will need to support yourself, and where you are and are not willing to live. You should

Figure 13.1
The best preparation for work in announcing is a combination of theory and practice. These students are meeting for discussion in a special classroom adjacent to the university radio studio. (Photo by Ellis Herwig, Stock Boston)

also ask yourself if you will be comfortable in a field in which there is really no job security.

The checklist presented here allows you to assess your potential for success as a broadcast performer. It consists of a number of questions that *only you* can answer. These questions are extremely personal, but the answers need not be shared with anyone. For this self-assessment to be of value to you, it is imperative that you dig deeply and not settle for superficial, hasty answers. This self-assessment should be undertaken at a number of points during your student years. Although you should keep these questions in mind from the very beginning, *your most important answers will come at or near the end of your studies*. Also remember that you should not be unjustifiably negative toward yourself, especially during your early years as a student. Be *honest*, but be *reasonable*. No one expects a beginner to perform at the level of a veteran!

The time to begin preparing for that first job is while you are still in school. This is the time to start making connections that may someday pay off. Join broadcast-related organizations such as College Students in Broadcasting, Alpha Epsilon Rho, and Women in Communication, Inc. (WICI).

During your final two semesters in college, you should serve internships at the kinds of stations where you would like to work. Ask for an internship only when you are ready to make an important contribution at a particular station; otherwise, you may wind up stuffing envelopes or answering the phone. On the other hand, if you can help a station in some significant way, your internship could very well turn into a job!

Job-Hunting Tools

For most announcing jobs, you will look for employment at radio or television stations. If you are interested in commercial announcing and narrating, you will almost certainly need to work through a talent agency. Whether you approach a station or a talent agency, there are two things you will need: a résumé (with a cover letter) and an audition tape.

Résumés

The **résumé** is an indispensable tool for those seeking employment in any announcing field. It lists, in an abbreviated manner, the most relevant facts about a job applicant. Employers can tell, almost at a

Checklist: Assessing Your Career Potential

As a communicator in the electronic media

1. Do I truly have talent as a performer?
2. Is my voice adequate for the career I seek? If not, is it improvable through exercises and practice? Am I prepared to work until the improvement has occurred?
3. (For television performance) Is my physical appearance appropriate to the kinds of positions I seek? If it is not, can my appearance be made acceptable or adequate through hair styling, makeup, and so forth?
4. Do I have an on-air personality that is engaging and unique?
5. What is there about me that makes me feel that I can succeed as an announcer?

As a radio announcer

1. Am I willing to start at the very bottom of the ladder?
2. Am I willing to work for very low wages?
3. Am I prepared to move anywhere at any time to further my career?
4. Can I live with the fact that any change in ratings, ownership, or format could cost me my job?
5. Do I perform well under pressure?
6. Does mic fright presently interfere with my performance? If so, what are the chances that I can eventually bring this under control?
7. Do I possess the manipulative skills necessary to perform in an effortless and error-free manner as a disk jockey?

As a voice-over announcer for commercials, industrials, and documentaries

1. Do I take direction well, responding quickly and sensitively to instructions?
2. Can I perform effectively under pressure?
3. Can I do a professional job of interpreting copy that requires accents, dialects, or character voices?
4. Am I prepared to live on an absolutely unpredictable and uncertain income?

As a reporter or anchor for radio or television news

1. Am I a quick judge of the newsworthiness of events as they happen?
2. Have I properly prepared myself to work as a journalist?
3. Can I remain reasonably detached at the scene of a wreck, fire, or other catastrophe where people have been badly injured or killed?
4. Can I maintain my composure and deliver a coherent live report from a location at which there are many ongoing distractions?

5. Have I adequately learned to operate basic items of audio and video equipment that most likely will be used by me on the job?

As a sports reporter or play-by-play announcer

1. Do I have a thorough grounding in all of the major sports, or am I a single-sport devotee?

2. Do I love sports enough to commit myself to becoming a sports announcer, despite the scarcity of jobs and the stiff competition?

3. Am I willing to spend years of frequent travel, often being away from family and friends for weeks at a time?

glance, if the applicant is appropriate for a vacancy or, at least, worthy of an interview. With so much at stake for you, the preparation of an attractive, factual, and to-the-point résumé is invaluable. Note, however, that even the best résumé cannot help you get a job unless you are truly capable, dependable, and punctual and an asset to any employer. The suggestions that follow take for granted that you have these qualities and that you deserve a position in broadcasting.

Before starting to prepare your résumé, visit the nearest career guidance or job counseling center. If you are a student, you will probably find such an office right on campus. If you are not attending school, you can still get help from the job center of almost any community college or four-year school. Some schools regularly offer résumé-writing clinics, sometimes for a small registration fee. Many college placement offices have free handouts on the subject of résumé writing. Arm yourself with as much information as you can find. The bibliography for this chapter lists some excellent books on the subject of résumés and job seeking.

Although campus placement offices can help you with useful information on résumés, cover letters, and interviews, do not expect personnel in these offices to have all the answers. The field of broadcast performance is so specialized, and so out of the ordinary, that few career guidance counselors have in-depth firsthand knowledge of it.

Types of résumés   There are two general types of résumés and a third type that is a hybrid of those two. All résumés provide some common items of information, including name, address, phone number, formal education, and references, but differ in certain important respects. The first type, the **chronological résumé**, lists relevant employment in reverse chronological order. The second type, the **competency-based**, or **functional, résumé**, lists the applicant's areas of competency. The **hybrid résumé**, as the name indicates, combines features of both the chronological and the competency-based résumé.

The chronological résumé is used by anyone with some professional experience. A sample of this type of résumé is shown in Figure 13.3.

The competency-based, or functional, résumé is preferable for students who are nearing graduation and are looking for their first job. Many graduating seniors can point only to the knowledge they have acquired in school, which includes skills learned on college radio and television stations or through internships at commercial or public broadcasting stations. A chronological listing of part-time jobs held while in school, such as bussing dishes or working in a car wash, is not likely to impress a prospective employer. However, if you earned half or more of your living expenses while in school, state this fact, together with a brief list of jobs held. This will tell a prospective employer that you are an industrious person who made a sacrifice to gain an education. If you have had bookkeeping, accounting, or sales experience, say so.

More important, though, is indicating that you can perform the functions expected of a person in the position for which you are applying. State, for instance, that you can operate all standard control room or EFP equipment, that you can do audiotape or videotape editing, or that you can operate studio cameras and switchers. These and similar competencies can be put forward as positive qualifications for an entry-level position. This is the thrust of a competency-based résumé, as the example in Figure 13.4 illustrates.

It is appropriate, on a competency-based résumé, to list positions held as a member of a college radio or television station staff and to provide information about work done as an intern. But it is crucial that such work be clearly identified. Applicants who list positions held as a member of a campus radio station in such a way as to make it seem that they were held at a commercial station will be seen as misrepresenting their backgrounds. And those who try to pass off an internship at a commercial or public broadcasting station as professional experience will be written off immediately. It is unlikely that a prospective employer would even schedule an interview or review an air check if that employer felt that the applicant was providing misleading information.

Figure 13.2
Even small schools, such as the College of St. Rose in Albany, New York are likely to be well-equipped for studio practice. A student nervously looks over her copy and listens to last-minute advice from the instructor before going "on-air" as a news anchor in a videotaped performance. (Source: Martin Benjamin, The Image Works)

The hybrid résumé is useful for students who have had some professional experience, either before or during school years, and who have also acquired knowledge and competencies as a student. An example of a hybrid résumé is shown in Figure 13.5.

Some tips on résumé preparation In most instances, you will want to list on your résumé your career aspirations—what kind of work you want to do, what growth opportunities you seek, whether or not you will relocate, etc. In this age of word processing, it is quite easy to prepare more than one résumé, each with a different personal statement. For instance, as a graduate of a department of radio and television, you may very well want to apply for positions in both fields; obviously, the same statement of career aspirations would not serve both purposes.

Résumés should be double-spaced and only one page long. Although you may feel you have more than a page of information to impart, remember that prospective employers want to see your qualifications in the briefest possible form.

In preparing your résumé, it is wise to make a first draft and then ask a qualified person—a teacher of broadcasting, a person working

```
                  Mary Ann Williams
                  586 Poplar Avenue
                  Huntington, WV 25704
                  (304) 883-6572

OBJECTIVE:        Radio station news anchor or reporter

EDUCATION:        Kimball University, Hays, Kentucky
                  B.A. in Radio and Television, 1989
                  Course work included news gathering; depth
                  reporting; legal aspects of journalism; newswriting;
                  and radio news production and performance.
                  Performed as news reporter and anchor on campus
                  radio station for three years.

EMPLOYMENT
1989-             News reporter, WBRE, Mount Embree, Kentucky
present           Cover local stories; report live from the field;
                  produce news packages at station; specialize in
                  education and environment

1988-1989         Paid news intern at WBRE-AM, Mount Embree,
                  Kentucky
                  Collected and edited wire-service copy; rewrote
                  stories; maintained files; performed as on-air
                  news anchor on weekends

1986-1988         Volunteer reporter at local NPR station, writing
                  and voicing reports on school board meetings,
                  local election issues, and impact of growth on the
                  community

1985-1988         Variety of part-time jobs to pay for my education

HONORS            Dean's list, all semesters in college; President,
                  College Students in Broadcasting, 1987; Adan
                  Marshall Scholarship, 1988; Albert Johnson Award
                  as outstanding graduating senior, 1989; graduated
                  cum laude, 1989

REFERENCES        Supplied on request
```

Figure 13.3 An example of a chronological résumé.

```
                    Ralph Wente
                    435 Livingston Street
                    Tacoma, Washington 98499
                    (206) 446-3790

OBJECTIVE           Initial objective: entry-level position in
                    television sports department
                    Ultimate objective: to become a television
                    sports reporter and play-by-play announcer

COMPETENCIES
Sports              Thorough knowledge of sports officiating and
Knowledge           scoring of gymnastics, diving, and other
                    competitive sports; six years' experience
                    scoring baseball; knowledge of football and
                    basketball strategies

Sports              Played baseball (second base and shortstop),
Experience          three years in high school and four in college;
                    played football (running back), three years
                    in college; manager, college basketball team,
                    two years

Other               Expert at both still and video camera work;
Competencies        considerable skill in both on- and off-line
                    videotape editing; two years' experience in
                    writing copy for sports newscasts on campus
                    closed-circuit television station; bilingual
                    in Spanish

AWARDS AND          Dean's list, 1987-88; member and president of
HONORS              University Block T Club (Sports Honor
                    Society); valedictorian

EDUCATION           B.A., Broadcasting, University of Tacoma, 1989
                    Specialized in television performance,
                    production, and writing for sports broadcasts.

REFERENCES          Supplied on request
```

Figure 13.4 An example of a competency-based résumé.

```
                    Charles Gonzalez
                    1616 South M Street
                    Callison, New Jersey 08110
                    (609) 777-5456

OBJECTIVE           To join dynamic, popular music station as on-air
                    talent

EXPERIENCE          Intern at WBCD-AM and FM, an MOR station: worked
                    with on-air talent in dubbing discs to carts;
                    produced jingles and station IDs; timed music cuts
                    and produced file cards of basic information
                    Three years' experience as DJ on campus radio
                    station featuring CHR and AOR music; managed
                    station in final year; two years as music director
                    Two years as standup comic at local comedy club

EMPLOYMENT          Manager of Callison Comedy Club, 1987-1989
                    Part-time sales associate, MusicLand, Callison,
                    New Jersey, 1985-1988
                    Worked at student union as audio engineer for
                    various performing groups, 1986-1989

EDUCATION           B.A. in Mass Communications, Genessee University,
                    Fountain, New Jersey, 1989
                    Graduated with honors

REFERENCES          Supplied on request
```

Figure 13.5 An example of a hybrid résumé.

in a career guidance or job placement center, or a broadcaster—to review and comment on it.

Omit from your résumé all of the following:

Height, weight, hair color, and eye color—*unless* you are applying for an on-air television position or a job as an on-camera commercial performer, where your physical features are of importance. In this case, supply all pertinent physical information and include photographs (see the subsection on p. 414).

Hobbies—unless they add to your qualifications. Listing the collecting of jazz records could be important if you were applying for a position as a DJ on a jazz station. Saying that you enjoy skateboarding or hiking is irrelevant.

Race, ethnic or national origin, sex, or physical condition—it is against the law for employers to discriminate against job applicants on the basis of any of these facts or conditions. If you have a disabling physical condition that calls for special facilities or other consideration, it should be mentioned in your cover letter.

Your high school or college academic transcript—unless it is requested. You may be asked to provide a list of courses you have taken that relate directly to the job for which you are applying, so be prepared to do so.

You should include information about the following in your résumé:

Your student record, if it was exceptional. For example, you may say "dean's list, 6 semesters," "graduated cum laude," or "3.87 grade point average during last 60 units."

Supplementary abilities that might be put to use at the station—including experience in sales, weather reporting, electronics, data processing, typing, and audio production of commercials and features (including writing, recording, editing, and mixing). If you can operate a word processor, say so, and state what systems you are qualified to use.

Leadership positions, such as student body officer, class president, commencement speaker, and so on

Membership in a national association that relates to broadcasting, such as College Students in Broadcasting, Alpha Epsilon Rho, Audio Engineering Society, Women in Communication, Inc. (WICI), or the National Academy of Recording Arts and Sciences

Contributions to your community, such as Little League coaching, charitable fund-raising, and similar activities

The ability to speak or read one or more languages, with an indication of the degree of your proficiency ("bilingual," "fluent," or "passable")

You may choose to list references, or you may prefer to state that references are available on request. If you are applying to a number of potential employers, giving names could inundate your recommenders. If you *do* provide names, list at least three, and include their titles and business addresses. Choose your recommenders wisely, avoiding close friends, family members, or employers—unless the employment was related to the job you are seeking and the former employer can attest to your dependability, punctuality, honesty, or other qualities that would make you a good employee. Your best references will come from teachers and those who supervised your work in an internship at a broadcast station. *Always* obtain permission before listing anyone as a reference. And, when you do ask recommenders to send letters to potential employers, *always* supply stamped and addressed envelopes.

Your final draft should be professionally typed, on either a high-quality typewriter or a word processor. When using a typewriter, make sure it features "pica" type. When using a word processor, use a standard type font, such as Times or Geneva. Do not use a novelty font of any kind. Type size should be 12 point. Your résumé will be more attractive if you pay to have it laser-printed. Any copying service can use this original to make an unlimited number of prints on good-quality 20-pound bond. When having your résumé duplicated, choose white, off-white, or buff paper, and use matching envelopes. Do *not* choose a garish or weird color.

Finally, despite all of the above suggestions of things to put in your résumé, if you find that you cannot comfortably fit your information on one page, omit the least important. If you must omit such items as community service, membership in organizations, leadership positions, or academic honors, you may put these on a supplemental résumé, sent as a second sheet.

Photographs   It is unwise to include a photograph when applying for a position at a radio station or as a freelance performer. The physical appearance of a person who does radio or voice-over work is totally irrelevant, because the sound of the voice is all-important. A photograph adds nothing: it can in fact work against you if a potential employer feels that you don't "look like you sound."

Photographs are essential when applying for an on-air position in television. Even if you are sending an audition videotape, it is wise to also send still photos. Two or three photos should be sent, showing you in different work environments. Photos may be black and white or in color and should be either 5 by 7 inches or 8 by 10 inches. Do not send "artsy" photos, provocative poses, or graduation photos. The best photos are those taken of you while you are performing as a reporter, anchor, program host, or other on-air role. You do not need to spend a lot of money on photos; producers and agents can see what they need to know by looking at high-quality snapshots.

The Cover Letter

All résumés should be accompanied by a cover letter. This letter is perhaps as important as your résumé. It gives you an opportunity to stress some accomplishment or quality that makes you uniquely qualified for the job. The function of the cover letter is to persuade a prospective employer to read your résumé; the objective of the résumé is to get that employer to listen to your audition tape; the goal of the tape is to gain an interview; the anticipated outcome of the interview is to get that job!

The nature of the cover letter will differ depending on whether you are asking to be interviewed for station employment or looking for an agent. A cover letter to station managers should be brief and to the point. Most such letters contain four short paragraphs. The first tells what position you are applying for, and why you are applying to this particular station. The second paragraph gives brief details on your qualifications. The third refers to the accompanying résumé and audition tape and underscores the most significant points. The last paragraph requests an interview and states when you will call to ask for it.

Cover letters to agents may be quite brief, because the audition tape counts for nearly everything. An opening statement of your qualifications and aspirations, a request that your tape be reviewed, and information as to how you may be reached are all you need to include.

Because cover letters should be an honest expression of *your* feelings, you should not look for a model cover letter to copy. If you cannot clearly and effectively state your case in a cover letter, you may need to attend a résumé-writing workshop in which cover letters are also discussed.

Never duplicate cover letters. Always create a separate letter for each person to whom you are sending a résumé. Type your letter on a typewriter or compose it with a word processor. Do *not* print it on a dot matrix printer—use a letter-quality printer. Poor-quality computer-generated letters give the impression that they are being produced in quantity. *Never* send a letter that has been duplicated by a copy machine. If you use a word processor, do *not* justify the right margin. Personalize each letter, so that you do not inadvertently give the impression that your applications are blanketing the nation. Personalized letters, which mention the employer's name, call letters, music format, news policy, or whatever is appropriate, tell the reader that the letter in hand is the only one of its kind. Above all, your letter should be neat, with no erasures, strikeovers, or other signs of sloppiness. Proofread your letter carefully.

Audition Tapes

An audition tape is a must for anyone seeking work as an announcer, whether at a station or as a freelance voice-over performer.

Producing audition tapes for employment at a broadcast station For station employment the audition tape may be a **presentation tape** or an **air check**. Strictly speaking, the term *air check* refers to an edited recording of a person's on-air performance. For most people looking for work at a station, this is the best kind of audition tape. Actually being on the air—even if it is only a local cable company's public

Figure 13.6
Although most beginning announcers will need only to prepare audio audition tapes, it's good practice to know how to put together a quality videotape. An announcer who specializes in industrial videos reviews her audition tape with a coach. (Photo by Spencer Grant, The Picture Cube)

access television channel, a cable company's radio channel, or a "wired wireless" campus setup—gives you a level of energy and a sound that is hard to duplicate when simply making a recording for audition purposes.

Most audition tapes produced by students are collections of radio or television performances compiled from recordings made in a media performance class or on news, entertainment, and information programs supplied by a college department of broadcasting to local broadcasters or cable companies. Some departments of broadcasting make resources available to students to edit, assemble, and duplicate their presentation tapes. If you have a good collection of videotaped performances, you can select 8 to 10 minutes of your best performances; for radio performance, limit the tape's length to no more than 3 minutes.

Radio audition tapes are inexpensive to produce. The audio recording equipment available in almost all college departments of broadcasting is adequate for this purpose. A typical audio audition tape for a position as a DJ will be only 3 minutes in length and will feature five or six different pieces: 10 seconds of an upbeat commercial; 10 or 15 seconds of a more subdued commercial; a 20-second news story, read at a rapid rate of delivery; a series of music introductions (or back-announcing of a music set); two or three 10-second PSAs; and an ad-lib performance, commenting on some event of the day.

Because making an audition tape for a popular music radio station is both simple and inexpensive, you are advised to make more than one tape. All music radio stations have an established **sound**, an overall mood and spirit. If you are applying for an announcing position at a station that expects its announcers to display wit, warmth, and congeniality, the material on your audition tape will be quite different from that prepared for a station whose announcers are instructed to keep their comments brief and matter-of-fact. Also, a given country music station may have a sound that differs considerably from a Top 40 station in the same market. Study the sounds of the stations in which you have an interest, and prepare audition tapes accordingly.

If your audio audition tape is going to an all-news station, it should present several short news stories of varying moods, plus at least one 30-second commercial. An audition tape for a position in sports should include samples of sports reporting, play-by-play, and play analysis. Gear your tapes as specifically as possible to the station(s) where you would like to work. If time permits, use the actual call letters of the station to which you are sending the tape.

Spotlight: Breaking into the Announcing Field

Denny Delk has loved radio as long as he can remember. His mother, when reading bedtime stories, used her voice to add sound effects. As early as age 4, he tried to emulate her. He started playing with a tape recorder when he was 13, varying sounds by speeding up and slowing down his recorded voice and trying out vocalized sound effects. Today, Delk does voice work for commercials, cartoons, and promos and narration for industrials and documentaries.

Delk enjoys voice work more than any other mode of performance. "Radio, as has been said many times, is the theater of the mind," he says. "You can do anything you want to do. You can be anyone you want to be. You can make the imagination of the listener work by the way you treat the microphone, by the things the producer does with you, by the way you react with people—you can't raise an eyebrow; you can't give a sidelong glance—you have to do those things with your voice. And it's fun to be able to play that way."

Originally from Oklahoma, Delk got his start at a small town radio station. There was a sign on the door that read "dollar a holler," meaning that each commercial message aired on the station cost only $1. It was a small beginning, but he loved radio. He later moved on to other jobs in broadcasting, all of them related to communication with an audience: camera operator, television director, studio engineer, sound technician for a television station, newspaper reporter, concert promoter, disc jockey, and radio talk show host—all before becoming a voice-over.

An English major who performed in many stage plays during his college days, Delk has worked in theater everywhere he's lived. He does improvisational comedy with the National Theatre of the Deranged. He calls this "lazy-man's theater—no need to memorize." Delk is convinced that doing theater helps a voice-over actor become a more complete performer. He urges students to become involved in college or community theater. Even behind-the-scenes work can teach you what communicating with an audience is all about.

Delk offers advice to aspiring announcers:

- How do you market yourself? Your first challenge is to get agents and producers to listen to your audition tape. Most likely, they are already working with a stable of regulars—outstanding voice-over people, with all types of personalities and ages—and you have to make them want to listen to your tape.
- The packaging of your tape can create a strong impression. Delk prefers to use a 5-inch open reel because its size allows him to include visual material. When agents are listening to a tape, there is absolutely nothing to do but listen. Delk includes visual material to help focus their attention on his performance. He encloses eight panels of humorous cartoons on a 10-by-20-inch sheet which, when folded, fit snugly inside his tape box. The cartoons relate to both announcing and his personality, and they catch the eyes of those who hire people to do voice work.
- Never include your photo for voice-over work. Your appearance has nothing to do with the job you are auditioning for. Casting agents and producers will expect you—or want you—to sound like you look. Don't give them a chance to say "No, this person doesn't look right for the part." Force them to judge you only by the sound of your voice and your interpretive abilities, which are the only things that are relevant.
- Delk uses three separate "packages": one each for straight announcing, cartoon and character voice work, and industrial narration. Creating separate portfolio packages allows you to tailor each one to a distinct style and market.
- After sending an audition tape, follow with a card and a note "hope you had a chance to lis-

ten." *Never* call the person. They don't have the time, and you really don't have anything to say. If you ask what was thought about the tape, you've put that person in an awkward and difficult position.

- Put on your tape as many different things you can do *well*. Do not include any voices or attitudes that are marginal or questionable. If you can't determine on your own what things you do well, ask a qualified person, such as your instructor, for help.
- Your tape must never be longer than 3 minutes—2½ is better. For industrial work or other types of voice-over narration, you may do a longer tape.
- You must have an attention-getter at the front. Use your best-sounding effort at the start. If you place it later, the agent may never hear it.
- Do not do complete spots—10 seconds is enough to establish any one thing.
- Show a variety of attitudes (better than accents): soft sell, snooty, seductive, downtrodden, and so on. Don't put them together in a haphazard or

random order. Work for variety. Do a soft sell, followed by a hard sell—in other words, break up the pieces. This makes each segment more impressive than it would be if it stood alone, or if it were surrounded by similar readings.

- Don't ask to have your tape returned. Audiotapes are inexpensive, and you want the tape to be sitting on producers' shelves. When the person they usually use is unavailable, perhaps they'll remember your tape and listen to it again—and then they may call you.
- Even if a producer likes your tape, you'll still have to audition for a job. Sometimes tapes are better than people are, and they want to know if you are as good as your tape.
- Finally, remember that you will not succeed without the help of many others—agents, writers, producers, directors, sound engineers, advertising agency personnel, secretaries, union officials, and so forth. The profession is a highly rewarding one in which cooperation is eventually as important as talent, and people have feelings and very long memories.

Denny Delk does more than send in his résumé; he gives potential clients something entertaining to look at while they review his audition tapes. (Cartoon by Charles Oldham, Wonderworks, © 1981. Reprinted by permission.)

If you cannot use broadcast department equipment to record and edit your audio audition tape, find a recording studio that provides an audition tape service. Audio recording studios are generally found only in larger cities, so you may have to travel to one if you live in a smaller community. The Yellow Pages of telephone directories list recording studios. You should get price quotations from at least three studios before choosing one.

Independent video production companies may be found in every medium to major market. Some will produce studio-based audition tapes; others will go into the field with you to cover some planned news event, such as a parade, a picket line, or a marathon. Most production companies will provide some guidance, including suggestions for improving your appearance or your performance. Production companies usually charge by the day, with a one-day minimum. There will be additional charges for editing the tape and making copies. You can expect to pay between $500 and $1,500 for a complete video presentation tape.

Producing audition tapes for employment as a freelance announcer   A very different kind of audition tape should be made for presentation to a talent agency. Most of the voice work obtained through agencies is for these specializations: radio commercials, voice-over narration for television commercials (both radio and television commercials are called voice-overs by freelancers), corporate videos (also called **industrials**), documentary narration, promos for stations, promos for radio and television special programs, cartoon voicing, and looping. **Looping** is also called **dubbing** (short for *post-production synchronous dubbing*). In this procedure a person's voice is dubbed onto a tape or film soundtrack to match the lip movements and the emotions of another person acting in the film. The most common use of looping in the United States and Canada is in the dubbing of foreign-language films in English.

To become a freelance performer, you almost certainly will need an agent. Agents notify their clients when work that suits their talent is available, help them prepare and tape the audition for the specific job, and negotiate payments with potential employers. Agents collect 10 percent of all payments earned, but good ones more than earn their fee. If you decide to seek an agent, your first audition tape should be planned to persuade an agent to "take you on."

The audition tape required for freelance work is different from that for radio station employment. Most important is that you show your ability to interpret copy. Unless you are convinced that your future lies in doing character voices or accents and dialects, you should concentrate on performing high-quality, imaginative, but basically standard, commercial copy. Select pieces that will demonstrate a range of approaches—thoughtful, concerned, upbeat, sultry, excited, laid back, and so on. Do only 10 to 15 seconds of each. As you assemble the bits, arrange them in a sequence that shows contrast; begin with a soft sell, follow with a hard sell, and so forth. The entire audition tape should run no longer than 3 minutes.

If you want to do character voices and your repertoire includes a variety of foreign accents or regional dialects, use samples of these in carefully selected bits of commercials. Put on your tape only those voices or accents that you do extremely well. Confine your voiced bits to 10 to 15 seconds each; take somewhat longer to demonstrate your ability to do straight narration for industrials. In short, provide the agent with as great a range of your vocal competencies as possible. Some freelance performers prepare as many as three audition tapes: one devoted to straight commercial announcing, one to characters and cartoon voices, and one to narration for industrials.

If you are serious about a career as a freelance announcer of commercials, industrials, documentaries, and/or cartoons, it may be desirable to take a workshop from a successful professional performer. Many reputable freelance performers conduct workshops with small enrollments and of brief duration that concentrate on developing the skills needed for this work and culminate in the production and packaging of an audition tape. To identify a potential coach, ask your instructors as well as professional announcers for suggestions. When contacting those who offer courses, ask for permission to sit in on a session before committing yourself to enrolling in a course. If you are satisfied that the performer is capable, that the workshop is compatible with your needs, and that the cost is not excessive, you could wind up with greatly enhanced performing abilities, as well as a professionally produced audition tape.

Other tips concerning audition tapes Nearly anyone can make an impressive audition tape if enough time and effort are expended. Working over a period of several days, doing take after take, and then selecting the best bits of your work and assembling them can result in a high-quality product. This may present a problem: if it is your tape that gets you an agent or a job, you will have to live up to its quality consistently. Make certain that your audition tape truly reflects what you can do under actual recording circumstances.

Do not send out audition tapes that are hastily made, that are made with inferior equipment, or that you made before you attained your current professional level of ability. Poor audition tapes can prejudice potential employers or agents against you.

Duplicate your audition tapes for voice performance, whether for radio station or freelance employment, on regular audio cassettes. Never record or duplicate on a used tape. Be sure to listen to every tape dub you make, and listen all the way through; oftentimes tapes are sent to stations with inaudible or distorted sections. Neatly type your identification both on the cassette itself and on its plastic box.

Answering Machine

A number of years ago, a survey of broadcast announcers asked how they got their first job. More than 85 percent said that they happened to be "in the right place at the right time." In other words, they were immediately available when an opening occurred. You cannot, of course, be at several radio or television stations at the same time, but you can be available by telephone at all hours—if you have an answering machine. Adequate answering machines may be bought for under $100, used ones for much less. Make certain that the machine you buy allows you to pick up messages on it by calling from another phone. Also, make sure that you have a businesslike message on your tape. A prospective employer will be turned off by a raucous, bawdy, or childish message.

Mailing Address and Phone Number

Because you may be away at school, without a permanent address, you should give some thought to the address and phone number you list on your résumé. For most job seekers it is best to list only one address, one that will remain accurate for some time (that of your parents perhaps). The telephone number given should be for the phone you use every day, which, as indicated above, should be connected to an answering machine.

Finding Job Openings

Colleges and universities are sites of intensive recruiting activity every spring semester. That's the good news. The bad news is that broadcasters almost never appear on college campuses to interview prospective announcers. However, this fact should not discourage you. Broadcast executives do not like to advertise job openings beyond the requirements of law. They are busy people, and they do not want to schedule interviews with dozens of job applicants. Many station executives, particularly those at small-market stations, make vacancies known to faculty members in college and university departments of broadcasting and request that no more than three to five students be told of each opening. If you have gained the confidence of a faculty member, ask to be notified of job openings in your field of interest.

Also, remember that jobs *are* available if you are willing to move to a small market, to accept an entry-level position, and to work for a subsistence salary. This is called **paying your dues**.

Table 13.1 and the accompanying map show the distribution of stations by region in the continental United States. Although it appears that limitless graduates could find jobs in the U.S. broadcast market, which has a total of 10,009 radio/television/cable stations, the fact is that many of these stations are shoestring stations in small markets, which rely on versatile freelance and staff employees. You can see that job opportunities vary by region; for example, radio stations predominate in the South Atlantic States, while there are more cable stations in the East North Central States than anywhere else.

The long-established and accepted practice of underpaying and overworking novices in the field of broadcasting is, to be sure, lamentable; however, the fact remains that this is the way it has been, now is, and (most likely) always will be. If you are committed to becoming a successful radio or television announcer, chances are great that you will have to begin at the proverbial bottom, and gradually work yourself into better and higher-paying positions.

Announcements of job openings are published in a number of trade magazines, including *Broadcasting* and *R&R (Radio & Records)*. To find your first job, however, you should not limit yourself to responding to ads for announcers. Most stations that advertise either cannot find anyone willing to work at their station, or are looking for people with at least a few years of appropriate experience. Announcing vacancies occur regularly at most stations, so you should apply for whatever position is open at every station you consider to be a good starting point or a second step for you. Begin with stations in your own area, unless you have compelling reasons to leave.

Table 13.1   Where the Jobs Are

Region	Number of Stations by Region		
	Radio	**TV**	**Cable**
Pacific States	849	150	109
Mountain States	522	111	60
West South Central States	871	160	121
East South Central States	687	114	71
South Atlantic States	1,452	228	106
West North Central States	670	156	105
East North Central States	1,104	193	127
Middle Atlantic States	730	93	78
New England	342	60	44
Totals for U.S.	7,227	1,265	821

Source: Map and table based on data from *Gale Directory of Publications and Broadcast Media*, 1990 Edition, Gale Research Inc., Publishers.

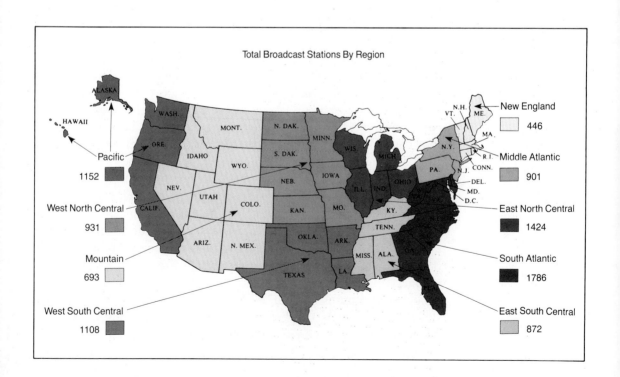

Applying for a Position as a Disc Jockey

With a completed résumé and audition tape, you are ready to apply for an announcing job. This section discusses applying for disc jockey work. Most of the suggestions apply as well to seeking jobs in broadcast news and sports reporting. The recommendations given can be followed by most first-time applicants for announcing positions.

To apply for a job as a disc jockey, first obtain the names of the program directors of those radio stations for which you would like to work. Names are listed in *Broadcasting Yearbook*, which can be found at many libraries and at nearly every radio and television station. Before writing to a program director, however, telephone the station to confirm that the person listed is still with the station and in the same position. There is a great deal of movement of executives in the broadcasting industry.

Send a brief letter, a résumé, and your audition tape to each program director. In your letter, state that you will call in a week to see if an interview can be arranged. Follow through with the telephone call, but don't be discouraged if few or none of the station managers express any interest in you. Even though announcing jobs are available, the number of persons applying for them far exceeds the availability of positions. *Perseverance is the most important quality a prospective disc jockey can possess.*

If you live in a major or secondary market, it is unlikely that you will be hired by a local station unless you have had years of on-air experience. Therefore, be prepared to look for work in a smaller market. *Broadcasting Yearbook* can be of real help to you in locating stations to which you may apply. It lists every radio station in the United States and Canada, indicates its signal strength (a clue to its audience size, and therefore its economic standing), gives names of chief administrative personnel, and tells the music format.

In addition to obtaining as much information as you can about a station, make sure you have actually listened to the one to which you are applying. It will be most uncomfortable for you if you have to admit that you know little or nothing about the station. If a station to which you are applying is far enough away from your home that you cannot receive its signal, you can compensate by learning what kind of music policy and format it has in *Broadcasting Yearbook* and spending at least a few hours on arrival in the area listening to the sound of the station. It will be to your advantage if you can intelligently discuss details of the station's music policy, the nature of the DJ's chatter (if any), etc. When listening to the station, make notes as to how the news is dealt with—whether there are national network cut-ins or local news only, who is responsible for reading the news, and so on. News reading may very well be a part of your air shift as a DJ.

Interviewing for a Job

The job interview is undoubtedly the most important element in your pursuit of a position as a radio or television station performer. A general manager, station manager, or program director may be impressed with your credentials, your audition tape, and your résumé, but an interview is usually the final test that puts you to work—or sends you away.

Before seriously seeking a job, you may want to discuss career possibilities and job seeking with an executive at a station where you are not applying for work. This is called an **informational interview**. Almost any college teacher of broadcasting can guide you to someone who will be happy to spend time with you exploring your employment prospects. Ask the professional to review your résumé and to discuss strategies for finding employment.

The suggestions and comments that follow are based on several assumptions: that you truly are ready for the position you seek, that you will honestly state your capabilities and competencies, and that you will be able to back up statements about your strengths with concrete examples.

Before you appear for an interview, practice being interviewed. A friend or an instructor may be willing to assist you and to critique your performance. Remember that an interview is not acting, but it *is* a form of performance.

When confirming an appointment for an interview by phone, do not ask how to find the station or where to park. To ask such questions is to give the impression that you can't find your way around.

Before going to another town for a job interview, take time to learn something about that community. The *Places Rated Almanac* (published by Rand McNally) and *Cities of the United States* (in four volumes, two of which—*The South* and *The West*—were available in 1990) are convenient sources of information about nearly every town and city in the United States.

When being interviewed, have with you all pertinent information about yourself that might be needed to complete an application form.

Figure 13.7
The job interview, the most important step in the path toward the right job, is extremely difficult to achieve in this competitive industry. Of two hundred applicants to the position of weathercaster at this television station in Washington, D.C., only eight finalists made the cut; prior to their interviews the station's weekend anchor offers a few pointers. (Courtesy of WJLA-TV)

This includes social security number, driver's license number, dates of graduating, dates of starting and ending various jobs, previous addresses, and so forth. Also bring a list of references, in case it is asked for.

Always be early for an interview, but not too early; 5 to 10 minutes ahead of your appointment is just about right. If you are being interviewed in an unfamiliar city or town, drive past the station sometime before the interview—preferably the day before and at the same time of day as your appointment. Not only will you learn the way to the spot, but this will tell you how much traffic there is at that time of day and where there is parking.

Dress neatly and conservatively for your interview. Although some on-air performers may dress casually, remember that they are established, and you are not. Chances are good that you will be interviewed by a person who is essentially a businessperson, not a performer. You cannot make a mistake by wearing a dress or a sport coat and tie.

Be yourself. Do not try to act the part of the person you assume the interviewer is looking for.

Be frank about your strengths and accomplishments, but take care not to come across as boastful.

Match your eye contact with that of the interviewer. Most interviewers maintain strong eye contact, but if you meet one who does not, act accordingly. Eye contact is not the same thing as staring. If the interviewer looks you in the eye, try to reciprocate. Take your cue from him or her.

Do not take chances by making small talk that might reveal ignorance. For instance, do not ask what tune is being played—it might be number one in that community. Do not venture opinions about broadcasting in general unless they are completely to the point of the interview. You can hurt your cause by stepping on the toes of your interviewer.

Be careful to avoid traps. Some interviewers will lead job applicants along, making somewhat outrageous suggestions, to see if the applicant is an unprincipled "yes person." Do not be argumentative, but think carefully before you respond to questions that seem to be "off the wall."

Do not misrepresent yourself or your abilities in any way! Even if you obtained a job through an exaggeration of your capabilities, you would not have it for long.

Stay away from politics, religion, and sex. If the interviewer tries to lead you into any of these areas, politely avoid them.

The law states that there are certain things you do not have to reveal, including national origin, religion, and physical condition. If you refuse to divulge such information, do it as tactfully as possible.

Although you are under pressure during a job interview, try to be relaxed, warm, open, and relatively energetic. Help the interviewer to enjoy spending time with you. Do not, however, try to entertain by taking over the interview and telling stories, anecdotes, or jokes.

Be ready to answer any questions the interviewer may have about statements made on your résumé. Also, be prepared to tell your life story—in an abbreviated form, of course. This might include where you were born, where you grew up, schools attended, significant travel, relevant job experience, and where you are headed in your career.

During an interview, find opportunities to ask questions. Most people like to feel they have something of value to communicate. If you feel comfortable doing so, ask the interviewer for advice. You may or may not get the job, but you will certainly get some tips from an experienced person and make that person feel your respect.

Mention any favorable opinions you have reached about the station and its music, its sound, and its on-air personnel. This is not the time to tell the interviewer what you don't like about the station or any plans you may have for changing things.

Never try to gain the sympathy of the person interviewing you by complaining about your problems. People will hire you for one or another of these reasons: (1) they believe you can help them or make them look good; (2) they believe you can make money for them; (3) they need someone and think that you are the best applicant. You will never be hired because a station executive feels sorry for you!

You may be asked to do an audition after an initial interview. You have already sent in an air check or audition tape. But this is an on-the-spot, under-pressure audition, and it can be very nerve-wracking and threatening. If you are truly prepared and well suited for an on-air position, this is your opportunity to really show off! The important point is that you should go into each job interview with the attitude that you will succeed. And this in turn means that you will be prepared for an on-the-spot audition.

If you are asked to audition, you may be given scripts full of words that are difficult to pronounce, sentences that feature plosive and sibilant sounds, announcements that contain foreign words and names, or pieces that require you to read at 190 to 200 words per minute. You must practice, in advance of job interviews, for these and similar possibilities.

If you are taken on a tour of the station, make note of the equipment being used, and be prepared to state whether or not you can operate it. When you are introduced to engineers, people in sales and traffic, on-air announcers, and others, show your genuine interest in them and what they are doing. If you feel no such interest, you are probably applying at the wrong station.

If you smoke, avoid it totally while you are at the station. Even if your host is a smoker, others who are influential at the station may take offense. It is all right to accept the offer of coffee, tea, or a soft drink, but under no circumstances should you accept the offer of an alcoholic beverage.

Toward the end of the interview, look for an opportunity to ask about salary and fringe benefits. A good interviewer will generally bring this up without your asking, but you cannot count on it. Almost without exception, the salary of a first-time station employee will be abysmally low, so you should be prepared. At the same time, it is extremely important for you to know whether health, dental, and/or vision plans are to be offered, and how long you must be employed before they are in effect.

Joining a Union

To work at a unionized station or to perform freelance at a high professional level, you will be obliged to join a union. The two unions for performers are the American Federation of Television and Radio Artists (AFTRA) and the Screen Actors Guild (SAG). Generally speaking, AFTRA represents performers who work live on radio or television, or whose performances are recorded on audio or videotape. SAG represents those who perform on film. Radio and television station and network announcers usually belong to AFTRA; freelance performers as a rule belong to both unions.

Joining a performers' union can be tricky. To be accepted by SAG, you must have worked as a film performer; the catch is that you are not likely to be employed as a film performer unless you already belong to SAG! A way around this dilemma is to join AFTRA, which does not require previous professional employment. Then, after having gained experience while a member of that union, you will be eligible for membership in SAG.

Going Where Your Career Takes You

If you live in a major or secondary market, you may have to leave for a smaller market to obtain that first job—unless, of course, you are willing to accept an entry-level job as a receptionist, a courier, or a clerk in the mail room. A few graduating seniors are so talented that they move directly from school to on-air positions at medium- or even major-market broadcast stations. For most, though, a career begins by moving to a smaller market, where there is less competition and, usually, less pay. Most radio and television stations in markets of over 200,000 hire only on-air performers who have gained experience and moved up through the ranks in smaller markets.

Unfortunately, a very negative and self-defeating phrase for gaining initial employment in a smaller market has been around for many decades. "Going to the sticks" implies that moving to, and working in, a small town is a regrettable necessity for most beginning broadcast performers. This attitude carries with it a feeling of contempt for life and work in markets outside of major metropolitan areas. It further carries with it a belief that, after suffering for several years in some sort of rural purgatory, all will be well if the individual is able to "move up" to a larger market. There are several reasons why this attitude should be shunned.

Figure 13.8
Your first job in broadcasting could be anywhere. Even the smallest radio stations are set up for professional sound. Although none of the equipment in the studio on the right is new, it is perfectly functional: an Auto Gram AC-7 console, an Otari reel-to-reel tape recorder, an International Tapetronics cart machine, two Technics turntables, and a Realistic microphone. (Left, photo by Richard Pasley, Stock Boston; right, photo courtesy of KNRY, Pacific Grove, CA)

First, by beginning your career in a smaller market, you can begin your on-air work at once, thereby accelerating your growth as a performer. Unlike those who start at a station in a major market as a receptionist or a runner, you do not have to wait for that break that may never come.

Second, life as a broadcaster in a small town can be very fulfilling. Knowing that you are able to help your community in significant ways through public service work can be very rewarding. Putting down roots, becoming a contributing member of society, and participating in town events can give you the assurance that you do make a difference!

Salaries do tend to be lower in smaller markets, and many stations are non-union. At the same time, the cost of living is lower, and you may very well find your standard of living higher in a small town than in a large city.

A final reason for avoiding a negative attitude about going to a smaller market is that the people who do the hiring there are quick to spot condescension on the part of any job applicant who communicates a "holier than thou" attitude. Would you hire applicants who acted as though they were making a sacrifice to come to work for you?

This chapter may help you find entry-level employment at a radio or television station. Most of the suggestions are applicable to other kinds of employment—doing voice-overs, industrials, and other freelance work, for example. There are several things this chapter *cannot* give you, however. It cannot give you talent, good work habits, or the perseverance that is required for success in the world of broadcasting. Remember that there *are* jobs out there, and you can obtain one if you have performance skills, if you are a reliable and hardworking person, and if you have a strong drive to succeed.

Practice: Drafting Your Résumé

Write a résumé, following the guidelines and examples given in this chapter. Bring copies for your instructor and each class member to discuss and compare.

Practice: Checking Out the Job Scene

Visit your nearest career guidance center and obtain any available handouts giving tips on résumés, job interviews, and other information that may help you find that first job. Using a current issue of *Broadcasting* magazine, compile a list of advertised job openings for on-air talent. Note the geographical areas where there are the greatest number of openings and the areas of specialization most in demand.

14

The International Phonetic Alphabet

The International Phonetic Alphabet (IPA) is a system for encoding the correct pronunciation of problem words, allowing efficient and accurate retrieval. The IPA may seem formidable at first, but it is actually easier to learn than the system of diacritical markings used in dictionaries. You will find many uses for the IPA, and if you intend to enter the field of broadcast performance, you should make a sincere effort to learn it. Because spoken language is the communication medium used by announcers, mastery of any aspect of human speech will benefit your work.

It is true that only a small number of professional announcers are familiar with the IPA, but it is also true that all would benefit from knowing and using it. Those who do not know the IPA usually follow the principles of wire-service phonetics, adding symbols of their own as necessity demands. Such a system is capable of handling most of the pronunciation problems that arise in a day's work, but it fails often enough to warrant being replaced by a more refined and accurate system.

The IPA has several advantages:

- It is an unvarying system of transcription in which one symbol represents only one speech sound.
- Every sound in any language, however subtle it may be, is given a distinctive symbol.
- Once the correct pronunciation of each sound is learned, there is almost no possibility of error because of regional dialect.
- The IPA is the most nearly perfect system of describing human speech sounds yet devised.

The IPA is widely used. The excellent *NBC Handbook of Pronunciation* (New York: Harper & Row, 1984) transcribes names of persons and places using IPA symbols. Many foreign language dictionaries and texts use the IPA to indicate correct pronunciation. Drama departments use it to help teach dialects, and music departments use it to teach singers foreign pronunciation. *A Pronouncing Dictionary of American English* by Kenyon and Knott (Springfield, Mass: G. & C. Merriam, 1953), transcribes exclusively with the IPA. Both it and the *NBC Handbook of Pronunciation* are excellent sources of correct pronunciation of American and foreign place names and the names of famous composers, authors, artists, scientists, and political figures.

Like any system for indicating correctness in speech sounds, the IPA defines each sound in terms of its use in a particular word. For example, the correct sound of the IPA symbol [i] is indicated by the information that it is pronounced like the vowel sound of the word *bee*. This poses no problem where the key word is pronounced uniformly throughout the United States and Canada, but a distinct problem arises when there are regional variations in the pronunciation of a key word. For example, in southern British, as well as in the speech of eastern New England, the sound [ɑ], as in *father*, is not used for words spelled with *o*, and the sounds [ɒ], as in the eastern New England *wash*, and [ɔ], as in *bought*, are not differentiated. Thus *bomb*, *wash*, and *bought* are all pronounced with the same vowel sound, which varies from [ɒ] to [ɔ]. The speech sounds and the key words used in describing them are as in General American, unless otherwise indicated. General American is defined as the speech of well-educated citizens of Canada and the United States in the Midwest and Far West. If you live in a region of the United States or Canada where General American is not spoken, you may experience some difficulty in learning the IPA symbols. If, for example, you live in the southeastern United States, and you pronounce the word *bait* as most Americans pronounce *bite*, then the key words used to explain the IPA may confuse you. But a little extra effort can make the IPA a useful tool.

Obviously, your use of the IPA will be reserved for the few names and words in your copy that require you to turn to a dictionary, gazetteer, or similar source of information. Once you have determined the correct pronunciation of a word, you can render it in IPA symbols directly above the problem word in your script. Having done so, you should be able to read it on the air with little chance of stumbling.

Here is a sample script:

THE MAYOR OF THE SMALL NORTH CAROLINA TOWN OF
[ˈkɪmb|tən]
KIMBOLTON SAID TODAY THAT HE IS SKEPTICAL ABOUT
REPORTS OF FLYING SAUCERS ABOVE HIS COMMUNITY.

A glance at *A Pronouncing Dictionary of American English* shows that *Kimbolton* is pronounced KIM-BOLT'-UN [kɪmˈboltn̩] in the Ohio community of that name, but in the town of the same name in North Carolina it is pronounced KIM'-BUL-TUN [ˈkɪmb|tən]. The correct pronunciation of the name of a town may seem of slight importance to some, but to a professional announcer it is a matter of pride to be as accurate as time and resources permit.

IPA symbols represent vowel sounds, diphthongs or glides, and consonants. This chapter covers only the sounds in American speech. Symbols for foreign speech sounds are discussed in Chapter 15.

Remember that IPA is used to transcribe *sounds*. Pronounce the word as you transcribe it, breaking it down into its component sounds. In transcribing the word *broken*, for example, say to yourself the first sound, "b," then add the second, making "br," then the third, forming "bro," and so on. Because one sound in a word may condition the sound that precedes or follows it, you should use an additive system, rather than one that isolates each sound from all others. Note, however, that this advice is meant for those in the early stages of learning to use the IPA. With practice and growing proficiency, you will be able to transcribe almost without conscious effort.

Vowel Sounds

Vowel sounds are classified as front vowels and back vowels, depending on where they are formed in the mouth. The front vowels are produced through vibrations of the vocal folds in the throat and are articulated by the tongue and teeth near the front of the mouth. The back vowels are produced in the same manner but are articulated by the tongue and the opening in the rear of the mouth.

The Front Vowels

The front vowels are summarized in Table 14.1. Note that [a] is pronounced "aah," as in the word *bath* as pronounced in parts of the

Table 14.1   IPA Symbols for the Front Vowels

Vowel Sound	IPA Symbol	Key Word	IPA Transcription of Key Word
"ee"	[i]	*beet*	[bit]
"ih"	[ɪ]	*bit*	[bɪt]
"ay"	[e]	*bait*	[bet]
"eh"	[ɛ]	*bet*	[bɛt]
"ah"	[æ]	*bat*	[bæt]
"aah"	[a]	*bath*	[baθ]*

*Eastern and British pronunciation only

northeastern United States. This sound is not usually heard in General American speech, but the symbol must be learned because it is a part of two diphthongs to be considered later.

If you pronounce each of these sounds in turn, beginning at the top of the table and running to the bottom, you will find your mouth opening wider as you move from one sound to the next. As your mouth opens, your tongue is lowered and becomes increasingly relaxed.

The two front vowels [i] and [ɪ] require some elaboration. If you look in an American or English dictionary, you may be surprised to discover that the final sounds of words such as *busy* and *worry* are given the pronunciation [ɪ], as in *ill*. Now there can be no doubt that in General American, as well as in the speech of most other sections of the country, these words have a distinct "ee" sound. Kenyon and Knott, in *A Pronouncing Dictionary of American English*, take note of this fact but indicate that minor variations in the pronunciation of this sound are too complex to pin down. Like most other American dictionaries, Kenyon and Knott's work uses the symbol [ɪ] for words in which the sound may actually be either [ɪ] or [i]. Thus they arrive at the pronunciation [ˈsɪtɪ] (SIH'-TIH) for *city*. Though it is doubtful that many Americans actually pronounce the word in this manner, most Americans *do* pronounce the final sound in the word somewhere between a distinct [ɪ] and a distinct [i].

It is worth noting at this point that the essential purpose of IPA is to help with pronunciation problems. The examples used here and throughout this chapter are included to make the IPA clearer to you, not because of any assumption that you actually have problems pronouncing words such as *busy* or *city*.

The Back Vowels

Table 14.2 presents the back vowels.[1] If you pronounce each of these vowel sounds in turn, you will find your mouth closing more and more and the sound being controlled at a progressively forward position in your mouth.

The Vowel Sounds "Er" and "Uh"

Only two other vowel sounds remain, "er" and "uh," which cause the most trouble to students of phonetics. Consider the two words *further* and *above*. In *further*, two "er" sounds appear. Pronounce this word aloud and you will discover that, because of a stress on the first syllable, the two "ers" sound slightly different. The same is true of the two "uh" sounds in *above*. Because the first syllable of this word is unstressed and the second is stressed, there is a slight but definite difference between the two sounds. The IPA makes allowances for these differences by assigning two symbols each to the "er" and "uh" sounds:

[ɝ] for a stressed "er," as in the first syllable of *further* [fɝðɚ]

[ɚ] for an unstressed "er," as in the *second* syllable of *further* [fɝðɚ]

Table 14.2   IPA Symbols for the Back Vowels

Vowel Sound	IPA Symbol	Key Word	IPA Transcription of Key Word
"ah"	[ɑ]	*bomb*	[bɑm]
"aw"	[ɔ]	*bought*	[bɔt]
"oh"	[o]	*boat*	[bot]
"ooh"	[ʊ]	*book*	[bʊk]
"oo"	[u]	*boot*	[but]

[1]The English language has many words with unsounded letters such as the final *b* in the key word *bomb* in the table. You may experience an unconscious tendency to include these in phonetic transcriptions. You should remember, however, that you are transcribing *sounds*, not letters, and should disregard all letters not sounded in a word.

[ʌ] for a stressed "uh," as in the *second* syllable of *above* [əbʌv]

[ə] for an unstressed "uh," as in the first syllable of *above* [əbʌv]

The unstressed "uh" sound is given a special symbol and name—[ə], the **schwa vowel**. Naturally, in a one-syllable word with an "uh" or an "er" sound, the sound is stressed. For this reason, in all one-syllable words, both "er" and "uh" are represented by their stressed symbols:

bird [bɝd]   church [tʃɝtʃ]   sun [sʌn]   come [kʌm]

Certain combinations of sounds may be transcribed in two ways, either of which is as accurate as the other. The word *flattery*, for example, may be transcribed either ['flætɚi] or ['flætəri]. The difference in the way [ɚ] and [ər] are pronounced is imperceptible to most ears.

Diphthongs

A diphthong is a combination of two vowel sounds, pronounced with a smooth glide from one sound to the other. If you say the "ow" of *how*, you will notice that it cannot be completed without moving the

Table 14.3   IPA Transcriptions for American English Diphthongs

Diphthong	Pronunciation*	Key Word	IPA Transcription of Key Word
[aɪ]	a rapid combination of the two vowels [a] and [ɪ]	*bite*	[baɪt]
[aʊ]	a rapid combination of the two vowels [a] and [ʊ]	*how*	[haʊ]
[ɔɪ]	a rapid combination of the two vowels [ɔ] and [ɪ]	*toy*	[tɔɪ]
[ju]	a rapid combination of the two sounds [j] and [u]	*using*	[juzɪŋ]
[ɪu]	a rapid combination of [ɪ] and [u]	*fuse*	[fɪuz]
[eɪ]	a glide from [e] to [ɪ]	*say*	[seɪ]

*Note the subtle difference in the sounds of the diphthongs [ju] and [ɪu].

lips. There is no way of holding the sound of the entire diphthong; you can hold only the last of the two vowels of which it is formed. The diphthong in *now* is actually a rapid movement from the vowel [a] to the vowel [ʊ].

The diphthongs of American English are summarized in Table 14.3. Note that the vowel [e], as in *bait*, is actually a diphthong, because its pronunciation in a word such as *say* involves a glide from [e] to [ɪ]. In other instances—in the word *fate*, for example—the [e] is cropped off more closely. Because it changes according to context, the [e] sound may be transcribed either as a pure vowel, [e], or as a diphthong, [eɪ]. It will be found both ways in various dictionaries and other works using the IPA.

Consonants

With only seven exceptions, the IPA symbols for consonant sounds are the same as the lowercase letters of the English alphabet. The consonants are therefore fairly easy to learn.

In general, consonants may be classified as either voiced or unvoiced. If you say aloud the letters *b* and *p*, adding the vowel sound "uh," to produce "puh" and "buh," you will notice that each is produced in exactly the same way, except that *b* involves phonation (a vibration of the vocal folds) and *p* is merely exploded air, with no phonation at all. Because most consonants are related this way, they are listed below in their paired relationships rather than alphabetically.

[p] is exploded air with no phonation, as in *poor* [pʊr].

[b] is a phonated explosion, as in *boor* [bʊr].

[t] is exploded air with no phonation, as in *time* [taɪm].

[d] is a phonated explosion, as in *dime* [daɪm].

[k] is exploded air with no phonation, as in *kite* [kaɪt].

[g] is a phonated explosion, as in *guide* [gaɪd].

[f] is escaping air with no phonation, as in *few* [fɪu].

[v] is escaping air with phonation, as in *view* [vɪu].

[θ] is escaping air with no phonation, as in *thigh* [θaɪ]. It is similar to the consonant [f] but has a different placement of the tongue and lips. The Greek letter theta is its symbol.

[ð] is escaping air but with phonation, as in *thy* [ðaɪ].

[s] is escaping air without phonation, as in *sing* [sɪŋ].

[z] is escaping air with phonation, as in *zing* [zɪŋ].

[ʃ] is escaping air without phonation, as in *shock* [ʃɑk].

[ʒ] is escaping air with phonation, as in *Jacques* (French) [ʒɑk].

[tʃ] is an unvoiced, or unphonated, combination of [t] and [ʃ]. It is pronounced as one sound, as in *chest* [tʃɛst].

[dʒ] is a voiced, or phonated, combination of [d] and [ʒ]. It is pronounced as one sound, as in *jest* [dʒɛst].

The following consonants have no pairings.

[h] is an unvoiced sound, as in *how* [haʊ].

[hw] is an unvoiced sound, as in *when* [hwɛn].

[m] is a voiced sound, as in *mom* [mɑm].

[n] is a voiced sound, as in *noun* [naʊn].

[ŋ] is a voiced sound, as in *sing* [sɪŋ].

[l] is a voiced sound, as in *love* [lʌv].

[w] is a voiced sound, as in *watch* [wɑtʃ].

[j] is a voiced sound, as in *yellow* ['jɛlo].

[r] is a voiced sound, as in *run* [rʌn].

Some Common Consonant Problems

A few consonants are potential sources of confusion and deserve special consideration.

The word *fire* is usually pronounced [faɪɚ] in the United States and Canada but is frequently transcribed as [faɪr] by the authors of dictionaries and phonetics texts. The problem here is that the "r" sound in a word such as *run* is really quite different from the "r" sound in the word *fire*; that is, the "r" sound differs depending on its position in a word. There is another difference: the r in *boor* is different from the r in *fire*, even though both are in the same position in the word and follow a vowel sound. This difference stems from the fact that it is easy to produce [r] after the vowel [ʊ] but difficult to produce [r] after the diphthong [aɪ]. If you transcribe *fire* in the conventional manner as a one-syllable word—[faɪr]—you must be careful to avoid having it become [fɑr], as it is often pronounced in the South.

Another potential source of trouble is the plural ending. Years of conditioning have taught us that most plurals end in an "s," though in actuality they end in a "z" sound—*brushes, masters, dozens, kittens,* and so on. Make certain, when transcribing into IPA, that you do not confuse the two symbols [s] and [z].

The common construction -*ing* tends to make one think of a combination of [n] and [g] when transcribing a word like *singing*. Many students transcribe this as ['sɪŋgɪŋ]. In IPA a distinct symbol, [ŋ], is used for the "ng" sound. The correct transcription of *singing* is ['sɪŋɪŋ]. Another common error is to add [g] after [ŋ]. To do so is incorrect.

The symbol [j] is never used to transcribe a word like *jump*. The symbol [dʒ] is used for the sound of the letter *j*. The symbol [j] is always pronounced as in *young* [jʌŋ], *yes* [jɛs], and *William* ['wɪljəm].

Note that many of the consonants change their sounds as they change their positions in words or are combined with different vowel sounds. You have already seen how the "r" sound does this. A similar change takes place in the "d" sound. Notice it in the first syllable of the word *dazed*. Because the initial *d* is followed by a vowel sound, [e], the *d* is sounded. But when the *d* appears in the final position of the word, it is merely exploded air and is only slightly different from the sound a *t* would make in the same position. The only way the final *d* could be sounded would be if a slight schwa sound were added.

Syllabic Consonants

Three of the consonants, [m], [n], and [l], can be sounded as separate syllables without a vowel sound before or after them. Though a word such as *button* may be pronounced [bʌtən], in colloquial speech the [ə] sound is often missing, and the word is represented [bʌtn̩]. In such a transcription, the **syllabic consonant** is represented by a short line under the symbol. Here are transcriptions for a few other words using syllabic consonants:

hokum [hokm̩]   *saddle* [sædl̩]   *apple* [æpl̩]

Accent Marks

Polysyllabic words transcribed into IPA symbols must have accent marks to indicate the relative emphasis to be placed on the various syllables. The word *familiar* has three syllables, [fə], [mɪl], and [jɚ]. In General American the first of these syllables receives little emphasis, or stress, the second receives the primary emphasis, the third receives about the same degree of emphasis as the first.

The IPA indication of primary stress in a word is a mark ['] *before* the syllable being stressed. In the word *facing* ['fesɪŋ], the mark indicates that the first syllable is to receive the primary stress. If the mark is placed below and before a syllable, as in *farewell* [ˌfɛrˈwɛl], it indicates that the syllable is to receive secondary stress. A third degree of stress is possible, but no mark is provided—this is an unstressed sound.

The word *satisfaction* will clarify the stressing of syllables. A continuous line drawn under the word indicates the degrees of stress placed on the syllables when uttering them:

sæt ɪs fæk ʃən

It can be seen that there are three rather distinct degrees of emphasis in the word. This word would be transcribed [ˌsætɪsˈfækʃən]. The primary mark is used for the syllable [fæk], and the secondary mark for the syllable [sæt]; there is no mark on the two unstressed syllables, [ɪs] and [ʃən]. Because secondary stress varies from slightly less than primary stress to slightly more than the unstressed syllables in a word, the secondary accent mark is used for a wide range of emphases, although it is used only once per polysyllabic word.

The following list of related words (related either in meaning or in spelling) shows how accent marks are used in IPA transcriptions to assist in representing the correct pronunciation.

consequence ['kɑnsəˌkwɛns]	*consequential* [ˌkɑnsəˈkwɛnʃəl]
overalls ['ovɚˌɔlz]	*overwhelm* [ˌovɚˈhwɛlm]
interim ['ɪntɚɪm]	*interior* [ɪnˈtɪriɚ]
mainspring ['menˌsprɪŋ]	*maintain* [menˈtaɪn]
contest (n.) ['kɑntɛst]	*contest* (v.) [kənˈtɛst]
Oliver ['ɑlɪvɚ]	*Olivia* [oˈlɪviə]
invalid (sick person) ['ɪnvəlɪd]	*invalid* (not valid) [ɪnˈvælɪd]

Because the schwa vowel, [ə], and the vowel [ɚ] are by definition unstressed, they need no further mark to indicate stress. Because the vowel sounds [ʌ] and [ɝ] are by definition stressed, they, too, need no additional mark when they appear in a transcribed word. For example, the words *lover* [lʌvɚ] and *earnest* [ɝnəst] are transcribed without accent marks of any kind.

Summary of the IPA

For handy reference, all the IPA symbols used to transcribe General American speech are listed in Table 14.4. Examples of words whose phonetic transcriptions contain each symbol are also given in the table.

Table 14.4   IPA Symbols for Sounds of General American

	IPA Symbol	Key Word	Other Words
Vowels	[i]	*beet* [bit]	*free* [fri] *peace* [pis] *leaf* [lif] *misdeed* [mɪs'did] *evening* ['ivnɪŋ]
	[ɪ]	*bit* [bɪt]	*wither* ['wɪðɚ] *pilgrim* ['pɪlgrɪm] *kilowatt* ['kɪləwɑt] *ethnic* ['ɛɵnɪk] *lift* [lɪft]
	[e]	*bait* [bet]	*late* [let] *complain* [kəm'plen] *La Mesa* [,lɑ'mesə] *coupé* [ku'pe] *phase* [fez]
	[ɛ]	*bet* [bɛt]	*phlegm* [flɛm] *scherzo* ['ʃkɛrtso] *Nez Perce* ['nɛz'pɚs] *pelican* ['pɛlɪkən] *bellicose* ['bɛlə,kos]
	[æ]	*bat* [bæt]	*satellite* ['sætlaɪt] *baggage* ['bægɪdʒ] *campfire* ['kæmp,faɪr] *Alabama* [,ælə'bæmə] *rang* [ræŋ]
	[ɝ]	*bird* [bɝd]	*absurd* [əbsɝd] *early* [ɝli] *curfew* [kɝfju] *ergo* [ɝgo] *hurdle* [hɝdl]
	[ɚ]	*bitter* [bɪtɚ]	*hanger* [hæŋɚ] *certificate* [sɚ'tɪfə,kɪt] *Berlin* [bɚ'lɪn] *flabbergast* ['flæbɚgæst]

Table 14.4   (Continued)

	IPA Symbol	Key Word	Other Words
Vowels (cont.)	[ɑ]	*bomb* [bɑm]	*body* [ˈbɑdi] *collar* [ˈkɑlɚ] *pardon* [ˈpɑrdn̩] *padre* [ˈpɑdre] *lollipop* [ˈlɑliˌpɑp]
	[ɔ]	*bought* [bɔt]	*fought* [fɔt] *longwinded* [ˈlɔŋˈwɪndɪd] *rawhide* [ˈrɔhaɪd] *Kennesaw* [ˈkɛnəˌsɔ] *awful* [ˈɔfl̩]
	[o]	*boat* [bot]	*closing* [ˈklozɪŋ] *Singapore* [ˈsɪŋgəpor] *tremolo* [ˈtrɛməlo] *odor* [ˈodɚ] *Pueblo* [ˈpwɛbˌlo]
	[ʊ]	*book* [bʊk]	*looking* [ˈlʊkɪŋ] *pull* [pʊl] *took* [tʊk] *tourniquet* [ˈtʊrnɪˌkɛt] *hoodwink* [ˈhʊdˌwɪŋk]
	[u]	*boot* [but]	*Lucifer* [ˈlusɪfɚ] *cuckoo* [ˈkuˌku] *losing* [ˈluzɪŋ] *nouveau riche* [nuvoˈriʃ]
	[ʌ]	*sun* [sʌn]	*lovelorn* [ˈlʌvlɔrn] *recover* [ˌrɪkʌvɚ] *chubby* [ˈtʃʌbi] *Prussia* [ˈprʌʃə] *hulled* [ˈhʌld]
	[ə]	*sofa* [sofə]	*lettuce* [ˈlɛtəs] *above* [əbʌv] *metropolis* [ˌməˈtrɑplɪs] *arena* [əˈrinə] *diffidence* [ˈdɪfədəns]
Diphthongs	[aɪ]	*bite* [baɪt]	*dime* [daɪm] *lifelong* [ˈlaɪfˈlɔŋ] *leviathan* [ləˈvaɪəθən] *bicycle* [ˈbaɪˌsɪkl̩] *imply* [ˌɪmˈplaɪ]

IPA Symbol	Key Word	Other Words
[aʊ]	*how* [haʊ]	*plowing* [ˈplaʊˌɪŋ] *endow* [ˌɛnˈdaʊ] *autobahn* [ˈaʊtoˌbɑn] *council* [ˈkaʊnsl̩] *housefly* [ˈhaʊsˌflaɪ]
[ɔɪ]	*toy* [tɔɪ]	*toiling* [ˈtɔɪlɪŋ] *oyster* [ˈɔɪstɚ] *loyalty* [ˈlɔɪˌti] *annoy* [əˈnɔɪ] *poison* [ˈpɔɪzn̩]
[ju]	*using* [ˈjuzɪŋ]	*universal* [junəˈvɝsl̩] *euphemism* [ˈjufəmɪzm̩] *feud* [fjud] *refuse* [rɪˈfjuz] *spew* [spju]
[ɪu]	*fuse* [fɪuz]	
[eɪ]	*say* [seɪ]	

Consonants

IPA Symbol	Key Word	Other Words
[p]	*poor* [pʊr]	*place* [ples] *applaud* [əˈplɔd] *slap* [slæp]
[b]	*boor* [bʊr]	*break* [brek] *about* [əˈbaʊt] *club* [klʌb]
[t]	*time* [taɪm]	*trend* [trɛnd] *attire* [əˈtaɪr] *blast* [blæst]
[d]	*dime* [daɪm]	*differ* [ˈdɪfɚ] *addenda* [əˈdɛndə] *closed* [klozd]
[k]	*kite* [kaɪt]	*careful* [ˈkɛrfəl] *accord* [əˈkɔrd] *attack* [əˈtæk]
[g]	*guide* [gaɪd]	*grand* [grænd] *aggressor* [əˈgrɛsɚ] *eggnog* [ˈɛgˌnɔg]
[f]	*few* [fɪu]	*finally* [ˈfaɪnl̩i] *affront* [əˈfrʌnt] *aloof* [əˈluf]
[v]	*view* [vɪu]	*velocity* [vəˈlɑsəti] *aver* [əˈvɝ] *love* [lʌv]

Table 14.4   (Continued)

	IPA Symbol	Key Word	Other Words
Consonants (cont.)	[θ]	*thigh* [θaɪ]	*thrifty* [ˈθrɪfti] *athwart* [əˈθwɔrt] *myth* [mɪθ]
	[ð]	*thy* [ðaɪ]	*these* [ðiz] *although* [ˌɔlˈðo] *breathe* [brið]
	[s]	*sing* [sɪŋ]	*simple* [ˈsɪmpl̩] *lastly* [ˈlæst͵li] *ships* [ʃɪps]
	[z]	*zing* [zɪŋ]	*xylophone* [ˈzaɪlə͵fon] *loses* [ˈluzɪz] *dreams* [drimz]
	[ʃ]	*shock* [ʃɑk]	*ashen* [æʃən] *trash* [træʃ]
	[ʒ]	*Jacques* [ʒɑk]	*gendarme* [ˈʒɑnˈdɑrm] *measure* [ˈmɛʒɚ] *beige* [beʒ]
	[tʃ]	*chest* [tʃɛst]	*checkers* [ˈtʃɛkɚz] *riches* [ˈrɪtʃɪz] *attach* [əˈtætʃ]
	[dʒ]	*jest* [dʒɛst]	*juggle* [dʒʌgl̩] *adjudicate* [əˈdʒudɪ͵ket] *adjudge* [əˈdʒʌdʒ]
	[h]	*how* [haʊ]	*heaven* [ˈhɛvən] *El Cajon* [ˌɛl͵kəˈhon] *cahoots* [ˌkəˈhuts]
	[hw]	*when* [hwɛn]	*Joaquin* [hwɑˈkin] *whimsical* [ˈhwɪmzɪkl̩]
	[m]	*mom* [mɑm]	*militant* [ˈmɪlətənt] *amusing* [əˈmjuzɪŋ] *spume* [spjum]
	[n]	*noun* [naʊn]	*nevermore* [ˌnɛvɚˈmɔr] *announcer* [əˈnaʊnsɚ] *sturgeon* [ˈstɚdʒən]
	[ŋ]	*sing* [sɪŋ]	*English* [ˈɪŋglɪʃ] *language* [ˈlæŋgwɪdʒ] *pang* [pæŋ]
	[l]	*love* [lʌv]	*lavender* [ˈlævəndɚ] *illusion* [ɪˈluʒən] *medial* [ˈmidil̩]

IPA Symbol	Key Word	Other Words
[w]	*watch* [wɑtʃ]	*wash* [wɑʃ] *aware* [ə'wɛr] *equestrian* [ɪ'kwɛstriən]
[j]	*yellow* ['jɛlo]	*William* ['wɪljəm] *Yukon* ['jukɑn]
[r]	*run* [rʌn]	*Wrigley* ['rɪgli] *martial* ['mɑrʃəl] *appear* [ə'pɪr]

Practice: Phonetic Transcription

For additional practice, transcribe any of the passages of this book into IPA symbols. When you have acquired some degree of proficiency with the IPA, begin transcribing from the daily news any names and words with which you are unfamiliar. Chapter 15 will help you determine correct pronunciation of names in some of the major languages, and gazetteers and dictionaries will give you correct pronunciations of unfamiliar words. To find the correct IPA transcriptions of unfamiliar words, use *A Pronouncing Dictionary of American English* or the *NBC Handbook of Pronunciation*.

¡5

Foreign Pronunciation

Despite the fact that nearly all Americans have their ethnic roots embedded in a foreign culture, most Americans are familiar with only one language—American English. This presents a problem to most American announcers, who must read words and names of foreign origin daily. News stories originating in any of a hundred different nations, featuring the names of places and people and organizations, must be read with accuracy and authority by professional news announcers. Announcers on classical music stations must deal with Spanish, Italian, French, German, and Russian names and music titles. Commercials for a variety of goods and services—international restaurants, foreign tours, exotic perfumes, foreign films, and Oriental rugs, to name a few—often require the ability to pronounce foreign names and words. It is no exaggeration to state that your career as a professional announcer will be seriously handicapped unless you develop skill and ease in pronouncing words from at least the major modern languages of the world.

Several years of study of every major language would prepare you ideally for your work, but because time and capacities do not usually permit such thoroughness, the next best solution is to learn the rules of pronunciation of the languages you are most likely to need. This chapter provides a detailed discussion of Spanish, Italian, French, and German pronunciation and briefly mentions other European and Asian languages. The practice section includes commercial and news copy drawing on several languages.

Although correct foreign pronunciation is stressed in this chapter, proper pronunciation for radio and television is not always the same as the correct pronunciation. Conventional pronunciations of foreign cities, nations, personal names, and musical compositions, though not correct, are usually preferred on radio and television. Here are some examples:

City	Correct pronunciation	Conventional pronunciation
Paris	PAH-REE' [pɑ'ri]	PAIR'-IS ['pɛrɪs or 'pærɪs]
Copenhagen	KOEBN-HAU'-N [købn̩'haʊn]	KOPE'-UN-HAIG'-UN ['kopən 'hegn̩]
Berlin	BEAR-LEEN' [bɛr'lin]	BER-LIHN' [bɚ'lɪn]

You are expected to use correct foreign pronunciation for certain words and to modify it for others. This amounts to knowing when it is correct to be incorrect.

There are three possibilities when you are pronouncing foreign or foreign-derived words:

1. You may pronounce them as the natives do in the country of origin.
2. You may modify them to conform to conventionally accepted American usage.
3. You may completely Anglicize them.

There are regrettably few rules to guide you. The absolutist position that the correct pronunciation is never wrong offers no help. Even the most extreme advocate of correct pronunciation would admit that an announcer who says PAH-REE', FRÄHS [pa'ri frãːs] is being affected.

This chapter discusses and illustrates the correct rules of foreign pronunciation. In each instance the correct pronunciation will be transcribed into IPA symbols as well as the less precise symbols of the radio and television wire services. Note that because most modern European countries comprise many formerly independent states, regional variations in pronunciation abound. The pronunciations given in this chapter follow those established by qualified natives as standard pronunciations. Deviations are not necessarily substandard.

Guidelines for Announcers

In the absence of ironclad rules, there are some suggestions that are in accord with the best practice among topflight announcers in the United States and Canada. These guidelines represent an attempt to impose order in a situation that is by definition disorderly, so they cannot guarantee answers to all pronunciation questions that may arise.

Give the names of cities and countries the familiar, conventionalized pronunciation current in the United States.   The citizens of Germany call their country *Deutschland*; the word *Germany* is not even a German word. If it were, its German pronunciation would differ considerably from that used by Americans. There is no point in either applying the German rules of pronunciation to the name *Germany* or calling Germany *Deutschland* in this country. Similarly, the correct Japanese pronunciation of Iwo Jima is EE-WAW´-DJEE-MAH [i ´wɔdʒimɑ], but it is customary in this country to say the technically incorrect EE´WO DJEE´-MUH [´i,wo ´dʒimə].

In most instances, we spell names of foreign cities as they are spelled in their own country but pronounce them in conventionalized ways that reflect neither their original pronunciations nor any rational system of Anglicization. This presents no problem when the name is in more or less constant use, as Paris, Berlin, and Copenhagen are. The problem arises when a city relatively unknown to Americans, such as Eleusis [ɛ´lusɪs], São Paulo [ˌsãu ´paʊlu], or Rheims [rɛ̃ːs], is suddenly thrust into the news. When pronunciation rules do not help, you should check a standard pronunciation guide. Several are to be found in almost every broadcast station, and at least one should be in the personal library of every announcer. Kenyon and Knott's *A Pronouncing Dictionary of American English* and the *NBC Handbook of Pronunciation* give conventional pronunciations of foreign place names for broadcast use.

Pronounce the names of American cities that have foreign namesakes as the natives pronounce them.   Vienna, Versailles, Marseilles, Cairo and Alhambra are all names of American cities, and not one of them is pronounced like its foreign counterpart. Pronunciation guides will give you the correct local pronunciations of these and other cities and towns.

In pronouncing the names of foreigners, adopt one of the following rules.   (1) If the person's preference is known, use the preferred pronunciation. (2) If the person is well-known and a conventional pronunciation has developed, use that pronunciation. (3) If the person is not well-known and you do not know the person's preference, follow the rules of pronunciation for his or her language.

In pronouncing the American names derived from foreign names, adopt one of the following rules. (1) If the person's preference is known, use that pronunciation. (2) If the person's preference is not known, pronounce the name the way other Americans of the same name do. For example, if the name is DuBois and the person is American, you will be safe pronouncing it DUE-BOYZ, rather than DUH-BWAH as if it were French.

In pronouncing the titles of foreign musical compositions, let the following rules guide you. (1) If the title is in common use and the customary pronunciation is quite close to the original, use that pronunciation. (2) If the title is little known and has no conventional pronunciation, pronounce it according to the rules in its country of origin. Although it may sometimes be desirable to soften some foreign words slightly for American ears, you cannot in this instance go wrong by being correct.

Spanish Pronunciation

Spanish, unlike English, is a strictly phoneticized language. Once you have mastered the rules of Spanish pronunciation, you will know how to pronounce any Spanish word you see in print. Although a few letters have more than one speech sound, the surrounding letters in the word provide an infallible guide to their pronunciation.

Stress

Spanish words have one strongly stressed syllable. All other syllables receive no stress at all. There is no such thing as secondary stress; every syllable in a word is either stressed or not, with no middle ground.

Many Spanish words carry an accent mark over one of the vowels—for example, *médico*—and in this case the syllable the accented vowel appears in receives a strong stress. Unlike the accent marks in French, the Spanish accent mark does not affect the pronunciation of the vowel.

Two general rules govern words that carry no mark:

1. Words ending in a consonant other than *n* or *s* are stressed on the last syllable, such as *usted* [uˈstɛd], *canal* [kɑˈnɑl], *señor* [seˈɲɔr].
2. Words ending in *n*, *s*, or a vowel are stressed on the penultimate

(next-to-last) syllable, such as *joven* ['xoven], *señores* [sen'jɔres], *hombre* ['ɔmbre].

Spanish Vowels

Spanish has five vowels: *a*, *e*, *i*, *o*, and *u*. Whether the vowel is stressed or unstressed, it seldom varies from its customary sound. The chief exceptions are *i* and *u* when they form part of a diphthong. No vowel ever becomes the schwa vowel [ə], as, for example, the letter *a* does in the English word *about*.

a	The vowel *a* is always pronounced "ah" [ɑ], as in *father*. Examples: *balsa* ['bɑlsɑ] (BAHL'-SAH); *casa* ['kɑsɑ] (KAH'-SAH).
e	The vowel *e* is pronounced "ay" [e], as in the English word *bait*, but it sometimes becomes more like "eh" [ɛ], as in *met*, depending on its context. When it has the "ay" sound, it is never prolonged and allowed to glide into an "ee" sound. Examples: *meses* ['meses] (MAY'-SAYS); *deberes* [de'beres] (DAY-BAY'-RAYS); *gobierno* [go'βjɛrno] (GO-BYEHR'-NOH).
i	The vowel *i*, except when part of a diphthong, is always pronounced "ee" [i], as in *machine*. Examples: *definitivo* [defini'tiβo] (DAY-FEE-NEE-TEE'-VO); *pipa* ['pipɑ] (PEE'-PAH).
o	The vowel *o* is usually pronounced "oh" [o], as in the English word *hoe*, but depending on its context it may become more like "aw" [ɔ]. Examples: *contrata* [kon'trɑtɑ] (KOHN-TRAH'-TAH); *pocos* ['pokos] (POH'-KOHS); *hombre* ['ɔmbre] (AWM'-BRAY).
u	The vowel *u*, when not part of a diphthong, is pronounced "oo" [u], as in *rule*. Examples: *luna* ['lunɑ] (LOO'-NAH); *público* ['publiko] (poo'-BLEE-KO).

Spanish Diphthongs

There are a number of diphthongs in Spanish. They are summarized in the following list.

ia, *ie*, *io*, and *iu*	If you pronounce the sounds "ee" and "ah" together very rapidly, they form a sound very much like "yah." A similar change occurs in rapidly saying aloud the two component sounds in *ie* ("yay"), *io* ("yo"), and *iu* ("you"). These sounds, called diphthongs because they are a combination of two vowels, are represented as follows in IPA: [jɑ], [je], [jo], [ju]. In pronouncing them, sound both component sounds but make sure that the *i* becomes [j]. Examples: *piano* ['pjɑno] (PYAH'-NO); *mientras* ['mjentrɑs] (MYAYN'-TRAS); *naciones* [nɑ'sjones] (NAH-SYONE'-AYS); *viuda* ['vjudɑ] (VYOO'-DAH).
ei	The Spanish *ei* is pronounced "ay" [e], as in the English word *rein*. Example: *seis* [ses] (SAYSS).
ai	The Spanish *ai* is pronounced "eye" [aɪ]. Example: *bailar* [baɪ'lɑr] (BY-LAHR'). (*Note:* At the ends of words, *ei* and *ai* are spelled *ey* and *ay*.)
oi	The Spanish *oi* is pronounced "oy" [ɔɪ], as in *loiter*. Example: *heroico* [ɛr'ɔɪko] (EH-ROY'-KO).
ua, *ue*, *ui*, and *uo*	In Spanish, *u* preceding another vowel is pronounced like *w* [w] in English. Examples: *cuatro* ['kwɑtro] (KWAH'-TRO); *puente* ['pwɛnte] (PWEN'-TAY); *cuidar* [kwi'dɑr] (KWEE-DAR'); *cuota* ['kwotɑ] (KWO'-TAH). (But note the exceptions under *gu* and *qu*.)
au	The Spanish *au* is pronounced "ow" [aʊ]. Example: *autobus* [aʊto'bus] (OW-TOE-BOOS').
eu	The Spanish *eu* is pronounced by running "eh" [ɛ] and "oo" [u] together rapidly. Example: *deuda* [dɛ'udɑ] (DEH-OO'-DAH).

Spanish Consonants

b	At the beginning of a word or after *m*, the Spanish *b* is pronounced like the English *b* [b]. Examples: *bueno* ['bweno] (BWAY'-NO);

nombre ['nombre] (NOHM'-BRAY). In other positions its sound is more like the English *v*, although it is produced with both lips instead of the upper teeth and lower lip. The IPA symbol for this sound is [β]. Example: *alabar* [ɑlɑ'βɑr] (AH-LAH-BAHR'). (*Note*: There is no way of indicating this sound with conventional type, so B is used in the wire-service example.)

c — The Spanish *c* has two values: (1) Before *e* or *i* it is soft. Castilian speech—fairly standard in most of Spain—pronounces this as *th* in *thin*. In southern Spain and in Latin America it is pronounced as *s* in *say*. You should base your choice on the origin of the person or title, unless a large Spanish-speaking audience in your area would consider Castilian pronunciation affected. Example: *ciudad* [sju'dɑd] (SYOU-DAHD') or [θju'dɑd] (THYOU-DAHD'). (2) In all other positions, *c* is pronounced as in *car*. Examples: *cura* ['ku rɑ] (KOO'-RAH); *acto* ['ɑkto] (AHK'-TOH). For the sound of "k" preceding *e* or *i* see *qu*.

cc — The first *c* is by definition hard, and because *cc* appears only before *e* or *i*, the second *c* is soft. Example: *acceso* [ɑk'seso] (AHK-SAY'-SOH) or in Castilian [ɑk'θeso] (AHK-THAY'-SO).

ch — The Spanish *ch* is pronounced as the *ch* [tʃ] in *church*. Example: *muchacha* [mu'tʃatʃɑ] (MOO-CHA'-CHA).

d — At the beginning of a word or after *n* or *l*, the Spanish *d* is much like the English *d* [d]. Examples: *dios* [djos] (DYOS); *caldo* ['kɑldo] (KAHL'-DO). In other positions it is more like a weak-voiced *th* [ð], as in *weather*. This sound is made by extending the tongue a short distance beyond the front teeth and thus weakening the sound. Example: *padre* ['pɑðre] (PAH'THRAY). (*Note*: This sound is still more [d] than [ð], so the [d] will be used in this chapter.)

f   The Spanish *f* is pronounced like the English *f* [f]. Example: *flores* ['flores] (FLO'-RAYS).

g   The Spanish *g* has two values: (1) Before *e* or *i*, a *g* is pronounced much like the German *ch* [x], as in *ach*, or the Scottish *ch*, as in *loch*. It is a guttural sound, with tightening and some rasp in the rear of the mouth but no vibration of the vocal folds. Examples: *general* [xene'rɑl] (KHAY-NAY-RAHL'); *gente* ['xente] (KHAYN'-TAY). (2) In all other positions, a Spanish *g* is hard, as in *gag*. Examples: *gala* ['gɑlɑ] (GAH'-LAH); *largo* ['lɑrgo] (LAHR'-GO). (*Note*: Because the sound [x] does not occur in English, the wire services have difficulty transcribing it. Sometimes they use CH and sometimes KH. When CH is used there is no way of knowing whether [x] or [tʃ] is intended. The sound is transcribed as KH in this chapter, but you should be alert to the frequent inconsistencies in transcribing it in the wire-service practice material later in this book.)

gu   When the sound of a hard *g* occurs before *e* or *i*, it is written *gu*. In this convention *u* is merely a marker and has no sound of its own. Example: *guia* ['giɑ] (GHEE'-AH).

gü   The two dots over *ü* when it is between *g* and *e* or *i* (*güe* or *güi*) indicate that *ü* is part of a diphthong, to be sounded like *w*. Example: *agüero* [ɑ'gwero] (AH-GWAY'-RO).

h   Except in the combination *ch*, the Spanish *h* is an unsounded letter—the only one in the language. Examples: *habas* ['ɑβɑs] (AH'-BAHS); *adhesivo* [ɑde'siβo] (AHD-AY-SEE'-BO).

j   The Spanish *j* has a sound exactly like the first pronunciation of *g* given above. Example: *junta* ['xuntɑ] (KHOON'-TAH).

l	The Spanish *l* is very similar to the English *l*, although the Spanish keep the rear of the tongue flat. Example: *labios* ['laβjos] (LAH′-BYOS).
ll	In Castilian Spanish, *ll* is pronounced much like *lli* [lj] in the English word *million*. However, in most parts of Latin America, *ll* is pronounced like *y* [j] in *yes*. Example: *calle* ['kalje] (KAH′-LYAY) or ['kaje] (KAH′-YAY).
m	The Spanish *m* is sounded just like the English *m*. Example: *cambio* ['kamβjo] (KAHM′-BYO).
n	Spanish has three pronunciations for the letter *n*. (1) Before *ca*, *co*, *cu*, *qui*, or *que* (that is, before any "k" sound) and before *g* or *j*, it is pronounced *ng* [ŋ] as in *sing*. Example: *tango* ['taŋgo] (TAHNG′-GO). (2) Before *f*, *v*, *p*, or *b*, it is pronounced like the English *m*. Example: *confiado* [komˈfjado] (KOM-FYAH′-DO). (3) In all other cases it is pronounced like the English *n*. Example: *manojo* [manˈoxo] (MAH-NO′-KHO).
nn	This combination is rare in Spanish. Both *n*'s are sounded. Example: *perenne* [peˈrenːe] (PAY-RAYN′-NAY).
ñ	The Spanish *ñ* is pronounced *ny* [ɲ], as in the English word *canyon*. Example: *señor* [seˈɲɔr] (SAY-NYOR′).
p	The Spanish *p* is pronounced like the English *p*. Example: *padre* ['paðre] (PAH′-THRAY).
qu	The combination *qu* occurs only before *e* or *i* and is pronounced like the hard *c*, with *u* never sounded. Examples: *qué* [ke] (KAY); *aquí* [aˈki] (AH-KEE′).
r	The Spanish *r* has two values, neither of which is like the English sound. (1) At the beginning of a word or after *l*, *n*, or *s*, the tongue is trilled against the roof of the mouth. Examples: *rico* ['riko] (RREE′-KO); *honrado* [onˈrado] (OWN-RRAH′-DO). (2) In other positions it is a single flip of the tongue

against the roof of the mouth. Example: *caro* ['kɑro] (KAH'-RO).

rr

The combination *rr* indicates a full trill rather than a single flip of the tongue.

s

There are two pronunciations of the letter *s*. (1) Before *b*, *d*, *g*, *l*, *m*, *n*, *r*, or *v*, it is pronounced like the English *z*. Example: *mismo* ['mizmo] (MEEZ'-MO). (2) In other cases it is pronounced like the English *s* in *sea*. Example: *cosa* ['kosɑ] (KOH'-SAH).

sc

An *s* and hard *c*, or [s] plus [k], are always pronounced separately in both Castilian and non-Castilian. Example: *disco* ['disko] (DEES'-KO). In non-Castilian, *s* and soft *c*, being identical sounds, are merged. Example: *discernir* [disɛr'nɪr] (DEE-SAIR-NEAR'). In Castilian, *s* and soft *c*, which is actually [θ], are pronounced separately. Example: *discernir* [disθɛr'nɪr] (DEES-THAIR-NEAR').

t

The Spanish *t* is much like English *t*. Example: *trato* ['trɑto] (TRAH'-TOE).

v

A *v* is sounded the same way as the Spanish *b*, with the same positional variations.

x

The Spanish *x* is normally sounded like the English *x* [ks] in the word *vex*. Example: *próximo* ['proksimo] (PROCK'-SEE-MO). When *x* occurs before a consonant, Castilians pronounce it like the Spanish *s*. Example: *expreso* [ɛs'preso] (ESS-PRAY'-SOH). The words for *Mexico* and *Mexican* are pronounced with the *j* [x] sound: *México* ['mexiko] (MAY'-KHEE-KO).

y

The letter *y* is sounded much like the English *y* in *year*. Example: *yerba* ['jɛrbɑ] (YEHR'-BAH). In certain instances, the letter *y* substitutes for the vowel *i*: (1) as the second element of a diphthong at the end of a word, as in *rey* [re] (RAY); (2) as the initial in a few proper names, as in *Ybarra* [i'bɑrɑ] (EE-BAH'-RAH); (3) as the word for *and*, as in *pan y vino* [pɑni'vino] (PAHN-EE-VEE'-NO).

z	The letter *z* follows the rules for the soft *c*. Examples: *jerez* [xeˈreθ] (KHAY-RAYTH′) (Castilian) or [xeˈres] (KHAY-RAYSS′) (Latin-American).

Italian Pronunciation

Italian, like Spanish, has a phonetically strict spelling system. Although not quite as thorough as the Spanish system, in which the spelling tells you everything about the pronunciation of a word, it is a very businesslike system. Italian conventional spelling does not consistently mark stress, and in the unmarked words certain vowel qualities are undifferentiated. Aside from this, Italian presents few difficulties.

Stress

Italian words have one strongly stressed syllable, and the other syllables are completely unstressed. Unlike English, Italian has no half-stresses. The relatively small number of words stressed on the last syllable are always marked with an accent over that vowel. Example: *sarà* [saˈra] (SAH-RAH′). Most Italian words are stressed on the penultimate syllable. Example: *infinito* [infiˈnito] (EEN-FEE-NEE′-TOE). Many words are stressed on the antepenultimate syllable.[1] Example: *medico* [ˈmediko] (MAY′-DEE-KOE). A few Italian printing houses mark such words with a grave accent over the vowel in the syllable to be stressed, but this is not the general rule. In this chapter, an accent mark will be used to show stress on some syllable other than the penultimate. The grave accent will also be used to indicate an open *e* [ɛ] or an open *o* [ɔ], but this should cause no confusion, because syllables containing open *e* or open *o* are always stressed in Italian.

Italian Vowels

Italian has seven basic vowel sounds but uses only the five letters *a*, *e*, *i*, *o*, and *u* to represent them. Stressed or unstressed, each keeps its distinctive quality, though stressed vowels tend to be lengthened before single consonants; the first vowel of *casa* is longer than that of *cassa*, for example.

[1]The antepenultimate syllable is the third from the end of a word.

a   The vowel *a* is always pronounced "ah" [ɑ], as in *father*. Examples: *là* [lɑ] (LAH); *pasta* ['pɑstɑ] (PAH'-STAH).

e   The Italian *e* varies from "ay" [e] to "eh" [ɛ]. Although there are ways of determining the correct pronunciation in each instance, the rules are too complex to be considered here. Most northern and southern Italians, including the best educated, use just one *e*, which may vary somewhat according to the consonants that precede or follow it. This pronunciation is understood and accepted everywhere. Where accent marks are given, the acutely accented *é* tells you that the pronunciation is [e], and the grave accent, *è*, tells you that the pronunciation is [ɛ]. Examples: *débole* ['debole] (DAY'-BO-LAY); *prèsto* ['prɛsto] (PREH'-STOE).

i   The Italian *i* is much like the English *i* in *machine*. Example: *pipa* ['pipɑ] (PEE'-PAH).

o   Speakers of Italian who distinguish between two *e* sounds also distinguish two qualities of *o*: a closed *o* [o], as in *go*, and an open *o* [ɔ], as in *bought*. Dictionaries sometimes indicate the closed *o* with an acute accent—*pólvere* ['polvere] (POHL'-VAY-RAY)—and the open *o* with a grave accent—*còsta* ['kɔstɑ] (KAW'-STAH). As with the open and closed *e*, the difference between the two varieties of *o* is minor, and most speakers who use only one *e* sound likewise use only one *o* sound.

u   The vowel *u* is like the English *u* in *rule*. Examples: *luna* ['lunɑ] (LOO'-NAH); *futuro* [fu'turo] (FOO-TOO'-ROH).

Italian Diphthongs

The Italian vowels *a*, *e*, *i*, *o*, and *u* form many different combinations to produce diphthongs. Although these may seem somewhat complex at first glance, they are quite easily mastered.

ia

The diphthong *ia*, except when it follows *c* or *g*, is pronounced with *i* becoming "y" [j] and *a* retaining its regular pronunciation. Example: *piano* ['pjɑno] (PYAN'-NOH). When *ia* follows *c*, the *i* serves as a silent marker to indicate that *c* is soft, [tʃ] like the *ch* in *chair*. Example: *Ciano* ['tʃɑn,o] (TCHAH'-NOH). When *ia* follows *g*, the *i* again serves as a silent marker to indicate that *g* is soft, [ʤ] like the *g* in *gem*. Example: *Gianinni* [ʤɑ'nini] (DGAH-NEE'-NEE).

ie

The diphthong *ie*, except for the few instances in which it follows *c* or *g*, is sounded with *i* becoming "y" [j] and *e* retaining its regular pronunciation. Examples: *pièno* ['pjeno] (PYAY'-NOH); *cielo* ['tʃɛlo] (TCHEH'-LOH). Like *ia*, *ie* following *c* or *g* serves to indicate that the soft pronunciation is to be used, and the *i* has no other function.

io

The diphthong *io*, except where it follows *c* or *g*, is pronounced with *i* becoming "y" [j] and *o* retaining its regular pronunciation. After *c* or *g*, the *i* serves as a silent marker to indicate that the soft pronunciation is to be used. Examples: *Mario* ['mɑrjo] (MAHR'-YO); *bacio* ['bɑtʃo] (BAH'-TCHOH); *Giorgio* ['ʤɔrʤo] (DGAWR'-DGOH).

iu

The diphthong *iu*, except where it follows *c* or *g*, is sounded with *i* becoming "y" [j] and *u* retaining its regular pronunciation. Following *c* or *g*, the *i* serves as a silent marker to indicate that the preceding sound is soft. Examples: *iuta* ['jutɑ] (YOU'-TAH); *acciuga* [ɑ'tʃugɑ] (AH-CHEW'-GAH); *giù* [ʤu] (DGOO).

ai, *oi*, and *ui*

These diphthongs are simply glides from *a*, *o*, or *u* to the "ee" sound. Examples: *mai* [maɪ] (MY); *pòi* [pɔɪ] (POY); *guida* ['gwidɑ] (GWEE'-DAH).

ua, *ue*, and *uo*	In these diphthongs *u* becomes *w* (as in *will*) and *a*, *e*, or *o* each retains its permanent sound. Examples: *guàio* [ˈgwajo] (GWAH′-YOH); *sàngue* [ˈsaŋgwe] (SAHNG′-GWAY); *cuòre* [ˈkwɔre] (KWAW′-RAY).
au	The diphthong *au* is pronounced like *ow* [aʊ] in the English word *how*. Example: *Làura* [ˈlaʊra] (LAU′-RAH).

Italian Consonants

A crucial feature of Italian pronunciation is the occurrence of both single (or short) and double (or long) consonants. In Italian, a written double consonant always means a spoken double consonant. The nearest thing in English is the effect produced in two-word expressions such as *ought to*, *guess so*, or *sick cat*, which have counterparts in the Italian words *òtto*, *messo*, and *seccare*. Note that this is not really a doubling of the sound as much as a prolonging of it. Before a double consonant (as in *canne*), a stressed vowel is perceptibly shorter than before a single consonant (as in *cane*). In the following discussion of the Italian consonants, many words will be listed without phonetic spellings for practice.

b	The Italian *b* is just like the English *b*. Examples: *barba*, *bianco*, *buòno*, *bambino*, *babbo*, *sàbbia*, *labbra*.
c	The Italian *c* has two values: (1) Before *e* or *i*, it is soft, like *ch* [tʃ] in *church*. Examples: *cena*, *cènto*, *fàcile*, *Lècce*, *spicci*, *accènto*. When the soft *c* sound [tʃ] occurs before *a*, *o*, or *u*, it is written *ci* (as in *ciò*), and *i* is a silent marker, with no sound of its own. Example: *bacio* [ˈbatʃo] (BAH′-TCHOH). (2) In all other positions, *c* is hard, like *c* [k] in *call*. Examples: *caldo*, *cura*, *clèro*, *bocca*, *sacco*, *piccolo*.
ch	The combination *ch* occurs only before *e* or *i*, where it represents a hard *c* [k]. Examples: *che* [ke] (KAY); *vècchio* [ˈvɛkːjo] (VEHK′-KYOH).
d	The Italian *d* is much like the English *d*. Examples: *dardo*, *càndido*, *freddo*, *iddio*.

f	The pronunciation of *f* is just as in English. Examples: *faccia, fiato, fiume, gufo, bèffa, ràffio, soffiare*.
g	The Italian *g* has two values; (1) Before *e* or *i*, it is soft, like the *g* in *gem* [ʤ]. Examples: *gènte, giro, pàgina, legge, viaggi, suggèllo*. When the soft *g* sound [ʤ] occurs before *a*, *o*, or *u*, it is written *gi* (as in *già*), and the *i* serves as a silent marker. Example: *Giovanni* [ʤoˈvɑnːi] (DGOH-VAHN′-NEE). (2) In all other positions, except as described below, *g* is hard, like the *g* in *good* [g]. Examples: *gamba, góndola, guèrra, lèggo, agganciare*.
gh	The combination *gh* occurs only before *e* or *i*, where it represents a hard *g* sound [g]. Example: *ghiàccio* [ˈgjatʃːo] (GYAHTCH′-OH).
gli	The Italian *gli* is like the *lli* in *million*. When another vowel follows, as it usually does (in the next word when *gli* appears as the definite article *the*), the *i* is a silent marker. When *gli* occurs within a word, the consonant sound is always double. Remember that the *g* in *gli* has no value whatsoever, and that, when *gli* is followed by another vowel, the *i* has no value. The entire sound, then, becomes [l] plus [j]. Examples: *figlio* [ˈfilːjo]) (FEE′-LYOH); *paglia* [ˈpalːja] (PAH′-LYAH); *pagliacci* [paˈljatʃːi] (PAH-LYAHCH′-CHEE); *gli altri* [ˈjaltri] (YAHL′-TREE).
gn	The combination *gn* is like the English *ny* [ɲ] in *canyon* (or the Spanish *ñ*). Within a word the sound is always double. Examples: *signore* [siˈɲːore] (SEEN-NYO′-RAY); *giugno* [ˈʤuɲo] (JOON′-NYOH).
h	Except in the combinations *ch* and *gh*, *h* is the only unsounded letter in Italian. In native words it occurs only at the beginning of four related forms of the verb *avere* (to have). The

word *hanno*, for example, is pronounced exactly like the word *anno* [ˈanːo] (AHN′-NO).

j   The letter *j* is not regularly used in Italian, except as a substitute for the letter *i* in proper names (*Jàcopo* for *Iàcopo*) or in a final position as a substitute for *ii* in plurals (*studj* for *studii*).

l   The letter *l* can be pronounced like the English *l*, though Italians pronounce it with the tongue flat and unraised in the back of the mouth. Examples: *lavoro, lièto, Itàlia, giallo, bèlla, nulla*.

m   The letter *m* is just like the English *m*. Examples: *mièle, mùsica, fame, mamma, gèmma, fiammiferi*.

n   The Italian *n* is pronounced like the English *n*, including [ŋ] (*ng* as in *thing*) where it precedes hard *c* or hard *g*. Examples: *nòno* [ˈnɔno] (NAW′-NOH); *bianco* [ˈbjaŋko] (BYAHNG′-KOH); *inglese* [iŋˈgleze] (ING-GLAYZ′-AY).

p   The pronunciation of *p* is much like the English *p*. Examples: *papa, prète, capo, dòppio, zuppa, appòggio*.

q   The letter *q* has the same sound as hard *c* and is always followed by *u*, which is always sounded [w] as part of a diphthong. Examples: *quadro, quindi, dunque, quèrcia*. When this sound is doubled, it appears as *cq*. Example: *acqua, nacque, acquistare*.

r   Where a single *r* appears, it is manufactured with a single flip of the tongue tip against the roof of the mouth. Where double *r* appears, it calls for a trill of the tongue tip, as in Spanish. Examples: *Roma, rumore, dramma, carro, burro, orrore*.

s   In most positions, the Italian *s* is pronounced like the English *s* in *sea*. Examples: *sole* [ˈsole] (SO′-LAY); *sfida* [ˈsfida] (SFEE′-DAH); *rosso* [ˈrosːo] (ROHS′-SOH). Before any of the voiced consonants, *b*, *d*, *g*, *l*, *m*, *n*, *r*, or *v*, the *s* is pronounced like *z* in *zoo*. Examples: *sbaglio* [ˈzbɑlːjo] (ZBAH'-LYOH); *disdegno* [diˈzdeɲo] (DEE-ZDAY'-NYOH); *slancio* [ˈzlɑntʃo] (ZLAHN'-CHOH). A single *s* between vowels is pronounced either [s] or [z], with [s] generally preferred in Tuscany and [z] elsewhere. Examples: *casa*, *francese*, *còsa*.

sc   Before *e* or *i*, *sc* is pronounced [ʃ] like *sh* in *shoe*. Within a word, it is pronounced twice. Examples: *scelto* [ˈʃelto] (SHAYL'-TOH); *pesce* [ˈpeʃːe] (PAYSH'-SHAY). Before *a*, *o*, or *u*, it appears as *sci*. In this convention, the *i* is a silent marker. Examples: *sciame* [ʃame] (SHAH'-MAY); *asciutto* [aˈʃːutːo] (AHSH-SHOOT'-TOH). The spelling *scie* is pronounced the same as *sce*. In all other positions, *sc* is pronounced like *sk* in *ski*. Examples: *scale* [ˈskɑle] (SKAH'-LAY); *tasca* [ˈtɑskɑ] (TAH'-SKAH).

sch   The combination *sch* occurs only before *e* and *i*, where it represents *s* as in *say* plus hard *c* as in *come*. Example: *schiavo* [ˈskjɑvo] (SKYAH'-VOH).

t   The Italian *t* is much like the English *t*. Examples: *tèsta*, *tòrto*, *triste*, *gatto*, *sêtte*, *prosciutto*.

v   The Italian *v* is like the English *v*. Examples: *vivo*, *Verona*, *vuòto*, *bevve*, *òvvio*, *avviso*.

z   The letter *z* is ambiguous in Italian, representing both [ts], like *ts* in *cats*, and [dz], like *ds* in *beds*. In the initial position, there is no firm rule for its pronunciation. Examples: *zèlo* [ˈdzɛlo] (DZEH'-LOH); *zio* [ˈtsio] (TSEE'-OH). Internally, [ts] is general after *r* and *l*. Example: *fòrza* [ˈfɔrtsɑ] (FAWR'-TSAH). A single *z* between vowels is [ts]. Example: *azione* [aˈtsjone] (AH-TSYOH'-NAY).

French Pronunciation

French, like English, uses complicated spelling conventions, including numerous superfluous letters, sequences of letters representing single sounds, several ways of writing one sound, and the use of one letter to represent several sounds. But on the whole, French spelling is more systematic than English, and with practice one can learn to read French words with an acceptable pronunciation.

Stress

French words, as well as entire phrases and sentences, have about equal accent on each syllable up to the last one, which is a little more heavily stressed. In the name of the French composer *Debussy* [dəbysi], the syllable *-sy* gets a slight extra stress if you pause or stop after it but not if you do not.[2] In the sentence *Debussy est bien connu* (*Debussy is well-known*), only the final sound of the phrase gets that extra bit of stress: [dəbysi ɛ bjɛ̃ kɔ'ny].

French Oral Vowels

French has three classes of vowel sounds: twelve oral vowels, four nasal vowels, and three semivowels. Because a single speech sound in French may have as many as six different spellings, the vowels, nasal vowels, and semivowels will be grouped by sound rather than alphabetically.

Many of the sample words include a sound somewhere between [o] (OH) and [ɔ] (AW). In IPA the symbol for this sound is [ǫ], but it is not much used in French dictionaries, so there is little point in using it here. Authoritative reference works use the symbol [ɔ] to describe *o* in *école* and *au* in *Paul*, even though the actual sound is probably closer to [o]. To avoid confusion, sample words will be transcribed as they are in standard reference works. As you become familiar with the French language, you may want to modify conventional transcriptions to suit your own standards of accuracy.

French has a number of speech sounds that do not occur in English,

[2]French *u* and German *ü* are both represented by the IPA symbol [y]. This sound does not occur in English, and no combination of English letters can approximate it phonetically. When sounds cannot be approximated with wire-service phonetics, no wire-service pronouncer is given.

and each has been given an IPA symbol. Most of them are described here, but two need special explanation. The French tend to prolong a final *l* or *r* in an unvoiced, recessive manner. These sounds are especially noticeable when the words they are in terminate a phrase or are sounded separately. The IPA uses a small circle—[l̥] and [r̥]— to distinguish these from other *l* and *r* sounds. These symbols differ from the English syllabic consonant symbols [l̩] and [r̩], and they sound quite unlike anything in the English language. There is no truly satisfactory way of approximating these sounds in wire-service phonetics, but in this book they are represented as in these examples: *siècle* [sjɛkl̥] (SYEH-KL(UH)); *mettre* [mɛtr̥] (MET-R(UH)).

Table 15.1 summarizes the pronunciation of the twelve French oral vowels.

The [ə] or "uh," sound occurs also in nine common little words consisting solely of a consonant plus this vowel: *ce*, *de*, *je*, *le*, *me*, *ne*, *que*, *se*, and *te*. These are usually prefinal in a phrase, as in *je sais* [ʒəse] (ZHUH-SAY) and *le roi* [lərwa] (LUH-RWAH). If you listen carefully to a French speaker, you may decide that the vowel sound in each of these short words is closer to [œ] than to [ə]. Despite what your ears tell you, all standard French dictionaries transcribe these words with the schwa vowel. This practice will be followed here to avoid confusion, but you should be careful not to give these words a fully Americanized [ə] (UH) sound.

At the end of many words, an extra *e* appears after another vowel. This so-called mute *e* has no effect on the pronunciation. Examples are *épée* [epe] (AY-PAY) and *craie* [krɛ] (KREH) or (KRAY).

Obviously, certain spellings fail to distinguish between pairs of vowel sounds: *a* represents both [a] and [ɑ]; *e* and *ai* represent both [e] and [ɛ]; *o* and *au* represent both [o] and [ɔ]; *eu* and *œu* represent both [ø] and [œ]. Following consonants often give clues—for example, [ɛ], [ɔ], or [œ] are always used before *r* in the same syllable and never [e], [o], or [ø]. However, there are few sure rules. Fortunately, it does not matter too much because the distinctions between two members of a given pair are rarely important in conversation, and many educated speakers of French do not scrupulously observe them.

French Nasal Vowels

In producing the nasalized French vowels, which have no counterpart in English, the breath passes through the mouth and nose simultaneously, giving a quality sharply distinct from that of the oral vowels.

Table 15.1 French Oral Vowels

IPA Symbol	Description of Sound	French Spelling	Examples
[a]	Between *a* in *father* and *æ* in *bat*	*a* *à*	*patte* [pat] (PAHT) *déjà* [deʒa] (DAY-ZHAH)
[ɑ]	Like *a* in *father*	*a* *â*	*phase* [fɑz] (FAHZ) *pâte* [pɑt] (PAHT)
[e]	Like *e* in *they* but without the final glide	*e* *é* *ai*	*parlez* [pɑrle] (PAR-LAY) *été* [ete] (AY-TAY) *gai* [ge] (GAY)
[ɛ]	Like *e* in *met*	*e* *ê* *è* *ei* *ai* *aî*	*mettre* [mɛtr̥] (MET-R(UH)) *bête* [bɛt] (BET) *frère* [frɛr] (FREHR) *neige* [nɛʒ] (NEHZH) *frais* [frɛ] (FREH) *maître* [mɛtr̥] (MET-R(UH))
[i]	Like *i* in *machine*	*i* *î* *y*	*ici* [isi] (EE-SEE) *île* [il] (EEL) *mystère* [mistɛr] (MEES-TAIR)
[o]	Like *o* in *hoe* but with the final glide toward an "oo" sound omitted	*o* *ô* *au* *eau*	*chose* [ʃoz] (SHOZ) *hôtel* [otɛl] (O-TEL) *haute* [ot] (OAT) *beauté* [bote] (BO-TAY)
[ɔ]	Like *ou* in *bought* but shorter	*o* *au*	*école* [ekɔl] (AY-KAWL) *Paul* [pɔl] (PAUL)
[u]	Much like *u* in *rule*	*ou* *où* *oû*	*vous* [vu] (VOO) *où* [u] (OO) *coûter* [kute] (KOO-TAY)
[y]	Pronounced with the tongue as for [i] but with the lips rounded as for [u]	*u* *û*	*lune* [lyn] *flûte* [flyt]
[ø]	Pronounced with the tongue as for [e] ("ay") but with the lips rounded as for [o] ("oh")	*eu* *œu*	*feu* [fø] *vœux* [vø]
[œ]	Pronounced with the tongue as for [ɛ] ("eh") but with the lips rounded as for [ɔ] ("aw")	*eu* *œu*	*seul* [sœl] *sœur* [sœr]
[ə]	The schwa vowel, a simple "uh" sound, like the sound of *a* in *about* (occurs mainly in prefinal syllables)	*e*	*semaine* [səmɛn] (SUH-MEN) *neveu* [nəvø]

Table 15.2 French Nasal Vowels

IPA Symbol	Description of Sound	French Spelling Before *m*	French Spelling Before *n*	Examples Before *m*	Examples Before *n*
[ɑ̃]	Nasalized [ɑ]	am	an	chambre [ʃɑ̃br̥] champagne [ʃɑ̃paɲ]	avant [avɑ̃] français [frɑ̃sɛ]
		em	en	temple [tɑ̃pl̥] semblable [sɑ̃blabl̥]	entente [ɑ̃tɑ̃t] pensée [pɑ̃se]
[ɛ̃]	Nasalized [ɛ]	im	in	simple [sɛ̃pl̥]	cinq [sɛ̃k]
		ym	yn	symphonie [sɛ̃fɔni]	syntaxe [sɛ̃tæks]
		aim	ain	faim [fɛ̃]	bain [bɛ̃]
		eim	ein	Rheims [rɛ̃ːs]	peintre [pɛ̃tr̥]
[ɔ̃]	Nasalized [ɔ]	om	on	sombre [sɔ̃br̥] rompu [rɔ̃py]	pont [pɔ̃] bonbon [bɔ̃bɔ̃]
[œ̃]	Nasalized [œ]	um	un	humble [œ̃bl̥]	lundi [lœ̃di]

There is no way to signify these sounds with wire-service phonetics, so the pronunciations of words containing nasalized vowels are transcribed only in IPA symbols.

The nasal vowels are the sounds that result when [ɑ], [ɛ], [ɔ], or [œ] precedes *m* or *n*. In such constructions, *m* or *n* is not pronounced but serves only to indicate that the preceding vowel sound is nasalized.

The nasal French vowels are summarized in Table 15.2.

Kenyon and Knott's *A Pronouncing Dictionary of American English* substitutes the symbol [æ̃] for [ɛ̃] and the symbol [õ] for [ɔ̃]. But most French dictionaries follow the practice given here. You should be aware, however, that the nasalized [ɛ] is actually closer in sound to the nasalized [æ] and that the nasalized [ɔ] is actually closer to the nasalized [o].

French Semivowels

In French, certain combinations of vowels or of vowels and consonants combine to form new sounds, summarized in Table 15.3.

The combination *ill* is ambiguous, because it represents either the diphthong [ij], as in *fille* [fij] or *sillon* [sijɔ̃], or the sequence [il], as in *mille* [mil] (MEEL) or *village* [vilaʒ] (VEE-LAZH).

In the diphthong [jɛ̃], the nasal vowel is written *en*. Examples: *ancien* [ɑ̃sjɛ̃]; *rien* [rjɛ̃].

The diphthong [wa] is written *oi*, as in *loi* [lwa] (LWAH). When it is followed by another diphthong beginning with [j], the letter *y* is used instead of *i*, as in *foyer* [fwaje] (FWAH-YAY) and *joyeux* [ʒwajø]. The diphthong [wɛ̃] is written *oin*, as in *point* [pwɛ̃] and *joindre* [ʒwɛ̃dr̥].

Table 15.3 French Semivowels

IPA Symbol	Description of Sound	French Spelling	Examples
[j]	Before a vowel, like English *y* in *yet*	*i*	*hier* [jɛr] (YEHR)
			Pierrot [pjɛro] (PYEH-ROH)
		ï	*païen* [paɪjɛ̃]
			aïeux [aɪjø]
		y	*payer* [pɛje] (PEH-YAY)
			yeux [jø]
	After a vowel, like *y* in *boy*	*il*	*travail* [trɑvaɪj] (TRAH-VAHYUH)
			soleil [sɔlaɪj] (SAW-LEHYUH)
			œil [œj]
		ill	*Marseille* [marsɛj] (MAR-SEHYUH)
		ll	*faillite* [fajit] (FAH-YEET)
			bouillon [bujɔ̃]
			fille [fij] (FEE-YUH)
			sillon [sijɔ̃]
[w]	Like the English *w* in *win*	*ou*	*oui* [wi] (WEE)
			ouest [wɛst] (WEST)
			avouer [ɑvwe] (AH-VWAY)
[ɥ]	Pronounced with the tongue as for [j] but with the lips rounded as for [w] (occurs mainly before the letter *i*)	*u*	*suisse* [sɥis]
			nuit [nɥi]
			cuir [kɥir]

French Consonants

With a few exceptions, the French consonants do not represent as many different sounds as the vowels do; for this reason, they are considered alphabetically in the following discussion.

The letters *b*, *d*, *f*, *m*, *n*, *p*, *t*, *v*, and *z* represent one sound each in French and are pronounced much the same as in English. With some exceptions doubled consonants (such as *nn*, *rr*, and *tt*) have the same values as the corresponding singles.

c   Before *e*, *i*, or *y* or with the cedilla (*ç*) before any vowel, *c* is soft as in *city* [s]. Examples: *cent* [sã]; *grâce* [grɑs] (GRAHSS); *cité* [site] (SEE-TAY); *précis* [presi] (PRAY-SEE); *ça* [sɑ] (SAH); *reçu* [rəsy]. Before *a*, *o*, *u*, or a consonant, or in a final position, or when it is without the cedilla, *c* is hard as in *cat* [k]. Examples: *calme* [kɑlm] (KAHLM); *encore* [ãkɔr]; *cri* [kri] (KREE); *siècle* [sjɛkl̩] (SYEH-KL(UH)); *sec* [sɛk] (SECK). Double *cc* represents [ks] or simply [k], depending on the following letter. Examples: *accident* [aksidã]; *accord* [akɔr] (A-KAWR).

ch   The combination *ch* is usually like *sh* in *shoe* [ʃ]. Examples: *chapeau* [ʃapo] (SHAH-POH); *Chopin* [ʃɔpɛ̃] *riche*; [riʃ] (REESH); *marché* [marʃe] (MAR-SHAY). In a few newer words of Greek derivation, *ch* stands for hard *c*. Example: *psychologie* [psikɔlɔʒi] (PSEE-KAW-LAW-ZHEE) or (PSEE-KOH-LOH-ZHEE).

g   Before *e*, *i*, or *y*, the French *g* is soft, like the English *z* in *azure* [ʒ]. Examples: *geste* [ʒɛst] (ZHEST); *mirage* [mirɑʒ] (MEE-RAZH); *agir* [aʒir] (AH-ZHEER). The combination *ge*, with a mute *e*, represents the soft English *g* before *a* or *o*. Example: *bourgeois* [burʒwɑ] (BOOR-ZWAH). Before other vowels or consonants (other than *n*), *g* is hard, as in *gag* [g]. Examples: *garçon* [gɑrsɔ̃]; *goût* [gu] (GOO); *règle* [rɛgl̩] (REG-L(UH)). The combination *gu*, with a mute *u*, represents a hard *g* before *e*, *i*, or *y*. Example: *vogue* [vɔg] (VAWG) or (VOHG).

gn   This combination is much like the English *ny* in *canyon* [ɲ]. Note that this represents a different sound from the similar [ŋ]. Examples: *mignon* [miɲɔ̃]; *Charlemagne* [ʃɑrləmɑɲ] (SHAR-L(UH)-MAH-NY(UH)).

h   Except in *ch* and *ph*, the letter *h* represents no sound at all. Examples: *histoire* [istwɑr] (EES-TWAHR); *honnête* [ɔnɛt] (AW-NET) or (OH-NET). Between two vowels, however, *h* indicates that the vowels form separate syllables rather than a diphthong. Example: *envahir* [ɑ̃vair] (three syllables, the nasalized "ah," followed by "vah," and completed with "eer").

j   The French *j* is pronounced like the English *z* in *azure* [ʒ], or the same as the French soft *g*. Examples: *jardin* [ʒɑrdɛ̃]; *Lejeune* [ləʒœn].

l   The letter *l* can be pronounced like the English *l*, although the French pronounce it with the tongue flat and not raised at the back. Examples: *lache* [lɑʃ] (LAHSH); *ville* [vil] (VEEL) (one syllable). (See also the earlier discussion of the final *l* [l̥].)

ph   This combination is the same as *f*. Example: *philosophie* [filɔzɔfi] (FEE-LAW-ZAW-FEE) or (FEE-LOH-ZOH-FEE).

q   The French *q* is pronounced like the English *k*. It is normally followed by *u*, which is always mute. Examples: *quatre* [kɑtr̥] (KAHT-R(UH)); *cinq* [sɛ̃k].

r   The letter *r* is pronounced by most speakers as a guttural sound, with tightening and vibration in the region of the uvula. Examples: *rose* [roz] (ROSE); *terre* [tɛr] (TEHR). (See also the earlier discussion of the final *r* [r̥].)

s   An *s* between vowels is pronounced like the English *z* in *crazy* [z]. Examples: *désir* [dezir]

(DAY-ZEER); *raison* [rɛzɔ̃]; *Thérèse* [terɛz] (TAY-REZ). A single *s* in other positions and double *s* are always like the English *s* in *sea* [s]. Examples: *Seine* [sɛn] (SEN); *message* [mɛsaʒ] (MEH-SAZH).

sc   Before *e*, *i*, and *y*, the combination *sc* is soft, as in *science*. Example: *descendre* [desɑ̃dr̥]. Elsewhere, it is pronounced as [s] plus [k]. Example: *escorte* [ɛskɔrt] (ES-KAWRT) or (ES-KORT).

x   The letter *x* is usually like the English *x* in *extra*. Example: *expliquer* [ɛksplike] (EX-PLEE-KAY). An initial *ex* before a vowel becomes [gz]. Example: *exercise* [ɛgzɛrsis] (EGGZ-AIR-SEES).

Consonants written at the ends of French words are often not sounded; examples are *trop* [tro] (TROH), *part* [pɑr] (PAR), *voix* [vwa] (VWAH), and *allez* [ale] (AH-LAY). An exception is *l*, as in *national* [nasjɔnal] (NAY-SYAW-NAHL) or (NAH-SYOH-NAHL). Often *c*, *f*, and *r* are sounded at the ends of words, as in *chic* [ʃik] (SHEEK), *chef* [ʃɛf] (SHEF), and *cher* [ʃɛr] (SHAIR). When a final *r* is preceded by *e*, the *r* is usually silent and the vowel is like *e* in *they* [e]. Example: *papier* [pɑpje] (PAH-PYAY).

All the consonant sounds are pronounced at the ends of the words when they are followed by mute *e*. Examples: *place* [plɑs] (PLAHS); *garage* [gɑrɑʒ] (GAH-RAZH); *rive gauche* [riv goʃ] (REEVE-GOASH). This includes *m* and *n*, which before a final mute *e* have their regular values and do not indicate that the preceding vowel is nasal. Examples: *aime* [ɛm] (EM); *pleine* [plɛn] (PLEN). Contrast these with *faim* [fɛ̃] (*f* plus nasalized *eh*) and *plein* [plɛ̃] (*pl* plus nasalized *eh*).

The addition of *s* (often the plural sign) after a consonant with or without a mute *e* has no effect on pronunciation. Thus *places* is the same as *place*, *parts* is the same as *part*, and *temps* is the same as *temp*. Likewise, the addition of *nt* (a plural sign in verbs) to a word ending in a mute *e* does not change anything—*chantent* and *chante* are both pronounced [ʃɑ̃t] (*sh*, as in *shoe*, plus the nasalized *ah*, plus a final *t*).

A liaison, or a linking, occurs in spoken French when the ordinarily silent consonant at the end of a word is sounded before a word beginning with a vowel sound. In liaison, *d* is pronounced [t], *g* is pronounced [k], *s* and *x* are pronounced [z], and nasalized *n* is sometimes denasalized. Examples: *grand amour* [grãtɑmur]; *sang impur* [sãkɛ̃pyːr]; *les autres* [lɛzotr̥] (LEH-ZOH-TR(UH)) or (LAY-ZOH-TR(UH)); *deux hommes* [døzɔm]; *mon ami* [mɔnəmi] (MOH-NAH-MEE).

German Pronunciation

The English spelling system contains a great many excess letters. French resembles English in this respect, but German, like Spanish and Italian, is economical in its spelling system, with every letter (or combination of letters) usually representing one sound.

German is actually easier to pronounce than it first appears to be. Most long German words are simply combinations of stem words with prefixes and suffixes. When you know how to identify these elements, you know where to break each word into syllables, and then pronunciation is quite simple. The formidable word *Arbeitsgemeinschaft*, for example, is easily divided into *Arbeits*, *gemein*, and *schaft* by anyone familiar with the way German words are put together. Also, all German nouns are capitalized, which should help you identify parts of speech, making for better interpretation of German titles and phrases.

Most German words are accented on the first syllable, such as *stehen* [ˈʃteːən] (SHTAY′-N), though not when they begin with a prefix, such as *verstehen* [fɛrˈʃteːən] (FER-SHTAY′-N). Words foreign to German are often accented on some syllable other than the first, to conform with their native pronunciation, for example, *Philosophie* [fiːloːzoːˈfi] (FEE-LOH-ZOH-FEE′). In compound words, the first component is usually accented, *Götterdämmerung* [ˈɡœtərˌdɛməruŋ].[3]

The German syllable *en*, when final in a word or word component, is deemphasized so that it is nearly lost. The IPA syllabic consonant [n̩] would be a fair way of representing this sound, but all standard German reference works transcribe it as [ən]. This practice will be

---

[3]This word is impossible to represent with wire-service phonetics because of the unique way Germans sound the syllable *er* at the ends of words or word components. This sound is transcribed [ər] in IPA, but rendering it UHR or UR would be misleading. In German speech, the "r" sound is almost completely lost, and the unaccented "uh" [ə] is nearly all that remains. The sound is quite different from the French [r̥], so the same wire-service phonetics cannot be used. Throughout this section, the German *er* will be transcribed as (UH(R)): *Götterdämmerung* is (GUH(R)-TUH(R)-DEM-MER-RUNG).

followed for IPA transcriptions, but in wire-service phonetic equivalents, N without a preceding vowel sound will be used. Example: *geben* [geːbən] (GAYB′-N).

At the end of a word and when otherwise unaccented (as, for example, when it appears in an unaccented prefix), the German letter *e* is pronounced as the schwa vowel—that is, as an unaccented "uh," the IPA symbol for which is [ə]. Examples: *sehe* [′zeːə] (ZAY′-UH); *gesehen* [gə′zeːən] (GUH-ZAY′-N).

German Vowels

German has four classes of vowel sounds: seven short vowels, seven long vowels, three diphthongs, and one special vowel that occurs only unaccented. Like the French vowels, they will be arranged according to sound rather than by their German spelling.

German short vowels   The seven German short vowels are summarized in Table 15.4.

Note that the German spelling generally indicates when an accented vowel is short by having two consonants or a double consonant after it.

German long vowels   Table 15.5 summarizes the seven German long vowels.

Note that German spelling has four ways of showing that an accented vowel is long. (1) The vowel is at the end of a word: *ja, je, schi.* (2) The vowel is followed by only one consonant: *Grab, haben, wen.* (3) The vowel is followed by an unpronounced *h*: *Kahn, gehen, ihn.* (4) The vowel is written double: *Staat, See, Boot.* (The long *i* is never doubled; *ie* is used as the lengthening sign, as in *Lieder.*) There are relatively few words in which long vowels are not indicated in one of these ways. Two exceptions are *Papst* [pɑːst] (PAHPST) and *Mond* [moːnt] (MOANT).

The double dot over *ä, ö,* and *ü* is called an umlaut. The old-fashioned spellings for these umlaut vowels are *ae, oe,* and *ue,* which still survive in a few names: *Goebbels, Goethe, Huebner.* You will also encounter these spellings when a type font (as, for example, on wire-service machines) has no special umlaut letters. Typewriters can simulate the umlaut with quotation marks, but wire-service machines cannot return, as a typewriter carriage can, to add the marks after the letter has been transmitted.

Table 15.4 German Short Vowels

IPA Symbol	Description of Sound	German Spelling	Examples
[a]	Like English *a* in *father* but much shorter	*a*	*Gast* [gast] (GAHST) *fallen* ['falən] (FAHL'N)
[ɛ]	Like English *e* in *bet*	*e*	*Bett* [bɛt] (BET) *essen* [ɛsən] (ESS'N)
	The spelling *ä* is used for this sound when the basic form is *a*	*ä*	*Gäste* [gɛstə] (GUEST'-UH) *fällt* [fɛlt] (FELT)
[ɪ]	Like English *i* in *hit*	*i*	*blind* [blɪnt] (BLIHNT) *Winter* ['vɪntər] (VIHN'-TUH(R))
[ɔ]	Like English *au* in *caught* but much shorter	*o*	*Kopf* [kɔpf] (KAWPF) *offen* ['ɔfən] (AWF'-N)
[œ]	Pronounced with the tongue as for "eh" [ɛ] but with the lips rounded as for "aw" [ɔ]	*ö*	*Köpfe* ['kœpfə] *öffnen* ['œfnən]
[ʊ]	Like English *u* in *put*	*u*	*Busch* [bʊʃ] (BUSH) *Mutter* ['mʊtər] (MUH'-TUH(R))
[y]	Pronounced with the tongue as for "ih" [ɪ] but with the lips rounded as for "oo" [u]	*ü*	*Büsche* ['byʃə] *Mütter* ['mytər]

German diphthongs   The German diphthongs are summarized in Table 15.6.

German Consonants

b	As in English, but see the discussion below on voiced and voiceless consonants.
c	Like English *k*. Rare in native German words.

Table 15.5   German Long Vowels

IPA Symbol	Description of Sound	German Spelling	Examples
[ɑ]	Like English *a* in *father*	*a* *ah* *aa*	*ja* [jɑː] (YAH) *Grab* [grɑːp] (GRAHP) *Kahn* [kɑːn] (KAHN) *Staat* [ʃtɑːt] (SHTAHT)
[e]	Much like English *e* in *they* but without the final glide When spelled *ä* or *äh*, the pronunciation usually is still "ay" [e]	*e* *eh* *ee* *ä* *äh*	*geben* [geːbən] (GAYB´-N) *gehen* [geːən] (GAY´-N) *See* [zeː] (ZAY) *Gräber* [ˈgreːbər] (GRAY´BUH(R)) *Kähne* [ˈkeːnə] (KAY´-NUH)
[i]	Much like English *i* in *machine*	*i* *ih* *ie*	*Schi* [ʃiː] (SHE) *Lid* [liːt] (LEET) *Ihn* [iːn] (EEN) *Lieder* [ˈliːdər] (LEE´-DUH(R))
[o]	Like English *ow* in *blow* but without the final glide	*o* *oh* *oo*	*so* [zoː] (ZO) *oben* [ˈoːbən] (OB´-N) *Lohn* [loːn] (LOAN) *Boot* [boːt] (BOAT)
[ø]	Pronounced with the tongue as for "ay" [e] but with the lips rounded as for "oh" [o]	*ö* *öh*	*Römer* [ˈrøːmər] *Löhne* [ˈløːnə]
[u]	Much like English *u* in *rule*	*u*	*du* [duː] (DOO) *Mut* [muːt] (MOOT)
[y]	Pronounced with the tongue as for "ee" [i] but lips rounded as for "oo" [u]	*ü* *üh*	*Brüder* [bryːdər] *rühmen* [ˈryːmən]

ch

In native German words, *ch* stands for two slightly different sounds. (1) After back vowels (*a, o, u,* or *au*), it is a sound like the *ch* in the Scottish word *loch*, in which the breath stream is forced through a narrow opening between the back of the tongue and the soft

Table 15.6 German Diphthongs

IPA Symbol	Description of Sound	German Spelling	Examples
[aɪ]	Like English *ai* in *aisle*	*ei*	*Leid* [laɪt] (LIGHT)
			Heine ['haɪnə] (HIGH'-NUH)
		ai	*Kaiser* ['kaɪzər] (KY'-ZUH(R))
		ey	*Meyer* ['maɪər] (MY'-UH(R))
		ay	*Bayern* ['baɪərn] (BUY'-URN)
[aʊ]	Like English *ou* in *house*	*au*	*Haus* [haʊs] (HOUSE)
			Glauben ['glaʊbən] (GLOUB'-N)
[ɔɪ]	Like English *oi* in *oil*	*eu*	*Leute* ['lɔɪtə] (LOY'-TUH)
		äu	*Häuser* ['hɔɪzər] (HOU'-ZUH(R))

palate. The IPA symbol for this sound is [x], and wire services transcribe it as either CH or KH. Examples: *Bach* [bɑx] (BAHKH); *Buch* [buːx] (BOOKH). (2) After front sounds, including the front vowels [i], [ɪ], [ɛ], and so on, the sound is produced by forcing the breath stream through a narrow channel between the front of the tongue and the hard palate. Many Americans make this same sound (although considerably weaker) in pronouncing the *h* of such words as *hue*, *huge*, and *human*. The IPA symbol for this sound is [ç], but the symbol [x] has been accepted by many authorities (including Kenyon and Knott) to represent both sounds, and it will be used here. Examples: *ich* [ix] (IHKH); *München* ['mynxən]; *Bräuche* ['brɔɪxə] (BROY'-KHUH); *Bäche* ['bɛxə] (BEKH'-UH). In a few foreign words, *ch* stands for [k]: *Charakter* [kə'rɑktər] (KUH-RAHKT'-TUH(R)).

chs Like English *ks*. Example: *wachsen* ['vɑksən'] (VAHKS'-N).

ck As in English. Example: *Stück* [ʃtyk].

d As in English, but see the discussion below on voiced and voiceless consonants.

dt	Like English *t*. Example: *Stadt* [ʃtɑt] (SHTAHT).
f	As in English. Example: *fahl* [fɑːl] (FAHL).
g	As in English except as noted below and when it appears in a final *ig*, where it becomes the "ch" [x] sound. Example: *hungrig* [ˈhʊŋrɪx] (HOONG´-RIHKH).
gn	Both letters are sounded, as in the English name *Agnes*. Example: *Gnade* [ˈgnɑːdə] (GNAH´-DUH).
h	As in English, when it occurs initially in a word or at the beginning of an element in a compounded word. Examples: *Haus* [haʊs] (HOUSE); *Rathaus* [ˈrɑɪt,haʊs] (RAHT´-HOUSE). As mentioned above, an unpronounced *h* is used as a mark of vowel length.
j	Like English *y* in *youth*. Example: *jung* [jʊŋ] (YOONG).
k	As in English.
kn	Both letters are sounded, as in *acknowledge*. Example: *Knabe* [ˈknɑːbə] (KNAH´-BUH).
l	Can be pronounced like the English *l*, although it is spoken with the tongue flatter in the mouth.
m	As in English.
n	As in English.
ng	Always like the English *ng* [ŋ] in *singer* and never like the English *ng* plus *g* [ŋg] in *finger*. Examples: *singen* [ˈziŋən] (ZING´-N); *Hunger* [ˈhuŋər] (HOONG´-UH(R)).
p	As in English.
q	Occurs only in the combination *qu*, pronounced [kv]. Example: *Quelle* [ˈkvɛlə] (KVEL´-LUH).
r	Pronounced with a slight guttural trill at the back of the tongue (although some northern and western dialects use the front of the tongue).

s	Like English *z*. Examples: *so* [zoː] (ZO); *Rose* [ˈroːzə] (ROH′-ZUH). See also the discussion below on voiced and voiceless consonants.
ss	As in English.
sch	Like English *sh* in *shoe*. Example: *schon* [ʃon] (SHOWN).
sp	At the beginning of a word or as part of a compound, *sp* is pronounced like English *sh* plus *p*. Examples: *springen* [ˈʃprɪŋən] (SHPRING′-N); *Zugspitze* [tsuːkʃpɪtsə] (TSOOK′-SHPITZ-UH).[4] Otherwise, it is pronounced like English *s* plus *p*. Example: *Wespe* [ˈvɛspə] (VES′-PUH).
st	At the beginning of a word or as part of a compound, *st* is pronounced like *sh* plus *t*: *Stück* [ʃtyk]; *Bleistift* [ˈblaɪʃtɪft] (BLY′-SHTIFT). Otherwise it is pronounced like English *st*. Example: *Westen* [ˈvɛstən] (VEST′N).
t	As in English.
th	Always like *t*. Example: *Thomas* [ˈtoːmɑs] (TOE′MAHS).
tz	Like *tz* in *Schlitz*.
v	In German words, *v* is pronounced like English *f*. Example: *vier* [fɪr] (FEAR). In foreign words, it is pronounced like the English *v*. Example: *November* [noːˈvɛmbər] (NO-VEM′-BER). See, however, the discussion below.
w	Always like the English *v*. Example: *Wein* [vaɪn] (VINE).
x	As in English.
z	Always like the English *ts*. Example: *zu* [tsu] (TSOO).

German has five pairs of voiced-voiceless consonants—that is, consonants produced in the same way except that the first of each pair is pronounced with some vibration of the vocal folds, whereas

[4]Some northern dialects pronounce *sp* and *st* in these positions as [sp] and [st], as in English.

the second of each pair is produced with the vocal folds open and not vibrating. These pairs are *b-p*, *d-t*, *g-k*, *v-f*, and *z-s*. Voiced *b*, *d*, *g*, *v*, or *z* occurs chiefly before vowels. When one of these vowels stands at the end of a word or part of a compound or before *s* or *t*, it is automatically replaced by the corresponding voiceless sound, although the spelling is not changed. This means that in these positions—finally or before *s* or *t*—the letters *b*, *d*, *g*, *v*, and *s* stand for the sounds [p], [t], [k], [f], and [s], respectively. Note the following examples.

Gräber ['greːbər] (GRAY'-BUH(R))	versus	*das Grab* [graːp] (GRAHP)
Räder ['reːdər] (RAY'-DUH(R))	versus	*das Rad* [raːt] (RAHT)
tragen ['traːgən] (TRAHG'-N)	versus	*du trägst* [treːkst] (TRAYKST)
Motive [moːˈtiːvə] (MO-TEE'-VUH)	versus	*das Motiv* [moːˈtiːf] (MO-TEEF')
lesen ['leːzən] (LAYZ'-N)	versus	*er las* [laːs] (LAHS)

Other Languages

News releases often feature names of people and places and other words in the languages of Asian, Middle Eastern, African, and Eastern European nations. As an announcer, you must be prepared to read names and other words from China, Japan, the USSR, and Israel, among others, with acceptable pronunciation and intonation. However, no extensive rules for pronouncing these languages are given here. The Chinese, Japanese, Hindustani, Arabic, Hebrew, and Russian languages use alphabets unfamiliar to most of us. When words from those languages appear in newspapers or in broadcast copy, they have been transliterated into the Latin (Roman) alphabet in some phoneticized version of the foreign original. For example, the Russian name РИМСКИЙ-КОРСАКОВ is meaningless and unpronounceable to people not familiar with the Cyrillic alphabet, but when it is transliterated into *Rimsky-Korsakov*, no announcer needs to rely on Russian rules to pronounce it correctly. It would not be necessary to learn the rules of French or Spanish pronunciation if *Bizet* were transcribed as "Bee-zay" or if *hombre* were spelled in English-speaking countries as "ohm'-bray." In transliterating words from non-Latin alphabets, we do this kind of phoneticizing. Because we do not phonetically transliterate Western European words, their spelling can confuse us if we are not familiar with the appropriate rules of pronunciation.

Broadcast announcers conventionalize the pronunciation of non-Western languages to a greater degree than those of Western Europe. During his career in politics, Nikita Khrushchev was called KROOS'-CHAWF by American announcers. But the correct Russian pronunciation requires a very different initial sound, one not possible to indicate by wire-service phonetics and not easily reproduced by most Americans. The initial sound of this name is represented by [x] in the International Phonetic Alphabet and is sounded as the final sound in the German word *ach* or Scottish *loch*. In the IPA, the name Khrushchev is represented as [xruʃ'tʃɔf]. When Mikhail Gorbachev became the leader of the Soviet Union, broadcast announcers began saying his last name as GAWR'-BUH-CHAWF, even though correct pronunciation places stress on the last syllable, GAWR-BUH-CHAWF'. Americans apparently have been conditioned to expect nearly correct pronunciation of Western European words, but to settle for far less authentic pronunciation of languages that do not use the Latin alphabet.

A few comments must be made about Chinese pronunciation. For many years, American announcers were about as casually inaccurate in the pronunciation of Chinese names and words as they were and are about the pronunciation of Japanese or Russian words. Since 1979, when the People's Republic of China adopted the Pinyin system of phonetic transcription, however, announcers have made serious efforts to pronounce Chinese words with some degree of authenticity. With the adoption of the Pinyin system, *Peking* became *Beijing*, *Szechwan* became *Sichuan*, and *Sinkiang* became *Xinjiang*. Former Chinese leader Mao Tse-Tung became *Mao Zedong*, while Hua Kuo-feng became *Hua Guofeng*. Most symbols used in the Pinyin system are easily mastered: *p*, *b*, *t*, *d*, *k g*, and *f*, for example, are pronounced as in English. There are, at the same time, some surprises: *q* represents the *ch* in *church*, and *x* represents the *sh* in *shoe*. Sounds that may cause trouble have been transcribed into wire-service phonetics and IPA symbols in Table 15.7.

The complete Chinese Phonetic Alphabet (CPA) is given in Table 15.8. You can say the Chinese alphabet by pronouncing the initial sounds, as listed in the first column, with the vowel given in parentheses after each one.

**Table 15.7   Transcription of Chinese Using the
Pinyin System**

Pinyin Symbol	Wire-Service Symbol	IPA Symbol
h	H (highly aspirated as in German *ach*)	[x]
q	CH (as in *chew*)	[tʃ]
x	SH (as in *she*)	[ʃ]
zh	J (as in *jump*)	[dʒ]
z	DS (as in *reads*)	[dz]
c	TS (as in *hats*)	[ts]
o	AW (as in *saw*)	[ɔ]
y	Y (as in *yet*)	[j]

Memorization of the Pinyin symbols would not be very helpful because they differ from wire-service phonetic symbols. It might, therefore, be more practical to use the table showing Pinyin symbols as the basis for your own transliteration into wire-service phonetics, as in the following examples. Note that each syllable gets equal stress.

Deng Xiaoping	(DUNG SHAU-PING)
Mao Zedong	(MAO DSUH-DUNG)
Hua Guofeng	(HWAH GWA-FUNG)
Guangdong	(GWUN-DUNG)
Beijing	(BAY-JING)
Qinghai	(TCHING-HY)
Zhejiang	(JAY-JUNG)

It also should be noted that some radio and television stations continue to use the older system of transliteration—the Wade-Giles system—so you should ask station management about local preference before attempting to read copy with Chinese names and words.

Table 15.8 The Chinese Phonetic Alphabet (CPA)

	CPA	IPA	Key Words*
Initial Sounds	*b* (o)	[b̥]	*b*ay (devoiced)
	p (o)	[p‘]	*p*ay
	m (o)	[m]	*m*ay
	f (o)	[f]	*f*air
	d (e)	[d̥]	*d*ay (devoiced)
	t (e)	[t‘]	*t*ake
	n (e)	[n]	*n*ay
	l (e)	[l]	*l*ay
	g (e)	[g̊]	*g*ay (devoiced)
	k (e)	[k‘]	*k*ay
	h (e)	[x]	*h*ay
	j (i)	[dʒ]	*j*eep (palatal)
	q (i)	[tʃ]	*ch*eer (palatal)
	x (i)	[ʃ]	*sh*e (palatal)
	zh (i)	[dʒ]	ju*dg*e (retroflex, devoiced)
	ch (i)	[tʃ]	*ch*ur*ch* (retroflex)
	sh (i)	[ʃ]	*sh*irt (retroflex)
	r (i)	[ʒ]	lei*s*ure (retroflex)
	z (i)	[dz]	rea*ds* (devoiced)
	c (i)	[ts‘]	ha*ts*
	s (i)	[s]	*s*ay
	y (i)	[j]	*y*ea
	w (u)	[w]	*w*ay
Final Sounds	*a*	[a]	f*a*ther
	o	[ɔ]	s*aw* (approximately)
	e	[ʊ]	h*er* (British)
	i (after *z, c, s,* *zh, ch, sh, r*)	[z,z̩]	

*Devoiced means the vocal cords do not vibrate. *Palatal* means the front of the tongue touches the hard palate.
Retroflex means the tip of the tongue is slightly curled.

Table 15.8 (*Continued*)

	CPA	IPA	Key Words
Final Sounds (cont.)	*i* (elsewhere)	[i]	see
	u	[u]	r*u*de
	ü†	[y]	French t*u*, German f*ü*hlen (*i* with rounded lips)
	er	[ər]	*err* (American)
	ai	[ai]	*eye*
	ei	[ei]	*ei*ght
	ao	[ɑu]	n*ow*
	ou	[ou]	*oh*
	an	[an]	c*an* (more open)
	en	[ən]	t*ur*n (British)
	ang	[ɑŋ]	G*ang* (German)
	eng	[ʌŋ]	s*ung*
	ong	[ʊŋ]	L*ung*e (German)
	ia	[ia]	Malays*ia*
	ie	[iɛ]	*ye*s
	iao	[iɑu]	*yow*l
	iu	[iou]	*yo*ke
	ian	[iɛn]	*yen*
	in	[in]	*in*
	iang	[iɑŋ]	*young* (approximately)
	ing	[iŋ]	s*ing*
	iong	[iuŋ]	*jüng*er (German) (approx.)
	ua	[ua]	g*ua*no
	uo	[uɔ]	w*a*ll
	uai	[uai]	w*i*fe
	ui	[uei]	*way*
	uan	[uan]	*one* (approximately)
	un	[uɛn]	w*en*t (approximately)
	uang	[uɑŋ]	*oo* + *ahng*
	üe†	[yɛ]	*ü* + *eh*
	üan†	[yan]	*ü* + *an*
	ün†	[yn]	gr*ün* (German)

†After j, q, x, y, the two dots above *u* are omitted.

Practice: Pronouncing Spanish Words

Practice pronouncing the following Spanish words:

Toledo	Ramírez	Cabezón
Guernica	San Sebastián	*Danzas españolas*
Falange	Albéniz	*Pepita Jiménez*
Cuernavaca	Manuel de Falla	Oviedo
Segovia	Granados	picante
García	Sarasate y Navascuez	servicio

Practice: Pronouncing Italian Words

Practice pronouncing the following Italian names and phrases.

Arcangelo Corèlli	*Il barbiere de Siviglia*
Giovanni Pierluigi Palestrina	*La cenerentola*
	L'Italiana in Algeri
Ottorino Respighi	*Tosca*
Gioacchino Rossini	*Chi vuole innamorarsi*
Doménico Scarlatti	*Il matrimonio segreto*
Giuseppe Tartini	*Le nozze di Figaro*
Beniamino Gigli	*La finta giardiniera*
Dusolina Giannini	*Cosi fan tutte*
Franco Ghione	*La gioconda*
Giàcomo Puccini	

Practice: Pronouncing French Words

Practice pronouncing the following French names and phrases.

Georges Bizet	Prosper Mérimée
Gabriel Fauré	Marcel Proust

Camille Saint-Saëns	*L'enfant prodigue*
Vincent d'Indy	*Danseuses del Delphes*
Maurice Chevalier	*Jardins sous la pluie*
Benoit Coquelin	*La demoiselle élue*
Rachel	*Le chant des oiseaux*
Guy de Maupassant	*Si mes vers avaient des ailes*

Practice: Pronouncing German Words

Practice pronouncing the following German names and words.

Wolfgang Amadeus[5] Mozart	Lebensgefährlich
Franz Neubauer	*Dass sie hier gewesen!*
Die schöne Müllerin	*Die Götterdämme- rung*
Dietrich Buxtehude	*O fröhliche Stunden*
Schmücke dich, o liebe Seele	*Ein' feste Burg*
Max Bruch	*Der fliegende Holländer*
Frühling übers Jahr	Die verklärte Nacht

Practice: Pronouncing Foreign Words

The following practice material consists of commercials featuring foreign words and names. Additional practice material for pronouncing foreign languages is found at the end of Chapter 11.

CLIENT: Cafe L'Europa

LENGTH: 60 seconds

ANNCR: When you think of good food, you probably think
          of Paris, Copenhagen, or Rome. But, now, right

[5]Amadeus, being a Latin name, does not follow German rules of pronunciation.

here in the center of America, you can find the
best of European and Asian cuisine at a price
that will surprise you. The Cafe L'Europa, on
Highway 40 at White's Road, is under the
supervision of Chef Aristide Framboise. Chef
Framboise earned his Cordon Bleu at the famous
Ecole des Quatre Gourmandes in Cannes, France.
The chef's staff of European and Asian cooks have
been personally trained for the exacting work of
pleasing you, regardless of your culinary
preferences. Whether you like poulet sauté
marseillais or gedämpfte Brust, spaghetti all'
amatricianna or calamares en su tinta, you'll
thrill to your candlelit dinner at Cafe L'Europa.
Dial 777-3434, and ask our maitre d' for a
reservation soon. That's 777-3434, the Cafe
L'Europa, at White's Road on Highway 40.

Pronunciation guide:

Aristide Framboise (AR-EES-TEED' FRAM-BWAH')

Ecole des Quatre Gourmandes (AY-KOHL' DAY KAT'
  GOOR-MAHND')

poulet sauté marseillais (POO-LAY' SO-TAY'
  MAHR-SAY-AY')

gedämpfte Brust (GEH-DEMFT'-UH BRUST)

spaghetti all'amatricianna (SPAH-GET'-EE AL
  AHM-AH-TREECH-YAH'-NAH)

calamares en su tinta (KAHL–AH–MAHR′–EES EN SU
  TEEN′–TAH)
maitre d' (MET′–RUH DEE)

CLIENT: Cafe L'Europa
LENGTH: 60 seconds

ANNCR: How long since you've enjoyed a special evening
           of your own creation? Not a birthday. Not an
           anniversary. Not a holiday. But an evening you've
           set aside to tell that special someone, "I
           appreciate you!" The Cafe L'Europa is the perfect
           restaurant for this and all other very special
           celebrations. The Cafe L'Europa features
           delicacies from around the world. Sukiyaki from
           Japan. Nasi goereng from Indonesia. European
           cuisine includes pfannekoeken from Holland,
           chochifrito from Spain, and ratatouille from
           France. Or, perhaps you'd prefer an English
           rarebit or a German sauerbraten. Whatever your
           taste, you're sure to enjoy candlelit dining at
           Cafe L'Europa. Make a date now, and call our
           maitre d' for a dinner reservation. Dial 777–
           3434, and prepare yourself for an unforgettable
           evening of dining at the Cafe L'Europa. Your
           significant other will appreciate your
           thoughtfulness.

<u>Pronunciation</u> <u>guide</u>:

sukiyaki (SKEE-AHK'-EE)

pfannekoeken (PFAHN'-KUK-UN)

ratatouille (RAT-UH-TOO'-EE)

nasi goereng (NAZ'-EE GEHR'-ING)

cochifrito (COACH-EE-FREE'-TOE)

sauerbraten (SOUR'-BRAHT-UN)

CLIENT: Kuyumjian's Rug Bazaar

LENGTH: 60 seconds

ANNCR: Kuyumjian's has just received a large shipment of
          new and used Oriental rugs which must be sold at
          once. These rugs are being sold to settle tax
          liens against a major import firm. So, their
          misfortune is your gain. Here is your chance to
          own a genuine Oriental rug at a fraction of its
          regular cost. Gulistan, Kerman, Sarouk, Shiraz,
          and Baktiary rugs at unheard-of prices. Time does
          not permit a complete listing, but here are a few
          specials: a five-by-seven Faridombeh in antique
          gold, only $288. A three-by-five Feraghan in
          ivory and pistachio, just $375. An extra-large,
          nine-by-fourteen virgin wool Ispahan in ivory,
          $1,000. Small Yezd, Oushak, and Belouj scatter
          rugs at less than $100. All sizes are
          approximate, and quantities of each style are

limited. Visit Kuyumjians's this week, and become
the proud owner of an original, hand-woven,
virgin wool Oriental rug. Kuyumjian's Rug Bazaar,
on the downtown mall opposite the State Theater.

Pronunciation guide:
Kuyumjian's (KY-OOM'-JUNZ)
Gulistan (GOO'-LIS-TAHN)
Kerman (KEHR'-MAHN)
Sarouk (SAH-ROUK')
Shiraz (SHEE'-RAHZ)
Baktiary (BAHK-TEE-AR'-EE)
Faridombeh (FAHR-EE-DOME'-BAY)
Feraghan (FEHR-AH-GAHN')
Ispahan (EES'-PAH-HAHN)
Yezd (YEZD)
Oushak (OO'-SHAHK)
Belouj (BELL-OODG')

CLIENT: Hough's House of Fabrics
LENGTH: 60 seconds

ANNCR: Hough's House of Fabrics announces its annual
spring fashion yardage sale. Beginning this
Thursday and running for one full week, you can
save dollars while you prepare for a colorful
spring and summer. Synthetic fabrics that never
need ironing, in a variety of textures and

patterns—appliqué puff, crêpe de chine, etched
peau di luna—your choice, only $2.49 a yard. Or
look for summertime sheers—batiste, voile, or
crushed crepe—at just $1.09 a yard. Hough's has
a complete collection of dazzling Hawaiian
prints, too. Wahini poplin, Kahului broadcloth,
or Niihau jacquard weave—with prices ranging ·
from 99¢ to $2.89 a yard. And, yes, Hough's has
patterns, notions, and everything else you need
to create your wardrobe for the coming season.
So, why don't you save money and get started on
your own versatile and original spring and summer
wardrobe right now? Remember, Hough's House of
Fabrics, in the Northfield Shopping Center, just
out of town on Marsh Road. That's Hough's—on
Marsh Road. Sale ends a week from Thursday.

Pronunciation guide:
Hough's (HUFFS)
appliqué puff (AP-LIH-KAY' PUFF)
crêpe de chine (KREP DUH-SHEEN')
peau di luna (PO DEE LUN-UH)
batiste (BA-TEEST')
voile (VOIL)
crepe (KRAYP)
Wahini (WAH-HEE'-NEE)
Kahului (KAH-HOO-LOO'-EE)
Niihau jacquard (NEE-EE-HOW' JUH-KARD')

Appendix A
Commercials
and PSAs

This appendix begins with a series of fact sheets for radio commercials. Fact sheets contain only the essentials about a particular product, service, or special occasion, such as a sale. They are sometimes sent to stations by advertising agencies, but most often are prepared by time sellers working for a station. Fact sheets can be used in two ways: (1) as the basis of an ad-lib delivery or (2) as the source of the information needed to write and perform scripts. You might want to produce some of these fact sheets as scripts, mixing music, sound effects, and voice to make a complete commercial package.

This appendix also provides scripts for radio commercials and public-service announcements. Some call for music or sound effects; it would be good practice to work with these audio elements whenever you can.

Only a few television commercial scripts are provided here. Nearly all television commercial productions require elaborate sets, complex graphics, or animation, none of which is available to most students. You may, however, adapt some of the radio scripts and public-service announcements for straight on-camera presentation.

The pronunciation of many uncommon or difficult words is given within the fact sheets and many scripts in wire-service phonetics and in the symbols of the International Phonetic Alphabet.

Radio Commercials

FACT SHEET 1

AGENCY: Kaplan Communications

CLIENT: The Home Improvement Center

OCCASION: Pre-inventory clearance of carpets and rugs

MERCHANDISE: Roll stock--Hi-Lo Long Wear Nylon--$4.95/yard

               Herculon (HER'-KYOO-LAHN) ['hɝkjulɑn] Rubberback, commercial
               grade--$4.49/yard

Summerdale by Barwick, polyester--$6.00/yard

Area rug sale--

Sarouk (SAH-REWK') [sɑ'ruk]

Kirman (KIHR'-MAHN) ['kɪrmɑn]

Bachtiar (BAHK-TEE-AHR') [bɑkti'ɑr]

Heriz (HAIR-EEZ') [hɛr'iz]

from $69.95 to $399.95

SALE DATES: Saturday and Sunday, Mar. 10-11, 9:00-9:00

FACT SHEET 2

AGENCY: Mills Advertising

CLIENT: S & F Drive-In

MERCHANDISE: Hot pastrami, chiliburgers, fishy-burgers, corny-dogs,
fries, onion rings, shakes

NOTHING OVER 88¢

ADDRESS: Just outside of town on Highway 44

NOTE: CLIENT WANTS A HUMOROUS COMMERCIAL.

FACT SHEET 3

CLIENT: Cafe International

OCCASION: Weekend features

MERCHANDISE: From Italy, stufato di manzo alla Genovese (STEW-FAH'-TOE
DEE MAHN'-TSOH AH'-LAH JEN-OH-VAY'-SAY)
[stu'fɑt,o di 'mɑnts,o 'ɑl,ɑ,dʒɛno've,se]

From Germany, gewürztes Rindfleisch (GEH-VIRTS'-ESS
RIHND'-FLYSCH) [ge'vɪrts,ɛs 'rɪnd,flaɪʃ]

From Mexico, carne in salza negra (KAR'-NAY EEN SAHL'-SAH
NAY'-GRAH) ['kɑr,ne in 'sɑlsə 'ne,grə]

From France, ratatouille (RAT-UH-TOO'-EE) [rætə'tu,i]

Wines of the week: Cabernet Sauvignon 1949 (KAB'-AIR-NAY
SO-VEEN-YAWN') ['kæbɛrne sovin'jɔn]

Gewürztraminer (GAY-VIRTS'-TRAH-MEEN'-ER) [geˈvɪrts traˈminɚ]

DATES: This Friday and Saturday evenings, Sunday noon to
            11:00 P.M.

ADDRESS: 118 Central, between Jefferson and Adams

NOTE: CLIENT EXPECTS YOU TO AWAKEN CURIOSITY ABOUT THESE
            DISHES. CORRECT PRONUNCIATION A MUST!

FACT SHEET 4

AGENCY: John Christian Services, Inc.

CLIENT: Allison's Pet Center

OCCASION: Christmas Sale

MERCHANDISE: Guppies and goldfish, 39¢ each

               Aquariums, 10-gal., with filter, $19.95

               White mice, $1.00 a pair

               Toucans, $95.00 each

DATES: Dec. 15th 'til Christmas Eve

ADDRESS: Corner Fulton and North Streets, Petaluma

NOTE: CLIENT WANTS HUMOROUS COMMERCIAL.

FACT SHEET 5

AGENCY: Paul C. Smith Communications, Inc.

CLIENT: Harmony Music

OCCASION: Semi-annual clearance sale, June 10-30

MERCHANDISE: Seventy-five new and reconditioned pianos to choose from.
               High trade-ins. 35% to 50% off.

               All world-famous piano and organ makes--Hammond, Kawai
               (KUH-WY') [kəˈwaɪ], Farfisa (FAR-FEE'-SUH) [fɑrˈfisə], Ibach
               (EE'-BACH) [ˈibɑx], Steinway, Chickering, and Sheidmeyer
               (SCHYD'-MY-ER) [ˈʃaɪd,maɪɚ].

ADDRESS: Cherry Hill Shopping Center

CREATION AND	
PRODUCTION:	Chuck Blore & Don Richman, Inc.
CLIENT:	AT&T
LENGTH:	60 seconds

CATHIANNE: (ON PHONE) Hello.

DANNY: Uh, hi. You probably still remember me, Edward introduced us at the seminar . . .

CATHIANNE: Oh, the guy with the nice beard.

DANNY: I don't know whether it's nice . . .

CATHIANNE: It's a gorgeous beard.

DANNY: Well, thank you, uh, listen, I'm gonna, uh, be in the city next Tuesday and I was, y'know, wondering if we could sorta, y'know, get together for lunch?

CATHIANNE: How 'bout dinner?

DANNY: Dinner? Dinner! Dinner's a better idea. You could pick your favorite restaurant and . . .

CATHIANNE: How 'bout my place? I'm my favorite cook.

DANNY: Uh, your place. Right. Sure. That's great to me.

CATHIANNE: Me too. It'll be fun.

DANNY: Yeah . . . listen, I'll bring the wine.

CATHIANNE: Perfect. I'll drink it.

BOTH: (LAUGH)

DANNY: Well, OK, then, I guess it's a date. I'll see you Tuesday.

CATHIANNE: Tuesday. Great.

DANNY: Actually, I just, uh, I called to see how you were and y'know, Tuesday sounds fine!

SOUND: PHONE HANGS UP

DANNY: (YELLING) Tuesday . . . AHHHH . . . she's gonna see me Tuesday. (FADE)

SUNG: REACH OUT, REACH OUT AND TOUCH SOMEONE

CREATION AND
PRODUCTION: Chuck Blore & Don Richman, Inc.

CLIENT: Hallmark Cards

LENGTH: 60 seconds

JOSH: My dad says we'll only be gone 4 to 5 weeks, tops.

NANCY: You're going to call me, aren't you?

JOSH: You know I'm gonna call you.

NANCY: I have a surprise for ya.

JOSH: Oh . . .

NANCY: Pick a hand

JOSH: Right hand

NANCY: Okay, see this?

JOSH: What is it?

NANCY: It's a charm. All you do is rub his stomach and you'll have luck for the rest of the day.

JOSH: Thanks, I have something for you also.

NANCY: You got me something?

JOSH: Here, it's a card.

NANCY: Ohhhh!

JOSH: It's a Hallmark card.

NANCY: (LAUGHS)

JOSH: You're gonna read it, aren't ya?

NANCY: Of course.

            Ohhh! I love you too. (LAUGHS)

JOSH: You don't have to get all choked up about it.

NANCY: Gimme a hug, man.

UNISON: (LAUGHING)

ANNCR: Sharing caring feelings, one-to-one, heart-to-heart. How
            could you give anything less than a Hallmark Card?
            Hallmark Cards. When you care enough.

AGENCY: Ketchum Advertising

CLIENT: The Potato Board

LENGTH: 60 seconds

ANNCR: The Potato Board wants to ask you a question: have you
            ever thought of the potato as a vegetable? The potato
            . . . as a vegetable? Most people only think of the
            potato as a starch—a filler food. They couldn't be more
            wrong, because The Potato Board reminds us that the
            potato is a vegetable that contains lots of good things
            like vitamins, minerals, complex carbohydrates, and, of
            course, fiber. But the potato is not full of calories.
            Only 100 in a medium-sized baked potato—and just 40 more
            with some butter. That 140 calories is less than a cup of
            green salad with two tablespoons of dressing. As a
            vegetable, the potato is the crown prince of versatility.
            And The Potato Board says you can serve potatoes in
            dozens of delicious ways, both as a side dish and an
            entree, for any meal of the day So next time you think

of the humble potato——please, please think of it first as a nutritious vegetable. Because that's exactly what the potato is.

AGENCY: Ketchum Advertising

CLIENT: Lindsay Olives

LENGTH: 60 seconds

MUSIC IN BACKGROUND.

YOUNG MAN: I was a homely looking olive when I was born. Not ugly,
(MID-20s)   but homeliness is next to nothingness if you're trying to be a handsome Lindsay Olive. So, I tried to change . . . to become one of the Beautiful Olives. I wore contact lenses. I had my pimiento styled by Mr. Joe. Nothing helped. So I turned to olive surgery. I mean, I was desperate to become a quality Lindsay Olive. Now, some surgeons wouldn't touch an olive that looked like me—— said it was too risky. But you can always find someone who'll take out a wrinkle here and inject an imitation of that great Lindsay Flavor there——if the price is right. What did I have to lose? So I tried it. The Lindsay People gave me a second look, and I <u>almost</u> got in. But, one inspector saw a scar, and I was through. I guess the Lindsay People were right after all . . . beauty is only skin deep, but ugliness goes all the way to the pit.

WOMAN ANNCR: An olive is just an olive, unless it's a Lindsay.

YOUNG MAN: Well, maybe another olive company will give me a break.
MUSIC OUT.

AGENCY: Millar Advertising, Inc.

CLIENT: Andre's International Bakery

LENGTH: 60 seconds

ANNCR: Hot fresh breakfast rolls, glistening with melting
             butter! Croissants (KRAH–SAHNTS′) [krɑ′sɑnts] and cafe au
             lait (KAHF′–AY–OH–LAY′) [′kæfe,o′le]. Raisin bran muffins to go
             with your poached eggs. Andre's has these delicacies, and
             they're waiting for you now. For afternoon tea, Andre
             suggests English biscuits, served with lemon marmalade.
             Or scones and plum jam. For after dinner desserts, what
             about baklava (BAHK–LAH–VAH′) [bɑklɑ′vɑ] the Persian
             delicacy made with dozens of layers of paper–thin pastry,
             honey, and chopped walnuts? Or, if your taste runs to
             chocolate, a German torte (TOR′–TUH) [′tɔrtə]? These and many
             other international delicacies are created daily by Andre
             and his staff. Made of pure and natural ingredients––
             grade A cream and butter, natural unrefined sugar, pure
             chocolate and cocoa, and pure spices. For mouth–watering
             pastries from around the world, it's Andre's
             International Bakery. We bring you the best from the
             gourmet capitals of the world. Visit Andre's today! In
             the Corte Madera Shopping Center. Andre's!

CREATION AND
PRODUCTION: Chuck Blore & Don Richman, Inc.

CLIENT: Campbell Soup

LENGTH: 30 seconds

DON: You're eating chunky chicken soup with a fork?

JOHN: Well, you've got to spear the chicken to get it into your mouth. Look at that. Look at the size of that. You gotta use a spoon for the noodles.

DON: You got some noodles on your fork.

JOHN: Yeah, but they slide through.

DON: Well, you use the spoon, you use the fork.

JOHN: That's right.

DON: Is chunky chicken a soup or a meal?

JOHN: I leave that up to the experts, but I personally . . .

DON: (OVER LAUGH) Why'd you say that?

JOHN: I know, but I mean, you know, I'm not a connoisseur on the food department but I would say it's a meal.

DON: But it's a soup.

JOHN: It's a meal within a soup can. Let's put it that way.

DON: Campbell's Chunky Chicken . . . it's the soup that eats like a meal.

CREATION AND
PRODUCTION: Chuck Blore & Don Richman, Inc.

CLIENT: Michigan Travel

LENGTH: 45 seconds

              (Note: This humorous commercial requires precise timing. Pauses must sound like natural hesitancies as the typed words catch up with the spoken words.)

SFX: TYPING BEHIND

BILL: Dear Mom . . .

              Skiing in Michigan is even cheaper than you . . .
              said it would be. I just hate the thought of you . . .
              missing all the fun, so I hit Mary Ruth . . .
              with the idea that you join us midweek. She said,

         "No, . . .

         time like the present to to tell her about Michigan's low

         mid . . .

         week rates." Mom, when you get here, you'll see your son

         going downhill . . .

         Your daughter-in-law going cross-country and you'll

         smell . . .

         the clean, pine-scented air. And the ski instructors . . .

         can spend more time with you midweek, which gives us more

         time to soak . . .

         up all the winter wonders of skiing Michigan with

         love . . .

         Your son, Hot Dog Billy.

SUNG: WINTER SPORTS OF ALL SORTS NEAR YOU

AGENCY: Grey Advertising, Inc.

CLIENT: Bank of America

LENGTH: 60 seconds

   SFX: OFFICE AMBIENCE. THEN UNDER THROUGHOUT

MAN #1: Hey partner of mine. Come over here and check out this
         ad.

MAN #2: Don't tell me. Another prospectus. For this you interrupt
         my calls?

MAN #1: Don't start, just read.

MAN #2: Alright. Alright. Says: Bank of America offers more of
         what small business needs to succeed. Hmmm . . . Can they
         do that?

MAN #1: They can do that. Keep reading--you impress me.

MAN #2:   Says Bank of America offers every banking service to help
            your small business make it in the marketplace. Gee . . .
            Can they do that?

MAN #1:   They can do that. (HE CONTINUES READING) Everything from
            business checking to unmatched worldwide capabilities.
            (HE STOPS READING) And what does our banker (your
            brother) do that's extra besides take us up skiing and
            tell corny jokes for two days?

MAN #2:   And look at this: Says Bank of America has over 1,000
            Business Bankers all over the state committed exclusively
            to small business? Can they do that?

MAN #1:   They can do that! In fact, I'm gonna call B of A right
            now. I bet someone will see us straight away.

MAN #2:   Can they do that?

MAN #1:   Let me put it this way . . . They can do that!

TAG: Bank on the leader. Bank of America.

AGENCY: Grey Advertising, Inc.

CLIENT: Bank of America

LENGTH: 60 seconds

SFX: FOOTSTEPS WALKING ACROSS HARD SURFACE

ANNCR: Bank of America would like to show you the way to get
            into a car. (FOOTSTEPS STOP) The key (KEYS JINGLE) is
            affordability. Bank of America has so many different auto
            loan options, one's bound to let you afford the car you
            want. Let's try (KEYS JINGLE AGAIN) this key. 100%
            financing—no down payment if you qualify. (KEY GOES INTO
            LOCK AND UNLOCKS CAR DOOR) Well that was good for
            openers. The next key gives you good rates on fixed rate

loans. (CAR DOOR OPENS) Now this key (KEYS JINGLE) gives you $\frac{1}{4}$% off for automatic payment from a B of A checking or savings account. While this key . . . (KEY GOES INTO IGNITION & CAR STARTS) . . . makes it easier to start with lower initial monthly (CAR DRIVES OFF UNDER) payments on variable rate loans. Or the "Almost-Like-A-Lease Loan." Now let's see if we can fuel the affordability with a variable rate loan that has fixed monthly payments and a rate cap.

ATTENDANT: Key please.

ANNCR: This should do. (BELL ON GAS PUMP RINGS AS TANK IS BEING FILLED) Come to California's lending leader. We'll show you the affordable way to get into a car.

SINGERS: Bank on the Leader.
Bank of America.

CLIENT: Houston Hearing Aid Center[1]

LENGTH: 60 seconds

ANNCR: Good evening, this is _____. Listen to me whisper this sentence. (WHISPERING) Do you have difficulty hearing someone speaking in a low voice? (NORMAL VOLUME) If you couldn't hear the previous statement because I was whispering, then you might need hearing assistance. Al Sawyers and associates at the Houston Hearing Aid Center are licensed hearing aid dispensers and offer a complete audiometric service. The Houston Hearing Aid Center on Starr Lane has been helping the hearing-impaired since 1947 with sales, service, and repairs on all brands of

[1]Courtesy Gerry Sher, Accounts Executive, KABL Radio.

hearing aids. Offering a senior citizens' discount, 30-day free trial, and credit terms, Al Sawyers of Houston Hearing Aid Center can assist you in creating a brighter outlook on life with the correct hearing aid. Call Al Sawyers at the Houston Hearing Aid Center, 555-3333, for an appointment, or for their free in-home service. This is _____ for the Houston Hearing Aid Center.

CLIENT: Eyes Have It[2]

LENGTH: 60 seconds

ANNCR: Where do you go when your eye doctor gives you a new prescription? If you live in the Willamette Valley, you should check out Eyes Have It in Eugene and Salem. As dispensing opticians for fifteen years, Eyes Have It has brought style to the necessity of wearing eyeglasses. You should look good if you wear glasses, and we'll see to it that you do. At Eyes Have It, you'll feel the family-owned warmth as you try on quality high-fashion eye wear. With our own lab and custom tinting, Eyes Have It is the complete dispensing optician for the entire family. Open weekdays from nine-thirty to five-thirty, and Saturday ten to one. Eyes Have It makes it easy for you who live away from Eugene or Salem. Look over the new look you'll get with sensational new high-fashion eye wear, from people who are homey, sensitive, pressureless, and fully knowledgeable to what's going on in the world of eye wear. We have Eyes Have It—you'll love the look!

[2]Courtesy Gerry Sher, Accounts Executive, KABL Radio.

CLIENT: Norwegian Designs[3]

LENGTH: 60 seconds

ANNCR: If I told you I have a hang-up for you, would that be
misleading? I'm _____ of Norwegian Designs. We're
the new and exclusive working wall system store in the
Financial District. At Norwegian Designs, our hang-ups
are leasable. It's probably the first time anyone has
offered your walls a new look with suspended furniture. I
could describe the file systems, or the hidden bar, or
many of the other features that space-saving wall units
offer your office, but I'd much prefer if you'd walk in
on me, and look at them in all their displayed beauty.
I'm at the corner of State and Michigan. Norwegian
Designs. Oh, I wasn't fooling about the leasing part—we
really do lease this office furniture. We carry major
systems of suspended furniture, with great varieties of
wood, tones, and colors. Your office may need just an
inexpensive facelift that's totally utilitarian. Stop by
and see us at Norwegian Designs. What a hang-up!

AGENCY: Ammirati & Puris, Inc.

CLIENT: Schweppes-Mixers

LENGTH: 60 seconds

SFX: WINTER SOUNDS (RAIN, SLUSH, ETC.)

BRITISH VO: Leave it to American ingenuity to take a rather bleak
time of year and transform it into a season full of
quaint but cheerful holiday traditions.

[3]Courtesy of Gerry Sher, Accounts Executive, KABL Radio.

SFX: HOLIDAY MUSIC

And leave it to British ingenuity to impart a rare
sparkle to these festivities--Schweppes.

For example, when feasting until immobilized on an
oversized bird, Schweppes Club Soda, bursting with
Schweppervescence, makes a lively dinner companion.

Your ritual of cramming as many people as possible into a
department store elevator, meanwhile, inspires a thirst
only Schweppes Ginger Ale with real Jamaican ginger can
quench.

And while transfixed to the telly watching a group of
massive, helmeted chaps smash into one another, what
could be more civilized than Schweppes Tonic Water with
essence of lime and Seville oranges?

And while many of your holiday traditions seem quite
curious to us, we certainly toast their spirit. And
suggest you do the same, with the purchase of Schweppes.
The Great British Bubbly.

AGENCY: Cunningham & Walsh, Inc.
CLIENT: Schieffelin & Co.
LENGTH: 60 seconds

ANNCR: Once again, Stiller and Meara for Blue Nun.
ANNE: Hello, I'm Frieda Beidermyer, your interior decorator.
JERRY: Oh, yes, come in. This is my apartment.
ANNE: Don't apologize.

JERRY: Huh?

ANNE: They didn't tell me you were color-blind. Plaid windows?

JERRY: I want decor that makes a statement about me, that exudes
         confidence, savoya fair. Where do we begin?

ANNE: The Last Chance Thrift Shop. Everything's gotta go.

JERRY: Everything?

ANNE: Everything.

JERRY: These are momentos my parents brought back from their
         honeymoon.

ANNE: They honeymooned in Tijuana?

JERRY: You noticed the terra-cotta donkey?

ANNE: I noticed. Out.

JERRY: So, where do we start?

ANNE: We start with a little Blue Nun.

JERRY: I want my apartment converted, not me.

ANNE: No, Blue Nun white wine. It'll lend you some style.

JERRY: I never tried Blue Nun.

ANNE: You have so much to learn, my naive nudnick. Blue Nun
         tastes terrific.

JERRY: I want good taste.

ANNE: That's why you can get Blue Nun by the glass or by the
         bottle at swank bars and restaurants.

JERRY: Gee, style, confidence, and taste. Will Blue Nun do all
         that for me?

ANNE: It's a bottle of wine, honey, not a miracle worker.

ANNCR: By the glass or by the bottle, there's a lot of good
         taste in Blue Nun. Imported by Schieffelin (SHIFF'-UH-LIN)
         & Co., New York.

Public Service Announcements

```
FACT SHEET
```

WHO: The Westside Community Club

WHAT: Annual Spring Flower Show

WHERE: Westside Community Club Clubhouse

WHEN: Thursday, April 28th, Friday, April 29th, 9:00 A.M.—7:00
         P.M.

WHY: This is one of two major fund—raising events held each
         year to support our public parks. Funds are used to help
         maintain gardens in three Westside parks.
         Admission is free. Handmade novelties and plants will be
         on sale. Evening barbecue starts at 5:00 P.M.

CLIENT: Amigos de las Americas

LENGTH: 60 seconds

ANNCR: Are you a teenager, sixteen years or older? Are you
         looking for the adventure of a lifetime? Why not check
         out Amigos de las Americas? Amigos is a non—profit
         organization, with chapters in cities all over America.
         Amigos spend the school year studying Spanish and
         paramedic work, and spend the summer working in a Latin
         American country. What do Amigos do? Well, last year
         Amigos administered over 230,000 dental treatments to
         60,000 children. They gave over 90,000 immunizations for
         polio and other diseases. And, they tested over 22,000
         people for tuberculosis. Amigos work in rural areas and
         big city slums. They are not on vacation. Assignments in
         Panama, Ecuador, Paraguay, and the Dominican Republic,

among others, call for dedicated, caring young people. If you think Amigos is for you, write for information. The address is: 5618 Star Lane, Houston, Texas, 77057. Or, use the toll-free number: 1-800-231-7796. Amigos!

CLIENT: Volunteer Center of Clark County

ANNCR: It took 3½ years to build and is on the market for 3.75 million dollars! It's the Clark County Designer Showcase house on Mount Hilary. Proceeds from tours go to the Volunteer Center of Clark County. Visit <u>your</u> dream house. Call 461-1986 for ticket information.

CLIENT: Project Family

ANNCR: Interested in adoption? Call Project Family at 775-1313. Project Family provides recruitment and preliminary screening of families interested in adopting. The Project seeks homes for children in need of permanent or temporary living situations. Make a difference in a child's life--and in yours--by adopting a child in need. Call 775-1313 today.

CLIENT: Ashland Chapter of American Diabetes Association

ANNCR: The Ashland Chapter of the American Diabetes Association proudly presents Dr. William M. Sloane, one of the nation's foremost diabetologists (DY-UH-BEET-AHL'-0-GISTS), as their guest speaker, Thursday, September 5, at 7:30 in the Ashland High School auditorium. There is no charge for this event.

Television Commercials

AGENCY: Ketchum Advertising
CLIENT: Safeway Stores, Inc.
LENGTH: 30 seconds

VIDEO	AUDIO
	SFX: MUSIC UNDER.
OPEN ON SAFEWAY LOGO. MOVE IN UNTIL ENTIRE SCREEN IS RED.	MALE VO: Safeway's international cheese experts invite your taste buds
DISS TO WHEEL OF WISCONSIN CHEDDAR WITH CRACKERS ON TOP AND PIECE OF BUNTING ON SIDE.[4]	
DISS TO LARGE SLICE OF DUTCH GOUDA WITH DUTCH FLAG.	and your taste budget to enjoy some of the world's finest cheeses.
DISS TO SLICES OF HAVARTI AND CRACKERS WITH HAVARTI ON THEM. DANISH FLAG IS STUCK IN ONE SLICE OF CHEESE.	So we feature them at low Safeway prices.
DISS TO SLICE OF JARLSBERG ON CUTTING BOARD, WHEEL OF JARLSBERG IS IN BACKGROUND. WOMAN'S HAND PLACES NORWEGIAN FLAG ON SLICE OF JARLSBERG.	A deliciously economical world taste tour that you can enjoy now.
DISS TO SQUARE OF SWISS CHEESE WITH SWISS FLAG. SMALL PIECES OF CHEESE ARE ON CUTTING BOARD. WOMAN'S HAND LIFTS PIECE OF CHEESE.	Quality world cheeses, low Safeway prices. No passport required; just an appetite.
	SFX: MUSIC ENDS.
DISS TO CU MAN BEING FED SWISS CHEESE BY WOMAN'S HAND.	MAN: Mmmmmm.
DISS TO SAFEWAY LOGO.	LOGO: Safeway. Everything you want from a store and a little bit more.

[4]DISS is an abbreviation for dissolve; "dissolve to" means to replace one picture with another.

AGENCY: Backer & Spielvogel, Inc.

CLIENT: Quaker

PRODUCT: Celeste Pizza

LENGTH: 30 seconds

SUPER: Giuseppe Celeste

Fictitious Little Brother

GIUSEPPE: I need your help. My big sister, Mama Celeste, she make a great crust for her pizza. But was Giuseppe's idea. I say, "Mama, you make perfect sauce, perfect toppings, make a perfect crust." She do it. But I think it. So my picture should be on the box, too, no? Which you like? (HOLDS UP PICTURES) Happy--"Hey, I think of great crust!"? Or serious--"Yes, I think of great crust."? Or it could be bigger? (HOLDS UP HUGE PICTURE)

ANNCR VO: Celeste Pizza. Delicious crust makes it great from top to bottom.

CLIENT: Herald Sewing Machines

TITLE: Pre-Holiday Sale

LENGTH: 60 seconds

VIDEO	AUDIO
OPEN ON SHOT OF ANNCR SEATED BEHIND SEWING MACHINE CONSOLE. ZOOM IN ON MACHINE, AND FOLLOW SEQUENCE OF SHOTS INDICATED BY ANNCR.	ANNCR: This is the famous Herald sewing machine. Notice the free arm, perfectly designed to allow you to sew sleeves, cuffs, and hems. Note, too, the stitch regulator dial. You move easily and instantly to stretch stitch, embroider, or zig-zag stitches.
ANNCR DEMONSTRATES THE REGULATOR DIAL.	

	The Herald has a drop feed for darning, appliquéing, and monogramming.
ANNCR DEMONSTRATES.	This advanced machine has a self-stop bobbin winder. Other standard features include a built-in light, a thread tension dial, and a snap-on extension dial for flat bed sewing.
ZOOM BACK TO MEDIUM SHOT OF ANNCR AND MACHINE.	Yes, there isn't a better or more versatile sewing machine available today.
ANNCR STANDS, AND WALKS AROUND MACHINE AND TOWARD CAMERA.	But, I've saved the best for last. The Herald Star model sewing machine is now on sale at dealers everywhere. The Star, the most advanced model Herald makes, is regularly priced at two hundred and forty-nine dollars.
ANNCR HOLDS UP SALE SIGN, WITH $249 CROSSED OUT AND $199 WRITTEN IN.	During this month, you can buy the Star for only one hundred ninety-nine dollars—a saving of fifty dollars. You can't beat a deal like this, so visit your Herald dealer soon, while you still have your choice of color. Check the yellow pages for the dealers in your area.

AGENCY: In-house

CLIENT: Madera Foods

LENGTH: 60 seconds

VIDEO	AUDIO
OPEN ON ANNCR STANDING BEFORE CHECKOUT STAND.	ANNCR: I'm here at Madera Foods, checking up on the specials you'll find here this weekend.
CUT TO PRODUCE SECTION. ANNCR WALKS INTO FRAME. ANNCR PICKS UP A GRAPEFRUIT. ANNCR POINTS TO LETTUCE.	There are excellent buys this weekend in fresh fruits and vegetables. Like extra fancy Indian River ruby red grapefruit, three for ninety-nine cents. Or iceberg lettuce, two heads for seventy-nine cents. And, don't overlook the relishes--green onions or radishes, two bunches for twenty-nine cents.
CUT TO MEAT DEPARTMENT, ANNCR WALKS INTO FRAME.	Meat specials include rib roast at two sixty-nine a pound, all lean center cut pork chops at two seventy-nine a pound, and lean ground chuck at only one thirty-nine a pound.
CUT BACK TO CHECKOUT STAND.	And, here I am, back at the checkout stand. Here's where you'll really come to appreciate Madera Foods. Their low, low prices add up to a total bill that winds down the cost

CUT TO ANNCR OUTSIDE FRONT ENTRANCE.	of living. So, pay a visit to Madera Foods this weekend. Specials are offered from Friday opening to closing on Sunday night. Madera Foods is located in the Madera Plaza Shopping Center. Hours are from 9:00 A.M. 'til 10:00 P.M., seven days a week.
DISS TO MADERA FOODS LOGO SLIDE. HOLD UNTIL CLOSE.	See you at Madera Foods.

AGENCY: Sherman Associates, Inc.
CLIENT: Bayview Health Club
LENGTH: 60 seconds

VIDEO	AUDIO
OPEN ON MCU OF TALENT.	Get ready! Swimsuit season is almost here! Now is the time to shed those excess pounds and achieve the body you know is hidden somewhere within you.
ZOOM OUT TO MEDIUM SHOT.	The Bayview Health Club will help you find the possible you. Bayview is a complete fitness club. We offer day
CUT TO STILL PHOTOS OF EACH FEATURE AS IT IS MENTIONED.	and evening classes in weight training, aerobic and jazzercise dance, full Nautilus equipment, tanning, Jacuzzi and sauna facilities.

CUT TO MCU OF TALENT.   In addition, we sponsor weight
                                   reduction clinics, jogging and
                                   running programs, and health and
CUT TO MCU OF TALENT.   beauty seminars, with a supportive
                                   staff to coach you in every facet of
                                   personal health care. Bayview is
                                   tailored for you--the modern man or
                                   woman--and, for this month only,
                                   we're offering new members an
                                   introductory price to join: Just half
                                   price! That's right, a 50 percent
                                   reduction during the month of April.
CUT TO MCU OF TALENT.   So, call now for a tour of our
                                   facilities. Meet the staff, and chat
                                   with satisfied members. Bayview
                                   Health Club, in downtown Portland.
                                   Join now. Don't lose time--instead,
                                   lose that waist, with a 50 percent
                                   reduction in membership costs.
MATTE IN ADDRESS AND PHONE NUMBER. Find the hidden you, and be ready for
                                   the beach! Bayview Health Club: we're
                                   ready when you are!

Appendix B
Pronunciation
Guide

This appendix consists of about 300 words, selected for one or more of these reasons: (1) The word is often mispronounced. (2) The word is unusual or new but might well appear in broadcast copy. (3) The word is of foreign origin but is widely used in the English-speaking world and may appear in commercial copy for fabrics, foods, or fashions.

The pronunciations given are those used in General American. All words are transcribed into the International Phonetic Alphabet (IPA), diacritics, and wire-service phonetics. The source of diacritical transcriptions is *The American Heritage Dictionary*.[1]

Because this is a pronunciation guide definitions are given only where necessary. Users should note that brief definitions given for words such as *gestalt* and *nihilism* are inadequate to explain these concepts fully. This appendix is not a substitute for a good dictionary.

It should be noted that many common words are omitted from this appendix because either of two common ways of pronouncing them is correct. In this category are words such as *economic*, *program*, and *pianist*.

accessory [æk'sɛsəri] (ăk-sĕs'ər-ē) (AK-SESS'-UH-REE)
Something supplementary; one who incites.

accompanist [ə'kʌmpənɪst] (ə-kŭm'pə-nĭst) (UH-KUM'-PUH-NIHST)

aegis ['idʒɪs] (ē'jĭs) (EE'-JIHS)
Protection; sponsorship; patronage.

almond ['ɑmənd] (ä'mənd) (AH'-MUND)
Note: The *l* is not sounded, and the first syllable is like the *a* in *father*.

amateur ['æmə,tʃʊr] (ăm'ə-chŏŏr) (AM'-UH-CHOOR)
An athlete or artist who participates without pay.

amoral [e'mɔrəl] (ā-môr'əl) (AM-MOR'-UL)
Not admitting of moral distinctions or judgments; neither moral nor immoral.

---

[1]William Morris, eds., *The American Heritage Dictionary of the English Language* (Boston: Houghton Mifflin, 1980).

a priori [ɑ priˈɔri] (ä prē-ōrˈē) (AH PREE-ORʹ-EE)
Made before or without examination; deductive; not based on an experiment or experience.

apropos [ˌæprəˈpo] (ăpʹrə-pōʹ) (A-PRUH-POʹ)
Appropriate.

archetype [ˈɑrkəˌtaɪp] (ärʹkə-tīpʹ) (ARʹ-KUH-TYPE)
An original model or type after which other similar things are patterned; a prototype.

Arctic [ˈɑrkˌtɪk] (ärkʹtīk) (ARKʹ-TICK)
Note: Both *c*'s must be sounded; the same is true for *Antarctic*.

argot [ˈɑrgo] (ärʹgō) (ARʹ-GO)
A specialized vocabulary or set of idioms used by a particular class or group.

art deco [ɑr deˈko] (är dā-koʹ) (AR DAY-KOʹ)
A highly decorative style of artistic design that was popular between the two world wars.

assuage [əˈswedʒ] (ə-swájʹ) (UH-SWAYJʹ)
To make less burdensome or less severe.

au gratin [o ˈgrɑtn̩] (ō grätʹn) (OH GRAHTʹ-UN)
Covered with bread crumbs or cheese and browned in an oven.

basalt [bəˈsɔlt] (bə-sôltʹ) (BUH-SALTʹ)
A hard, dense, volcanic rock.

baud [bɔd] (bôd) (BAWD)
A unit of speed in data processing, equal to one binary digit per second.

bestial [ˈbɛstʃəl] (bĕsʹchəl) (BESSʹ-CHUL)
Behaving in the manner of a brute; savage.

Bethesda [bɪˈθɛzdə] (bĭ-thĕzʹdə) (BIH-THEZʹ-DUH)
An urban center in Maryland; the name of a famous government hospital.

bijou [ˈbiˌʒu] (beˈzhōō ʹ) (BEEʹ-ZHOO)
A small, exquisitely wrought trinket; the name of many American movie houses.

bivouac [ˈbɪvuˌæk] (bĭvʹōō-ăk) (BIHVʹ-OO-ACK)
A temporary encampment made by soldiers in the field.

blasé [blɑˈze] (blä-zāʹ) (BLAH-ZAYʹ)
Having no more capacity or appetite for enjoyment.

B'nai B'rith [ˈbne ˈbrɪə] (bnäˈbrĭthʹ) (BNAYʹ-BRITHʹ)
A Jewish international fraternal society, perhaps best known for its sponsorship of the Anti-Defamation League.

boatswain [ˈbosən] (bōʹsən) (BOʹ-SUN)
A warrant officer or petty officer in charge of a ship's deck crew.

bouclé [bu'kle] (bōō-klā') (BOO-KLAY')
A type of yarn or a fabric knitted from this yarn.

bouquet [bo'ke] (bō-kā') (BO-KAY')

bourgeois [bʊr'ʒwɑ] (bōōr-zhwä') (BOOR-ZHWAH')
One belonging to the middle class.

boutique [bu'tik] (bōō-tēk') (BOO-TEEK')
A small retail shop that specializes in gifts, fashionable clothes, or accessories.

brooch [brotʃ] (brōch) (BROTCH)

buoy ['bu,i] (bōō'ē) (BOO'-EE)

cache [kæʃ] (kăsh) (kash)
A place for concealment and safekeeping, as of valuables; a store of goods hidden in a cache.

caisson ['kesɑn] (kā'sŏn') (KAY'-SAHN)
A watertight structure within which construction work is carried on; a large box used to hold ammunition.

calm [kam] (käm) (KAHM)
The *l* is not sounded.

camembert ['kæməm,bɛr] (kăm'əm-bâr) (KAM'-UM-BEAR)
A creamy, mold-ripened French cheese.

canapé ['kænəpe] (kän'ə-pā) (KAN'-UH-PAY)
An appetizer. *Note*: In broadcast copy, there is likely to be no acute accent mark over the *e*.

caramel ['kærəməl] (kăr'əməl) (KARE'-UH-MUHL)

carcinogen [kɑr'sınədʒən] (kär-sĭn'ə-jən) (KAR-SIN'-UH-JUN)
A cancer-causing substance.

Cassiopeia [,kæsiə'piə] (kăs'-ē-ə-pē'ə) (KASS-EE-UH-PEE'-UH)
A constellation visible in the Northern Hemisphere.

cataclysm ['kætə,klızm] (kăt'ə-klĭz'əm) (KAT'-UH-KLIZ-UM)
A violent upheaval.

catarrh [kə'tɑr] (kə-tär') (KUH-TAHR')
Inflammation of mucous membranes, especially of the nose and throat.

caulk [kɔk] (kôk) (KAWK)

chaise longue [,ʃez'lən] (shāz'lông') (SHAYZ LONG')

chamois ['ʃæmi] (shăm'ē) (SHAM'-EE)

chartreuse [ʃɑr'truz] (shär-trooz') (SHAHR-TROOZ')
A liqueur; a greenish yellow color

Charybdis [kə'rɪb,dɪs] (kə-rīb'dĭs) (KUH-RIB'-DISS)
A whirlpool off the Sicilian coast, opposite the rock of Scylla. (To be "between Scylla and Charybdis" implies that one is between two serious dangers.)

Chianti [ki'ɑnti] (kē-än'tē) (KEE-AHN'-TEE)
A dry, red Italian wine.

chiaroscuro [ki,ɑr-ə'skjuro] (kē-är'ə-skyōor'o) (KEE-AR-UH-SKYUR'-O)
The arrangement of light and dark elements in a pictorial work of art.

chic [ʃik] (shēk) (SHEEK)

chiropodist [kə'rɑpədɪst] (kə-rŏp'ə-dĭst) (KUH-RAHP'-UH-DIST)

ciao [tʃau] (chou) (CHOW)
An Italian greeting, meaning both hello and goodbye.

Cinzano [tʃɪn'zɑno] (chĭn-zän'-o) (CHIN-ZAHN'-O)
An Italian liqueur.

circa ['sɝ·kə] (sûr'kə) (SUR-KUH)
About; used before approximate dates or figures.

claque [klæk] (klăk) (KLACK) -
A group of persons hired to applaud at a performance; any group of adulating or fawning admirers.

cliché [kli'ʃe] (klē-shā') (KLEE-SHAY')
Note: In broadcast copy, this word may appear without the accent mark.

cloche [kloʃ] (klōsh) (KLOSH)
A close-fitting woman's hat.

cognac ['konjæk] (kōn'yăk') (KOHN'-YAK)
A French brandy.

coiffure [kwɑ'fjur] (kwä-fyoor') (KWAH-FYUR')

colloquial [kə'lokwiəl] (kə-lō'kwē-əl) (KUH-LO'-KWEE-UHL)

coma ['komə] (kō'mə) (KO'-MUH)

comatose ['komə,tos] (kō'mə-tōs') (KO'-MUH-TOESS)

comparable ['kampərəbl̩] (kom'pər-ə-bəl) (KAHM'-PUHR-UH-BUL)

comptroller [kən'trolɚ·] (kən-trō'lər) (KUN-TRO'-LER)
An officer who audits accounts and supervises the financial affairs of a corporation or governmental body. *Note*: the *p* is not sounded, and the *m* has the *n* sound.

conch [kɑŋk] (kängk) (KAHNK)
Any of various large marine mollusks.

concierge ['kɑnsiɚ·ʒ] (kŏn'sē-ûrzh) (KAHN-SEE-URZH')
A person who attends the entrance of a building.

conglomerate (v.) [kən'glamə,ret] (kən-glŏm'ərāt') (KUN-GLAHM'-UH-RAYT)
To collect into an adhering or rounded mass.
(n.) [kən'glamərɪt] (kən-glŏm'ərĭt) (KUN-GLAHM'-UH-RIHT)
A collected heterogeneous mass; a cluster.
Note: The noun frequently is used to denote a large corporation made up of several different types of businesses.

conjugal ['kɑndʒʊgl̩] (kŏn'jōō-gəl) (KAHN'-JYU-GUL)
Of marriage or the marital relationship.

consortium [kən'sɔrʃiəm] (kən-sôr'-shē-əm) (KUN-SAWR'-SHEE-UM)
Any association or partnership.

corps [kɔr] (kôr) (KAWR)

cortege [kɔr'tɛʒ] (kôr-tĕzh') (KAWR-TEHZH')
A train of attendants; usually refers to a funeral procession.

coup [ku] (kōō) (KOO)

coxswain ['kɑksn̩] (kŏk'sən) (KAHK'-SUN)

crepe [krep] (krāp) (KRAYP)
A light, soft, thin fabric; also a type of crinkled tissue paper.

crêpe [krɛp] (krĕp) (KREHP)
Note: In its French usages—crêpe de Chine is a type of cloth, and a crêpe is a thin pancake—this word is pronounced as indicated. This word will probably not have the circumflex over the *e* in broadcast copy, so you must remember to use the French pronunciation when the context so indicates.

crescendo [krə'ʃendo] (krə-shĕn'dō) (KRUH-SHEHN'-DOH)

crevasse [krə'væs] (krə-văs') (KRUH-VASS')
A deep fissure, as in a glacier.

crevice ['krɛvɪs] (krĕv'ĭs) (KREHV'-ISS)

crinoline ['krɪn'əlɪn] (krĭn'ə-lĭn) (KRIN'-UH-LIHN)
A coarse, stiff cotton fabric.

cryogenics [,kraɪo'dʒɛnɪks] (krī'o-jĕn'iks) (KRY-OH-JEN'-IKS)
The science of low-temperature phenomena.

cuisine [kwɪ'zin] (kwĭ-zēn') (KWIH-ZEEN')
A characteristic manner of preparing food.

culottes [ku'lɑts] (kōō-lŏts') (KOO-LOTS')
A divided skirt.

cupola ['kjupələ] (kyōō'-pə-lə) (KYOO'-PUH-LUH)

cybernetics [,saɪbɚ'nɛtɪks] (sī'bər-nĕt'ĭks) (SY-BER-NET'-IKS)

cynosure ['saɪnə,ʃʊr] (sī'nə-sho͝or') (SY'-NUH-SHOOR)
A center of interest or attraction.

dachshund ['dɑks,hʊnt] (däks'hoont') (DAHKS'-HUHNT)
Note: The word ends with a *t* sound, and the vowel sound in the second syllable is as in *took*.

Dacron ['dekrɑn] (dā'krŏn) (DAY'-KRAHN)

dais ['deɪs] (dā'ĭs) (DAY'-ISS)
A raised platform.

demise [dɪ'maɪz] (dĭ-mīz') (DIH-MYZ')
Death.

demur [dɪ'mɝ] (dĭ-mûr') (DIH-MUHR')
To take exception.

denier [də'nje] (də-nyā') (DUH-NYAY')
A unit of fineness for rayon, nylon, and silk yarns. *Note*: This word is spelled the same as that which means "one who denies"; the context should make clear which of its meanings is intended.

despot ['dɛspət] (dĕs'pət) (DES'-PUHT)

détente [de'tɑnt] (dā-tänt') (DAY-TAHNT')

dialysis [daɪ'æləsɪs] (dī-ăl'ə-sĭs) (DY-AL'-UH-SIS)

dichotomy [daɪ'kɑtəmi] (dī-kŏt'ə-mē) (DY-KAHT'-UH-MEE)
Division into two (usually contradictory) parts or opinions.

diminution [,dɪmə'njuʃən] (dim'ə-nyoo'shən) (DIM-UH-NYOO'-SHUN)
The act or process of diminishing.

diocese ['daɪəsɪs] (dī'əsĭs) (DY'-UH-SIHS)

diphtheria [dɪf'əɪriə] (dĭf-thîr'ē-ə) (DIFF-THIR'-EE-UH)
Note: The *ph* is pronounced *f*.

diphthong ['dɪfəɔŋ] (dĭf'thông') (DIFF'-THONG)
A combination of two vowel sounds; a glide.

diva ['divə] (dē'və) (DEE'-VUH)
An operatic prima donna, or leading singer.

dossier ['dɑsi,e] (dŏs'ē-ā') (DAHS'-EE-AY)

dour [dʊr] (door) (DUHR) (*Note*: rhymes with *poor*)
Silently ill-humored; gloomy.

drought [draʊt] (drout) (DRAWHT) (*Note*: rhymes with *snout*)

dysentery ['dɪsəntɛri] (dĭs'ən-tĕr'-ē) (DISS'-UN-TARE-EE)

dyspepsia [dɪs'pɛpʃə] (dĭs-pĕp'shə) (DISS-PEP'-SHUH)
Indigestion.

eczema ['ɛksəmə] (ĕk'sə-mə) (EK'-SUH-MUH)
An inflammation of the skin.

Eire ['ɛrə] (âr'ə) (AIR'-UH)
The Gaelic name for the Republic of Ireland.

emollient [ɪ'mɑljənt] (ĭ-mŏl'yənt) (IH-MAHL'-YUNT)
An agent that softens or soothes the skin.

Empire (ɑm'pɪr) (ŏm-pîr') (AHM-PEER')
Note: Pronounced as indicated when referring to the dress or the artistic style of the first Empire of France, 1804–1815.

encephalitis [ɛn,sɛfə'laɪtɪs] (ĕn-sef'ə-lī'tĭs) (EN-SEFF-UH-LY'-TISS)
Inflammation of the brain.

endocrine [ɛndə'krɪn] (ĕn'də-krĭn) (EN'-DUH-KRIHN)
Glandular; a gland.

ennui ['ɑn'wi] (än'wē') (AHN'-WEE')
Listlessness and dissatisfaction resulting from lack of interest; boredom.

en route [ɑn 'rut] (än rōōt') (AHN ROOT')

ensemble [ɑn'sɑmbl̩] (än-säm'bəl) (AHN-SAHM'-BUHL)

ensign Two pronunciations:
['ɛn,saɪn] (ĕn'sīn) (EN'-SYN) A flag.
['ɛnsən] (ĕn'sən) (EN'-SUN) A naval officer.

entourage [,ɑntu'rɑʒ] (än'tōō-räzh') (AHN-TOO-RAZH')

entrée ['ɑntre] (än'trā) (AHN'-TRAY)

envoy ['ɛnvɔɪ] (ĕn'voi) (EN'-VOY)
Note: Do not make the first syllable AHN, unless you are going to give the word its correct French pronunciation.

Epiphany [ɪ'pɪfəni] (ĭ-pĭf'ə-nē) (IH-PIFF'-UH-NEE)
A Christian festival held on January 6.

epitaph ['ɛpə,tæf] (ĕp'ə-tăf') (EP'-UH-TAFF)
An inscription on a tombstone; a tribute to a deceased person.

epitome [ɪ'pɪtəmi] (ĭ-pĭt'ə-mē) (IH-PIT'-UH-MEE)
One that is representative of an entire class or type; embodiment.

era ['ɪrə] (îr'ə) (IHR'-UH)

err [ɚ] (ûr) (ER)
Note: Do not pronounce this as the word *air*.

erudite ['ɛrju,daɪt] (ĕr'yōō-dīt') (AIR'-YOU-DYT)
Deeply learned.

euphemism ['jufə,mɪzm̩] (yōō'fə-mĭz'əm) (YOU'-FUH-MIZ-UM)
A term substituted for one considered offensively explicit.

exacerbate [ɛg'zæsɚ,bet] (ĕg-zăs'ər-bāt') (EGG-ZASS'-ER-BAYT)
To increase the severity of.

exquisite ['ɛkskwɪzɪt] (ĕks'kwĭ-zĭt) (EKS'-KWIH-ZIT)
Note: Do not place the stress on the second syllable.

extraordinary [ɛk'strɔrdə,nɛri] (ĕk-strôr'də-nĕr'ē)
(EK-STROR'-DUH-NARE-EE)

façade [fə'sɑd] (fəsäd') (FUH-SAHD')
Note: In broadcast copy, the cedilla on the *c* is usually lacking.

faux pas [fo 'pɑ] (fō pä') (FOH PAH')
A social blunder; a breach of etiquette.

fiduciary [fɪ'duʃiˌɛri] (fĭ-dōō'shē-ĕr'ē) (FIH-DOO'-SHEE-AIR-EE)
Of, pertaining to, or involving one who holds something in trust for another.

finite ['faɪˌnaɪt] (fī'nīt) (FY'-NYT)
Having boundaries; limited.

foible ['fɔɪbl̩] (foi'bəl) (FOY'-BUL)
A minor weakness or failing of character.

forecastle ['foksl̩] (fōk'səl) (FOKE'-SUL)
The section of the upper deck of a ship located at the bow.

forehead ['fɔrɪd] (fôr'ĭd) (FOR'-IHD)
Note: The *h* is not sounded.

forte Two words, spelled the same, but pronounced differently:
[fɔrt] (fôrt) (FORT) A person's strong point.
['fɔrte] (fôr'tā) (FOR'-TAY) Music direction, meaning "loudly."
Note: Do not say, "This is my FOR'-TAY."

frijoles [fri'holes] (frē-hō'lās) (FREE-HO'-LAYS)
Beans prepared as in parts of Latin America.

fungi ['fʌndʒaɪ] (fŭn'jī) (FUN'-JY)
Plural of *fungus*. *Note*: The letter *g* is sounded differently in the two words.

garage [gə'rɑʒ] (gə-räzh') (GUH-RAHZH')

gauche [goʃ] (gōsh) (GOOSH)
Note: This word rhymes with the first syllable of *lotion*.

geisha ['geʃə] (gā'shə) (GAY'-SHUH)
A Japanese woman trained to provide entertainment, especially for men.

genre ['ʒɑnrə] (zhän'rə) (ZHAHN'-RUH)
Type; class.

gestalt [gə'ʃtɑlt] (gə-shtält') (GUH-SHTAHLT')
A unified configuration that cannot be explained merely as the sum of its parts.

Gethsemane [gɛθ'sɛməni] (gĕth-sĕm'ə-nē) (GETH-SEM'-UH-NEE)
The garden outside Jerusalem where Jesus was arrested.

gherkin ['gɝkɪn] (gûr'kĭn) (GUHR'-KIHN)
A small pickle.

Gila The name of a monster, national park, and river. ['hilə] (hē'lə)
(HEE'-LUH)

gist [dʒɪst] (jĭst) (JIST)
The central idea of some matter.

googol [ˈɡu͵ɡɔl] (gōō′gôl′) (GOO′-GAHL)
The number 10 raised to the power 100; the number 1 followed by 100 zeros (from the new math).

grosgrain [ˈɡro͵ɡren] (grō′grān′) (GROW′-GRAIN)
A heavy silk or rayon fabric with narrow horizontal ribs.

gunwale [ˈɡʌnl̩] (gŭn′əl) (GUN′-UL)
The upper edge of a ship's side.

habeas corpus [ˈhebiəs ˈkɔrpəs] (hā′bĕ-əs ˈkôr′pəs) (HAY′-BEE-US KAWR′-PUHS)
A writ that may be issued to bring a person before a court or judge, having as its purpose the release of that person from unlawful restraint.

hasten [ˈhesn̩] (hās′ən) (HAYS′-UN)
Note: The *t* is not sounded.

hearth [hɑrə] (härth) (HAHRTH)

hegemony [hɪˈdʒɛməni] (hĭ-jĕm′ə-nē) (HIH-JEM′-UH-NEE)
Predominant influence of one state over others.

Hegira [hɪˈdʒaɪrə] (hĭ-jī′rə) (HIH-JY′-RUH)
The flight of Mohammed from Mecca to Medina; any flight, as from danger.

height [haɪt] (hīt) (HYT)

heinous [ˈhenəs] (hā′nəs) (HAY′-NUS)
Grossly wicked or reprehensible.

hiatus [haɪˈetəs] (hī-ā′-təs) (HY-AY′-TUS)
A gap or missing section.

hierarchy [ˈhaɪə͵rɑrki] (hī′ə-rär′-kē) (HY′-UH-RAR-KEE)

hors d'oeuvre [ɔr ˈdɝv] (ôr dûrv′) (OR DURV′)

hyperbole [haɪˈpɝbə͵li] (hī-pûr′bə-lē) (HY-PER′-BUH-LEE)
An exaggeration or extravagant statement used as a figure of speech. *Note:* Do not confuse this word with the geometric term *hyperbola*.

impotent [ˈɪmpətənt] (ĭm′pə-tənt) (IHM′-PUH-TUNT)
Note: Do *not* place stress on the second syllable.

imprimatur [͵ɪmprəˈmetɚ] (ĭm′-prə-mā′tər) (IHM-PRUH-MAY′-TUR)
Official approval or license to print or publish.

impugn [ɪmˈpjun] (ĭm-pyōōn′) (IHM-PYOON′)
To oppose or attack as false; criticize; refute.

integer [ˈɪntədʒɚ] (ĭn′tə-jər) (IN′-TUH-JUHR)
Any member of the set of positive whole numbers (1, 2, 3, . . .), negative whole numbers (−1, −2, −3, . . .), and zero (0).

integral [ˈɪntəɡrəl] (ĭn′tə-grəl) (IN′-TUH-GRUHL)
Note: Do not place stress on the second syllable.

Io [ˈaɪo] (īˈo) (EYE′-OH)
A satellite of Jupiter, named for a maiden in Greek mythology who was loved by Zeus.

irony [ˈaɪrəni] (īˈrə-nē) (EYE′-RUH-NEE)
Note: Avoid EYE′-ER-NEE.

jeroboam [dʒɛrəˈboəm] (jĕr-ə-bōˈəm) (JEHR-UH-BO′-UM)
A wine bottle holding about ⅕ of a gallon.

juvenile [ˈdʒuvənl] (jo͞oˈvə-nəl) (JOO′-VUH-NUHL)
Note: JOO′-VUH-NYL is acceptable, but the word is seldom given that pronunciation by professional announcers.

kibbutz [kɪˈbuts] (kī-bo͞otsˈ) (KIH-BOOTS′)
A collective farm or settlement in modern Israel.

lamé [læˈme] (lă-māˈ) (LA-MAY′)
A fabric having metallic threads in the warp or in the filling. *Note*: In broadcast copy, the accent mark may be missing—the context should tell you whether the copy refers to a cloth or to the condition of being lame.

liaison [ˌliˌeˈzɑn] (lēˈā-zŏnˈ) (LEE-AY-ZAHN′)

libation [laɪˈbeʃən] (lī-bāˈshən) (LY-BAY′-SHUN)
The pouring of a liquid offering as a religious ritual; an intoxicating beverage (informal usage).

llama [ˈjɑmə] (yäˈmə) (YAH′-MUH)
Note: In broadcast speech, it is helpful to use the Spanish pronunciation, as given here, to avoid confusion with *lama*, a Buddhist monk of Tibet or Mongolia.

lozenge [ˈlɑzɪndʒ] (lŏzˈĭnj) (LAHZ′-INJ)

macabre [məˈkɑbrə] (mə-käˈbrə) (MUH-KAH′-BRUH)
Gruesome; ghastly

Magi [ˈmedʒaɪ] (māˈjī) (MAY′-JY)
The "wise men from the East" who traveled to Bethlehem to pay homage to the infant Jesus.

mandamus [mænˈdeməs] (măn-dāˈməs) (MAN-DAY′-MUS)
A writ used by a superior court ordering a public official or body or a lower court to perform a specified duty.

Maya [ˈmɑjə] (mäˈyə) (MAH′-YUH)
A member of a race of native peoples in southern Mexico and Central America.

measure [ˈmɛʒɚ] (mĕzhˈər) (MEHZH′-UR)
Note: Avoid MAYZH′-UR.

melee [ˈmele] or [meˈle] (māˈlā) or (mālāˈ) (MAY′-LAY) or (MAY-LAY′)

meringue [mə'ræŋ] (mə-răng') (MUH-RANG')

mien [min] (mēn) (MEEN)
One's bearing or manner.

mnemonic [nɪ'mɑnɪk] (nĭ-mŏn'ĭk) (NIH-MAHN'-IK)
Relating to, assisting, or designed to assist the memory. *Note*: The *m* is not sounded.

moisten ['mɔɪsn̩] (mois'ən) (MOYS'-UN)
Note: The *t* is not sounded.

Moog [mog] (mōg) (MOHG)
A music synthesizer. *Note*: It is *not* pronounced MOOG.

mores ['mɔrez] (môr'āz) (MAWR'-AYZ)
The accepted traditional customs and usages of a particular social group; moral attitudes.

mot [mo] (mō) (MO)
A witticism or short, clever saying.

mousse [mus] (moos)) (MOOS)
Any of various chilled desserts.

myopia [maɪ'opiə] (mī-ō'pē-ə) (MY-O'-PEE-UH)
A visual defect; nearsightedness.

naivete [nɑ,iv'te] (nä'ēv-tā') (NAH-EEV-TAY')

naphtha ['næfθə] (năf'thə) (NAF'-THUH)
Note: The *ph* is sounded as an *f*.

née [ne] (nā) (NAY)
Born (used when identifying a married woman by her maiden name).

niche [nɪtʃ] (nĭch) (NITSCH)
Note: Rhymes with *rich*.

nihilism ['naɪəl,ɪzm̩] (nī'əl-ĭz'əm) (NY'-UHL-IZ-UM)
In ethics, the rejection of all distinctions in moral value. Also, the belief that destruction of existing political or social institutions is necessary to ensure future improvement; extreme radicalism.

Nisei ['nise] (nē'sā) (NEE'-SAY)
One born in America of immigrant Japanese parents.

nonpareil [,nɑnpə'rɛl] (nŏn'pə-rĕl') (NAHN-PUH-RELL')
Without rival; matchless; peerless; unequaled.

non sequitur [nɑn 'sɛkwɪtɚ] (nŏn sĕk'wĭ-toor') (NAHN-SEK'-WIH-TOOR)
An inference or conclusion that does not follow from established premises or evidence.

nouveau riche [nuvo 'riʃ] (nōō-vō rēsh') (NOO-VOH REESH')
One who has recently become rich.

nuclear ['nukliɚ] (nōō'klē-ər) (NOO'-KLEE-UHR)

nuptial ['nʌpʃəl] (nŭp'shəl) (NUHP'-SHUL)

objet d'art [abʒe 'dɑr] (ôb-zhĕ där') (AHB-ZHAY DAR')
An object valued for its artistry.

obsequies ['absəkwiz] (ŏb'sə-kwēz) (AHB'-SUH-KWEEZ)
A funeral rite or ceremony.

often ['ɔfən] (ô'fən) (AWF'-UN)
Note: The *t* is not sounded.

oregano [ə'rɛgəno] (ə-rĕg'ənō') (UH-REG'-UH-NO)
An herb. *Note*: The first syllable may be sounded as (O).

paean ['piən] (pē'ən) (PEE'-UN)
A song of joyful praise or exultation.

Pago Pago ['pæŋgo 'pæŋgo] (päng'gō päng'gō) (PANG'-GO PANG'-GO)
The capital of American Samoa.

Pall Mall ['pɛl 'mɛl] (pĕl'mĕl') (PELL'MELL')
A street in London.

palm [pɑm] (päm) (PAHM)
Note: In this word, alone or in combinations such as Palm Beach or palm oil, the *l* is not sounded. The *l is* sounded in *palmetto*, a small tropical palm.

papier-máché ['pepɚ mə'ʃe] (pä'pər mə-shä') (PAY'-PER MUH-SHAY')
Note: This word is almost universally Anglicized in broadcast speech.

papyrus [pə'paɪrəs] (pə-pī'rəs) (PUH-PY'-RUSS)

paradigm ['pærədaɪm] (păr'ə-dīm') (PARE'-UH-DYM)
Any example or model. *Note*: The first *a* is sounded as in *pat*.

paroxysm ['pærək,sɪzm̩] (păr'ək-sīz'əm) (PAR'-UK-SIZ-UM)
A sudden outburst of emotion or action; a spasm or fit.

passé [pæ'se] (pă-sā') (PA-SAY')
Note: This word may appear without the accent mark in broadcast copy.

pâté [pɑ'te] (pä-tā') (PAH-TAY')
A meat paste (may appear without the accent marks).

patent Two pronunciations:
['petn̩t] (pā t'ənt) (PAYT'-UNT) Obvious.
['pætn̩t] (păt'ənt) (PAT'-UNT) Right or title.

pejorative [pɪ'dʒɔrətɪv] (pī-jôr'ə-tĭv) (PIH-JOR'-UH-TIV)
Disparaging; downgrading.

per se ['pɝ 'se] (pûr' sā') (PER' SAY')
In or by itself.

perseverance [,pɝsə'vɪrəns] (pûr'sə-vîr'əns) (PER-SUH-VEER'-UNS)

pestle ['pɛsl̩] (pĕs'əl) (PES'-UHL)

petit ['pɛti] (pĕt'ē) (PET'-EE)
Note: This word, meaning "small" or "minor," is pronounced as shown in combinations such as *petit larceny*, *petit four*, and *petit mal*.

phlegm [flɛm] (flĕm) (FLEM)
Thick mucus.

picot [ˈpiko] (pēˈkō) (PEEˈ-KO)
An ornamental edging on ribbon or lace.

pieta [pjeˈtɑ] (pyā-täˈ) (PYAY-TAHˈ)
A depiction of Mary with the Dead Christ.

piety [ˈpaɪəti] (pīˈə-tē) (PYˈ-UH-TEE)
Religious devotion.

pincers [ˈpɪnsɚz] (pĭnˈsərz) (PINˈ-SERZ)

piqué [pɪˈke] (pĭ-käˈ) (PIHˈKAYˈ)
A fabric. *Note*: This word may appear without accent marks in scripts, so do not confuse it with *pique*, which is pronounced *peek*.

placebo [pləˈsibo] (plə-sēˈbō) (PLUH-SEEˈ-BO)
A substance containing no medication, administered to humor a patient.

potable [ˈpotəbl] (pōˈtə-bəl) (POˈ-TUH-BUL)
Fit to drink; drinkable.

potpourri [popʊˈri] (pōˈpo͞o-rēˈ) (PO-PUH-REEˈ)

primer—Two pronunciations:
[ˈprɪmɚ] (prĭmˈər) (PRIMˈ-ER) A textbook.
[ˈpraɪmɚ] (prīmˈər) (PRYMˈ-ER) An undercoat of paint; an explosive.

pseudo [ˈsudo] (so͞oˈdō) (SOOˈ-DO)

purée [pjʊˈre] (pyo͞o-räˈ) (PYOO-RAYˈ)

Purim [ˈpʊrɪm] (po͞orˈĭm) (POORˈ-IHM)
A Jewish holiday celebrating the deliverance of the Jews from massacre by Haman.

Qiana [kiˈɑnə] (kē-änˈə) (KEE-AHNˈ-UH)
A particular synthetic fabric.

quay [ki] (kē) (KEE)
A wharf.

ragout [ræˈgu] (ră-go͞oˈ) (RA-GOOˈ)
A meat and vegetable stew.

recoup [rɪˈkup] (rĭ-ko͞opˈ) (RIH-KOOPˈ)

regime [reˈʒim] (rā-zhēmˈ) (RAY-ZHEEMˈ)

reprise [rəˈpriz] (rə-prēzˈ) (RUH-PREEZˈ)
Repetition of a phrase, verse, or song.

respite [ˈrɛspɪt] (rĕsˈpĭt) (RESˈ-PIT)
A temporary cessation or postponement.

ribald [ˈrɪbl̩d] (rĭbˈəld) (RIBˈ-ULD)
Pertaining to or indulging in vulgar, lewd humor.

riboflavin ['raɪboflevɪn] (rī'bō-flā'vĭn) (RY'-BO-FLAYV-IHN)
The principal ingredient in vitamin B₂.

rodeo ['rodi,o] (rō'dē-o') (RO'-DEE-O)
Note: The Spanish pronunciation, RO-DAY'-O, is heard less and less in the United States.

roof [ruf] (rōof) (cannot be accurately indicated with wire-service phonetics)
Note: *Roof*, like *room* and *root*, uses the same vowel sound as the word *boot*.

roué [ru'e] (rōo -ā') (ROO-AY')
A lecherous and dissipated man. *Note*: The accent mark may be missing in broadcast copy.

rouge [ruʒ] (rōozh) (ROOZH)

sachet [sæ'ʃe] (să-shā') (SA-SHAY')
A small bag containing perfumed powder.

sake ['sɑki] (sä'kē) (SAH'-KEE)
A Japanese rice wine.

salve [sæv] (săv) (SAV)
Note: The *l* is not sounded.

sauté [so'te] (sō-tā') (SO-TAY')
Note: The accent mark may be omitted in broadcast copy.

schism ['sɪzm̩] (sĭz'əm) (SIHZ'-UM)

schizoid ['skɪt,sɔɪd] (skĭt'soid') (SKIT'-SOYD)

sciatica [saɪ'ætɪkə] (sī-ăt'ĭ-kə) (SY-AT'-IK-UH)
Neuralgia of the sciatic nerve; a pain in the area of the hip or thigh.

scion ['saɪən] (sī'ən) (SY'UN)
A descendant or heir.

Scylla ['sɪlə] (sĭl'ə) (SILL'-UH)
A rock on the Italian side of the Straight of Messina, opposite Charybdis.

segue ['sɛg,we] (sĕg'wā) (SEG'-WAY)
A transition from one program element to another (usually music) without overlap or pause.

skein [sken] (skān) (SKAYN)
A loose coil of thread or yarn.

slough [slu] (slōo) (SLEW)
A marsh.

soften ['sɔfən] (sôf'ən) (SAWF'-UN)
Note: The *t* is not sounded.

sophomore ['sɑfə,mɔr] (sŏf'ə-môr') (SAHF'-UH-MOR)
Note: Sound all three syllables.

soufflé [su'fle] (sōo -flā') (SOO-FLAY')

succinct [sək'sɪŋkt] (sək-sĭngkt') (SUK-SINGKT')

Succoth ['sukot] (sook'ōt) (SOOK'-OT)
A Jewish harvest festival.

sukiyaki [ski'ɑki] (skē-äk'ē) (SKEE-AHK'-EE)
A Japanese dish of meat and vegetables.

superfluous [sʊ'pɝfluəs] (soo-pûr'floo-əs) (SU-PER'-FLU-US)

synod ['sɪnəd] (sĭn'əd) (SIN'-UD)
A church council.

taffeta ['tæfətə] (tăfə-tə) (TAF'-UH-TUH)
A glossy fabric.

Tagalog [tə'gɑlɔg] (tə-gä'lôg) (TUH-GAH'-LOG)
A people native to the Philippines; their language.

Terpsichore [tɝp'sɪkəri] (tûrp-sĭk'ə-rē) (TERP-SIK'-UH-REE)
The Muse of dancing.

tertiary ['tɝʃi,ɛri] (tûr'shē-ĕr-ē) (TER'-SHEE-AIR-EE)
Third in place, order, degree, or rank.

testosterone [tɛs'tɑstəron] (tĕs-tŏs'tə-rōn') (TES-TAHS'-TUH-ROHN)
A male sex hormone.

Thames [tɛmz] (tĕmz) (TEMZ)
A river of England.

thyme [taɪm] (tīm) (TYM)
An herb.

tiara [ti'ɑrə] (tē-är'ə) (TEE-AHR'-UH)
A crownlike headpiece.

tortilla [tɔr'tijə] (tôr-tē'yə) (TAWR-TEE'-YUH)
A thin, unleavened Mexican pancake.

touché [tu'ʃe] (too-shā') (TOO-SHAY')
Note: The accent mark may be missing in broadcast copy.

toward [tɔrd] (tôrd) (TAWRD)
Note: This is a one-syllable word.

treacle ['trikl̩] (trē'kəl) (TREE'-KUL)
Molasses.

trestle ('trɛsl̩] (trĕs'əl) (TRESS'-UL)

tricot ['triko] (trē'kō) (TREE'-KO)
A soft cloth.

troche ['troki] (trō'kē) (TRO'-KEE)
A small lozenge.

trough [trɔf] (trôf) (TRAWF)

tulle [tul] (tool) (TOOL)
A fine starched net of silk, rayon, or nylon.

tzar [zɑr] (zär) (ZAHR)
Former ruler of Russia. The word is sometimes spelled *czar*, but both are pronounced the same.

unguent [ˈʌŋgwənt] (ŭng′gwənt) (UNG′-GWUNT)
A salve.

urethane [ˈjurəθen] (yo͞or′ə-thān′) (YOUR′-UH-THANE)

valance [ˈvæləns] (văl′əns) (VAL′-UNS)
A short, ornamental drapery hung across the top of a window or along a bed, shelf, canopy, or the like. *Note*: Do not confuse this word with a term from chemistry, *valence*, which is pronounced VAY′-LUNS.

venal [ˈvinl̩] (vē′nəl) (VEE′-NUL)
Open or susceptible to bribery.

venire [vɪˈnaɪri] (vĭ-nī′rē) (VIH-NY′-REE)
A panel of prospective jurors from which a jury is selected.

vicar [ˈvɪkɚ] (vĭk′ər) (VIK′-ER)

victual [ˈvɪtl̩] (vĭt′l) (VIT′-UL)
Food.

vicuña [vəˈkunjə] (və-ko͞on′yə) (VUH-KOON′-YUH)
A mammal of the Andes; the fleece of this animal. *Note*: The tilde may be missing in broadcast copy.

vigilante [ˌvɪdʒəˈlænti] (vĭj′ə-lăn′tē) (VIDG-UH-LAN′-TEE)
A member of an informal council exercising police power.

vin ordinaire [vɛ̃ ɔrdiˈnɛr] (văn ŏr-dē-nâr′) (VAN AWR-DEE′-NARE)
Note: The first *n* should be nasalized.

virulent [ˈvɪrjələnt] (vîr′yə-lənt) (VIHR′-YUH-LUNT)
Extremely poisonous.

vis-à-vis [ˌvizəˈvi] (vē′zə-vē′) (VEEZ-UH-VEE)
Face-to-face.

viscount [ˈvaɪˌkaʊnt] (vī′kount′) (VY′-KOUNT)
A British peer.

viscous [ˈvɪskəs] (vĭs′kəs) (VISS′-KUSS)

voile [vɔɪl] (voil) (VOYL)
A sheer fabric.

waistcoat [ˈwɛskɪt] (wĕs′kĭt) (WESS′-KIHT)

worsted [ˈwustɪd] (wo͞os′tĭd) (WUHSS′-TIHD)

yeoman [ˈjomən] (yō′mən) (YO′-MUN)

Yom Kippur [ˌjom kɪˈpur] (yōm′ kĭ-po͞or′) (YOOM KI-POOR′)
The holiest Jewish holiday.

Yosemite [joˈsɛməti] (yō-sĕm′ə-tē) (YO-SEHM′-UH-TEE)

Appendix C
Revised Job Titles from the U.S. Department of Labor

For generations, users of English and American English have tacitly assumed that certain jobs were appropriate only for persons of a particular group. One who held a low position in management was a *junior executive*, one who held a certain position in a police department was a *head matron*, and a person who delivered letters was a *mailman*. Recognizing that occupational titles are often discriminatory, the U.S. Department of Labor published a handbook titled *Job Title Revisions to Eliminate Sex- and Age-Referent Language from the Dictionary of Occupational Titles*. This publication preceded a thorough overhaul of the *Dictionary of Occupational Titles*, 4th ed. (Washington, D.C.: U.S. Department of Labor, 1977).

In revising the *Dictionary*, the Labor Department reviewed all recognized job categories and made changes in nearly 3,500 job titles. It is important for broadcast announcers to become familiar with this terminology.

The titles do not please everyone, and it is likely that some will undergo further change as people react to them. A *bellman* will not object to the new title *bell hop*, inasmuch as bell hops have used the "new" title for many years. *Farm boys* will undoubtedly be pleased to learn that they now are *farm hands*, just as *city hostesses* may be pleased with their new title, *goodwill ambassadors*. But some practitioners of ancient and honorable professions will take their new titles as an affront. An *animal husbandman* is now an *animal scientist*; a *bat boy* is now a *bat keeper*; a *brewmaster* is now a *brewery director*; and a *ring master* is a *ring conducter*.

Some of the new job titles will undoubtedly be easy to live with once we get used to them. Among these is *repairer*, now used for many different kinds of *repairmen*. This term makes grammatical sense, though it is somewhat difficult to articulate in a clear and unaffected manner. It is to the credit of the people who prepared the revised list that they avoided almost completely the temptation to replace *man* with *person*. Thus we do not have to contemplate titles such as *repairperson*, *longshoreperson*, or *fireperson*. In avoiding *person*, however, they came up with some titles that are either awkward or subject to misinterpretation, such as *servicer* for *serviceman* and *braker* for *brakeman*.

A few titles that reflect sexual identification were left unchanged. *Leading man* and *leading woman* remain as they always have been; here "sex is a bona fide occupational requirement." Similarly, *juvenile* has been left untouched, because age in the dramatic arts is a valid criterion. Some jobs were exempted from name change because they are fixed by legislation, international treaties, or other binding legal agreements; these include *ship master*, *able seaman*, and *masseur* and *masseuse*.

Some of the revised titles are less successful than others. It is unlikely that anyone in television will accept the term *property handler* for *floorman*. *Floor director*, *floor manager*, and *stage manager* are the terms most commonly used today. Also, it would have been simpler (and more logical) to remove unnecessary *-ettes* and *-esses* from such terms as *drum majorette*, *sculptress*, and *stewardess* than to change the terms to something altogether different. *Drum major* and *sculptor* may be used for people of either sex.

The following is a selected list of the job titles approved by the U.S. Department of Labor. For the complete list, see *Job Title Revisions to Eliminate Sex- and Age-Referent Language from the Dictionary of Occupational Titles* (Washington, D.C.: U.S. Department of Labor, 1977). Occupations marked with an asterisk (*) were changed by the Department of Labor at an earlier date.

Old Occupational Title	Revised Occupational Title
Advance man	Advance agent
Advertising lay-out man	Advertising lay-out planner
Airplane steward	(title deleted)
Airplane stewardess	Airplane flight attendant
Alteration woman	Alterer
Animal husbandman	Animal scientist
Animal man	Animal keeper
Appliance repairman	Appliance repairer
Art lay-out man	Art lay-out planner
Audio man*	Audio operator
Audio-video repairman	Audio-video repairer
Automobile-body repairman	Automobile-body repairer
Automobile radiator man	Automobile radiator mechanic
Automobile radio man	Automobile radio repairer
Automotive-parts man	Automotive-parts stock clerk
Bakery girl	Bakery clerk
Ballet master	Ballet master-mistress
Bar boy	Bartender helper
Barmaid	Waiter-waitress, tavern
Barman	Bar attendant
Bat boy	Bat keeper
Bellman	Bell hop
Bomb disposal man	Bomb disposal specialist
Bondsman	Bonding agent
Boom man	Log sorter
Border patrolman	Border guard
Brakeman (any industry)	Brake holder
Brakeman, automobile	Brake repairer
Brakeman, passenger train	Braker, passenger train
Brakeman, road freight	Brake coupler, road freight

Old Occupational Title	Revised Occupational Title
Brakeman, yard	Yard coupler
Brewmaster	Brewing director
Bridal consultant	Wedding consultant
Bus boy	Dining room attendant
Bus boy, dishes	Dish carrier
Bus boy, room service	Room service assistant
Bus girl	(title deleted)
Cable man (tel. and tel.)	Cable installer
Cable repairman (tel. and tel.)	Cable repairer
Camera girl	Photographer
Camera repairman	Camera repairer
Cameraman (television)	Camera operator
Cameraman, animation (mo. pict.)	Camera operator, animation
Cameraman, assistant (television)	Dolly pusher
Cameraman, first (mo. pict.)	Camera operator, first
Cameraman, second (mo. pict.)	Camera operator, second
Cameraman, special effects (mo. pict.)	Camera operator, special effects
Cameraman, title (mo. pict.)	Camera operator, title
Camp watchman	Camp guard
Carburetor man	Carburetor mechanic
Carpenter foreman, stage (mo. pict.)	Carpenter supervisor, stage
Cart boy (medical services)	Cart attendant
Cattle-ranch foreman	Supervisor, cattle ranch
Cellarman (hotel and rest.)	Cellar clerk
Chambermaid	Room cleaner
Charwoman	Charworker
Checkroom girl	Checkroom attendant
Cigarette girl	Cigarette vendor
Circus foreman	Circus supervisor
City hostess	Goodwill ambassador
Clean-up man (agriculture)	Clean-up hand
Clergyman	Clergy
Club boy (hotel and rest.)	Club attendant
Clubhouse boy (amusement and rec.)	Clubhouse attendant
Coachman	Coach driver
Coffee girl	Coffee maker
Comedian	Comedian-comedienne
Contact man	Song plugger
Control-room man (radio and TV)	Control operator
Control supervisor, junior (radio and TV)	Control supervisor I
Control supervisor, senior (radio and TV)	Control supervisor II
Copy boy	Messenger, copy
Copy cameraman	Copy-camera operator

Old Occupational Title	Revised Occupational Title
Correction man (print. and pub.)	Proofsheet corrector
Counter bus boy	Counter dish carrier
Countergirl	Counter attendant
Counterman (retail trades)	Salesperson
Credit man	Credit-mail clerk
Dairy husbandman	Dairy scientist
Day watchman	Day guard
Delivery boy	Deliverer, merchandise
Deliveryman II	Delivery driver
Depot master	Depot supervisor
Display man (any trade)	Sign painter, display
Display man (retail trades)	Merchandise displayer
Dock watchman	Dock guard
Dockman I	Stevedore, dock
Doorman	Doorkeeper
Draftsman	Drafter
Dredgemaster	Dredge operator
Electrical appliance repairman	Electrical appliance repairer
Electrical appliance serviceman	Electrical appliance servicer
Electrical propman (mo. pict.)	Electrical prop handler
Electrical repairman	Electrical repairer
Engineman	Engine operator
Exploitation man (amuse. and rec.)	Exploitation writer
Farm boy	Farm hand, general I
Farm foreman	Farm supervisor
Farm housemaid	Houseworker, farm
Fire patrolman (govt. serv.)	Fire ranger
Fireman*	Fire fighter
Fireman, diesel locomotive	Firer, diesel locomotive
Fireman, electric locomotive	Firer, electric locomotive
Fireman, locomotive	Firer, locomotive
Fireman, marine	Firer, marine
Fireman, stage	Fire inspector, stage
Fireworks man	Fireworks display artist
Fisherman	Fisher
Flagman	Flagger
Flight stewardess	(title deleted)
Floorlady	Floor supervisor
Floorman* (TV)	Property handler
Flyman (amuse. and rec.)	Flyer
Footman	Butler, second
Forelady	Supervisor (followed by specialty)
Foreman	Supervisor (followed by specialty)
Foster mother	Foster parent
Fountain girl	Fountain server

Old Occupational Title	Revised Occupational Title
Fountain man	Fountain server
Furnaceman	Furnace installer
Garbageman*	Garbage collector
Gateman (any industry)	Gate tender
Gateman (amuse. and rec.)	Gate attendant
General foreman	General supervisor
Governess	Child mentor
Groceryman, journeyman	Grocer
Hand propman (mo. pict.)	Hand prop handler
Hat-check girl	Hat-check attendant
Headmaster	Principal, private school
Headwaiter	Headwaiter-headwaitress
Herdsman, dairy	Cattle herder, dairy
Herdsman, swine	Herder, swine
High-rigging man (amuse. and rec.)	High-rigging installer
Highway-maintenance man	Highway-maintenance worker
Homicide-squad patrolman	Homicide-squad police officer
Horseman, show	Horse breeder, show
Host	Host-hostess
Hostess, hotel	Social director, hotel
House repairman	House repairer
Houseman (dom. serv.)	Caretaker, house
Housemother	Cottage parent
Iceman	Driver, ice route
Inkman	Inker
Installment man	Installment collector
Interior-display man	Merchandise displayer, interior
Junior executive	Executive trainee
Knock-up man (woodworking)	Knock-up assembler
Laundress (dom. serv.)	Launderer I
Laundry routeman	Driver, laundry route
Laundryman (dom. serv.)	Launderer II
Lay-out man (print. and pub.)	Lay-out planner
Lineman (amuse. and rec.)	Line umpire
Lineman (tel. and tel.)	Line installer-repairer
Longshoreman	Stevedore
Maid, general	Houseworker, general
Maid, hospital	Cleaner, hospital
Mail boy	Messenger, mail
Mailman*	Mail carrier
Maintenance man, building	Maintenance repairer, building
Make-up man (amuse. and rec.; mo. pict.)	Make-up artist
Master of ceremonies	Master-mistress of ceremonies

Old Occupational Title	Revised Occupational Title
Matron, head (govt. serv.)	Police sergeant
Messman	Mess attendant
Midwife	Birth attendant
Milkman	Driver, milk route
Motel maid	Motel cleaner
Motion-picture-equipment foreman	Motion-picture-equipment supervisor
Motorcycle patrolman	Motorcycle police officer
Motorman II (r.r. trans.)	Streetcar operator
Mounted policeman	Mounted police officer
New car salesman	New car sales associate
Newsboy	Newspaper vendor
Night watchman	Night guard
Nursemaid	Child monitor
Nursery governess	Child mentor, nursery
Nurseryman	Manager, nursery
Office boy	Office helper
Office girl	Office helper
Ordnanceman	Ordnance artificer
Outside-property man (mo. pict.)	Outside-property agent
Page boy	Page
Park foreman	Park maintenance supervisor
Park watchman	Park patroller
Parlor matron	Parlor chaperon
Patrolman (govt. serv.)	Police officer I
Paymaster	Pay agent
Personal maid	Lady's attendant
Pin boy	Pin setter
Policeman*	Police officer
Policewoman	Police officer
Produce man	Produce seller
Product-development man	Product-development worker
Production man (radio and TV)	Production coordinator
Property man (amuse. and rec.)	Property coordinator
Property man (mo. pict.)	Property handler
Property master (mo. pict.)	Property supervisor
Public-address serviceman	Public-address servicer
Public relations man	Public-relations practitioner
Public-relations woman	Public-relations practitioner
Radio patrolman	Radio police officer
Radio repairman	Radio repairer
Repairman	Repairer
Rest-room maid	Rest-room attendant
Rewrite man	Rewriter
Ring master	Ring conductor

Old Occupational Title	Revised Occupational Title
Salad girl	Salad maker
Salad man	Salad maker
Salesman	Sales associate (sales agent, sales representative, soliciter, driver)
Sandwich girl	Sandwich maker
Sandwich man	Sandwich maker
Sculptress	(title deleted)
Seamstress	Sewer, custom (mender, alterer)
Shoe repairman	Shoe repairer
Shop foreman	Shop supervisor
Song and dance man	Song and dance person
Sound-effects man	Sound-effects technician
Special-effects man (mo. pict.)	Special-effects specialist
Special-events man (radio and TV)	Special-events coordinator
Stage-door man	Stage-door attendant
Stage man	Stage hand
State-highway patrolman	State-highway police officer
Station master	Station manager
Steward	Steward-stewardess
Stewardess	Steward-stewardess
Television-installation man	Television installer
Television service and repairman	Television-and-radio repairer
Traffic patrolman	Traffic police officer
Used car salesman	Used car sales associate
Valet	Gentleman's attendant
Video man	Video installer
Waiter	Waiter-waitress
Waitress	Waiter-waitress
Wardrobe mistress	Wardrobe supervisor
Watchman, crossing	Crossing tender
Watchman I (any industry)	Guard II
Wine steward	Wine steward-stewardess

Appendix D
Nations and Citizens
of the World

Prior to the Second World War, much of Africa and Oceania and some parts of Asia were colonies or possessions of European nations. These were given names convenient to their occupiers: Tanganyika, Palau, and New Hebrides, to name three. Upon achieving independence, many of these nations immediately changed their names: Tanganyika became Tanzania, Palau became Belau, and New Hebrides became Vanuatu. Other nations, long independent, have changed their names in recent years, including Kampuchea (Cambodia), Burkino Faso (Upper Volta), Myanmar (Burma), and Benin (Dahomey). Because of such changes, announcers—and especially news reporters and anchors—must have available an up-to-date source of correct terminology for every nation of the world.

Additionally, as stated at the end of Chapter 5, it is important for announcers to know how to refer to citizens of all nations of the world. It may come as a surprise to learn that a citizen of the Ivory Coast is an Ivorian, a citizen of Lesotho is a Masotho (plural Basotho), and a citizen of the Seychelles a Seychellois. This appendix presents the Americanized name of every nation of the world and gives both usage and pronunciation for these nations and their citizens. Where they differ, both noun and adjective used to denote a nation's inhabitants are given.

Nation	Pronunciation	Person from the Nation	Pronunciation
Afghanistan	[æf'gænəstæn] (AF-GAN'-UH-STAN)	Afghan	['æfgæn] (AF'-GAN)
Albania	[æl'beniə] (AL-BAY'-NEE-UH)	Albanian	[æl'beniən] (AL-BAY'-NEE-UN)
Algeria	[æl'dʒɪriə] (AL-JEER'-EE-UH)	Algerian	[æl'dʒɪriən] (AL-JEER'-EE-UN)
Andorra	[æn'dɔrə] (AN-DOOR'UH)	Andorran	[æn'dɔrən] (AN-DOOR'-UN)
Angola	[æn'golə] (AN-GO'-LUH)	Angolan	[æn'golən] (AN-GO'-LUN)
Antigua	[æn'tigwə] (AN-TEEG'-WUH)	Antiguan	[æn'tigwən] (AN-TEEG'-WUN)

Nation	Pronunciation	Person from the Nation	Pronunciation
Argentina	[ɑrdʒən'tinə] (AR-JUN-TEE'-NUH)	Argentine	['ɑrdʒən,tin] ('AR-JUN-TEEN) or ['ɑrdʒən,taɪn] ('AR-JUN-TYNE)
Australia	[ɔ'streljə] (AW-STRAYL'-YUH)	Australian (*Aussie* is slang, but not bad taste)	[ɔ'streljən] (AW-STRAYL'-YUHN)
Austria	['ɔstriə] (AWS'-TREE-UH)	Austrian	['ɔstriən] (AW'-STREE-UN)
Bahamas	[bə'heməz] (BUH-HAY'-MUZ) [bə'hɑməz] (BUH-HAH'-MUZ)	Bahamian	[bə'hemiən] (BUH-HAY'-MEE-UN) [bə'hɑmiən] (BUH-HAH'-MEE-UN)
Bahrain	[bɑ'ren] (BAH-RAIN')	Bahraini	[bɑ'reni] (BAH-RAY'-NEE)
Bangladesh	['bɑŋglədɛʃ] (BAHNG'-GLUH-DESH)	*n.* Bangladeshi *a.* Bangladesh	[bɑŋglə'dɛʃi] (BAHNG-GLUH-DESH'-EE) (same as name of nation)
Barbados	[bɑr'bedoz] (BAR-BAY'-DOZ)	Barbadian	[bɑr'bediən] (BAR-BAY'-DEE-UN)
Belau	[be'laʊ] (BAY-LAU')	Belauan	[be'laʊn] (BAY-LAU'-UN)

(The Republic of Belau was formerly known as Palau.)

Nation	Pronunciation	Person from the Nation	Pronunciation
Belgium	['bɛldʒəm] (BEL'-JUM)	Belgian	['bɛldʒən] (BEL'-JUN)
Belize	[bɛ'liz] (BEH-LEEZ')	Belizean	[bɛ'liziən] (BEH-LEEZ'-EE-UN)
Benin	[bɛ'nin] (BEH-NEEN')	Beninese	[bɛnə'niz] (BEN-UH-NEEZ')
Bermuda	[bɚ'mjudə] (BER-MYOO'-DUH)	Bermudian	[bɚ'mjudiən] (BER-MYOO'-DEE-UN)
Bhutan	[bu'tɑn] (BOO-TAHN')	Bhutanese	[butɑ'niz] (BOO-TAH-NEEZ')
Bolivia	[bo'lɪviə] (BO-LIV'-EE-UH)	Bolivian	[bo'lɪviən] (BO-LIV'-EE-UN)
Botswana	[bɑt'swɑnə] (BAHT-SWAN'-UH)	Motswana (sing.) Batswana (pl.)	[mɑt'swɑnə] (MAHT-'SWAN-UH) [bɑt'swɑnə] (BAHT-SWAN'-UH)

(Batswana and Botswana receive the same pronunciation.)

Nation	Pronunciation	Person from the Nation	Pronunciation
Brazil	[brə'zɪl] (BRUH-ZIL')	Brazilian	[brə'zɪljən] (BRUH-ZIL'-YUN)
Brunei	[bru'naɪ] (BRUH-NY')	Bruneian	[bru'naɪən] (BRUH-NY'-UN)

Nation	Pronunciation	Person from the Nation	Pronunciation
Bulgaria	[bʊl'gɛriə] (BUHL-GARE'-EE-UH)	Bulgarian	[bʊl'gɛriən] (BUHL-GARE -EE-UN)
Burkina Faso (formerly Upper Volta)	[bʊr'kinə'fas,o] (BOOR-KEEN'-UH FAH'-SO)	Burkinan	[bʊr'kinɑn] (BOOR-KEEN'-UN)
Burundi	[bʊ'rʊndi] (BUH-RUHN'-DEE)	*n.* Burundian	[bʊrʊndiən] (BUH-RUHN'-DEE-UN)
		a. Burundi	(same as name of nation)
Cameroon	[kæmɚ'un] (KAM-ER-OON')	Cameroonian	[kæmɚ'uniən] (KAM-ER-OON'-EE-UN)
Canada	['kænədə] (KAN'-UH-DUH)	Canadian	[kə'nediən] (KUH-NAY'-DEE-UN)

(French Canadians pronounce it [,kɑ,nɑ'dɑ] (KAH-NAH-DAH'), with a slight stress on the last syllable. Females are Canadienne [,kɑ,nɑ'djɛn] (KAH-NAH-DYEHN'), and males are Canadien [,kɑ,nɑ'djẽ] (KAH-NAH-DYEH').)

Nation	Pronunciation	Person from the Nation	Pronunciation
Cape Verdi	['kep'vɛrdi] (KAYP'-VEHR'-DEE)	*n.* Cape Verdean; *a.* Cape Verdian	both pronounced ['vɛrdiən] (VEHR'-DEE-UN)
Central African Republic		Central African	
Chad	[tʃæd] (TCHAD)	Chadian	['tʃædiən] (TCHAD'-EE-UN)
Chile	['tʃɪli] (TCHIL'-EE)	Chilean	['tʃɪliən] (TCHIL'-EE-UN) or [tʃɪ'leən] (TCHI-LAY'-UN)
China	['tʃaɪnə] (TCHY'-NUH)	Chinese	[tʃaɪ'niz] (TCHY-NEEZ')

(Mainland China is the People's Republic of China; the Republic of China is on Taiwan and nearby islands.)

Nation	Pronunciation	Person from the Nation	Pronunciation
Colombia	[ko'lʌmbiə] (KO-LUM'-BEE-UH)	Colombian	[ko'lʌmbiən] (KO-LUM'-BEE-UN)

(Most dictionaries give KUH-LUM'-BEE-UH, but current radio and television usage favors the more nearly Spanish pronunciation.)

Nation	Pronunciation	Person from the Nation	Pronunciation
Comoros	[kə'mɔr,oz] (KUH-MOR'-OHZ)	Comoran	[kə'mɔr,ən] (KUH-MOR'-UN)
Congo	['kɑŋgo] (KAHNG'-GO)	Congolese	[kɑŋgə'liz] (KAHNG-GUH-LEEZ')

(The Republic of Congo is not the former Belgian Congo, but a part of what was once French Equatorial Africa.)

Nation	Pronunciation	Person from the Nation	Pronunciation
Cook Islands	[kʊk] (KOOK)	Cook Islander	
Costa Rica	['kostə'rikə] (KOST'-UH REE'-KUH)	Costa Rican	['kostə'rikən] (KOST'-UH REEK'-UN)

Nation	Pronunciation	Person from the Nation	Pronunciation
Cuba	['kjubə] (KYOO'-BUH)	Cuban	['kjubən] (KYOO'-BUN)
Cyprus	['saɪ,prəs] (SY'-PRUSS)	Cypriot	['sɪp,riət] (SIP'-REE-UT)
Czechoslovakia	[,tʃɛkoslo'vɑkiə] (CHECK-OH-SLO-VAHK'-EE-UH)	Czechoslovakian	[,tʃɛkoslo'vɑkiən] (CHECK-OH-SLO-VAHK'-EE-UN)
Denmark	['dɛn,mɑrk] (DEN'-MARK)	*n.* Dane	[den] (DAYN)
		a. Danish	['denɪʃ] (DAYN'-ISH)
Djibouti	[dʒɪ'buti] (JIH-BOOT'-EE)	Citizen of Djibouti	
Dominica	[də'mɪnɪkə] (DUH-MIN'-IK-UH)	Dominican	[də'mɪnɪkən] (DUH-MIN'-IK-UN)
Dominican Republic	[də'mɪnɪkən] (DUH-MIN'-IK-UN)	Dominican	
Ecuador	['ɛkwə,dɔr] (EK'-WUH-DOOR)	Ecuadorean	[ɛkwə'dɔriən] (EK-WUH-DOOR'-EE-UN)
Egypt	['idʒɪpt] (EE'-JIPT)	Egyptian	[i'dʒɪpʃən] (EE-JIP'SHUN)
El Salvador	[ɛl'sælvədɔr] (EL SAL'-VUH-DOOR)	Salvadoran	[sælvə'dɔrən] (SAL-VUH-DOOR'-UN)
Equatorial Guinea	[ɛkwə'tɔriəl'gini] (EK-WAH-TOR'-EE-UL GIN'-EE)	Equatorial Guinean	[ɛkwə'tɔriəl'giniən] (EK-WAH-TOR'-EE-UL GIN'-EE-UN)

[There are three Guineas in Africa: Equatorial Guinea (once known as Spanish Guinea), Guinea, and Guinea-Bissau. GIN should be pronounced like the last syllable of *begin*.]

Nation	Pronunciation	Person from the Nation	Pronunciation
Eritrea	[,ɛrɪ'treə] (AIR-IH-TRAY'-UH)	Eritrean	[,ɛrɪ'treən] (AIR-IH-TRAY'-UN)
Ethiopia	[,iθi'opiə] (EE-THEE-O'-PEE-UH)	Ethiopian	[,iθi'opiən] (EE-THEE-O'-PEE-UN)
Falkland Islands	['fɔk,lənd] (FAWK'-LUND)	Falkland Islander	
Faroe Islands	['færo] (FA'-RO)	Faroese	[,færo'iz] (FA-RO-EEZ')
Fiji	['fidʒi] (FEE'-JEE)	Fijian	['fidʒiən] (FEE'-JEE-UN)
Finland	['fɪnlənd] (FIN'-LUND)	*n.* Finn	[fɪn] (FIN)
		a. Finnish	['fɪ,ɪʃ] (FIN'-ISH)
France	[fræns] (FRANS)	*n.* Frenchman or Frenchwoman	['frɛntʃmən], ['frɛntʃwʊmən] (FRENTSH'-MUN), (FRENTSH'-WUH-MUN)
French Guiana	[gi'ænə] (GEE-AN'-UH)	*a.* French	
		n. French Guianese	[giə'niz] (GEE-UH-NEEZ')
		a. French Guiana	(same as name of nation)
French Polynesia	[pɑlə'niʒə] (PAHL-UH-NEEZH'-UH)	French Polynesian	[pɑlə'niʒən] (PAHL-UH-NEEZH'-UN)
Gabon	[gɑ'bɔn] (GAH-BAWN')	Gabonese	[,gɑbə'niz] (GAH-BUH-NEEZ')

(Gabon Republic was once part of French Equatorial Africa.)

Nation	Pronunciation	Person from the Nation	Pronunciation
Gambia	['gæmbiə] (GAM'-BEE-UH)	Gambian	['gæmbiən] (GAM'-BEE-UN)
Germany	['dʒɝməni] (JER'-MUH-NEE)	German	['dʒɝmən] (JER'-MUN)
Ghana	['gɑnə] (GAH'-NUH)	Ghanaian	[gɑ'neən] (GAH-NAY'-UN)

[Some dictionaries list *Ghanian* (GAH-NEE-UN) as an alternative to *Ghanaian*, but the Documentation and Terminology Service of the United Nations does not suggest this usage.]

Nation	Pronunciation	Person from the Nation	Pronunciation
Gibraltar	[dʒɪ'brɔltɚ] (JIH-BRAHLT'-ER)	*n.* Gibraltarian	[dʒɪbrɔl'tɛriən] (JIH-BRAHL-TARE'-EE-UN)
		a. Gibraltar	(same as name of nation)
Greece	[gris] (GREES)	Greek	[grik] (GREEK)
Greenland	['grin,lənd] (GREEN'-LUND)	*n.* Greenlander	['grin,ləndɚ] (GREEN'-LUND-ER)
		a. Greenland	(same as name of nation)
Grenada	[grɔ'nedə] (GRUH-NAY'-DUH)	Grenadian	[,grə'nediən] (GRUH-NAY'-DEE-UN)
Guadeloupe	[gwɑdə'lup] (GWAH-DUH-LOOP')	*n.* Guadeloupian	[gwɑdə'lupiən] (GWAH-DUH-LOO'-PEE-UN)
		a. Guadeloupe	(same as name of nation)
Guatemala	[gwɑtə'mɑlə] (GWAH-TUH-MAHL'-UH)	Guatemalan	[gwɑtə'mɑlən] (GWAH-TUH-MAHL'-UN)
Guinea	['gɪn,i] (GIN'-EE)	Guinean	['gɪn,iən] (GIN'-EE-UN)
Guinea-Bissau	[bɪs'aʊ] (BISS-OW')	Guinean	['gɪn,iən] (GIN'-EE-UN)
Guyana	[gaɪ'ænə] (GUY-AN'-UH)	Guyanese	[gaɪə'niz] (GUY-UN-EEZ')
Haiti	['he,ti] (HAY'-TEE)	Haitian	['heʃən] (HAY'-SHUN)
Honduras	[hɑn'dʊrəs] (HAHN-DUHR'-US)	Honduran	[hɑn'dʊrən] (HAHN-DUHR'-UN)
Hong Kong	[hɔŋ 'kɔŋ] (HAWNG'KAWNG')	Citizen of Hong Kong	
Hungary	['hʌŋgəri] (HUNG'-GUH-REE)	Hungarian	[hʌŋ'gɛriən] (HUNG-GARE'-EE-UN)
Iceland	['aɪslənd] (EYES'-LUND)	*n.* Icelander	['aɪsləndɚ] (EYES'-LUND-ER)
		a. Icelandic	[aɪs'lændɪk] (EYES-LAN'-DIK)
India	['ɪndiə] (IN'-DEE-UH)	Indian	['ɪndiən] (IN'-DEE-UN)
Indonesia	[,ɪndo'niʒə] (IN-DO-NEEZH'-UH)	Indonesian	[,ɪndo'niʒən] (IN-DO-NEEZH'-UN)
Iran	[ɪ'rɑn] (IH-RAHN')	Iranian	[ɪ'rɑn,iən] (IH-RAHN'-EE-UN)
Iraq	[ɪ'rɑk] (IH-RACK')	Iraqi	[ɪ'rɑki] (IH-RACK'-EE)

Nation	Pronunciation	Person from the Nation	Pronunciation
Ireland	['aɪɚlənd] (EYE'-ER-LUND)	*n.* Irishman; Irishwoman	['aɪrɪʃ] (EYE'-RISCH)
		a. Irish	['aɪrɪʃ] (EYE'-RISCH)
Israel	['ɪzriəl] (IZ'-REE-UL)	Israeli	[ɪz'reli] (IZ-RAY'-LEE)

(Dictionaries and announcers prefer IZ'-REE-UL and IS-RAY'-LEE, but more nearly correct IZ'-RY-EL' and IZ-RY-AY'-LEE are heard more and more often. Use *Israelite* when referring to Biblical times.)

Italy	['ɪtəli] (IT'-UH-LEE)	Italian	[ɪ'tæljən] (IH-TAL'-YUN)
Ivory Coast	['aɪvri 'kost] (EYE'-VRY KOST)	Ivorian	[aɪ'vɔriən] (EYE-VOR'-EE-UN)
		Ivoirien	[ɪvwarjɛ̃] (IH-VWAR'-YEN)

(République du Côte d'Ivoire; French *Ivoirien* is interchangeable with Anglicized *Ivorian*.)

Jamaica	[dʒə'mekə] (JUH-MAKE'-UH)	Jamaican	[dʒə'mekən] (JUH-MAKE'-UN)
Japan	[dʒə'pæn] (JUH-PAN')	Japanese	[ˌdʒæpə'niz] (JAP-UH-NEEZ')
Jordan	['dʒɔrdən] (JAWR'-DUN)	Jordanian	['dʒɔr'deniən] (JAWR-DAYNE'-EE-UN)
Kampuchea	[kɑmpu'tʃiə] (KAHM-POO-CHEE'-UH)	Kampuchean	[ˌkɑmpu'tʃiən] (KAHM-POO-CHEE'-UN)

(Kampuchea was formerly known as Cambodia.)

Kenya	['kɛnjə] (KEN'-YUH)	Kenyan	['kɛnjən] (KEN'-YUN)

(The pronunciation KEEN'-YUH is of British colonial origin, and Kenyans dislike that pronunciation.)

Kiribati	[kɪrɪbɑti] (KEER-IH-BAHT'-EE)	*n.* Kiribatian	[ˌkɪrɪ'bɑtiən] (KEER-IH-BAHT'-EE-UN)
		a. Kiribati	(same as name of nation)
Korea	[kɔ'riə] (KAW-REE'-UH)	Korean	[kɔ'riən] (KAW-REE'-UN)

(South Korea is the Republic of Korea; North Korea is the People's Democratic Republic of Korea.)

Kuwait	[ku'et] (KOO-WAYT')	Kuwaiti	[ku'eti] (KOO-WAYT'-EE)
Laos	['lɑ,os] (LAH'-OSS)	*n.* Lao	['lɑ,o] (LAH'-O)
		a. Laotian	[le'o,ʃən] (LAY-OH'-SHUN]
Lebanon	['lɛbə,nɑn] (LEB'-UH-NAHN)	Lebanese	[lɛbə'niz] (LEB-UH-NEEZ')
Lesotho	[lɛ'soto] (LEH-SO'-TOE)	*n.* Mosotho (sing.), Basotho (pl.)	[mo'soto] (MO-SO'-TOE) [bɑ'soto] (BAH-SO'-TOE)
		a. Basotho	
Liberia	[laɪ'bɪriə] (LY-BEER'-EE-UH)	Liberian	[laɪ'bɪriən] (LY-BEER'-EE-UN)
Libya	['lɪbiə] (LIB'-EE-UH)	Libyan	['lɪbiən] (LIB'-EE-UN)
Liechtenstein	['lɪktan,staɪn] (LIK'-TUN-STYN)	*n.* Liechtensteiner	['lɪktan,staɪnɚ] (LIK'-TUN-STYN-ER)
		a. Liechtenstein	

Nation	Pronunciation	Person from the Nation	Pronunciation
Luxembourg	['lʌksəmbʊrg] (LUKS'-UM-BOORG)	n. Luxembourger	['lʌksəmbʊrgɚ] (LUKS'-UM-BOORG-ER)
		a. Luxembourg	(same as name of nation)
Macau	[ma'kaʊ] (MAH-KOW')	n. Macanese	[makan'iz] (MAH-KAHN-EEZ')
		a. Macau	(same as name of nation)
Madagascar	[mædə'gæskar] (MAD-UH-GAS'-KAHR)	Malagasy	[malə'gasi] (MAHL-UH-GAHS'-EE)
Malawi	[ma'la,wi] (MAH-LAH'-WEE)	Malawian	[ma'la,wiən] (MAH-LAH'-WEE-UN)
Malaysia	[mə'leʒə] (MUH-LAY'-ZHUH)	Malaysian	[mə'leʒən] (MAH-LAH'-ZHUN)
Maldives	['mældaɪvz] (MAL'-DYVEZ)	Maldivian	[mæl'dɪviən] (MAL-DIV'-EE-UN)
Mali	['mali] (MAH'-LEE)	Malian	['ma,liən] (MAH'-LEE-UN)
Malta	['mɔltə] (MAWL'-TUH)	Maltese	[mɔl'tiz] (MAWL-TEEZ')
Martinique	[martæn'ik] (MAHR-TAN-EEK')	Martiniquais	[martæni'ke] (MAHR-TAN-EE-KAY')
Mauritania	[mɔrɪ'teniə] (MAWR-IH-TAYN'-EE-UH)	Mauritanian	[mɔrɪ'teniən] (MAWR-IH-TAYN'-EE-UN)
Mauritius	[mɔ'rɪt,iəs] (MAW-RIHT'-EE-US)	Mauritian	[mɔ'rɪt,iən] (MAW-RIHT'-EE-UN)
Mexico	['mɛksɪ,ko] (MEHX'-IH-KO)	Mexican	['mɛksɪkən] (MEHX'-IH-KUN)
Monaco	['manɪ,ko] (MAHN'-IH-KO)	Monacan or Monegasque	['manɪkən] or [manɪ'gask] (MAHN'-IH-KUN) or (MAHN-IH-GAHSK')
Mongolia	[man'goliə] (MAHN-GO'-LEE-UH)	Mongolian	[man'goliən] (MAHN-GO'-LEE-UN)
Morocco	[mə'rak,o] (MUH-RAHK'-O)	Moroccan	[mə'rakən] (MUH-RAHK'-UN)
Mozambique	[mozæm'bik] (MO-ZAM-BEEK')	Mozambican	[mozæm'bikən] (MO-ZAM-BEEK'-UN)
Myanmar	[mi'an,ma] (MEE-AHN'-MAH)	Citizen of Myanmar	
Namibia	[nə'mɪbiə] (NUH-MIB'-EE-UH)	Namibian	[nə'mɪbiən] (NUH-MIB'-EE-UN)
Nauru	[na'u,ru] (NAH-OO'-ROO)	Nauruan	[na,uruən] (NAH-OO-ROO'-UN)
Nepal	[nɛ'pal] (NEH-PAHL')	Nepalese	[nɛpə'liz] (NEH-PUH-LEEZ')
Netherlands	['nɛðɚləndz] (NETH'-ER-LUNDZ)	Netherlander	[nɛðɚ'lændɚ] (NETH-ER-LAND'-ER)

Nation	Pronunciation	Person from the Nation	Pronunciation
Netherlands Antilles	[æn'tɪl,iz] (AN-TIL'-EEZ)	Netherlands Antillean	[æn'tɪliən] (AN-TIL'-EE-UN)
New Caledonia	[kælə'doniə] (KAL-UH-DON'-EE-UH)	New Caledonian	[kælə'doniən] (KAL-UH-DON'-EE-UN)
New Zealand	['zilənd] (ZEE'-LUND)	*n.* New Zealander	['ziləndɚ] (ZEE'-LUND-ER)
		a. New Zealand	(same as name of nation)
Nicaragua	[nɪkə'rɑg'wɑ] (NIK-UH-RAHG'-WAH)	Nicaraguan	[nɪkə'rɑgwən] (NIK-UH-RAHG'-WUN)
Niger	['naɪdʒɚ] (NY'-JER)	*n.* Nigerien	[nɪʒɪr'jɛ̃] (NIH-ZHIHR-YEHN')
		a. Niger	(same as name of nation)

(*Nigerian* applies only to citizens of Nigeria. Use the French *Nigerien* and the anglicized *Niger* for citizens of the Republic of Niger.)

Nation	Pronunciation	Person from the Nation	Pronunciation
Nigeria	[naɪ'dʒɪriə] (NY-JEER'-EE-UH)	Nigerian	[naɪ'dʒɪriən] (NY-JEER'-EE-UN)
Norway	['nɔrwe] (NAWR'-WAY)	Norwegian	[nɔr'widʒən] (NAWR-WEEJ'-UN)
Oman	[o'mɑn] (OH-MAHN')	Omani	[o'mɑni] (OH-MAHN'-EE)
Pakistan	['pɑkɪ,stɑn] (PAHK'-IH-STAHN)	Pakistani	[,pɑkɪ'stɑni] (PAHK-IS-TAHN'-EE)
Panama	['pænə,mɑ] (PAN'-UH-MAH)	Panamanian	['pænə'meniən] (PAN-UH-MAYNE'-EE-UN)
Papua New Guinea	['pæpjuə] (PAP'-YOU-UH)	Papau New Guinean	['gɪniən] (GIN'-EE-UN)
Paraguay	['pɑrəgwaɪ] (PAHR'-UH-GWY)	Paraguayan	[pɑrə'gwyən] (PAHR-UH-GWY'-UN)
Peru	[pə'ru] (PUH-ROO')	Peruvian	[pə'ruviən] (PUH-ROO'-VEE-UN)
Philippines	['fɪləpinz] (FIL'-UH-PEENZ)	*n.* Filipino	[fɪlə'pino] (FIL-UH-PEEN'-O)
		a. Philippine	
Poland	['polənd] (PO'-LUND)	*n.* Pole *a.* Polish	[pol] (POL) ['polɪʃ] (PO'-LISH)
Portugal	['pɔrtʃəgəl] (PAWR'-CHUH-GUL)	Portuguese	[pɔrtʃə'giz] (PAWR-CHUH-GEEZ')
Qatar	[kɑ'tɑr] (KAH-TAHR')	Qatari	[kɑ'tɑri] (KAH-TAHR'-EE)
Reunion	[ri'junjən] (REE-YOON'-YUN)	Reunionese	[rijunjən'iz] (REE-YOON-YUN-EEZ')
Romania	[ro'menjə] (RO-MAYNE'-YUH) [ro'meniə] (RO-MAY'-NEE-UH)	Romanian	[ro'menjən] (RO-MAYNE'-YUN) [ro'meniən] (RO-MAY'-NEE-UN)

(*Romania* is also *Rumania* and may be pronounced with an initial ROO.)

Nation	Pronunciation	Person from the Nation	Pronunciation
Rwanda	[ru'ɑndə] (ROO-AHN'-DUH) ['rwɑndə] (RWAN'-DUH)	Rwandan	[ru'ɑndən] (ROO-AHN'-DUN) ['rwɑndən] (RWAN'-DUN)
St. Christopher-Nevis-Anguilla	['sent'krɪstəfɚ-'nɛvɪs-æŋ'gwilə] (SAYNT KRIS'-TUH-FUR-NEHV'-ISS-ANG-GWEE'-LUH)	Kittsian, Nevisian, Anguillan	['kɪtsiən], [nɛ'vɪsiən], [æŋ'gwilən] (KITS'-EE-UN), (NEH-VISS'-EE-UN), (ANG-GWEE'-LUN)
St. Lucia	['luʃə] (LOOSH'-UH)	St. Lucian	['luʃən] (LOOSH'-UN)
St. Vincent and the Grenadines	['vɪnsənt, grɛnə'dinz] (VIN'-SUNT, GREN-UH-DEENZ')	St. Vincentian	[vɪn'sɛntiən] (VIN-SENT'-EE-UN)
San Marino	['sæn mə'rin,o] (SAN MUH-REEN'-O)	Sanmarinese	[san mɑrin'ese] (SAN MAHR-EEN-AY'-SAY)
São Tomé and Principe	[sãʊ'tomɛ, 'prinsi,pɛ] (SAUNG-TOE'-MEH, PREEN'-SEE-PEH)	São Toméan	[sãʊ 'tomɛən] (SAUNG-TOE'-MEH-UN)
Saudi Arabia	[sɑ'u'di] (SAH-OO'-DEE)	*n.* Saudi *a.* Saudi Arabian	(same as name of nation)
Senegal	[sɛnə'gɑl] (SEHN-UH-GAHL')	Senegalese	[sɛnəgə'liz] (SEHN-UH-GUH-LEEZ')
Seychelles	[se'ʃɛlz] (SAY-SHELZ')	*n.* Seychellois *a.* Seychelles	[seʃɛl'wɑ] (SAY-SHEL-WAH') (same as name of nation)
Sierra Leone	[si'ɛrə li'on] (SEE-AIR'-UH LEE-OWN')	Sierra Leonean	[li'oniən] (LEE-OWN'-EE-EE-UN)
Singapore	['sɪŋgəpɔr] (SING'-GUH-PAWR)	*n.* Singaporean	[sɪŋgə'pɔriən] (SING-GUH-PAWR'-EE-UN)
Solomon Islands	['sɑləmən] (SAHL'-UH-MUN)	Solomon Islander	
Somalia	[so'mɑljə] (SO-MAHL'-YUH)	Somali	[so'mɑli] (SO-MAHL'-EE)
South Africa		South African	
Soviet Union	[sovi'ɛt] (SO-VEE-ET') ['sovjɛt] (SOV'-YET)	Russian	['rʌʃən] (RUSH'-UN)

(*Russian* is correct for only about half the Union of Soviet Socialist Republics, or U.S.S.R. *Soviet* means *council*, even though it is often used to mean "Citizen of the U.S.S.R." Formal usage calls for "Citizen of the Soviet Union" or "Citizen of the U.S.S.R."; less formal usage, *Soviet citizen*; informal, *Russian*.)

Nation	Pronunciation	Person from the Nation	Pronunciation
Spain	[spen] (SPAYN)	*n.* Spaniard	[ˈspænjɚd] (SPAN'-YERD)
		a. Spanish	[ˈspænɪʃ] (SPAN'-ISH)
Sri Lanka	[sri ˈlɑŋkə] (SREE LAHNGK'-UH)	Sri Lankan	[sri ˈlɑŋkən] (SREELAHNGK'-UN)
Sudan	[suˈdæn] (SOO-DAN')	Sudanese	[sudəˈniz] (SOO-DUH-NEEZ')
Surinam	[ˈsurɪˌnɑm] (SOOR'-IH-NAHM)	*n.* Surinamer	[surɪˈnɑmɚ] (SOOR-IH-NAHM'-ER)
		a. Surinamese	[surɪnɑˈmiz] (SOOR-IH-NAH-MEEZ')
Swaziland	[ˈswɑziˌlænd] (SWAZI'-LAND)	Swazi	[ˈswɑzi] (SWAH'-ZEE)
Sweden	[ˈswidən] (SWEED'-UN)	*n.* Swede	[swid] (SWEED)
		a. Swedish	[ˈswidɪʃ] (SWEED'-ISH)
Switzerland	[ˈswɪtzɚlənd] (SWITZ'-ER-LUND)	Swiss	[swɪs] (SWISS)
Syria	[ˈsɪriə] (SIHR'-EE-UH)	Syrian	[ˈsɪriən] (SIHR'-EE-UN)
Taiwan	[taɪˈwɑn] (TY-WAHN')	Taiwanese	[taɪwɑnˈiz] (TY-WAHN-EEZ')
		Chinese	[tʃaɪˈniz] (CHY-NEEZ')

(Only 14 percent of the population of Taiwan is from mainland China; 84 percent is native Taiwanese.)

Nation	Pronunciation	Person from the Nation	Pronunciation
Tanzania	[tænzəˈniə] (TAN-ZUH-NEE'-UH)	Tanzanian	[tænzəˈniən] (TAN-ZUH-NEE'-UN)
Thailand	[ˈtaɪˌlænd] (TY'-LAND)	Thai	[taɪ] (TY)
Togo	[ˈtoˌgo] (TOE'-GO)	Togolese	[ˌtoˌgoˈliz] (TOE-GO-LEEZ')
Tonga	[ˈtɔŋgə] (TAWNG'-GUH)	Tongan	[ˈtɔŋgən] (TAWNG'-GUN)
Trinidad and Tobago	[ˈtrɪnədæd, təˈbego] (TRIN'-UH-DAD, TUH-BAY'-GO)	Trinidadian	[trɪnəˈdædiən] (TRIN-UH-DAD'-EE-UN)
		Tobagonian	[təbəˈgoniən] (TUH-BUH-GOHN'-EE-UN)
Tunisia	[tuˈniʒə] (TOO-NEEZH'-UH)	Tunisian	[tuˈniʒən] (TOO-NEEZH'-UN)
Turkey	[ˈtɝki] (TERK'-EE)	*n.* Turk	[tɝk] (TERK)
		a. Turkish	[ˈtɝkɪʃ] (TERK'-ISH)
Tuvalu	[tuˈvɑlu] (TOO-VAHL'-OO)	Tuvaluan	[tuvəˈluən] (TOO-VUH-LOO'-UN)
Uganda	[juˈgændə] (YOU-GAND'-UH)	Ugandan	[juˈgændən] (YOU-GAND'-UN)
United Arab Emirates	[emˈmɪrɪts] (EH-MIHR'-ITS)	Emirian	[ɛˈmɪriən] (EH-MIHR'-EE-UN)

Nation	**Pronunciation**	**Person from the Nation**	**Pronunciation**
United Kingdom		*n.* Briton *collective plural,* British *a.* British	['brɪtən] (BRIHT'-UN) ['brɪtɪʃ] (BRIHT'-ISH)

United States
(*American* for a U.S. citizen is resented by some North and South Americans because they are Americans, too. Despite this, the term is widely used to mean a person who lives in or is a citizen of the United States.)

Upper Volta	['vʊltə] (VOLT'-UH)	Upper Voltan	['vʊltən] (VOLT'-UN)
Uruguay	['ʊrəgwaɪ] (OOR'-UH-GWY)	Uruguayan	[ʊrə'gwaɪən] (OOR-UH-GWY'-UN)
Vanuatu	[ˌvɑn‚u'ɑ‚tu] (VAHN-OO-AH'-TOO)	Vanuatuan	[ˌvɑn‚uɑ'tuən] (VAHN-OO-AH-TOO'-UN)
(formerly New Hebrides, in South Pacific)			
Vatican City State	['vætəkən] (VAT'-UH-KUN)	Citizen of . . .	
Venezuela	['vɛnə'zwelə] (VEN-UH-ZWAY'-LUH)	Venezuelan	['vɛnə'zwelən] (VEN-UH-ZWAY'-LUN)
Vietnam	[ˌvi'ɛt‚nɑm] (VEE-ET'-NAHM)	Vietnamese	[ˌvi'ɛtnə'miz] (VEE-ET'-NUH-MEEZ')
Wallis and Futuna	['wɑlɪs, fu'tunə] (WALL'-US, FOO-TOON'-UH)	Wallisian Futunan or Wallis and Futuna Islander	[wɑ'lisiən] (WAH-LEES'-EE-UN) [fu'tunən] (FOO-TOON'-UN)
Western Sahara	[sə'hɛrə] (SUH-HARE'-UH)	Saharan	[sə'hɛrən] (SUH-HARE'-UN)
Western Samoa	[sæ'moə] (SA-MO'-UH)	Western Samoan	[sæ'moən] (SA-MO'-UN)
Yemen	['jɛmən] (YEHM'-UN)	Yemeni	[jɛ'mɛni] (YEH-MEN'-EE)
Yugoslavia	[jugo'slaviə] (YOU-GO-SLAV'-EE-UH)	Yugoslav	['jugo'slav] (YOU'-GO-SLAV)
Zaire	[zɑ'ɪr] (ZA-EAR')	Zairian	[ˌzɑ'ɪriən] (ZAH-EAR'-EE-UN)
Zambia	['zæmbiə] (ZAM'-BEE-UH)	Zambian	['zæmbiən] (ZAM'-BEE-UN)
Zimbabwe	[zɪm'babwe] (ZIM-BOB'-WAY)	Zimbabwean	[zɪm'babwiən] (ZIM-BOB'-WEE-UN)

Appendix E
Suggested
Readings

•Chapter 1: Broadcast Announcing

Rivers, William L., Schramm, Wilbur, and Christian, Clifford G. *Responsibility in Mass Communication*. 3rd ed. New York: Harper & Row, 1980.

U.S. Department of Labor. *Occupational Outlook Handbook*. Published periodically. Available at U.S. Government bookstores and most college libraries.

Chapter 2: The Announcer as Communicator

Blythin, Evan, and Samovar, Larry A. *Communicating Effectively on Television*. Belmont, CA: Wadsworth, 1985.

Duerr, Edwin. *Radio and Television Acting: Criticism, Theory and Practice*. Westport, CT: Greenwood Press, 1972.

Tedlock, Dennis. *The Spoken Word and the Work of Interpretation*. Philadelphia: University of Pennsylvania Press, 1983.

Chapter 3: Performance

Hawes, William. *The Performer in the Mass Media*. New York: Hastings House, 1978.

Malandro, Loretta A., and Barker, Larry. *Nonverbal Communication*. New York: Random House, 1983.

McConkey, Wilfred J. *Klee as in Clay*. Lanham, MD: Hamilton Press, 1986.

NBC Staff. *NBC Handbook of Pronunciation*. 4th ed. New York: Harper & Row, 1984.

Zannes, Estelle, and Goldhaber, Gerald. *Stand Up, Speak Out*. 2nd ed. Reading, MA: Addison-Wesley, 1983.

Chapter 4: Voice and Diction

Cooper, Morton. *Change Your Voice Change Your Life*. New York: Macmillan, 1984.

Keith, Michael C. *Broadcast Voice Performance*. Chicago: Bonus Books, 1986.

Moncur, John P., and Harrison, M. Karr. *Developing Your Speaking Voice*. 2nd ed. New York: Harper & Row, 1972.

Rizzo, Raymond. *The Voice as an Instrument*. 2nd ed. New York: Odyssey Press, 1978.

Sprague, Jo, and Stuart, Douglas. *The Speaker's Handbook*. 2nd ed. San Diego: Harcourt Brace Jovanovich, 1988.

Uris, Dorothy. *A Woman's Voice: A Handbook to Successful Public and Private Speaking*. Chelsea, MD: Scarborough House, 1974.

Chapter 5: American English Usage

Follett, Wilson. *Modern American Usage: A Guide*. Edited by Jacques Barzun. New York: Hill & Wang, 1966.

Newman, Edwin. *Strictly Speaking*. New York: Warner Books, 1982.

Safire, William. *I Stand Corrected*. New York: Times Books, 1984.

Chapter 6: Broadcast Equipment

Alten, Stanley R. *Audio in Media*. 2nd ed. Belmont, CA: Wadsworth, 1990.

Compesi, Ronald J., and Sheriffs, Ronald E. *Small Format Television Production*. 2nd ed. Boston: Allyn and Bacon, 1990.

Nisbett, Alec. *The Use of Microphones*. 2nd ed. Stoneham, MA: Focal Press, 1983.

Woran, John, and Kefauver, Alan P. *The New Recording Studio Handbook*. Rev. ed. Plainveiw, NY: ALAR, 1989.

Zettl, Herbert L. *Television Production Handbook*. 5th ed. Belmont, CA: Wadsworth, 1991.

Chapter 7: Commercials and Public-Service Announcements

Baker, Georgette. *You Too Can Be in Television Commercials*. Diamond Bar, CA: Talented, 1988.

Blu, Susan, and Mullin, Molly Ann. *Word of Mouth: A Guide to Commercial Voice-Over Excellence*. Los Angeles: Pomegranate Press, 1987.

Fridell, Squire. *Acting in Television Commercials for Fun and Profit*. New York: Crown, 1987.

Heighton, Elizabeth J., and Cunningham, Don R. *Advertising in the Broadcast and Cable Media*. 2nd ed. Belmont, CA: Wadsworth, 1984.

Peacock, James. *How to Audition for Television Commercials and Get Them*. Chicago: Contemporary Books, 1982.

Chapter 8: Interview and Talk Programs

Blythin, Evan, and Samovar, Larry A. *Communicating Effectively on Television*. Belmont, CA: Wadsworth, 1985.

Cohen, Akiba A. *The Television News Interview*. Newbury Park, CA: SAGE Publications, 1987.

Nathan, Harriet. *Critical Choices in Interviews*. Berkeley, CA: University of California Institute of Governmental Studies, 1986.

Chapters 9 and 10: Radio News and Television News

Fang, Irving. *Television News, Radio News*. 4th revised ed. St. Paul, MN: Rada Press, 1985.

Gans, Herbert J. *Deciding What's News: A Study of CBS Evening News, NBC Nightly News, Newsweek and Time*. New York: Random House, 1980.

Graber, Doris A. *Processing the News*. 2nd ed. New York: Longman, forthcoming.

Hewitt, John. *Air Words: Writing for Broadcast News*. Mountain View, CA: Mayfield, 1988.

MacDonald, R. H. *Broadcast News Manual of Style*. New York: Longman, 1987.

Tuchman, Gaye. *Making News: A Study in the Construction of Reality*. New York: Free Press, 1980.

Chapter 11: Music Announcing

Apel, Willi. *Harvard Dictionary of Music*. 2nd ed. Cambridge: Harvard University Press, 1969.

Crofton, Ian, and Fraser, Donald. *A Dictionary of Musical Quotations*. New York: Schirmer Books, 1989.

Cross, Milton. *New Milton Cross' Stories of the Great Operas*. New York: Doubleday, 1955.

Cross, Milton, and Kohrs, Karl. *The New Milton Cross' More Stories of the Great Operas*. New York: Doubleday, 1980.

Keith, Michael C., and Krause, Joseph M. *The Radio Station*. 2nd ed. Boston: Focal Press, 1989.

Sadie, Stanley, ed. *The New Grove Dictionary of Music and Musicians*. 6th ed. 20 vols. London: Macmillan Publishers Ltd., 1980.

Wong, Michael. *A Day in the Life of a Disc Jockey*. Mahwah, NJ: Troll Association, 1987.

Chapter 12: Sports Announcing

Gunther, Marc, and Carter, Bill. *Monday Night Mayhem: The Inside Story of ABC's Monday Night Football*. New York: William Morrow, 1988.

Harwell, Ernie. *Tuned to Baseball*. South Bend, IN: Diamond Communications, 1986.

Odums, R.I., et al. *Career Guide to Sports Broadcasting*. Rita Tessman, ed. Cleveland, OH: Guidepost, 1986.

Smith, Curt. *Voices of the Game: The First Full-Scale Overview of Baseball Broadcasting*. South Bend, IN: Diamond Communications, 1987.

Spence, Jim, and Diles, Dave. *Up Close and Personal: The Inside Story of Network Television Sports*. New York: Macmillan, 1988.

Chapter 13: Starting a Career in Broadcasting

Ellis, Elmo. *Opportunities in Broadcasting*. Lincolnwood, IL: National Textbook, 1986.

Pearlman, Donn. *Breaking into Broadcasting*. Chicago: Bonus Books, 1986.

Reed, Maxine K., and Reed, Robert M. *Career Opportunities in Television, Cable, and Video*. Rev. ed. New York: Facts on File, 1986.

Chapter 14: The International Phonetic Alphabet

Kenyon, John S., and Knott, Thomas. *A Pronouncing Dictionary of American English.* 2nd ed. Springfield, MA: G. & C. Merriam, 1953.

NBC Staff. *NBC Handbook of Pronunciation*. 4th ed. New York: Harper & Row, 1984.

Chapter 15: Foreign Pronunciation

Bras, Monique. *Your Guide to French Pronunciation*. New York: Larousse, 1975.

Bratus, B. V. *Russian Intonation*. Elmsford, NY: Pergamon Press, 1972.

Cox, Richard G. *The Singer's Manual of French and German Diction*. New York: Schirmer Books, 1970.

Jackson, Eugene, and Geiger, Adolph. *German Made Simple*. New York: Doubleday, 1985.

Jackson, Eugene, and LoPreato, Joseph. *Italian Made Simple*. New York: Doubleday, 1960.

Jackson, Eugene, and Rubio, Antonio. *Spanish Made Simple*. New York: Doubleday, 1984.

McConkey, Wilfred J. *Klee as in Clay*. Lanham, MD: Hamilton Press, 1986.

NBC Staff. *NBC Handbook of Pronunciation*. 4th ed. New York: Harper & Row, 1984.

Glossary

Terms are defined here only as they are used in this book. Many of the terms have additional uses and meanings not explained here.

A/C   Abbreviation for *Adult Contemporary,* a radio station format and the type of popular music played by such a radio station.

account executive   A person who sells broadcast time for a radio station or an agency.

actuality   A term used in radio news to refer to a report featuring someone other than broadcast personnel (politician, police inspector, athlete, or eyewitness) who provides an actual statement rather than one paraphrased and spoken by a reporter.

Adult Contemporary   Descriptive of a format or type of music played on some radio stations, consisting of soft to moderate rock, ballads, and current hits.

affricates   Speech sounds that combine a plosive (release of air as in saying the letter *p*) with a fricative (friction of air through a restricted air passage as in saying the letter *s*); an example is the "ch" sound in *choose.*

AFTRA   Abbreviation for American Federation of Radio and Television Artists, the union made up of radio and television announcers whose work is either live or taped.

aircheck   An audition tape, usually a portion of an actual broadcast.

Album-Oriented Rock   A radio station format featuring all styles of rock music.

allusion   An indirect but pointed, or meaningful, reference; "he is as subtle as Dirty Harry" is an allusion.

alveolus   The upper gum ridge.

ambient noise   Unwanted sounds in an acoustical environment (such as air conditioners, traffic noises, airplanes).

ambient sounds   Normal background sounds that do not detract from the recording or the program and may even add to the excitement of the broadcast (such as crowd sounds at a sports event).

amplitude   The strength of a radio wave.

anchor   The chief newscaster on a radio or television news broadcast.

announcer   Anyone who speaks to an audience through a broadcasting medium: radio or television transmission over the public airways, cable or other closed-circuit audio or video distribution, or electronic amplification, as in an auditorium or a theater. Announcers include newscasters, reporters, commentators, sportscasters, narrators, "personalities," disc jockeys, program hosts, and people who deliver commercial messages (as contrasted with those who act in dramatized commercials).

AOR   Abbreviation for *Album-Oriented Rock.*

articulation   The physical formation of spoken words by means of teeth, tongue, and lips working together with the soft palate, gum ridges, and each other to break up phonated sounds into articulate (or even inarticulate) speech sounds.

aspirate   To release a puff of breath, as in sounding the word *unhitch.* Overaspiration results in a popping sound when sitting or standing close to a microphone.

attenuator   A volume control on an audio console.

attitude   An announcer's position or bearing, made up of mind set, stance, point of view, and beliefs; similar to mood, but going deeper and connoting a relationship between the announcer and persons being addressed.

audience demographics   See *demographics.*

audio console   The control board that receives, mixes, amplifies, and sends audio signals to a recorder or a transmitter.

AWRT   Abbreviation of American Women in Radio and Television.

back-announce   To identify songs and artists after the music has been played.

barbarism   A blunder in speech; similar to a solecism.

barter   The exchange of airtime for goods or services.

BB   Script symbol for *billboard,* used to indicate to an announcer that an upcoming feature or event should be promoted.

BEA   Abbreviation for Broadcast Education Association.

beat check   Using a telephone to search for and tape news stories from a list of agencies, including the FBI, police and fire departments, local hospitals, the weather bureau, and airport control towers; also called the *phone beat.*

Beautiful Music   A radio station format that features gentle or restful music from motion picture soundtracks, instrumental arrangements of old standards, and some stage musicals and operettas.

bed   See *music bed.*

beeper   Electronic beeping tones placed on the audio track of a videotape for cuing. Eight beeps are laid down, 1 second apart. The last 2 seconds of the electronic leader are silent, and the director, responding to the rhythm of the eight beeps, allows 2 more seconds to elapse before giving the next instruction to the technical director.

beeper reports   News reports, either recorded or live, telephoned to a station, during which an electronic beep is sounded to let the person speaking know that a recording is being made. The beep is not used when station personnel are recorded and need not be used for others if they are told that they are being recorded or being broadcast.

bending the needle   Causing the swinging needle of a VU or VI meter on an audio console to hit the extreme right of its calibrated scale, indicating to the operator that the volume of the sound being sent through the console is too high.

Best Time Available   A radio station advertising package that schedules commercials at the station's discretion, with a promise to broadcast them at the best available time slots.

BG   Script symbol for *background,* referring most often to background music.

bidirectional   The pickup pattern of a microphone that accepts sounds from two of its sides.

bilabial   Sounds articulated primarily by both lips, for example, the consonants *p* and *w;* also called *labial sounds.*

billboard   To promote an upcoming feature or event on the air.

billing log   The name given by the sales and business departments to a radio station's program log, a listing, in sequence, of each element of the broadcast day, including commercials.

blocking   Instructing performers in a television production as to when and where to stand, walk, and so on.

BM   Abbreviation for *Beautiful Music,* a radio station format.

board   In radio, an audio console; in television news operations, a large Plexiglas sheet on which the elements of a newscast are entered throughout the day.

board fade   A lowering of the volume on an audio console, usually to the point of losing the sound altogether.

boom   Short for *audio boom,* a device for moving a microphone without allowing either its operator or the mic to be seen on the television screen. Most booms are mounted on movable dollies and have controls for moving the microphone in or out, up or down, or sideways. Television camera cranes are sometimes called booms.

boosting   Strengthening an audio signal by means of an amplifier.

brain   The computer used to program an automated radio station; also called a *controller.*

BTA   Abbreviation for *Best Time Available.*

bulletin font   The oversized type produced by a printer or typewriter that prints scripts for television news broadcasts.

bumper   The device used to move a television program from one element to another, as in a transition from the program to a commercial or from one segment of the program to another.

calling the game   Giving a play-by-play description of a sports event.

camera consciousness   The awareness on the part of a performer of the capabilities and limitations of the television cameras.

cardioid   A type of microphone pickup pattern that is heart-shaped.

cart   Short for *audiotape cartridge;* a loop of tape encased in a plug-in cartridge that automatically recues.

cart machine   An electronic audio device that records and plays back (or sometimes only plays back) material for broadcast.

cart with live tag   A commercial that begins with a recorded announcement, often with musical background, and ends with a live closing by a local announcer.

carted commercials   Commercials dubbed to audiotape cartridges.

carting   The act of dubbing, or recording on, an audiotape cartridge.

CD   Abbreviation for *compact disc.*

CG Abbreviation for *character generator.*

chain A group of broadcast stations owned by one company or by a network.

channel selector switch A control on an audio console that enables the operator to select from two or more inputs.

character generator An electronic device used for creating titles, bar graphs, and many other graphics for the television screen.

cheating to the camera Positioning oneself to create the impression on-screen of talking directly to another person, while presenting a favorable angle to the camera.

CHR Abbreviation for *Contemporary Hit Radio.*

chroma-key An electronic system that makes it possible for one television scene to be matted in behind another. Chroma-keying is used to show a slide or some other graphic aid behind a news anchor, for instance. Blue is generally used for chroma-key matting.

chronological résumé A résumé that presents basic information on work experience in chronological order.

clichés Overused and worn out expressions.

clock See *hot clock.*

cluster Two or more radio commercials played without intervening comment or program material; also called *commercial cluster* or *spot set.*

CNN Abbreviation of Cable News Network.

co-anchors Two or more announcers who share the role of chief newscaster on a radio or television program.

cold copy A script not seen by an announcer until the moment to read it has arrived.

color Comments made by a member of an announcing team to add an extra dimension to a live broadcast; usually consist of human-interest anecdotes and informative, amusing, or unusual facts.

combo operator A radio disc jockey who does his or her own engineering.

commercial cluster See *cluster.*

communicaster Used by some radio stations to identify the host of a telephone call-in show.

competency-based résumé A résumé that stresses the skills an applicant possesses.

condenser microphone A type of microphone that features a diaphragm and an electrode as a backplate.

console An audio control board.

Contemporary Hit Radio A radio station format that features the current top rock hits, sometimes interspersed with a few golden oldies; also known as *Top 40.*

continuity book A loose-leaf compilation of radio commercials in the order they are to be read or introduced (if on tape) by the announcer on duty; sometimes called *copy book.*

continuity writers Writers of broadcast scripts other than news scripts.

controller   The computer that controls the programming of an automated radio system; also called the *brain*.

cooperative commercials   Commercials used on both radio and television, whose cost is divided between a national and a local advertiser.

copy book   See *continuity book*.

copy sets   Multipart forms, complete with one-use carbon papers, used widely in television newsrooms to create as many as six duplicate scripts of a program.

corporate media   See *industrial media*.

cover letter   The letter written to accompany a résumé or an audition tape.

cover shot   A television shot that gives a picture of a medium-to-large area. On an interview set, a cover shot would include both interviewer and guest(s).

crank up the gain   To increase the volume of sound going through an audio console.

crescendo   An increase in the volume or intensity of an announcer's voice.

cross fade   Manipulating the volume controls of an audio console so that one program sound fades out while another simultaneously fades in.

crossplug   A pitch made by a disc jockey or talk program host to promote another program on the same station.

CU   Television script symbol for *close-up*.

cue box   Small speaker in an audio control room or on-air studio that allows an audio operator to hear program elements as they are being cued up or previewed; sometimes called a *cue speaker*.

cue cards   Cards used in television to convey information or entire scripts to on-camera performers.

cumes   Short for *cumulative ratings,* which indicate the number of people listening to or viewing a particular station at a given time.

cut sheet   In radio, a listing that tells an engineer how to edit one or more cuts from an audiotape to a tape cartridge; in television news operations, a form on which information about taped material is entered during editing by videotape engineers.

cutaway shots   Reaction shots, usually of a reporter listening to a newsmaker, recorded at the time of an interview and later edited into a package to avoid jump cuts at points in the report where parts of the speaker's comments have been omitted.

daypart   A term used by music radio stations to identify specific portions of the broadcast day, which may be *dayparted* into morning drive time, afternoon drive time, midday, nighttime, and overnight.

debriefing log   A record kept by radio and television stations of information about the performance of guests and the degree of audience interest in them.

decrescendo   A decrease in the force or loudness of an announcer's voice.

demographics   The profile of an actual or intended audience, including information on age, sex, ethnic background, income, and other factors that might help a broadcaster attract or hold a particular audience.

denasality   A quality of the voice due to speaking without allowing air to pass through the nasal passage.

depth of field   The area in front of a camera lens in which everything is in focus.

desk   A name used for the assignment editor in broadcast news operations.

diacritical marks   The marks used by dictionaries to indicate pronunciation.

diaphragm   The muscular membrane that separates the stomach from the lungs.

diphthongs   Speech sounds that consist of a glide from one vowel sound to another, for example, the "oy" sound in the word *joy*.

disc jockey   The person who identifies the music and provides pertinent comments on a popular music radio station.

DJ   Abbreviation for *disc jockey;* sometimes spelled *deejay*.

donut commercial   A commercial with a recorded beginning and end and live material read by a local announcer in the middle.

double out   A term used in radio production to warn an engineer that a speaker repeats the out-cue in a particular tape. A sports coach, for example, may say "early in the year" both in the body of his comments and at the end of the cut; the warning *double-out* is given so that the engineer will not stop the cart prematurely.

drive time   Hours during which radio stations receive their highest audience ratings, usually 6–10 A.M. and 3–7 P.M.

drugola   The acceptance of illegal drugs in exchange for such favors as promoting a recording produced by the supplier of the drugs.

dubbing   Transferring audio- or videotaped program material to another tape; also, recording another person's voice onto the soundtrack to replace the voice of the person who is seen on the screen.

DVE   Abbreviation for *digital video effects*.

DVE machine   A device that can turn a video picture into a mosaic, swing it through space, make it shrink or grow in size, and achieve many other visually interesting effects.

dynamic microphone   A rugged, high-quality microphone that works well as an outdoor or hand-held mic; also known as a *pressure mic*.

ear training   Developing a sensitivity to sounds, especially spoken words, and the ability to detect even slight variations from accepted standards of pronunciation, articulation, voice quality, and other aspects of human speech. Ear training is an essential part of voice improvement.

easy listening formula   A system for judging the clarity of a script that is to be broadcast.

EBS   Abbreviation for *Emergency Broadcast System*.

EFP   Abbreviation for *electronic field production*.

egg-on-face look   The strained look of a performer who is trying to hold a smile while waiting for the director to go to black.

elasped time clock   A clock that shows how much time has been used up, rather than time remaining, in a broadcast segment.

electronic field production   Any kind of videotaping using minicams and portable recorders and done on location.

electronic news gathering   Producing news reports for television in the field, using the same kind of portable equipment employed in electronic field production.

electrostatic microphone   An alternative term for a *condenser mic.*

ELF   Abbreviation for *easy listening formula.*

Emergency Broadcast System   A notification system developed by the U.S. government and requiring broadcast licensees to provide information about emergencies, such as floods, hurricanes, earthquakes, and tornadoes.

ENG   Abbreviation for *electronic news gathering.*

equal time   A provision of the Communications Act that requires broadcast licensees in the United States to provide time on an equal basis for legally qualified candidates for office.

ESPN   Abbreviation of Entertainment and Sports Programming Network.

ET   A script symbol for *electrical transcription,* which was an early term for a certain type of phonograph record, now used for any kind of disc recording.

fact sheet   An outline of information about a product or an event, from which a writer prepares a script for a commercial or public-service announcement.

fader   A control on an audio console enabling an operator to increase or decrease the volume of sound going through the board.

fairness doctrine   A policy of the FCC that requires broadcast licensees to devote air time to the discussion of public issues.

FCC   Abbreviation for *Federal Communications Commission.*

Federal Communications Commission   The governmental agency that oversees broadcasting and other telecommunications industries in the United States.

feedback   A howl or squeal created when a microphone picks up and reamplifies the sound from a nearby loudspeaker.

fidelity   Faithfulness to an original sound, as in a recording of a live music performance.

flaring   Flashes on the television screen caused by reflection of studio lights or sunlight off some shiny object, such as jewelry.

format   (1) A type of script used in television, usually a bare script outline; (2) the type of programming provided by a radio station (for example, an MOR format); (3) the layout of a radio or television script, or the manner in which dialogue, sound effects, music, and other program elements are set forth on the page.

freeze   To remain motionless, usually at the end of a television scene.

fricatives   Sounds created by the friction of air through a restricted air passage; an example is the sound of the letter *f.*

functional résumé   See *competency-based résumé.*

future file   A set of 31 folders (one for each day of the month) holding information about coming events so that they may be considered for news coverage by an assignment editor.

gaffer's tape   The tape used to hold cables in place in television studios. (A *gaffer* is the chief electrician on a motion picture set.)

gain   The degree of sound volume through an audio console.

gain control   A sliding vertical fader or rotating knob used to regulate the volume of sound through an audio console.

General American   The speech of educated citizens of the Midwest and Far West of the United States and of most of Canada; also called *broadcast speech.*

general assignment reporter   A radio or television reporter who does not have a regular beat, or assignment.

glottal consonant   The letter *h,* when uttered without vibration of the vocal folds.

glottal stop   A speech sound produced by a momentary but complete closure of the throat passage, followed by an explosive release of air.

graveyard shift   Working hours that extend from midnight until 6:00 A.M.

hand signals   Signals developed to communicate instructions to performers without the use of spoken words.

happy talk   A derogatory term for a newscast featuring news personnel who ad-lib, make jokes, and banter with one another.

hard news   Important stories that are usually unanticipated by a broadcast news department.

headline   To *tease* upcoming music selections on a radio show.

headlines signal   A hand signal given by an announcer to tell the engineer that headlines will follow the news item currently being read.

headphone jack   A receptacle on a tape recorder or audio console for connecting a headset.

hemispheric   The pickup pattern of a microphone that accepts sounds within a half globe.

hitting marks   Moving to an exact spot in television performance, usually indicated by tape placed on the floor or the ground.

homers   Sports play-by-play announcers who show an obvious bias for the home team.

horizontal spots   Radio commercials scheduled at about the same time across the days of the week.

hot change   Words created by a character generator that jump from one word or phrase to another on the television screen.

hot clock   A wheel used by music, satellite, and news radio stations to schedule the playing of certain types of musical selections (up-tempo, golden oldie, current hit, etc.), to indicate precisely when local insertions (commercials, weather reports, or local news) may be made, or to specify the timing of headlines, news stories, weather reports, commercials, and other program elements; also called the *clock.*

hybrid résumé   A résumé that combines the features of a chronological and a competency-based résumé.

hypercardioid   A microphone pickup pattern.

I & I   Script symbol for *introduce and interview*.

IDs   Brief musical passages used to identify an upcoming sports report, business report, or other feature; also called *sounders* or *logos*.

IFB   Abbreviation for *interrupted foldback*.

in the mud   Expression used when the volume of sound going through an audio console is so weak that it barely moves the needle of the VU meter; the needle is said to be *in the mud*.

industrial media   Audiovisual presentations made for (and often by) corporations, government agencies, and similar entities and intended for internal use, usually for training purposes; usually referred to as *industrials*.

inflection   The variation of the pitch of a human voice.

informational interview   A conversation with an experienced broadcast executive for the purpose of gaining information about job-seeking.

input selector switch   Control on an audio console that allows more than one program input (several microphones, for example) to be fed selectively into the same preamp.

interdental   A speech sound made with the tongue between the upper and lower teeth, for example, the "th" sound in *thin*.

International Phonetic Alphabet   A system of phonetic transcription that employs special symbols to denote pronunciations.

interrupted foldback   A miniaturized earphone worn by news reporters and anchors and sportscasters. Instructions and cues are given over the IFB by producers and directors.

IPA   Abbreviation for *International Phonetic Alphabet*.

jock   Short for *disc jockey*.

jump cut   A noticeable "jump" in the television picture when a portion of taped material has been edited out.

labial   A speech sound made primarily with the lips, for example, the sound of the letter *p*.

labiodental   A speech sound requiring the lower lip to be in proximity to the upper teeth. Labiodental sounds are associated with the letters *f* and *v*.

larynx   The part of the body connecting the trachea (or windpipe) and the pharynx (the area between the mouth and the nasal passages) and containing the vocal folds.

lavaliere microphone   A small microphone clipped to the dress, tie, or lapel of a performer.

lead-in   The opening phrases of a taped or live report or the words used by a reporter to introduce a taped actuality or voicer.

lead-out   The closing phrases of a taped or live report or the words used by a reporter in adding a conclusion to a taped actuality or voicer.

LED   Abbreviation for *light-emitting diode*.

level indicator   A device that shows graphically the amount of volume being sent through an audio console or to an audio or videotape recorder.

libertarian theory   A theory concerning the media that maintains that, except for defamation, obscenity, or wartime sedition, there should be no censorship of the news whatsoever.

light-emitting diode   A device that indicates audio volume through the activation of a series of small lights.

linear notes   Notes prepared by a radio station executive, from which a disc jockey will promote a contest, an upcoming feature, or another disc jockey's show; sometimes called *liner cards*.

lingua-alveolar   A speech sound made with the tip of the tongue (or lingua) placed against the upper gum ridge (or alveolus), for example, the sound of the letter *t*.

linguadental   A speech sound made with the tongue between the upper and lower teeth, for example, the initial sound in *thin*.

linguapalatal   A speech sound made with the tip of the tongue nearly touching the upper gum ridge, for example, the sound of the letter *r*.

linguavelar   A speech sound made when the rear of the tongue is raised against the soft palate (or velum) and the tip of the tongue is lowered to the bottom of the mouth, as in sounding the letter *k*.

lip synch   Matching, or synchronizing, the movement of the lips with the speech sounds of the performer. This is achieved automatically with video equipment but is difficult when dubbing one performer's voice to the lip movements of another who is seen on-screen.

live coverage   Reporting on a story as it happens, most often from the scene of the event.

logo   An aural or visual symbol used to identify a program, product, company, or similar entity. The famous CBS eye is the logo for that network. An aural logo is also called a *sounder*.

looping   The dubbing of one person's voice onto the soundtrack of a tape to replace the voice of the person who is seen on the screen.

major market   A city or metropolitan area with a potential viewing or listening audience of over 1,000,000.

market   The reception area of a radio or television station, classified as major, secondary, or smaller.

marking copy   Making notations on scripts as reminders of when to pause or to stress a word or phrase or to show phonetic transcriptions of difficult words.

marks   Positions for television performers, usually indicated by small pieces of gaffer's tape on the floor of the studio or the ground at an exterior location.

master pot   A control on an audio console, capable of raising and lowering simultaneously all sounds going through the board; *pot* is short for *potentiometer*.

matte in   To combine electronically two pictures on the television screen without superimposing one over the other; see also *chroma-key*.

MERPS Abbreviation for *multi-event recorder/player systems,* which are audio/video electronic cart machines.

message design and testing The process of determining in advance the objectives of a given program and then rating its degree of success after.

mic fright A fear of performing in front of a microphone.

microphone consciousness An awareness of the capabilities and shortcomings of microphones.

Middle-of-the-Road A radio station format characterized by the playing of songs and orchestrations of moderate volume, tempo, and performance style.

minicam A small, lightweight, portable television camera and its associated equipment.

minidoc A short documentary, usually produced as a series for a radio or television news program.

minus out To eliminate the announcer's voice from the sound relayed back from a satellite to the announcer's IFB so that the $1\frac{1}{2}$-second delay will not confuse the announcer.

mixer An audio console.

moiré effect A wavering or shimmering of the picture on a television screen, due to patterns of small checks or narrow stripes on performers' clothing.

monitor pot A control on an audio console enabling the operator to adjust the volume of sound coming from a monitor speaker without affecting the volume of sound being broadcast or recorded.

monitor speaker Speaker in an audio control room that enables the operator to hear the material being broadcast or recorded.

mood A state of mind or emotion projected by a performer. Some typical moods are gloomy, joyous, cynical, elated, and festive. See also *attitude.*

moonlighting Working at odd jobs, usually at night, while holding down a permanent position.

MOR Abbreviation for *Middle-of-the-Road.*

morgue A collection of magazine and newspaper clippings, organized by topic and used for gathering background information for news stories and interviews.

MOS Script abbreviation for *man-on-the-street interview.* (Despite efforts to avoid gender-specific references in broadcast terminology, this term is still used.)

multidirectional microphone A microphone that can be adjusted to employ more than one pickup pattern.

music bed The musical background of a radio commercial, usually laid down before voices are added.

music sweep Several music recordings played back-to-back without interruption or comment by the DJ.

musical IDs Musical logos that identify a program or a program segment.

muting relays Devices that automatically cut off the sound from a monitor speaker when an announce mic in the control room is opened.

NAB Abbreviation for National Association of Broadcasters.

nasality A quality of the voice due to allowing air to exit through the nose, rather than the mouth, when speaking.

nasals Speech sounds that employ nasal resonance, such as *m, n,* and *ng.*

National Public Radio A network of noncommercial radio stations, established by the Corporation for Public Broadcasting.

newswheel An hourly *clock* that shows when headlines, commercials, weather and traffic reports, etc., are to be broadcast.

NRP Abbreviation for *National Public Radio.*

O & O Abbreviation for *owned and operated;* refers to radio or television stations owned and operated by a parent network.

off hours The portion of a broadcast day, usually late night and very early morning, when the audience is least likely to be tuned in.

omnidirectional A microphone pickup pattern in which all sides will accept sound signals.

on-air studio The studio in which radio disc jockeys and news anchors perform.

opening up to the camera Positioning oneself at a slight angle from a second person to present a favorable appearance to the camera.

optimum pitch The pitch at which a speaker feels most comfortable while producing the most pleasant speech sounds.

orbiting spots See *rotating spots.*

out-cue The words that conclude a recorded and carted program segment, alerting the engineer and the announcer that the carted segment has come to its conclusion.

overmodulation Excessive volume that distorts an audio signal.

package (1) A complete news report prepared by a field or special assignment reporter, needing only a lead-in by an anchor; (2) a series of programs marketed to television stations as a unit.

pan pot Short for *panoramic potentiometer.*

panic button A control that allows a producer to cut off obscene or defamatory comments by a caller on a telephone talk show.

panoramic potentiometer A volume control that allows an operator to change the volume balance between two audio channels.

payola The accepting of money in return for playing certain songs on the air.

peripheral vision The ability to see out of the corners of the eyes, to see a hand signal, for example, without looking at the person giving it.

personality A term sometimes used for a disc jockey, program host, or other popular entertainer.

pharynx The area between the mouth and the nasal passages.

phonation   The utterance of speech sounds; articulation breaks up these sounds into recognizable speech.

phone beat   See *beat check*.

phone screener   A person, usually a producer or assistant producer, who receives telephone calls from listeners or viewers who want to talk with a program host and attempts to eliminate those from people who are obviously cranks or drunks or are too-frequent callers.

phoneme   The smallest unit of distinguishable speech sound.

pickup arm   The arm on a turntable that contains the stylus; also called the *tone arm*.

pickup pattern   The three-dimensional area around a microphone from within which sound is transmitted most faithfully, also referred to as the *polar pattern*.

pitch   The property of a tone that is determined by the frequency of vibration of the sound waves. For humans, the slower the vocal folds vibrate, the lower the pitch of the voice.

pitchman   A type of announcer whose style is reminiscent of sideshow barkers and old-time medicine shows.

play analyst   An announcer, usually a former star athlete, who works with a play-by-play announcer, providing insight and analysis of a game.

play-by-play announcer   A sportscaster who describes the action of a game.

playlist   Music approved by radio station management for playing at stipulated times.

plosive   A speech sound manufactured by the sudden release of blocked-off air. In English, the plosives are *p, b, t, d, c,* and *g*.

plugola   The free promotion of a product or service in which the announcer has a financial interest. (Reading or playing commercials that have been paid for is not illegal, even when the announcer has an interest in the product being advertised.)

polar pattern   See *pickup pattern*.

popping   The sound made when a plosive is spoken too closely to a sensitive mic.

postmortem   A meeting held after a broadcast to discuss what worked, what did not, and why.

postproduction   Editing and other electronic manipulation of audio- or videotapes after they have been recorded.

pot   Short for *potentiometer*.

potentiometer   A volume control on an audio console.

preamplifier   An electronic device that boosts the strength of an audio signal and sends it to the program amplifier; often shortened to *preamp*.

presentation tape   An audition tape.

pressure microphone   A rugged professional microphone that features a molded diaphragm and a wire coil suspended in a magnetic field; also called a *dynamic microphone*.

pressure zone microphone A type of microphone that eliminates time lags between direct and reflected sounds.

prime time That part of the broadcast day during which the radio or television audience is most likely to be tuned in.

production studio A radio studio in which music is dubbed from discs to carts, station promos are recorded, and other program elements requiring a sophisticated audio setup are produced.

program amplifier An electronic device that collects, boosts, and sends sounds to a transmitter or tape recorder.

program log A listing of all commercials, public-service announcements, ·and program material broadcast by a station.

promo Short for *promotion;* any prepared spot that promotes viewing or listening to a station or a program broadcast by the station.

prompter Any of several machines that display a script before a broadcast performer; also called *prompting devices* or *teleprompters* (however, TelePrompTer is the brand name of one prompting system).

pronouncer The phoneticized pronunciation for a word or name included on wire-service copy.

prop Short for *property;* any article other than sets or costumes used in a television production.

PSA Abbreviation for *public-service announcement.*

public-service announcement A radio or television announcement that promotes a charitable or nonprofit organization or cause.

PZM Abbreviation for *pressure zone microphone.*

Q & A session Questions-and-answer session, a brief on-air discussion of a news story between an anchor and a reporter in the field.

recurrent A term used in music radio to indicate selections that are just off the playlist.

redundancy Repetition of ideas or words or phrases, which is sometimes appropriate, as in repeating a telephone number to be called, and sometimes excessive, as in the term "joint partnership."

resonance The intensification of vocal tones during speech as the result of vibrations in the nose and cheekbones.

reveal Words or phrases produced by a character generator and "revealed" one at a time on the television screen to match the points being made by an announcer.

ribbon microphone A sensitive, professional microphone that has a metallic ribbon suspended between the poles of a magnet; also referred to as a *velocity mic.*

rip and read To take copy directly from a wire-service printer and read it on the air without editing it, marking it, or prereading it.

roll Words or phrases produced by a character generator and moved from bottom to top on the television screen.

ROS   Abbreviation for *Run of Station.*

rotating potentiometers   Knobs on an audio console that are turned clockwise or counterclockwise to raise or lower the volume of sound; see also *vertical faders.*

rotating spots   Commercial announcements whose time of broadcast varies throughout the week; also called orbiting spots.

rule of three   A theory that the impact of a statement is diluted by going beyond three words or phrases in a sequence.

Run of Station   A system of scheduling radio commercials on a random basis at available times.

running log   A listing of the times at which every program element will be broadcast by a radio station.

SAG   Abbreviation for the Screen Actors Guild, the union for those actors and announcers whose work is filmed (as opposed to taped).

SAT PIC   Abbreviation for *satellite picture,* a view of the Earth's weather sent from a satellite.

scener   A live or taped radio news report on a breaking event.

secondary market   An area with a potential braodcast audience of between 200,000 and 1,000,000 viewers or listeners.

segue   To broadcast two elements of a radio program back-to-back without overlap or pause. The first sound is faded out, and the second is immediately faded in.

semivowels   Speech sounds similar to true vowel sounds in their resonance patterns. The consonants *w, r,* and *l* are the semivowels.

set   Two or more songs played back to back without intervening commentary by the DJ.

SFX   Script symbol for *sound effects.*

sibilance   The sound made when pronouncing the fricatives *s, sh,* and sometimes *z.* Excessive sibilance is exaggerated by sensitive microphones.

signature   Same as a *logo* or *ID.*

simulcast   The simultaneous broadcasting of the same program over an AM and an FM station, or over a radio and a television station.

slate   An audio and/or visual identification of a taped television program segment that is included at the beginning of the tape and provides information about the segment—its title, the date of recording, the intended date of showing, and the number of the take.

slip start   A method of starting to play a cued-up phonograph record by allowing the turntable to rotate while the operator's hand holds the disc motionless and then releasing the disc.

slug commercial   A hard-hitting commercial, usually characterized by high volume, rapid reading, and frenetic delivery.

slug line   The shortened, or abbreviated, title given to a news event for identification purposes.

smaller market   An area with a potential audience of fewer than 200,000 viewers or listeners.

social responsibility theory   A theory concerning the media that charges journalists with considering the potential consequences of their coverage of the news.

soft news   News stories about scheduled events, such as meetings, briefings, hearings, or news conferences, that lack the immediacy and urgency of hard news.

solecism   A blunder in speech.

SOT   Script symbol for *sound on tape*.

sound bite   A brief statement made on-camera by someone other than station personnel; equivalent to an *actuality* on radio.

sounder   A short, recorded musical identification of a particular radio program element, such as a traffic, sports, or weather report; also referred to as an *ID* or *logo*.

sounds   Recorded statements introduced as part of radio news stories. Sounds include actualities, wraps, sceners, and voicers.

speech personality   The overall quality of a person's voice, that which makes one instantly recognizable to friends when speaking on the telephone.

spilling over   Another expression for *bending the needle*.

spot   Another term for a commercial.

spot set   See *cluster*.

stand-up   A direct address made to a camera by a television reporter at any time within a news package, but almost always for the closing comments.

stash   A term used for songs that are not on a radio station's current playlist but are occasionally played.

station ID   Short for *station identification*.

station logo   A symbol, either aural or visual, by which a station identifies itself.

status-conferral function   The concept that the media of radio and television confer exalted status to those who appear on them.

studio cards   Cards used in television to convey information or entire scripts to on-camera performers.

stylus   Part of a tone arm pickup cartridge, the needle.

super   Short for *superimposition*, the showing of one picture over another on the television screen.

sweep   The playing of several songs consecutively, without intervening comment by the DJ.

sweetening   Electronically treating music, during recording and in postproduction, to improve the sound quality.

switcher   (1) The video console that allows an operator to cut, dissolve, and perform other electronic functions; (2) the title given to the person who operates such a console.

tag   To make closing comments at the end of a scene or program segment.

take a level   To speak into a microphone prior to broadcast or recording so that an audio engineer can adjust the volume control.

takes   Any number of attempts to record a program segment successfully.

taking camera   In a multiple-camera television production, the camera that is "on" at a specific moment.

talk-back microphone   The mic located in a control room that allows the audio operator to speak to people in other production areas, such as studios or newsrooms.

talking head   A derogatory term for a television shot featuring a close-up of a speaker addressing the camera.

tally light   A red light mounted on the top of a television camera that, when lit, indicates the *taking camera*.

TAP   Abbreviation for *Total Audience Plan*.

tape cart   A cartridge of ¼-inch audiotape that rewinds and recues itself.

target audience   The intended audience for a program or a commercial.

tease   A brief promotion of a program or an upcoming segment of a program.

telegraphing a movement   A subtle indication by a television performer who is about to move, stand, or sit. Directors and camera operators need such warnings to follow movements effectively.

tempo   A speaker's rate of delivery.

tight shot   A close-up shot.

time-delay system   A means of delaying material being broadcast live (such as a call-in talk show) to permit intervention if someone uses profanity or makes other unacceptable comments.

Top 40   A radio station format that rotates the top hits of the day, usually interspersed with golden oldies; also called *Contemporary Hit Radio*.

toss   To turn the program over to a co-anchor, a weather reporter, or another member of the broadcast team with a brief ad-libbed transitional statement.

total audience plan   A system for distributing commercial messages over three or more dayparts.

trachea   The windpipe.

traffic department   The personnel at a broadcast station who schedule the placement of commercials.

transduction   The conversion of sound waves into electrical energy.

trash television   Television talk shows that regularly use intimidation, obscenity, vulgarity, and controversial and unsubstantiated statements to attract an audience that seeks cheap thrills.

UC   Abbreviation for *Urban Contemporary*.

unidirectional   A microphone pick-up pattern in which sound is accepted from only one direction.

uplink   A transmitter that sends a signal to a satellite and is often part of a mobile van.

Urban Contemporary   A radio station format that features music by African-American artists.

variable equalizer   A filter that enables an audio console operator to eliminate undesirable frequencies, such as those associated with scratches on a record.

velocity microphone   See *ribbon microphone.*

velum   The soft palate.

vertical fader   A sliding lever on certain audio consoles that is moved up or down to raise or lower the volume of sound.

vertical spots   Radio commercials scheduled at various times on a given day.

VI meter   Short for *volume indicator meter,* which registers the volume of sounds through an audio console.

virgule   A slash, used by some announcers to indicate a pause when marking broadcast copy for delivery.

vitality   The enthusiasm and high energy level of a performer.

voice-overs   Taped performances in which the announcer is not seen.

voicer   A carted report from a radio news reporter.

vowel   A pure phonated tone that can be held indefinitely without moving the articulators, for example, the sound "ah" in *father.*

VTR   Abbreviation for *videotape recorder.*

VTR SOT   Abbreviation for *videotape, sound on tape.*

VU meter   Short for *volume unit meter,* a part of an audio console that shows, by means of a swinging needle, the volume of sound going through the board.

wheel   Another term for a *clock,* or *hot clock.*

wild spots   Radio commercials guaranteed by a station to be played at some point within a designated block of time.

wipe   An electronic effect in which one picture appears to push another off the television screen.

woodshedding   The careful study, marking, and rehearsing of broadcast copy before performance.

working combo   Performing both announcing and engineering functions for a radio broadcast.

wowing   The distorted sound when a record or tape is run at an incorrect or inconsistent speed.

wrap   A recorded report from the field in which a radio news reporter provides a lead-in and a lead-out, "wrapped around" an actuality; also called a *wraparound.*

WX   Script symbol for *weather report.*

Index

Abbreviations, for television scripts, 318
Abstraction, avoiding, 251–253
Accent marks, 441–442
Actuality, 250, 287–288
Ad-lib announcing, 44–49, 52–54
Adult Contemporary (A/C) format, 338
Adverbs, misuse of, 160, 163
Advertising agencies, 203–204
Advertising practices, 200–205. *See also* Commercials
Affectation, in pronunciation, 111
Affricates, 130
Age referents, 149–150
Aircheck, 348, 416
Album-Oriented Rock (AOR) format, 340
Allege, correct use of, 161–163
Allusions, 39–40
American English
  changes in, 167–176
  clichés in, 154–157
  jargon in, 150–152
  nonstandard expressions of, 158–167
  plurals, 157–158
  speech sounds of, 112–120
American Heritage Dictionary, The, 92
Anchors
  radio, 282–290, 294–298
  television, 322–326
Announce microphones, 184
Announcer. *See also* Disc jockey
  and commercials, 205–219
  definition of, 4–5
  delivery style of, 20
  employment opportunities as, 7–9
  radio talk show, 270–274
  responsibilities of, 15–19, 274, 323–324
  roles of, 3–7
Announcing
  ad lib, 44–49, 52–54
  classical music, 353–357
  of commercials, 205–219
  education and training for, 9–15, 404–405
  modes of, 21
  of news, 282–298, 322–326
  specializations in, 5–6
  on radio talk shows, 267–274
AOR stations, 340
Articulation, 111, 129–135
Ashton, Betsy, 331
Aspiration, 108

Associated Press (AP), 283–286
Athletes, interviewing, 376–379
Attention signal, 81
Attenuator, 186
Audience demographics, 200
Audio consoles, 185–191
Audio recorder, for practice, 2
Audition tapes, 348, 416–422
Automated radio stations, 195–197
Azurin, Nerissa, 68, 70

Bach, Alwyn, 169
Back vowels, 113, 115, 437
Back-announcing, 335
Background, need for, 43
Beat check, 285
Best Times Available (BTA), 202–203
Bias, avoiding, 251–253
Bidirectional pickup pattern, 183
Biel, Michael, 169
Big Band format, 341
Billboarding, 276
Billing log, 272
Book of States, 254
Boosted signals, 187
Box graphics, 319
Break signal, 83
Breathing, correct, 128
Broadcast equipment
  audio consoles, 185–191
  in automated radio stations, 195–197
  cart machines, 191–192
  CD players, 192–193
  for the future, 197–198
  microphones, 180–184
  turntables, 193–195
Broadcast ethics, 16–17, 272
Broadcast journalism
  philosophies of, 329–331
  specializations in, 5
Brokaw, Tom, 197
Brown, Walt, 391
Bumpers, 319
Bus (phone), 271, 295

Camera
  addressing, 68–70
  cheating to, 67–68
  consciousness, 64–77
  depth of field of, 65
  fright, 56, 58–62
  movement while on, 66–67
  opening up to, 67
  robot, 197
  sitting while on, 66

standing while on, 65, 66
  taking, 68
Caray, Harry, 400–401
Cardioid pickup pattern, 183
Carlo, Laura, 126–127
Carts
  cuing and playing of, 191–192
  definition of, 191
  hand signal for, 84
  with live tag, 203
  for sports broadcasts, 383–385
Casselman, Chet, 290
CD player, 192–193
Chang, Caroline, 11, 314
Character generator, 317
Character voices, for commercials, 220–221
Characterizations, 44
Chinese, pronunciation of, 481–484
Chroma-keying, 72
Chronological résumé, 407–408, 410
Classical music announcing, 353–357
Clichés, 154–157
Clothing, on television, 72–73
Co-anchor, 296
Code of Broadcast News Ethics, 17
Cold copy, 21
Collins, Al "Jazzbeaux," 350–351
Colon, 35–36
Color, 7
Comma, 38
Commercial cluster, 271–272
Commercial log, 215–216
Commercials
  announcer's role in, 205–219
  character voices in, 220–221
  conveying interest in, 41–42
  cooperative, 227
  donut, 204, 220
  hand signal for, 84
  in-house production of, 204–205
  language misuse in, 167
  mood of, 209–212
  nonstandard speech styles used in, 222
  versus public-service announcements, 199
  radio, 200–205
  recording, in studio, 214–215
  specialization in, 6
  structure of, 31–33, 206–209
  television, 225–230
  timing for, 219–220
  working with, on-air, 215–220
Communication, effective, 22–24
Compact disc player, 192–193
Competency-based résumé, 408, 411

Computer information banks, 48
Computers, at broadcast stations, 13, 197–198, 328
Condenser microphones, 181–182
Consonants
  classification of, 129–130
  common problems with, 440–441
  French, 470–473
  German, 475–480
  Italian, 461–464
  medial, 131, 134
  pronunciation of, 439–441
  Spanish, 453–458
  syllabic, 441
Contemporary Hit Radio (CHR) format, 339–340
Continuity book, 216, 295
Continuity writers, 204
Controller, 196
Conversational style, 96
Cooke, Alistair, 153
Cooperative commercial, 227
Copy. *See also* Scripts
  analysis of, 25, 33–38, 206–212
  conveying interest in, 41–42
  determining organization of, 31–33
  employing characterizations in, 44
  getting general meaning of, 24–25
  hard, 75
  marking, 38, 212–214
  mood of, 27–31
  for news broadcasts, 290–294
  purpose of, 25–26
  reading aloud, 40–41
  verifying meaning and pronunciation of, 38–40
Copy book, 216
Copysets, 75, 325
Cornelsen, Howard, 355
Corporate media, 8, 420
Correspondents, 314
Country format, 339
Cover letter, 415–416
Cover shot, 68
CPA, 481–484
Cronkite, Walter, 55
Cue box, 190
Cue cards, 73–74
Cue signal, 81
Cue speaker, 190
Cues, 77–78. *See also* Hand signals
Cuing
  of cart machine, 191–192
  of CD player, 192–193
  of records, 194–195
Cumes, 346
Cut, 192

Cut signal, 81
Cutaway shots, 317

Dash, use of, 36–37
Daypart, 202, 203, 345
Dead air, 192
Deasey, Jim, 34
Debriefing log, 270
Defamation, 16, 17
Delivery, 20, 108–109
Delk, Denny, 418–419
Denasality, 122–124
Depth of field, 65
Design computer, 318
Diacritical marks, 92–93
Dictionary of Occupational Titles, 173–174
Dimitrova, Ghena, 105
Diphthongs, 112–113
  distortion of, 120
  German, 475
  Italian, 459–461
  pronunciation of, 117, 120, 438–439
  Spanish, 452–453
Disc jockey (DJ), 333
  announcing style of, 343
  applying for position as, 425–426
  preparing for career as, 347–353
  working conditions of, 333–338, 343–347
Donahue, Phil, 151
Donner, Stanley T., 24
Donut commercials, 204, 220
Drop-report signal, 83
Drugola, 17
Dubbing, 420
Dynamic microphones, 181

Ear training, 2
Eason, Jim, 269–270
Easy Listening format, 340–341
Easy listening formula (ELF), 294
EBS, 18
Education, for announcing, 9–15
Edwards, Bob, 303, 304
Effective communication, principles of, 22–24
Elapsed-time clock, 295
Electronic field production (EFP), 227
Electronic news gathering (ENG), 315
Electrostatic microphones, 181–182
Ellipses, 37
Emergency Broadcast System, 18
Emergency notification, 15–18
Emphasis, marking copy for, 38

Employment opportunities, in announcing, 7–9, 422–424
English. *See* American English; General American
Equal time, provision of, 273
ESPN, 368
Ethics, 16–17, 272
Ethnicity, terms concerning, 168–173
Europa Yearbook, 254
Exclamation point, 34
Eyewear, on television, 72–73

Facts on File, 304
Fade-out, 306
Fader, 186
Fairness doctrine, 273
Fang, Irving, 294
Fear of failure, 59–60
Federal Communications Commission, 17
Fessenden, Reginald, 197
Fidelity, 182
Field reporting
  for radio, 298–308
  for television, 314–322
Fifteen-second signal, 82
File, future, 314
Finlayson, Andrew, 276
Five-to-zero signal, 82
Flaring, 72
Fong, Cheryl, 72
Foreign languages. *See* Chinese; French; German; etc.
Format sheet, 276
Formats, of popular music stations, 338–343
French, pronunciation of, 465–473
Fricatives, 129–130
Front vowels, 113, 115, 435–437
Future file, 314

Gain control, 186
Gender, terms concerning, 173–175
General American, 110, 169–170
German, pronunciation of, 473–480
Glasses, on television, 72–73
Glottal consonant, 130
Golden Oldies format, 340
Graveyard shift, 268
Greek plurals, 157–158
Green room, 277
Greene, Eric, 67, 272, 276–278
Gundlach, Del, 350

Hall, Arsenio, 46–47
Hand signals, 80–85
Hand-held microphones, 184

Hard copy, 75
Hart, Al, 253
Hayakawa, S. I., 251
Headlines signal, 84
Headlining, 335
Headphone jack, 190
Headset microphones, 184
Heinrich, Don, 7
Hemispheric pickup pattern, 183
Homers, 392
Horizontal spots, 203
Hosting talk shows, 267–278
Hot change, 317
Houlberg, Rick, 55–56
Huskiness, 124
Hybrid résumé, 408, 412
Hypercardioid pickup pattern, 183

IDs, 84
IFB, 75, 77, 322
Impairment, physical, and
    pronunciation, 111
Industrial media, 8, 420
Inflection, 107
Information retrieval services, 302
Informational interview, 426
In-house production, of
    commercials, 204–205
Input selector switches, 187
Instructions, on-air, 77–85
Interdental consonants, 130
Interest, conveying, 41–42
International Phonetic Alphabet
    (IPA)
    accent marks in, 441–442
    advantages of, 93, 433
    consonant sounds in, 439–441
    diphthong sounds in, 438–439
    symbols of, 436, 437, 439, 443–
        447
    vowel sounds in, 435–438
Interrupted foldback (IFB), 75, 77,
    322
Interviews
    of athletes, 376–379
    avoiding abstraction and bias in,
        251–253
    control in, 257
    ending, 266–267
    informational, 426
    job, 426–429
    questions for, 261–263, 265–266
    recording of, 305–309
    research for, 254
    treatment of guest, 254–257, 270
    topic of, 257, 260
Introduce-report signal, 83
Intros, 288

IPA. *See* International Phonetic
    Alphabet
Italian, pronunciation of, 458–464

Jacobs, Jeffrey, 57
Jargon, 150–152, 266
Jazz format, 341
Jennings, Cheryl, 78
Jennings, Peter, 59
Jewelry, on television, 72
Job interviews, 426–429
Job openings, 7–9, 422–424
Job-hunting tools, 405–422
Jump cut, 317

Keys, graphic, 317
King, Bill, 387
King, Larry, 252
Klein, Don, 7, 383–384, 385, 390
Koppel, Ted, 60
Kreiling, Ernie, 254

Labial consonants, 130
Labiodental consonants, 130
Laquidara, Charles, 17
Latin plurals, 157–158
Lazarsfeld, Paul, 18
LED, 188
Lehrer, Robert, 21
Leigh, Katie, 44
Level indicator, types of, 188–189
Libertarian theory, 329, 330, 331
Light-emitting diode, 188
Liner notes, 345
Lingua-alveolar consonants, 130
Linguadental consonants, 130
Linguapalatal consonants, 130
Linguavelar consonants, 130
Live coverage, 3–4
Logos, 84
Loop, 218
Looping, 420
Lopez, Maria, 334
Louder signal, 83
Lowry, Terry, 65, 66, 70, 71, 272,
    277
Luttrell, Buzz, 84

MacNeil, Jim, 21
Makeup, 73
Markets, types of, 334
Marking copy, 38, 212–214
Marks, hitting, 64–65
Master pot, 189
McCarthy, Bob, 10
Medial consonants, 131, 134
Melkonian, Lois, 292
Mellish, Kirk, 327

Mental preparation, for
    performance, 61
Merton, Robert K., 18
Message design and testing, 8
Mic fright, 58–62, 106
Microphone consciousness, 62–64
Microphones
    internal structure of, 180–182
    pickup patterns of, 182–184
    positioning of, 62–64, 296
    types of, 184–185
Middle-of-the-Road (MOR) format,
    339
Mills, Cindy, 204
Minicams, 320
Minidocs, 298, 302–308
Misreading, 111
Mixer, 186
Moiré effect, 72
Monihan, Bill, 223
Monitor pot, 190
Monitor select switch, 190
Monitor speakers, 190
Mood, 27–31, 209–212
Moonlighting, 228
Morgue, 45, 48
Moses, Bessie, 29
Move-back-from-the-mic signal, 83
Move-closer-to-the-mic signal, 83
Movement, telegraphing of, 66–67
Multidirectional pickup pattern, 183
Multi-images, in commercials, 228
Municipal Yearbook, 254
Music announcing
    classical, 353–357
    popular, 333–353
    specializations in, 5
Music bed, 204–205
Music sweep, 335
MusicScan, 198
Muting relay, 189

Narration, 6
Nasality, 122–124
Nasals, 130
National Public Radio, 303–304
Nations, terms for, 175–176
NBC Handbook of Pronunciation,
    433–434
News
    hard versus soft, 314
    radio, 282–298
    sources of, 283–287
    television, 310–331
News log, 289–290
News runners, 313
News script, 295
Newswheel, 282–283, 285

Nichols, Mary Ann, 126, 127
Nonverbal communication skills, practice of, 2
NPR, 303–304

Obscenity, 17
Ocean, Bobby, 349
Off-mic, 183
Omnidirectional pickup pattern, 183
On-air studio, 334
One-minute signal, 82
Optimum pitch, 105–107
Out cues, 288
Outros, 288
Overmodulation, 189

Packages, 299–302, 315–319
Panic button, 274
Parentheses, 37
Paris, Samantha, 218–219
Payola, 16, 17, 273
Performances
    checklists for, 95, 100–101
    evaluating, 99
    preparing for, 94–95
    skills for, 94–101
Period, 33–34
Peripheral vision, 72
Personal attacks, 273
Philosophies, of broadcast journalism, 329–331
Phone beat (check), 285
Phone numbers, 96–97
Phone screener, 268
Phonetic transcription, 85–93. See also International Phonetic Alphabet
Photographs, 414–415
Pickup arm, 193–194
Pickup cartridge, 194
Pickup patterns, of microphones, 182–184
Pinyin system, 481–482
Pitch, 104–107
Pitchmen, 27, 103
Play analyst, 398–402
Playback machine. See Cart machine
Play-by-play announcer, 373–376, 385–392
Playlist, 337
Plosives, 129
Plugola, 17, 273
Plurals, Latin and Greek, 157–158
Polar patterns, of microphones, 182–184
Popping, 80, 108
Postmortem, 278, 313
Postproduction, 228

Potentiometers (pots), 186, 189–190
Preamplifiers, 187–188
Preparation, for performing, 58–59, 61
Presentation tape, 415
Pressure microphones, 181
Pressure zone microphones, 181–182
Prime time, 288
Production consoles, 185
Production studio, 179
Profanity, 17, 274
Program amplifier, 188
Program clock, 282–283, 284, 337
Program log, 272
Prompters, 73, 74–77
Pronouncer, 76
Pronouncing Dictionary of American English, A, 434, 436
Pronunciation, 91, 449–451
    of American English, 112–120
    of Chinese, 481–484
    of diphthongs, 438–439
    of French, 465–473
    of German, 473–480
    of Italian, 458–464
    of Russian, 480–481
    of Spanish, 451–458
    phonetic transcription for, 85–93
    problems in, 110–112
    verifying, in copy, 38–40
    of vowel sounds, 435–438
Props, 70–71
Public affairs, specialization in, 5
Public-service announcements, 199, 221–225
Punctuation, 33–38

Quality, voice, 121–128
Question mark, 34
Question-and-answer session, 321–322
Quotation marks, 34–35
Quotations, incorrect, 156–157

Radio
    advertising practices of, 200–205
    automated stations, 195–197
    field reporting for, 298–308
    hand signals for, 81–82, 83–85
    news, 281–290
    station formats, 338–343
    talk, 267–274
    writing news for, 290–294
Raw sound, 288
Reader's Guide to Periodical Literature, 254, 304
Reading aloud, 40–41
Real time, 268

Records, cuing up, 194–195
Redundancies, avoiding, 152–154
Remoted cart, 191
Reporters
    radio field, 298–308
    sports, 379–382
    television field, 314–322
    weather, 326–329
Resonance, 105, 124–125, 128, 139–140
Résumés, 405–407
    preparation of, 409–414
    types of, 407–409
Reveal, 317
Ribbon microphones, 180–182
Rip-and-read operations, 90, 281
Roll, 317
Rotating table, 193
Roth, J. D., 276
Rule of three, 206–208
Running log, 294
Run of Station (ROS), 202–203
Russian, pronunciation of, 480–481

Sanchez, Don, 78
Savitch, Jessica, 127
Scener, 288
Schaub, Jeffrey, 283
Schwa vowel, 438
Scott, Marvin, 48
Scripts, 49–51, 71. See also Copy symbols used in, 217–218
Selector, 198
Self-esteem, and performing, 60–61
Semicolon, 35
Semivowels, 130, 469
Set, 350
Shaer, Pat, 300
Shaw, Bernard, 175
Shaw, George Bernard, 86
Sibilance, 80, 108, 132
Similies, 154
Simmons, Lon, 383
Simulcast, 344
Single-sponsor programs, 200–201
Slang, 158–159
Slip starting, 193
Slow-down signal, 81–82
Social responsibility theory, 330–331, 332
Softer signal, 83
Solecisms, 159–166
Sound, 417
Sound bite, 250, 316
Sounders, 84, 85
Sounds, 287
Spanish, pronunciation of, 451–458
Spanish radio stations, 341–342

Speech personality, 104
Speed-selector switch, 194
Speed-up signal, 82
Sports announcing, 368–369
  calling the game, 391–392
  interviewing athletes, 376–379
  play analyst, 398–402
  specializations in, 5
  tips on, 392–398
  working conditions for, 369–376
Sports director, 371–372, 382–385
Sports reporter, 370–371
Sports reporting, 379–385
Sportscaster, 372–373
Spots (advertising), 199, 203
Spotters, role of, 386–388
Stand microphones, 184
Standby signal, 81, 82
Stand-up, 314
Stash, 345
Status-conferral function, 18
Steelman, Rohn, 6
Steinman, Harvey, 253
Stone, Steve, 401
Stretch signal, 81–82
Studio cards, 249
Styluses, 194
Supercardioid pickup pattern, 183
Supers, 256, 396
Sweetening, 185
Switch-camera signal, 82–83
Switcher, 275, 313, 319
Syllabic consonants, 441

Take-a-level signal, 83
Takes, 214–215
Talk stations, 271–274
Talk shows, 251, 274–278
Talking heads, 382
Target audience, 200
Tease, 325
Telegraphing movement, 66–67
Telephone numbers, 96–97

Television
  anchoring news on, 322–326
  clothing and makeup on, 72–73
  commercials on, 225–230
  field reporting for, 314–322
  hand signals for, 81–83
  news programs, 310–314
  sports reporting for, 379–382
  talk programs, 274–278
Tempo, 108–109, 137–138
Ten-to-zero signal, 82
Thirty-second signal, 82
Three-minute signal, 82
Time, developing sense of, 97–98
Time code, 319
Time-delay system, use of, 268
Timing, on commercials, 219–220
Tone arm, 193–194
Toss, 325
Total Audience Plan (TAP), 202
Trademarks, use of, 166
Traffic department, 215
Trash television, 257
Turntables, 193–195
Two-minute signal, 82

Unidirectional pickup pattern, 183
Unions, 430
United Press International (UPI),
  283–285
United States Criminal Code, 17
Unvoiced consonants, 129
Uplink equipment, 316
Urban Contemporary (UC) format,
  340

Variable equalizers, 194
Velocity microphones, 180–182
Vertical spots, 203
VI (volume indicator) meter, 188
Virgule, 38
Vision, peripheral, 72

Vocal folds (chords), 58, 106, 128
Voice
  inflection of, 107
  pitch of, 104–107
  quality of, 121–128
  vitality of, 109–110
  volume of, 107–108
Voice level, taking, 79–80
Voiced consonants, 129
Voice-overs, tips on, 218–219
Voicer, 288, 299–302
Volume, 107–108, 188
Vowels, 112
  back, 113, 115, 437
  classification of, 113–117
  distortion of, 112, 114, 116–117,
    118–119
  French, 465–469
  front, 113, 115, 435–437
  German, 474
  Italian, 458–459
  pronunciation of, 435–438
  Spanish, 452
VU (volume unit) meter, 188

Weather reporting, 326–329
Webster's Collegiate Dictionary, 92
Wheeler, Patsy, 84
Who's Who, 254
Wild spot, 203
Williams, Bruce, 258–259
Williams, Jerry, 269
Windscreens, 63
Winfrey, Oprah, 57–58
Wipe, 319
Wireless microphones, 184
Wire-service phonetics, 87–92
Woodshedding, 209
Working combo, 185, 334
Wrap, 288, 301
Wrap-up signal, 82

Zappala, Janet, 68, 69